SAP PRESS Books: Always on hand

Print or e-book, Kindle or iPad, workplace or airplane: Choose where and how to read your SAP PRESS books! You can now get all our titles as e-books, too:

- ▶ By download and online access
- ▶ For all popular devices
- ▶ And, of course, DRM-free

Convinced? Then go to **www.sap-press.com** and get your e-book today.

SAP® Performance Optimization Guide

 **PRESS**

SAP PRESS is a joint initiative of SAP and Galileo Press. The know-how offered by SAP specialists combined with the expertise of the Galileo Press publishing house offers the reader expert books in the field. SAP PRESS features first-hand information and expert advice, and provides useful skills for professional decision-making.

SAP PRESS offers a variety of books on technical and business related topics for the SAP user. For further information, please visit our website: *www.sap-press.com*.

Thomas Schneider

SAP® Performance Optimization Guide

Galileo Press

Bonn • Boston

Galileo Press is named after the Italian physicist, mathematician, and philosopher Galileo Galilei (1564–1642). He is known as one of the founders of modern science and an advocate of our contemporary, heliocentric worldview. His words *Eppur si muove* (And yet it moves) have become legendary. The Galileo Press logo depicts Jupiter orbited by the four Galilean moons, which were discovered by Galileo in 1610.

Editor Florian Zimniak
English Edition Editor Kelly Grace Harris
Translation Lemoine International, Inc., Salt Lake City, UT
Copyeditor Ruth Saavedra
Cover Design Graham Geary
Photo Credit Getty Images/Steve Bloom
Layout Design Vera Brauner
Production Manager Kelly O'Callaghan
Production Editor Graham Geary
Typesetting Publishers' Design and Production Services, Inc.
Printed and bound in the United States of America, on paper from sustainable sources

ISBN 978-1-59229-368-1

© 2013 by Galileo Press Inc., Boston (MA)
6th edition 2011, 1st reprint 2013
6th German edition published 2010 by Galileo Press, Bonn, Germany

Library of Congress Cataloging-in-Publication Data
Schneider, Thomas.
  [SAP.-Performanceoptimierung. English]
  SAP performance optimization guide / Thomas Schneider. — 6th ed.
      p. cm.
  Original ed. titled: SAP R/3 performance optimization. 1999.
  ISBN-13: 978-1-59229-368-1
  ISBN-10: 1-59229-368-9
  1. SAP R/3. 2. Business — Computer programs. 3. Accounting — Computer programs.
  4. Client/server computing. I. SAP R/3 performance optimization. II. Title.
  HF5548.4.R2S3416 2011
  650.0285'53 — dc22
  2010035939

Contents at a Glance

Dear Reader,

Now in its sixth edition, *SAP Performance Optimization Guide* is one of the best-selling and most frequently updated books at SAP PRESS. Although the information contained in previous editions is hardly obsolete, the constantly evolving world of SAP necessitates a reference that is up-to-date for the latest versions of applications, all of which impact the performance of others.

Thanks to the work of Thomas Schneider, this book has evolved along with the ever-changing landscape of SAP. In each new iteration, he has expanded the content to include a new SAP application — and this book is no exception. For this sixth edition, the topic at hand is SAP NetWeaver BW, a crucial application that can help businesses makes decisions and take actions critical to their very survival as a company.

We always look forward to praise, but are also interested in critical comments that will help us improve our books. We encourage you to visit our website at *www.sap-press.com* and share your feedback about this work.

Thank you for purchasing a book from SAP PRESS!

Kelly Grace Harris
Editor, SAP PRESS

Galileo Press
100 Grossman Drive, Suite 205
Braintree, MA 02184

kelly.harris@galileo-press.com
www.sap-press.com

Contents

5   Hardware Sizing and System Distribution 247

6   Workload Distribution and Interfaces 281

Foreword

At SAP, our first priority is to ensure that the SAP software solutions in your enterprise run successfully and at minimal cost. This *lowest cost of ownership* is achieved with fast and efficient implementation, together with optimal and dependable operation. SAP Active Global Support is actively and consistently there to help you with the new SAP Solution Management Assessment service. Throughout the entire lifecycle of a solution, SAP offers customers all of the necessary services, first-class support, a suitable infrastructure, and the relevant know-how. The new service is backed up by three powerful support programs: SAP Safeguarding (in other words, risk management), Solution Management Assessment, which aims to optimize the customer's IT solution, and empowering, which ensures a targeted, effective transfer of knowledge from SAP to the customer.

One of the key goals of this book is to impart knowledge. It provides a detailed overview of technical aspects and concepts for managing SAP software solutions.

Whether you are new to SAP system management or want to become further qualified, you will benefit from the wealth of practical experience and first-hand information contained in this book. Additionally, SAP endeavors to help prepare you to qualify as a certified technical consultant. Please note, however, that books cannot (nor do they attempt to) replace personal experience gained from working with the various SAP solutions. Rather, the authors offer suggestions to help your day-to-day work with the software.

Innovations in SAP solutions always bring with them new challenges and solutions for system management. Demands made on the customer's organization or external support organizations also increase. The expertise and knowledge of these organizations can be a great help in avoiding problems when using the software. Therefore, one of the core tasks of this series of books is to teach problem-solving skills.

Even in this Internet age, books prove to be an ideal medium for imparting knowledge in a compact form. Furthermore, their content complements the new service and support platform, SAP Solution Manager, and other new services offered by SAP. This series provides background knowledge on the operation and functions of new SAP solutions and contributes to customer satisfaction.

Gerhard Oswald

Executive Board Member, SAP

Uwe Hommel

Executive Vice President, SAP
SAP Active Global Support

Acknowledgments

As a result of the huge success of the first editions of this book, one can say without a doubt that it has become a cornerstone in performance training not only for customers, but also for many SAP employees. Therefore, once again the need has arisen for an updated and extended edition, and it is a great pleasure to write this sixth revised edition. For the most part, the topics have been selected and presented based on the experiences my colleagues and I encountered in real-life situations when working with many SAP systems in production operations — whether in SAP EarlyWatch® Check and SAP GoingLive™ Check services, training courses for performance analysis, or during on-site analysis of systems with critical performance problems. Based on these experiences, we are confident that this book covers a broad range of important performance-related topics.

In the fifth edition, the sections that dealt with performance analysis of the SAP J2EE Engine and Java programs were revised or added to on the basis of SAP Solution Manager Diagnostics 7.0. This sixth edition has been supplemented with chapters on SAP NetWeaver® Business Warehouse (BW) and TREX including SAP NetWeaver BW Accelerator. Moreover, the database sections were migrated to the Database Administrator (DBA) Cockpit, and the sizing chapter was supplemented with extensive examples.

This book would not have been possible without the support of many competent partners. First, I would very much like to mention our colleague and mentor Augustinus Wohlfahrt, whose sudden and untimely death left us all deeply shaken. As one of the initiators of this series of books, he played a central part in putting together this publication. I would like to dedicate this book to him.

I would also like to thank the following colleagues who have provided suggestions over many years and helped with proofreading and much more: Christian Bartels, Kai Baumgarten, Thomas Becker, Hartwig Brand,

Jens Claussen, Ralf Czekalla, Guido Derwand, Anja Gerstmair, Manfred Hirsch, Brigitte Huy, Susanne Janssen, Anja Kerber, Christian Knappke, Kerstin Knebusch, Mandy Krimmel, John Landis, Claudia Langner, Ulrich Marquard, Manfred Mensch, Kai Morich, Dirk Müller, Christian Niedermayer, Jens Otto, Volker Sauermann, Marko Schmidt, Sebastian Schmitt, Gerold Völker, and Liane Will. In addition, I would like to thank Tomas Wehren and Florian Zimniak at Galileo Press for their outstanding support.

Dr. Thomas Schneider

Introduction

Why is the performance of your business IT application important? Users will only be motivated and work efficiently with an application if response times are good. A slow system leads to downtime and frustration. If the situation deteriorates further, in the worst case, you no longer have the throughput necessary for running business processes. The results are overtime, delays in production, and financial loss. In contrast, the systematic, proactive optimization of performance considerably increases the value of your business application.

A data-processing system's performance is defined as the system's ability to fulfill requirements in response time and data throughput. The system might, for example, be required to achieve a throughput of 10,000 printed invoices in one hour or a response time of under one second for the creation of a sales order. Good performance is, however, not an absolute characteristic of a business application. Rather, it should always be viewed as relative to the demands made on the application.

Proactive Performance Management

In this book, *performance optimization* refers to a process that always includes five phases. The first two phases are *understanding the business processes* and *setting and quantifying performance goals*. These steps involve all participating parties — that is, technicians and application experts. Optimization can only be successful on the basis of these prerequisites. Phases three to five involve the *systematic monitoring, identification, and analysis* of problems; *implementation of optimization measures;* and further analysis to *verify the success* of the measures introduced (Figure 1). We warn against randomly tinkering with configuration parameters and similar impulsive tuning measures. Rather, this book's objective is to enable you to identify and analyze performance problems to deal with them effectively.

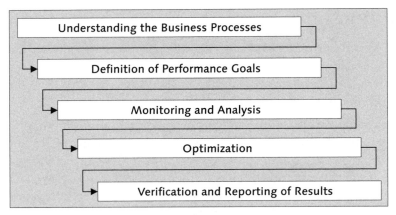

Figure 1 Performance Optimization in Five Phases

Technical optimization From a technical point of view, a business application is made up of many different components. These include the logical components: processes such as services, threads or work processes, and memory areas such as buffers and user contexts. Then there are the physical components such as the processors (CPU), main memory (RAM), hard disks, and network segments. Each of these components allows for maximum throughput and optimal response time. If the interplay between the components is not appropriately balanced or if an individual component has reached its performance limit, wait situations can occur that have a negative effect on throughput and response times. In this book, *technical optimization* refers to the identification, analysis, and solution of these problems by tuning the components and distributing the system's workload.

Application optimization The second important task of performance optimization is to prevent unnecessary workload. Inefficient programs or their suboptimal use can weaken performance. The optimization of individual programs is referred to as *application optimization*.

The goal of optimization is first to improve the system settings and applications to achieve the desired performance, based on existing hardware resources. If the existing resources are not sufficient, they must be extended according to the knowledge gained by analysis.

How much tuning is necessary? How much effort is involved in the performance analysis and tuning of an SAP solution? The answer to this question depends largely on the size of the system. For a small or medium installation that has no modifications to the SAP standard or customer developments, it is normally sufficient to do performance optimization just before and shortly after the start of production and after large-scale changes, for example, after upgrades, large data transfers or client transports, or when new SAP solutions or additional users are introduced into the system. Of course, it is also necessary to intervene when acute performance problems occur. The tuning potential, and its inherent effort in analysis and optimization, increases proportionately with the size of the system. Experience has shown that many performance bottlenecks are caused by customer developments and modifications to the standard SAP software. The most common reason for this is insufficient testing, but problems can also arise as a result of time constraints or lack of experience on the part of the developer. The extreme case would be a large, constantly developing installation with several hundred users, complicated process chains, a dozen or more developers (often from different consulting firms, working on the system at different times and in different places), and outsourced system management. In such a system environment, it is absolutely necessary that a small group of administrators and developers has an overview of the entire system and keeps an eye on performance.

SAP's remote services offer help with performance analysis and tuning — namely, SAP GoingLive Check, which enables your system to make a smooth transition to production operation, and SAP EarlyWatch Check, which monitors your system and suggests additional optimizations.

How does *proactive performance management* help you attain the objective of successfully running a business application? You should keep two influencing factors in mind if you're going to achieve this objective: the satisfaction of users and the costs of running the business application. Operating costs come, on one hand, from the cost of hardware (infrastructure, CPU, main memory, hard disks, and networks) and personnel (administration, maintenance, fault analysis). However, you should not overlook the costs that arise if an application is not available or does not achieve the required performance. In these cases, losses incurred in a few hours or days can exceed one year's average investment for proactive performance optimization. You must compare these costs to the

Proactive performance management

costs of proactive performance management. Table 1 shows the value of proactive performance management with two concrete examples.

Proactive Measure	Effect on System	Immediate Value, Owing to Increased User Satisfaction	Immediate Value, Owing to Lower Operating Costs	Diminished Risk of Deterioration
Optimizing SQL statements	Reduction of database load	Faster response times for certain transactions	Hardware investments (database server, memory system) can be stretched	Overloading of the database system can be avoided
Proactive data management (data avoidance, archiving, reorganization)	Database growth reduced Shorter times for maintenance work on the database (backup/recovery, upgrade, migration, system copy)	Faster response times for certain transactions Shorter downtime during maintenance work	Hardware investments can be stretched Fewer personnel requirements for maintenance work	Database size remains manageable

Table 1 Examples of the Value of Proactive Performance Management

Challenges posed by the Internet and intranet

With the development of the Internet, there has been a paradigm shift in the world of business software: Software is no longer aimed at highly specialized employees; rather, it is aimed at Internet or intranet users. With SAP R/3, the traditional strategy of process automation was based on highly specialized users who accessed their SAP ERP system) from fixed work centers via installed SAP GUIs. The role of these specialized agents, who had to be trained to use the software, is becoming unnecessary in many cases. Instead, the end user can have direct access to the enterprise's SAP ERP systems via the Internet or intranet. Today, for example, in many enterprises, employees can enter their work and absent times, travel expenses, and so forth into the system themselves via the Internet, whereas this would have previously been done by central users. Increasingly, customers order products directly over the Internet and no longer by means of letters, faxes, or telephone calls to sales centers.

User expectations concerning the usability and performance of an e-business solution are disproportionately higher than the traditional employee's expectations regarding their SAP ERP system. The employee relies on his own SAP ERP system, and if it normally helps to make day-to-day work easier, it is accepted, and minor errors or weak points in performance are tolerated. The Internet user is quite different: If applications offered over the Internet do not work easily and effectively, users can immediately switch to the competition and, for example, make their purchases there — the competition is only a mouse-click away. In addition, the Internet does not finish work at 5:00 p.m.; an e-business solution on the Internet has to be available and efficiently working 365 days a year, 24 hours a day.

The demand for an open, flexible software architecture requires specialized, independently running software components that are linked via interfaces, which means a business process involves several software components. The constantly growing number of solutions and components presents an administrative challenge for data centers. The number of components has grown from the manageable SAP R/3 (with SAP instances, database, hardware/operating system) to a constantly increasing range of technologies — including products that SAP does not produce but offers as a reseller.

IT services

Consistent with this trend, business process operators are increasingly integrating more and more service partners into the service and support processes. Outsourcing might involve only hardware (computer performance, hard disk memory, network resources, and so on), or it might also involve the application (*application service providing* [ASP]). For example, the services of an Internet product catalog can be completely allocated to a service provider instead of being operated by the catalog software in the enterprise. Therefore, not only is it necessary to monitor hardware and software components, but monitoring must also go beyond company and component boundaries.

Overall, completely new requirements arise for administration and monitoring of SAP solutions — requirements that you cannot deal with using previously held concepts.

About this Book

The methods for performance analysis and optimization presented in this book reflect those initially used by experts in the *EarlyWatch® service* and SAP *GoingLive Check*, and they are included in the SAP Basis training courses ADM315 Workload Analysis and ADM490 Optimization of ABAP Programs. This is the sixth edition of this book, and with each new edition, we take opportunity to thoroughly describe current trends in product development at SAP and, wherever relevant, consider developments in the IT world in general. In particular, the fifth edition describes the SAP Solution Manager Diagnostics functions for end-to-end workload and runtime analysis. Additional innovations are, for example, the performance analysis of Web Dynpro for ABAP applications, the integrated Internet Transaction Server, and double-stack installations. This edition includes revisions of the database-related topics, and the topics SAP NetWeaver Business Warehouse (SAP NetWeaver BW) and TREX applications were newly added.

Figure 2 gives an overview of the chapters of this book and suggests a possible sequence in which to read them.

Chapter 1, Performance Management of an SAP Solution, is directed at SAP administrators, SAP consultants, application developers, and SAP project leads. It deals on a nontechnical level with the fundamental questions about performance analysis:

▶ Which preventative measures must you take to guarantee the optimal performance of an SAP solution?

▶ What performance tuning measures should you take into consideration?

▶ Who is involved in the tuning process?

The service provided for the user frequently turns out to be a combination of a number of different services carried out by a network of partners. Parts are provided by many different, sometimes external, service providers. To master this complexity, many service providers and customers implement *service-level management* (SLM). SLM calls for a structured, proactive method to ensure an adequate service level for the IT application users, taking into account both cost efficiency and customer's business objectives. In this book, we'll describe the tools and methods used to implement SLM for an SAP solution.

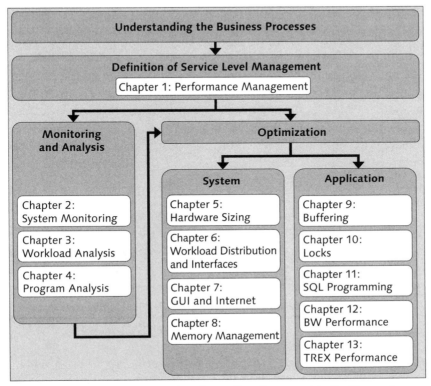

Figure 2 The Chapters in this Book and How They Correspond to the Phases of Performance Optimization

Performance analysis is presented in **Chapters 2** through **4**. After having read these chapters you should be prepared to carry out a systematic performance analysis.

In this book, we initially follow the bottom-up analysis strategy, starting in **Chapter 2**, Monitoring Hardware, Databases, and SAP Basis, with an examination of the operating system, database, SAP memory management, and SAP work processes. At the same time, solution proposals are provided that should enable the administrator or consultant to solve the most important performance problems. For small and medium-size installations, this level of tuning is often sufficient.

Then **Chapter 3**, Workload Analysis, discusses the more complex workload analysis as an example of top-down analysis. In **Chapter 4**, Identifying Performance Problems in ABAP and Java Programs, you will find methods for analyzing individual programs using tools such as SQL trace, ABAP runtime analysis, and Introscope runtime analysis, among others.

The remaining nine chapters, 5 to 13, present information necessary for a more in-depth performance analysis. They are intended for SAP consultants responsible for the efficient functioning of large systems who need to reach the full tuning potential of their systems. These chapters are independent units to a large extent, and you can read them in any order once you are familiar with the content of the first four chapters.

The topics are:

▶ **Chapter 5: Hardware Sizing and System Distribution**
Optimally designed hardware is the prerequisite to avoiding hardware bottlenecks on the one hand and limiting keeping the costs of unnecessary hardware on the other hand. Server consolidation — that is, the bundling of all services on a few powerful machines — has become an important IT market trend in recent years. We'll describe what you must take into account to use these technologies efficiently.

▶ **Chapter 6: Workload Distribution and Interfaces**
Optimal workload distribution of web, dialog, update, and background requests helps ensure efficient use of hardware and the avoidance of bottlenecks brought about by suboptimal configurations. Interface performance between software components also contributes greatly to the efficiency of the entire solution. E-business solutions that consisted solely of a monolithic R/3 systems were rarely used, even in the past. Rather, open solutions that comprise several components connected to each other via interfaces are the standard.

▶ **Chapter 7: SAP GUI and Internet Connection**
Analysis and configuration recommendations demonstrate the optimization potential of linking GUIs (classical SAP GUI or web browser) with the application. The chapter discusses performance aspects of

SAP GUI controls, Internet Transaction Server (ITS), Business Server Pages, Web Dynpro for ABAP, and Web Dynpro for Java in detail.

▶ **Chapter 8: Memory Management**
The configuration of the memory areas allocated by the SAP system has a considerable influence on performance. In this context, we'll pay special attention to the implementation of the 64-bit memory allocation technology.

▶ **Chapter 9: SAP Buffering**
Buffered tables on the application servers speed up access to frequently read data and help ease the load on the database.

▶ **Chapter 10: Locks**
Database and SAP locks ensure data consistency. You can avoid bottlenecks in throughput with an optimized administration of locks (for example, with the ATP server or by buffering number ranges).

▶ **Chapter 11: Optimizing SQL Statements**
Ineffective SQL statements make heavy demands on the database and can hamper the performance of the entire application. We therefore devote an entire chapter to optimizing SQL statements.

▶ **Chapter 12: Optimizing Queries to SAP NetWeaver Business Warehouse**
SAP NetWeaver Business Warehouse queries are special SQL statements that usually process large quantities of data. Special optimization options exist for this type of queries.

▶ **Chapter 13: Optimizing Search Queries Using TREX**
You can use TREX for optimizing text-based and attribute-based search queries and SAP NetWeaver Business Warehouse queries (SAP NetWeaver BW Accelerator) instead of traditional database indexes and aggregation tables.

Knowledge of performance optimization of SAP systems and applications us highly beneficial for SAP administrators, SAP application managers, SAP developers, and SAP project leads, and these are the target groups of this book. Every chapter first provides an introduction, which is followed by a short section, "When Should You Read this Chapter?," which specifies the target group of the chapter.

Target groups

We have already differentiated between technical optimization and application optimization. Chapters 2, 5, 6. 7, and 8 deal with technical optimization and are mainly aimed at SAP system administrators and technical consultants. Chapters 4, 9, 10, and 11 deal with the analysis and tuning of individual programs (or applications) and as such form part of application optimization. This part of the analysis is also of interest to those responsible for SAP applications (employees in the department, application consultants, and developers). Chapters 1 and 3 are relevant to both areas.

Prerequisites   Chapters 2 and 6 through 13 assume both theoretical and practical knowledge of SAP component administration. You should be familiar with the use of the Computer Center Management System (CCMS), in particular. SAP NetWeaver Application Server ABAP System Administration (see Appendix G, Information Sources) should serve as good preparation. Parts of this book (for instance, Chapters 4, 9, 10, 11, and 12) assume familiarity with the ABAP programming language, the functioning of relational databases, and SQL.

Limitations of this book   The book does not cover the following topics:

- ► **Hardware and network tuning**
  Although this book helps you identify bottlenecks in the CPU, main memory, I/O, or network, a detailed analysis requires hardware or network provider tools. In view of the enormous number of products offered, we cannon include this subject (especially tuning hard disks).

- ► **Databases**
  In the Computer Center Management System (CCMS), SAP offers tools that standardize most administrative and analysis tasks for different database systems. However, if you want to do more in-depth database tuning, you need to be familiar with the different database system architectures. It is not possible for this book to go into sufficient detail on the fine points of all seven database systems that can be used in conjunction with SAP Business Suite. In addition, this information is not necessary, because reference material on tuning is available for all database systems. This book cannot replace these

materials, nor does it endeavor to do so. Rather, the emphasis is on the SAP-specific context of database tuning and on explaining concepts common to all database systems. The concrete examples used always refer to individual database systems. In Appendix B, you will find an overview of the most important monitors for analyzing database systems.

▶ **Application tuning**
Many problems with performance can only be solved with detailed knowledge of the application and the individual SAP system modules. A change in customized settings often solves the problem. This book does not provide the know-how for tuning individual SAP system modules. However, it does provide you with analysis strategies so you can narrow performance problems down to certain applications and then consult the appropriate developer or consultant.

One question that was heatedly discussed prior to this book's publication is the extent to which release-dependent and time-dependent information should be included, for example, menu paths, recommendations for configuration parameters, and guide values for performance counters. Factors such as a new version, patches (for the SAP system component, database, or operating system), or a new generation of computers, among others, could render previous information obsolete overnight. In the worst-case scenario, outdated recommendations could even have negative effects on performance. We are aware of this risk. Nevertheless, we have decided to include time-dependent information and rules. Only in this way can you use this book as a reference for daily work in SAP administration. On the other hand, it is clear that this is not a book of fixed rules and regulations, and anyone who views performance optimization as mechanical rule-following is mistaken. This book cannot replace direct analysis of the solution, SAP online help, or up-to-date SAP Notes on the SAP Service Marketplace. It only aims to support these.

Release dependency

All details on menu paths, references to performance monitor screens, and guideline values for performance counters refer to SAP NetWeaver 7.10 if not otherwise noted.

SAP NetWeaver 7.10

[+]   You will find important notes and tips in sections marked with this symbol.

[Ex]   This symbol is an example.

[!]   Caution sections are marked with this symbol to warn of potential errors and pitfalls.

UNIX Windows   Sections that refer to specific features of the UNIX or Windows operating systems will be marked as such.

www.sap-press.com   As with previous editions, we'll provide current information and additional texts relating to the topics on the book's page at *www.sap-press. com*.

1 Performance Management of an SAP Solution

Customers who implement SAP solutions expect them to be reliable and easy to maintain. They assume that the standard-setting levels of excellence achieved with SAP R/3 have been maintained in more recent SAP solutions, such as SAP Customer Relationship Management (CRM), SAP Supply Chain Management (SCM), and SAP NetWeaver BW. In addition, SAP not only offers its tried-and-tested platform for SAP ERP and other business solutions with the most high-performance architecture on the market, but according to analysts, it also offers an innovative service concept.

In this chapter, we will present the architecture and the service concept. In the first section, we will deal with the architecture in which SAP solutions are constructed and outline the potential for system optimization. At this stage, we deliberately dispense with technical details. In the second section, we deal with organizational questions regarding the running of an SAP solution, such as the creation of a monitoring and optimizing plan with SAP Solution Manager. Two elements play key roles here: On the one hand is a plan for the continuous monitoring of availability and performance of the business process, and on the other hand is the service level management method.

When Should You Read this Chapter?

You should read this chapter if you want to develop a monitoring and optimization plan for an SAP solution. We recommend that you read this chapter first to get an overview of the contents of this book before getting into more detail in subsequent chapters.

1.1   SAP Solution Architecture

The architecture of the SAP Business Suite is described below. First, we will look at the different SAP solutions and components. A section on client/server architecture follows.

1.1.1   SAP Solutions and SAP Components

Makeup of an SAP solution landscape

SAP Business Suite provides integrated business software solutions for communication with customers (represented by SAP Customer Relationship Management [CRM]), suppliers (SAP Supplier Relationship Management [SRM]), and employees (SAP ERP Human Capital Management [HCM]) and solutions for logistics (SAP Supply Chain Management [SCM]) and accounting and controlling (SAP ERP Financials). You can use these solutions to map the entire business, from marketing, sales, and service to invoicing, delivery, and collection to production and employee planning and the appropriate processes of procurement including the necessary accounting and controlling. Figure 1.1 shows the disciplines of business software and the relationships with the most important business partners: customers, employees, suppliers, and owners.

SAP Business Suite products consist of the technology components of the SAP NetWeaver technology platform and application components that form the following core applications:

- SAP ERP or SAP R/3 Enterprise (up to version 4.7), which comprises SAP ERP Financials, SAP ERP Human Capital Management, and — under the name SAP ERP Operations — operative components for sales, service, production, logistics, and purchasing (formerly known as "SAP module" SD, PP, MM, and so on)
- SAP Customer Relationship Management (SAP CRM)
- SAP Supply Chain Management (SAP SCM) with the SAP Advanced Planning & Optimization (SAP APO)
- SAP Supplier Relationship Management (SAP SRM)
- SAP Product Lifecycle Management (SAP PLM)

You can find a complete overview of the SAP Business Suite solutions at *http://www.sap.com/solutions/business-suite/index.epx*.

The SAP Business Suite applications run on various systems. Through-out this book, the term *SAP systems* will refer to applications with SAP technology components and a separate database instance (including the three-digit database ID that must be unique within an SAP landscape). The installation of one or more SAP products as SAP systems forms an SAP solution landscape.

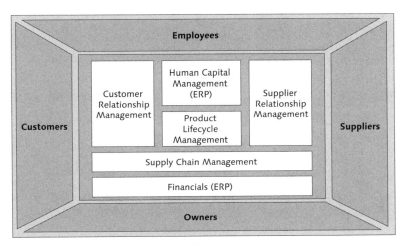

Figure 1.1 Solutions of SAP Business Suite

In the past SAP software was built on a single technological component, *SAP Basis*, which served as the base for SAP R/3. By contrast, SAP Business Suite is implemented on various technology components whose combination forms the SAP NetWeaver technology platform. Figure 1.2 shows the technology components of SAP NetWeaver. These include:

SAP NetWeaver

▶ Advanced Business Application Programming (ABAP) development and runtime environment: SAP NetWeaver Application Server ABAP, the successor to SAP Basis (from SAP R/3), which contains the Development Workbench and basic tools such as the Computing Center Management System (CCMS)

▶ Java 2 Platform, Enterprise Edition (J2EE) development and runtime environment: SAP NetWeaver Application Server Java (also referred to as the SAP J2EE Engine)

▶ Database and operating system platform

- ▶ SAP liveCache

- ▶ SAP Internet Transaction Server (SAP ITS)

- ▶ SAP NetWeaver Business Warehouse (BW)

- ▶ SAP NetWeaver Process Integration (PI)

- ▶ SAP NetWeaver Business Process Management (BPM)

- ▶ SAP NetWeaver Portal with collaboration and knowledge management

- ▶ SAP NetWeaver Enterprise Search with TREX

This list is by no means complete, but is intended to introduce the components presented in this book. You can find the complete component overview of SAP NetWeaver at *http://www.sap.com/platform/netweaver/index.epx*.

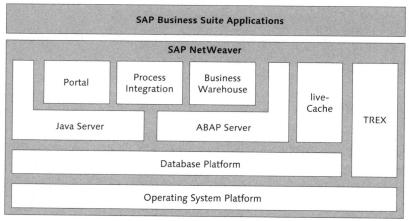

Figure 1.2   Technology Components of SAP NetWeaver

Bundling all technology components into the SAP NetWeaver product strategy, technically integrates these components to such an extent that the cost of implementing and operating the software can be reduced drastically. However, SAP's challenge is to find an ideal balance between fast integration (which could result in incompatibility between different versions of software components) and protecting the investment in the existing system (which again raises the issue of required compatibility and rules out fast integration in some cases).

When the first version of SAP NetWeaver (that is, SAP NetWeaver 2004) was introduced, the various versions of the technology components had to be harmonized; therefore, today we speak of a uniform SAP NetWeaver product. Furthermore, there were consolidations, such as the integration of the ABAP and J2EE runtime environments, the integration of SAP NetWeaver BW into the ABAP runtime environment (so that, for instance, you can operate an SAP ERP and SAP NetWeaver BW system in one SAP NetWeaver instance), and the integration of SAP ITS into the C kernel of the ABAP runtime environment.

Initial integration efforts were also made in the area of administration tools, for instance, the integration of monitoring data into CCMS and the development of a central workload analysis. We'll describe both subjects later.

Administration tools

Every SAP system can run independently. For example, it can be started, stopped, and maintained independently of others. But there are, of course, dependencies to consider. Data is exchanged between components using *remote function calls* (RFCs) or via Web services. With RFCs or Web services, systems and components of different versions can communicate with each other.

Linking systems with RFC

For an SAP ERP system and, for example, an SAP APO or SAP NetWeaver BW system to work together, you must implement software transports, known as plug-ins, in the SAP ERP system.

The interfaces the user employs to log onto to the system (GUI interfaces) are the *SAP GUI for Windows environment*, the *SAP GUI for Java environment*, and the *SAP GUI for HTML*. Specialized users use the SAP GUI for Windows or Java environments. The disadvantage of the SAP GUI for Windows environment is that it must be installed on the desktop computer. (The Java GUI must also be installed on the desktop computer, but its installation is much easier than SAP GUI for Windows.) Typical Windows or Java GUI users are controllers, planners, and employees in sales centers such as telesales.

User connection

Occasional users (Internet or intranet) log on using a web browser. The advantage here is that no special GUI program needs to be installed on the desktop computer. All input and output screens are presented in HTML format via the web browser. Communication between the web browser and the SAP application level is effected on the Internet level (see the paragraph on SAP NetWeaver Portal).

A third possible means of access uses *mobile clients* — laptop computers or handheld devices that are not continuously linked to the central system but that exchange data with the system periodically. This method is useful, for example, for field sales or service employees. Access can take place via an SAP CRM server and a distributed component object model (DCOM) connector.

SAP NetWeaver Portal | SAP NetWeaver Portal standardizes access to all systems within the landscape. A user logs on to the portal only once, and the portal server creates a *portal page* for that user on which all access information this user needs for day-to-day work is recorded. This includes reference to transactions on the SAP components and non–SAP components, Internet and intranet links, and additional information called *iViews*. From this portal page, users can execute all day-to-day tasks without having to log on to different systems. With SAP NetWeaver Portal you can create portal pages for employees and for customers and business partners.

1.1.2 Client/Server Architecture

The technology of an SAP component is based on a multilayer client/server architecture, as shown in Figure 1.3. The presentation level consists of the frontend and is where the users perform data input and output. Actual processing is carried out on the application level, which represents the business process. The database level is for the permanent storage and preparation of data.

Presentation level | Presentation servers are normally set up as PCs. The GUI program is the traditional SAP GUI (SAP GUI for Windows or Java environments), which must be installed on the desktop computer or via a web browser.

Application level | Once a user has ended a data entry, the presentation server sends this data to the *application level,* which contains the application logic and the presentation logic. The application level also forms the integrated Internet connection of the SAP NetWeaver Application Server (SAP Web AS, until Release 6.40 referred to as SAP Web Application Server or SAP Basis).

Application logic is encapsulated in transactions, screens, reports, or function modules.

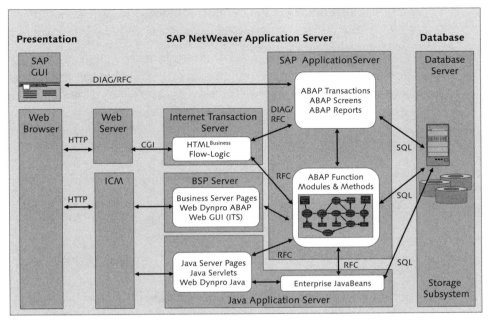

Figure 1.3 Client/Server Architecture (SAP NetWeaver Application Server)

There are three ways to connect Internet users to the SAP application level. The first is to use the SAP Internet Transaction Server (SAP ITS) and a Web server provided by a third party. This technique is available beginning with SAP R/3 3.1. SAP no longer recognizes applications based on the ITS as of SAP R/3 4.6C. Given that SAP and their customers have made substantial investments in ITS applications, SAP still maintains ITS and integrates it into the SAP NetWeaver Application Server. It is available in two versions: external ITS, an independent installation, and ITS integrated into the kernel of the ABAP server.

Connecting Internet users

Business Server Pages (BSP) are the second programming model. With BSPs, you can dynamically generate HTML pages using ABAP or JavaScript as the script language. The technical advantage of this programming model is that you don't need to install other software components; Business Server Pages are generated directly in the normal SAP application instances. A special Web server is not absolutely necessary. However, from a security point of view, it is recommended that you install a separate Web server as a security buffer. Business Server Pages form part

39

of SAP Basis 6.10. An example of this technology's use is found in SAP CRM 5.0. The further development of Business Server Pages is referred to as Web Dynpro for ABAP.

The third option for connecting Internet users to the SAP application level is to use a JavaServer Page (JSP) server or a Java Application Server. The languages used are HTML and Java, and the programming models are JavaServer Pages)(JSP) or Java Servlets. Because of Java's compatibility, you can replace the SAP Java Application Server with a third-party Java application server (such as from BEA or IBM) once this has been authorized by SAP. Examples of solutions that use this programming model for realizing presentation logic are SAP NetWeaver Portal and (as of SAP NetWeaver 2004) SAP Web Dynpro applications, such as the employee applications (employee self-service [ESS]: time recording, travel accounting, and so forth) and manager applications (manager self-service [MSS]) in SAP ERP.

Also, parts of the application logic can be done in Java in a Java Application Server (such as *Enterprise JavaBeans* (EJBs)). When this book went to press, large applications had not been created using this technology.

Database level   If data is required to process a user request, and this data is not yet in the application server's main memory, the data is read from the database server. The relational database is the medium used for permanently storing data. In addition to SAP's own database (MaxDB), SAP also supports the use of databases from other large producers (IBM, Oracle, Microsoft).

Figure 1.4 shows the structure of SAP NetWeaver Application Server as a double-stack installation. As of SAP Web AS 6.10, the Internet Communication Server (ICM) became a component of SAP Basis. The integration of "classic" SAP Basis and the J2EE Engine occurred with SAP Web AS 6.20, and when SAP Web AS 6.30 was released, the external Internet Transaction Server (ITS) was also integrated. The integrated ITS version has been available since SAP Web AS 6.40. The SAP Web dispatcher is responsible for distributing inbound Web requests. The message server centrally stores information about the availability and utilization of individual instances and therefore is continuously connected to the instances and SAP Web dispatcher. In an Internet scenario, the external ITS Web server and SAP Web dispatcher are in the *demilitarized zone* (DMZ).

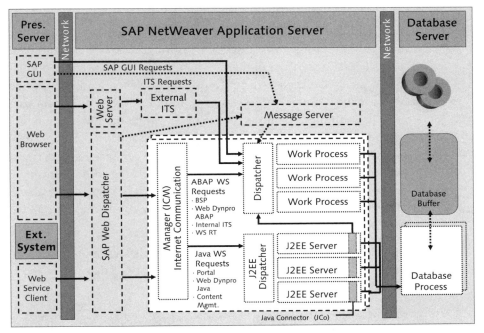

Figure 1.4 SAP NetWeaver Application Server as a Double-Stack Installation

Because presentation servers are normally set up as PCs, no further tuning is required on this level once the hardware conforms to the current recommendations for the SAP release being used.

Aspects of performance and tuning potential

The situation is different for the other levels in the client/server architecture, where requests share processes and memory areas.

We'll use the application server example to explain process configuration: Requests from users or other systems are processed in the application server by *SAP work processes*. SAP systems are typically configured to enable an average of 5 to 10 active users to share one SAP dialog work process. This assumes that users need about 10 times as long to enter data on the screen and interpret the results as the SAP system needs to process the users' requests. Therefore, enough free work processes

Process configuration

should always be available to allow the processing of user requests without delay. If individual users start reports with very long response times (perhaps even several at the same time), they can occupy work processes for several minutes. This results in there being not enough remaining work processes to handle other users' requests quickly, and wait times will occur. The SAP system does not prioritize users. If a bottleneck occurs, all users, regardless of their corporate role or the urgency of their requests, must wait their turn in the queue. However, load distribution methods make it possible to reserve application servers for certain user groups. In addition to requests for dialog or online transactions, an SAP component also processes background, update, and print tasks. There is a different type of SAP work process for each of these request types. Appropriate tuning in this area enables the workload to be distributed optimally in line with system requirements. For Internet and database-level servers, the processes must also be suitably configured for parallel request processing.

Buffers (caches) On all levels, *buffers* (also called *caches*) ensure that once data has been loaded into a server, it is held in the main memory of that server and is available for future requests.

Background: Buffer Types in the SAP System

The first three of the following buffers store pages or blocks with a size specified by the operating or database system, for instance, 8KB, without further knowledge of the contents. These are:

▶ Storage subsystem buffer
This buffer is only available if you use a storage subsystem.

▶ Operating system buffer

▶ Data buffer of the database instance

The other buffers store the data based on the application's data or object model:

▶ Data model–oriented buffers for row-based buffering of tables in the SAP application instance (table buffer) or column-based buffering of tables in TREX (attribute indexes)

▶ Object-oriented application buffers that can buffer structured objects

---

These buffers form a buffer hierarchy; that is, the system queries the buffers that are close to the application before it accesses the database instance data buffer, the operating system buffer, and the storage subsystem buffer. The general rule is that the further down the buffer is in the hierarchy, the more generic its usage area is; the higher it is in the hierarchy, the higher the performance gain for the application must be. If this is not the case, you can omit the buffer. The following example illustrates this situation: Reading data from the table buffer of the SAP application instance is approximately 10 to 100 times faster than reading data from the database server.

If you want to optimize a buffer, you must understand how it behaves in case of changes or displacement. If buffered data is changed, you must notify the buffer about this and invalidate the buffered data. If a second process uses the data at the same time, the buffer can ensure read consistency; that is, as long as the process is in a transaction, it can still access the data prior to the change to obtain a consistent view of the data. Alternatively, there are also buffers that don't ensure this read consistency; that is, the program must anticipate that data changes in case of multiple read processes in a transaction. Provided that multiple instances of the buffer exist, you must consider how the synchronization between the buffers is performed if data is changed.

The second point where the behaviors of the buffers differentiate is the displacement behavior. Some buffers displace data from the buffer either in a time-controlled manner or in case of lack of space. For the displacing buffers, you must query the displacement algorithms.

Ultimately, you must determine how a buffer behaves when the application or database instance is restarted. Some buffers periodically save information on the buffered content and restore the buffered data when the instance is restarted to avoid a cold start, that is, a start with an empty buffer.

On the application level, for example, programs, table and field definitions, and data about configuration tables are held in the buffers. When optimally configured, these buffers ensure that a minimum amount of data needs to be read directly from the database server.

Database tuning comprises three areas. The first is the optimal setting of database buffers and other database parameters. The second area involves optimizing the layout of the database's hard drives to distribute the workload as evenly as possible across the disks to avoid wait situations when writing to or reading from the disks. The third aspect of database tuning is the optimization of expensive (that is, long-running) SQL statements.

Database tuning

Network Network transfer speed and data throughput between the different levels of the client/server architecture are very important. They can affect the performance of the entire SAP solution.

The SAP architecture is structured so that most data communication occurs between the application and database levels. This amount can be reduced by optimizing expensive SQL statements. However, in practice, the application and database levels will be linked by a *local area network* (LAN).

Data transfer between presentation and application, on the other hand, is as low as possible, because the network connection can be achieved with either a LAN or a *wide area network* (WAN).

Internet When using a web browser as a GUI, take care when programming to ensure that as little data as possible is transferred between the presentation and Internet levels. If elaborate HTML pages are generated, there is a greater risk that the user will be limited by network runtimes than if the classic SAP GUI is used, because it uses SAP's own DIAG protocol. Tuning potential depends greatly on the programming model. Given that the Internet level is used purely as a transfer level between the presentation and application levels (such as SAP GUI for HTML), optimizing potential is limited to configuration. The more logic that is stored on the Internet level (for example, field checking), the greater will be the need for program analysis on this level.

Hardware You should check hardware on both the database server and the application servers; that is, sufficient hardware (CPU and main memory) should be available to manage the existing load. Also ensure that the operating system parameters and network parameters are optimally set to achieve good hardware performance. You should refer to the tools and literature provided by the manufacturer on this matter.

> **Background: Scalability of the Client/Server Infrastructure**
>
> SAP components are scalable client/server systems. *Vertical scalability* means the software components on all levels can be installed either centrally on one computer (server) or distributed over several computers. (However, because not all software components are authorized for all operating systems, the centralized installation of all components is only possible on certain platforms.)

Within the client/server level, the load that occurs can be distributed over several logical instances, which can run on different computers. This is known as *horizontal scalability*. Presentation levels are therefore generally distributed on PCs or terminal servers. The application level is achieved by SAP instances, and the Internet level by ITS instances and Web server instances. In principle, for some database systems (for example, Oracle and DB2), it is possible to arrange several database instances in parallel to form the database level. However, this approach is rarely used in practice.

With client/server architecture, it is possible to increase the number of application, Internet, and presentation servers to almost as many as you want to cope with the increasing demand produced by growing numbers of users. The database level is formed by a database server. (Oracle Parallel Server and DB2, which are exceptions, are not discussed here.) In principle, certain processes on the database server cannot be distributed, for example, lock management. Experience has shown that performance problems in large SAP ERP installations with more than 10 application servers are usually caused by bottlenecks in the database server. As a result, tuning the database becomes increasingly important as the system grows. When a system has been running in production operation for some time, most tuning settings, such as buffer settings and load distribution, will have been satisfactorily optimized and will require no further change. In contrast, the tuning of expensive SQL statements becomes more important as the data volume grows; and the tuning process will be ongoing.

1.2 Monitoring and Optimization Plan for an SAP Solution

The following sections deal with a monitoring and optimization plan for an SAP solution. First, however, we should discuss the requirements of this plan.

1.2.1 Requirements of a Monitoring and Optimization Plan

To meet the expectations of an SAP user, it is necessary to have a monitoring and optimization plan (Figure 1.5). Just as SAP has presented itself to customers as a solution provider, rather than as a software provider, the task of monitoring has also changed. Instead of traditional system monitoring, today we speak of solution monitoring, which no longer covers merely the individual system components, but the business process as a whole.

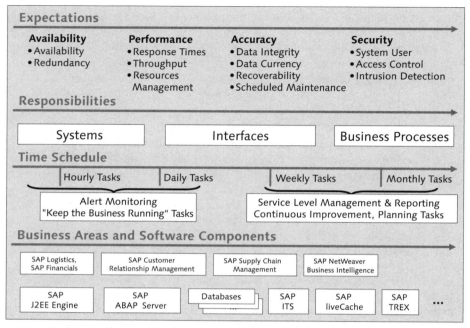

Figure 1.5 Requirements for Monitoring an SAP Solution (Solution Monitoring)

User expectations SAP application users are either employees, customers, or partners (for example, suppliers) of the enterprise that owns the application. As a result, user satisfaction is one of the first objectives to be achieved in the operation of the application. We therefore require that our monitoring plan meets user expectations.

Ask yourself what exactly are your expectations for an Internet application that you use to order goods or conduct bank transactions, for example. You will come up with four requirements: First, the application should be available when you need it; second, performance should be reasonable; third, it should run correctly (for example, products must be delivered and invoiced the same as presented on the Internet); and fourth, you want to ensure that the application is secure; that is, nobody can manipulate your data.

Availability To guarantee availability — the first expectation users have of an application — most system management platforms on the market offer hardware and software component monitoring. However, this is not enough to guarantee that the business process is available. For a user, an application is also unavailable if communication is interrupted between components or a serious application error prevents entering or requesting data. An availability monitor must therefore guarantee that the entire business process is available — not just individual components.

Poor performance in a business application is a sure way to annoy customers. Here, performance refers to the dialog part of the application, that is, how data is entered and saved and the automatic background processing that processes data, even if the customer is not online. Poor performance in the dialog application affects the customer as soon as they enter data, whereas poor performance in the associated background applications affects the customer indirectly when, for example, products ordered are prevented from being delivered by the agreed date.

Performance

As a rule, the performance of dialog applications and background applications should be evaluated separately. The distribution of resources according to need forms part of performance monitoring if both types of application run on a technical IT system (which is usually the case). Normally, dialog applications are given higher priority than background applications. However, there are exceptions to this rule: Background applications with strict deadlines should be given the highest priority. For example, consider the printing of shipping documents (delivery note, address labels, invoices, etc.). If these are not completed by a specific time, there might be up to a 24-hours (that is, missed mail pickup) delay!

To guarantee the integrity (or correctness) of an application, you should consider the following areas for the monitoring plan:

Integrity

▶ **Integrity of data**
Violations of data integrity can include corrupt data in the database, network errors, or errors in interfaces.

▶ **Software components and data are up-to-date and consistent**
If software components or master and configuration data are not correctly updated, there may be inconsistency between documents. For example, an Internet catalog might display a price that is not the same as that recorded in the billing system, and as a result, the bill the customer receives will be incorrect.

> ▶ **Backup of databases and file systems and their recoverability**
> If the content of a production database is irretrievably damaged due to a hardware or software defect, you must be able to retrieve it by using a backup.

Backup Monitoring backup is generally as time-consuming as the backup plan itself. We won't treat this area will not be treated in detail.

At best, traditional system monitoring checks each software component individually. Given the number of components that are involved in a solution, however, even if each component functions correctly by itself, the overall business process might not work well, optimally, and securely for the end user. This can be due to poor communication between components. As a result, solution monitoring must have a specific section to monitor the overall business process, beyond the boundaries of individual components (see Figure 1.5 under Responsibilities).

In Figure 1.5 under Time Schedule, you can see that a monitoring plan must address different time horizons. In other words, alert information is dealt with on different timescales. For example, when a production component goes down, alert information is necessary within a minutes. On the other hand, an alert that informs you of a backup going wrong the previous night can be dealt with in hours. Another type of alarm might inform the administrator that the extrapolated database growth will exhaust the hard drive space in four weeks. Whereas this is also useful information that should persuade the administrator to deal with the problem (perhaps the administrator can start archiving rather than ordering extra hard drive capacity), nobody needs a red light displayed in the alert monitor for four weeks. Therefore, a monitoring plan must provide for short-term (checking on exceptional situations), medium-term, and long-term reporting and optimization.

Central monitoring and extensibility Finally, the fourth area of Figure 1.5, Business Areas and Software Components, comprises the monitoring plan's constantly growing number of solutions and components, which presents an administrative challenge for computing centers. This number has grown from the manageable SAP R/3 system (with SAP instances, database, and hardware/operating system) to a constantly increasing number of technologies, including products that SAP does not produce itself but offers as a reseller. As a result, each computing center manager requires a monitoring method that is both centralized (all information in one tool) and can be expanded to include new components.

So far, we have presented the following requirements for a monitoring and optimizing plan (see Figure 1.5):

Summary

▸ A monitoring and optimizing plan has to cover the areas of availability, performance, correct functioning, and backup.

▸ A monitoring and optimization plan should not only take individual hardware and software components into account. Rather, it must monitor and optimize the information flow of business processes between components.

▸ Different timescales should be taken into account for monitoring — from error situations you must deal with as soon as possible to long-term planning and the analysis of trends.

▸ If possible, the plan should cover all business processes and components in one central tool.

1.2.2 Service Level Management

Service-level management (SLM) is used for long-term monitoring and optimization. Many IT organizations have already implemented it to manage the relationships between individual service providers and the owner of the business process. Service-level management refers to a structured, proactive method that strives to guarantee an adequate level of service to IT application users in accordance with the business objectives of the client and at an optimal cost. Clearly defined, verifiable goals and clear communication must exist between the business process holder and the operators of a solution. (For servers, databases, networks, and so on, there may be several internal or external operators.) First, service-level management requires a service-level agreement that defines the goals (availability, performance, correctness, and security). It also clearly spells out how the achievement of these objectives will be measured and communicated. Service-level reporting describes how objectives will be attained within a certain period of time. The first goal of service-level reporting, therefore, is to determine whether or not the operating goals have been achieved and to indicate potential for optimization.

In addition, the business process holder wants to achieve end-user satisfaction at an optimal cost of ownership. In addition to monitoring availability, performance, correctness, and security, service-level management should also make costs transparent (for example, hardware and personnel costs) (Figure 1.6). Another requirement of service-level management is to monitor communication between business process holders and service providers, which in practice can often be difficult.

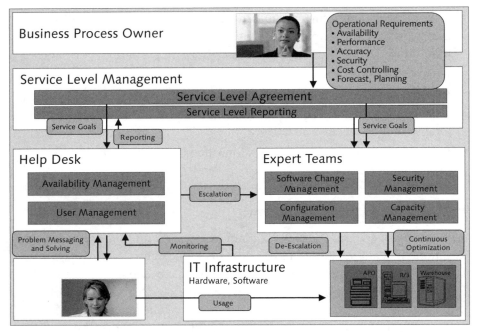

Figure 1.6 The Interconnection Between Service-Level Management, Alert Monitoring, and Continuous System Monitoring

Arranging Service-Level Management

To achieve successful service-level management in your SAP project, you should first prepare a service-level agreement in which objectives to be attained by the individual service partners are recorded. Specify measures that should be put in place if objectives are not met and how the achievement of these objectives will be measured and presented. A service-level agreement should cover the following issues:

- Definition of business hours
- Database backup and recovery
- Performance
- Content of reports

Note that our observations are not a model for a legally watertight contract.They are merely useful items that should be included.

Start the service-level agreement with a description of business hours. For example, you may want to define three different types of business hours: A, B, and C. For each set of hours, define:

> **Definition of business hours**

- **Period of application**
  Example: Monday to Friday, 8:00 a.m. to 5:00 p.m. for A business hours.

- **Availability of service personnel**
  Example: During A business hours, a help desk is available with sufficient capacity to manage requests from end users. In addition, all experts necessary for operation and any necessary problem solving are also available. During B and C business hours, only emergency service is available. During B business hours, experts are on call.

- **Availability for planned and unplanned downtimes**
  Example: During A business hours, planned downtimes are not possible; unplanned downtimes can be a maximum of two hours in one day, with a maximum of four hours per month. During B business hours, planned downtimes are only possible after consultation with business process holders; unplanned downtimes can be a maximum of 4 hours per day, with a maximum of 12 hours per month. During C business hours, downtimes are possible at any time. (Exceptions to this are special situations such as software upgrades, which may lead to extended downtimes.)

All planned and unplanned downtimes must be included in the service-level report, with details on the reasons for the downtimes.

The service-level agreement should set down responsibilities for backup and recovery of databases and, if necessary, file systems. You should set out the scope of the backup to be carried out. Define a procedure

> **Backup and recovery**

for the recovery of databases and file systems in the event of error, in accordance with regulations. The maximum time necessary for this is calculated from the maximum time allowed for unplanned downtime.

Performance

Service providers often give guarantees for average dialog response times. A generally accepted rule of thumb is that good performance is indicated by an average response time of one second or less. This kind of broad generalization is not always valid for all of the different requirements of SAP components.

Rather, agreements should be reached on the monitoring of SAP dialog transactions. You can analyze SAP dialog transaction response times with both the central Alert Monitor and the workload monitor. To reach a useful service-level agreement, proceed as follows:

1. Choose 10 to 20 critical transactions whose performance should be monitored. You can decide whether or not a transaction is critical using the following criteria:

   ▶ If a transaction performs poorly, do you suffer immediate economic damage such as contract penalties, lost orders, and so on?

   ▶ Does the poor performance of a transaction mean that your company's image is seriously damaged? Is the transaction directly accessible by your customers or partners (via the Internet, for example), or is the transaction used in direct dealings with customers or partners (such as in telesales)?

   ▶ Is it one of the most frequently executed transactions? (You can check this in the transaction profile of the workload monitor.)

   Please note that it will not be possible to agree on a complete performance monitoring of business processes in a service-level agreement. Nevertheless, the selected transactions should form the most representative sample possible of your most important applications.

2. Measure the average response time of the transaction in production operation over a given period of time (in the transaction profile of the workload monitor). At the same time, find out if the user is satisfied with this response time. If so, give the measured response time a margin of about 50% as a threshold value for good performance.

3. Agree that weekly details on the response times for selected transactions will be included in service-level reporting.

4. Link the selected transactions to the CCMS monitor (see Chapter 2, Section 2.8, Continuous Monitoring Using CCMS).

5. Agree that if the set threshold value is exceeded, an analysis will be carried out on all persons involved with the transaction. A general action plan should be drawn up, and the people named in it should apply assigned measures to restore stable performance.

Errors in regular operation come to the system or application manager's attention in two ways: either a user reports the errors, or errors become evident through active monitoring.

Troubleshooting

In the service-level agreement, priorities should be spelled out for problem-solving errors and reaction times.

For communication between SAP and customers, four priorities are used (SAP Note 67739):

▶ Very high (negative impact, which causes the entire system or a critical process to stop responding)

▶ High (considerable impact on a critical process)

▶ Medium (impact on a process)

▶ Low (small problem, additional questions)

You should also fix the initial reaction time, that is, when error analysis is started and the entire processing time (the time it will take to deal with an error).

You should also describe which error situations the monitoring team will monitor. These include:

▶ Interrupted updates

▶ Interrupted background processes

▶ Interrupted interface processes (transactional RFC, queued RFC, IDoc or ALE, Web service, and SAP NetWeaver PI messages)

Define what problem solving should look like. Interrupted or unexecuted updates can lead to situations where documents entered or changed by users are not saved in the corresponding application table (that is, they disappear). The daily check of updating tasks is therefore an important task for the SAP system administrator. If interrupted updates are not investigated immediately, there is little chance of finding the cause of the error after a few days have passed. In the following example, we describe the problem-solving process for interrupted updating: The monitoring team monitors interrupted updates in all production systems. For A business hours, one hour is set as an initial reaction time (in this case, the time between the error's occurrence and when the monitoring team notices the error). The monitoring team passes the error information on to the relevant expert. To do this, they use a list of transaction codes and corresponding used. The specialist contacts the user for whom the error has occurred, resolves the interrupted updating in the system, and clears up any other necessary steps in the department so similar error situations do not recur. A maximum processing time can be set for this, which once again depends on the importance of the transaction to the operation of business. As a guideline value, we suggest eight hours of working time (during A business hours) for business-critical transactions.

Finally, you should specify that the number of interrupted updates over a given period of time be recorded in the service level report.

The same procedure applies to the background and interface processes listed.

Escalation procedure If you can foresee at a particular time that a problem cannot be resolved within the agreed service target, the problem must be *escalated,* which means someone in a higher position of authority must decide how to proceed with this problem.

In the service-level agreement you should detail who will be notified in the event of escalation and when. If necessary, define several escalation levels. The *escalation procedure* should cover all hierarchy levels within both the customer enterprise and the service provider. Establish that the details of an escalation must be included in the service-level report.

Service-level reporting In the service-level report (aside from the key figures already mentioned), you should include other key figures that are characteristic of the SAP system. Examples are:

- Number of users logged on and number of transaction steps
- Average response time for dialog and update tasks
- Average response time during the hour with the greatest system load
- CPU and main memory load during the hour with the greatest system load
- Size of the database and its rate of growth

You can often trace medium- and long-term trends from this information, which in turn enables timely intervention, for example, archiving measures in the event of high database growth.

Record how often a service-level report should be written (we recommend weekly) and to whom it should be distributed.

Service-level management in SAP Solution Manager (which we'll describe in the last section of this chapter) covers the previously described issues. Its setup allows you to enter the different parameters of your service-level agreement (for example, hours of business or critical transactions that should be monitored carefully). Based on this data, SAP Solution Manager draws up a service-level report each week. Service-level reporting in SAP Solution Manager includes the following functions:

SAP Solution Manager

- Automated setup, for example, for starting critical transactions
- Presentation of selected performance indicators, error messages, and optimization advice for all SAP solution components, based on the results of SAP EarlyWatch Alert services
- Presentation of performance indicators, error messages, and optimization recommendations grouped according to system and business area
- Graphical presentation of the time spans for selected performance indicators (trend analysis), for example, hardware load
- Automatic generation of instructions and references to other SAP services

1.2.3   Plan for Continuous Performance Optimization

You can gather optimization potential from the service-level management and feedback from continuous monitoring. Performance optimization measures can be divided into two categories:

► **Technical tuning actions**
With technical tuning, all components belonging to the system are set up in such a way that the system can optimally process user loads, and no performance bottlenecks occur. The operating system, database, SAP application server, and networks are all subject to technical tuning.

► **Application tuning measures**
Application tuning works at the program level. The main emphasis is on checking application-specific procedures for requirements and effectiveness. The goal is to minimize the use of main memory and CPU resources, network transfers, and hard drive accesses.

Typical application tuning actions include the effective use of SAP transactions or performance-tuning of customer-developed ABAP programs. Technical tuning is necessary for each IT application, and this need grows proportionally with the size of the installation — in particular with regard to data volume and the number of users and customer-developed programs and modifications.

Whereas technical tuning optimally distributes the load generated by applications on the system, application tuning strives to keep system resources low, such as CPU consumption, main memory consumption, and I/O activity on the database server and application servers. This is usually a matter of setting applications as efficiently as possible to avoid unnecessary load on the system in the first place.

Therefore, within the context of workload analysis, a list is initially drawn up that shows transactions and programs that place heavy loads on the system and which of them could be optimized. These programs are then examined according to the following criteria:

► Which programs or transactions consume the most resources?

► Which SQL statements are putting a high load on the database? From which programs do these statements come?

The first tuning measure in application tuning is the efficient use of *standard SAP functions*. As a rule, there are many similar options for portraying business processes in SAP components. Among these (which only differ in technical implementation), some solutions are more and others less powerful, and their effects will result in higher or lower response times for the user. Any customizing done to the SAP component will also influence subsequent performance.

Another tuning measure is *program optimization*. This measure is mainly used for customer-developed programs, modifications of SAP standards, and user exits. Unfortunately, performance quality control for customer-developed programs is hardly ever done in SAP projects. More often than not, programs are written during the implementation phase, often by inexperienced developers or under a lot of time pressure, and tested with a completely unrepresentative dataset. As the dataset grows in production, the performance of these programs continuously deteriorates, finally leading to problems for the entire system. When this happens, the original developer is often not available, and any subsequent performance optimization involves extensive work.

Future performance must be considered, for both customizing and customer-developed programs and modifications, starting with the implementation of the SAP system. If a consultant partner carries out development work, this partner must be responsible not only for the functionality of developments, but also their performance.

There are also SAP Notes for SAP standard programs on adjusting coding to improve performance. You should consult the SAP Service Marketplace regularly to see if up-to-date error corrections or recommended modifications for your most important transactions are available. Search the SAP Service Marketplace for notes on your performance-critical transactions by using the key word "performance" and the corresponding transaction code program or table name.

Other options for reducing database load are the correct use of the SAP buffer and the definition of suitable database indexes (secondary indexes), which can greatly reduce the database load for read operations. Table buffering and indexes are already set when SAP components are installed. To optimize the runtime of individual programs, however, it

Optimizing standard SAP functions

Program optimization

Table buffering and indexing

may be necessary to change these default settings. The developer of customer-developed tables must always establish these settings.

Summary: It is better to avoid workload than distribute it.

Table 1.1 presents an overview of the most important tuning measures. The Person column lists the party responsible for each activity. M: IT management; S: those responsible for the system (administrators, basis expert); A: application consultant (employee of the department, application administrator, developer); U: user.

In general, there are several solutions for resolving a performance problem. When deciding which measures should be carried out and in what order, one rule of thumb is, It is better to avoid workload than distribute it. There are, of course, exceptions. In certain cases (or as a temporary solution), it might be better to compensate for inefficient customizing and inefficiently written customer programs with technical measures such as creating indexes, increasing the size of the buffer, or installing better and faster hardware. The actual list of measures for performance tuning must therefore be adapted according to the results of a performance analysis and by taking local circumstances into account.

Technical tuning	Person
Setting system parameters for operating system, database, and SAP Basis system (database buffer, SAP buffer, number of work processes, and so on)	S
Optimization of the database layout (I/O balancing)	S
Definition of daily, weekly, and monthly workload distribution (for example, background processing, logon groups)	A, S, U, M
Installation of additional and more powerful hardware	S, M
Application tuning	
Looking for and applying SAP Notes from the SAP Service Marketplace (patches, error correction, or recommended modifications)	A, S
Optimizing the customizing of standard SAP transactions to improve performance	A
Optimizing coding for customer-developed programs and modifications	A
Defining table buffering	A, S
Creating, changing, or deleting secondary indexes	A, S

Table 1.1 Tuning Measures

Example: Technical Tuning and Application Tuning

The following example explains the interplay between technical and application optimization. It shows a performance analysis and a range of possible measures for optimization. The technical details of the analysis are purposely omitted.

Imagine a situation where SAP ERP system users are complaining of massive performance problems in Production Planning (PP), for example, in the creation of requirement and stock lists. **[Ex]**

A performance analysis has come up with the following results:

▶ The SAP work process overview shows that several programs repeatedly spend a long time reading from table RESB.

▶ An analysis of the database shows that all tables with transaction data reside on one hard drive. Together, all transaction data amounts to 8GB, of which table RESB accounts for 2 GB.

▶ The operating system monitor shows that the hard drive on which (among other things) the RESB table resides is fully loaded (80 to 100% load; and response times of over 100 ms per access).

System administrators and application consultants sit down together to solve the problem. From the system administrator's point of view, they need to discuss the following technical solution strategies:

▶ They could make the data buffer on the database server so that it would be able to hold a large part of the RESB table on the main memory of the database server. **Measures for system support**

▶ They could place the RESB table on a separate hard drive. They could also change the database hard drive layout so that the RESB table can be distributed over several hard drives.

▶ Using the available-to-promise (ATP) server would make it possible to buffer partial RESB table results on the application server main memory and thereby reduce database accesses to this table.

▶ As a last resort, they could consider installing faster hard drives.

The RESB table contains the reservation and dependent requirements of materials, components, and assemblies used in production planning. It is read during availability checks, in particular. Skillful customizing of the **Measures for application support** availability check might reduce the size and read frequency of the RESB table. From the application administrator's point of view, the following issues must be examined:

▸ Could the availability check be simplified for some materials? Examples of this are screws, cable ties, and other small parts that are used in all products. Is it really necessary to check the availability of these materials for each production order, or can an individual check for this type of material be deactivated? This measure would reduce the expansion of the RESB table and the frequency of accesses to it and as a result increase the performance of the availability check.

▸ How often is the content of the RESB table archived and deleted? Is there still very old planning data in the table?

▸ The RESB table also contains future planning data. Is the excessive table growth due to planning that goes too far into the future?

It is evident that, given the many possible measures, system administrators and application consultants must work out a solution together. The most effective method for optimizing performance is often to deactivate unnecessary application functions. The application administrator needs the system administrator's analyses to know what should be deactivated or simplified by customizing. Therefore, a joint effort is necessary to find the best solution.

1.2.4 Tools and Methods for the Monitoring and Optimization Plan

The SAP Basis system includes a range of powerful programs for monitoring and analysis, which are constantly being added by SAP. These include component-specific, local tools that experts (of the respective components at SAP) have developed for experts (for use in the field).

They are complemented by central tools that are indispensable for the standardized and cost-efficient operation of larger landscapes: central SAP Alert Monitor, central SAP NetWeaver Administrator, and SAP Solution Manager.

The *expert monitors* for performance analysis of the ABAP server are available in the performance menu (Transaction STUN) of the Computer Center Management System (CCMS):

Performance analysis expert monitors

ADMINISTRATION • SYSTEM ADMINISTRATION • MONITOR • PERFORMANCE or ADMINISTRATION • CCMS • CONTROL/MONITORING • PERFORMANCE

You can find the monitors for the SAP J2EE Engine in the SAP management console and in the local SAP NetWeaver Administrator at *http://<sapserver>:<port>/nwa*, where *<sapserver>* is the name of an application server on which the SAP J2EE Engine is running, and *<port>* is the TCP/IP port to which the dispatcher answers.

Table 1.2 lists the performance monitors available for analyzing SAP Basis and other applications.

Monitors for Technical Analysis	
Operating system monitor (ST06)	Monitors the utilization of the CPU and the physical main memory.
Database monitor (ABAP: ST04; Java: SAP NetWeaver Administrator)	Monitors the utilization of the database buffer; database locks, and other wait situations; write and read accesses to hard drives; monitoring of SQL statements.
SAP memory configuration monitor (setup/buffers, ST02)	Monitors the load on the SAP buffer and other memory areas and SAP work processes
Work process overview (SM50)	Monitors the load on SAP work processes.
Workload monitor (ST03, ST03N, ST03G)	Overviews load distribution in the SAP system. In a technical analysis, for example, problems on the database, in SAP memory management, or SAP buffers can be identified and analyzed.
SAP Management Console (SAP MC)	Load and memory requirement (garbage collection) of the work processes in the Java Virtual Machine.
ICM monitor (SMICM)	Load, memory requirement, and HTTP trace of the Internet Communication Manager.
ITS monitor (SITSPMON)	Load and memory requirement of the Internet Transaction Server.

Table 1.2 SAP Performance Monitors

Monitors for Technical Analysis	
Workload monitor (ST03, ST03N, ST03G) and single record statistics (STAD, STATTRACE)	Overviews load distribution in the SAP system. In an application analysis, transactions, programs, and users that place heavy loads on the system can be identified and analyzed.
Application monitor (ST07, ST14)	Monitors the use of resources according to SAP modules.
SQL Trace (ABAP: ST05; Java: SAP NetWeaver Administrator) ABAP Trace (SE30) Java Trace (Introscope)	Trace functions for a detailed analysis of ABAP and Java programs.

Table 1.2 SAP Performance Monitors (Cont.)

Central SAP monitor and SAP NetWeaver Administrator

Continuous system monitoring checks that all components are available and working well. If this is not the case, an alarm is triggered. You can automate continuous monitoring using the central monitoring architecture. You can use the central Alter Monitor (Transaction RZ20) in CCMS. Define one SAP system as the central monitoring system, and error reports from all SAP components will be sent to this system. Until now, data on the ABAP instances, the SAP J2EE Engine, databases, operating systems, and other SAP components such as the ITS have been linked in the *central Alert Monitor*. Other data suppliers are also available for non-SAP components. As of SAP NetWeaver 2004, the central Alert Monitor has been integrated into the user interface of the central SAP NetWeaver Administrator and can now be used directly from there.

Interfaces

All SAP performance monitors have open *interfaces* that enable SAP partners to call up SAP system–related performance data. This means that if you use external system management software for monitoring, you can access SAP performance data, so you can monitor your SAP solution system-wide. Examples of monitoring tools that can access SAP performance data include OpenView (HP), Tivoli (IBM), and Patrol (BMC Software). Note that only system monitoring is possible with these products (we call this the *outside-in* approach). With these products, it is not possible to monitor applications. We will deal with this in greater detail in the next section.

1.2.5   SAP Solution Manager

SAP Solution Manager provides SAP customers and partners with tools and procedures to support all SAP solutions over their entire lifecycles. In this way, customers can use SAP Business Suite to its full potential.

SAP Solution Manager for Monitoring

From day-to-day life, you know that even the best tool kit is of no use if the person using it does not have the necessary skill to use those tools. In addition to the well-known SAP media that has educated customers and partners up to now (including SAP online help, training courses, SAP Service Marketplace with SAP Notes, other documentation — and, of course, this book), since 2001, SAP has also provided partners and customers with service procedures. These let you implement SAP solutions efficiently and put them to productive use.

SAP Solution Manager is the portal for accessing these services, and it gives you centralized access to tools and service procedures for performance monitoring and optimization. In technical terms, SAP Solution Manager (in its current version 7.0) consists of an SAP NetWeaver Application Server, an SAP CRM system preconfigured for the IT service operation, and a service add-on with additional functionality for IT service and application management. The diagnostics functions, which we will describe in great detail in this section, run on the Java part of SAP NetWeaver Application Server. With SAP Solution Manager, you can monitor and optimize SAP systems (starting with SAP Basis 3.1).

A core element of SAP Solution Manager is solution monitoring, which makes it possible to monitor SAP solutions. Unlike classic system monitoring, which is limited to hardware elements and software components, solution monitoring checks the functionality of the entire business process. The solution monitoring method comprises three steps: The first step covers the most important business processes and the implementation of these as an SAP solution to identify which hardware and software components participate in the solution. In the second step, it is determined which indicators (for example, response times or error messages) should be monitored to ensure problem-free operation. To this end, SAP delivers templates for each business process with a standardized moni-

Solution monitoring

toring plan. These templates can be downloaded from the SAP Service Marketplace to SAP Solution Manager and adapted to the needs of the customer so that an individual monitoring plan can be created with minimum effort. In the third step, a monitoring plan suited to the customer's business processes emerges. Figure 1.7 displays a graphical representation of a business process and its status in the form of alarm symbols (in this case, green checkmarks and red lightning bolts). The business process graphics make it easier to find your way around a monitor, and you can see at first glance whether or not a particular business process is affected by an error. For the Create Outbound Delivery step, a (red) lightning bolt symbol is displayed that indicates a serious error has occurred in this component. You can then navigate to the corresponding expert monitor via the graphic.

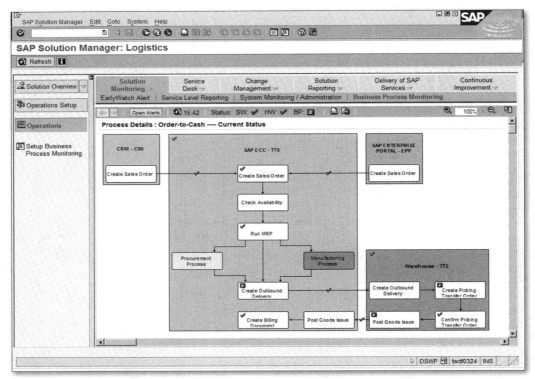

Figure 1.7 Business Process Graphic in SAP Solution Manager with Error Messages

The SAP EarlyWatch Alert service, already used by most customers, is also an element of solution monitoring, as is service-level management based on monitoring data. One important feature that differentiates solution monitoring in SAP Solution Manager from monitoring in previous system management programs is that SAP Solution Manager focuses on the business process. It considers the network of relationships that exists between software components when a business process runs over several software components. Previously, system management only monitored components individually, without recognizing the relationships between them. Therefore, we could say that SAP Solution Manager monitors a business process practically from the inside, whereas previous system monitoring only provided monitoring from the outside.

SAP Solution Manager for Analysis

As of version 7.0, SAP Solution Manager provides cross-component workload analysis and tracing using the search term "end-to-end diagnostics." The cross-component workload analysis summarizes the performance data of all components participating in a solution and displays it in the user interface. For cross-component tracing, it is possible to centrally activate a trace for a transaction in the user interface, in other words, in the web browser or SAP GUI, which is then distributed to the participating components via the data flow. So if a user activates a trace, each component activates its trace locally and stores it under a specific ID. SAP Solution Manager then collects the trace data and provides it for central evaluation. You can activate different trace levels for this purpose.

End-to-end diagnostics

Cross-component tracing has numerous benefits over local tracing:

Cross-component tracing vs. local tracing

► The person implementing the tracing doesn't have to be familiar with the specific properties of the trace, because activation and deactivation, as well as reading, are done by a central tool.

► When transferring requests via the components, the user might change, for example, to a service user. Consequently, for traditional tracing, activation of the trace is only possible to a limited extent or not at all. Cross-component traces are activated specifically for the request, independent of the technical user.

► If you use load distribution during the creation of the trace, you won't know to which instances the request will be distributed; this particularly applies if the request runs across multiple components. In traditional tracing, you usually have to activate tracing for all instances and then manually select the instances on which the request has been processed. In this case, tracing is very laborious or sometimes even impossible. In cross-component tracing, the traces are activated for the instances on which the request is processed.

SAP Solution Manager for Optimization

SAP Solution Manager helps you not only with performance monitoring, but also with performance optimization. For example, let's assume that monitoring has found numerous, expensive SQL statements that are placing a high load on your database, frequently leading to bottlenecks. The SAP EarlyWatch Alert service identifies the statements in question and recommends a service that should be carried out to optimize SQL statements. This service can also be downloaded from SAP Service Marketplace to SAP Solution Manager and executed there. SAP Solution Manager interacts with your system landscape on the one hand to load the necessary statistics and other data, and on the other hand, it interacts with the agent that carries out the service. Using a repetitive procedure, it finds ways to improve performance. Clearly, this type of service program can be much more detailed than (for example) this book or a training course. The service mentioned here for optimizing SQL statements covers over 500 individual optimization possibilities — beginning with common pitfalls and misused features in database software — with recommendations for everything from optimizing indexes to reformulating SQL statements. From these 500 cases, the agent will certainly be able to find those that apply to the problem at hand.

In addition to service procedures that help you optimize during production, other service procedures help achieve an optimal setting for your system landscape, right from implementation. In this case, SAP Solution Manager also works with both the system and the agent, which can achieve optimal configuration with the help of the service.

Carrying out services After you have downloaded the service procedures from SAP Service Marketplace onto SAP Solution Manager, you can in principle carry out these services yourself. Alternatively, you can have them provided by SAP or your service partner as remote or on-site services. Depending on your needs, you can decide to either build up specific know-how within your organization or acquire it externally. For example, this choice exists for SAP EarlyWatch Alert, which has been available as a remote service since 1984. It is provided by SAP and numerous service partners (including the most critical hardware partners of SAP). Since 2001, employees of SAP customers have also been able to take part in a training course and qualify for certification in SAP EarlyWatch Alert so they can perform the service in their own enterprises. As a result, customers can choose to build up this know-how in-house or, as in the past, use external providers. Your service and support center can give you details on service provision.

Summary: SAP Solution Manager

Table 1.3 explains the most important services in SAP Solution Manager as regards performance monitoring and optimization. Your service and support center can give you further details, or you can find more information online at *http://service.sap.com/solutionmanager*.

Service	Objective	Prerequisites	See Also Chapters
Solution monitoring	Monitoring an SAP solution	Certified technical consultant (recommended)	1, 2
Service-level management	Reporting on whether or not objectives regarding availability, performance, and error situations are achieved	Certified technical consultant (recommended)	1, 3
End-to-end diagnostics	Cross-component workload analysis and tracing (end-to-end)	Certified technical consultant (recommended)	3, 4, 7
SAP EarlyWatch Alert	Identifying medium- and long-term optimization potentials	Certified technical consultant (recommended)	1, 2, 3

Table 1.3 SAP Solution Manager Services in the Area of Performance Monitoring and Optimization

Service	Objective	Prerequisites	See Also Chapters
SAP EarlyWatch	Detailed system analysis and optimization	Service-specific certification (SAP EarlyWatch)	All
Customer program optimization	Optimization of customer-developed programs	Service-specific certification	4, 9, 10, 11
SQL statement optimization	Optimizing SQL statements	Service-specific certification	2, 9, 11
System administration	Optimization of system administration, including service-level management and monitoring	Service-specific certification	1, 2, 3
Storage subsystem optimization	Optimization of the storage system with regard to configuration and data distribution		
Interface management	Optimization of interfaces	Service-specific certification	6, 7
Data management and archiving	Reduction of occurring data by avoiding data (optimized customizing) and archiving	Service-specific certification	
Business process performance optimization	Optimizing performance of processes	Service-specific certification	
Business process management	Optimization of business processes	Service-specific certification	
SAP GoingLive Check	Checking transition to production operation	Service-specific certification	All
SAP GoingLive Functional Upgrade Check	Verify production operation after a software upgrade	Service-specific certification	All

Table 1.3 SAP Solution Manager Services in the Area of Performance Monitoring and Optimization (Cont.)

1.3   Summary

There are two essential prerequisites for sound system performance:

► The cooperation of everyone involved in setting up an SAP solution and in the execution and administration of customizing or developments.

► Long-term planning of performance monitoring and optimization. For this you can use service-level management methods and the central monitoring architecture of CCMS in SAP Solution Manager.

What are the concrete advantages of a structured monitoring and optimization plan? First, clearly defined and measurable goals and communication structures improve the IT organization's understanding of the requirements of end users and business process owners. The quality of the IT organization's service improves, because it can work in a more purposeful way; and as a result, customer satisfaction also increases. Indirectly, service-level reporting makes the current cost structure (for example, use of hardware and IT) transparent and allows for forecasting. Finally, well-executed service-level management should have a positive effect on IT employee motivation because, given clear objectives, they can see that they are doing everything possible to achieve a high level of customer satisfaction. (Anyone who has experienced the often-indiscriminate finger-pointing in IT organizations knows the frustration employees feel when they have subjectively done their best and can well understand this point!)

The tasks of performance monitoring and optimization are carried out by very different people. Employees who carry out error monitoring and generate service-level reports generally have a good basic understanding of the technology and applications but don't normally have specialized knowledge. This is because system monitoring must be maintained 24 hours per day, 7 days per week, and specialists from all areas cannot be available for these tasks at all times. During monitoring or service-level reporting, a help desk employee or manager must be in a position to decide whether a specialist should be consulted. In other words, you should not need a database expert to decide whether a database expert is needed.

The planning or arrangement of monitoring and the continuous optimization of the application, on the other hand, generally require more extensive, specialized knowledge. Technical tuning requires knowledge of the operating system, the database, and the SAP Basis system. Consequently, it is usually carried out by an SAP Basis administrator or SAP Basis consultant. If necessary, database and network administrators are available to help.

Application tuning requires broader knowledge of the SAP solution and SAP technology:

▶ Knowledge of the database will help in the decision to create additional database indexes or how to formulate SQL statements effectively.

▶ Knowledge of SAP Basis (ABAP runtime environment) will help you buffer tables optimally.

▶ Knowledge of SAP Basis (J2EE runtime environment) will help you optimize the creation of dynamic HTML pages with regard to the network load and rendering time.

▶ Knowledge of the ABAP programming language will help you use ABAP commands effectively.

▶ Knowledge of the SAP solutions will help ensure that SAP programs and transactions are used effectively.

▶ Knowledge of business processes within the enterprise will help you recognize time-critical processes and adapt important transactions to suit users.

It is generally impossible for one person to have such broad expertise in the SAP system. Therefore, it is important to form teams. For a large SAP project, it is necessary to set up a *performance forum* to ensure regular meetings between people who represent the various aspects of performance optimization.

Important Concepts in this Chapter

After reading this chapter, you should be familiar with the following concepts:

- SAP solutions and SAP software components
- Client/server technology and SAP NetWeaver Application Server
- SAP Solution Manager
- Central CCMS Alert Monitor
- Service-level management

2 Monitoring Hardware, Databases, and SAP Basis

This chapter provides the basic information on how to monitor and analyze the performance of your hardware, database, SAP memory configuration, and SAP work processes of the ABAP runtime environment, as well as the Java virtual machine of the Java runtime environment. Procedure roadmaps at the end of each section summarize the most important analysis paths and clarify when to use the various monitors. The last section describes the central Alert Monitor, which integrates the performance indicators from all areas.

This chapter will provide simple recommendations to help you optimize each component, except where in-depth explanations are required (these are given in subsequent chapters). Unnecessary background information is intentionally kept to a minimum so that even application consultants or system administrators with limited experience in performance analysis can use this chapter to improve the performance of their system. For example, we describe monitoring and customizing SAP extended memory without explaining SAP extended memory in detail. You can find more detailed information in Chapters 5 through 9. Our experience suggests that you can solve many performance problems in the operating system, database, and SAP Basis by using simple instructions, without delving into technical details.

When Should You Read this Chapter?

You should read this chapter if you want to use your SAP system to technically monitor and optimize the performance of your SAP system, database, or operating system.

2.1 Basic Terms

This section explains how the terms *computer, server, application server, SAP instance, database, database server,* and *database instance* are used throughout this book:

Computer will always mean a physical machine with a CPU, main memory, IP address, and so on.

SAP application instance

An *SAP application instance,* also referred to as an *SAP instance,* is a logical unit. It consists of a set of SAP work processes that are administered by a dispatcher. It also includes a set of SAP buffers located in the host computer's shared memory and accessed by the work processes. An SAP application instance can be an ABAP or Java application instance (SAP J2EE Engine). There can be multiple SAP instances on one computer. As a result, there will be multiple dispatchers and sets of buffers. An *application server* is a computer with one or more SAP instances.

Database

Every SAP system has only one database. The term *database* refers to a set of data that is organized into files, for example. The database can be thought of as the passive part of the database system.

The active part of the database system is the *database instance,* a logical unit that allows access to the database. A database instance consists of database processes with a common set of buffers in the shared memory of a computer. A *database server* is a computer with one or more database instances. A computer can be both a database server and an application server if a database instance and an SAP instance run on it.

In the SAP environment, there is normally only one database instance for each database. Examples of database systems where multiple database instances can access a database are DB2 and Oracle Parallel Server. This book does not cover the special features of these *parallel database systems.*

SAP systems

We refer to SAP software components as *SAP systems,* which are based on SAP Basis. These are SAP ERP, SAP NetWeaver BW, SAP APO, SAP SRM, and SAP NetWeaver Portal.

According to this terminology, an SAP ERP system can consist of one or two systems, depending on whether the Java and ABAP parts run on a joint system with one database (for example, SAP NetWeaver double stack) or on two systems with separate databases. This terminology also applies to SAP Solution Manager.

SAP documentation and literature use the term *server* in both a hardware sense and a software sense. Therefore, the term can refer to a computer, for example, in the term *database server,* and to a logical service, such as in the terms *message server* and *ATP server*.

2.2   Hardware Monitoring

The operating system monitor analyzes hardware bottlenecks and operating system problems. To start the operating system monitor for the application server you are currently logged on to, select: TOOLS • ADMINISTRATION • MONITOR • PERFORMANCE • OPERATING SYSTEM • LOCAL • ACTIVITY or enter Transaction ST06. The main screen of the operating system monitor will appear.

The operating system monitor was revised for SAP Basis version 7.10.   **[+]**
Since the revision, the Transactions OS06, OS07, and ST06 open a monitor that you can use to monitor both the local and remote computers. Up to version 6.20, the revision is available as a preliminary correction with SAP Note 994025. For versions prior to 7.10, the new transactions are available under Transactions OS06N, OS07N, and ST06N; with Transactions OS06, OS07, and ST06 you can still access the older transactions. All information discussed in this book is also available in the old transactions. You can view the detail analyses by clicking the DETAIL ANALYSIS MENU button.

Alternatively, you can call the operating system monitor from the server overview using Transaction SM51 or by selecting TOOLS • ADMINISTRATION • MONITOR • SYSTEM MONITORING • SERVER (Transaction SM51). Mark the application server you want and select GOTO • SERVER • OS MONITOR.

The operating system monitor screen (Figure 2.1) is divided into three areas. In the top-left window, you can view the list of computers that are monitored and select a computer for analysis. In the lower-left window, you select the analysis data. The window on the right contains data on the selected computer and the selected analysis. Table 2.1 explains the fields on this screen in more detail.

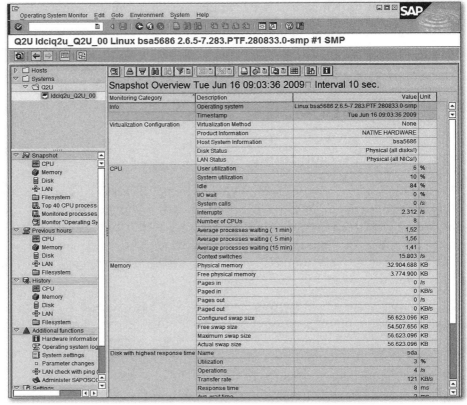

Figure 2.1 Main Screen of the Operating System Monitor

Field	Explanation
User Utilization	CPU workload caused by user processes (SAP system, database, etc.)
System Utilization	CPU workload caused by the operating system
Idle	Free CPU capacity; this value should be at least 20%, optimally 35%
Number of CPUs	Number of CPU threads
Average Processes Waiting	Number of processes waiting for CPUs, averaged over 1, 5, or 15 minutes
Physical Memory	Available physical main memory (RAM) in KB

Table 2.1 Operating System Monitor Fields

By default, the selection list shows all machines on which SAP instances with ABAP servers have been installed. Essentially, any computer can be integrated into the remote operating system monitor, provided a monitoring agent has been installed in that machine. We strongly recommend installing monitoring agents on machines that run a stand-alone database, an SAP J2EE Engine, TREX, or an ITS.

You should install this monitor even if you use a tool from a different vendor to monitor utilization of your computers. If you need support from SAP, an SAP expert can analyze the computers only with the SAP-proprietary monitor.

[!]

2.2.1 Analyzing a Hardware Bottleneck (CPU and Main Memory)

Under SNAPSHOT in the analysis selection, you can find an overview of the most critical operating system and hardware data. All data is refreshed every 10 seconds by the auxiliary program, `saposcol`. To update the data on the screen (after 10 seconds or longer), you need to click the corresponding button.

CPU workloadUnder the header CPU in the operating system monitor initial screen, you'll find the fields USER UTILIZATION, SYSTEM UTILIZATION, and IDLE. These values indicate the percentage of total CPU capacity currently being used by user processes (the SAP system, database, and other processes), the percentage being used by the operating system itself, and the percentage not being used. The NUMBER OF CPUs field indicates the number of CPU threads. AVERAGE Processes Waiting is the average number of work processes waiting for a free processor and is indicated for the previous minute, 5 minutes, and 15 minutes. The other values listed under CPU are less significant for analyzing system performance.

> **Background: Processors, Cores, and Threads**
>
> As a description of the computer equipment, you can find the following specifications, for example: "2 processors, 8 cores, 16 threads, processor of manufacturer X with 2.93 GHz clock speed." But what does this information on the number of processors, cores, and threads mean for the SAP system?

The term *processor* refers to the *central processing unit* (CPU) of a computer, which is capable of executing programs. Here, a distinction is made between single-core processors and multicore processors. Multicore processors have multiple fully developed processing cores on one chip. The individual cores only share the bus; that is, they are considered as full CPUs. Multithreaded CPUs have *one* CPU but register as *multiple* CPUs to the operating system. As a result, various queues exist for these cores between which the core switches. To optimize this switching, each thread has its own register set, including a stack pointer and program counter so you can switch between the threads without additional processor cycles. These hardware-based threads should not be confused with the threads that generate the application processes (user or software threads). Within a process of the database or the ABAP, Java, or TREX server, you can generate multiple (software) threads that the operating system executes in time slices. The switch between the (software) threads is referred to as a *context switch*. Considering this, it can be assumed that additional (hardware) threads promote context switches between (software) threads and therefore support a better utilization of the existing core; however, the increase in performance doesn't fully come up to an additional core.

Main memory workload

Under the MEMORY header in the operating system monitor initial screen, you'll find the amount of available physical main memory (PHYS-ICAL MEMORY field), the operating system paging rates, and paged data quantities.

Swap space

Under the header SWAP, the amount of currently allocated *swap space is listed*. The swap space must be greater than the total of the configured memory area.

[+] If the sum of the physical memory and swap space is smaller than the total amount of memory required by the SAP system, database, and other programs, this may cause program terminations or even operating system failure. You should therefore ensure that there is sufficient swap space.

History: CPU and main memory

To display the CPU workload over the previous 24 hours, select the analysis PREVIOUS HOURS • CPU.

The PREVIOUS HOURS CPU screen is displayed. The column headers are the same as in the fields under CPU in the operating system monitor initial screen, except that the values are for one hour. A similar overview is available for main memory usage (PREVIOUS HOURS • MEMORY), for the swap space, and so on.

When Is There a CPU or Main Memory Bottleneck?

The unused CPU capacity (idle) should normally average at least 20% per hour. This enables the system to accommodate temporary workload peaks. A reading of 35% idle CPU capacity is even better. For the paging rate, the following guideline values apply:

▶ For computers that contain a database, an SAP J2EE Engine, or TREX, only very minor paging rates should occur; that is, they should be dimensioned in such a way that the available main memory corresponds to the configured memory areas.

▶ For computers that only include ABAP instances, you can tolerate moderate paging rates of up to 20% of the physical main memory per hour.

For operating systems that page asynchronously (for example, Windows), the value indicated in the operating system monitor as paged-in rate is the key statistic on paging performance. For other operating systems that page only when necessary (such as most UNIX derivatives), the key statistic is the *paged-out rate*.

If the operating system monitor sometimes shows values that exceed these guideline values, this does not automatically mean you have a hardware bottleneck. Rather, you should use the workload monitor to check whether the high CPU workload or the paging rate is associated with poor response times. Corresponding analyses can be found in Chapter 3, Section 3.4.1, Analyzing General Performance Problems.

If you observe high paging rates on several computers, calculate the virtual main memory allocated to the SAP instances and the database. (To calculate the virtual memory, see Sections 2.4.3, Displaying Allocated Memory, and 2.3.1, Analyzing the Database Buffer) Compare this with the available physical main memory. As a rule of thumb, there should be approximately 50% more virtual memory than physical memory.

Main memory bottleneck

In Windows and Solaris operating systems, the analysis of the paging rate on the database server can lead to misinterpretation, because in

[Ex]

these operating systems, read/write operations (I/O) can sometimes be counted as paging. For more information on this issue, please refer to SAP Notes 124199 (Solaris) and 689818 (Windows).

Causes of Hardware Bottlenecks

If you detect a hardware bottleneck on one or more SAP system computers, it may be due to one or more of several causes.

Nonoptimal load distribution
In a distributed system with multiple computers, if you discover a hardware bottleneck on at least one computer, whereas other computers have unused resources, the workload is probably not optimally distributed. To improve performance, redistribute the SAP work processes and the user logons.

It is extremely important that the database server has enough resources. A CPU or main memory bottleneck on the database server means the required data cannot be retrieved quickly from the database, which causes poor response times in the entire system.

CPU load of individual programs
In the operating system monitor (Transaction ST06) select the analysis SNAPSHOT • TOP CPU PROCESSES. The overview of the operating system processes is displayed. Here you can see all processes currently active and their demands on resources. Figure 2.2 shows such an overview for a system in which an ABAP server, an SAP J2EE Engine, a MaxDB database, and TREX are installed on a Linux operating system. You can identify the following processes:

- **"dw_<instance>"**
  SAP work process of the ABAP Server on a UNIX operating system. On Windows operating systems, the name is "disp+work."

- **"jstart ... "**
  Work process of the SAP J2EE Engine/

- **"TREX ... "**
  TREX process. The server type is indicated in the process name, for instance, index server, preprocessor, and so on

- **"icman ... "**
  Process of the Internet Communication Manager (ICM).

▶ **"Kernel ... "**

Database process of the MaxDB database. The processes of other databases normally carry the brand name (such as Oracle or Informix), which appears in the process or user name.

▶ **"saposcol ... "**

Auxiliary program, which collects the data for the operating system monitor, for example.

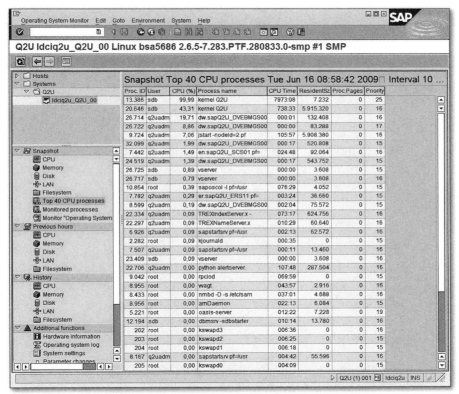

Figure 2.2 Analysis of the Top CPU Processes in the Operating System Monitor

To check whether individual processes are placing a heavy load on the CPU for long periods of time, refresh the monitor periodically and observe any changes in the value CPU (%). If the processes that place a heavy load on the CPU entail processes of SAP Basis or the database, the subsequent monitors provide further information on the processes' activities. Start the monitor in a second mode, identify the process with the heavy CPU load using the process ID, which you can also find in the corresponding basis monitors, and check the monitors to determine which program or tables, queries, and so on are being processed by the process.

▶ **SAP work processes**
Open a new user session and call the local work process overview (see Section 2.5, Analyzing SAP Work Processes). From the work process overview, note the name of the ABAP program and the user corresponding to the process identifier (PID).

▶ **Work process of the SAP J2EE Engine**
Open the SAP Management Console (see Section 2.6, Analyzing Java Virtual Machine (JVM) Memory Management and Work Processes). Use a thread dump to obtain process-internal information.

▶ **TREX processes**
Open the TREX administration tool (see Chapter 13, Section 13.2, Implementing the Performance Analysis on TREX). You can find details on the TREX services in the SERVICES monitor.

▶ **ICM**
Open the ICM monitor (see Section 2.7, Analysis of the Internet Communication Manager (ICM)).

▶ **Database processes**
Open the database process monitor in the Database Administration (DBA) Cockpit (see Section 2.3.2, Identifying and Analyzing Expensive SQL Statements) to identify the SQL statements that are being processed by the database.

Using the operating system monitor in conjunction with the monitors mentioned, you can fairly easily identify programs, transactions, and SQL statements that cause high CPU load.

External processes   *External processes* can also cause a CPU bottleneck. In the operating system monitor, if you find external processes (that is, processes that are not part of the SAP system) with high CPU consumption that cause a CPU bottleneck, you should find out whether these processes are really necessary for your system or whether they can be switched off or moved to another computer. Examples of external processes are administrative software, virus scanners, backups, external systems, screen savers, and so on.

Suppose you notice a CPU bottleneck during times of peak user activity. The process overview in the operating system monitor reveals a single SAP work process that is causing a CPU load of 30% over several minutes. At the same time, the SAP work process overview shows a long-running background program. You should try to see if the background program could be run at a time when the dialog load is lighter.

[Ex]

To identify programs with high memory requirements that may be causing a main memory bottleneck, you can use a method similar to that previously described for CPU bottlenecks (see also Chapter 8, Memory Management).

Memory requirement of individual programs

Operating systems normally administer their own *file system cache*. This cache is located in the main memory, where it competes for memory space with the SAP system and the database. If the cache is too large, it causes high paging rates, even though the physical main memory is more than large enough to accommodate both the SAP system and the database. SAP recommends reducing this cache to between 7 and 10% of the physical memory.

Minimize file system cache

The operating system parameters for configuring the file system cache include `dbc_max_pct` for HP-UX, `ubc-maxpercent` for Digital UNIX, and `maxperm` for AIX.

UNIX

To reduce the size of the file system cache for Windows, from the screen (symbol: NETWORK) in the control panel of your Windows operating system, select the Services tab and the Server service, and click the Properties button. In the following screen, under the screen area OPTIMIZATION, select the MAXIMIZE THROUGHPUT FOR NETWORK APPLICATIONS option, and confirm by clicking OK. You must reboot the computer to activate the file cache's new settings.

Windows

A main memory bottleneck creates excessive paging, which in turn requires more processor use and can lead to a CPU bottleneck. Removing the cause of excessive paging usually makes the CPU bottleneck disappear.

2.2.2 Identifying Read/Write (I/O) Problems

In the operating system monitor (Transaction ST06), in the analysis view (SNAPSHOT • DISK), you'll find, among other things, information on hard disk load and (if the operating system makes it available) information on the disks' wait and response times.

By double-clicking a row in the hard disk monitor (listed in Table 2.2), you can display an overview of the average response times over the previous 24 hours for the selected hard disk.

Field	Explanation
Disk	Operating system name of the hard disk
Utilization (%)	Load on the hard disk (in %)
Queue Length	Number of processes waiting for I/O operations
Wait Time (ms)	Wait time (in msec)
Service Time (ms)	Service time (in msec)
Transfer (Kbyte/s)	Transfer rate (in Kbyte/second)
Operations (per Sec)	Number of I/O operations (per second)
Response Time (ms)	Average response times of the hard disk (in msec)

Table 2.2 Fields of the Hard Disk Monitor

I/O bottleneck

In the hard disk monitor, a heavy load on an individual disk is signified by a value greater than 50% in the UTILIZATION (%) column. This may indicate an *I/O bottleneck*. However, you can only get limited information about I/O problems from the SAP system. To perform a more detailed analysis, you need tools provided by the hardware manufacturer.

An I/O bottleneck is particularly critical if it is on the hard disk where the operating system's paging file resides. Monitoring is particularly recommended for the database server disks. To prevent bottlenecks during read or write operations to the database, use the database performance monitor and the hard disk monitor. For further details on these problems, please see Section 2.3.3, Identifying Read/Write (I/O) Problems.

2.2.3   Other Checks with the Operating System Monitor

For UNIX operating systems, the SAP system logs all operating system parameter changes. To display the log of these changes, from the operating system monitor, select OTHER FUNCTIONS • PARAMETER CHANGES. Place the cursor over the name of a server and click the HISTORY OF FILE BUTTON. This log lets you determine whether the start of performance problems can be linked to the time when particular parameters were changed.

Parameter changes

With the OTHER FUNCTIONS • LAN CHECK BY PING tool, you can carry out a quick test on the network. Select any database server, application server, or presentation server and test the network connection, for example, response times or whether there was any data loss. Although the analysis is incorrectly called LAN check, you can also address computers in WAN. You can find an example of an analysis with this tool in Chapter 7, Section 7.1.2, Analyzing and Optimizing the Performance of GUI Communication.

Network check

2.2.4   Summary

Performance problems may be indicated if:

▶ The average idle CPU capacity is less than 20% every hour.

▶ More than 20% of the physical main memory is paged every hour.

▶ Utilization of individual hard disks is more than 50%.

Excessive utilization of the hard disks, particularly on the database server, can cause system-wide performance problems. To check whether the high CPU load or the high paging rate significantly damages response times in the SAP system or the database, use the workload monitor (see Chapter 3, Section 3.4, Performing Workload Analyses).

Figures 2.3 and 2.4 show the procedure for analyzing a hardware bottleneck. A common solution for resolving bottlenecks is to redistribute the workload (for example, move work processes). Possible causes of a CPU bottleneck include inefficient applications, which can usually be identified in the database process monitor and the work process overview, and external processes that do not belong to an SAP instance or the database instance. You should always perform a complete performance analysis before deciding whether the existing hardware is sufficient for SAP system demands.

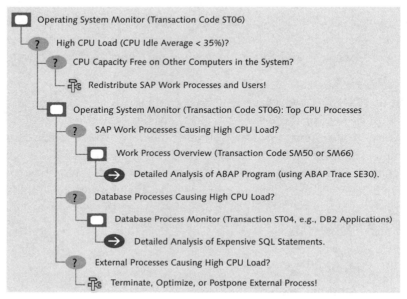

Figure 2.3 Detailed Analysis of a (CPU) Hardware Bottleneck

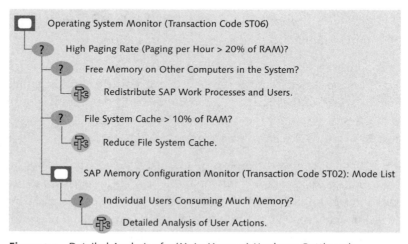

Figure 2.4 Detailed Analysis of a (Main Memory) Hardware Bottleneck

The roadmaps in Figures 2.3 and 2.4 show the procedure to follow in the event of a hardware bottleneck within the CPU and main memory, respectively. They refer to monitors and analyses described later in this book (which will have similar procedure roadmaps throughout). You can find a collection of all the roadmaps and an explanation of the symbols used in them in Appendix A.

2.3   Database Monitoring

The SAP system currently supports seven relational database systems, each of which has a different architecture. Many performance problems, however, occur independently of the type of database system implemented. To help customers analyze and tune their databases, the SAP system has its own database performance monitor with basic functions that work independently of the database system used.

The most important functions that you require for performance monitoring of the database include the following:

Basic functions of the database monitor

- ▶ Overview of the database buffers' status
- ▶ Overview of the currently running database operations, particularly the SQL statements
- ▶ Statistics on the SQL statements executed and their costs
- ▶ Overview of the distribution of read and write accesses at the logical (*tablespaces*) and physical level (for instance, *container* in DB2 for LUW or *datafiles* in Oracle) and therefore about the hard drives
- ▶ Overview of the current lock situations
- ▶ Overview of whether the database indexes and optimizer statistics are up to date
- ▶ Access to the database's error log and logging of parameter changes

The database performance monitor collects performance data from two sources:

- ▶ The monitor relies on performance data collected by the relevant database system. It also uses analytical functions. Every database user has access to these functions in a stand-alone database, and the results

Data sources

are only displayed in the SAP system. Functions developed by SAP or partner companies for monitoring SAP system performance can also be used to a certain extent.

▶ A portion of the performance data is entered and collected directly by the SAP system, for example, in the database interface for the SAP work processes.

You can find the database performance monitor in the Database Administration Cockpit, which you start with Transaction DBACOCKPIT or via the SAP menu Tools • CCMS • DB Administration • DBA Cockpit.

The DBA Cockpit: System Configuration Maintenance screen is displayed (see Figure 2.5). The Database Administration (DBA) Cockpit screen is divided into three areas. The upper-left area includes buttons to navigate to the system configuration and to select databases for monitoring, because from the DBA Cockpit you can manage various databases, for instance, the database of the ABAP system, SAP J2EE Engine, or liveCache.

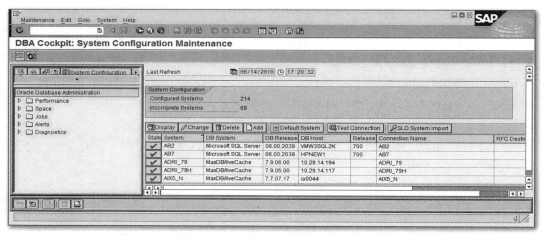

Figure 2.5 DBA Cockpit: System Configuration Maintenance

The lower-left area includes a navigation tree that takes you to the individual monitoring and administration functions. Besides the performance-relevant monitors in the Performance branch, you can find additional database administration functions, for instance, for data management. The area on the right comprises the monitor that you've selected via the navigation tree.

The database monitor has been completely revised for Basis version 7.0. **[+]**
It replaces the old transaction codes for database performance (ST04),
database locks (DB01), data management (DB02), and planning calendar
and database jobs (DB12, DB13, DB13C, and DB24). This section presents the new monitor as an example for Oracle databases (Figure 2.6).
Appendix B provides information and notes on the other databases and
the database monitors on the SAP J2EE Engine.

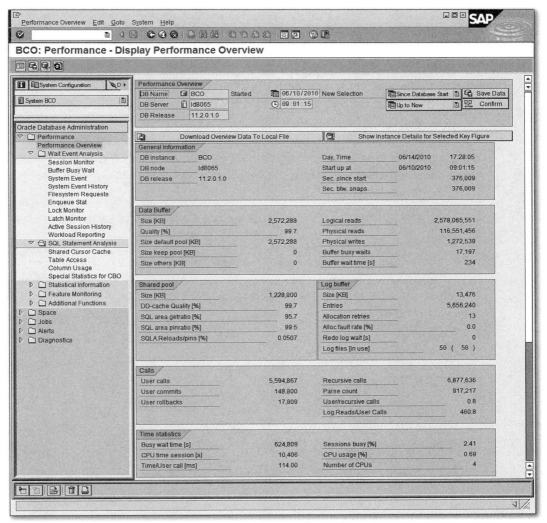

Figure 2.6 Main Screen of the Database Monitor for an Oracle Database

2.3.1 Analyzing the Database Buffer

Every database has various *buffers* that enable user data (for example, from tables) and administrative information from the database to be stored in main memory and, as a result, reduce the number of accesses to the hard disk. Accessing buffers in main memory is normally 10 to 100 times faster than accessing the hard disk. If the buffers are too small, the data volume will be too large for the buffer. Data will be forced out of the buffer and must be read again (reloaded) from the hard disk. Therefore, monitoring buffer activity is an important element of performance analysis. You can find the information needed for monitoring the buffer analyzing all databases.

Data buffer
The most important buffer in a database is the *data buffer,* also referred to as the *data cache* or *buffer pool*. It stores parts of the most recently read database tables and their indexes. It is first stored temporarily in the data buffer. The data buffer is divided into *blocks* or *pages,* which can be 2 to 32KB in size, depending on the database and operating system. Data is read from the hard disk in blocks or pages and then stored in the data buffer.

The following values characterize the quality of data buffer accesses:

- **Physical read accesses**
  Number of read accesses to the hard disk. This value indicates how many blocks or pages must be loaded to satisfy user queries being processed in an SAP work process.

- **Logical read accesses**
  Total number of read accesses. This figure indicates how many blocks or pages are read from the buffer *and* the hard disk.

- **Buffer quality or hit ratio**
  This value is derived by the following equation:

Buffer quality = (logical accesses – physical accesses) ÷ logical accesses × 100%

The smaller the number of physical accesses in relation to the number of logical accesses, the higher the buffer quality. A buffer quality of 100% is ideal and means that no database tables are read from disks. Instead, all required objects reside in the main memory of the database instance.

If the database instance has just been started, the buffer will have been just loaded, and the hit ratio will be low. Therefore, when you evaluate the buffer quality, ensure that the database has been running for several hours. In production systems, the size of the data buffer normally varies between 500MB and 4GB, depending on the size of the database. However, for large installations, the data buffer can be significantly larger.

The next section explains the memory areas for a Oracle database. You can find information on other types of database systems in Appendix B.

An Oracle database instance allocates memory in three areas:

▶ **Data buffer**
(DATA BUFFER: SIZE field in the PERFORMANCE OVERVIEW screen of the DBA Cockpit)

▶ **Shared pool**
(SHARED POOL: SIZE field) The data buffer and the shared pool form the System Global Area (SGA).

▶ **Program Global Area (PGA)**
Allocated as variable local memory by Oracle database processes. As a guideline, you can allocate from 2 to 5MB for each database process. You can find out the number of Oracle database processes in the DBA Cockpit under PERFORMANCE • WAIT EVENT ANALYSIS • SESSION MONITOR.

The total size of the allocated memory in an Oracle database equals the sum of the sizes of these three areas.

The size of the Oracle data buffer is defined by the parameter DB_BLOCK_BUFFERS (usually in 8KB blocks) in the file *init_<SID>.ora* or in Server Parameter File (SAP Note 601157). Under the header Data Buffer in the initial screen of the database performance monitor (Transaction ST04), the number of logical read accesses to the data buffer is indicated as Reads. The number of physical read accesses is indicated as Physical Reads. Table 2.3 shows the key figures for evaluating the performance of Oracle database buffers.

Data buffer

The quality of the data buffer (indicated as Quality %) is optimal if it is at least 96%.

Oracle uses the *shared pool* to store administrative information. The shared pool consists of the row cache and the *shared cursor cache*:

▶ The row cache contains, for example, the names and characteristics of tables, indexes, extents, fields, and users.

▶ The shared cursor cache stores the execution plans for SQL statements so they do not have to be continuously recalculated.

Under the header Shared Pool in the initial screen of the database performance monitor (Transaction ST04), the Size field indicates the allocated size of the shared pool in kilobytes. The size of the shared pool is defined in bytes by the parameter SHARED_POOL_SIZE.

There are two indicators for the buffer quality of the shared pool. One is the buffer quality of the shared SQL area, indicated in Transaction ST04 under the header SHARED POOL as PINRATIO. This value should be at least 98%. The other indicator is the quality of the row cache, indicated as the ratio of user calls to recursive calls (in Transaction ST04 under the header Calls). *User calls* is the number of queries the SAP system has sent to the database. To respond to each query, the database requires administrative information from the row cache. If the database cannot obtain this information from the row cache, it performs a *recursive call* to import the information from the hard drive. Therefore, the ratio of user calls to recursive calls should be as large as possible and should not be less than 2:1. A typical size for the shared pool in a production SAP system is between 300 and 600MB.

Name of Buffer	Key Figure and Assessment	Parameter
Data buffer	Data buffer: quality 96%	DB_BLOCK_BUFFERS
Shared pool	The ratio of user calls to recursive calls should be at least 2:1	SHARED_POOL_SIZE
	Pinratio 98%	SHARED_POOL_SIZE

Table 2.3 Key Figures for Evaluating the Performance of Oracle Database Buffers

Summary

Appendix B lists the key figures considered when evaluating database buffers for different database systems in the SAP environment. Poor buffering normally has two possible causes:

▸ *Poorly optimized and expensive SQL statements* are the main cause of poor buffering in the buffer pool. They should be identified and must be dealt with as a high priority. Proceed with the next section, Checkpoints and Savepoints, and analyze your system to find expensive SQL statements.

▸ The other main cause is a *buffer pool that is too small*. If your database server still has sufficient main memory reserves, you can increase the buffer, for example, by 10 to 20%. Check whether the quality of buffering significantly improves as a result. If it does, you can try increasing the buffer some more. However, if this initial increase to the buffer has no effect, look elsewhere for a cause of poor buffer quality. For some databases, you have the option to page tables, which can be identified as the main cause of poor buffer quality, to own tablespaces with appropriate buffer quality in order to obtain a better buffer quality for the remaining ones.

[!] Note that these buffer quality values are only guidelines. In some cases, a database instance can still run well with apparently low buffer quality. Therefore, to avoid unnecessary investment in time and energy in optimizing the buffer quality, check the database response times using the workload analysis.

Checkpoints and savepoints

The buffer pool of a database instance not only reduces the time required by database read accesses, but it also speeds up database change operations. When a record is in the buffer, a database change operation initially involves only changes to the data block in the buffer pool. These changes are saved to the hard disk asynchronously, that is, at a later time, so several change operations can be collected on a data block in the buffer before that block is saved to the hard disk. However, the database instance must write *all* of the changed data blocks to the hard disks within a certain interval, defined by a *checkpoint* or *savepoint*.

[+] For all database systems, you can strategically define the frequency of checkpoints or savepoints by setting certain parameters. To find out which parameter defines the checkpoint for your database system, consult the online help documentation for the database performance monitor. You should change SAP's default parameter settings only after consulting SAP.

2.3.2 Identifying and Analyzing Expensive SQL Statements

Expensive SQL statements are long-running statements and one of the main causes of performance problems. In addition to creating long runtimes in the programs that call them, they also indirectly cause performance problems in other transactions.

Effects
Expensive SQL statements can have the following effects on the entire system:

► They cause high CPU utilization percentages and high I/O loads. This can lead to an acute hardware bottleneck on the database server and reduce the performance of other programs.

► They block SAP work processes for a long time, which means user requests cannot be processed immediately; they have to wait for free work processes. This can mean waiting in the SAP dispatcher queue.

► They read many data blocks into the data buffer of the database server, which displaces data required by other SQL statements. This data must then be read from the hard disk. As a result, the execution times of other SQL statements also increase.

It is not uncommon for a few expensive SQL statements to cause more than half of the entire load on the database server. Identifying these statements is therefore an important part of performance analysis.

Analyzing Currently Running SQL Statements

First, we want to present a strategy for identifying expensive, currently executing SQL statements. All database systems have a monitor for analyzing SQL statements currently being processed on the database: the *database process monitor*. This monitor, which is also referred to as the *session monitor* in Oracle, displays the currently active database processes, which are called *shadow processes* in Oracle. You can find this monitor in the DBA Cockpit under PERFORMANCE • WAIT EVENT ANALYSIS • SESSION MONITOR.

The monitor displays the SQL statements that are being processed and can indicate the SAP work processes to which a database process is allocated.

Moreover, in the Event column the Oracle session monitor shows the current event of the database process. Important events, which you can view in Figure 2.7, which shows the session monitor, include:

▶ CPU, which indicates that the database CPU currently executes an operation, for instance, sorting

▶ DB File Sequential Read for a file access

▶ SQL*Net Data More Data to Client (or also ... More Data from Client), which means data from the shadow process is transferred to the SAP work process (or vice versa)

▶ Enq: TX – Row Lock Contention, which shows that a shadow process is waiting for a lock

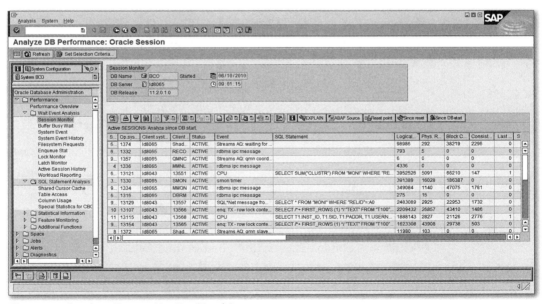

Figure 2.7   Database Process Monitor (Oracle)

You can find statistics on the events, in which the shadow processes currently are, via the menu path PERFORMANCE • WAIT EVENT ANALYSIS • SYSTEM EVENT. Typically, the already mentioned events CPU Used by this Session and DB File Sequential Read will be at the top of the statistics. You can obtain a detailed description of the Oracle process states in SAP Note 619188.

Open a second user session and start the system-wide work process overview parallel to the database process monitor (see Section 2.5, Analyzing SAP Work Processes). To identify long-running SQL statements, continually refresh the monitors of both user sessions. Because both monitors display the application server and the PID of the related SAP work process for the database processes, you can see which database process corresponds to which SAP work process. From the two monitors, you can determine:

▶ Program name and transaction code of the executed program (from the work process overview)

▶ Table name (from the work process overview and the database process monitor)

▶ The user who started the program (from the work process overview)

▶ WHERE conditions of the SQL statement (from the database process monitor)

From the database performance monitor, it is also possible to create an execution plan for the SQL statement by using the Explain function. You can find more details in Chapter 11, Optimizing SQL Statements.

This is all the information you require to perform a detailed analysis of an SQL statement.

Analyzing Previously Executed SQL Statements (SQL Statistics)

For almost all database systems, you can monitor statistics for the previously executed SQL statements. Statistics cover, for example, the number of executions of an SQL statement, the number of logical and physical read accesses per statement, the number of rows that were read, and the response times. For some database systems, these statistics are collected from the time the database was started; for other database systems, you must explicitly switch on these statistics. These statistics on the shared SQL area help you analyze expensive SQL statements. For Oracle databases, monitoring statistics on previously executed SQL statements is commonly referred to as monitoring the *shared SQL area* (also referred to as the *shared cursor cache* or the *shared SQL cache*). In this book, *SQL statistics* is also the collective term used for the previously executed SQL statements in various database systems.

You can find Oracle's shared cursor cache (see Figure 2.8) in the DBA Cockpit under PERFORMANCE • SQL STATEMENT ANALYSIS • SHARED CURSOR CACHE.

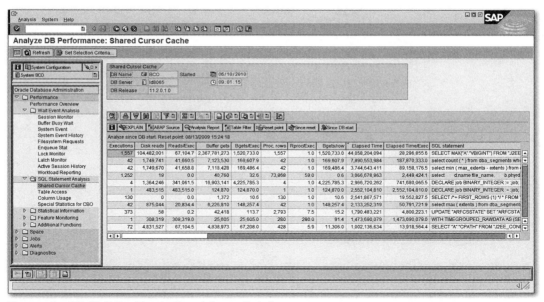

Figure 2.8 SQL Statistics (Oracle Shared Curser Cache)

For each SQL statement, the statistics contain the details in Table 2.4, among other things.

Field	Explanation
Executions	Number of times the statement has been executed since the start of the database
Disk Reads	Number of physical read accesses required for all executions of the statement; a high value indicates that there were a lot of read accesses to the hard disks
Reads/Execution	Number of physical read accesses required, on average, for one execution of the statement
Buffer Gets	Number of logical read accesses required for all of the executions of the statement; the ratio of buffer gets and disk reads indicates whether many accesses are possible from the buffer
Buffer Gets/ Execution	Number of logical read accesses required, on average, for one execution of the statement
Processed Rows	Number of rows read for all of the executions of the statement
Processed Rows/ Execution	Average number of rows read for an execution of the statement
Buffer Gets/Row	Average number of logical read accesses per row read; a high value indicates an inefficient search strategy (except for aggregating accesses, for instance, summation)
Elapsed Time	Time required for all of the executions of the statement
Elapsed Time/ Execution	Average time required for an execution of the statement

Table 2.4 Fields in the Shared Cursor Cache (Oracle)

In Oracle, the SQL statistics are collected by the database, and they are active by default.

Expensive SQL statements

Expensive SQL statements are indicated by a long execution time. Therefore sort the list by the numbers in the column Elapsed Time, Buffer Gets, or Disk Reads. This organizes expensive SQL statements in the order of required analysis and possible optimization. You should also take the number of executions into account here.

You can also obtain the following information from the monitor:

▸ Table name

▸ `WHERE` clause in the SQL statement

▸ Procedure roadmap of the SQL statement

An *analysis of the SQL statistics* is a powerful tool for analyzing perfor- **Analysis of the**
mance. However, considerable experience is required when deciding **SQL statistics**
which of the expensive SQL statements to optimize.

To identify the most expensive SQL statements, compare the indicated
number of read accesses of a particular SQL statement with the number
of read accesses for the entire database, as follows:

1. Sort the SQL statistics by the column Elapsed Time, Buffer Gets, or
   Disk Reads.

2. Open a second user session and start the main screen of the database
   performance monitor. Buffer Gets in the SQL statistics corresponds to
   Reads in the main screen of the database performance monitor. Similarly, Disk Reads in the SQL statistics corresponds to Physical Reads in
   the main screen of the database performance monitor.

3. To calculate the percentage of all logical accesses made by an SQL
   statement, divide the number of buffer gets in the shared SQL area
   by the reads in the main screen of the database performance monitor.
   Similarly, to calculate the percent of all physical accesses made by an
   SQL statement, divide the disk reads in the SQL statistics by the physical reads in the main screen of the database performance monitor.

4. If there are SQL statements that cause more than 5% of the total logical or physical accesses on the entire database, tuning these statements usually improves database performance significantly.

If you use the Explain function for displaying the SQL execution plan **[+]**
in an Oracle database in the SQL statistics and in the SQL trace (Transaction ST05), this may result in different results in exceptional cases.
For displaying the execution plan in the SQL trace, the optimizer recal-
culates the execution plan. Due to changed statistics, for example, this
plan may deviate from the execution plan that was available during the
actual execution. In the SQL statistics, in contrast, the internal database
view V$SQLPLAN of the Oracle database is accessed, which displays the
actual execution plan.

[+] For detailed analysis and optimization of SQL statements, see Chapter 11, Optimizing SQL Statements. First, however, you should look for SAP Notes on the particular expensive SQL statements identified. Use the search term "performance" and the table name.

SAP also has monitors for other database systems on SQL statistics. You can find further information in Appendix B.

Another way to identify expensive SQL statements is with an SQL trace, which is discussed in Chapter 4, Identifying Performance Problems in ABAP and Java Programs.

2.3.3   Identifying Read/Write (I/O) Problems

To achieve optimal database performance, I/O activity (read/write accesses) should be evenly distributed on the database's hard disks. You should avoid *hot spots*.

You can find important key figures on the I/O performance for an Oracle database in the DBA Cockpit via the menu path PERFORMANCE • WAIT EVENT ANALYSIS • FILESYSTEM REQUESTS. A particularly high number of file system accesses are to be expected in Oracle to redo log files, the PSAPROLL tablespace, and the directory for offline redo log files (SAPARCH).

I/O bottleneck   In the database server operating system monitor (Transaction ST06) under SNAPSHOT • DISKS, you'll find information about the load on the hard disks and wait times and response times for I/O operations on these disks. There is a risk of an I/O bottleneck if individual disks show very high levels of utilization (UTIL. > 50% for hourly average), if frequently accessed data files reside on those disks, or if wait situations occur when you access those files.

You can resolve an I/O bottleneck by improving the table distribution on the file system. In particular, ensure that the disks with high load contain no additional, frequently accessed files that could be relocated. The components listed in Table 2.5 are some of the most frequently accessed database objects. As a general rule, these objects should not reside on the same hard disk as the database files; nor should they reside on a hard disk array such as a RAID-5 system.

Database System	File or Database Object
Independent	Operating system swap space (high priority)
MaxDB	Log area, system devspace
DB2	Online log directory (high priority)
	Offline log directory (medium priority)
Informix	Dbspaces ROOTDBS, PHSYDBS, and LOGDBS
Oracle	Redo log files (high priority)
	Tablespace PSAPROLL (medium priority)
	Directory for the offline redo log files (SAPARCH) (medium priority)
SQL Server	Transaction log (high priority)
	Tempdb (medium priority)

Table 2.5 Examples of Files and Database Objects with High Read/Write Activity

However, you can gain only limited information about I/O problems from the SAP system. For a more detailed analysis, the hardware manufacturer's tools are necessary.

2.3.4 Other Database Checks

Database Lock Monitor

An exclusive database lock occurs when a user locks a row in a table, for example, with the SQL statement UPDATE or SELECT FOR UPDATE. If another user also tries to lock this row, that user has to wait until the first user releases the row. This wait situation is called an *exclusive lock wait*.

All database systems have a monitor for displaying exclusive lock waits. In an Oracle database, you can find this monitor in the DBA Cockpit under PERFORMANCE • WAIT EVENT ANALYSIS • LOCK MONITOR.

You can also enter Transaction DB01 to navigate directly to this monitor.

The following information is displayed for both the process holding the lock and the process waiting for its release:

- ID of the database process.

- Client host and client PID: name of the application server and the process ID of the related SAP work process. This helps you find the related SAP work process in the SAP work process overview, thereby identifying the program and the user holding the lock.

- Database-specific information such as the time the lock began, information about the locked table and row, and the last SQL statement executed.

Refresh this monitor several times to observe the progress of wait situations brought about by database locks. With the help of the Client Host and Client PID fields in the work process overview, you can determine which programs and users hold locks.

Exclusive
database locks

The following is a checklist for the elimination of exclusive database locks:

- If the work process overview shows that the lock is being held by a database process that is not related to an SAP work process, you can use operating system tools to terminate the database process. This applies if, for example, an external program that is not related to the SAP system is holding a lock or if an error caused an SAP work process to terminate, and the related database process is not properly closed.

- If a program holds a lock for several minutes, you can contact the user who started the program. Together with the user, check whether the program is still working properly. If not, end the program after consulting the user.

- Determine whether the lock wait is due to users concurrently using programs in a way that ultimately causes the programs to lock resources from each other. In this case, the user should study the documentation of the affected program and modify the way it is being used so lock waits can be avoided in future.

- If none of the previous points apply, check whether there are other database performance problems that prevent SQL statements from being processed quickly and cause relatively long holds on database locks. After resolving the other database performance problem, check whether the database locks are released more quickly.

[+] Database locks are absolutely necessary to safeguard data consistency on the database. Therefore, short waits due to database locks should not be regarded as performance problems. The situation becomes critical if locks are held for a long time and cannot be resolved. This leads to a chain reaction in which an increasing number of users have to wait because of locks. You can find more detailed information on database locks in Chapter 10, Locks.

Database Error Log File

Database error or message files contain important information on errors and the general condition of the database. The log should be checked regularly. In an Oracle database, you can find the log in the DBA Cockpit under DATABASE MESSAGE LOG or DATABASE ALERT LOG. For more detailed information about the error messages, refer to the manuals for your specific database.

Parameter Changes

The SAP system logs all changes made to database parameters. You can view the change log in the DBA Cockpit under CONFIGURATION • PARAMETER CHANGES. From the indicated dates of parameter changes, you may be able to detect correlations between parameter changes and subsequent performance problems.

Number of Database Processors

For some database systems, you can specify the maximum number of processors that the database instance can use. For example, this parameter is MAXCPU for MaxDB and NUMCPUVPS for Informix. It is important that this parameter has the correct setting, because if it is set too small, there will not be enough CPU capacity available for the database instance, even if CPU resources are still free.

[Ex] Suppose an SAP installation has a total of five computers. On the database server, there are four available processors. Both the database instance and the central SAP instance with enqueue and dialog work processes are located on the database server. The Database Profile parameter, which limits the number of processors that the database instance can use, is set to one. Therefore, the database instance can only use one processor. Assume that the central SAP instance also requires only one processor. The operating system monitor (Transaction ST06) shows that there is an average CPU utilization of 50%, so there are no bottlenecks. However, you may see high database times with this configuration, because one processor is normally insufficient for processing database queries in a system with five computers.

If the Database Profile parameter that limits the number of processors used by the database instance is set too large, this can also limit performance.

[Ex] Suppose the Database Profile parameter is set to four, and the database instance, therefore, has all of the processors to itself. The operating system and the SAP instance with the enqueue work process would then suffer from a CPU bottleneck, causing the enqueue queries of all SAP instances to be processed very slowly.

[+] On computers with more than two processors, the maximum number of processors the database instance can use is normally smaller than the number of physically available processors. Chapter 6, Workload Distribution and Interfaces, provides guidelines on how many processors should be reserved for a database instance in an SAP system.

Table Statistics for the Database Optimizer (Update Statistics)

All database systems that can be used in conjunction with the SAP system use a *cost-based optimizer*. Therefore, up-to-date statistics on the sizes of tables and indexes must be generated regularly. The optimizer needs these statistics to create the correct access plans for SQL statements. The administrator should regularly schedule the relevant update-statistics program. If the statistics are missing or obsolete, the optimizer may suggest inefficient access paths, which can cause significant performance problems. Update statistics do not need to be generated for a rule-based optimizer.

To check whether the relevant update-statistics program has been scheduled, open the DBA Planning Calendar by selecting DBA Planning Calendar in the DBA Cockpit.

If the update-statistics program is scheduled, you will see the entry `AnalyzeTab` (for Oracle), `RUNSTATS` (for DB2), or `Update Statistics` (for SQL Server). View the logs regularly to check that the update-statistics program runs were successful.

To generate update statistics, it is essential to use SAP tools from CCMS. The statistics generated through these tools are specifically adapted to SQL statements used by the SAP system.

[+]

For more information about the different optimizers and update statistics, see Chapter 11, Optimizing SQL Statements, and the SAP Notes listed in Appendix C.

Missing Database Indices

Missing database indices can lead to a significant reduction in system performance. To check the consistency of the indices between the ABAP Dictionary and the database, from the initial screen of the database performance monitor, in the DBA Cockpit select DIAGNOSIS • MISSING TABLES AND INDEXES A screen appears that displays indices defined in the ABAP Dictionary but missing from the database or vice versa.

The display of missing indices is divided into primary and secondary indices. If a primary index is missing, the consistency of the data is no longer ensured. There is a danger that duplicate keys can be written. Furthermore, a missing primary index causes ineffective database accesses; for large tables, it can lead to massive performance problems. This status is critical for the system and requires immediate intervention by the database administrator. For instructions on creating indices, see Chapter 11, Section 11.2.2, Administration for Indexes and Table Access Statistics.

[+]

Database Not Responding

If the database instance does not respond, the entire SAP system will soon stop responding. The database instance stops responding particularly when critical memory areas of the database are full, such as the file system or *log areas* such as the redo log files (for Oracle), the archive log files (for DB2), or the transaction log (for SQL Server). Database errors that can cause the database to stop responding are especially likely to occur when a large volume of data is updated on the database, for example, when data transfers or client copies are performed. Consider the following examples that describe how an error situation on the database can cause the SAP system to stop responding.

[Ex] **Example 1:** Database and SAP system are not responding because of full log areas:

1. Because of an administration error or incorrect capacity planning, the log areas of the database are full (for example, the redo log files for Oracle). When that happens, no further database operations are possible. In the DB2 for Linux, Unix, and Windows (DB2 for LUW) and the Oracle environment, this situation is called *archiver stuck*. The database instance writes an error message in the database error log file, such as *db2diag.log*: "SQL0964C The transaction log for the database is full," (for DB2 for LUW) or "All online log files need archiving" (for Oracle).

2. Every SAP work process that tries to execute a database change operation will be unable to complete it. You can view this process in the work process overview.

3. Soon no more SAP work processes will be available. The SAP system will stop responding. All users who send a request to the SAP system will have to wait.

4. Normally, this error situation can be resolved without having to stop the SAP system or the database. The data in the log area must be archived.

5. After archiving is completed, the database instance can resume work and process the accumulated requests.

[Ex] **Example 2:** Database file overflow:

1. During an attempt to write data into a database table via an Insert operation, an error occurs in the database because a database file is full or the hard disk is full. The database instance then returns an

error message to the SAP work process that called it, and the error message is (by default) written to the database error log file.

2. If the error occurs during an SAP update, the work process deactivates the entire SAP update service. At that point, SAP update requests receive no response. To determine whether the update service has been deactivated, display the update records. To do this, follow the menu path Tools • Administration • Monitor • Update or use Transaction SM13. See if the field below Update System displays the message "Updating by system deactivated." If so, find the associated error message and user by looking at the SAP system log (Transaction SM21).

3. When updates are no longer being completed, dialog work processes that are waiting for the updates to finish will gradually stop responding. You can view this process in the work process overview.

   Normally, you can resolve the error situation without having to stop the SAP system or the database. First, resolve the database error, for example, by expanding the file system. Then activate the SAP update service manually by opening the update monitor (SM13) and selecting Administration • Activate.

4. Now the SAP update service can resume work and process the accumulated requests.

The update service was stopped to enable the database administrator to correct a database error without terminating the updates. If the update service was not stopped, other update work processes would also be affected by the same database error. If the database error is not found quickly enough, hundreds of terminated updates may result, all of which must then be individually updated by the users.

Ensuring that the database remains operational is a database adminis- **[+]**
tration task, rather than a matter for performance optimization, and is therefore not explicitly covered in this book. Refer to the literature on database administration and create a contingency plan tailored to your company that, for example, provides procedures to:

▸ Ensure that a potential overflow of the log area or file system is detected well in advance.

▶ Determine which database error has occurred if the SAP system is not responding. Spell out how to locate the database error log file and which error messages are critical.

▶ Determine what must be done if an error occurs and whether the R/3 system or the database must be restarted. Simulate error situations and response procedures in a test system.

2.3.5 Summary

Performance problems in the database instance affect the performance of the entire SAP system. Therefore, performance monitoring has high priority and consists of the following tasks (listed in order of importance):

▶ Keep your database engine running! The database is the heart (engine) of your SAP system. If the database instance does not respond, the entire SAP system will soon stop responding. Regularly monitor the fill level of the *database log area* (for example, the redo log files for Oracle, the online log files for DB2 for LUW, or the transaction log for SQL Server) or the file system.

▶ Ensure that the database server has sufficient CPU and storage capacity. More than 20% of the CPU should be idle, and the paging rate should be low.

▶ If your database system has a profile parameter that limits the maximum number of physical processors that the database instance can occupy, ensure that this parameter's setting is neither too small nor too large.

▶ Ensure that individual hard disks are not showing more than 50% utilization.

▶ Check that the configuration and performance of the database buffers are adequate, as previously outlined.

▶ Identify any SQL statements that put a heavy load on the database server. An extremely expensive SQL statement is one that takes up more than 5% of the entire database load in the shared SQL area (measured in reads or gets).

▶ Remove the causes of frequent exclusive lock waits.

▶ Ensure that update statistics for the cost-based optimizer are updated frequently, and regularly check the consistency of the database and look for missing indexes.

2.4   Analyzing SAP Memory Configuration

To start the SAP memory configuration monitor for the SAP instance to which you are currently logged on, select TOOLS • ADMINISTRATION • MONITOR • PERFORMANCE • SETTINGS/BUFFER • BUFFER or use Transaction ST02. The main Tune Summary screen appears, as shown in Figure 2.9.

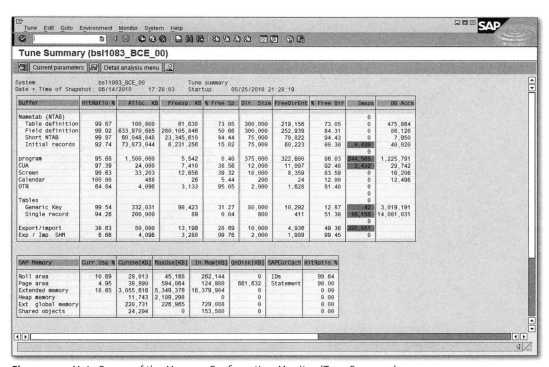

Figure 2.9   Main Screen of the Memory Configuration Monitor (Tune Summary)

The main memory configuration monitor screen displays information on the configuration and utilization of the SAP buffer, the SAP extended memory, and the SAP heap memory. All data shown corresponds to the period since the last startup of the specific SAP instance.

2.4.1 Analyzing SAP Buffers

You can find details on the various SAP buffers in the Buffer section of the SAP memory configuration monitor. Table 2.6 explains the columns corresponding to these buffers.

Field	Explanation
HitRatio	The definition of the SAP buffer hit ratio is identical to that given for database buffers.
Allocated	Memory space allocated to the respective buffer. Every SAP buffer is normally characterized by two parameters: the size of the buffer and the maximum number of buffered entries.
Free Space	Currently unoccupied memory space in the buffer.
Dir. Entries	Maximum number of entries in the buffer.
Free directory entries	Difference between the current number of objects stored in the buffer and the maximum possible number of objects.
Swaps	Number of buffer objects displaced from the buffer.
Database accesses	Number of database accesses (which is also the number of data transfers from the database into the buffer).

Table 2.6 Fields in the Memory Configuration Monitor

Like the database buffer, the SAP buffer must also achieve a minimum buffer quality to ensure smooth SAP system operation. If the buffers are too small, data is displaced, and the database has to be accessed (unnecessarily) to reload the data. When an object is loaded into the buffer and the free space in the buffer is too small to completely store the object, other objects must be displaced from the buffer to make space available. For example, Figure 2.9 shows the number of swaps for the field description buffer in the Swaps column.

When monitoring SAP buffers, consider the following guidelines:

▶ The hit ratio for SAP buffers should generally be 98% or higher. (Exception: For the program buffer, the single record buffer, and the export/import buffer, lower hit ratios are acceptable.)

▶ There should be no swaps (displacements) in the buffers of a production system. If there are swaps, the buffer size or the maximum number of entries should be increased. Here again, the exception is the program buffer, for which approximately 10,000 swaps per day represents an acceptable number of buffer displacements.

▶ To help avoid subsequent displacements, ensure that each buffer has sufficient memory (indicated as Free Space) and free entries (indicated as Free Directory Entries).

If you see in the memory configuration monitor that there have been displacements in an SAP buffer, proceed as follows:

Buffer settings

1. First, check whether the buffer is too small (Free Space field) or if the maximum number of possible buffer entries is too small (Free Directory Entries field).

2. Depending on the results of these checks, increase either the buffer size or the maximum number of allowed entries by 10 to 50%. To determine the relevant SAP profile parameters, select Current Parameters from the main screen of the memory configuration monitor (as described in more detail a little later in this chapter). Before increasing the buffer size, ensure that the computer still has sufficient main memory reserves; otherwise, you run the risk of a memory bottleneck.

Do not confuse *displacements* (swaps) with *invalidations*, which are not indicated in the Swaps column. Invalidation is when a buffered object such as a program or table is declared invalid because it has been changed. Invalidations lower the hit ratio and cause objects to be reloaded from the database, but they cannot be identified using the memory configuration monitor. Invalidations can occur when programs or customizing settings have been transported into a production system or have been changed in production operation. Therefore, it is recommended that transports be scheduled once or twice per week when the system load is low. Tables that are too large for buffering can also lead to problems with table buffers. Chapter 9, SAP Buffering, deals with this subject .

Displacements and invalidations

All SAP buffers and related SAP profile parameters are listed in Appendix C. You can view the current settings in the SAP memory configuration monitor by clicking the Current Parameters button.

Parameters for buffer settings

2.4.2 Analyzing SAP Extended Memory, SAP Heap Memory, and SAP Roll Memory

The SAP Memory section of the SAP memory configuration monitor (see Figure 2.9) lists data on the SAP memory areas Roll Area, Page Area, Extended Memory, Heap Memory, Ext Global Memory, and Shared Objects. Table 2.7 explains these fields.

Field	Explanation
Current Use	Amount of memory currently used in the memory area, given in KB and %.
Max. Use	Maximum amount of this memory area that has been used since the SAP instance was started (also known as the high water mark).
In Memory	Amount of main memory allocated to this area at system startup. For the roll area and the paging area, this space corresponds to the SAP roll buffer and SAP paging buffer.
On Disk	For the roll area and the paging area, SAP roll and paging files are located on the hard disk of the application server. The size of these files is indicated here.

Table 2.7 Fields in the Memory Configuration Monitor

When monitoring the SAP memory areas, consider the following guidelines:

► For Roll Area, the Max. Use value should not exceed the corresponding amount in the In Memory column. In other words, the role file should not be used.

► For Extended Memory, the Max. Use value should be at least 20% smaller than the corresponding value in the In Memory column. This ensures that there will continue to be sufficient free extended memory.

In Figure 2.9 you can see that almost 100% of the SAP extended memory is in use. In addition, more roll memory is being used than is available in the roll buffer; Max. Use in the Roll Memory column is greater than the corresponding amount in In Memory.

If you detect that the roll memory or SAP extended memory requires all of the memory allocated to these areas at SAP instance startup, you can increase the values in the SAP profile parameters `rdisp/ROLL_SHM` or `em/initial_size_MB` (provided there is sufficient physical memory on the computer). Check whether this solves, or at least eases, the problem. If the problem persists, see Chapter 8, Memory Management, for further information on SAP memory management.

Experience has shown that performance is dramatically reduced when SAP extended memory is full, making it impossible to work productively in the SAP instances. Therefore, high priority should be given to monitoring the SAP extended memory. You can generally afford to allocate extended memory generously. Unused extended memory is swapped out by the operating system. As a rule of thumb:

[+]

1. About 6 to 10MB of extended memory is allocated for each user.

2. Approximately 70 to 120% of the physical main memory can be allocated as extended memory.

These guidelines do, of course, depend on the release and the application module. Ensure that the swap space on the operating system level is large enough. Ensure also that the operating system can administer the preferred memory size. You can find more details in Chapter 8, Memory Management.

To display the current system settings, choose Current Parameters in the Roll, Extended and Heap Memory section. Appendix C lists all of the relevant SAP profile parameters for memory area configuration.

Parameters for memory area configuration

With R/3 release 4.0, SAP introduced *Zero Administration Memory Management,* which made manual setting unnecessary. Zero Administration dynamically allocates memory based on the hardware available to the SAP instance and adapts memory management settings automatically (SAP Note 88416 in the SAP Service Marketplace). Zero Administration Memory Management requires only one SAP profile parameter: `PHYS_MEMSIZE`. This parameter defines how much of the computer's main memory should be used for the SAP instance. If no value is entered in the instance profile for `PHYS_MEMSIZE`, the full amount of physical main

Zero Administration Memory Management

memory is automatically set. All other SAP memory management settings are automatically calculated on the basis of PHYS_MEMSIZE.

2.4.3 Displaying Allocated Memory

To analyze performance, it is important to have an overview of current memory allocation. For this purpose, you use the monitor located in the SAP memory configuration monitor under DETAIL ANALYSIS MENU • STORAGE. The STORAGE USAGE AND REQUIREMENTS screen appears. Figure 2.10 shows an example of this screen, and Table 2.8 explains its key figures.

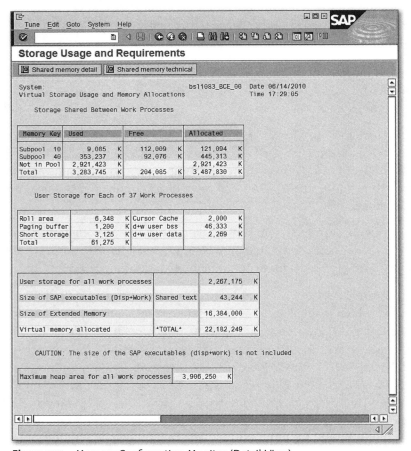

Figure 2.10 Memory Configuration Monitor (Detail View)

Field	Explanation
Storage Shared between Work Processes	The value for the Allocated column in the Total row shows the total memory allocated to the SAP buffers. (For UNIX operating systems, this section also displays the values for the allocated, used, and free memory space for each shared memory pool.)
User Storage for All Work Processes	The size of the memory allocated for the SAP work processes.
Size of Extended Memory	The size of the memory allocated to the SAP extended memory.
Virtual Memory Allocated	The size of the total memory allocated at instance startup to the SAP buffer, SAP work processes, and extended memory. This is the critical value for assessing whether main memory bottlenecks are likely to occur.
Maximum Heap Area for All Work Processes	The size of the SAP heap memory that can be allocated as local memory by the SAP work processes, if required. This value corresponds to the parameter `abap/heap_area_total`.

Table 2.8 Fields for Determining Allocated Memory

To ensure that the total memory allocated by SAP is not significantly disproportionate to the physically available main memory, compare allocated and physical memory. Begin by calculating the allocated memory, as follows:

Allocated and physical memory

- Find the amount of memory allocated by an SAP instance since startup. This value is indicated as Virtual Memory Allocated. If there are multiple instances on the computer, the values for all of the SAP instances are added.

- If the instance is on the same computer as the database, add the memory requirement of the database. To find out the database memory requirement, see the database performance monitor (Transaction ST04).

- Add about 50 to 100MB for the main memory requirements of the operating system.

To determine the amount of physically available memory on the computer, see the operating system monitor (Transaction ST06).

Normally, the amount of allocated memory is significantly greater than the amount of physically available memory. Normally, however, we assume that no critical paging should occur when the allocated memory is more than 50% greater than the physically available memory. If this limit is exceeded, use the operating system monitor to check the paging rates and the workload monitor to analyze the response times to determine whether there is a memory bottleneck.

You can also use the memory configuration monitor to determine whether there is sufficient swap space at the operating-system level. First, calculate the maximum memory that can be allocated by the SAP system; add the Virtual Memory Allocated and Maximum Heap Area values. When added to the memory requirements of any other systems on the same computer — such as a database, the operating system, and possibly other systems — the maximum allocatable memory area should be smaller than the sum of the physically available main memory and the swap space. Otherwise, system failure may occur.

2.4.4 Other Monitors in the Memory Configuration Monitor

SAP Parameter Changes

The SAP system logs all changes to SAP parameters. You can view the change log in the SAP memory configuration monitor via DETAIL ANALYSIS MENU • PARAMETERS.

Select an application server, and select HISTORY OF FILE. Note that very recent changes may not yet appear in the log. This monitor enables you to check for parameter changes that are linked to performance problems.

Other Monitors

In the Detail Analysis menu of the memory configuration monitor, you can call other SAP buffer allocation monitors by clicking the Call Statistic and Buffer Synchron buttons. These monitors are discussed in greater detail in Chapter 9, SAP Buffering.

2.4.5 Summary

When you set the profile parameters for SAP memory management, you define how much virtual memory can be allocated by an SAP instance. You can allocate more virtual memory than is physically available.

The memory configuration monitor enables you to monitor the size and use of SAP memory areas. Displacement should not occur in the SAP buffers (with the exception of the program buffer, which may have up to 10,000 displacements each day). Ensure that neither the extended memory nor the roll buffer become full.

Make it a top priority to monitor the extended memory. If this memory is used up completely, production work ceases, and immediate action is required to solve the problem. One solution is to increase the size of extended memory. You should also check whether there are programs with excessive memory consumption that can be terminated or optimized (see Chapter 8, Memory Management).

If you detect displacements in the following buffers, adapt the corresponding parameters with medium priority, that is, within a few days:

▸ TTAB, FTAB, SNTAB, and IRDB buffers
▸ Roll buffers, program buffers, and table buffers

The settings of the following buffers have a somewhat lower priority:

▸ CUA buffer and screen buffer
▸ SAP paging buffer

Note that the size of allocable memory is affected by operating system–specific limitations such as the maximum size of allocable shared memory and the maximum address space. If you change the memory configuration, check whether the new parameters allow the SAP instance to start without error (see Figure 2.11).

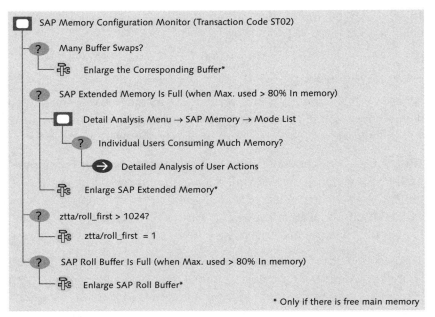

Figure 2.11 Detailed Analysis of SAP Memory Configuration

2.5 Analyzing SAP Work Processes

The SAP work process overview is available to analyze the SAP work processes. To call the work process overview for the current application server (local work process overview), select TOOLS • ADMINISTRATION • MONITOR • SYSTEM MONITORING • PROCESS OVERVIEW or enter Transaction SM50. The Process Overview screen is displayed.

To display the work processes of any application server, call the server overview by following the menu path TOOLS • ADMINISTRATION • MONITOR • SYSTEM MONITORING • SERVER (Transaction SM51).

Place the cursor on the application server you want and select GOTO • PROCESSES.

To see a system-wide overview of all work processes in the SAP system, start the system-wide work process overview via TOOLS • ADMINISTRATION • MONITOR • PERFORMANCE • EXCEPTIONS/USERS • ACTIVE

Users • Global Process Overview. Alternatively, you can enter Transaction SM66. The Global Work Process Overview screen is displayed.

If a performance problem has escalated to such an extent that you can no longer the work process overview from the SAP system, you can start the SAP Management Console or the auxiliary program dpmon on the operating system level instead. The work process overview can also be found under menu option L.

2.5.1 Work Process Overview Fields

Table 2.9 describes the columns that appear in the local work process overview.

Field	Explanation
No.	Work process number (unique for each SAP instance). This number and the SAP instance name (or the computer name and the process ID) uniquely identify an SAP work process in an SAP system.
Type	DIA, dialog, BTC: background, UPD: update, ENQ: enqueue, SPO: spool.
PID	Process ID for the operating system (unique for each computer). Using this number, you can deal with the process using operating system commands (for example, terminated).
Status	This field displays the status of a work process.
	The status Waiting shows that the process is available for user requests. Normally, there should always be sufficient work processes displaying this status; otherwise, users will experience poor response times.
	The status Running means the work process is processing a user request. To determine which action the work process is currently executing, check the column Action/Reason for Waiting.
	The status Ended means hat the process was terminated because of an error in the SAP kernel.
	The status Stopped means hat the process is waiting for a message.

Table 2.9 Work Process Overview Fields

Field	Explanation
Reason	For work processes with the status Stopped, this column explains the reason for the wait time. You can find an overview of the most important reasons for waiting and their causes in Appendix C.
Start	This column tells you whether, for a given work process, the dispatcher is set to restart the work process if it terminates.
Err	Number of times the work process has been terminated.
Sem	Number of the semaphore. A number with a green background shows that this work process is holding a semaphore. A number with a red background shows that the work process is waiting for the semaphore.
CPU	The CPU time used by the work process so far in minutes:seconds.
Time	The elapsed processing time for the current request (in seconds).
Clie	Client.
User	Name of the user whose request is currently being executed.
Report	Name of the report currently being executed.
Action/ reason for waiting	For work processes with the status Running, this field displays the current action.
Table	The database table that was last accessed by the work process.

Table 2.9 Work Process Overview Fields (Cont.)

Process ID

The combination of computer and *process ID* enables you to clearly identify an SAP work process in an SAP system. The process ID is also used in the following monitors:

► Process overview in the operating system monitor (Transaction ST06): SNAPSHOT • TOP CPU PROCESSES. This monitor enables you to determine how much CPU load a specific work process is currently generating.

▶ Database process monitor (Transaction DBACOCKPIT): PERFORMANCE • APPLICATIONS (for DB/2). This monitor enables you to determine which SQL statement is currently being processed by a work process.

▶ Database lock monitor (Transaction DBACOCKPIT): PERFORMANCE • WAIT SITUATIONS FOR LOCKS. This monitor enables you to determine whether a work process is currently holding a database lock or waiting for a lock to be released.

▶ SAP Management Console: J2EE Processes.

▶ TREX server overview (Transaction TREXADMIN): Services.

A combination of the information contained in these monitors — the work process overview, the process overview in the operating system monitor, the database process monitor, and the database lock monitor, as well as the SAP Management Console and the TREX server overview — provide you with an extensive overview of the current work process situation in your SAP system.

Every application server has resources that can be used by only one work process at a time. If a work process needs to use these resources, it sets a *semaphore*. If other processes also require this resource, they have to wait until the process that is holding the semaphore has completed its action. For example, if an entry in an SAP buffer needs to be changed, a semaphore is set, because only one process can perform changes in the buffer. If several processes are waiting for a semaphore, this is called *serialization*. Another operation that requires a semaphore to be set is *roll-in* or *roll-out*, which means only one process at a time can perform a roll-in or roll-out. You can obtain a complete list of SAP semaphores by pressing ⌈F1⌉ for help on the SEM field.

Semaphores

2.5.2 Analyzing Work Processes

If you watch the work process overview for several minutes and repeatedly click the Refresh button to update the display, you can usually determine whether there is a current performance problem related to work processes in the SAP instance; and if there is a problem, you can roughly estimate its cause. The main indication of a performance problem is that all of the work processes of a particular type (such as dialog or update) are occupied.

Problem: Long database response times

There is a problem in the database area if the work process overview in the Action column shows numerous database-related actions, such as Sequential Read, Direct Read, Update, Commit, or Waiting for DB Lock. In this case, start two additional user sessions. Start the database process monitor and the database lock monitor *(exclusive lock waits)* to search for expensive SQL statements or database locks.

Problem: deactivated update service

If all update work processes (UPDs) are occupied, you have a problem. Use Transaction SM13 to check if the update service has been deactivated. Establish whether you can find the message Updating by System Deactivated. If so, find the associated error message and user by looking at the SAP system log (Transaction SM21). As soon as the underlying problem is resolved, for example, a database error, you can reactivate the update work process with Transaction SM13.

Problems with SAP memory management

Problems with SAP memory management are often indicated in the work process overview as follows:

► The Action/Reason for Waiting field frequently displays Roll-in or Roll-out (accompanied by a type 6 semaphore).

► Many work processes are in PRIV mode (the Status field displays Stopped and the Reason field displays PRIV).

[Ex] Figures 2.9 and 2.12 are screenshots that were taken at the same time and indicate how a performance problem can be evident. The problem is more evident in the local work process overview (see Figure 2.12). We can see that almost all work processes are in the roll-out phase. Furthermore, the memory configuration monitor (Figure 2.9) shows that the cause for the wait situation is that both the SAP extended memory and the roll buffer are completely full. Increasing the size of the extended memory (parameter `em/initial_size_MB`) will likely solve the problem in this case.

If a work process listed in the local work process overview has the status Stopped, the cause is indicated in the Reason column. To obtain a list of the possible reasons, access Help for this column.

Stopped work processes

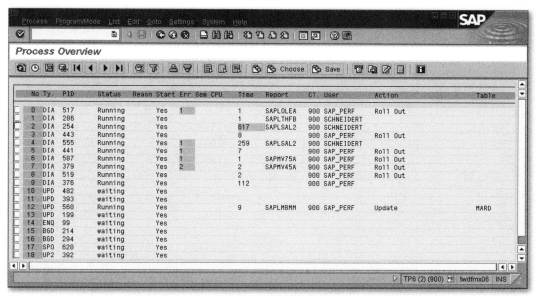

Figure 2.12 SAP Work Process Overview – All Work Processes Occupied and Almost All on "Roll Out"

Normally, it is not a problem if some work processes have the status Stopped for short periods of time. However, if the number of work processes that are stopped for the same reason exceeds 20%, or if these work processes continue to have the status Stopped for a long time, you should analyze the situation in detail. A single ineffective or defective work process often starts a chain reaction that stops other work processes. You can often assume that the work process with the longest runtime (indicated in the Time column) caused the problem. If the problem is acute, consider manually terminating the defective work process.

In the local work process overview, if you detect numerous terminated work processes (indicated as Complete in the Status column) and find

Completed work processes

that you cannot restart them, it is likely that there is a problem with the SAP kernel or with logging onto the database. Examine the relevant trace file by marking the appropriate work process and selecting PROCESS • TRACE • DISPLAY FILE. The trace file will be overwritten when the work process is restarted, so save the trace file to a secure location to enable subsequent troubleshooting. Look for SAP Notes referring to the problem at the SAP Service Marketplace or consult SAP.

Problem: nonoptimal load distribution

In a distributed system with several computers, you may find that all work processes on one or more computers are busy and are keeping users waiting, while other computers have idle work processes. Check how many users are logged onto each SAP instance. On the workload monitor, you can also check how many dialog steps have been executed on each server. If you discover a very uneven distribution load, you should optimize your logon distribution. Use Transaction SMLG to check whether all of the servers are available for logon distribution or whether there are any relevant error messages. Then proceed with reorganizing the logon distribution.

For an overview of current user distribution, see the logon group distribution: TOOLS • ADMINISTRATION • CCMS • CONFIGURATION • LOGON GROUPS (Transaction SMLG) • GOTO • LOAD DISTRIBUTION

Problem: Too few work processes

As you can see from the problems described in the previous sections, there are many reasons why all work processes of a given type might be busy. If you have ruled out all of the problems discussed so far yet still have a work process bottleneck, it may be that you have not configured enough work processes. In this case, you should increase the number of work processes. However, before doing so, check whether the computer has sufficient CPU and main memory resources. If the CPU is already being 80% utilized, an increase in the number of work processes will more likely further decrease, rather than increase, performance.

Further information

Table 2.10 summarizes the sections of this book that explain how to deal with problems that can be identified through the local work process overview.

Problem	Section/ Chapter	Title
Long database response times	2.3.2	Identifying and Analyzing Expensive SQL Statements
	10	Locks
	11	Optimizing SQL Statements
SAP memory configuration	2.4	Analyzing SAP Memory Configuration
	8	Memory management
Nonoptimal load distribution, too few work processes	5	Hardware Sizing and System Distribution

Table 2.10 References to Problems that Can Be Detected Using the Work Process Overview

2.5.3 System-Wide Work Process Overview

To monitor a system with multiple SAP instances, use the system-wide work process overview (Transaction SM66). By navigating with the → button, you'll see the following fields in the system-wide work process overview:

For a dialog work process:

▶ **Tcod**
Code for the transaction that is currently running

▶ **CUA Rep.**
Name of the program from which the user started the currently running transaction (also known as the main program)

▶ **Dynp**
Name of the dynpro last processed

▶ **Fcod**
Code for the last function called in the current program

For a background work process:

▶ **Job**
Name of the executed background job

Dialog work processes

Background work processes

For both cases:

▶ **Ext. Mem**
Current extended memory utilization

▶ **Priv. Mem**
Current heap memory utilization

In the system-wide work process overview, you can change the following options.

Using the Settings button:

▶ **Display the connections and status in the status line**
Selecting this option displays the current server connection or other status issues in the status line at the bottom of the screen. This is helpful if, for example, the connection is problematic or takes a long time. By default, this option is not selected.

▶ **Display only abbreviated information, avoid RFC**
If you select this option, the system-wide work process overview gets its information from the message server rather than from each application server (through RFC). Because application servers report the status of their work processes to the message server only after a delay, the message server is not always up to date. By deselecting this option, an RFC connection to each application server is established for a check on the current status of the work processes. The information is therefore up to date; however, this takes more time. By default, this option is selected, that is, only abbreviated information is displayed. If you require a complete overview of work processes for a performance analysis, deselect this option and refresh the display frequently.

▶ **Do not take personal work processes used for analysis into account**
For a complete analysis (see next bullet point), an RFC connection is made to each server, each of which runs one work process. These work processes are not displayed if this option is selected. By default, this option is selected.

▶ **Do not look for exclusive database locks**
With this option, the monitor program looks for exclusive locks on the database and, if it finds any, displays them in the Action/Reason for waiting field (Stopped DB Lock or Waiting for DB Lock).

Using the Select Process button:

▶ A specific group of work processes can be found and displayed. This is especially necessary for large installations with hundreds of work processes. By default, waiting work processes are not shown.

2.5.4 Monitoring the Dispatcher Queue

Occasionally, it may be useful to monitor the dispatcher queue. You can see statistics on dispatcher activities by selecting TOOLS • ADMINISTRATION • MONITOR • SYSTEM MONITORING • SERVER (Transaction SM51) in the Server Overview.

Then mark an SAP instance with the cursor and select GOTO • QUEUE INFO. A list appears, showing information for each work process type on the requests currently waiting, the maximum number of user requests since the SAP instance was started, the maximum possible number of user requests for each queue, and the number of requests read and written.

The information about the dispatcher queue is especially important when the system is not responding because the number of requests in the queue is much larger than the number of work processes. In this situation, the SAP system does not have any more work processes available to perform an analysis. To obtain the queue data, use the auxiliary program `dpmon`.

2.5.5 Summary

To monitor the actions of SAP work processes, use the local work process overview. In particular, refer to the Time, Status, Reason, Action/Reason for Waiting, and Table columns. Note the following points:

▶ Are enough work processes of all types available (status Waiting) for each SAP instance?

▶ Is there a program that uses a work process for too long (Time field)? If this is the case, the user should check this program and see if it has any errors. A detailed program analysis may also be necessary.

▶ Check the Status, Reason, Action/Reason for Waiting, and Table fields to see whether more than 20% of the work processes are performing the same action. The main problems with this can be:

▶ If more than 20% of the work processes are in PRIV mode, or in the roll-in or roll-out phase, this indicates a problem with SAP memory management.

▶ If more than 40% of work processes are performing a database action, such as sequential read or commit, this indicates a database problem.

▶ If more than 20% of work processes are reading the same table at the same time, there may be a problem with an expensive SQL statement or exclusive lock waits in the database.

You can call the local work process overview at the operating system level with the `dpmon` program. This is particularly necessary if the performance problem is so massive that no work processes can be used for the analysis.

Figures 2.13 and 2.14 show the analysis procedure for SAP work processes.

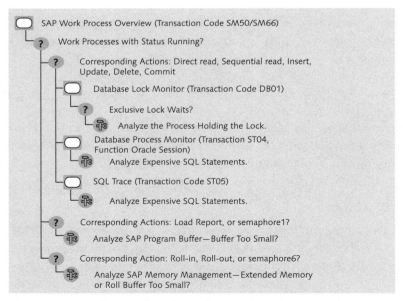

Figure 2.13 Procedure Roadmap for Analyzing SAP Work Processes (I)

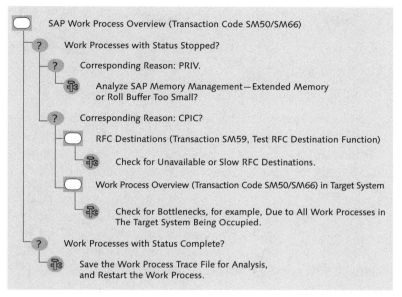

Figure 2.14 Procedure Roadmap for Analyzing SAP Work Processes (II)

2.6 Analyzing Java Virtual Machine (JVM) Memory Management and Work Processes

The SAP J2EE Engine currently supports *Java Virtual Machines* (JVMs) manufactured by IBM, HP, and Sun. For operating SAP NetWeaver 7.10, you can now use SAP JVM, which offers various benefits in the support area, for example, for transferring user contexts to other JVMs in case of an error (session failover) or improved monitoring functionality. You can perform the JVM analysis either in the SAP Management Console or in SAP Solution Manager Diagnostics, regardless of the JVM used. The monitoring views for memory management and work processes described in the following sections are only available in the SAP Management Console for SAP JVM.

2.6.1 Analyzing Garbage Collection

To understand the following analysis, it is essential to know that garbage collection is one of the most critical performance aspects of a Java Virtual

Garbage collection

Machine. In this process, objects that are no longer required (that is, no longer referenced by other objects) are removed from memory. In the JVMs permitted for SAP systems, we differentiate between partial garbage collection and full garbage collection. In partial garbage collection, only a small percentage of the entire Java machine memory is searched and removed; this part is called the *young* objects. Objects that are still used are successively moved to the *old* memory, which grows over time. Objects in the old memory are not examined during partial garbage collection. If the old memory has exceeded a specified value, it must be cleared as well. This process is known as *full garbage collection*.

Partial garbage collection is carried out within split seconds, whereas full garbage collection takes several seconds. During this time, the JVM pauses, and users have to wait. For users of an ABAP system, this is an unusual situation, because this behavior is not common in an ABAP engine, provided it is not overloaded and is configured correctly.

To monitor the garbage collection, you need to set the `-verbose:gc` parameter. Only then will the data be written in the log file of the JVM processes via the garbage collections.

Developer trace
You can view garbage collection details in the developer trace of a J2EE process. To do so, select the process list in the SAP Management Console. Then select a process and right-click the Developer Trace entry in the menu. Figure 2.15 shows an excerpt of the developer trace, including the log of the garbage collection.

The Type: Partial entry indicates that a partial garbage collection was implemented, and the Duration: 63.99 ms entry shows that the process took approximately 64 milliseconds.

Analyzing garbage collections
As previously mentioned, the garbage collection process is an integral part of the JVM operation. However, if many full garbage collections are performed, you should analyze them in more detail. For this, you have several options:

▶ If you use the SAP JVM deployed for operation (as of SAP NetWeaver 7.10), you can find a list containing the simple evaluation of garbage collections in the SAP Management Console. Figure 2.16 shows this list, where you can see that, for example, a full garbage collection takes 12 to 20 seconds and how often it occurs.

▶ On the Internet, you can find products to visualize this data. However, SAP recommends performing the evaluation in SAP Solution Manager, which we'll describe in the following sections.

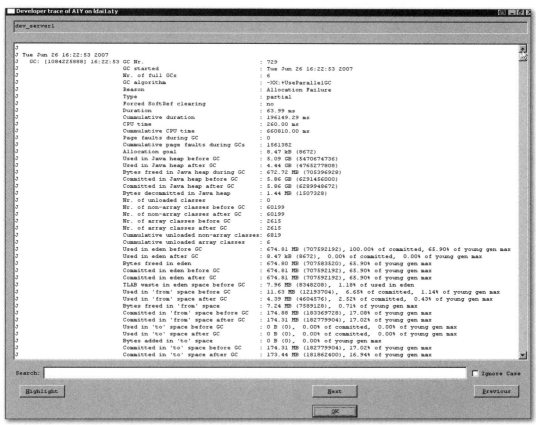

Figure 2.15 Developer Trace, Including Details About the Partial Garbage Collection in the SAP Management Console

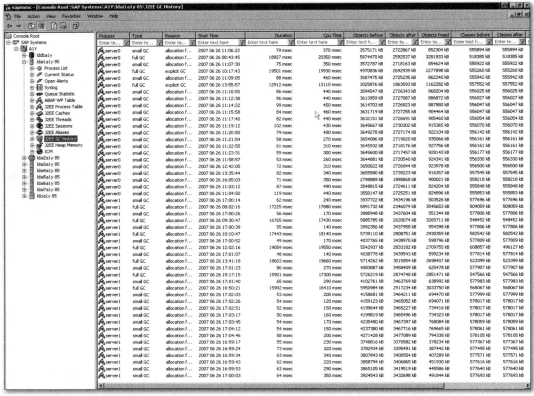

Figure 2.16 History Display of Garbage Collection in the SAP Management Console Using the SAP JVM

Analyses in SAP Solution Manager

You can find the monitor for analyzing the memory management of the J2EE Engine in SAP Solution Manager (Transaction DSWP) under GOTO • START SOLUTION MANAGER DIAGNOSTICS. In the diagnosis application of SAP Solution Manager, select WORKLOAD • E2E WORKLOAD ANALYSIS. Then select your solution and all components. Select the tab with the name of the J2EE Engine that you want to analyze. Click the Memory Analysis button to navigate to the memory analysis.

SAP Solution Manager analyzes the log files of the J2EE Engine and summarizes the information in key figures, which are listed in Table 2.11.

Key Figure	Evaluation
The time that the J2EE Engine requires to clear the memory (Garbage Collection, GC), in percent	5%
Growth rate of the requested memory (allocation rate) in bytes per second	
Ratio of full garbage collection (FGC) and partial garbage collection (GC)	<<10%
Growth rate of old memory space (OGR)	Show decrease to zero in times with low load
Rate of the data moved in the old memory area, in bytes per second	

Table 2.11 Key Figures for Evaluating Memory Behavior of the J2EE Engine

Via manually triggered garbage collections you can determine the memory requirement of a Java program as described in the following. A prerequisite for the measurement is that no other programs are executed in parallel, that is, this measurement can de facto be run only on a test system.

Determining memory requirement for a Java program

1. Manually trigger a garbage collection five times in a row.

2. Execute the program to be examined.

3. Manually trigger a garbage collection five times in a row.

4. The memory requirement of the Java program results from the memory released in the garbage collection.

5. Repeat steps 1 through 4 five times to ensure a stable measurement value.

2.6.2 Analyzing Work Processes

You can implement the analysis of JVM work processes directly in the SAP Management Console or in prepared form in SAP Solution Manager Diagnostics.

In the SAP Management Console, you analyze the state of the work process and its threads by forcing the process to write the state of its threads into the log file. For this, select the process list in the SAP Management Console. Then select a process and right-click the Dump Stack Trace entry in the menu.

You can find the analysis result in the log file, which you can display by selecting the process and right-clicking the Developer Trace entry in the menu.

[+] To create a thread dump, the JVM is stopped; this means that every thread must pass a savepoint. You can only reach a savepoint at specific points in the Java code, for example, during return operations or when requesting locks. Implementing locks means they are increasingly displayed in thread dumps, and you could easily get the impression that something is wrong and that the threads spend too much time waiting for locks, which is only due to the previously mentioned admission time point. You should only worry about your system if too many lock wait situations are displayed, the CPU load of the machine is considerably low, or if many requests are simultaneously sent to the server and take a long time to be processed.

The JVMs usually automatically detect deadlocks (as of version 1.4.2) if a thread dump is triggered. In this case, a warning message is sent.

Analyzing the developer trace Developer trace analysis is very complex for a large production system. Therefore, you have the following options:

▶ If you use the SAP JVM deployed for operation as of SAP NetWeaver 7.10, in the SAP Management Console under J2EE Threads, you can find a simple evaluation of the work processes and their threads. Figure 2.17 shows this evaluation. In this list, you can find, for example, the user, the runtime, and additional information, making this monitor similar to the work process monitor of the ABAP runtime environment.

▶ You can also implement the analysis in SAP Solution Manager, which we'll describe next.

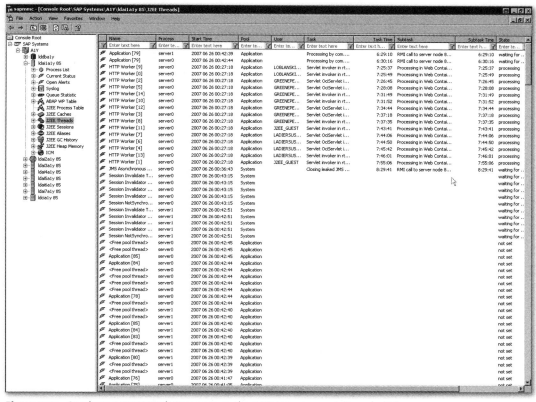

Figure 2.17 Displaying JVM Work Processes in the SAP Management Console Using the SAP JVM

You can find the monitor for analyzing the work processes of the Java Virtual Machine in SAP Solution Manager (Transaction DSWP) under GOTO • START SOLUTION MANAGER DIAGNOSTICS. In the diagnosis application of SAP Solution Manager, select EXCEPTIONS • APPLICATION SELECTION • JAVA. Then choose your solution and trigger the analysis via Trigger Dump. Click the Analysis button to navigate to the analysis.

Analyses in SAP Solution Manager

You can start a JVM work process analysis in the same cases for which you would carry out an analysis of the ABAP work processes:

▶ The system is stuck or offers very poor performance.

▶ The system processes individual applications very slowly.

▶ The system exhibits signs of age, meaning it becomes slower and slower until it has to be restarted.

In the latter two cases, we recommend performing a series of work process analyses using SAP Solution Manager.

The different tables of the work process analysis are listed in Table 2.12. Figure 2.18 shows thread details in the JVM work process analysis in SAP Solution Manager.

Table	Explanation
Summary	Lists all implemented work process analyses. This list also provides information on how long a J2EE node already runs. Restarts and deadlocks are indicated using alarm symbols.
All Dumps	Shows the trend analysis of the statuses of the threads in the JVM work processes. The table rows display the process and status; the columns show the number of threads with their current status for continuous analyses.
	The In Object.wait() status indicates that a thread is available; in other words, it waits for a new request. Sufficient threads should be available in this state.
	The Runable status indicates that an application is currently executed. Provided you carry out a series of analyses and identify long-running threads, you can monitor the threads.
	The Waiting for Monitor Entry status indicates that the system is currently waiting for a lock. These threads want to execute an application that is locked by another thread. This is a critical situation and impacts the response time.
Threads Activity	Shows an overview of the critical thread for continuous analyses.
Single Dump	Shows an overview of the threads in a work process.
Threads Details	Lists the thread details, in particular, the complete stack trace, based on which you can determine the current activity of an application.

Table 2.12 JVM Work Process Analysis

Table	Explanation
Locks	Lists the relations between the threads containing a lock and the threads waiting for a lock. Note: Locks in the JVM work process analysis correspond approximately to the semaphores of the SAP work process, and you shouldn't mix these locks up with the database locks or SAP enqueues.
Customer Code	Lists all non-SAP Java programs that are active at the time of analysis. You can use this information to find the correct person group for a detailed program analysis.

Table 2.12 JVM Work Process Analysis (Cont.)

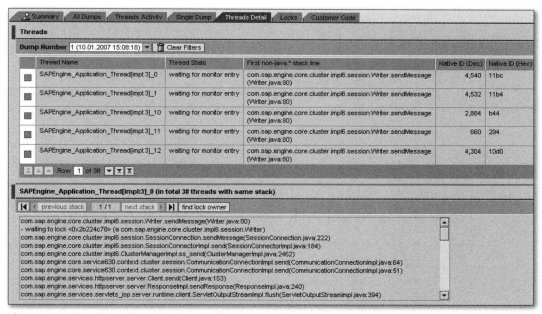

Figure 2.18 Thread Details in the JVM Work Process Analysis in SAP Solution Manager

2.6.3 Summary

Frequent full garbage collections constitute serious performance problems for users, because the J2EE Engine "stands still" during the collection. Reasons can include an engine overload, for example, due to suboptimal load distribution or an application problem.

Besides frequent garbage collection, an overload of the JVM work processes is another critical performance problem. Here as well, the reasons can be an engine overload, for example, due to suboptimal load distribution or an application problem.

2.7 Analysis of the Internet Communication Manager (ICM)

The *Internet Communication Manager* (ICM) provides communication between the web browser and SAP work processes of the SAP J2EE Engine or the ABAP server. It does not process business logic or generate web pages, which means the load it has to manage is less than that of SAP work processes. Regarding the operating system, the ICM is a process (icman.exe). Internally, the ICM is scalable, which means it has several threads.

To monitor ICM load, call the ICM monitor (Transaction SMICM): TOOLS • ADMINISTRATION • MONITOR • SYSTEM MONITORING • ICM MONITOR. In the initial monitor screen, you can see the status of individual ICM threads. The upper part of the screen shows statistical information on the status of the threads (Threads Generated row), the connections (CONNECTIONS USED row), and the queue (USED QUEUE ENTRIES row). You can recognize a bottleneck in the ICM if the value Peak is the same as the value Maximum for these three parameters.

Memory pipes

To monitor the load on memory pipes in the ICM monitor, select GOTO • MEMORY PIPES • DISPLAY DATA. Among other things, you will find information here on the number of memory pipe buffers (Total #Mpi Buffer field) and their loads (Peak Buffer Usage field). If the value for Peak is the same as the value for Maximum, then there is a bottleneck.

Cache mechanisms

The ICM has a cache in which it records web pages or parts of web pages such as image files. You can find an overview of the data in the ICM monitor cache under GOTO • HTTP SERVER CACHE • DISPLAY. You can get statistical data on the fill level and efficiency of the cache by selecting GOTO • HTTP SERVER CACHE • DISPLAY STATISTICS. Interesting values here include the absolute size of the cache (Cache Size (Bytes) field) and the occupied space in the Occupied Cache Memory (Bytes) field.

The ICM is activated with the SAP profile parameter, `rdisp/start_` `icman = true`. (By default, the ICM is active after installation of the SAP NetWeaver Application Server.) In Appendix C, you will find an overview of the SAP profile parameters relevant to performance and used in the configuration of the ICM, memory pipes, and cache.

2.8   Continuous Monitoring Using CCMS

The CCMS *(Computing Center Management System)* contains a monitor called the Alert Monitor with which you can monitor all aspects of your SAP solution. Together with SAP Solution Manager, this forms a complete solution for the continuous monitoring of your system. The monitor offers:

▸ Complete, detailed monitoring (performance indicators) of SAP software components, servers, databases, and third-party (non-SAP) components

▸ Status indicators (alerts: green, yellow, red) for performance indicators if threshold values are exceeded or not met

▸ Alert tracking and administration

▸ Expansion possibilities, thanks to the open structure (also for non-SAP software components)

▸ Together with SAP Solution Manager, a graphical interface for monitoring and follow-up of errors

After introducing the Alert Monitor, this section presents concrete recommendations such as how to adapt the tree in the monitor to suit your SAP solution, how to organize an escalation procedure (for example, messaging by email or pager), and how to link the Alert Monitor to the graphical interface of SAP Solution Manager. Used together, these measures define a complete monitoring solution.

The status of an IT solution is illustrated by *performance indicators*. Performance indicators can be:

Performance
indicators

139

▶ **Counters**
For example, average response times, throughput statistics, degree of process workload, or the fill level of memory areas.

▶ **Text information**
For example, error messages (an error message "processing of document X has been terminated" is also an indicator of poor performance in a system). In this sense, performance refers not merely to runtime performance; it also evaluates availability and error situations.

The task of solution monitoring is to generate, record, aggregate, and evaluate performance indicators. The SAP central Alert Monitor integrates performance indicators from dozens of *expert monitors* and brings them together in monitoring trees. These expert monitors act as suppliers of data to the Alert Monitor. The advantage of the central Alert Monitor is that you only need to use the expert monitors in exceptional situations, and not for the normal monitoring of components. The expert monitors linked to the indicators can be started in the central Alert Monitor by clicking the name of an *analysis method*. Therefore, from the Alert Monitor, you can go directly to the corresponding expert monitor (also if you are logged onto a remote system).

The Alert Monitor automatically generates alerts if an indicator threshold value is exceeded or not reached. Standards are supplied for threshold values, which you can individually adapt to suit your needs.

Not all performance indicators are of equal importance in evaluating whether or not your SAP solution is running optimally. As you gain experience, some indicators will emerge as being of particular importance. We refer to these as *key performance indicators* (KPIs). Therefore, one objective when putting together a monitoring plan is to filter out the KPIs relevant to you from the wealth of information available. We'll provide you with some instructions to help you do this.

2.8.1 Working with the Alert Monitor

Using the Alert Monitor, you can work in SAP GUI or in the Web user interface of the central SAP NetWeaver Administrator. In this section, we describe the user interface in the SAP GUI; the Web user interface is self-explanatory. In the SAP GUI, you can call the Alert Monitor as follows:

1. Select Tools • CCMS • Control/Monitoring • CCMS Monitor Collections (Transaction RZ20). The system displays the CCMS monitor collections.

2. Display the Entire System monitor in the SAP CCMS Monitor Templates collection by placing the cursor over it and selecting Load Monitor. The monitor displays the tree in the presentation last used. The monitoring tree is a hierarchical display of the monitor objects (system components) and monitor attributes (information on types of object) in the system. The Entire System monitoring tree displays all objects and attributes presented in the expert view and objects from other views for which there are alerts. Expand the tree if the entire hierarchy is not displayed. Place the cursor in the Entire System row and select Process • Tree • Expand tree • Expand sub-tree.

In addition to the Entire System monitor, there are other predefined monitors for special purposes. For example, a database administrator can open the Database monitor instead of the Entire System monitor. CCMS Self Monitoring is one of the special monitors in the SAP CCMS Technical Expert Monitors collection. This monitor displays possible problems in the Alert Monitor and in the monitoring architecture. In this monitor, you can check that all data collection methods started by the Alert Monitor are running properly. If no data is given for a monitoring element, the monitoring tree is displayed in gray (see Figure 2.19).

[+]

Check the current status of your SAP components by displaying the current system status in your monitor. From the list of buttons, select Current Status. (If the button does not appear in the list, then this view is already displayed.) In the Current Status view, you can see the latest performance values and status information reported to the control monitor. Older alerts that are still open (meaning they have not been dealt with) are not displayed in color. To view a legend of the colors and symbols used in the Alert Monitor, select Extras • Legend. The Alert Monitor gives the highest alert level in the monitoring tree. For example, if the monitoring object with the name of your SAP component is green, all components in the monitoring tree of the SAP component have Green status; that is, the Alert Monitor has not found any problems in this component.

Alert propagation

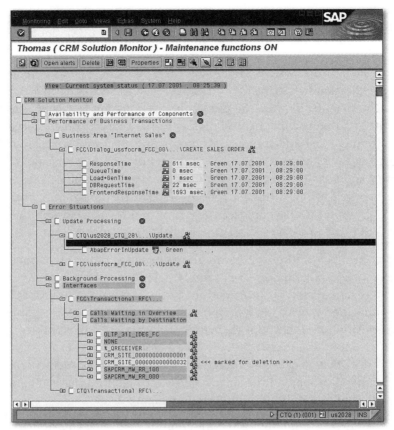

Figure 2.19 Central CCMS Alert Monitor for an SAP CRM Solution – Alerts on the Performance of Business Process Steps and Error Situations Within Update, Background, and Interface Processing

Refresh display

You can set the display to refresh automatically. To do so, select EXTRAS • DISPLAY OPTIONS and select the General tab. Within Refresh Display, select the option Yes, Interval and enter a refresh interval. The suggested value is 300 seconds or longer. If automatic refresh is not activated, the Alert Monitor displays the data that was available when the monitor was started.

Current status and open alerts

In the Open Alerts view check to see what has happened in the system recently. The color code in this view does not tell you the current status of the system; it tells which alerts are open. Open alerts are those that have not yet been analyzed. At the beginning of your workday or after lunch, you can check the Open Alerts view to see what has happened in the system in your absence. The monitor records the alerts for you, even if the circumstances that triggered the alert have since improved.

If you see yellow or red entries in the monitoring tree, there is a warning (yellow) or an error (red). First, ensure that you are in the Open Alerts view. The monitor now displays how many alerts there are for each monitoring object. It also displays the most important waiting alert messages.

Reacting to an alert

Place the cursor over a yellow or red monitoring tree element and select Display Alerts. The system opens the alert browser and displays the open alerts for the corresponding monitoring object. The alert browser shows all alerts in the branch of the tree you have marked. Move the cursor further up the monitoring tree to display a larger range of alerts. If you position the cursor on a monitoring object on the lowest level, only alerts on this monitoring object will be displayed.

Each row in the alert browser gives overview information on an alert, including the message. The browser offers two further sources of information. To begin, select an alert, and then:

Methods of analysis

▶ Double-click a monitoring object to start the corresponding analysis method. The analysis methods are expert tools for performance analysis (discussed in detail in other chapters).

▶ Select Display Details to view details of the monitoring tree element. These include the most recent values or status reports, the alert threshold values, and performance data for the latest control period (only for performance monitoring tree elements). You can represent performance data graphically by marking the corresponding row and selecting Display Performance Values Graphically.

When you have analyzed and resolved the problem or ensured that it can safely be ignored, set the Alert to "resolved." Mark the alert and select Complete Alert. The Alert Monitor deletes it from the list of open alerts.

Dealing with alerts

143

2.8.2   Arranging Monitoring Trees

In principle, the CCMS Alert Monitor is ready for use immediately after installation. However, its configuration should be optimized and adapted to suit your solution. You can also define and change monitoring objects and trees. Any changes made can also be transferred between systems.

This section describes the most important performance indicator categories you should take into account for daily monitoring and for which you should adjust the CCMS Alert Monitor. In Appendix C, you can find a detailed description of individual performance indicators for various components.

Performance indicators can be subdivided into three groups:

▶ **Availability and performance of components**
The objective in monitoring these indicators is to ensure the availability and system performance of hardware and software components that participate in the SAP solution. In other words, an alert in this area indicates that a component is not working at all or is working very slowly. All components are included in the monitoring, regardless of whether or not they come from SAP.

▶ **Performance of business transactions**
The performance of SAP online transactions is monitored. The transaction-based monitoring of response times has the advantage that it is possible to react to performance problems flexibly and individually. This means, for example, that you can react to a transaction in the sales area with a higher priority than to a transaction in accounts. In particular, you should monitor the transactions for which a service-level agreement has been reached.

▶ **Error situations**
Errors in the regular operation are monitored here.

Availability and performance of SAP systems

By default, the Alert Monitor examines the SAP component in which it is started. However, you can examine several SAP components with a single control monitor.

To do this, identify an SAP component in your central system for monitoring. The central system should have the most up-to-date version of SAP Basis possible so that you always have access to the latest monitoring tools. Depending on the size of your installation, you may need to use a dedicated SAP system for this. If you use SAP Solution Manager, assign it and the central CCMS monitoring to one system.

Make the other SAP components known to the Alert Monitor. You will find a more detailed description of how to link an SAP system to the Alert Monitor in SAP online help.

Monitoring remote components occurs via an RFC connection. From a single system, you can monitor as many SAP components as you want. Technical factors such as the speed of and traffic in your network limit the number of systems that can be monitored. This becomes particularly noticeable if a component in your system landscape is already down or if the performance is already particularly bad. In these cases, it is neither useful nor desirable to generate all performance indicators. Here, to be able to react, the central Alert Monitor offers a special form of control function availability with which you can monitor the availability of remote SAP components and their application servers. By monitoring availability, you can determine whether or not a component and its server are running and available for work.

The availability control uses the alert and display functions included in the monitoring architecture. It uses an *agent* for data entry (to determine whether a remote system is active and available). An agent is an independent program that runs external to the SAP component. By using an agent, you can check the availability of several remote systems and various other components from one central system without the risk that a nonactive system will cause the Alert Monitor to display "system crash." An RFC connection to the remote systems is not necessary. The Alert Monitor does not have to log on to a remote component to check its availability. As a result, the data entry procedure, with which you can check the availability of even hundreds of systems from a central CCMS Alert Monitor, is extremely fast. The availability monitor also has a short wait time in case a component is not available.

With the CCMS Alert Monitor, you can check the availability and performance of any computer in your system landscape — not only those running SAP systems. To do this, you need to install what is known as a *monitoring agent* on the computers you want to monitor.

Computers without SAP software

Software components without SAP Basis

You can also monitor SAP components that are not based on an ABAP server using SAP monitoring agents and include them in the central monitor. The procedures are described in detail in SAP Notes (for example, SAP Note 498179 for SAP J2EE Engine and other notes in Appendix G). The monitoring agents are a prerequisite for the central workload analysis and central single-record statistics described in Chapter 3, Workload Analysis, and Chapter 4, Identifying Performance Problems in ABAP and Java Programs.

External software components

The open structure of the CCMS monitoring architecture means that you can stipulate your own data supplier for the Alert Monitor and monitor software components that do not come from SAP.

For further information on SAP monitoring agents and their enhancements, see the SAP Service Marketplace under *http://service.sap.com/systemmanagement*.

Summary of component monitoring

Figure 2.19 shows the *component monitoring* in the central monitor as it would be arranged for SAP Customer Relationship Management (SAP CRM). In the Availability and Performance of Components, Software Components branch, the monitoring of three SAP instances in the CTQ system (R/3 back end) and FCC (CRM Server) hangs, as do other components of the Internet Transaction Server (ITS) solution, Internet Pricing & Configurator (IPC), and the Index Management Server (IMS). In the Hardware Components branch, you can find performance indicators for the computers on which SAP systems CTQ and FCC run and a computer (P37221) on which SAP ITS runs. (This is monitored by agents, as previously described.)

Performance-specific transactions

You can track the response times of certain clients or SAP transactions with the Alert Monitor. This is of particular importance for transactions you have included in the service-level agreement. As of SAP Basis 4.6C, the Alert Monitor contains the Transaction-Specific Dialog monitor in the *CCMS Monitors for Optional Components* collection. Further information is available at SAP online help. In our example (Figure 2.19), the transaction Create Sales Order is included in the check.

Error situations

The most important error situations you should constantly check for in all SAP components are:

▶ Interrupted updates.

▶ Interrupted background processes.

▶ Interrupted interface processes (transactional RFC, queued RFC, IDoc). Important alerts for interrupted interface processes are located in the monitoring branch, Transactional RFC.

The Error Situations branch in Figure 2.19 shows which error situations should be monitored in our SAP CRM example.

2.8.3 Arranging Automatic Alert Messaging

As of SAP Basis 4.6, you can allocate *auto-reaction methods* to critical performance indicators so you will be informed of an alert by email, fax, or pager — even if you are not currently working with the Alert Monitor. The Alert Monitor can automatically dial a pager or send an email or fax to the following addressees:

▶ A business workplace user in Client 000. The email is sent within five minutes of the alert's occurrence and is delivered immediately.

▶ A distribution list or external email address; the email is sent within five minutes of the alert's occurrence. Depending on the settings in SAPconnect, there can be a delay before mail is sent to external email addresses (that is, user addresses that are not defined in Client 000 or in the SAP system). You should set the time delay for the SAPconnect send process to less than one hour.

The email message text contains the same information displayed in the Alert Monitor: what the problem is, where and when it occurred, and the degree of urgency of the alert (a red alert indicates a problem or an error; an amber alert is a warning). Further information is available at SAP online help and in SAP Note 176492.

2.8.4 Graphical User Interface in SAP Solution Manager

SAP Solution Manager includes a graphical interface for presenting your business processes and the corresponding alert situations. This makes monitoring considerably simpler, particularly for complex processes and software landscapes, and it illustrates the connection between business process and software. An example of the graphical presentation of business processes and their states is shown in Figure 1.6 (Chapter 1, Performance Management of an SAP Solution).

2.8.5 Summary

In principle, the CCMS Alert Monitor is ready to use immediately upon installation of your SAP system. In practice, however, you should adapt it to suit your specific SAP solution. Monitoring includes:

- ▶ Central monitoring of availability and performance of all hardware and software components participating in the SAP solution via the SAP monitoring agent (The agent can easily be extended to cover non-SAP software.)

- ▶ Monitoring of the performance of the most important SAP online transactions

- ▶ Monitoring of error situations in online transactions, updates, background processing, and interfaces

For alerts identified as particularly critical, you can define automatic reaction procedures; for example, emails or SMS messages are sent so that constant monitoring is guaranteed, even if you are not constantly physically reviewing the Alert Monitor.

In Appendix C you will find an overview of the most important performance counters in the central Alert Monitor for all SAP components.

2.9 Summary

You will find a summary at the end of each section in this chapter.

Important Concepts in this Chapter

After reading this chapter, you should be familiar with the following concepts:

- ▶ Hardware bottleneck

- ▶ Logical and physical database read accesses (buffer gets and disk reads)

▶ Expensive SQL statements

▶ Exclusive database locks

▶ Allocated and physical memory

▶ SAP work process bottleneck

▶ Semaphores

▶ Garbage collection and Java Virtual Machine (JVM)

▶ Performance indicators and alarms in central CCMS monitoring

Questions

1. Which of the following can cause a CPU bottleneck on the database server?

    a) External processes that do not belong to the database or an SAP instance running on the database server.

    b) The SAP extended memory is configured too small.

    c) Work processes that belong to an SAP instance running on the database (for example, background or update work processes) require CPU capacity.

    d) There are expensive SQL statements, for example, those that contribute 5% or more of the entire database load in the shared SQL area.

    e) The database buffers are set too small; therefore, data must be continuously reloaded from the hard drives.

2. Which of the following are necessary to achieve optimal database performance?

    a) Table analyses (using a program such as Update Statistics) must be regularly scheduled.

    b) The number of SAP work processes must be large enough that there are enough database processes to process the database load.

    c) The database buffers must be sufficiently large.

    d) You should regularly check whether expensive SQL statements are unnecessarily consuming CPU and main memory resources.

    e) The database instance should be run only on a separate computer without SAP instances.

3. Which points should you take into consideration when monitoring SAP memory management?

   a) The total memory allocated by the SAP and database instances should not be larger than the physical main memory of the computer.

   b) The extended memory must be sufficiently large.

   c) If possible, no displacements should occur in the SAP buffers.

4. In the local work process overview, the information displayed for a particular work process over a considerable time period is as follows: Running, Sequential Read, and a specific table name. What does this tell you?

   a) There may be an expensive SQL statement that accesses the table and can be analyzed more closely in the database process monitor.

   b) There may be a wait situation in the dispatcher, which is preventing a connection to the database. The dispatcher queue should be analyzed more closely.

   c) There may be an exclusive lock wait that can be analyzed in the monitor for exclusive database locks.

   d) There may be a network problem between the application server and the database server.

5. Your JEE Engine frequently runs full garbage collections. What does this tell you?

   a) The garbage collection is a background process of the Java virtual machine; as long as there is no CPU bottleneck, performance problems won't occur.

   b) During a full garbage collection run, the Java applications are stopped. Consequently, frequent runs considerably impact the system. You should perform a detailed analysis of the memory consumption.

   c) During a full garbage collection run, all Java applications are terminated, the main memory of the JVM is deleted, and the applications are reloaded. You should perform a detailed error analysis of the programs involved.

3   Workload Analysis

Workload analysis provides reliable data on throughput, load, and response times for SAP systems and their components. As described in the Introduction, an experienced performance analyst begins by using a workload analysis to reveal areas of an SAP system that have noticeable performance problems and then proceeds with a more detailed top-down analysis.

Example: Assume you have systematically performed the analyses **[Ex]** explained in Chapter 2 and have discovered several problems both in the database area and in the SAP memory configuration. How can you determine which problem is the most serious and requires urgent attention? Workload analysis can provide the answer.

Workload analysis examines the various response times measured by the system. The kinds of performance problems identified by workload analysis are those that negatively affect throughput and response time and are known as *bottlenecks*. Bottlenecks can critically affect production operations and therefore require speedy removal. Workload analysis can also be used to prioritize performance problems.

In addition, workload analysis reveals the load distribution for each application's programs or transactions and indicates which of these are placing the greatest load on the SAP system. Workload analysis should therefore be the starting point for a detailed application analysis.

Following an introduction to the basics of workload and runtime analyses for the various SAP components, we'll present the basic concepts of workload analysis based on an ABAP server. After an introduction to the workload monitor, we'll explain which statistics the SAP system measures in units of time and how you can use these measurements to identify performance problems. The second section of this chapter provides recommendations on how to monitor your system's performance regularly. In the last section, we'll apply the detailed methods, which are based on the ABAP server, to the SAP J2EE Engine.

When Should You Read this Chapter?

Read this chapter when you want to monitor, analyze, and interpret the response time of the SAP system or the individual programs and transactions. If you want to technically monitor and optimize the performance of the SAP system, you can read this chapter either before or after Chapter 2, Monitoring Hardware, Databases, and SAP Basis. If you want to monitor and optimize the performance of programs and transactions, read this chapter and then read Chapter 4, Identifying Performance Problems in ABAP and Java Programs. Understanding workload analysis is a precondition for successful performance optimization.

3.1 Basics of Workload Analysis and Runtime Analysis

Statistics such as response times, memory use, and database accesses are collected and stored for all transaction steps for all SAP components. The data collected for a request is called a *statistics single record*.

Passport and distributed statistics records
If multiple SAP components are involved in the processing of a user request, each component writes its data record. In the communication flow between the components, a unique identifier (a GUID, also referred to as a passport) is included and stored in each record so that the single records can be merged across individual components. The first component of a transactional step generates this passport (technically speaking, this is a GUID that is used to uniquely identify the transactional step) and transfers it to the next component that is part of the transactional step. For performance reasons, only passport data is transferred in the communication flow during a transaction step; the actual statistical data is first saved locally by the respective components and then transferred asynchronously to the central monitoring system or SAP Solution Manager. Based on their passports, the statistics records involved in a transactional step can be identified and displayed. In SAP Help, this technology is also referred to as *distributed statistics records* (DSRs).

Data in the statistics record
In principle, one or more statistics records are written for every request. The content of these records can be differentiated by key figures and characteristic parameters. *Key figures* are measurement values, for instance,

specific runtimes, transferred data volumes, and the number of calls of specific actions in a program. They specifically indicate the time a component required for processing and the time the component waited for the subsequent request to be processed. Information about the point of time, user, instance name of the component, computer, type of service, and program executed are *characteristic parameters*. You can find detailed information about the meanings and interpretations of this data in this and the following chapters.

We differentiate two different use cases for statistics records:

Use cases

▶ The workload analysis (this chapter), in which you evaluate the performance data of your system periodically or via event-driven management. For this purpose, the single records are organized in *load profiles* that can be displayed in the workload monitor. The workload monitor enables you to obtain a comprehensive overview of load distribution between and within SAP components (which is the subject of this chapter).

▶ The runtime analysis of individual requests (see Chapter 4), in which you create an event-driven runtime analysis of specific requests. Here, the statistics records of the calls to be analyzed are compiled in an analysis transaction according to their call sequence. This single-record analysis enables you to determine the time elapsed in individual components and operations and which detail trace needs to be switched on next or analyzed if it has already run simultaneously.

3.1.1 ABAP Server Statistics

The statistics records of the ABAP server are written by the server's C kernel. In principle, a record is written for every request processed by the server. In addition to the main record, which is always generated, the ABAP server writes *subrecords* for specific actions. Examples are subrecords for database calls or database procedure calls, which are intensively used, for instance, in SAP liveCache, RFC calls, and HTTP calls.

Functionality

For performance reasons, the statistics records are initially stored in the main memory and then written to the file system on the hard drive. In a background process that runs every 60 minutes (SAP performance collector), the data is organized in load profiles based on characteristic parameters; these can be time profiles, server profiles, or transaction profiles. The single records are deleted after a predefined period of time, and the aggregated data is stored in the database (Table MONI).

Workload Monitor
You can use the workload monitor (Transaction ST03N) to evaluate the aggregated data. To display the single records stored in the file system, use Transaction STAD (which we'll detail in Chapter 4, Identifying Performance Problems in ABAP and Java Programs). At the same time, you can transfer the data to an SAP NetWeaver Business Warehouse (BW) system and create your own analysis reports based on the SAP NetWeaver BW content provided by SAP. In practice, this is only an option for large IT departments; therefore we won't detail it in this book. If you use SAP Solution Manager, it reads the data from the connected systems via a remote function call and stores it in the business warehouse system of SAP Solution Manager. There, the evaluation reports are preconfigured, and you can use them directly after installation.

The statistics main record and its subrecords cover the following programming models and components (if they are not detailed in this chapter or Chapter 4, we'll indicate where the information can be found):

► "Normal" ABAP transactions and reports

► ABAP transactions with SAP GUI controls (Chapter 7, SAP GUI and Internet Connection)

► ABAP Web services such as Business Server Pages, Web Dynpro for ABAP, and the internal Internet Transaction Server (ITS), (Chapter 7, SAP GUI and Internet Connection)

► SAP NetWeaver BW reporting

► Remote function calls between SAP systems (Chapter 6, Workload Distribution and Interfaces)

► SAP liveCache

► SAP Virtual Machine Container (VMC), (Chapter 6, Workload Distribution and Interfaces)

3.1.2   SAP J2EE Engine Statistics

The SAP J2EE Engine uses two technologies: statistics records written by the SAP J2EE Engine itself and statistics from Wily Introscope, an external tool.

Just like the ABAP server, the SAP J2EE Engine creates statistics records that include comparable key figures and characteristic parameters. They are also stored in the SAP J2EE Engine file system. You can display the data either in the central monitoring system or in SAP Solution Manager. In the former case, the CCMS agent transfers the data to the central monitoring system and displays it in the central workload monitor (Transaction ST03G) and the central single record display (Transaction STATTRACE). In these monitors, you can see data for both the SAP J2EE Engine and the ABAP server, provided the central monitoring system has been configured accordingly. If you use SAP Solution Manager, the Solution Manager Diagnostics (SMD) agent provided in SAP Solution Manager transfers the data to SAP Solution Manager. There, it is stored in the business warehouse system and can be displayed along with ABAP server data.

Functionality of Java statistics

The Java workload and runtime analysis, via Introscope, has been integrated into SAP Solution Manager as of version 4.0. This includes a license to use Computer Associates' Wily Introscope in the functional scope delivered with SAP Solution Manager. (The use of Wily Introscope beyond this functional scope requires a separate license.)

Functionality of Introscope

Wily Introscope technology enables you to dynamically instrument the Java code. To do so, you need to define measuring points in Java code, so-called *probes* that are stored in the configuration files. When you start a Java application, an agent combines the probes with the original program to create a program with dynamic measuring points. This process is also referred to as *injecting* probes. At runtime, the probes collect the specified data.

Data from the Wily Introscope byte code agent, which runs as part of the monitored JVM, is recorded. The SMD agent automatically installs this agent. Every 15 seconds, the collected statistics are transferred from the monitoring system to the Central Introscope Enterprise Manager *(Smart-*

Stor), which is usually installed in SAP Solution Manager. By default, the data is stored for 30 days and then deleted.

Evaluation

Wily Introscope statistics are used for both workload and runtime analyses. In both cases, the data is evaluated using a Java presentation server program *(Introscope Workstation)* or the Web user interfaces of Wily Introscope. Moreover, aggregated statistics are stored in the BW system of SAP Solution Manager. SAP Solution Manager carries out the evaluation within an end-to-end workload analysis or end-to-end runtime analysis.

Compared to the static performance measurements, this dynamic instrumentation has the benefit of reacting extremely flexibly to new developments. You can still carry out a validation of the Java applications if the product has already been implemented and delivered, and it does not have to anticipate where the measuring points must be set, as is the case for statistics single records.

The disadvantage of measurements using Wily Introscope is, however, that information on the user who performed the operation is not stored; that is, no user profile is created.

Java Application
Resource
Measurement
(JARM)

In the past, SAP had developed its own solution for creating detailed statistics, *Java Application Resource Management* (JARM). The project was stopped, however, because implementation was too static. Therefore, the corresponding section on this subject (contained in the fourth edition of this book) is omitted in this edition.

3.1.3 SAP Strategy for an End-to-End-Workload and Runtime Analysis

Creating statistics

The creation of statistics and load profiles is always activated on the ABAP server to enable monitoring of the system. The process is critical for performance and has constantly been improved by SAP, so the creation and processing of statistics has grown even in SAP systems with very high throughput. SAP license agreements even specify that these statistics are required for ensuring support.

The continuous use of statistics records in workload analyses of the SAP J2EE Engine is not mandatory. However, SAP stipulates the use of Wily

Introscope statistics in the context of SAP Solution Manager to support Java-based SAP solutions.

To monitor a request across SAP components and to coherently display it, the end-to-end (E2E) runtime analysis uses the statistics records on both components. For this purpose, the unique identifier (GUID) is used, which connects the records of the SAP J2EE Engine and ABAP server. Provided they are not activated on the SAP J2EE Engine by default, they are specifically activated for the runtime analysis (see Chapter 4, Identifying Performance Problems in ABAP and Java Programs). For detailed analysis, the statistics records are used on the ABAP server and the Wily Introscope trace on the SAP J2EE Engine. As an option, you can also activate the ABAP runtime analysis and SQL trace on the ABAP server, and the Java logging and SQL trace on the SAP J2EE Engine.

E2E runtime analysis

3.2   Workload Monitor

This section describes the workload monitor. First, we'll deal with the functions and availability of the monitor and then describe how to work with it. Finally, we'll look at its technical settings.

3.2.1   Functions and Availability

The workload monitor (as of SAP Basis 4.6C; Transaction ST03N; for earlier versions, Transaction ST03) has been a part of SAP software since the first release of SAP R/3 (in the Computer Center Management System [CCMS]). In the central version of the workload monitor, it is possible to display statistical data from all SAP components in complex system landscapes, even from non-R/3 systems (Transaction ST03G). The statistical data from remote components can be accessed using RFC. The central workload monitor is available with SAP Basis 6.10. The system to be monitored must be at least SAP Basis 4.0 and have the corresponding support packages installed.

In the following section, we'll refer to mapping and menu paths for the local workload monitor in SAP Basis 4.6C and higher. We'll present the central workload monitor in Section 3.6, Central Workload Monitor.

3.2.2 Working with the Workload Monitor

To access the workload monitor initial screen, follow the menu path Tools • Administration • Monitor • Performance • System Load • Aggregated Statistics Records—Local. Alternatively, you can also use Transaction ST03. The main screen of the workload monitor appears, Workload in System PB5, as shown in Figure 3.1. The main screen is divided into three windows.

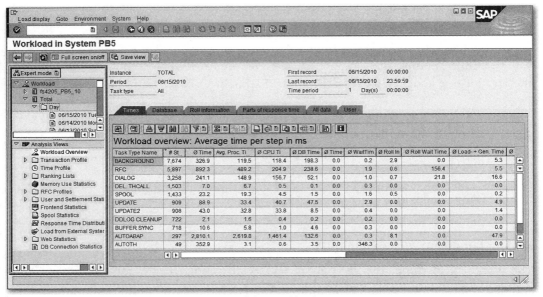

Figure 3.1 Main Screen of the Workload Monitor

In the top-left corner of the window, you will find a button with which you can choose a role. There are three roles:

▶ **Administrator**

This is the standard user mode. It enables fast access to the system load statistics of the current day and gives an overview of system load distribution. In addition, in this mode, you can display functions related to the data collector.

▶ **Service Engineer**

This mode gives you the system load statistics for the current day and the previous week, an overview of the history and distribution of the workload, and a detailed analysis of system load. By default, the system displays all of the statistics for all application servers.

▶ **Expert**
This mode gives users all of the functions available in Transaction ST03N. You can display all available system load data (daily, weekly, and monthly).

Also in the upper left, you can select the SAP instance you want to analyze or Total if you want to analyze the entire SAP system. You can also select the period of time to include in the analysis.

You will find administration information in the top-right portion of the window. The Instance field displays the name of the SAP instance, or select Total if you are analyzing the entire SAP system. Using the data for Period, First record, and Last record, you can check to see if the collection and compression of data for the selected time period has been done accordingly.

Further down, you will see statistical data on the performance of the SAP system and information on possible causes of performance problems. If you select the Workload Overview analysis view in the lower left, a breakdown of statistics on response times and throughput according to different task types will be shown. For the most part, the task types correspond to the work process types Dialog, Update, Update2, Background, and Spool. The Dialog work process type is further subdivided into Dialog, RFC, AutoABAP, and Buffer Sync.

The first important values are the number of *transaction steps* (Number of Steps column) and the average response time (Av. Response Time). In a dialog task, a transaction step corresponds to a screen change, that is, to a request that the SAP component executes for a user. The term *dialog step* might be misleading, because workload monitor dialog steps are performed not only for dialog tasks (immediate responses to input from online users), but also for background tasks, update tasks, and spool tasks. Processing an update request or spool request is counted as one dialog step by the workload monitor. Similarly, a background program may involve one or more dialog steps. To avoid ambiguity, this book will use the term *transaction step* for the processing step referred to in the workload monitor as a *dialog step* to differentiate it from a background

Transaction step

dialog step. We'll refer to the number of transaction steps per unit of time as *system activity* or *throughput*.

The *average response time for a transaction step* in a dialog task (Av. Response Time) is seen by many SAP users as the criterion for acceptable performance in an SAP component. Another generally accepted rule of thumb is that good performance in the SAP R/3 system is indicated by an average response time of one second or less. As we will see in this chapter, however, this broad generalization is practical when the variety of different SAP components, and the demands made on each, is considered.

In addition to the average response time, many other statistics such as database time, CPU time, and so on enable you to understand performance problems and their possible causes. We'll explain these statistics in the next section.

Using the tabs in the menu interface, you can select other screens with information about database accesses and so on. Use the Save View function to save user-specific views. The next time you call up Transaction ST03N, the system will automatically display the view you saved.

Load profiles (or analysis views) enable you to perform a detailed analysis of load distribution and response times. In addition to the Workload Overview previously mentioned, in the lower-left window, you can select other analysis views: Transaction Profile and Time Profile, which we'll discuss in greater detail in later sections.

If you are interested in the current statistics for the server you are connected to, from the initial screen of the workload monitor, select THIS APPLICATION SERVER • LAST MINUTE LOAD. Then specify over how many minutes the response times should be given (for example, the past 15 minutes). You are then taken to the main screen of the workload monitor, Performance: Recent Workload for Server.

The main screen of the workload monitor is divided into three sections. The first section, Instance, contains administrative information. The fields, SAP System, Server, and Instance No, show the names of the SAP component and server selected (or Total if you are analyzing the entire SAP system). Using the data for First Record and Last Record, you can check to see if the collection and compression of data in the selected time period has been done accordingly. The lower section, Task Types, tells you which task type has been chosen (Current field), and displays buttons that enable you to choose other task types. The central section of the screen (Workload) contains statistical data.

From the main screen of the workload monitor, go to the load profile by selecting GOTO • PROFILES. There, you can select profiles for the technical analyses such as Task Type Profile, Time Profile, Computer Profile, and Memory Profile, as well as profiles for application analyses such as Transaction Profile, User Profile, Client Profile, and Accounting Profile.

3.2.3 Technical Settings for the Workload Monitor

To ensure that the single statistical records generated and recorded for each transaction step are regularly collated in profiles, the RSCOLL00 program must be scheduled to run every hour as a background job (generally under the name SAP_COLLECTOR_FOR_PERFORMANCE). The compressed statistics are stored in the SWNCMONI table. You can display and modify the parameters that affect profile creation in the workload monitor. In the Expert role, select COLLECTOR AND PERFORMANCE DB • PERFORMANCE DATABASE • MONITORING DATABASE • REORGANIZATION. Under Standard Retention Periods, you can enter the retention periods for profiles, that is, the length of time before they are automatically deleted. Under Time Comparison Data, you can enter the retention period for data displayed under the workload monitor menu option Load History.

Protocols are set for each run of the RSCOLL00 program, which you can use for troubleshooting. You can view the log in the workload monitor under COLLECTOR AND PERFORMANCE DB • PERFORMANCE MONITOR COLLECTOR • LOG. You can find explanations of the functions and settings of the data collector in SAP Online Help and in the SAP Notes listed in Appendix C.

3.3   Workload Analysis

To examine workload analysis more closely, we'll now discuss the sequence of events in a transaction step and the times measured during it, with the help of Figures 3.2 and 3.3.

3.3.1 Transaction Step Cycle

Once an SAP user completes an entry, the presentation server sends the request to the dispatcher on the application server. The response time (Av. Response Time) is measured from the moment the request from the presentation server reaches the dispatcher in the application server (step ❶ in Figure 3.2). The response time ends when the request is processed, and the last data is sent back to the presentation server.

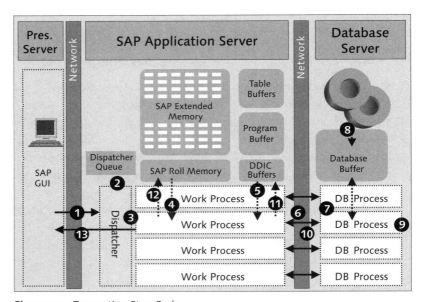

Figure 3.2 Transaction Step Cycle

Dispatcher wait time

When the dispatcher receives a processing request, it looks for a free SAP work process of the required type (dialog, update, etc.) and then sends the request to this work process, which begins the work. If all SAP work processes of the required type are busy when the request initially reaches the dispatcher, the request is placed in the dispatcher queue ❷.

In the dispatcher queue, the request waits until a work process of the required type is free. As soon as a work process is free, the dispatcher sends the request to it ❸. The time the request spends in the dispatcher queue is indicated as the Av. Wait Time. Note that many other kinds of wait times are involved in processing, for example, waiting for RFC calls, locks, CPU access, database access, and so on. To differentiate the wait time discussed here from others, it will be referred to as *dispatcher wait time*.

An SAP transaction normally extends over several transaction steps (screen changes). During these steps, data such as variables, internal tables, and screen lists are built up and stored in the main memory of the application server. This data is known as *user context*. Different transaction steps are normally processed by different dialog work processes. For example, the first transaction step may be processed by work process number three, the second transaction step by work process number four, and so on. At the beginning of a transaction step, the user context is made available to the appropriate work process. This procedure is called *roll-in* ❹. The technical processes comprising a roll-in, such as copying data to the local memory of the work process, are described in detail in Chapter 8, Memory Management. The opposite process, *roll-out*, saves the current user-context data to virtual memory at the conclusion of a transaction step ⓬. The duration of roll-in is referred to as *roll-in time*, and the duration of roll-out is known as *roll-out time*. The average roll times are indicated as Time per Roll In or Time per Roll Out in the workload monitor in Release 3. To obtain the average roll times in Release 4, divide the values of Roll In Time or Roll Out Time by the number of roll-ins or roll-outs, respectively. Please note that the roll-out time is not part of the transaction step response time. At roll-out, when the user context is copied from the local memory of the work process to the roll memory, the processed data has already been returned to the presentation server.

Roll-in, roll-out

All ABAP programs and screens that are required but not yet available in the application server buffers must be loaded or generated. The time it takes to do this is indicated as Av. Load+Gen Time. Loading a program also entails accessing database tables that store the ABAP programs, for example, the tables D010S and D010L.

Load time

When data is read or changed in the database, the time required is known as *database time* and is indicated as Av. DB Request Time. Database time is measured from the moment the database request is sent to the database server and runs until the moment the data is returned to the application server ❻ – ❿. Because database time is measured by the

Database time

application server, it includes not only the time required by the database to produce the requested data, but also the time required for network transfer of that data. Therefore, a network problem between the database and the application server will result in a greater database time.

Before accessing the database, the database interface of the work process checks whether the required data is already in the SAP buffers. If so, the buffers are accessed directly, because buffer use is up to 100 times faster than database access (❺, ⓫). Buffer access does not contribute to database time.

DB procedure time

Since release 4.6C, it has been possible to gather statistics separately on DB procedure calls. DB procedure calls are particularly relevant in APO systems, because communication between APO instances and liveCache are done via DB procedures (also called *COM routines*). For analysis purposes, a new subrecord type, the *DB procedure subrecord,* was introduced, which contains the name of a DB procedure and the name of the logical DB connection as a key field, along with the number of calls and the total execution time as the data section. By default, these subrecords are not written. To activate writing, you must set the profile parameter stat/ dbprocrec. This is also possible in a workload monitor running instance in expert mode. In the workload monitor, the time needed to execute DB procedures is identified as DB Procedure Time. The database time in the workload monitor and in the single record statistics only contains times for calls to the actual database.

Roll wait time

Roll wait time occurs in remote function calls (RFCs), in other words, when there is communication between software components or (beginning with SAP Basis 4.6) when there is communication with the presentation level.

GUI time

Up until SAP Basis 4.5, the duration of communication between the presentation and application servers (that is, network transfers and the creation of images on the presentation server) was not included in the workload analysis data. Starting with SAP Basis 4.6, these times are included in the response time (for the main part, at least) as *GUI time*. Roll wait time and GUI time are explained in Chapter 6, Workload Distribution and Interfaces, and Chapter 7, SAP GUI and Internet Connection.

Enqueue time, indicated as Av. Enqueue Time, is the time during which a work process sets an enqueue request.

Processing time is the total response time minus the sum of all times previously mentioned (except GUI time).

All of the statistics discussed concern actions that form part of an SAP work process; that is, whenever the action in question runs, it is timed. With Av. CPU Time, on the other hand, at the end of a transaction step, the SAP work process asks the operating system how much CPU time has expired during that step. CPU time is determined by the operating system and is not an additive component of transaction response time (like the times mentioned above) but is consumed during load time, roll time, and processing time (see Figure 3.3).

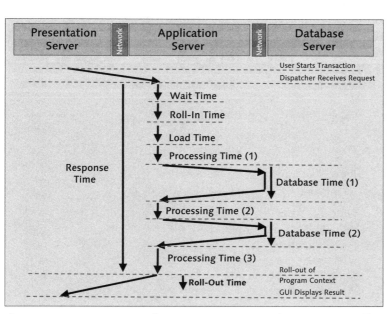

Figure 3.3 Response Time and Its Components: Dispatcher Wait Time, Roll-in Time, Roll Wait Time, Load Time, Database Time, Processing Time, and CPU Time

3.3.2 Interpreting Response Times

To analyze response times for dialog processing, use the guideline values in Table 3.1. The *update* task type value can be about 50% higher than indicated in the table. The Problem Indicated column specifies what problem may arise if the guideline values are significantly exceeded.

Time	Guideline Value	Problem Indicated	See Chapter
Dispatcher wait time (Wait time)	<10% of response time; <50 ms	General performance problem with many possible causes	
Load time (Load+gen time)	<50 ms	Program buffer too small or CPU bottleneck	2
Roll-in time, Roll-out time (in Release 4.0: Roll-in time/ Roll-ins; in Release 3.0/3.1: time per roll-in, etc.	<20 ms	SAP roll buffer or SAP extended memory too small, or CPU bottleneck	2, 8
Roll wait time	<200 ms	Problem with frontend communication (together with higher GUI time) or with communication with external component	4, 6, 7
GUI time	<200 ms	Problem with frontend communication (together with higher roll wait time)	4, 6, 7
Enqueue time	<5 ms	Problem with enqueue or network problems	4
Processing time CPU time	Processing time <2 × CPU time	CPU bottleneck or communication problem	5
Database time (DB request time)	<40% of response time minus dispatcher wait time; Guideline value: 200–600 ms	Database problem, network problem, or CPU bottleneck	3, 4, 11
Time per DB request	<5 ms	Database problem	3, 4, 11
Direct reads	<2 ms	Database problem	3, 4, 11
Sequential reads	<10 ms	Database problem	3, 4, 11
Changes and commits	<25 ms	Database problem	3, 4, 11

Table 3.1 Guideline Values for Analyzing Average Response Times for Task Type Dialog

If the values you observe in the workload monitor are significantly outside the guideline range indicated in Table 3.1, there may be a performance problem in the relevant area (for example, in the database). Note that these values are based on standard situations and may differ in some SAP components.

[+]

In addition to comparing your statistics with the guideline values, you should perform the following analysis, which could be referred to as the "search for time lost." As previously mentioned, there are two different sources of time statistics. All times, except for CPU time, are measured from the perspective of the SAP work process. CPU time is measured from the perspective of the operating system. The lost time analysis checks whether the two statistics can be brought together. To do so, we subtract from the total average response time all times for which the SAP work process does not require any CPU time, namely, dispatcher wait time, database time, enqueue time, and roll wait time. (As of Release 4, to find the average roll wait time in the workload monitor, divide the Roll Wait Time by the Dialog Steps.)

Lost time

Generally, programs are processed during processing time, and CPU capacity is normally consumed during this time. Therefore, processing time and CPU time should be more or less the same. As a rule of thumb, the difference between processing time and CPU time should not be more than 10%. Greater lost times indicate performance problems.

What are the possible causes of a significant difference between processing time and CPU time?

▶ The first possible cause is a CPU bottleneck, which means there is not enough CPU capacity available for the SAP work processes, which must therefore wait until the CPU becomes available. In this case, processing time is measured in the work process while no CPU time is used, and this processing time is considerably greater than CPU time.

▶ Another reason for a difference between processing time and CPU time can be wait times in the SAP work process. Whenever the SAP work process has a Stopped status, processing time is measured without out CPU time being used. This type of wait situation can be identified in the work process overview.

3.3.3 Activity, Throughput, and Load

Activity, throughput
The concepts system activity, throughput, and load can best be explained using the Workload Overview analysis view (see Figure 3.1): The number of transaction steps can be seen in the second column (Number of Steps). The number of transaction steps per unit of time can be defined as *system activity* or *throughput*. In our example, the highest level of activity (2,614 transaction steps) corresponds to dialog processing; that is, the user has performed 2,614 screen changes in dialog processing mode during the specified period of time.

Load
If two users each executed 100 transaction steps within a given time period, they created equal activity. This does not mean, however, that they produced the same *load* on the system. If, for example, the first user (entering financial documents) has executed 100 transaction steps with an average response time of 500 ms, this user has occupied the system for 50 seconds. If a second user (creating auditing reports) performs 100 transaction steps with of an average response time of 5 seconds, this user has occupied the system for 500 seconds. The second user has created a system *load* that is 10 times greater than the first user, with the same amount of *activity*. As can be seen from this example, the product of the number of transaction steps and the average response time is a way of measuring the load generated. (To be more precise, subtract dispatcher wait time and roll wait time from the total response time, because a request does not create system load while it waits in the dispatcher queue or while it waits for an RFC to be carried out.) Similarly, you can determine the database load created by the different task types using the total database time (transaction steps multiplied by average database time). CPU load on the application server can also be measured in this way. The distribution of times (database time, CPU time, and so on) therefore reflects the distribution of load on the system better than just the number of transaction steps.

Active users
The simplest and most graphic measure of an SAP component's size is its number of users. Unfortunately, the *number of users* is also an imprecise measure; its meaning varies according to context. For example, the number of users can mean either the number of licenses or the number of user master records, to mention just two possible definitions.

For components that are mainly characterized by background or interface load, the number of users is no longer relevant as an indication of size. To avoid confusion, this book distinguishes three types of users, as follows:

▶ **Occasional user**
On average, this type of user performs fewer than 400 transaction steps (screen changes) per week. For a 40-hour workweek, this corresponds to an average of one transaction step every six minutes. This user typically only uses the SAP component now and then.

▶ **Transactional user**
On average, a transactional user performs up to 4,800 transaction steps per week. This corresponds to less than one transaction step every 30 seconds. These users use the SAP component regularly and continuously.

▶ **Data entry, telesales, or high-volume power user**
Power users perform more than 4,800 transaction steps per week. They use the SAP component regularly and at high volume.

In this book, the term *active user* corresponds to either the transactional user or power user category.

The user profile gives information about users' activities. You can call the user profile in the workload monitor by selecting LOAD DISTRIBUTION • USERS PER INSTANCE.

3.4   Performing Workload Analyses

In general, the first input for a performance analysis comes from observations made by users. The workload monitor helps you verify users' subjective comments and narrow down the causes of performance problems. We can distinguish between two types of problems:

▶ **General performance problems**
A *general performance problem* results in poor response times and unsatisfactory throughput in *all transactions*. This type of problem can have a negative impact on business processes and lead to financial loss.

▶ **Specific performance problems**
If the throughput or response time of *individual transactions* is unsatisfactory, then we can experience *specific performance problems*. Specific performance problems can have a negative impact on business processes if the transaction in question is key to the business process (such as ordering/delivering goods).

With the help of the seven questions in the following sections, you can further limit performance problems. Guideline values and examples are provided to help you answer these questions. You should, however, bear in mind that a simple yes or no answer is not always possible.

3.4.1 Analyzing General Performance Problems

Is There a General Performance Problem?

Users can often identify a general performance problem. You can use the workload monitor to verify users' observations and check whether response times that affect all transactions are high. The following criteria, which apply to dialog tasks, may help you decide if there is a problem:

▶ **Dispatcher wait time >>50 ms**
A significantly large dispatcher wait time always affects all transactions. It implies that programs are too slow and are blocking work processes for lengthy periods — or that too few work processes have been configured.

▶ **Database time >>40% (response time minus dispatcher wait time); and database time >400 ms**
A high database time slows performance for all transactions.

▶ **Processing time >2 × CPU time**
High processing time slows performance for all transactions. This can be caused by a CPU bottleneck or a problem with communication between systems.

▶ **Average response time greater than the system-specific guideline value**
Average response time for a dialog task is seen by many SAP users as the decisive criterion for acceptable performance in an SAP component. A guideline value must be defined for each individual SAP

component. A generally accepted rule of thumb is that good performance is indicated by an average response time of one second or less. This kind of broad generalization is not always valid for all of the different requirements of SAP components.

Since SAP Basis 4.6, the response times displayed in the workload monitor have included time data regarding communication between the application and presentation levels (as part of GUI time and as time for network transfer and processing in the presentation server). This means time elements are created that were not included in measurements in older versions. Due to the change in measuring techniques, the workload monitor for an SAP R/3 4.6 system or a younger SAP ERP system generally displays average response times of around 100–200 milliseconds higher than the older versions, even though performance has not changed from the user's point of view. This should be kept in mind when negotiating service-level agreements.

[+]

Is the Performance Problem Temporary or Permanent?

After verifying that there is a general performance problem, try to find out how frequently the problem occurs. The following questions may help:

▶ Is the problem permanent or temporary?

▶ Does this problem occur at regular time intervals, for example, at particular times of the day?

▶ Is it a nonrecurring problem?

▶ At what times (database time, CPU time, or processing time) does the problem occur?

▶ Does the problem occur following only specific system activities, for example, when background programs run on the system?

To examine these questions more closely, compare the workload statistics for recent days.

In workload monitor expert mode, in the upper-left window, select LOAD HISTORY AND DISTRIBUTION • LOAD HISTORY • TOTAL. Compare the performance values for several days to find out if the problem only occurs on certain days (see Figure 3.4).

Then generate the *day or time profile* by selecting the Time Profile analysis view in the lower left of the workload monitor window. In a day or time profile, the transaction steps and response times for all of the hours in one day are presented.

Using the time profile, you can analyze the daily loads on the system. If you find that the average response time increases dramatically only at particular periods of high load, you can infer that the system is overloaded at these times. If the average response times are also unsatisfactory at times of low system load, the performance problem is load-independent.

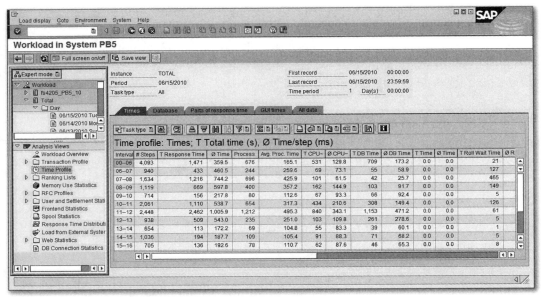

Figure 3.4 Time Profile for Dialog Processing

[Ex] You can diagnose a general performance problem using the workload analysis. By comparing the workload data for different days, you can narrow the problem down to a particular period of time in which there is conspicuously high database usage, especially changes and commits. For example, a closer examination of the error log file in the database reveals that an *archiver stuck* occurred overnight. (An archiver stuck occurs in an Oracle database if the directory for redo log files is full, which means no further redo information can be written; the database and the SAP instances stop responding. Once the problem has been eliminated, the database and SAP instances continue working without error.) The database administrator resolves the problem the next morning. In the middle of the day, the archiver stuck leads to higher database response times for this day (especially for changes and commits). An analysis on the workload monitor would suggest poor database performance, although the performance is actually good, which becomes evident once this problem has been eliminated.

Time profiles enable you to determine whether excessive background processing during periods of peak system load has a negative impact on dialog processing. To create time profiles for dialog processing and background processing, click the Task Type button and select the task types Dialog or Background. Use the Total Response Time (s), Total CPU Time Total (s), and Total DB Time Total (s) fields to determine what time of day the dialog or background load occurs. These profiles enable you to determine whether excessive use of background processing during periods of peak system load has a negative impact on dialog processing. Try to ensure that the background processing load remains low during these peak periods, particularly if there are performance problems.

Dialog versus background load

You may also find it helpful to compare the time profile per day in the workload monitor with the time profile per day for CPU load and paging (both indicated in the operating system monitor). This comparison enables you to determine whether deteriorating response times correlate with a large CPU load or a high paging rate. If so, a temporary hardware bottleneck is indicated (see the next question).

In the SAP EarlyWatch Alert report (in the DB Load Profile section), you can get a weekly overview of the dialog, background and RFC load for each day. The tables in the SAP EarlyWatch Alert report are a compressed version of the daily profile.

SAP EarlyWatch Alert

Is There a Hardware Bottleneck?

A CPU bottleneck or main memory bottleneck can be detected as follows:

1. Find out if the hourly averages for the CPU load or paging rate are large. As a rule of thumb, the risk of a hardware bottleneck is regard-

ed as high when the hourly average of free CPU capacity (indicated as CPU Idle) is less than 20% or the paging rate per hour exceeds 20% of the physical main memory (see also Chapter 2, Section 2.2.1, Analyzing a Hardware Bottleneck (CPU and Main Memory).

2. Check whether the large CPU load or high paging rate really does negatively affect SAP component response times.

   To check for a hardware bottleneck on an application server, look at the processing time. If the processing time is much greater than double the CPU time, this indicates that the work processes are waiting for CPU resources. (However, an increased processing time may have other causes. See also Section 3.3, Workload Analysis.) A further indication of a hardware bottleneck on the application server is increased load, roll-in, and dispatcher wait times.

   To check for a hardware bottleneck on the database server, establish whether the database time is too large. Compare, for example, the average database times in the daily time profile at times of high and low loads.

3. To check for a main memory bottleneck, determine whether the virtual allocated memory is significantly greater than the physical available main memory. As long as virtual memory is less than 1.5 times the physical main memory, there is usually no risk of a main memory bottleneck.

You can be fairly certain that there is, in fact, a hardware bottleneck only if all three of these checks indicate a problem (the first two apply to CPU and memory, the final one only to memory).

The three possible causes of a hardware bottleneck are as follows:

▶ **Poor load distribution**
The load is not optimally distributed across the servers. There may be servers with free CPU or main memory capacity. Alternatively, load distribution may become less than optimal at certain times of the day, for example, when several background processes run in parallel during periods of peak system load. You should be able to reschedule these programs to run when there is low system load.

▶ **Individual processes cause high CPU load**
Individual processes with high CPU loads may be running when there is a high system load. These can include database processes (with expensive SQL statements), SAP work processes (with programs running as background jobs), or processes external to SAP. To improve performance, you may be able to tune, reschedule, or (in the case of external processes) cancel these processes.

▶ **Insufficient hardware capacity**
If the two previously mentioned causes of hardware bottlenecks do not apply, the hardware capacity may be too small for your system load.

If you have correctly identified a hardware bottleneck, proceed as described in Chapter 2, Section 2.2.1, Analyzing a Hardware Bottleneck (CPU and Main Memory).

Is There a General Database Performance Problem?

A general database performance problem is indicated by increased database times. The following guideline values for dialog tasks in the workload monitor can indicate a general performance problem:

▶ Database time >>40% (response time minus dispatcher wait time); database time >400 ms

▶ Direct reads >>2 ms

▶ Sequential reads >>10 ms

▶ Changes and commits >>25 ms

A database performance problem can have many possible causes. Proceed as described in Chapter 2, Section 2.3, Database Monitoring.

Is the Load Distribution Optimal?

You can detect a performance problem caused by nonoptimal load distribution by comparing the CPU load and paging rates for the various servers (in the operating system monitor). You should also compare response times for the various application servers in the workload monitor.

To display the *server profile* from the workload monitor initial screen, follow the menu path GOTO • PERFORMANCE DATABASE • ANALYZE ALL SERVERS • COMPARE ALL SERVERS. You can then enter the period of analysis by selecting EDIT • CHOOSE PERIOD TYPE and clicking the Period+ and Period- buttons.

The server profile shows the transaction steps and related response times for each server. If there are several SAP instances on one application server, the statistics indicated for the server are the totals for all instances on that server. To obtain details on the individual servers' task types, double-click a row in the list of servers.

Dispatcher wait time

In the server profile, check the load distribution across your servers. For example, if the *dispatcher wait time* occurs only on one server or on a small number of servers, this implies either that too many users are working on these servers or that too few work processes are configured on these servers.

CPU time

Total *CPU time* (indicated as CPU Time Total) on all application servers should be roughly equal if all servers have the same CPU capacity. If you have servers with different CPU capacities, CPU times should differ accordingly.

One cause of poor load distribution may be a nonoptimal configuration of logon groups or work processes. To optimize load distribution, see Chapter 6, Section 6.2, Load Distribution Within the ABAP Application Instances.

Database time

If the average *database times* (indicated as DB Time Avg.) for the various servers differ greatly, this may indicate a network problem. You can assume that application servers are configured with the same work processes and that users on the various application servers are, on average, using the same transactions. Therefore, there is no obvious reason, other than a network problem, for the database to serve one application server slower than another application server. This argument applies only to servers that are configured with the same work processes. For background servers, update servers, or servers mainly used for reporting, the average database time will be greater than that for dialog servers.

**Is There a Performance Problem Caused
by SAP Memory Management?**

Performance problems caused by SAP memory management (see Chapter 2, Section 2.3, Database Monitoring) may be the result of SAP buffers or SAP extended memory being too small. These problems would be seen in the workload monitor, as follows:

▸ If the program buffer, CUA buffer, or screen buffer are too small, there will be an increase in average load time (average load time >>50 ms).

▸ If the extended memory or roll buffer are full, the roll-in or roll-out times may increase (average roll-in or roll-out times >>20 ms).

These guideline times apply to dialog tasks.

You should also monitor the *memory profile*. In the old workload monitor (Transaction ST03 in SAP Basis 4.6 and earlier), this could be found under GOTO • PROFILES • MEMORY PROFILE.

Memory profile

The memory profile shows memory usage per program. Utilization of extended memory and heap memory (Priv. Mem.) are indicated. The monitor also shows how often work processes entered PRIV mode (in the column Workproc. Reservations) and how often a work process was restarted after its use of heap memory exceeded the value of the `abap/heaplimit` parameter (indicated in the column Workproc. Restarts). If you notice higher roll or load times, proceed with the analysis described in Chapter 2, Section 2.4, Analyzing SAP Memory Configuration.

With SAP Basis 6.10, the memory profile is integrated into the new workload monitor (Transaction ST03N).

3.4.2 Analyzing Specific Performance Problems

The workload monitor is an analysis tool used for both technical analysis and application analysis.

Is There a Performance Problem with a Transaction?

The *transaction profile* is of primary importance for application analysis. To change over to the transaction profile, in the lower-left window of the workload monitor under Analysis Views, select Transaction Profile.

The transaction profile contains a list of all transactions (or programs) started in the selected period. The number of transaction steps for each transaction is recorded (Number of Steps) and is a measure of the activity of a transaction. Other columns in the transaction profile show the total and average response times and the proportions of CPU time, dispatcher wait time, and database time. Using the tabs in the menu interface, you can select other screens with information about database accesses and so on.

Activity From the number of transaction steps (Number of Steps), you can estimate how frequently the transaction was executed if you know how many transaction steps (screen changes) each regular user requires on average per procedure. For example, if a regular user requires an average of 5 transaction steps to create a sales order (Transaction VA01), and the transaction profile shows 100,000 transaction steps for the selected time period, you can calculate that 20,000 sales orders were created. To see which transaction had the most activity, sort by the Number of Steps column.

Load The Total Response Time column displays a measure for the entire load on the system (see Section 3.3.3, Activity, Throughput, and Load). To find out which transactions produced the most load on the system, sort the list by the columns Total Response Time, Total CPU Time, and/or Total DB Time. After each sort, the programs at the top of the list are likely candidates for performance optimization.

[Ex] In Figure 3.5, Transaction VA01 is executed twice as often as Transaction VA03 (1,208 steps compared to 604); however, due to the higher average response time, Transaction VA01 generates 10 times as much load as Transaction VA03 (9,429 seconds compared with 968 seconds).

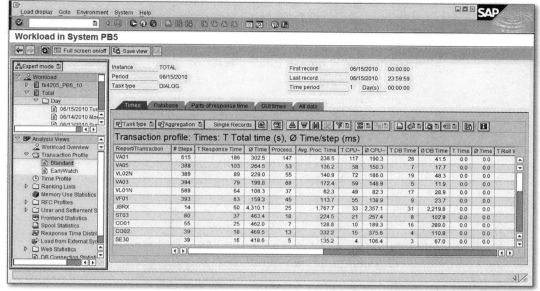

Figure 3.5 Transaction Profile

For users, the *average response time* of transactions is an important index of performance. Monitor and create guideline values for the average response times of core transactions, that is, transactions in which performance is central to business operations.

Average response time

In general, when analyzing the transaction profile, consider the following questions:

- Sort the transaction profile according to Total DB Time. Which transactions cause the greatest database load?

- Sort the transaction profile according to Total CPU Time. Which transactions cause the greatest CPU load?

- Are there transactions for which the proportion of database time or CPU time is significantly higher than 60% of the total response time? Analyze these transactions using an SQL trace or ABAP trace. The procedure for analyzing individual programs and transactions is described in Chapter 4, Identifying Performance Problems in ABAP and Java Programs.

- Are there any customer-developed programs or transactions that produce a large load?

Monitor and save a copy of the transaction profile at regular intervals. This enables you to determine whether the response times of individual transactions grow continuously over time or whether there is a sudden worsening of response times after a program modification. By recognizing these trends early in the transaction profile, you can initiate a detailed program analysis before a program causes bottlenecks for the entire process chain — or worse, reduces the performance of the entire SAP system due to heavy CPU or database loads.

Table 3.2 provides explanations and guideline response times for common system transactions. In general, these programs can be ignored during performance analysis.

Transaction/ Program	Description/Comment	Acceptable Response Time
MainMenu	Actions in the menu. MainMenu frequently appears near the top of the list if sorted according to Dialog Steps.	<100 ms
Login_Pw/ Logoff	Logon or logoff screen.	
AutoABAP	The AutoABAP runs periodically in the background and executes actions like those required by the Alert Monitor.	<1,000 ms
Buf.Sync	Display table buffer (buffer synchronization).	<1,000 ms
Rep_Edit	Actions in the ABAP Editor.	
(B)SCHDL	The batch scheduler runs periodically and checks whether background programs are due to be started.	
RSCOLL00	The performance collector runs periodically and collects data on performance. If you sort the transaction profile according to Response Time Total, this program is often near the top of the list. However, the CPU Time Total and DB Time Total columns indicate that this program produces little CPU or database time. Most of the response time for this program occurs when it is waiting in work processes for performance data.	
RSM13000	The update program is used to summarize all update module statistics that cannot be ascribed to a transaction.	<3,000 ms

Table 3.2 System Programs in the Transaction Profile

3.5   Application Monitor

Another important instrument for workload analysis is the Application Monitor (Transaction ST07), which you can use to create a load profile for each SAP module. To call this monitor, select: TOOLS • ADMINISTRATION • MONITOR • PERFORMANCE • WORKLOAD • APPLICATION • APPLICATION MONITOR.

All screens of the Application Monitor show performance-relevant data according to the SAP application module. The monitor takes advantage of the fact that each transaction, program, and table can be found in the SAP component hierarchy. For example, you can see statistics in the Create Sales Order transaction (Transaction VA01) under the SAP hierarchy branch SALES & DISTRIBUTION • SALES • CREATE SALES ORDER. (To see an outline of the full SAP component hierarchy structure, use Transaction HIER.) Many screens in the Application Monitor show data that is also displayed in other monitors, such as the workload monitor, the SAP Storage Configuration Monitor (Transaction ST02), and the Table Call Statistics (Transaction ST10). The advantage of using the Application Monitor is that the data is grouped according to the SAP application component hierarchy; from an initial overview, you can drill down to increasingly detailed views of particular modules, submodules, and transactions that might be consuming excessive system resources.

3.5.1   User Profile

The initial screen of the Application Monitor shows the current number of users for different SAP modules. The user profile for each listed application consists of the number of logged-on users, active users, and users currently waiting for a request to be processed. To descend to a lower level of the SAP application component hierarchy and see the user profile for a more specific area, double-click the appropriate modules.

For example, double-clicking the Sales & Distribution module displays   **[Ex]**
the distribution of users in the submodules Sales, Shipping, Billing, and Basic Functions. A subsequent double-click on Sales shows the user profile for transactions belonging to Sales, such as VA01 and VA02.

Looking at the user profile in the Application Monitor is a convenient way of finding out the number of logged on and active users (Figure 3.6). An active user is one who has performed a transaction step in the past 30 seconds. You can change this time period by selecting the menu option USER DISTRIBUTION • CHANGE ACTIVE TIME. To analyze user distribution on the application servers, select USER DISTRIBUTION • CHOOSE APP. SERVER. The user profile in the Application Monitor is especially useful when you want to check whether group logons are functioning correctly; that is, users are logging on to application servers independently of one another.

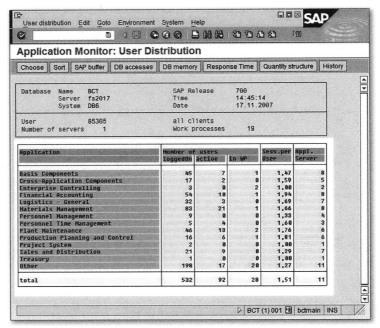

Figure 3.6 User Profile in the Application Monitor

3.5.2 Load per SAP Application Module

From the Application Monitor initial screen, select Response Time to display the load profile for each SAP application module.

In the dialog boxes that appear, specify the relevant server and time period — similar to the procedure used with the workload monitor.

The data on this screen matches data in the transaction profile and includes transaction steps, response times per transaction step, CPU times, wait times, and database times. Click the TOTAL→AVG button to toggle between the average response times per transaction and the total response time for all transaction steps. All data on this screen is grouped according to SAP application module. By double-clicking the appropriate module, you can navigate to statistics on more specific component areas.

You can use the Application Monitor the same way as the transaction profile in the workload monitor. The advantage of using the Application Monitor is that data is grouped according to the SAP application component hierarchy; from an initial overview, you can access increasingly detailed views of particular modules and submodules that are consuming the most system resources.

The Application Monitor can create graphs and diagrams that illustrate load distribution. Click the TOTAL→AVG button to show total response times (that is, Resp. Time Total (s), CPU Time Total (s), and so on), and then click the Graphic button. The resulting pie charts illustrate the distribution of transaction steps and the response times according to SAP application module. The distribution of transaction steps on the module corresponds to activity distribution, the distribution of total response time corresponds to load distribution among all SAP components, the distribution of database time corresponds to load distribution on the database, and the distribution of CPU time corresponds to load distribution on the application servers.

In the Workload by Application Module section of the SAP EarlyWatch Alert report, you can get a weekly overview of workload distribution per SAP component. The tables in the SAP EarlyWatch Alert report present a condensed version of data from the Application Monitor.

SAP EarlyWatch Alert

3.5.3 SAP Buffer

On the Application Monitor initial screen, click the SAP Buffer button to access an application of the SAP buffer, differentiated according to SAP modules (for example, program buffer, CUA buffer, screen buffer, and table buffer for generic buffering and single record buffering). To access statistics for more specific areas within an SAP application module (following the SAP component hierarchy), double-click the appropriate rows in the Application column until you get down to the individual programs and tables.

3.6 Central Workload Monitor

In a classic SAP ERP system, a transactional step usually consists of one action within a system. In a more complex system environment, a single transactional step can involve actions in several systems. Examples of these transactional steps include:

▸ ITS applications such as SAP GUI for HTML, easy web transactions (EWTs), and so forth, which involve actions on the ITS and in the ABAP runtime environment during a single transactional step.

▸ Applications such as SAP CRM Internet Sales, Portal-iViews, and Web Dynpro applications, in which the frontend communication takes place via the SAP J2EE Engine, and the backend functionality is implemented via the ABAP server.

▸ Applications that involve two or more ABAP systems coupled via RFC, for example, sales transactions in the SAP ERP system that use the available-to-promise (ATP) function in SAP APO for availability checks.

For all of these cases, SAP NetWeaver technology enables you to carry out a cross-system workload analysis that links the performance statistics of the various components with each other.

Availability   The central workload monitor is available as of SAP Basis 6.20. The ABAP-based components to be monitored need at least version 4.0 of SAP Basis. In addition to ABAP-based components (SAP ERP, SAP NetWeaver BW, SAP APO, and so on) you can use the workload monitor to analyze the SAP J2EE Engine, SAP ITS, and SAP Business Connector. Monitoring agents must be installed and running on the respective machines.

To use the central workload monitor, you must set up an SAP component (with ABAP Basis 6.20 or later) as a central monitoring system. This system should be the same as the one used for the central CCMS

Monitor. Typically, this is SAP Solution Manager. The components to be monitored must be made known to the central monitoring system in the CCMS System Component Repository (SCR) (see Chapter 2, Section 2.8, Continuous Monitoring Using CCMS).

You can find more information on the CCMS SCR and the SAP monitoring agents and their enhancements in the SAP Service Marketplace at *http://service.sap.com/systemmanagement*.

Whereas the global workload monitor displays aggregated data, central single-record statistics (which we'll describe in Chapter 4) provide a more detailed view; single statistics records are displayed so you can trace actions that belong to a transactional step or business process across system boundaries. The central workload monitor (ST03G) is therefore an enhancement of the workload monitor (ST03N), whereas the central single-record statistics (STATTRACE) is an enhancement of single-record statistics (STAD).

Central single-record statistics and the central workload monitor

Working with the Central Workload Monitor

To access the central workload monitor initial screen, follow the menu path Tools • Administration • Monitor • Performance • System Load • Aggregated Statistics Records — Global. Alternatively, you can also use Transaction ST03. This takes you to the main screen of the workload monitor, Global System Load Analysis. The design of this monitor is very similar to that of the workload monitor for a single SAP system. The screen is divided into three window panes.

The top-left pane contains the Workload node, where you can find the components for which load information is available. The load data is structured in the following hierarchy:

▶ **Component type**
Describes the type of component. For an ABAP-based component, SAP R/3 is displayed; for the ITS, the short name ITS; for the SAP J2EE Engine, SAPJ2ENode; and for the database to which the J2EE Engine is connected, SAPJDBI. For ABAP-based components, the SID is also displayed.

> ► **Component**
> Describes an actual component, such as the instance name of an ABAP-based component or the instance name of an ITS.

> ► **Period**
> You can view workload data on a daily, weekly, or monthly basis. To do this, expand the relevant time unit and select the concrete period by double-clicking it.

Analysis views   The lower-left pane contains a list of analysis views. The analysis views for the ABAP server are similar to those analysis views already introduced in the context of the local workload monitor. The analysis views of other components are similar to those of the ABAP server; this means they also contain system load profile, time profile, transaction profile, and so on. Table 3.3 describes the individual profiles for non-ABAP components.

Profile	Description
Workload overview	Shows the aggregation of the statistics records according to task types; on the SAP J2EE Engine, for example, Web Request, EJB Request, System
Action profile	Shows the aggregation of statistics records according to actions; on the SAP J2EE Engine, for example, specific actions in Web Dynpro, RFC calls, and so on (Figure 3.7)
Time profile	Shows the aggregation of statistics records according to the hours of the day
User profile	Shows the aggregation of statistics records according to users
Load from external systems	Shows the aggregation of statistics records according to external systems
Response time distribution	Shows the distribution of response times
Availability	Shows the distribution of components' availability, measured by the CCMS agents

Table 3.3   Load Profiles in the Central Workload Monitor for Non-ABAP Components

Analysis data   The right-hand pane, which presents the analysis data, also has the same structure as the one you already know from the local workload monitor: The upper part of the right-hand pane contains administration information, the instance name of the component, and the period for which statistical data is available.

The lower part of the right-hand pane displays the actual workload data, depending on the analysis view selected in the lower-left pane. In the first columns, you can find the dimensions of the load profile; the Action Profile in Figure 3.7 shows the action and the action type. The other columns contain performance key figures. These include:

▶ Number of dialog steps

▶ Response time

▶ CPU time

▶ Call or roll wait time

▶ Wait time in the components

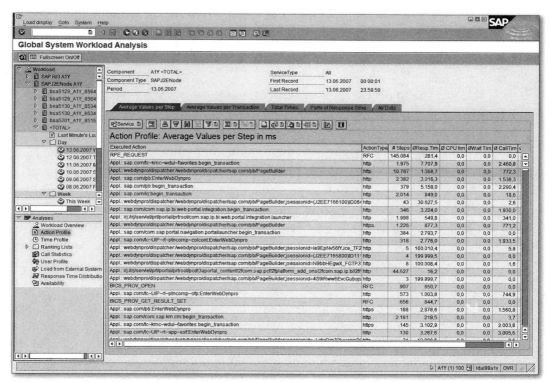

Figure 3.7 Action Screen of the Central Workload Monitor

With this information, you can quickly find out which components had long wait times. High CPU time means the application on this component must be analyzed further. A high wait time in the component means an overload situation exists. Depending on the type of component (ABAP server, J2EE Engine, or ITS), you must carry out a component-based analysis. We'll describe that analysis in more detail in the following chapters. A high call/roll wait time means the performance problem cannot be found in this component but can be found in a component that has been called by this one.

Publishing components for central workload analysis

When you call the central workload monitor in your SAP system, you may only find statistical data for the ABAP component you are currently logged onto. To access statistics data for other components from a specific system, you must make these components known centrally. Proceed as follows:

1. Expand the Setting & Log subtree in the upper-left pane of the central workload monitor.

2. Select System Selection. The screen Last Saved Dataset is now displayed.

3. To display a list of systems, select the entry you want in the Systems dropdown menu.

4. If necessary, you can make changes to the list displayed.

5. To start the consistency analysis for a system list, click the Apply button. The analysis is then performed for each activated entry. Prior to that, the system carries out a consistency check of the destination to the monitoring system. If the consistency check fails for a specific entry, this entry is deactivated, and a message for the application log is generated. The list specified when you click the Apply button therefore contains the systems that the global system load monitor displays.

Last Minute's Load

Under the Workload node in the upper-left pane, you can find the Last Minute's Load function. The workload monitor essentially determines the workload data once per hour on the basis of statistical data for the individual components. Therefore, you cannot view any data that is less than one hour old, because it hasn't been written to the database yet. The Last Minute's Load function, however, enables you to request data that refers to a specific period within the last hour, such as the past 15 minutes. Note, however, that this can take several minutes, depending on the size of the system.

For the global workload monitor, as for every system-monitoring tool, you must also find an optimal solution somewhere between the requirement for an exact monitoring of the system and the requirement for monitoring that doesn't affect overall system performance. The parameters that control statistics data management are located under the Control Data and Settings & Log subtrees. (You can find further information on this subject in the online Help.)

Technical settings for the workload monitor

Figure 3.7 shows the action profile for an SAP J2EE Engine on which the portal and Web Dynpro for Java run. Actions starting with `irj/servlet/...` are portal actions, and actions starting with `webdynpro/dispatcher...` are Web Dynpro actions. Let's discuss the `/webdynpro/dispatcher/sap.com/pb/PageBuilder` action, which represents the call of an application built with Web Dynpro for Java (highlighted in the figure). The average response time for a call of these applications is 1,368.7 milliseconds; 772.3 milliseconds are then required for the call of the ABAP server (Call Time column). The remaining time is required for processing in the SAP J2EE Engine. In the CPU Time column, our example does not provide any values, because the appropriate statistics was not available on the operating system. By default, the values in the Wait Time column are always zero in the SAP J2EE Engine, because a request that cannot be processed immediately is denied with a corresponding error message.

[Ex]

The RFC action type includes the calls of the ABAP server; here, the RFCs, RPE_REQUEST, BICS_PROV_OPEN, and BICS_PROV_GET_RESULT are significant. The Response Times column indicates the time for calls. The Call Time column is not used.

3.7 The Java Workload Monitor in SAP Solution Manager and the Introscope Monitor

In this section, we'll present user interfaces for Java workload analysis in SAP Solution Manager and Introscope.

3.7.1 Working with the Java Workload Monitor in SAP Solution Manager

End-to-end workload analysis

The end-to-end workload analysis in the diagnostics part of SAP Solution Manager provides functions for a workload analysis of ABAP and Java applications on SAP NetWeaver.

The ABAP part of the workload analysis in SAP Solution Manager uses functions that are also available in ABAP Basis. An additional benefit is the centralization of the solution view of the analyses. Provided you are familiar with the workload monitors of the ABAP server, you can easily orient yourself in the ABAP part of the workload analysis of SAP Solution Manager. Therefore, we won't go into detail here.

Java part

The Java part of workload analysis in SAP Solution Manager, however, provides new functions that would not be available without SAP Solution Manager. Workload analysis of Java applications uses a Wily product (owned by Computer Associates), which is licensed for applications with SAP Solution Manager.

You can find the end-to-end workload analysis in SAP Solution Manager (Transaction DSWP) under Goto • Start Solution Manager Diagnostics. In the diagnosis application of SAP Solution Manager, select Workload • E2E Workload Analysis. Then select your solution and all components. Select the tab with the name of the J2EE Engine that you want to analyze (Figure 3.8).

You can then navigate to the different load profiles via the tabs. As was previously mentioned, load profiles are preconfigured SAP NetWeaver BW reports. You can change the selection criteria of the load profiles in the Navigation subscreen.

Profiles

In addition to a workload overview, time profile, storage profile (described in Chapter 2, Monitoring Hardware, Databases and SAP-Basis), and CPU profile (which shows the data of the [local] operating system monitor), you can find several profiles listing the applications that generated the highest load within their categories. Table 3.4 describes the "top" profiles.

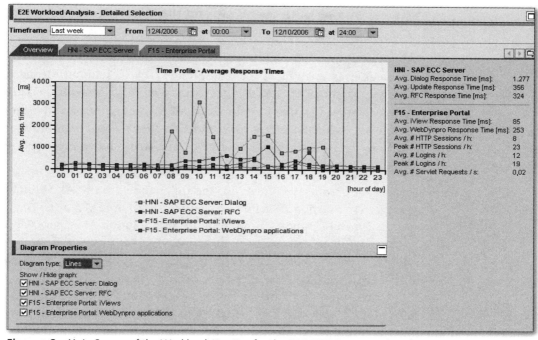

Figure 3.8 Main Screen of the Workload Monitor for the SAP J2EE Engine with Wily Introscope Data in SAP Solution Manager

Profile	Description
Top iViews	Shows the most expensive iViews. iViews are parts of portal pages in which the applications run.
Top servlets	Shows the most expensive servlets. Servlets are specific Java applications that run on the SAP J2EE Engine.
Top Web Dynpro applications	Shows the most expensive Web Dynpro for Java applications. These are UI applications that were built using Web Dynpro for the Java programming environment.
Top KM methods	Shows the most expensive methods of the knowledge management system.
Top SQL statements	Shows the most expensive SQL statements that the SAP J2EE Engine directly (that is, without any detours via the ABAP server) executes on the database.
Top JCo calls	Shows the most expensive JCo calls. JCo calls are calls via the JCo connector to the ABAP server. The name of the JCo calls includes the name of the RFC that is called on the ABAP server.

Table 3.4 Load Profiles in SAP Solution Manager for Analyzing the SAP J2EE Engine

3.7.2 Working with WebView and the Wily Introscope Workstation

If you were able to limit the performance problem on the SAP J2EE Engine after an analysis of the load profiles in SAP Solution Manager, and if you require more detailed data from Wily Introscope for the analysis, you can access the data stored in Introscope Enterprise Manager directly via two user interfaces: Introscope WebView (a web browser interface) and Introscope Workstation (a Java Swing–based presentation server application).

Start
To start Introscope WebView, use the following path in SAP Solution Manager (Transaction DSWP): GOTO • START SOLUTION MANAGER DIAG-NOSTICS. In the diagnosis application of SAP Solution Manager, select WORKLOAD • WILY INTROSCOPE. Or you can start Introscope WebView via *http://<server>:<port>/webview,* where *<server>* is the server on which Introscope Enterprise Manager runs, and *<port>* is the TCP/IP port of Introscope Enterprise Manager (default is 8081). Introscope Workstation starts via Java web start and the URL *http://<server>:<port>/workstation.*

Introscope WebView and Introscope Workstation have two different analysis views: the console that compiles the predefined analysis views for different application cases *(dashboards)* and the investigator view in which you have direct access to detailed data. You can navigate to one of the analysis views via WORKSTATION • NEW CONSOLE or NEW INVESTIGATOR.

Dashboards
In the upper part of the investigator view, first select the time range and resolution of the analysis. In Figure 3.9, you can see that the Time Range selection box was set to two days; on the left side, the 10th and 11th calendar days of the current month were selected, and on the right, the resolution was set to 48 minutes. In the Time Rangeselection box, you can also select the value Live; in this case, the system shows the current data reported by the server every 15 seconds. In the left-hand window, you can select the server to be analyzed and the measured metric. In our case, the executed servlets were chosen as the metric.

The corresponding analysis is displayed in the main window of the screen. In the upper part of the window, you can see a list of the executed servlets, and the chronological sequence of the executions is displayed in the lower part of the window. The analyses provided depend on the selected metric. For more information on this subject, refer to the training documents in SAP Solution Manager.

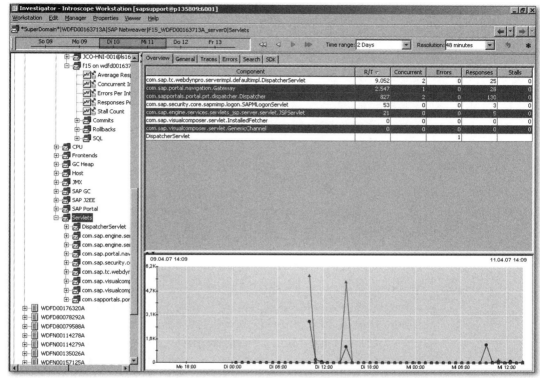

Figure 3.9 Investigator View in Introscope Workstation for Workload Analysis of the SAP J2EE Engine

The tabs above the main screen provide the following additional functions:

Functions

▶ **Traces**

Introscope Workstation has a trace mode. For more details, refer to Chapter 4, Identifying Performance Problems in ABAP and Java Programs.

▶ **Search**

Enables the search according to any term, for example, the name of a table in SQL statements or part of a program name.

▶ **Errors**
Displays the errors in the communication flow, for instance, programming or authorization errors.

Errors in communication flow can also be essential for performance analysis if, for example, due to an error, the program waits for a timeout and only continues its work after a wait time. In this case, the user may not even notice the error, because the application can react to the timeout appropriately. However, the user may notice a long response time.

3.8   Performing Workload Analysis for the SAP J2EE Engine

For workload analysis in the SAP J2EE Engine, we'll consider the same questions as for our analysis of the ABAP server: Is there a general or a specific performance problem? Is the performance problem permanent or temporary? Is there a problem in a specific application?

Is There a General Performance Problem?

Time profile   The time profile is particularly suitable for evaluating whether there is a general performance problem. A general performance problem exists if the response times for iViews, servlets, and Web Dynpro applications (provided they are implemented at all) increase considerably within a specific time interval and if you can't specify an individual application in the top profiles for this time interval that is responsible for the increased response times. An additional indicator of a general performance problem is if response times increase while the throughput (that, is the processed calls) decrease, in other words, if the accumulating load can no longer be processed.

Is the Performance Problem Temporary or Permanent?

A permanent performance problem exists if the response times don't improve for off-peak loads. In extreme cases, you need to restart the SAP J2EE Engine to achieve a good performance again. There is a temporary performance problem if the response times return to the normal level again after a load peak.

Is the Performance Problem Due To the SAP J2EE Engine or an Underlying Component, for Example, the ABAP Server?

To determine whether the performance problem is due to the SAP J2EE Engine or whether only the performance problem of an underlying system is redirected or intensified, you must compare the response times of the iViews, servlets, and Web Dynpro applications with the response times of the JCo calls. If only the response times for the first three applications increase, and the response times of the JCo calls remain constant, the performance problem is probably due to the SAP J2EE Engine. But if the response times of the JCo calls increase more than those of the iViews, servlets, and Web Dynpro applications, then you can assume there is a performance problem on the underlying component and continue the performance analysis there.

Figure 3.10 shows how general, temporary performance problems can impact the time profile. You can see that the response times increase several times within the selected periods, whereas the throughput decreases considerably during the same time. After the load peaks, the system recovers again. Now note the difference between the first load peak at 10:00 a.m. and the one some hours later.

[Ex]

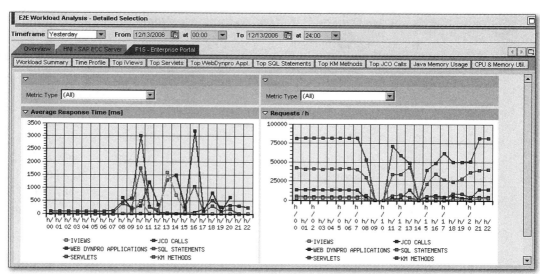

Figure 3.10 Time Profile of the Workload Analysis for the SAP J2EE Engine in SAP Solution Manager

During the first peak, the response times for the JCo calls increases more than for all other response times — a clear sign that there is a problem in the underlying component. For load peaks after 1:00 p.m., however, the response times of JCo calls only change slightly, which means the SAP J2EE Engine itself should be analyzed more closely.

Is the Load Distribution Optimal?

To answer this question, limit the load profile — in particular, the time profile based on which you determined a general performance problem — to the different computers of your system landscape. If you can only establish high response times on one or a few computers, and if the number of calls is distributed unevenly, you can assume a less-than-optimal load distribution.

Is There a Hardware Bottleneck?

There is a hardware bottleneck on a computer if the operating system analysis determines a high CPU load or main memory workload on the same computer parallel to high response times (see Chapter 2, Monitoring Hardware, Databases, and SAP Basis).

Is There a General Database Performance Problem?

There is a general database problem if additional key figures of the database analysis (Chapter 2, Monitoring Hardware, Databases, and SAP Basis) are critical and parallel to the high response times for database accesses.

Is There a Performance Problem Caused by Garbage Collection?

If you determine that there are frequent, full garbage collections (Chapter 2, Monitoring Hardware, Databases, and SAP Basis) parallel to the high response times of the SAP J2EE Engine, and if you can exclude a nonoptimal load distribution, there is a problem in the garbage collection of the JVM.

Is There a Specific Performance Problem?

There is a specific performance problem if individual applications account for a large proportion of the load in the top profiles, that is, if the total of the average response time and the number of calls is high or if individual applications have very high average response times. To further analyze a specific performance problem, implement the necessary runtime analyses of the applications to reveal the optimization potential of these applications.

Top profiles

3.9 Summary

Workload analysis enables you to make detailed statements about the distribution of response times not only across different system components such as the database, hardware, and ABAP and Java servers, but also across different transactions and programs. By performing a workload analysis, you can determine the system areas in which you require further analysis and tuning. Always remember to compare the results of your workload analysis with the observations of users. This helps you avoid jumping to wrong conclusions if a superficial analysis of the workload monitor indicates a performance problem where, in fact, there is no real problem. It also avoids the opposite situation of not noticing that the workload monitor is indicating a performance problem that is readily apparent to users.

Figure 3.11 summarizes a workload analysis for a general performance problem on the ABAP server. You can find the corresponding detailed analyses for hardware, databases, and SAP memory configuration in Section 3.2, Workload Monitor; Section 3.3, Workload Analysis; and Section 3.4, Performing Workload Analyses.

Figure 3.12 summarizes the workload analysis of the SAP J2EE Engine for a general performance problem. You can find the corresponding detailed analyses for hardware, database, and Java Virtual Machine in Section 3.2, Workload Monitor; Section 3.3, Workload Analysis; Section 3.8, Performing Workload Analysis for the SAP J2EE Engine; and Appendix B.

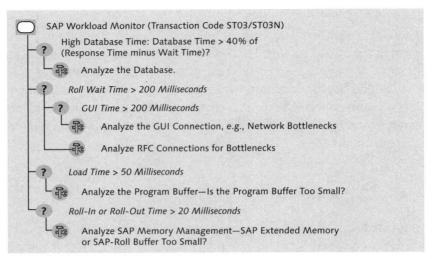

Figure 3.11 Summary of the Most Critical Steps in Workload Analysis on the ABAP Server for a General Performance Problem

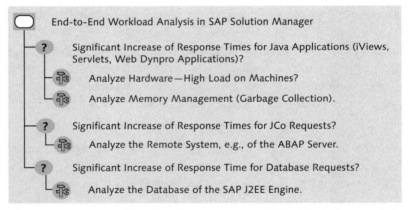

Figure 3.12 Summary of the Most Critical Steps in Workload Analysis on the SAP J2EE Engine for a General Performance Problem

Important Concepts in this Chapter

After reading this chapter, you should be familiar with the following concepts:

► Dispatcher wait time, load time, and database time

► Roll-in time and roll-out time

▶ Processing time and CPU time

▶ Activity, throughput, and load

▶ Performance measuring using SAP statistics records and Wily Introscope

Questions

1. Which of the following statements are correct?

   a) CPU time is measured by the operating system of the application server.

   b) Database time is measured by the database system.

   c) High network times for data transfers between the presentation server and the application server are reflected in an increased response time in the workload monitor.

   d) High network times for data transfers between the application server and the database server are reflected in an increased response time in the workload monitor.

   e) The roll-out time is not part of the response time, because the roll-out of a user occurs only after the response has been sent to the presentation server. Nevertheless, it is important for the performance of SAP components to keep roll-out time to a minimum, because during roll-outs, the SAP work process remains occupied.

2. How is the term *load* defined in this book?

   a) *Load* is defined as the amount of load on the CPU of a computer, expressed as a percentage. It can be monitored in the operating system monitor (CPU Utilization).

   b) In this book, load is the sum of response times. Therefore, total load refers to the Response Time Total, CPU load refers to the CPU Time Total, and database load refers to the DB Time Total.

   c) The term *load* refers to the number of transaction steps per unit of time.

3. The workload monitor displays increased wait times for the dispatcher such that Av. Wait Time is much greater than 50 ms. What does this tell you?

a) There is a communication problem between the presentation servers and the dispatcher of the application server, for example, a network problem.

b) There is a general performance problem, for example, a database problem, hardware bottleneck, or insufficient SAP extended memory; or there are too few SAP work processes. This statement does not provide enough information to pinpoint the exact problem.

c) An increased dispatcher wait time is normal for an SAP component. It protects the operating system from being overloaded and can be ignored.

4. In the workload analysis for the SAP J2EE Engine, you determine that the response times for Web Dynpro applications increase considerably, whereas the response times for JCo calls don't change very much at all. What do you have to do?

a) Because Web Dynpro applications are always linked with business-relevant applications on an ABAP server, you should carry out an analysis on the ABAP server.

b) There is a problem on the SAP J2EE Engine. Therefore, you should check whether the load distribution is unfavorable, whether there is a hardware bottleneck on the SAP J2EE Engine's computer, or whether the SAP J2EE Engine has problems with garbage collection.

4 Identifying Performance Problems in ABAP and Java Programs

This chapter explains how to perform a detailed performance analysis for programs and transactions that you have already identified as expensive. In other words, you have performed a workload analysis and consulted users and discovered that the performance of these programs is not satisfactory.

To begin the analysis, examine the single statistical records, which will give you an overview of the response times of a transaction. For more in-depth analysis, use Performance Trace for detailed analysis of database accesses, RFCs, and lock operations (enqueues). If after using these methods you still cannot find the problem, you can attempt to identify it by using ABAP trace and ABAP debugger.

In the fifth and sixth editions of this book, sections were added that detail Wily Introscope trace, end-to-end trace with SAP Solution Manager, and Code Inspector.

When Should You Read this Chapter?

You should read this chapter if you have identified a program or transaction as being critical for performance and you now want to perform a detailed analysis of it.

4.1 Single-Record Statistics

For every transaction step executed in the SAP system, a *record with statistical information* is generated and saved in files on the application servers. This statistical information includes response times, memory requirements, database accesses, and so on. By default, there are 48 files, which each contain data for one hour; that is, after 48 hours the oldest file is overwritten again. Via the `stat/maxfiles` parameter you can configure a maximum of 99 statistics files so that the single-record statistics are held for a longer period of time.

These records are collected hourly by the collector program `RSCOLL00` and are deleted after approximately one day. (See also Chapter 3, Section 3.2.3, Technical Settings for the Workload Monitor.)

Displaying statistical records

Beginning with SAP Basis 4.6, you can display *statistical records* using Transaction STAD, provided they have not been deleted. (For versions older than SAP Basis 4.6, you can view the single statistical records using Transaction STAT.) The single-record statistics in SAP Basis 4.6 are much more complete than in earlier versions, and as a result, it is now possible to evaluate all SAP application servers. (Previously, it was only possible to get an overview of the server that one was logged on to.) The statistical records can be grouped and evaluated according to transaction, and the values displayed can be personalized. You will find further information on these options in the following sections.

Once you have called Transaction STAD, a dialog box appears in which you should specify a user, transaction or program name, and the period of time you want to analyze. In the selection mask, you can also establish how the single statistics will be presented. Choose between the options Show All Statistic Records, Sorted by Start Time (standard option), Show All Records, Grouped by Business Transaction, or Show Business Transaction Summ.

A screen with the statistical records that match your selection criteria will then be displayed. Click the Sel. Fields button to select which statistical values you want displayed in the list.

Figure 4.1 shows an example of statistical records related to a user's SD transactions. Show Business Transaction Summ has been selected as the presentation mode, which means that all records belonging to one transaction are grouped together. Under Transaction VA01, you can see a sequence of four dialog steps and one update step.

With single-record statistics you can identify problems that might not be visible in the average values of the transaction profile. For example, single records enable you to determine whether the response times for all transaction steps are equally high or whether they are generally low but occasionally extremely high (in which case the averages would be deceptively high). For example, the Fcod column, which displays the function code within a transaction, helps determine whether observed high response times are always associated with a particular transaction screen. In the example in Figure 4.1, the response times for the transaction are generally less than 1 second in the first three steps, but the last transaction step in the dialog task (marked with function code SICH) displays a high response time of 49 to 62 seconds. These records should be examined in greater detail.

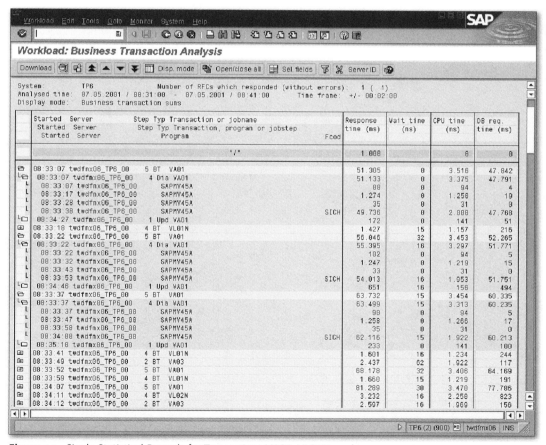

Figure 4.1 Single Statistical Records for Transactions VA01, VL01N, and so on

To display more details on an individual record, double-click it, select Record, and then click the All Details button to display all of the details of a single record, as shown in Figure 4.2, where Avg. Time/Row (ms) = 217.7 for Sequential Read. The optimal read time is 1 ms per data record for Sequential Read.

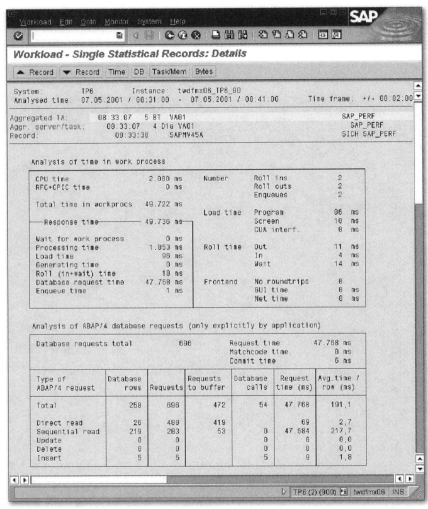

Figure 4.2 Single Statistical Record with High Database Time Due to High Read Time per Data Record

The following list provides an overview of typical problems you can recognize with the help of single-record statistics:

▶ High database times usually indicate a database problem you can analyze using an SQL trace. Using the values for kBytes Transferred
(Figure 4.1) or Database Rows (Figure 4.2), you can distinguish two
types of database problems:

  ▸ Database time is high even though relatively little data is transferred. Figure 4.2 shows a single statistic for which 47,684 ms are
  needed for 219 records (in the Sequential Read area), which implies
  an average read time of 217.7 ms per record. According to the classification of SQL statements presented in Chapter 11, Optimizing
  SQL Statements, this represents an expensive SQL statement of
  type 2.

  ▸ Database time is high because the quantity of data transferred is
  large, but the data transfer speed is optimal. An optimal rate of data
  transfer is around 1 ms per record. This observation indicates an
  expensive SQL statement of type 1 according to our classification.

  For more information on the interpretation and analysis of database
  times and other analyses, see Section 4.3.2, Evaluating an SQL Trace,
  and Chapter 11, Optimizing SQL Statements.

▶ If you find high database times only sporadically, check individual
records to see whether the message "NOTE: TABLES WERE SAVED IN THE
TABLE BUFFER" is displayed. This entry means that tables transferred
from the database have been saved in the table buffer. If the SAP system has been running for some time with high load since the start, all
necessary tables should be located in the table buffer and do not have
to be reloaded. If this entry occurs frequently in production operation, a problem with displacements or the invalidation of table buffers
is indicated. In this case, proceed with the analysis in Chapter 9, SAP
Buffering.

▶ High roll wait times and high GUI times indicate communication
problems, which you can analyze with the RFC trace. We'll discuss
the analysis of these problems in greater detail in Section 4.3.5, Evaluating an RFC Trace; Chapter 6, Workload Distribution and Interfaces;
and Chapter 7, SAP GUI and Internet Connection.

- High CPU times indicate either time-consuming calculations in the ABAP coding or frequent access to table buffers. Programs with over 50% CPU time can be examined in greater detail with the ABAP trace or debugger.

- Other problems that can be located using single statistics include those with program buffer load procedures, SAP lock administration (enqueue), or RFC calls.

4.2   Central Single-Record Statistics

As described in Chapter 3 in Section 3.6, Central Workload Monitor, several components are involved in a transactional step in complex system landscapes, for instance, via RFC calls across several components (multiple ABAP instances, J2EE Engine, or ITS). The *central single-record statistics*, also referred to as *functional trace* in SAP Help, enables you to perform a centralized analysis of the statistics records of several components that are involved in a transactional step. The basis for this is the *distributed statistics records* (DSRs), which were described in Section 3.6, Central Workload Monitor, and the *passport* that is forwarded among the components during the communication process for cross-component identification of statistics records involved in a transactional step. To maintain performance, only the passport data is transferred in the communication flow during a transactional step. The actual statistical data is first saved locally by the respective components, read out asynchronously via RFC or the monitoring agent (SAPCCMSR), and then transferred to the monitoring system. Based on their passport, the statistics records involved in a transactional step can be identified and displayed in the central monitoring system.

The same terms of availability apply for single-record statistics as for the workload monitor. See Chapter 3, Workload Analysis, for more information.

Working with the central single-record statistics

You can call the central single-record statistics using Transaction STAT-TRACE. The functional trace screen consists of a navigation area in the left-hand pane that can be shown or hidden via Full Screen On/Off, and an analysis area in the right-hand pane.

The following functions are available in the navigation area:

- Using the system selection, you can select those systems for which you want to analyze statistics records and, if necessary, traces. You can restrict this analysis to the local system or to several systems within a system landscape or business process. You can also create system lists.

- In the data selection, you can define a period for reading the statistics records. For this period, statistics records are read for the components you previously specified in the system selection.

- In addition, you can specify parameters in the data selection for filtering statistical records. For example, you can filter the records by initial user or initial system. The filtered statistics records are displayed in the analysis view.

- In case of an error, you can view the application logs of the functional trace to find its cause.

- Several options are available for displaying and analyzing data. For example, you can display the statistics records in chronological order in a call hierarchy or in a list.

- In addition to statistics records, you can display traces for ABAP systems (SQL trace and runtime analysis) and DSR traces in the analysis view. SQL traces can be switched on directly from the functional trace.

Once you have performed an analysis and the required statistics records are displayed, the right-hand pane in which the analysis data is presented displays the following information in the upper half of the screen:

- Analyzed period (date, time)
- Analyzed components
- Components that provided no data
- Time zone
- Date and time of the first and last statistics records in the period analyzed

The lower part of the right-hand pane also displays the actual statistics records, depending on the analysis view selected in the left-hand pane. The statistics records that belong to a dialog step are displayed in a tree structure, together with the most-important performance information. These include:

▶ Response time: the total response time for an action within a component

▶ CPU time

▶ Call/roll wait time

▶ Step wait time

With this information, you can quickly find out which component had long wait times. High CPU time means the application on this component must be analyzed further. A high wait time in the component means an overload situation exists. Depending on the type of component (ABAP server, SAP J2EE Engine, or ITS), you must carry out a component-based analysis. We'll describe that analysis in further detail in the following chapters. A high call/roll wait time means the performance problem cannot be found in this component but can be found in a component that has been called by this one, so another statistics record with a high response time must exist for a called component.

In addition to this important statistical data, the statistics records contain further, component-dependent data for analysis. To the extent that this detailed data has not already been described in Chapter 3, Workload Analysis, or in Section 4.1, Single-Record Statistics, we'll provide descriptions in subsequent chapters.

4.3   Performance Trace

Runtime analysis of ABAP programs

Performance Trace is a powerful tool for analyzing the runtime of ABAP programs. It enables you to record a program runtime for the following operations: database access (that is, SQL user statements), RFC calls, enqueue operations, and accesses to SAP buffers. Performance Trace was developed by SAP and is identical for all database systems, except in the fine details.

To enter the initial screen of Performance Trace, select System • Utilities • Performance Trace or use Transaction ST05. On this screen, you will find buttons to start, stop, and evaluate Performance Trace. You can also find checkboxes for selecting the trace modes SQL trace, Enqueue trace, RFC trace, http Trace (as of Basis version 7.10), and Buffer trace. In the default setting, only SQL trace is activated. For standard analysis, you should select SQL trace, Enqueue trace, and RFC trace.

The SAP J2EE Engine also provides you with an SQL trace that has functionality comparable to the SQL trace of the ABAP server. We'll describe its use in Appendix B.

Java SQL trace

4.3.1 Activating a Performance Trace

You can start and stop a performance trace by clicking the Trace On and Trace Off buttons, which you will find in the previously mentioned screen. You can only create one performance trace per application server at a time. In the State of Trace field, you can see whether a trace is already being processed and which user has activated the trace. When you start a trace, a selection screen appears where you can enter users for whom the trace should be activated. The name with which you logged on is usually the user name entered here. Use a different name if you want to trace the actions of another user. The user who activates the trace does not have to be the same one whose actions are being traced.

Keep in mind the following points when generating a trace:

[+]

▸ Ensure that the user whose actions are to be recorded only carries out one action during the trace; otherwise the trace will not be clear. You should also ensure that no background jobs or update requests are running for this user.

▸ The performance trace is created in the application server. For each database operation, data is written to a trace file in the file system on the application server. You must therefore ensure that you have logged on to the same application server as the user to be monitored. This is particularly important if you want to record an update request or a background job and are working in a system with distributed updating or distributed background processing. In this case, you will not know where the request will be started and, as a result, will have to start the trace on all application servers with update or background work processes.

▶ The SQL trace only displays accesses to the database. SQL statements that can be satisfied from data in the SAP buffer do not appear in the trace. If you want to analyze buffer accesses, activate the SAP buffer trace.

▶ However, buffer load processes are also recorded in the SQL trace. Because you are normally not interested in recording the buffer load process in the SQL trace, first execute a program once without activating the trace to allow the buffers to be loaded (that is, the SAP buffers and database buffers). Then run the program again with the SQL trace activated, and use the results of this trace for evaluation.

▶ During the trace, look at the following monitors: the work process overview (for general monitoring), the operating system monitor of the database server (for monitoring possible CPU bottlenecks on the database server), and the database process monitor for direct monitoring of the executed SQL statements. It makes no sense to watch these monitors during the trace if you are logged on as the user being traced. The SQL statement of the monitors would appear in the trace.

▶ The default trace file name is set with the SAP profile parameter `rstr/file`. In the initial screen, you can assign a different name to the trace file. Writing to the trace file is cyclical in the sense that when the file is full, the oldest entries are deleted to make room for new entries. The size of the trace file (in bytes) is specified by the SAP profile parameter `rstr/max_diskspace`, for which the default value is 16,384,000 bytes (16MB).

▶ You can also store recorded traces. For this purpose, select PERFORMANCE TRACE • SAVE TRACE or PERFORMANCE TRACE • DISPLAY SAVED TRACE TO OPEN A SAVED TRACE.

▶ As of SAP Basis version 7.10, you can select GOTO • TRACE ANALYSIS USING THE CODE INSPECTOR to navigate from the performance trace to the Code Inspector, which is described later in this chapter.

4.3.2   Evaluating an SQL Trace

To evaluate a performance trace, select List Trace in the initial screen. A dialog box displays, and in the Trace Mode field, you can specify which part of the trace to analyze. In this and subsequent sections, we'll first discuss the evaluation of an SQL trace and then look at the RFC trace and enqueue trace. (In practice, you can analyze all three trace modes together.) Table 4.1 lists other fields you can use to restrict SQL trace analysis.

Field	Explanation
Trace Filename	Name of the trace file. Normally this name should not be changed.
Trace Mode	Default trace mode setting is SQL trace. To analyze an RFC trace or enqueue trace, select the corresponding checkboxes.
Trace Period	Period in which the trace runs.
Username	User whose actions have been traced.
Objectname	Names of specific tables to which the display of trace results is to be restricted. Note that by default, the tables D010*, D020*, and DDLOG are not shown in the trace results, because these tables contain the ABAP code of the program being traced and the buffer synchronization data.
Duration	Restricts the display to SQL statements that have a certain execution time.
Operation	Restricts the trace data to particular database operations.

Table 4.1   Fields in the Dialog Box for Evaluating a Trace

Next, click the Execute button. The basic SQL trace list is displayed. Table 4.2 explains the columns displayed in an SQL trace (the last three columns are only displayed if you click the More Info button). Figure 4.3 shows an example of a basic trace list.

Field	Explanation
Duration	Runtime of an SQL statement, in microseconds. If the runtime is more than 150,000 microseconds, the corresponding row is red to identify that SQL statement as having a "long runtime." However, the value 150,000 is a somewhat random boundary.
Object	Name of the database table or database view.
Oper	Operation executed on the database, for example Prepare: preparation ("parsing") of a statement, Open: open a database cursor, Fetch: transfer of data from the database, and so on.
Hits	Number of records read from the database.
RC	Database system-specific return code.
Statement	Short form of the executed SQL statement. The complete statement can be displayed by double-clicking the corresponding row.
hh:mm:ss.ms	Time stamp in the form hour:minute:second:millisecond.
Program	Name of the program from which the SQL statement originates.
Curs	Database cursor number.

Table 4.2 Fields in an SQL Trace

Direct Read   One SQL statement that appears in Figure 4.3 accesses the table DD01L. The fields specified in the Where clause are key fields in the table. The result of the request can therefore only be either one record (Hits = 1) or no record (Hits = 0), depending on whether a table entry exists for the specified key. SQL statements that use the equals (=) sign to specify all key fields of the table are called *fully qualified accesses or direct reads*. Normally, a fully qualified database access should not last longer than 2–10 ms. However, in individual cases, an access may last up to 10 times longer, such as when blocks cannot be found in the database buffer and must be retrieved from the hard drive.

The database access consists of two *database operations*, one `Open/Reopen` operation, and one `Fetch` operation. The `Reopen` operation transfers the concrete values in the `Where` clause to the database. The `Fetch` operation locates the database data and transfers it to the application server.

HH:MM:SS.		Durtn	Program Name	Object name	Operation	Curs	Arr	Hits	RC	Co	Statement
17:54:18.923		7	ZTS_SQL_TEST2	DD01L	REOPEN	216	0	0	0	R/3	SELECT WHERE "DOMNAME"= 'AREA' AND "AS4LOCAL"= 'A' AND "AS4VERS"= 0000
17:54:18.923		723	ZTS_SQL_TEST2	DD01L	FETCH	216	291	1	1,403	R/3	
17:54:18.923		5	ZTS_SQL_TEST2	MONI	REOPEN	20	0	0	0	R/3	SELECT WHERE "RELID"= 'OS'
17:54:18.923		1,546	ZTS_SQL_TEST2	MONI	FETCH	20	43	43	0	R/3	
17:54:18.925		1,177	ZTS_SQL_TEST2	MONI	FETCH	20	43	43	0	R/3	
17:54:18.926		1,259	ZTS_SQL_TEST2	MONI	FETCH	20	43	43	0	R/3	
17:54:18.928		1,444	ZTS_SQL_TEST2	MONI	FETCH	20	43	43	0	R/3	
17:54:18.929		2,680	ZTS_SQL_TEST2	MONI	FETCH	20	43	43	0	R/3	
17:54:18.932		3,401	ZTS_SQL_TEST2	MONI	FETCH	20	43	43	0	R/3	
17:54:18.936		2,638	ZTS_SQL_TEST2	MONI	FETCH	20	43	43	0	R/3	
17:54:18.938		1,654	ZTS_SQL_TEST2	MONI	FETCH	20	43	43	0	R/3	
17:54:18.940		2,844	ZTS_SQL_TEST2	MONI	FETCH	20	43	43	0	R/3	
17:54:18.943		1,496	ZTS_SQL_TEST2	MONI	FETCH	20	43	43	0	R/3	
17:54:18.944		1,344	ZTS_SQL_TEST2	MONI	FETCH	20	43	43	0	R/3	
17:54:18.946		1,234	ZTS_SQL_TEST2	MONI	FETCH	20	43	43	0	R/3	

Figure 4.3 Basic Performance Trace List with Entries from SQL Trace and RFC Trace

A second object accessed in Figure 4.3 is table MONI. Not all key fields in the `Where` clause are clearly specified with this access. As a result, multiple records can be transferred. However, in our example, only one record was transferred (`Rec = 1`). The data records are transferred to the application server in packets, in one or more fetches (*array fetch*). An array fetch offers better performance than transferring individual records in a client/server environment.

Sequential read

The maximum number of records that can be transferred in a `Fetch` operation is determined by the SAP database interface, as follows: Every SAP work process has an input/output buffer for transferring data to or from the database. The SAP profile parameter `dbs/io_buf_size` specifies the size of this buffer. The number of records transferred from the database by a fetch is calculated as follows:

Number of records = dbs/io_buf_size ÷ length of one record in bytes

The number of records per fetch depends on the Select clause of the SQL statement. If the number of fields to be transferred from the database is restricted by a Select clause, more records fit into in a single fetch than when Select * is used. The default value for the SAP profile parameter dbs/io_buf_size is 33,792 (bytes) and should not be changed unless recommended by SAP.

The guideline response time for optimal array fetches is under 10 ms per selected record. The actual runtime greatly depends on the Where clause, the index used, and how well the data is stored.

Declare, Prepare, Open

Other database operations that may be listed in the SQL trace are Declare, Prepare, and Open. The Declare operation defines what is known as a *cursor* to manage data transfer between ABAP programs and a database, and also assigns an ID number to the cursor. This cursor ID is used for communication between SAP work processes and the database system.

In the subsequent Prepare operation, the database process determines the access strategy for the statement. In the Statement column, instead of the correct values of the WHERE clause, a variable is indicated (INSTANCE =:A0, not shown in Figure 4.3). Prepare operations can be time-consuming. To reduce the need for them, each application server's work process retains a certain number of already parsed SQL statements in a special buffer (*SAP cursor cache*) and buffers the operations Declare, Prepare, Open, and Exec in its SAP cursor cache. Once the work process has defined a cursor for a Declare operation, the same cursor can be used repeatedly until, after a specified time, it is displaced from the SAP cursor cache, because the size of the cache is limited.

The database does not receive the concrete values of the Where clause (Mandt =100, and so on) until the Open operation is used. A Prepare operation is only necessary for the first execution of a statement, as long as that statement has not been displaced from the SAP cursor cache. Subsequently, the statement, which has already been prepared (parsed), can always be reaccessed with Open or Reopen.

[Ex] Figure 4.3 shows the second SQL trace run for a report. Given that the Declare, Prepare, and Open operations are executed only in the report's first run, our example shows only the Reopen operation.

If through an SQL trace you identify an SQL statement with a long runtime, you should perform second and third SQL traces to deepen your
analysis. It is useful to perform the trace at a time of high system load
and again at a time of low system load. If you find that the response
times for database accesses are high only at particular times, this indicates throughput problems in the network or in database access (for
example an I/O bottleneck). If, on the other hand, the response times
for database access are poor in general (not only at particular times),
the cause is probably an inefficient SQL statement, which should be
optimized.

When evaluating database response times, remember that the processing times of SQL statements are measured on the application server.
The runtime shown in the trace includes not only the time required by
the database to furnish the requested data, but also the time required to
transfer data between the database and the application server. If there is
a performance problem in network communication, the runtimes of SQL
statements will increase.

You can best recognize network problems between the database and
the application server by comparing traces, as follows. First, execute the
same SQL trace at least twice — once on the application server that is on
the same computer as the database and directly connected to the database and once on an application server that is connected to the database
through the TCP/IP network. Compare the SQL traces. If there are significantly higher response times (greater by 50% or more) on the application
server connected through the network, you have a network problem.
Perform this test at a time of low system load, and repeat it several times
to rule out runtime differences due to the buffer-load process on the
database and application servers. This test works only when your application server is connected to the database through IPC.

4.3.3 Other Tools in the SQL Trace

Using the Summary function of the SQL trace you can get an overview of
the most expensive SQL accesses: GOTO • SUMMARY • COMPRESS.

A list appears. Table 4.3 explains the columns (for every table) in the list. Sort the list according to the runtimes of the SQL statements. The SQL statements with the longest runtimes should be optimized first.

Field	Explanation
SQL-Op	Database operation: Select, Update, Insert, or Delete
Accesses	Number of accesses per table
Records	Number of records read per table
Time	Runtime per table in milliseconds
Percent	Runtime per table in percentage

Table 4.3 Fields in the Compressed Summary of an SQL Trace

Identical selects

Programs that reduce performance often read identical data from the database several times in succession. To help you identify these identical SQL statements, the SQL trace offers the following functions: Goto • IDENTICAL SELECTS.

A list of identical selects is displayed that tells you how often each identical select was executed. By using this function in conjunction with the compressed data, you can roughly see how much of an improvement in performance can be gained by optimizing the programming for identical SQL statements.

Other functions

After this preliminary evaluation using the SQL trace, you have all of the information necessary for a more detailed analysis:

▸ Program name and transaction code of the executed program. Using the ABAP DISPLAY button in the trace list, you can jump directly to the code location that executes the SQL statement.

▸ Table name. The DDIC Info button gives a summary of the most important dictionary information for this table.

▸ Where clause in the SQL statement.

▸ Detailed analysis of the SQL statement, for example, Explain function.

You can find more information about these functions in Chapter 11, Optimizing SQL Statements.

For customer-developed ABAP programs, perform (at least) the following checks as a form of program quality control:

1. For each customer-developed ABAP program, perform an SQL trace either on the production system or on a system with a representative volume of test data.

2. From the basic trace list display, create a compressed summary to find the SQL statements with the longest runtimes: GOTO • SUMMARY • COMPRESS.

3. Display a list of identical accesses to find SQL statements that are executed several times in succession: GOTO • IDENTICAL SELECTS.

4. Use these lists to decide whether the program should be approved or whether it needs to be improved by the responsible ABAP developer.

5. Save a copy of the lists along with the program documentation. If program performance diminishes at a later date (whether due to a modification or due to the growing data volume), perform another SQL trace and compare it to the earlier one. Monitor performance in this way after each significant program modification.

These measures can be used not only to monitor customer-developed programs, but also to regularly monitor frequently used, standard SAP transactions that are critical to performance. If the runtimes of particular SQL statements grow over time, you may need to archive the corresponding table.

[+]

4.3.4 Evaluating a Buffer Trace

Table 4.4 explains the fields that are displayed in a buffer trace. The last three columns are only displayed if you click the More Info button. You can find more detailed explanations on the SAP table buffering in Chapter 9, SAP Buffering.

Field	Explanation
Duration	Runtime of the enqueue/dequeue statement in microseconds
Object	Name of the database table or database view
Oper	Name of the function that was executed on the buffer
Hits	number of records read from the buffer
RC	Return code: 0: function executed correctly 64: no further records available 256: records not available in the buffer 1024: record not available in the buffer, buffer is loaded (for parallel read accesses)
Statement	In the Open operation, the buffering type is indicated: G: generic buffering P: single-record buffering R: full buffering S: export/import buffer C: CUA buffer O: OTR buffer E: export/import buffering in shared memory
hh:mm:ss.ms	Time stamp in the form hour:minute:second:millisecond
Program	Name of the program that has triggered the buffer call

Table 4.4 Fields of a Buffer Trace

4.3.5 Evaluating an RFC Trace

Table 4.5 lists the columns displayed in an RFC trace. The last three fields are only displayed if you click the More Info or Extended List button.

Like the SQL trace, the RFC trace provides several detailed analysis functions:

▶ By double-clicking a line of the RFC trace or by clicking the Details button, you can obtain complete information on the RFC, including the names and IP addresses of the sender and recipient, the name of the RFC module, and the transferred data quantity.

▶ By clicking the ABAP Display button, you can view the source text of the corresponding ABAP program.

Field	Explanation
Duration	RFC runtime in microseconds.
Object	Name of the recipient, for example, the SAP instance called.
Oper	If "Client" is entered: RFC sent, which means the instance on which the trace is executed is the client (sender). If "Server" is entered: RFC received, which means the instance on which the trace is executed is the server (recipient).
Hits	Not used.
RC	Return code (for successful execution: 0 [zero]).
Statement	Additional information on the RFC, including the names of the sender and recipient, name of the RFC module, and amount of data transferred. You can view all information on the RFC by double-clicking the corresponding row in the RFC trace.
hh:mm:ss.ms	Time stamp in the form hour:minute:second:millisecond
Program	Name of the program from which the RFC statement originates.

Table 4.5 Fields in an RFC Trace

4.3.6 Evaluating an HTTP Trace

Table 4.6 explains the fields that are displayed in an HTTP trace. The last three columns are only displayed if you click the More Info button. You can find more detailed descriptions on HTTP calls in Chapter 7, SAP GUI and Internet Connection.

Field	Explanation
Duration	Runtime of the HTTP call in microseconds
Program name	Name (logical path) of the executed HTTP call

Table 4.6 Fields of an HTTP Trace

Field	Explanation
Object name	Name of the recipient, for example, the SAP instance called.
Operation	If "Client" is entered: HTTP sent, which means the instance on which the trace is executed is the client (sender). If "Server" is entered: HTTP received, which means the instance on which the trace is executed is the server (recipient).
RC	HTTP return code (200 for successful execution, 401 for failed authentication, and so on)
Statement	Additional information on the HTTP, including the names of the sender and recipient, name of the HTTP call, and amount of data transferred. You can view all information on the HTTP call by double-clicking the corresponding row in the HTTP trace.
hh:mm:ss.ms	Time stamp in the form hour:minute:second:millisecond.
Program	Name of the program from which the HTTP call originates.

Table 4.6 Fields of an HTTP Trace (Cont.)

4.3.7 Evaluating an Enqueue Trace

Table 4.7 explains the fields that are displayed in an enqueue trace. The last three columns are only displayed if you click the More Info button. You can find more detailed explanations of the SAP enqueue concept in Chapter 10, Locks.

Field	Explanation
Duration	Runtime of the enqueue/dequeue statement in microseconds.
Object	Name of the enqueue object. To see details on the object, call the ABAP dictionary (using Transaction SE12) and enter the object name in the field under Lock Objects. To view the features of the objects, select Display.

Table 4.7 Fields in an Enqueue Trace

Field	Explanation
Oper	ENQUEUE operation: Enqueue(s) set. DEQUEUE operation: Individual enqueues are released. DEQ ALL operation with specific object entry in the Object column: All enqueues for the object in question are released. DEQ ALL operation with no object entry in the Object column (entry "{{{{{{{{{{"): All enqueues for the transaction in question are released (end of a transaction).
Oper	ENQPERM operation: At the end of the dialog part of a transaction, enqueues are passed on to update management.
Hits	Number of enqueues that are set or released.
RC	Return code (for successful execution: 0 [zero]).
Statement	More detailed information on the enqueue: Entries "Excl" or "Shared": exclusive or "shared" locks; name of locked unit (such as "MARC 900SD000002" for a lock in table MARC, in client 900 and material SD000002). The entries in this row correspond with the features of the enqueue object defined in the ABAP dictionary.
hh:mm:ss.ms	Time stamp in the form hour:minute:second:millisecond.
Program	Name of the program from which the Enqueue statement originates.
Curs	Not used.

Table 4.7 Fields in an Enqueue Trace (Cont.)

4.4 Performance Analysis with ABAP Trace (Runtime Analysis)

You should use an ABAP trace when the runtime of the programs to be analyzed consists mainly of CPU time. An ABAP trace measures not only the runtime of database accesses (SELECT, EXEC SQL, and so on), but also the time required by individual modularization units (such as MODULE, PERFORM, CALL FUNCTION, SUBMIT), internal table operations (APPEND, COLLECT, SORT, READ TABLE), and other ABAP statements.

4.4.1 Activating an ABAP Trace

1. Use the following menu path to access the initial screen of the ABAP trace: SYSTEM • Utilities • RUNTIME ANALYSIS • EXECUTE, or select Transaction SE30.

[+] In the initial screen, a traffic light indicates whether the runtime measurement can determine reliable times. If the traffic light is red, it means this isn't possible because of nonsynchronized CPUs in a machine with multiple processors. Therefore, you must carry out the time measurements with low accuracy (SETTINGS • MEASUREMENT ACCURACY • LOW). You can find further operating system–specific information in SAP Notes 20097 and 87447. If you want to perform a runtime analysis in parallel mode, please refer to SAP Note 729520.

2. In the upper part of the screen, under Measure, enter a transaction code, program name, or function module, and select Execute to start the measuring process. You can also click the In Parallel Mode button to access a process list, where you can activate the ABAP trace for the currently active work process.

3. The system starts to measure the runtime and creates a file with the resulting measurement data.

4. When you want to return to the initial runtime analysis screen, simply exit the program, function module, or transaction as normal, or start the runtime analysis again. The initial runtime analysis screen will show the newly created Measurement Data File in the lower part of the window.

When you are activating an ABAP trace, filter functions enable you to restrict the trace to a particular function module or group of ABAP statements or to adjust an aggregation. Section 4.4.3, Using Function Variations, explains how to use these options.

When you activate an ABAP trace, bear the following points in mind (which are similar to those that apply to an SQL trace):

▶ Because you are normally not interested in recording the buffer load process in the trace, you should first execute a program once without activating the trace, thereby allowing the buffers to be loaded (that is, the SAP and database buffers). Then run the program again with the ABAP trace activated, and use the results of this trace for evaluation.

▸ Perform the trace at a time of high system load and again at a time of low system load. Ensure that the measured times are not influenced by a temporary system overload (for example, a CPU overload).

▸ To enable runtime analysis, the system requires the SAP profile parameters `abap/atrapath` and `abap/atrasizequota`. These parameters are set when the system is installed. The profile parameter `abap/atrapath` indicates in which directory the trace files are written. You can restrict the maximum size of all ABAP trace files by using the parameter `abap/atrasizequota`. The trace files are deleted after 30 days. With the single-transaction analysis (Transaction ST12) described in Section 4.4.6, you can permanently store ABAP trace files.

4.4.2 Evaluating an ABAP Trace

To display the results of an analysis, select the file you want. In the initial screen of the runtime analysis, click the Analyze button to display an overview of the analysis. The runtime analysis presents different views of the results in list form, as follows:

▸ Click the Hit List button to view a list that displays the execution time (in microseconds) for each statement. This list is sorted in decreasing order of gross times.

▸ The Hierarchy is a chronological procedure of your transaction or program.

▸ Other buttons will display specific analyses that, for example, categorize database tables or modularization units.

If the ABAP trace was recorded in aggregate form, only the hit list is available as an evaluation.

If you have generated an ABAP trace, first display the hit list. Sort the hit list according to net time to get an overview of statements with the highest net runtimes.

[+]

The runtime analysis establishes the gross and/or net times of individual program calls in microseconds. Gross time is the total time required for

Gross and net time

the call. This includes the times of all modularization units and ABAP statements in this call. The net time is the gross time minus the time required for the called modularization units (MODULE, PERFORM, CALL FUNCTION, CALL SCREEN, CALL TRANSACTION, CALL DIALOG, SUBMIT) and separately specified ABAP statements. For "elementary" statements such as APPEND or SORT, the gross time is the same as the net time. If the gross and net times for a call differ, this call contains other calls or modularization units. For example, if a subroutine shows a gross time of 100,000 ms and a net time of 80,000 ms, this means 20,000 ms are used for calling the routine itself, and 80,000 ms are used for assigning further statements to the routine.

The runtime analysis involves a lot of work; generating the analysis can as much as double the runtime of a program (compared to a program run without runtime analysis activated). The runtime analysis takes this into account and displays correspondingly adjusted runtimes in the lists. However, if you look at the statistical record created while the runtime analysis was active, you will see that it is clearly distorted when compared to a program run without runtime analysis. In contrast, letting a performance trace run simultaneously does not involve much extra load; the additional load is less than 5%.

4.4.3 Using Function Variations

The ABAP trace function offers variants you can use to adjust how the trace is carried out. It is particularly advisable to try out these options when analyzing a complex program, because data quantities of several megabytes can be generated very quickly, much of which is often completely irrelevant to the analysis. Using variants, you can determine more precisely what you want to analyze.

You can see the currently selected variant in the initial screen of the runtime analysis under Measurement restrictions. The DEFAULT variant is already set in the system. You can save your personal settings as your own variant.

Settings   The Display Variants or Change Variants button takes you to the screen where you can enter the settings for a variant:

▶ On the Program Parts tab, you can set which parts of the program to analyze. Entries in the table enable you to limit the trace to selected function modules and form routines and other modularizing units. If you select the Specific Units option, the ABAP trace doesn't start when the object to be analyzed is called, but it can be activated from a subsequent dialog step via the menu path SYSTEM • UTILITIES • RUNTIME ANALYSIS • ACTIVATE.

▶ Moreover, on the Program Parts tab, you specify whether RFCs and update calls are supposed to be recorded as well. If you activate the corresponding option, this information is forwarded to the corresponding processes. To be able to record an RFC in another system, that system must accept foreign trace calls. You configure this using the `rstr/accept_remote_trace` parameter, which you must set to `true`. The trace file is then written to the foreign system. If you use the E2E trace in SAP Solution Manager, this function is activated automatically, and the E2E trace automatically reads all trace files.

▶ The settings on the Statements tab determine which operations will be monitored in the runtime analysis. Tip: If you want to analyze operations on internal tables such as `Append`, `Loop`, or `Sort`, you should activate the Read Operations and Change Operations checkboxes under Int. Tables. These settings are not activated in the default variant.

▶ On the Duration + Type tab, you can, among other things, set the type of aggregation. Aggregation is always relevant when a statement is called numerous times in a program, for example, an SQL statement within a loop. If aggregation is not activated, an entry will be written to the trace measurement file each time the SQL statement is called. If aggregation is activated, only one entry will be recorded, in which the runtimes for each execution are added together. On the Duration + Type tab, you are offered three options:

▶ **No Aggregation**
An entry is written to the measurement file each time the statement is called.

▶ **Full Aggregation**
The runtimes for individual executions of a statement are added

225

together in one entry; therefore, one entry is written to the measurement file for each statement.

▶ **Aggregation According to Call Location**
The runtimes for individual executions of a statement are added together in one entry. However, if a statement appears several times in a program at several locations in the program text, one entry is written for each time it appears in the program text.

In general, activating aggregation dramatically reduces the size of the measurement file, and in many cases, an analysis of long program flows is only possible with aggregation. When you use aggregation, some evaluation functions (for example, the hierarchy list) are lost and therefore no longer available for evaluation. In production systems, full aggregation is set as the default.

[+] How should you carry out an analysis of more complex programs? We recommend that you first carry out an analysis of the entire program with aggregation, according to call location and without analyzing operations on internal tables. The objective of this analysis is to find the modularization units with the highest runtimes. After this initial analysis, sort the hit list according to net times and identify the modularization units or statements with high runtime.

If you cannot deduce recommendations for optimizing the program from this first analysis, proceed to perform a more detailed analysis, setting variants to limit the analysis to these modularization units. Simultaneously, activate the trace for operations from internal tables and deactivate the aggregation.

4.4.4 Activating the Runtime Analysis for BSP and Web Dynpro ABAP Applications

To start a runtime analysis for BSP and Web Dynpro ABAPapplications, call Transaction SICF (Service Maintenance). Select the service to analyze in the navigation tree and activate the runtime analysis via EDIT • RUNTIME ANALYSIS • ACTIVATE.

Beginning in version 6.40, you can restrict the procedure to a user name during activation and specify a variant to use for recording. Here, it is also possible to specify the measurements' level of precision.

4.4.5 Outlook: Single Transaction Analysis

The *single-transaction analysis* (Transaction ST12) is part of SAP Solution Manager and is provided along with the add-on for connecting production systems to SAP Solution Manager (Add-on ST-A/PI, see SAP Note 69455). SAP support employees and their partners are the primary target audience for this type of analysis, but system administrators and developers can also use it. Compared to ABAP trace, this tool provides the following enhancements:

▶ **Better support for an aggregated trace**
ABAP trace without aggregation is not provided in the single-transaction analysis. However, the single-transaction analysis provides better support for the aggregated trace According to Call Location. Hierarchy functions enhance this aggregated trace to such an extent that usually you can do without any laborious aggregated measurement. The upward hierarchy from an entry can help you identify expensive loops or user exits in the superordinate hierarchy. The downstream *time-flow hierarchy* indicates how time is distributed to the underlying routines and which routines belong together. In both cases, the hierarchies are displayed in a diagram that illustrates the various call relationships. A diamond symbol indicates an outgoing call relationship, whereas a small triangle represents an incoming one. The little arrows between the two represent the connection lines. The new view, According to Modularization Unit, provides a highly aggregated overview with only one line per routine, but you can also expand the lines to view the commands processed in the respective lines. This is useful if you want to modify larger source texts of a routine.

▶ **New options to switch on ABAP trace**
You can activate ABAP trace with the single-transaction analysis for a different user, which means the ABAP trace operation and the execution of the dialog transaction to be analyzed can be done by two people from now on. Moreover, you can switch on ABAP trace sys-

tem-wide using the single-transaction analysis to catch incoming RFCs. To do this, a specific kernel-patch level is required.

▶ **ABAP trace summary**
The summary shows whether the program runtime is caused by known expensive functions. In particular, the time component of user exits and customer programs is determined. For this purpose, we use customizing, which is maintained by SAP and delivered with the single-transaction analysis.

▶ **Integration of SQL trace**
You can switch SQL trace and ABAP trace on and off using the single-transaction analysis. To start the analysis, you go directly to the SQL trace display by pressing any key.

▶ **Convenience and additional information**
Transaction ST12 stores ABAP trace in the database so that it is permanently available to the entire system. You can enter and save your own notes, especially results from the SQL trace analysis, in an amodal text box. A top-500 filter enables faster display of large ABAP traces. Compared to ABAP trace, you get valuable additional information. When you are using commands such as `Read Table` or `Append`, the name of the internal table from the source text is displayed. Short texts from the ABAP repository are useful for functional analyses, and the indication of the last person who performed changes supports you in tracing user exits or program modifications.

In addition to the new options for switching the analysis on and off and the simplified usage, the new analysis options represent a big advantage in the single-transaction analysis.

4.4.6 Using Single-Transaction Analysis

In the following list, you will find the most important tips for analyzing an ABAP trace using the single-transaction analysis:

1. **Local optimization of individual statements with high net time**
Sort the ABAP trace According to Call Location in descending order with regard to the net time, and search for expensive statements.

2. **Optimization in the superordinate hierarchy**

   Place the cursor on the expensive statement and view the superordinate hierarchy. Analyze the hierarchy levels to determine where the number of executions suddenly increases, because that's where loops are located. Check, for instance, whether the problem can be solved by implementing mass-processing at a higher level, or whether there are modules that are called too often or in nonoptimal ways.

3. **Optimizing larger net-time aggregations**

   Go to the aggregation view According to Modularization Unit. In particular, if the trace was recorded using internal tables, it is easier to identify large net-time aggregations in this highly aggregated mode. Sort by net time in descending order. Expand modularization units with high net-time values to view the statements contained in them. Based on the number of executions, it is sometimes possible to estimate the size of internal tables or judge the selectivity of filters.

4. **Gross-time optimization**

   Sort the trace According to Call Location by the gross time in descending order. Use the downward time-flow hierarchy to form groups. The most noteworthy medium hierarchy level is the one where the process is divided into disjunct functions with more than 5% gross time. Read the names of the modularization units and, if necessary, show the short texts to estimate (exactly) what the modularization units do. The objective of gross-time optimization is to identify and switch off superfluous, negligible, or identical processes, for example, data collected for viewing and tabs not used or hidden, screen controls that refresh more often than needed, a wrong flag in customizing that activates unneeded functions, a user exit that reads the same document hundreds of times, and so on.

5. **Functional analysis according to gross time**

   Based on the gross time view previously described, and using the time-flow hierarchy and the ABAP trace summary, you can determine how much time was spent for each functionality and how much room for improvement exists if you want to implement functional optimization. The frequency with which modules and statements are executed gives you an idea of the number of involved documents, materials, or other items. This information enables you to determine the document throughput and the scaling behavior.

4.5 Analyzing Memory Usage with ABAP Debugger and in the Memory Inspector

In addition to expensive SQL statements, one of the most important causes of performance problems is internal tables with many entries. Large internal tables consume massive amounts of memory and CPU, for example, during copy, sort, or search operations.

Using the ABAP debugger, you can create an overview of all internal tables of a program. ABAP debugger is a tool for performing functional troubleshooting in programs. You can find more detailed descriptions of the debugger in SAP literature under ABAP programming. Performance analysis using the ABAP debugger is not a standard procedure and is best performed by an ABAP developer.

[!] Take the following advice into account when working with the ABAP debugger. During the debugging process, the ABAP program may terminate and display the error message Invalid Interruption of a Database Selection, or the system may automatically trigger a database commit. In either case, an SAP logical unit of work (LUW) has been interrupted, and this may lead to inconsistencies in the application tables. Therefore, you should only debug on a test system or in the presence of someone who is very familiar with the program being analyzed and who can manually correct inconsistencies in the database tables if necessary. See Debugging Programs in the Production Client in SAP Online Help for the ABAP debugger.

1. Begin performance analysis with the debugger by starting the program to be analyzed. Then open a second session. Here you can monitor the program to be analyzed in the work process overview (Transaction SM50). Enter the debugger from the work process overview by selecting Debugging. By using the debugger several times in succession, you can identify the parts of the program that cause high CPU consumption. Often, these sections consist of LOOP ... ENDLOOP statements that affect large internal tables.

2. To display the current memory requirements, from the menu (of the "old" debugger), select GOTO • OTHER SCREENS • MEMORY USE. Check for cases of unnecessary memory consumption that may have been

caused by a nonoptimal program or inefficient use of a program. As a guideline, bear in mind that a program being used by several users in dialog mode should not allocate more than 100MB.

3. From version 6.20 on, you can use the old debugger to create a list of program objects located in the memory by selecting GOTO • STATUS DISPLAY • MEMORY USE. The MEMORY CONSUMPTION • RANKING LISTS tab contains a list of objects and their memory consumption.

   In versions 4.6 and 6.10, you can obtain a memory consumption list by following the menu path GOTO • SYSTEM • SYSTEM AREAS. Enter "ITAB-TOP25" in the Area field. This way, you will obtain a list of the 25 largest internal tables.

4. In the "new"" debugger, you first display the memory analysis tool by clicking the button for the new tool and then selecting Memory Analysis in the Special Tools folder. The initial screen then displays how much memory is allocated or used by the analyzed internal mode. Click the Memory Objects button to go to the list of the largest memory objects, which can be the internal tables, objects, anonymous data objects, or strings.

Moreover, you can create and then analyze a memory extract, in other words, an overview of the objects that occupy memory space. You can create a memory extract in the ABAP debugger via DEVELOPMENT • MEMORY ANALYSIS • CREATE MEMORY EXTRACT. You can also select SYSTEM • UTILITIES • MEMORY ANALYSIS • CREATE MEMORY EXTRACT in any transaction or simply enter function code /HMUSA. The third option is to create a memory extract from program coding. (Refer to SAP Help for a description of the system class.)

Memory Inspector

To evaluate the memory extract, start the Memory Inspector (Transaction code S_MEMORY_INSPECTOR) via MEMORY ANALYSIS • COMPARE MEMORY EXTRACTS in the ABAP debugger or SYSTEM • UTILITIES • MEMORY ANALYSIS • COMPARE MEMORY EXTRACTS in any transaction. The Memory Inspector lists all memory extracts in the upper part of the screen. In the lower part of the screen, you can find details about the individual memory extract. Here, a distinction is made *between* the object types, programs, classes, dynamic memory request of a class, table bodies, strings, and types of anonymous data objects. You are provided with

Evaluating the memory extract

different ranking lists, according to which you can sort the objects. For each memory object, you are provided with the values of bound allocated, bound used, referenced allocated, and referenced used memories. You can find a detailed description of the ranking lists and the displayed values in SAP Help.

The Memory Inspector is particularly useful for examining transactions over a long period of time, as is the case in a customer interaction center. Here, users frequently enter a transaction at the beginning of their workday and exit it when they go home. In these "long-term" transactions, data often remains, and therefore memory consumption continuously increases.

Common performance problems

There are three common programming errors that cause large memory or CPU requirements for programs:

▶ **Missing REFRESH or FREE statements**
The ABAP statements REFRESH and FREE delete internal tables and release the memory that was allocated to them. If these statements are missing, memory resources may be unnecessarily tied up, and the operations being executed (READ or LOOP) will require an unnecessarily large amount of time. Please note that the CLEAR statement only deletes the header line in internal tables.

▶ **Inefficient reading in large internal tables**
The ABAP statement READ TABLE ... WITH KEY ... enables you to search internal tables. If you use this statement by itself for a standard table, the search is sequential. For large tables, this is a time-consuming process. You can significantly improve search performance by adding the statement ... BINARY SEARCH, thereby specifying a binary search. However, the table must be sorted (see ABAP Help for the statement READ TABLE).

You can optimize the performance of operations on large tables by using sorted tables (SORTED TABLE) or hash tables (SORTED TABLE). If a READ statement is executed on a sorted table, the ABAP processor automatically performs a binary search. It is important that the key fields used for the search correspond to the sort criteria for the table. For a sorted table, the search effort increases logarithmically with the size of the table. For hash tables, constant access costs exist if the

ABAP statement READ TABLE ... WITH TABLE KEY is used. However, efficient access to hash tables is only possible if you enter the complete key.

► **Nested loops**

Nested loops are frequently used for processing dependent tables (for example, header and position data), for example:

```
LOOP AT HEADER INTO WA_HEADER.
  LOOP AT POSITION INTO WA_POSITION
        WHERE KEY = WA_HEADER-KEY.
   "Processing ...
  ENDLOOP.
ENDLOOP.
```

If HEADER and POSITION are standard tables in this case, then for each entry in the HEADER table, the ABAP processor loops across all entries in the POSITION table and checks if the WHERE clause is fulfilled for all entries. This is especially time-consuming if the tables HEADER and POSITION contain many entries. However, if you use SORTED-type tables, the ABAP processor determines the data to process by performing a binary search and only loops across those areas that fulfill the WHERE clause. Sorting is only useful, however, if the WHERE clause contains the first fields of the sort key.

Loop via each entry

As an alternative, you can use index operations that are much less time-consuming. To use index operations, it is necessary to sort the internal tables HEADER and POSITION by the Key field, as follows:

```
I = 1.
LOOP AT HEADER INTO WA_HEADER.
  LOOP AT POSITION INTO WA_POSITION FROM I.
   IF WA_POSITION-KEY <> WA_HEADER-KEY.
    I = SY-TABIX.
    EXIT.
   ENDIF.
   "  ...
  ENDLOOP.
ENDLOOP.
```

You can find further information in the SAP online Help for the ABAP programming environment and in Transaction SE30 under Tips and Tricks.

> **Background: Scalability of a Program**
>
> Scalability of a program refers to the dependency of a program's runtime from the data quantity.
>
> Many operations linearly depend on the data quantity ($t = O(n)$), that is, the runtime increases the runtime linearly to the data quantity. Examples include the database selections in large tables without or with inappropriate index support and loops via internal tables in the program. Linear scalability is acceptable for the processing of medium data quantities. If they cannot be avoided in programs that are supposed to process large data quantities, you must consider parallelization.
>
> Of course, constant runtimes ($t = O(1)$) or a logarithmic dependency ($t = O(\log n)$) is better for performance than a linear scalability. Logarithmic dependencies occur, for example, in large tables with optimal index support for database selections or in internal tables with binary search for read operations. Because the logarithm function increases only very slowly, in real life you don't need to differentiate between constant and logarithmically increasing runtimes.
>
> Quadratic dependencies ($t = O(n \times n)$) and anything beyond are inacceptable for the processing of medium and large data quantities. However, problems with quadratic dependencies through intelligent programming can usually be traced back to dependencies of $t = O(n \times \log n)$. An example is the comparison of two tables that both grow with a factor of n. A comparison of the unsorted tables would result in a quadratic dependency, a comparison with sorted tables in dependency $t = O(n \times \log n)$. Because the logarithm function increases only very slowly, in real life you don't need to differentiate between an increase of $t = O(n \times \log n)$ and a linear increase.

4.6 Code Inspector

The Code Inspector is a tool that checks ABAP programs and other repository objects statically for problems. Its meaning for the quality analysis of ABAP programs goes far beyond the meaning for the performance analysis, to which the following description is restricted. The Code Inspector performs a static analysis, that is, the code doesn't need to be executed and is therefore independent of test or production data. It has been generally available as of SAP Basis version 6.10. A preliminary version exists for version 4.6C (SAP Note 543359).

You call the Code Inspector from the development tools of the ABAP Workbench for programs, function modules, or ABAP classes (Transaction codes SE38, SE37, or SE24) using the PROGRAM/FUNCTION MODULE/ CLASS • CHECK • CODE INSPECTOR menu path or directly using Transaction code SCII.

Table 4.8 summarizes which checks are performed in the performance category and where you can find further information on the checks. The checks reveal standard errors and problems. They cant indicate how seriously the actual effects will impact the performance. For this purpose, you require the runtime checks described previously. The verification of these checks should nevertheless be part of the quality control of ABAP programs.

Check	Description
Analysis of the WHERE clause	Checks that the SQL statements include a WHERE clause and that they have index support. Buffered tables, joins, and views are not covered with this check. For more information refer to Chapter 11, Optimizing SQL Statements.
Analysis of table buffer accesses	Checks whether SQL statements to buffered tables will access the database past the buffer. For more information, refer to Chapter 9, Section 9.2.2, Buffer Accessing.
SELECT statements with CHECK	Checks whether SELECT/ENDSELECT loops include a CHECK statement. This statement can often be integrated with the WHERE clause and thus reduce the read data quantity from the start. For more information, refer to Chapter 11, Optimizing SQL Statements.
SQL statements in loops	Checks whether SQL statements are in loops. These result in an increased communication effort and can possibly be replaced by bundled accesses. For more information refer to Chapter 11, Optimizing SQL Statements.
Nested loops	Checks the system for nested loops where nonlinear runtime behavior can occur.

Table 4.8 Performance Checks in the Code Inspector

Check	Description
Copying large data objects	Sends alerts on high copy costs for large data objects, for instance, nested internal tables. However, this check only refers structures with a width of more than 1,000 bytes; it cannot consider how long a table will be at runtime.
Low-performance operations on internal tables	Sends alerts on low-performance read accesses to internal tables.
Low-performance parameter transfers	Examines whether there is a better way to transfer parameters when you call a form, function module, method, or event.
EXIT or no ABAP commands in the SELECT/ENDSELECT loop	Checks whether SELECT/ENDSELECT loops include an EXIT statement or no ABAP coding at all. With this type of code you often check the existence of records in a database table, which can be designed with higher performance. For more information refer to Chapter 11, Optimizing SQL Statements.
Instance generation of BAdIs	As of SAP Basis version 7.0 you should use the GET BADI statement instead of the method call, CALL METHOD cl_exithandler=>get_instance, for performance reasons.
Check of table properties	Examines the technical settings such as transportability, buffering, and indices of database tables.

Table 4.8 Performance Checks in the Code Inspector (Cont.)

4.7   Introscope Trace

The Introscope trace is a powerful tool for analyzing the runtime of Java programs on the SAP J2EE Engine.

Starting the Introscope trace

You start the Introscope trace analysis using Introscope WebView or Introscope Workstation. To start Introscope WebView, use the following path in SAP Solution Manager (Transaction code DSWP): Goto • Start Solution Manager Diagnostics. In the diagnosis application of SAP Solution Manager, select Workload • Wily Introscope. You can also start Introscope WebView via *http://<server>:<port>/webview,* where *<server>* is the server running Introscope Enterprise Manager, and *<port>* is the TCP/IP port of Introscope Enterprise Manager (default is 8081). Start Introscope Workstation via the following URL: *http://<server>:<port>/workstation.*

In Introscope WebView, you can create a new trace view via TRANSAC-TION VIEWER • NEW TRACE..., or in Workstation via WORKSTATION • NEW TRACE SESSION.

Creating an Introscope trace

Once you've created a new trace view, you can restrict the trace view parameters, for example, to the user for whom the trace is being created. You can also specify that only calls with a specific duration or of specific types will be recorded. In trace mode, Introscope records all calls that correspond to the filter criteria. This differs from workload mode, in which samples that have already been averaged via the calls are extracted every 15 seconds.

After you determine the trace parameters and perform the transaction analysis, you can evaluate the trace. For this purpose, select from three views, which you can navigate via specific tabs. The Summary View tab displays all recorded statements in a table, including the number of executions, the overall duration of the executions, and the minimum, maximum, and average response time of each statement's execution. The Trace View tab displays recorded statements as a time axis, and the Tree View tab shows a hierarchy.

Analyzing the Introscope trace

On the SAP J2EE Engine, the Introscope probes for the following calls are implemented:

▶ iViews

▶ Servlets

▶ Web Dynpro applications

▶ KM methods

▶ JCo calls

▶ SQL statements

Additional examples are Web service calls, LDAP accesses, SAP NetWeaver PI messaging, SAP CRM Struts actions, and postal content directory (PCD) accesses.

For more details on these terms, refer to Chapter 3, Section 3.7, The Java Workload Monitor in SAP Solution Manager and the Introscope Monitor, and Chapter 7, Section 7.6, Java Server Pages and Web Dynpro for Java.

4.8 End-to-End Runtime Analysis in SAP Solution Manager

When you start a program from a web browser, difficulties can arise that make program analysis using statistical records and traces difficult or even impossible in large system landscapes. Often, it is not clear in advance which components are involved in a Web request. As a result, on many components, traces need to be activated and statistics searched during the analysis to find the correct data. It is also possible that a user that is a non-person-related service accesses components that many users use at the same time, and this makes identification of statistics and traces in the system impossible.

Target-oriented analysis

To activate statistics and traces for Web transactions in a target-oriented manner, the end-to-end trace in SAP Solution Manager offers a suitable solution. Here, the previously described traces and additional traces of the frontend are activated in a target-oriented manner and are then centrally evaluated. In this context, target-oriented means that information, statistics, and traces are written and forwarded via the different components of the SAP NetWeaver Application Server, and between the various SAP systems, so that analysis data is collected on all involved components. This data includes requests specifically sent by the monitored web browser.

4.8.1 Activating the Runtime Analysis

You can activate the end-to-end runtime analysis for a Web transaction, but also for an SAP GUI transaction if it is required, for instance, because the SAP GUI transaction runs across several systems.

To activate statistics and traces for a Web transaction, you require the **SAP HTTP plug-in**
SAP HTTP plug-in for Microsoft Internet Explorer. It is an integral part of
the SAP Solution Manager installation, but you can also install it separately via SAP Note 1041556. After this application is installed on your
presentation server, call it using the `ie-https.cmd` command. Microsoft
Internet Explorer and a separate application are started as displayed in
Figure 4.4. You now carry out the application in the web browser; the
plug-in logs the requests to the Web server and modifies the HTTP flow
so that SAP NetWeaver Application Server is notified about the traces to
be activated.

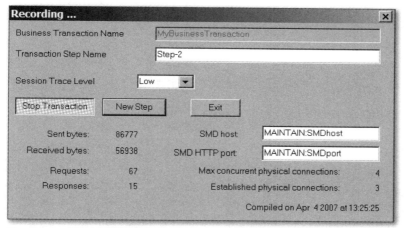

Figure 4.4 SAP HTTP Plug-In for Target-Oriented Activation of Statistics and Traces
on the SAP NetWeaver Application Server and the Presentation Server

When you reach the point in the Web transaction at which you want
to start the analysis, enter an analysis name in the Business Transaction
Name field and then start the trace by clicking the Start Transaction button. Each time you perform a new step in the web browser, you also
start a new analysis step via the New Step button. You can also stipulate
names for the transaction steps by entering the name in the Transaction
Step Name field. If you don't do so, the analysis application automatically assigns the names Step-1, Step-2, and so on.

Transaction /SDF/
E2E_TRACE
For an SAP GUI transaction you activate the end-to-end runtime analysis using Transaction /SDF/E2E_TRACE. This transaction offers functions comparable to those of the SAP HTTP plug-in for Web transactions. However, you don't need to manually select the steps; each operation in the SAP GUI is automatically handled as a new step.

Trace level
In the analysis application, you can also set the trace level of the SAP NetWeaver Application Server. Table 4.9 indicates the traces you can set. In addition to traces, statistical records are always written.

Trace/Trace Level	None	Low	Medium	High
Internet Communication Manager (ICM): HTTP log)	Off	Active	Active	Active
J2EE: SQL trace	Off	Off	Active	Active
J2EE: Logging	Off	Off	Off	Active
J2EE: Introscope trace	Off	Active	Active	Active
ABAP: SQL trace	Off	Off	Active	Active
ABAP: RFC trace	Off	Off	Active	Active
ABAP: Runtime analysis	Off	Off	Aggregated	Not aggregated
ABAP: Enqueue and buffer trace	Off	Off	Off	Active
ABAP: Authorization trace	Off	Off	Off	Active
Web service trace (SRTUTIL)	Off	Off	Active	Active
ESF trace (ESFUTIL)	Off	Off	Performance trace active	Data trace active
SAP NetWeaver BW statistics	Off	Off	Active	Active
Application log	Off	Off	Off	Active
VMC trace	Off	Off	Active	Active

Table 4.9 Overview of the Traces that Can Be Activated for End-to-End Analysis

When you have completed the part of the transaction for analysis, click Stop Transaction. After you have entered the corresponding connection data for SAP Solution Manager in the SMD Host and SMD http Port fields, the analysis transaction sends the data collected on the presentation server to SAP Solution Manager and displays it with data collected on the SAP NetWeaver Application Server.

4.8.2 Displaying an End-to-End Runtime Analysis in SAP Solution Manager

You can find the function for displaying a cross-component analysis in SAP Solution Manager (Transaction code DSWP) under GOTO • START SOLUTION MANAGER DIAGNOSTICS. In the diagnostics application of SAP Solution Manager, select TRACES • END-TO-END TRACE ANALYSIS. From the Business Transactions table, select the transaction for which you want a runtime analysis displayed. Then, in the lower part of the table, select the step to be displayed and open the analysis by clicking the Display button.

The analysis display provides three views: an analysis overview of the HTTP requests (Summary), a display of the statistical records, including references to the created traces (Messages Table), and a graphical overview of the statistical records (Message Graphics).

Views

The graphics show you the data discussed in the section on the presentation server trace (Chapter 7, SAP GUI and Internet Connection). In addition, the interaction of the presentation server trace and HTTP logs on the SAP NetWeaver Application Server is used to calculate the runtime of the presentation server (Client Time), the network runtime (Network Time), and the runtime of the SAP NetWeaver Application Server. We'll discuss analysis of high browser-generation time and high network time in Chapter 7, SAP GUI and Internet Connection.

The Requests Tree tab enables a detailed analysis of the runtime distribution within SAP NetWeaver Application Server. Figure 4.5 shows an example. In the tree, statistics records are displayed in hierarchical form. At the topmost level are HTTP requests that were recorded by the analysis application on the presentation server. In our example, you can see the requests with IDs 0, 1, 29, and 35. The requests in between were answered from the buffer of the browser and are filtered in the analysis display. The request with ID 29 is now further expanded. Below the HTTP request is a request to the SAP J2EE Engine, and further down are five requests to the ABAP server. The net times indicated in the table can be interpreted as follows. The processing of the request in the SAP NetWeaver Application Server took 1,537 milliseconds, 952 of which make up the pure processing in the SAP J2EE Engine, and 21 millisec-

Detailed analysis

onds were required to establish five connections to the ABAP server. The processing of RFCs on the ABAP server took 564 milliseconds. You can view the runtimes of the individual RFCs in the table.

Traces   The icons in the other table columns display the created traces, provided that they have been activated. The clock icon represents the Introscope trace on the SAP J2EE Engine or the aggregated ABAP runtime analysis on the ABAP server. (If you create a nonaggregated runtime analysis, detailed data is not transferred to SAP Solution Manager for performance reasons. To display this data, you need to log onto the system.) The database icon indicates an SQL trace, and the sheet with the glasses icon represents SAP J2EE Engine logs.

End2End Trace data

Display 20 rows ▼

		Id	Prop.	Type	Metric Name	System	Net	Gross			
▶		0	2%	HTTP	..jQ%253D%253D&sap-wd-cltwndid=WID1168357342000	F15	41	41			
▶		1	4%	HTTP	..P2005&HistoryMode=0&windowId=WID1168357342000	F15	80	80			
▼		29	92%	HTTP	...F15_30)ID0799852750DB0116236934553615 4185End	F15	1532	1532			
▼		29	92%	J2EE	... sap.com/tc~wd~dispwda:begin_transaction	F15	952	1537	⊛	📇	📄
▼		29	35%	J2EE	5 call(s) of type RFC to system HNI	F15	~21	585			
▼		29	34%	ABAP	At least 5 incoming call(s)	HNI	564	564	⊛	📇	
•		29	2%	ABAP	RHXSS_SER_GET_EMPLOYEE_DATA	HNI		37			
•		29	15%	ABAP	PT_ARQ_CUSTOMIZING_GET	HNI		258			
•		29	1%	ABAP	PT_ARQ_EECALE_GET	HNI		25			
•		29	14%	ABAP	PT_ARQ_REQUEST_PREPARE	HNI		242			
•		29	0%	ABAP	HRXSS_SER_INITSERVICE	HNI		3			
▶		35	0%	HTTP	...ok=init&guid=61a746e09ff811db85ce003005c546d8	F15	0	0			

Figure 4.5 Detailed View of the Cross-Component Runtime Analysis in SAP Solution Manager

4.9 Summary

Monitors enable detailed analysis of individual ABAP programs.

Single-statistics records   Analyzing *single-statistical records* lets you narrow down the causes of performance problems in individual programs to one of the following problem areas:

▶ Inefficient table buffering

▶ Expensive SQL statements

▶ High CPU consumption of ABAP statements

▶ Long runtimes of Java programs

SQL trace is the recommended tool for analyzing SQL statements in ABAP programs. Evaluating the trace enables you to identify network problems or throughput bottlenecks in the database. You will find further information on optimizing SQL statements in Chapter 11, Optimizing SQL Statements.

SQL trace

You use RFC trace to analyze the performance of sent and received RFCs. With SAP Basis version 7.10, you also have an HTTP trace at hand to record HTTP statements. For further information on this subject, see Chapter 6, Workload Distribution and Interfaces, and Chapter 7, SAP GUI and Internet Connection.

The enqueue trace is a means for selecting analyses of lock operations (enqueue/dequeue operations). You will find further information in Chapter 10, Locks.

For high CPU consumption problems, use an ABAP trace. In contrast to an SQL trace, an ABAP trace enables time measurements for operations on internal tables, such as LOOP, READ, SORT, and so on. As an alternative, you can monitor CPU-consuming programs using the ABAP debugger, which you can call from the work process overview. However, only developers should perform this analysis.

You should examine ABAP programs proactively using the Code Inspector, which implements static checks of the program and sends alerts on standard performance errors and problems.

Code Inspector

To analyze Java programs, you can use single-record statistics (on the SAP J2EE Engine), or you can directly implement an end-to-end runtime analysis. You can start the latter on the presentation server using the SAP Solution Manager *HTTP plug-in*. An evaluation of the central single-record statistics or end-to-end runtime analysis enables you to determine whether the lion's share of the response time can be allotted to the presentation server, the network, the SAP J2EE Engine, or the ABAP server.

End-to-end runtime analysis

For high runtimes in the Java part of the program, you can use an Introscope trace for the SAP J2EE Engine or SQL trace for the SAP J2EE Engine.

Figure 4.6 summarizes the procedure for analyzing an individual program or transaction.

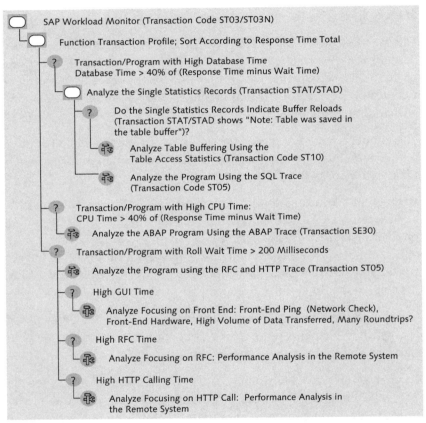

Figure 4.6 Performance Analysis Procedure for an ABAP Program

You can activate and evaluate the statistics records and each trace individually. However, this can create difficulties in larger production systems because of their complexity. To facilitate the analysis, SAP Solution Manager standardizes the activation and analysis of statistics records and traces in the end-to-end runtime analysis.

Questions

1. Which statements can be made on the basis of SAP statistics records?

   a) If a user action involves several SAP components (for example, ABAP, J2EE, ITS, etc.), an action ID (referred to as the passport) enables you to trace the user action across the components.

   b) The statistics records contain information on the response time of individual program components (function module calls, or methods in the case of ABAP, classes in the case of Java).

   c) The global statistics records contain the response time of a corresponding component (for example, ABAP, J2EE, ITS, etc.), the CPU time needed by the component, and the response time of additional components that are called by the component that writes the statistics record.

   d) On the basis of the statistics records, you can make statements on the performance of the business processes, such as cash flow in financials or delivery reliability in logistics.

2. What do you have to consider when you perform an SQL trace?

   a) There is only one trace file in each SAP system. Therefore, only one SQL trace can be created per SAP system.

   b) The user whose actions are being traced should not run multiple programs concurrently.

   c) You should perform the SQL trace on a second execution of a program, because the relevant buffers will already have been loaded.

   d) SQL traces are useful on the database server, but not on application servers, which yield inexact results due to network times.

3. When should you perform an ABAP trace?

   a) If a problem occurs with the table buffer.

   b) For programs with high CPU requirements.

   c) An ABAP trace is useful for analyzing I/O problems on hard drives.

5   Hardware Sizing and System Distribution

Hardware sizing entails the calculation of the hardware that is presumably necessary for an SAP system, that is, the required CPU power and size of main memory, I/O, and hard drive. Sizing for SAP systems follows clear guidelines that are worked out between SAP and its certified hardware partners and are constantly being improved.

Every performance expert should be familiar with the fundamentals of hardware sizing. The first section of this chapter presents the sizing of a new system (initial sizing) by discussing the basics of a concrete sample project and introducing the *SAP Standard Application Benchmarks*. The second section outlines the different sizing situations that you encounter in already existing systems: load increase, version change, Unicode conversion, and so on. The last section of this chapter then considers questions about the system, database, and server consolidation.

Background: Linearity Assumptions in Sizing

All considerations on sizing and on landscape planning are based on two assumptions concerning linearity and scalability, which basically go through the entire book and are now briefly summarized at the beginning of this chapter:

The resource requirement of a single transaction — after a certain "training period" of the system — neither depends on the data quantity managed in the system nor on the number of transactions processed in parallel in the system.

You can draw two conclusions:

- A sizing, which is determined for a specific number of users or for a specific throughput, still applies after the system has been in use for some time.

- The resource requirement of an application scales linearly with the number of users or the throughput according to the following formula: $R = \sum a_i \times L_i$. Here, R stands for resource requirement, L_i represents the load — either expressed by the number of users or the number of documents processed in this period of time — and ai is an application-dependent parameter. To calculate the overall load, you must add up the product of $a_i \times L_i$ for all applications that are represented by the index $_i$.

If you are going to make these assumptions, the underlying applications must be scalable. For this and the next assumption, also refer to the textbox, Background: Scalability of a Program, in Chapter 4, Section 4.5, Analyzing Memory Usage with ABAP Debugger and in the Memory Inspector.This linear approach only applies within specific limitations. Other sections of this book provide detailed examples for the limitations of this approach. Performance optimization in the various areas aims at recognizing the limitations of this linear behavior and expanding them as much as possible.

The second linearity assumption that forms the basis of sizing is the following: The system scales compared to a distribution to computers, that is, if the load increases, the system can be distributed to multiple computers. Chapter 1, Section 1.1.2, Client/Server Architecture, already discussed the terms *vertical scalability* and *horizontal scalability*.

When Should You Read this Chapter?

You should read this chapter to obtain detailed knowledge on hardware sizing and the distribution of your SAP system or your systems to computers, databases, and application instances.

5.1 Initial Hardware Sizing

Sizing decisions must draw on detailed figures gained through experience about the resource requirements of users and transactions. These values quickly become obsolete in view of new application and computer generations; therefore, this chapter focuses on processes and tools. In a sizing project, you should always bear in mind that the actual sizing is done by the hardware partners — in consultation with SAP, if necessary. However, as a project leader or employee, you will need a basic understanding of the sizing process to competently compare and evaluate different sizing options and reports and to understand all of the possible risks and limits. These are discussed in this chapter.

Figure 5.1 shows the steps involved in the sizing process. On the horizontal axes, you can see the phases of a project. Important milestones include going into live production operation, subsequent version changes, and production operation starts for additional functions or users. The bold, black curve shows the growing workload on the system and, with it, the growing demands made on the hardware.

Initial sizing is done before live operation begins. It involves hardware partners (with their corresponding sizing options) and SAP (with SAP Quick Sizer and SAP GoingLive Check). System hardware requirements can grow even after the initial start of production operation. As a result, planning for additional capacity is also necessary during these phases. SAP assists you here with its service program and hardware partners.

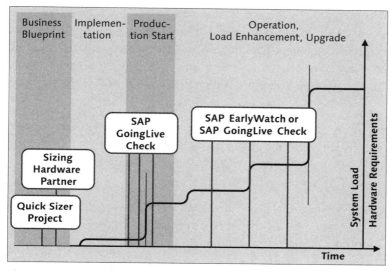

Figure 5.1 Hardware Sizing in the Lifecycle of an SAP Project

5.1.1 Overview of the Project for Initial Sizing

There are different approaches to implement sizing. For many processes, SAP offers *Quick Sizer* in the SAP Service Marketplace — a browser-based application in which you can create sizing projects, enter data, and calculate the hardware requirement. You can find Quick Sizer in the SAP Service Marketplace at *http://service.sap.com/sizing*. In addition to documentation about Quick Sizer, you can also find information here on sizing SAP solutions. This chapter presents a detailed example.

As an alternative to sizing using Quick Sizer, SAP often offers *T-shirt sizing*. For this type of sizing, typical hardware configurations are described that correspond to size categories such as small, medium, large, and extra large — hence the term T-shirt sizing. For this configuration, it is speci-

T-shirt sizing

fied how many users or how much throughput a specific configuration can handle. An example of T-shirt sizing is the sizing for SAP Enterprise Point-of-Sale (POS). You can find the sizing guideline in the SAP Service Marketplace under *http://service.sap.com/sizing* • SIZING GUIDELINES • SOLUTIONS AND PLATFORMS. There, among other things, you can find the following specifications for a medium-sized installation with 100 connected terminals: 800 SAPS (SAP Application Performance Standard) and 1GB main memory for the application server, 100 SAPS and 1GB main memory for the messaging middleware and 400 SAPS and 1GB main memory for the database instance. Note that these figures are only an example. They may become obsolete and only present a small part of the sizing instruction. Therefore, they must not be used as the basis for sizing.

The third alternative for an initial sizing is the direct use of sizing formulas, which you can find in the sizing instructions in the SAP Service Marketplace. The document "Sizing SAP E-Recruiting" is an example of sizing instruction with explicit sizing formulas.

When sizing begins, calculating the hardware necessary is based on data about the users (user-based sizing) and/or transactions (throughput-based sizing). Output parameters of sizing include the following:

▶ CPU requirement for database server, application server (ABAP or Java), TREX, SAP liveCache (the requirements are output separately irrespective of the option to install or distribute the components on a computer)

▶ Main memory requirement for database server, application server, TREX, SAP liveCache

▶ Disk space requirement on the database server

▶ Requirement for input and output capacity (I/O) on the database server

User-based sizing On the one hand, data about the number of users in different SAP applications serves as sizing input. Using detailed values based on past experience of the hardware requirements of SAP applications, you first calculate the hardware requirement for each application (the product of the number of users and application-specific load factors, and possibly a constant basic requirement). Then, you calculate the total hardware requirements as a sum of the individual requirements of each application. User-based sizing always delivers reliable data if the main system load is created by dialog users and if the SAP standard has not been changed significantly. When you interpret the result, you must take into account that the user-based sizing in Quick Sizer assumes a target utilization of 100% with regard to the main memory and 33% with regard to the CPU. Chapter 2, Monitoring Hardware, Databases, and SAP Basis, already discussed that you cannot utilize a CPU at 100% if you want to ensure good response times on a computer with dialog users. The target utilization that is set relatively low also considers a relatively high security factor that you must take into account in user-based sizing.

Data input for throughput-based sizing can involve what is referred to as the *quantity structure*, for example, data on the number of business operations that need to be processed within particular time frames or the number of sales orders, deliveries and production orders, or printed documents. The advantage of this method is that data transfer in background processes (for example, batch input or ALE), the distribution of the document throughput over the day, and a sizing for peak load times are taken into consideration. The throughput-based approach should always be selected if a considerable amount of the load is created by background processes or interfaces. Examples of this include SAP retail solutions (transfer of sales data in point-of-sale inbound processing) and banking, utilities, or telecommunications solutions. In practice, a combination of both forms of sizing is usually selected. For a throughput-based sizing, a CPU target utilization of 65% is assumed in Quick Sizer.

Throughput-based sizing

In Quick Sizer, user-based and throughput-based sizing are calculated separately, so you can perform sizing for the user-based approach and the throughput-based approach in parallel in Quick Sizer. However, you must take into consideration that the two sizing types aren't offered for all processes. If parallel sizing is possible, you can compare the two results with one another for a consistency check, but you cannot add up the results in this case. The alternative would be to have the system calculate some processes based on the users and others based on the throughput, and then add up the result. Because of the consistency check, we recommend using the first variant.

As a project proceeds, you will receive one or more offers from *hardware partners*. The hardware partners are ultimately responsible for the sizing of a project, because only they can guarantee the performance of their hardware. Where necessary, the hardware partners can get support from SAP sizing experts via their SAP Competence Center.

To simplify the sizing process, SAP has defined the following standard procedures:

1. Compile a sizing plan for your implementation project in SAP Quick Sizer in the SAP Service Marketplace. Enter the data necessary for sizing there. If Quick Sizer doesn't support sizing for the processes selected, use the appropriate sizing guideline.

2. Next, give any hardware partners from whom you want to receive a sizing offer access to this sizing plan in the SAP Service Marketplace; give them the password for the plan. You will also find links to the websites of hardware partners in SAP Quick Sizer.

3. Finally, on the basis of the data you enter, hardware partners can create a concrete hardware offer.

If you want to receive offers from several hardware partners, do not forget to check the data on hardware performance in SAPS. Only then can you compare offers from different manufacturers. You should also ask about the benchmark certificates of the hardware offered (also be found on the Internet).

As part of their software maintenance contract (TeamSAP Support), SAP offers all customers the *SAP GoingLive Check* service. To carry out this service, SAP employees or their service partners log on to your system remotely at several different times (sessions) and check the system. This service is carried out within a period of two months after the start of production operation. SAP GoingLive Check contains a sizing plausibility check. This does not involve a new sizing plan; rather, it rates how the already installed or planned hardware can deal with the estimated load. Three ratings can be given:

▶ **Green**
Based on the results of SAP GoingLive Check and data on the hard-

ware and forecast load, there is no fear of any hardware bottlenecks occurring.

▶ **Yellow**

Based on the results of SAP GoingLive Check and data on the hardware and forecast load, the hardware complies with the minimum requirements. Therefore, bottlenecks are possible or even probable in situations of high workload.

▶ **Red**

Based on the results of SAP GoingLive Check and data on the hardware and forecast load, the hardware will not be able to cope with the workload. Performance bottlenecks will probably occur. SAP recommends that you do not go into production operation with the existing hardware.

You can find further information on SAP GoingLive Check in the SAP Service Marketplace at *www://service.sap.com/goinglivecheck*.

When sizing for Internet applications, you can only roughly estimate the number of users and throughput at times of peak workload in advance. If your applications are not available and performing well at these times, grave consequences might result:

Special challenges from the Internet

▶ *Financial damage* can occur, because after unsuccessful attempts to access or use a site, many potential customers won't try again.

▶ *Image damage* can occur, because unsuccessful potential customers may feel that the website operator is incompetent and the application is unsafe.

▶ *Legal damage* is also possible. For example, a bank's home pages and call centers must be available at all times to all customers using online banking. In fact, in Germany, federal authorities have warned banks that they are obliged to make reasonable access available continuously if they offer online banking services.

In all of these cases, several thousand users are possible at peak workload times. Given that benchmark results are available, the relevant people at the hardware partner's company can carry out hardware sizing to meet peak demand.

Unfortunately, however, the hardware necessary for times of peak workload will be unused for perhaps 350 days of the year. In the future, there will be an increasing number of business scenarios of this type for which active capacity management is required.

Summary of the initial sizing Why do hardware partners and SAP offer their customers this threefold security? To put it another way, what are the strengths and limitations of this three-step sizing? The advantages of Quick Sizer or T-shirt sizing based on sizing guidelines are its constant availability and ease of use by project employees. However, because only standard applications are accounted for, this procedure soon reaches its limits.

A hardware offer from a manufacturer can clearly examine the individual requirements of a project in greater detail. For example, an experienced sizing consultant can estimate the additional investment necessary to deal with interfaces, individually developed functions, and requirements of availability or down time and performance, even in situations of high workload. The disadvantage is that individual sizing offers are costly and therefore cannot be run as often as you might desire.

SAP GoingLive Check takes into account the same influencing factors as does sizing by hardware partners. Whereas the hardware partner's sizing can often be several months old, SAP GoingLive Check is done immediately before the start of production. As a result, any changes that have been introduced to the project plan and the latest knowledge can be included in the analysis. In addition, if necessary, service employees can analyze business-critical transactions in detail. In this way, it is possible to see if inefficient customizing or customer enhancements (user exits) cause additional load, something that may not be taken into consideration in standard sizing.

[+] To be able to generate a sizing report, the experts need information about project-specific key values that will determine the sizing. In particular, these include the software versions used, the expected number of users, and the expected number of transactions (throughput) in the different applications. In Quick Sizer, you will first find questionnaires on these key values. Then hardware partners will send you relevant questionnaires as part of SAP GoingLive Check. You should consider the following rules when working with these questionnaires:

▶ Treat these questionnaires as very important. Only if the data is entered correctly can you ensure that you will receive reliable sizing information.

▶ Constantly evaluate the figures as the project proceeds. If changes are made to the project plan during the implementation phase, and data in the sizing questionnaire is changed, you should inform your hardware partner immediately so you can discuss the possible effects on the planned hardware.

Incorrect sizing and the resulting conflicts usually occur because of imprecise forecasts of the expected number of users and documents. Taking responsibility for the quality of these forecasts is the project leader's most important task in the sizing process. The experts among the hardware partners are available to offer advice on this matter.

5.1.2 Implementing a Sizing Project in Detail

The example provided shows a sizing project form the customer's perspective. The methods presented don't enable you to perform a hardware sizing. The hardware partner is responsible for this. The numbers in this example are fictitious. You cannot use them for a real sizing.

[+]

To prepare the sizing project, open the sizing page of the SAP Service Marketplace at *http://service.sap.com/sizing*. Follow the link SIZING GUIDELINES • SOLUTIONS AND PLATFORMS. This page includes a list of sizing instructions on standard and industry solutions from SAP and on technology components of SAP NetWeaver. Select your relevant instructions, load them into your computer, and study them in detail. The instructions inform about how to perform sizing, whether using a Quick Sizer project, a T-shirt sizing, or a different procedure described in the instructions. The instructions also provide an overview of the architecture and address solution-specific or industry-specific characteristics.

Preparation

The document "Sizing SAP CRM, Version 7.0" is relevant for this example of sizing for a SAP CRM project in the following ways.

Let's assume for this practical example that the sizing is supposed to be implemented using Quick Sizer. Now proceed as follows:

Implement a Quick Sizer project

1. Open the sizing page in the SAP Service Marketplace at *http://service. sap.com/sizing*. Follow the navigation path QUICK SIZER TOOL • START THE QUICK SIZER. Quick Sizer starts in a new browser window.

2. Enter your customer number and a project name, and then create the project by clicking the Create Project button.

3. For this sample project, select the CRM • SALES solution in the left-hand navigation area.

4. In the right-hand window, the system now displays tables for entering users and documents. Table 5.1 lists the numbers of users that you've entered in Quick Sizer for this example.

5. In the left-hand navigation area, select Master Data and Interaction Center. Table 5.1 also lists the numbers of users that you've entered in Quick Sizer for these categories.

User Type	Low	Medium	High
Master data	0	50	0
Activity management	200	150	50
Opportunity management	200	150	0
Sales transactions	200	150	50
Interaction center	0	100	100

Table 5.1 Sizing Entries for the Sample Project

After you've entered the data, click the Calculate Result button to calculate the sizing's result. The system takes you to the Quick Sizer result page, in which you can find the results in the tables that are provided in the All, CPU, and Memory and Disk tabs. Table 5.2 presents selected results of this sample project. For more information for interpretation and the basic use of Quick Sizer, refer to the documentation that you can find via the Documentation link in Quick Sizer.

The main memory and the disk space requirements are indicated in MB and the requirements of I/O capacity in accesses per second, that is, in typical units. For the CPU capacity, Quick Sizer provides the result in SAPS so you can compare the different CPU architectures with one another. Hardware partners can inform you about the SAPS performance of your computer. The next section describes the definition of the SAPS unit in detail.

Field	Result	Explanation
Solution Release	CRM 7.0	Indicates the SAP product version to which the sizing applies. In principle, you can use Quick Sizer only for sizing the current version of an SAP product.
SAPS (total)	30,300	CPU requirement in SAPS.
Release Memory (total, MB)	76,800	Main memory requirement in MB, total.
DB Memory	8,192	Main memory requirement in MB for the database.
App. Mem. (ABAP)	68,608	Main memory requirement in MB for the application server, in this case ABAP server.
DB Disk (MB, total)	785,000	Hard disk memory required (for more information refer to the link Information LifeCycle Management).
I/Os per s	11,800	Requirement for input/output capacity in I/O per second

Table 5.2 Sizing Result for the Sample Project (Selected Data; the Categories Specified are Left Out)

After you've completed your sizing project, you can obtain a hardware offer on the project from hardware partners of your choice. For this purpose, select Hardware Vendors in Quick Sizer. An Internet page opens that provides a list of participating hardware partners. Follow the link of the hardware partner you want. You're redirected to the hardware partner's Internet page, where you can request a hardware offer. For this purpose, the hardware partner asks for your customer number and the name of the sizing project so they can access it. To be able to compare competing offers of the hardware partners, it is important that all hardware partners use the same data and don't deploy different questionnaires on your project. The fact that the hardware partners access your sizing project in Quick Sizer is not only due to the convenience of

Obtain and evaluate a hardware offer

not having to enter data multiple times in different questionnaires, but it also ensures the comparability of results.

The hardware partners now create their offers on the sizing project, from which you must select. For this sample project, it would be possible to cover the requirements with one computer. Alternatively, the hardware requirement can be distributed across multiple computers. Let's assume for this project that you decide on an offer that includes three computers with a capacity of 12,000 SAPS and 32GB main memory each according to the manufacturer's information. In total, the solution has a performance of 36,000 SAPS and a main memory capacity of 96GB. The database and a central SAP instance are supposed to be installed on one computer, and the other two computers are supposed to include SAP instances for the majority of the dialog, background, and update load. With this distributed installation it is assumed that you can maintain a restricted operation and reduce the risk of a total failure even if one of the computers fails. For further considerations on the topic of load distribution, refer to the last part of this chapter and the next chapter.

Alternatively or in parallel, you can obtain information on the performance of the offered hardware based on the published benchmark results. The following section discusses this option.

5.1.3 SAP Standard Application Benchmarks

SAP Standard Application Benchmarks are automated and standardized executions of business processes with defined customizing and master data. They have various purposes: verify the scalability of hardware, database, SAP Basis, and tested SAP applications; determine factors for comparing the performance of various computers; determine factors for comparing different SAP applications.

SD benchmark SAP provides benchmarks for more than 20 application scenarios. The *SD benchmark* (for Sales and Distribution) is the most popular SAP benchmark. The SD benchmark comprises the creation and display of sales documents, the creation and change of deliveries, posting of goods issue, and the creation of an invoice for the sales documents created. More benchmarks are offered for the modules of SAP ERP (Financial Accounting [FI] Materials Management [MM], and so on) for SAP CRM components, for APO components, for SAP NetWeaver Portal, and for SAP NetWeaver Business Warehouse, as well as for some industry solutions that depend on a high throughput, for instance, *retail*, banking, and *utilities*. All details on a benchmark's process are available at SAP's public web site (*www.sap.com/benchmark*).

Hardware partners can have benchmark runs certified by SAP. For this purpose, they send data about the benchmark process to SAP. SAP precisely defines this data, and they publish certified benchmarks on the Internet. A distinction is made between benchmark runs that are implemented on one computer (two-tier) and those that are implemented in a distributed computer landscape (three-tier). Three-tier benchmarks impressively demonstrate the scalability of hardware, database, SAP Basis, and tested SAP applications. Every year, particularly for the two-tier SD benchmark, several dozens of benchmark runs are certified that are primarily aimed at demonstrating the performance of the computer used.

For all other benchmarks, certifications are basically to be found for the time of the scenario's rollout. Moreover, many internal benchmark runs are implemented by SAP and hardware partners to obtain data for the sizing process.

You can use benchmark runs to determine the computers' performance. Let's take a look at the two following specifications on computer equipment:

- ▶ 2 processors/12 cores/12 threads; 6-core processor of manufacturer A with 2.6GHz clock speed, 128KB L1 cache, and 512KB L2 cache per core; 6MB L3 cache per processor

- ▶ 2 processors/8 cores/16 threads; processor of manufacturer B with 2.93GHz clock speed, 64KB L1 cache, and 256KB L2 cache per core; 8MB L3 cache per processor

From the analytical perspective, it is not possible to forecast which of the two computers offers a higher performance with regard to SAP applications because the process architecture, clock speed, and main memory areas close to the CPU (L1 cache, L2 cache, and so on) are highly significant in addition to the number of processors. So the performance can

SAPS

only be determined using a benchmark. For the throughput generated in an SD benchmark, SAP has developed the SAPS unit which stands for *SAP Application Performance Standard*. A value of 100 SAPS corresponds to 2,000 fully processed order items per hour, 6,000 dialog steps (screen changes) with 2,000 updates, or 2,400 SAP SD transactions. The SAPS data is specific to the tested version.

Strictly speaking, the SAPS unit is a measure of CPU performance according in an SAP SD benchmark. However, comparing benchmarks shows that this statement can be transferred to all SAP applications — also to Java-based applications despite the different architecture. Therefore, SAPS data is an effective way to compare different manufacturers' hardware.

Determining performance

If you want to obtain information on the performance of current computers based on certified benchmark results, proceed as follows:

1. Open SAP's benchmark page at SAP's publicly accessible website at *http://www.sap.com/benchmark*. Follow the navigation path SALES AND DISTRIBUTION (SD) ... • TWO-TIER .... A list is displayed that includes the published two-tier SD benchmarks. (The list goes back to 1995.)

2. The columns of the list are split into four groups of information on each benchmark: The first group informs about the certification date, the hardware partner that performed the benchmark, and a reference to the benchmark certificate. The second group provides information on the throughput achieved that is indicated with the benchmark users, documents processed, dialog steps and — decisively — SAPS. Ultimately, each of these key figures can be converted into the others as a result of the definition of the SAPS unit. The third group of information refers to the software used: operating system type and version, database type and version, and SAP product version. Finally, you are provided with information on the hardware itself, that is, on CPU and main memory.

3. Based on the benchmarks published, you can obtain information on the hardware's performance. For example, let's assume that you find a benchmark for computer X with 32GB RAM, which you're interested in. This benchmark indicates a performance of 12,000 SAPS. In this

case, three computers of this type would cover the specified hardware requirement.

For the evaluation of the hardware, the question arises to what extent the database system, operating system, and SAP version play a role. SAP makes no statements on the first two influencing factors; that is, the database and operating systems used should not differ in their performance. For the SAP version, however, information is provided if the hardware requirement changes from one version to the other. This means you can consider differences if the SAP version that you want to use in production doesn't correspond to the version for which the benchmark was performed. The next section discusses the differences in the hardware requirements of different versions.

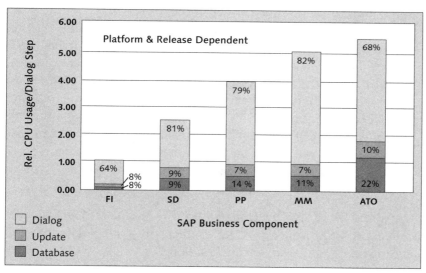

Figure 5.2 CPU Requirement for Dialog, Update, and Database Services for Different SAP Applications

To be able to implement a sizing, it is not sufficient to be able to compare the computers' performance; you also require factors for comparing the various scenarios among one another. Figure 5.2 shows the CPU requirement for dialog, update, and database services for the SAP applications FI, SD, PP, MM, and the ATO scenario. This figure is the result of numerous SAP benchmark tests (SAP Standard Application Benchmarks). The bar chart level for the FI application is therefore standardized at one user as a reference point. The number of FI users that can be served by one processor depends mainly on the processor build type and the SAP system version and cannot be ascertained from the graphic.

Conclusions You can draw the following conclusions regarding the sizing and the system configuration from comparing SAP benchmarks:

► SAP benchmarks provide cutoff values for CPU requirements for different SAP applications. The heights of the individual bars in Figure 5.2 show the drastic differences in CPU requirements for different applications. We can see that an MM application user needs five times more CPU capacity than an FI user. Accordingly, the number of configured work processes also depends strongly on the applications running on the corresponding SAP instance.

► In addition, SAP benchmarks give information on the CPU requirements of individual services. The lower part of the bars in Figure 5.2 shows the CPU requirement of the database instance. Depending on the SAP application, this accounts for between 8 and 22% of the entire SAP systems' CPU requirements. The middle section of the bars shows the CPU capacity required by update services, also accounting for around 8 to 10% of the entire requirement. The remaining 68 to 84% corresponds to the requirements of the dialog service. The ratio of dialog work processes to update work processes can also be estimated.

Simulations with SAP benchmarks provide useful results that help configure real SAP systems. However, there are some points that SAP benchmarks cannot take into consideration.

The benchmarks illustrated in Figure 5.2 only consider the *online transaction processing* (OLTP) of the corresponding application because this is usually considered more critical for performance than reporting (*online analytical processing* (OLAP). (Posting sales orders, deliveries, and invoicing is more important than reports on these processes.) Reporting activities normally place a high load on the database. As a result, in real SAP systems, the database workload is normally higher in relation to the dialog and update loads; the share of the database instance would typically be between 10 and 30%. The ratio of dialog work processes to the number of update work processes depends on the actual requirements of the system.

The benchmarks shown in Figure 5.2 do not take into account any background workload. However, in a real system, the bars shown in Figure 5.2 as Dialog would be split into a dialog segment and a background segment. The relationship between the dialog workload and background workload, therefore, depends on the actual implementation of the business process.

In the SAP benchmark for the SD application, sales orders, deliveries, and invoices are generated in dialog mode. In your SAP system, however, perhaps only sales orders are created in dialog mode, whereas deliveries and invoices are created in background mode by what is referred to as collective processing for delivery notes and invoices. If you want to create a workload profile for this example and compare it with the profile of the SAP Standard Benchmark in Figure 5.2, the relationship between the database and update workloads would not change. The part marked Dialog would, however, be divided into a dialog section and a background section.

[Ex]

5.2   Sizing to Deal with Increased Workload, Change of Release, or Migration

Only very rarely do large projects go live with one "big bang." More often, an SAP system is rolled out in several stages. Before workload is increased, you should always carry out a review of capacity planning. The same applies for a change in the SAP software version (upgrades), a migration to a different hardware or database platform, or a Unicode migration.

5.2.1   Overview of a Sizing Project in the Environment of an Installation that is Already Used

Before a planned increase in workload, you should employ an SAP service that determines current hardware load and evaluates the effects of the planned increase in workload. SAP recommends that you use the SAP EarlyWatch service for planned workload increases of up to 30%

Recommended services

and SAP GoingLive Check for larger increases in workload. Special SAP GoingLive Checks are also available for changes in SAP release or changing database or hardware platforms (see Table 5.3).

These services measure and evaluate the current load on hardware. Additional hardware requirements are determined based on data from the planned project steps. Previously planned changes to the hardware landscape are included in the evaluation. The free, automatic SAP EarlyWatch Alert service also determines the current hardware workload and presents it in a summary report.

Given that production usage already exists, the current utilization data is used for the sizing project. It would be a wrong decision to implement an initial sizing for the new overall load and ignore the current utilization data.

Project	Appropriate Sizing Strategy	Recommended SAP Services
Re-sizing: Increase the load with the same application profile	Determine the existing load in the production system and re-sizing with load factor	SAP GoingLive Check
Delta sizing: Increase the load with the changed application profile (new applications)	Determine the existing load in the production system and delta sizing with Quick Sizer for the new applications	SAP GoingLive Check
Upgrade sizing: Change of the SAP version (upgrade)	Determine the existing load in the production system and upgrade sizing with load factor	SAP GoingLive Functional Upgrade Check
Changeover to Unicode	Determine the existing load in the production system and sizing with load factor	SAP GoingLive Functional Upgrade Check
Migration: Change of database or hardware platform (changing operating system or manufacturer)	Determine the existing load in the production system	SAP GoingLive Migration Check
Continuous monitoring of capacity	Determine the existing load in the production system	SAP EarlyWatch, SAP EarlyWatch Alert

Table 5.3 Strategies for Sizing in the Environment of Installations Used in Production

5.2.2 Implementing Sizing in the Environment of Installations Used in Production

As you can see in Table 5.3, a sizing process in the environment of installations used in production consists of two steps: the determination of the existing load in the production system and the determination of the load increase. The first step is identical for all types of sizing. The second step depends on the project.

Determine the Existing Load in the Production System

You determine the existing load based on the histories in the operating system monitor (Transaction code ST06), which is described in Chapter 2, Section 2.2, Hardware Monitoring. The hourly average values of the CPU utilization and the main memory utilization (in percentage) of the available capacity are used as load values. We do not recommended using average values for shorter periods of time because then too much emphasize would be on the evaluation of temporary load peaks. It is a problem to select the right hourly average value from the load distribution of the past days and weeks. To generally use the maximum often leads to excessive load values, for example, if processes such as backup or reorganizations occupy the CPU or if individual programs allocate a lot of main memory that is hardly used and can therefore be paged. We therefore recommend to analyzing the load profiles for unusual peaks and ignoring them if it can be proven that these were indeed untypical operating situations.

In parallel, you can determine the main memory requirements from the system. To do so, proceed as follows:

Main memory requirements

► **ABAP server**
In the main memory configuration monitor (Transaction code ST02), you can find a list of all memory areas that are allocated by the ABAP server — including the usage histories. As a rule of thumb, you can subtract one-third because moderate over-allocation by the ABAP server is usually uncritical (see Chapter 2, Section 2.4.3, Displaying Allocated Memory).

265

▶ **SAP J2EE Engine**
You specify the main memory requirements of the SAP J2EE Engine based on the logs of the garbage collection runs (see Chapter 2, Section 2.6.1, Analyzing Garbage Collection).

▶ **Database**
You can find the main memory requirements of the database in the DBA Cockpit (see Chapter 2, Section 2.3.1, Analyzing the Database Buffer, and Appendix B).

▶ **TREX**
You determine the main memory requirements of TREX based on the data in the TREX server overview (Section Chapter 13, 13.2.1, Monitoring the Utilization of the TREX Servers).

On the one hand, this analysis is useful as a consistency check of data that is provided by the operating system monitor. For this purpose, add up the main memory requirements and compare the result with the values that you determine in the operating system. If the values strongly deviate, you must analyze whether there are processes that don't directly belong to the SAP system. On the other hand, you can also determine on the database server how much main memory is required by the database instance and by the SAP instance, for example.

CPU workload   To implement the corresponding cross-check for the CPU utilization, you proceed as follows:

▶ **ABAP server**
In the workload monitor, call the time profile. Take the entire CPU time for an hour with a high load from this profile. Divide this value by 3,600 seconds and then by the number of CPUs. This results in the average CPU utilization for the ABAP server in this specific hour.

▶ **SAP J2EE Engine**
For the SAP J2EE Engine you can implement this analysis with Wily Introscope in SAP Solution Manager.

▶ **Database**
Some databases analyze the CPU time; others don't.

▶ **TREX**
For TREX, you can determine the CPU utilization from the load file. Because the load file logs the CPU times per minute, you must first

aggregate the data by the hour. Then you can use the same procedure as for the ABAP server.

Let's return to the sizing example. You determine the utilization key [Ex] figures indicated in Table 5.4 for the database server and the two application servers. The main memory utilization of 71,000MB is slightly below the value of 76,800MB that was determined in sizing. The measured CPU utilization in percentage was converted in the CPU utilization in SAPS. When you compare the actual utilization with the value that was determined in sizing, you must take into account that the user-based sizing calculates the CPU requirement in a way that results in a target CPU utilization of 33%. In this example, the value measured is therefore above the sizing value.

Based on the user overview in the workload monitor (Transaction code ST03N), you should check whether the actual user number corresponds to the sizing data.

Server	Main Memory Utilization in Percentage	Main Memory Utilization in MB	CPU Utilization in Percentage	CPU Utilization in SAPS
Database instance on the database server	47	15,000	41	4,920
Application instance on the database server	38	12,000	15	1,800
Subtotal database server	85	27,000	56	6,720
Application server 1	62	20,000	37	4,444
Application server 2	73	23,000	36	4,320
Total	73	70,000	43	15,484

Table 5.4 Result of the Load Analysis

Increase the Load While Keeping the Application Profile

In this example, you are now supposed to increase the load while keeping the application profile; that is, more users are supposed to use the applications Activity Management, Opportunity Management, and Sales and Distribution. Assume that the number of users is supposed to increase by 20% in this example. The resizing assumes that this reflects proportionately in the load increase. In total, you have a main memory utilization of 87.6% and a CPU utilization of 51.2%, which means the existing hardware is not sufficient for the load increase.

In a distributed installation, however, it is necessary to consider not only the summarized load, but also the future distribution of the load to the servers. In this example you can see that the utilization of the database server is considerably higher than the utilization of the application server. Because an SAP instance is located on the database server, you must reduce the load caused by this instance and distribute it to the two application servers.

Increase the Load with a Changed Application Profile

In the next case, you are supposed to activate another application for live operation on the same system; in this example, 150 users are supposed to use the service application of the SAP CRM system.

In this case, the sizing involves three steps:

1. First, you determine the existing load in the production system.
2. Then you perform an initial sizing for the additional load using Quick Sizer.
3. Finally, you convert the result of the sizing using Quick Sizer into the main memory and CPU load of your system and add the additional amounts to the existing load. The result shows whether the existing hardware installation can include the additional load.

[Ex] Let's perform these steps based on a concrete example. The first step was already described; Table 5.4 shows the result. In the second step, you create a Quick Sizer project as described in Section 5.1.2, Implementing a Sizing Project in Detail. For this purpose, in the Service category enter 100 users of the Medium category and 50 users of the High category. Click the Calculate Result button to navigate to the result page, and then select System Extension. Assume that the result reveals an additional main memory requirement of 2,048MB for the database instance and 10,240MB for the SAP instances and a CPU requirement of 6,200 SAPS. In this case, the main memory utilization after the planned load increase is 82,300MB or 85.7%. To calculate the CPU utilization, add 33% of the requirement that you've determined using Quick Sizer (2,046 SAPS or 5.6%) to the current CPU utilization (15,484 SAPS or 43%), which results in a utilization after the load increase of 17,530 SAPS or 49%.

The factor 33% is included in the formula because the user-based sizing in Quick Sizer anticipates a target utilization of 33%. If you determine the additional load with the throughput-based approach that anticipates a target utilization of 65%, the factor 65% is included in the calculation. **[+]**

Change the SAP Version (Upgrade or Update) and Changeover to Unicode

In the SAP Notes, which you can find in Appendix G, SAP provides information on the additional hardware requirement for changing the SAP version. The statements about the additional requirement are implemented based on the SAP Standard Application Benchmarks and comparison measures of other important transactions.

For the version change from SAP ERP 6.0 to SAP ERP 6.0 Enhancement Package 4 (SAP Business Suite 7), SAP Note 1311835 includes the information about an additional CPU and main memory requirement of 5% maximum, depending on the application used. **[Ex]**

The information on the additional hardware requirement in the SAP notes only applies if no new functionality is used. Check carefully if this applies to your project. **[!]**

After the version change, an increased hardware requirement may temporarily arise, which decreases again after a couple of days. There are three reasons for this effect: **[+]**

▸ Even some time after the version change, the system still generates new objects or changes data if required.

▸ There may still be performance errors in the SAP programs for which corrections already exist but have not been implemented yet. Or there are performance errors in customer or partner programs that still need to be remedied.

▶ Particularly if the user interfaces change, the users must get used to these changes. They will possibly try out the new functions.

These aspects make clear that the performance monitoring should be performed with particular care after a version change.

Unicode
If you still need to changeover your system to Unicode, you must also take into consideration a higher resource requirement that results from the fact that data structures for character type variables require more main memory space and that more CPU capacity is required for computing with these broader variables. SAP Note 1139642 specifies the additional requirement between 10 and 30% for the CPU and 40 to 50% for the main memory. Note that these specifications are average values that may be exceeded or fallen below in concrete installations. The memory space of the database also changes depending on the code used. The database size can increase or decrease in certain cases.

You can find detailed information in the SAP Service Marketplace at *http://service.sap.com/unicode* and in SAP Note 790099 (Parameter Recommendations for Unicode Systems). We highly recommend obtaining a verification via the SAP GoingLive Functional Upgrade Check service.

The sizing for an SAP version change or a changeover to Unicode involves two steps:

1. First, you determine the existing load in the production system.

2. Based on the corresponding SAP Notes, you determine the factor or the load that is to be expected additionally after the version change and/or the changeover to Unicode. If a change involving multiple versions is performed in one step, you must cumulate the upgrade factors. Even if the Unicode conversion is performed in combination with an upgrade, you must cumulate the factors, too. Multiply the factors determined for CPU and main memory with the current utilization values. The result shows whether the existing hardware installation can accommodate the additional load.

[+]
For a version change — especially if this change involves multiple versions — and for the Unicode conversion you have to pay special attention if older hardware is used. Even if the upgrade sizing formally has the result that the existing hardware should be sufficient for the target sta-

tus, in rare cases, customers have found that the performance drastically deteriorates after the upgrade or the Unicode conversion. This can be due to the following factors, for example:

▶ The load is distributed to too many, small computers, but on the individual computers, the main memory is no longer sufficient for an effective buffering.

▶ Computers are used with many processors and a low clock speed. The SAPS key figure informs about the throughput that can be achieved on a computer. The same throughput can be achieved with few faster processors or with many slow processors. To obtain a good response time in the dialog, we recommend using a few fast processors. Particularly if legacy database servers with many processors that are slow compared to today's standards are rededicated to application servers because a new database server is commissioned, the result may be disappointing. As you can see in Figure 5.2, the CPU time on the application server constitutes 80 to 90% of the response time, and the database CPU time only 10 to 20%. A slow application server has a higher impact on the dialog response time than the database server.

▶ The change of the SAP version often involves a change of the operating system version. If the SAP kernel and the new operating system version are optimized for the current processor types, this can have a negative influence on the performance of older processors.

▶ SAP Note 1139642 explicitly indicates that after a Unicode conversion older processors require more CPU than newer processors that are already optimized for Unicode.

Change of Database or Hardware Platform

When you change the database or hardware platform, that is, you change the operating system or the hardware manufacturer, a migration is necessary. There are no general statements that the CPU or main memory requirement changes with such a change, but this is possible nevertheless. No resizing is performed for such a change, but you should analyze the existing load in the production system to ensure that the system to be migrated is not running almost to the capacity limits.

5.3   Planning the System Landscape

Now that you've gotten to know the methods of load distribution and hardware sizing, we'll answer the question of how many system databases, application instances, and servers are required to handle the load. In particular, with the introduction of SAP Business Suite, the project team is faced with the challenging task of not letting the amount of work involved in the maintenance and administration of hardware, databases, SAP instances, and other software explode. Against this backdrop, many projects strive for consolidation, which means reducing the software instances to a few powerful computers. Hardware partners support this consolidation with innovative concepts in technology and marketing.

In this context, this section attempts to address the following approaches:

▶ **Server consolidation**

   ▶ Consolidation of SAP application instances: Over how many SAP instances and servers should the SAP application level be distributed? Can the number of SAP instances be reduced by designing larger instances?

   ▶ Hardware consolidation (SAP systems): Can the use of several production systems on the same server help reduce the number of servers?

▶ **System and database consolidation**
   With the integration of SAP Basis components in SAP NetWeaver, it is possible to consolidate systems and databases to operate, for example, ABAP and Java, an OLTP system and SAP NetWeaver Business Warehouse, an SAP APO server and SAP liveCache, each in a system and a database, technically speaking in a <SID>. We will deal with these questions in greater detail in the next section.

Apart from the main objective of this section, there is the closely linked matter of system consolidation, or harmonization, which is mainly a matter of business consulting.

▶ **System consolidation or harmonization**
   Over how many SAP systems should business processes be distributed? Can business processes that are currently running in several

systems be merged into one system? How many production clients should be set up in an SAP system?

5.3.1 Distribution of SAP Application Instances

Over how many SAP instances and servers should the SAP application level be distributed?

Basically, you should not set up too many servers and instances, because each additional server or instance brings with it increased administration and monitoring work. The following lines of reasoning, however, support setting up several instances:

Reasons for multiple instances

▶ If one server or instance goes down, the remaining servers or instances must absorb the additional workload. The fewer servers or instances you have configured, the more severe the effects will be.

▶ As we have seen before, logon groups are an important way to distribute workload. However, logon groups can only be implemented if several instances have been configured.

▶ Some older arguments in favor of distributing the application level of a system over many SAP instances have since been dealt with by enhancements in the SAP kernel. Nevertheless, we would like to address the following points here:

  ▶ With 32-bit technology, the physical main memory cannot be correctly addressed because of operating system–specific limitations and therefore cannot be used, or at least not optimally. This limitation has been eliminated with the introduction of 64-bit technology. For further details on this matter, see Chapter 8, Memory Management.

  ▶ With very large instances, the dispatcher, roll administration, or buffer administration can exhibit performance bottlenecks. However, each of these must be checked individually. You can, however, assume that with 64-bit technology, it is possible to have instances for 500 users or more.

Therefore, for distributing the application level over instances, the rule of thumb should be this: Install as many instances as necessary, but as few as possible.

5.3.2 Hardware Consolidation

When selecting hardware, you must consider two seemingly contrary trends. Some data centers will decide to consolidate their servers, that is, concentrate all services on a few very powerful servers. This has been, without a doubt, an important trend in the IT market in recent years. The benefits that hardware partners promise customers include lower hardware costs; however, these often result less from procurement than from reduced hardware maintenance costs after production begins. The technology developed by SAP supports this trend in many respects.

The contrary trend is to use less expensive servers with lower performance and to invest in the maintenance standardization of this server farm. Both trends are significant; however, we won't discuss them in detail within the scope of this book.

Background: Virtualization

Hardware consolidation is closely linked with hardware virtualization. Virtualization is the decoupling of application software instances from hardware via an abstraction layer. The decoupling has the following goals:

- In case of load fluctuations or hardware failures, the instances can be moved or parked flexibly if they are not used without having to change the instances' configuration.
- Physically existing hardware resources can be distributed across instances (logically partitioned) or combined in a logical hardware. The latter, however, is insignificant in the SAP environment.

To achieve virtualization, there are approaches at three different levels:

- Solutions that are at the level below the actual operating system enable you to virtualize entire instances of the operating system; that is, you can even operate instances of different operating systems on one computer. VMware and XEN are examples for such solutions.
- Operating systems themselves also offer virtualization solutions; with these solutions, you can set up multiple partitions in the operating system. On these partitions, in turn, you can operate application software instances (for example, IBM Dynamic LPAR and Micropartitioning LPAR, HP Integrity Virtual Machines).

► The SAP software also provides virtualization at the level above the operating system. Thanks to the consistent usage of virtual server names within the SAP system, you can flexibly manage SAP instances using the *Adaptive Computing Controller;* for example, they can be moved within a very short period of time.

SAP supports virtualization solutions at all three levels. All of these solutions offer major advantages in the flexible management of systems, but they also entail specific disadvantages.

Deciding whether server consolidation or virtualization are the best approach for a project does not depend on the costs of hardware procurement and maintenance. Consolidation can incur costs in other areas of the production operation, which you must be take into account.

Cost aspects

► Many different user groups have to accept maintenance schedules (for example, upgrades). A maintenance level may have to be applied for a system, which implies downtime for all systems.

► To achieve high availability in a consolidated landscape, the server must be configured in high-availability clusters, which means that if one server goes down, the various services are automatically started in other servers *(failover recovery)*. These recovery scenarios have to be configured and tested.

► Sometimes additional licensing costs are incurred for the virtualization and resource management software.

► You have to define and monitor resource access for the various systems. The costs of training and use of the corresponding software for virtualization and resource management must also be taken into account.

Benchmark studies of various hardware manufacturers show that running several SAP systems on one server is possible without any performance problems. In practice, however, the question of resource management remains to be resolved. A discussion of the possible solutions offered by hardware partners in this respect goes beyond the scope of this chapter. You can, however, evaluate the different solutions using the following checklist:

Checklist for
evaluation

▶ Do the different applications (SAP instances, database instances, and so on) run in different operating system instances (windows); that is, are they virtually disconnected?

▶ Can the CPU, main memory, and drive I/O resources be administrated using the methods of the operating system manufacturer?

▶ Can resource management be regulated with a fixed allocation of CPU, main memory, and drive I/O or by prioritizing requests?

▶ Can resources be dynamically redistributed (that is, without having to restart the operating system) to adapt to current requirements?

You can fine up-to-date information from SAP on these matters in SAP Note 21960. If you want to run several SAP systems on a single server, you should do this in close collaboration with your hardware partner, and a corresponding consultancy project should also be agreed upon.

5.3.3 System and Database Consolidation

With the integration of SAP Basis components in SAP NetWeaver, it is possible to consolidate systems and databases. SAP supports this consolidation if specific prerequisites are met.

ABAP and
Java — separate
or double stack

The first topic for consolidation is whether ABAP and Java are to be operated in a system and a database. The architecture of this *double-stack* solution is shown in Chapter 1, Figure 1.4. In previous versions, a double-stack installation was also possible for SAP Business Suite systems. Now, however, this is no longer available for systems of SAP Business Suite 7 (SAP Note 855534).

The goal of a double-stack installation, is to configure a Java and ABAP application instance on each computer, and not configure any additional load distribution between the Java and ABAP instances; in other words, the ABAP instance processes the requests of the Java instance on the same computer. The load distribution is carried out exclusively in the Java instances. Of course, you can also implement more elaborate distribution scenarios.

In a separate installation, you can set up an ABAP system without Java and an SAP J2EE Engine as an independent system, that is, with its own <SID> and an "upstream" database. In this case, you would provide another load distribution via logon groups between the SAP J2EE Engine and the ABAP system.

Each SAP NetWeaver–based system is provided with the data warehouse software SAP NetWeaver BW, and SAP supports BW; that is, the online analytical processing (OLAP) is operated in the same database as the online transaction processing (OLTP).

OLTP and OLAP on one database

If you operate a database for OLTP and OLAP (BW), the consolidated solution could constitute a problem, because some database platforms differ in their parameterization recommendations for BW and OLTP systems. The relevant notes are listed in Appendix G of this book. Furthermore, you should consult your hardware or database partner or an SAP consultant.

liveCache and SAP APO server can also be operated in a database. However, this option is limited, because you can only use MaxDB as the database platform, because SAP liveCache is only implemented in MaxDB.

SAP liveCache and SAP APO server on a database

ITS doesn't have to be operated as separate software. It's available as an integrated version in the kernel of the ABAP server, which we'll discuss in Chapter 7, SAP GUI and Internet Connection.

External or integrated ITS

With SAP NetWeaver 7.0, IPC (which previously was operated as separate Java software) is now integrated into the kernel of the ABAP server — the *Virtual Machine Container* (VMC) — which we discuss in Chapter 6, Section 6.4, SAP Virtual Machine Container.

Internet Pricing and Configurator (IPC)

For performance reasons, there are practically no preferences for or against a consolidated solution, provided you observe this rule: Always implement sizing in an additive manner. In other words, sizing must interpret the consolidated solution as two separately operated components. For double stacks, this means the server must be large enough to carry the Java and ABAP instance, for example, via four CPU kernels and 16GB main memory. The same applies to other consolidation solutions. The amount of hardware can't be reduced considerably.

Evaluating the consolidation

Performance considerations usually don't take center stage when you decide on a consolidation strategy. Rather, the focus will be on whether you can compile a maintenance strategy for a consolidated solution that meets the expectations of all involved requestors within the enterprise.

5.4   Summary

We strongly recommend hardware planning before the start of production operation, load increases, version changes, and migrations. SAP and their hardware partners offer you clearly defined processes and services (SAP GoingLive Check). The quality and results depend largely on attention to project planning (planned users and throughput figures). You can get continuous statistics on the workload of your hardware using the SAP EarlyWatch Alert service.

You can operate SAP software both on very large and on smaller, more cost-efficient servers. Provided you implemented sizing correctly and distributed the load appropriately, you can achieve very good performance with both hardware strategies.

SAP pays close attention to the linear scaling of its software. Therefore, there is practically no reason (from a performance point of view) to use multiple SAP systems of the same type in parallel (that is, multiple SAP ERP systems, multiple SAP NetWeaver BW systems, and so on). With the continuous integration of SAP NetWeaver in a system and database, you can partly also use SAP components that previously had to be operated in their own systems (for example, ABAP and Java, OLAP and OLTP, ITS, IPC, and so on). This will help you reduce operating costs.

Important Concepts in this Chapter

After reading this chapter, you should be familiar with the following concepts:

▶ Sizing process: Quick Sizer, integration of hardware partners, SAP GoingLive Check

▶ Sizing methods for initial sizing: user-based, throughput-based

▶ Sizing methods for sizing in the environment of installations used in production: resizing, delta sizing, upgrade sizing

▶ SAP NetWeaver double-stack installation

Questions

1. In an SAP ERP system, 300 users are already active in the SD area and 50 users are in the FI area. You now plan the go-live of 150 users in the MM area and 25 users in the FI area. What do you have to do for sizing?

   a) You implement the sizing with a new sizing project in Quick Sizer, where you calculate the sizing on the basis of 300 SD, 150 MM, and 75 FI users.

   b) You determine the current hardware utilization and add 50% for the load that the newly added users will cause.

   c) You determine the current hardware utilization and run a new sizing project in Quick Sizer with 150 MM and 25 FI users. You then add up the hardware requirements.

   d) You require special tools from the hardware partner to implement a delta sizing.

2. You plan to use different system components, such as ABAP server, SAP J2EE Engine, SAP liveCache, and so on. Are these components supposed to be operated on one or multiple computers?

   a) Every component should be operated on one computer. Due to displacement effects in the main memory and more context changes in the CPU, you cannot achieve good performance otherwise.

   b) Components can be operated together on computers. However, you must add the hardware requirement of every component in the dimensioning of the computer.

   c) Components can be operated together on computers. In practical use, you can assume that the operation of components together on one computer results in considerable CPU and main memory savings (thanks to synergy effects because the load is usually evenly distributed for all components).

6 Workload Distribution and Interfaces

To achieve optimal performance, it is necessary to distribute SAP system load across the CPU resources of all available servers. This helps the CPU resources cope with demands on the system, for example, the number of users and their activities and the number of background programs. In addition to improving performance, optimizing workload distribution also protects performance-critical processes and gives these processes priority in accessing resources.

In the first section of this chapter, we'll present the services of SAP NetWeaver Application Server and the two central services for distributing requests: the *message server* and the *SAP Web Dispatcher*. The second section is dedicated to options available for distributing the load within ABAP application instances.

RFCs are used for implementing interfaces to external systems, parallelizing within a system, and communicating with frontend services. After a general introduction to RFC technology, the third section of this chapter will present the options for performance optimization for the first two application areas mentioned. The next chapter then deals with frontend technologies.

This chapter concludes with a brief introduction to the Virtual Machine Container, the second SAP Java technology.

When Should You Read this Chapter?

You should read this chapter if you want detailed suggestions for optimizing workload distribution within the SAP system and interfaces to external systems.

6.1   Services of the SAP NetWeaver Application Server

An important task of an SAP system is the creation and processing of business documents such as sales orders and financial documents. There are four ways that documents are found and processed in the system:

▶ **Processing by dialog (or online) users**
Users logged on to the SAP system create or process documents in dialog mode. An example of this type of processing is a call center, where employees take orders from customers over the telephone and enter them directly into the system. Here, the SAP system can be accessed via the SAP GUI or web browser.

▶ **Processing by background programs**
With this type of processing, documents are created or processed by programs that work without continuous communication with dialog users — hence the term *background*. For example, during multiple background-processing of delivery notes, all existing sales orders are analyzed, and deliveries are automatically created for these orders within the specified time. A second example of a background program is automatic salary calculation, which is based on personal master data stored in the system and time data entered by employees. Background processing, therefore, is characterized by a corresponding program that reads data already in the system and uses this information to create new documents — in our examples, delivery notes and pay slips.

▶ **Background input processing (batch input)**
Often, data needed for the SAP system to create documents is already in electronic form, for example, as existing files. It would make no sense for dialog users to manually reenter this data. Rather, with the SAP system, this data can be imported into the system using interface programs that run in the background. This type of processing is also referred to as *batch input* and is a special type of background processing. It is often used as a communication interface between the SAP system and external data processing systems. Take, for example, a project in which sales orders are created and saved in decentralized computers with local software. When required, these computers send

orders to a central office, where these files are imported into the SAP system as a batch input.

▶ **Processing using interfaces**
An SAP system can not only communicate with another IT system indirectly via files, as previously described, but there can also be direct data exchange. This takes place via *remote function calls* (RFCs) or *Web services*. RFCs and Web services can exchange data between SAP systems, and between an SAP system and an external system, provided that the latter can handle the corresponding protocol. With this type of processing, an external DP system can transfer data into the SAP system and remotely execute a program there, and vice versa. With RFCs or Web services, for example, a warehouse management system can be linked to the SAP system. The SAP system creates the transfer orders for stock movements and sends this transfer order to an external system via RFC or Web services. When the warehouse management system has carried out the transfer order, it executes a transaction by RFC or Web services to inform the SAP system of the movement of goods.

Processes of the SAP NetWeaver Application Server

The SAP NetWeaver Application Server provides logical services for processing the workload mapped through operation system processes (see Figure 6.1).

These include the dispatcher and work processes of the ABAP server, which are each implemented on UNIX derivatives as separate operating system processes (*disp+work.exe*) and on Windows operating systems through what are known as *threads* within a process. The work processes of the ABAP server are configured to provide one of the following services: dialog service, background service, update service, spool service, or enqueue service. In addition, the work process can also offer available-to-promise (ATP) or VMC services.

The SAP J2EE Engine also provides a dispatcher process and one or multiple work processes (server processes), which process the requests. They are implemented as Java processes (*dispatcher.exe* and *server.exe*) that scale internally via multiple threads.

Services on the Java side

This is supplemented by database service processes and (optionally) by SAP liveCache and TREX.

Operating system processes

Furthermore, additional services are available in the SAP NetWeaver Application Server that are implemented in their own operating system processes: Internet Communication Manager (ICM) service (*icman.exe*), message service, gateway service, and SAP Web Dispatcher service.

Figure 6.1 shows an overview of all SAP NetWeaver Application Server processes. It displays a consolidated *double-stack* installation in which ABAP and Java run on one instance. You can also install Java and ABAP individually; in this case, however, the respective other part is missing.

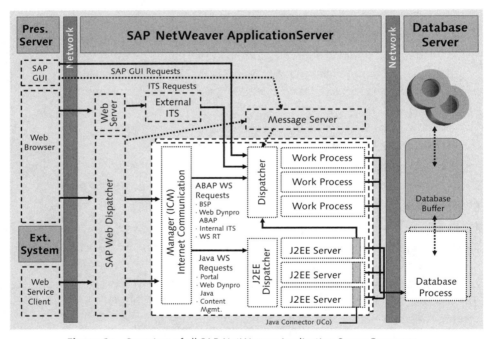

Figure 6.1 Overview of all SAP NetWeaver Application Server Processes

Dispatch methods

Dispatch methods distribute the inbound load to all available processes; they are supposed to ensure an optimal load distribution on the system. The SAP Web Dispatcher (for Web requests) and message server (for dialog, background, and update requests) are responsible for the dispatching and the dispatcher processes of the respective Java or ABAP application instances.

Within an SAP NetWeaver Application Server, there is a message server located on one SAP NetWeaver AS computer. The message server controls communication between the different instances of an SAP Basis system and places free process resources on the SAP instance level. The individual application instances constantly inform the message server about their availability and current load so that the message server can carry out its work. The message server is responsible for dispatching the following request types:

Message server

▶ **Online users that have logged on via SAP GUI**
Distributed to an ABAP application instance once upon logon. By default, the message server considers the current average dialog response time for distribution. This mechanism can be influenced via configuration parameters. For more details, refer to Section 6.2.4, Dynamic User Distribution: Configuring Logon Groups.

▶ **RFC requests**
Distributed like online users. As long as the RFC client keeps the connection, all other RFCs are processed on the same instance. If a client closes the connection, the next request is newly distributed.

▶ **Background requests**
Distributed according to free background work processes.

▶ **Update requests**
Distributed according to free update work processes. For more information, see the section on updates later in this chapter.

▶ **Web requests**
You can also distribute Web requests via the message server. For this purpose, the browser sends a request to the SAP system's message server. This distributes the load and sends the browser the logon address of the application server. If a user has logged on once to an application server with his browser, he remains logged on until the end of the session. This procedure is very similar to logon balancing with the SAP GUI. However, it has several disadvantages and is therefore not recommended by SAP.

SAP Web
Dispatcher

SAP recommends distributing Web requests via the SAP Web Dispatcher. The SAP Web Dispatcher is based on the same technology as the Internet Communication Manager (ICM) but offers additional functionality. It can be installed as separate SAP software for Web dispatching.

Functions

The SAP Web Dispatcher provides the following functions:

▶ Distribution of requests to ABAP or Java application instances, both for HTTP and HTTPS requests.

▶ Request filtering: The SAP Web Dispatcher can deny unwanted requests.

▶ Buffering of Web requests.

▶ Unchangeable Web addresses: Independent of the application instance's name, the SAP Web Dispatcher ensures that users can always access the system via one address.

▶ Security: Provided that security restrictions between the Internet and SAP NetWeaver Application Server require a *demilitarized zone* (DMZ) that is bordered by two firewalls, the SAP Web Dispatcher runs within this DMZ.

Process

For distributing requests, the SAP Web Dispatcher initially checks whether the request already belongs to a transactional context that can be referred to as *stateful*; in this case, the request is sent to the application instance on which the transaction context already exists. Then the SAP Web Dispatcher checks whether the request is intended for a Java or ABAP application instance. The SAP Web Dispatcher selects an instance from a list of available Java or ABAP application instances and sends the request to the ICM of the corresponding instance. The SAP Web Dispatcher provides different methods for dispatching; for example, you can specify that certain URLs are only distributed to specific instances, or you can assign capacities to the instances that are considered for distribution. The SAP Web Dispatcher receives information about the available ABAP and Java application instances from the message server and the individual instances. For further details, refer to Section 6.2.4, Dynamic User Distribution: Configuring Logon Groups.

The distribution concept for Web requests differs from the dialog requests from the SAP GUI. For the SAP GUI, user requests are processed without any further dispatching in the application instance to which the user was assigned during logon. When Web requests are dispatched, instance processing is only ensured for one transaction for that instance; a new transaction may already be processed on another instance. Moreover, requests without transactional context, also referred to as *stateless*, are always newly distributed.

Java and ABAP application instances differ in their architectures, but there are also similarities. Table 6.1 presents the most important similarities and differences.

Java and ABAP application instances

ABAP Application Instances	J2EE Application Instances (SAP J2EE Engine)
SAP ABAP system.	J2EE cluster (SAP Java system).
ABAP application instance.	J2EE server (Java application instance).
ABAP work process.	Work thread (Java work process).
Message server (one per system) and dispatcher (one per instance).	J2EE dispatcher (one per system).
User contexts are in the shared memory of an SAP instance; that is, users are "tied" to an instance.	User contexts are in the local memory of a J2EE server; that is, users are "tied" to a server.
SAP GUI or web browser as presentation server.	Web browser as presentation server.
Upon logon, user requests are distributed by the message server to an instance with a low load (if logon balancing is activated). Then the presentation server and the SAP instance communicate with each other.	User requests are distributed to a server by the J2EE dispatcher. If a user context already exists, then users are distributed to the same server that has that user context. The presentation server and J2EE server basically communicate with each other only via the dispatcher.

Table 6.1 Comparison of ABAP and Java Application Instances

If a request has reached the J2EE server, it is processed by one of its threads. You can configure the maximum number of threads. If this maximum number has been reached, the J2EE server sends an error message; queuing (that is, the temporary storage of requests) is not possible.

The ABAP application instance, however, provides specialized work processes that enable fine-tuned control of the load and queuing of requests. The next section will deal with these methods in greater detail.

6.2 Load Distribution Within the ABAP Application Instances

The services listed in Table 6.2 exist on the ABAP application instance level. An ABAP instance can fulfill several functions, such as a message, enqueue, dialog, or server update, all at the same time.

Service	Number of Processes per SAP System	Number of Processes per ABAP Application Instance
Message	1	0 or 1
Enqueue	≥1 on one ABAP instance	0 or ≥1 on one ABAP instance
Dialog	≥ 2, or equal or greater than the sum of nondialog work processes	≥2
Background	≥1	≥0
Update (V1 and V2)	≥1	≥0
Batch	≥1	≥0
Spool	≥1	≥0
Dispatcher	1 per SAP application instance	1
Gateway	1 per application server	1

Table 6.2 Rules for the Type and Number of ABAP Application Instance Processes

Enqueue service

The *enqueue service* manages SAP locks (*SAP enqueues*). It is provided by one ABAP instance. The instance containing the enqueue service is often called the *enqueue server*. On this instance (usually one, or in exceptional cases, multiple), enqueue work processes are installed. Enqueue management in Java has been available since SAP Web AS 6.30, which means the locks are centrally set via the enqueue service of the ABAP instance.

With this, at least you can avoid the inconsistency problems regarding the locks in Java and ABAP. You will find further details on SAP enqueues and the ATP server in Chapter 10, Locks.

Dialog, update, background, and *spool services* are provided by one or several SAP work processes. These services can be distributed over several ABAP instances. If update or background processing takes place on only one SAP instance, this is referred to as a *central update* or *background processing*. If they are located on more than one SAP instance, we refer to a *distributed update* (or again, *background processing*). The service provided by each SAP work process is determined by the dispatcher of the corresponding SAP instance. The dispatcher process coordinates the work of the other work processes and, therefore, the services they offer. Each ABAP instance has just one dispatcher. The dispatcher coordinates the work done within each ABAP instance, whereas the message server manages communication between the ABAP instances.

Dialog, update, background, spool

How should the *SAP services* be represented in a *hardware landscape?* In a *central installation*, the database instance and all SAP services (in particular, message, enqueue, dialog, update, background, and spool services) are configured on a single computer. This type of installation is typically found in development, testing, and small production systems (with up to around 100 active users).

SAP services and hardware landscape

In a *distributed installation*, the services are distributed over several servers. The following sections describe how this should be done with regard to *high availability* of the SAP system and performance.

The workload monitor (Transaction ST03N or ST03), the logon groups monitor (Transaction SMLG), and the work process overview (Transaction SM66 or SM50) are tools available for monitoring workload distribution. In Chapter 2, Section 2.5, Analyzing SAP Work Processes, and Chapter 3, Section 3.4.1, Analyzing General Performance Problems, you will find descriptions of the analyses that you can use to check whether or not the workload is optimally distributed over the system. If you find a bottleneck in the workload distribution, redistributing work processes can be an effective way to solve the problem. In the following sections, you will find detailed recommendations for distributing work processes.

Monitoring tools

6.2.1 Distributing Message, Enqueue, and ATP Services

Message, *enqueue*, and *ATP services* work closely together. For performance reasons, they should always be run on the same instance. The corresponding SAP profile parameters are:

- ▶ `rdisp/mshost`: <Server>
- ▶ `rdisp/enqname`: <Server>_<Instance>_<Nr>
- ▶ `rdisp/atp_server`: <Server>_<Instance>_<Nr>

From the point of view of *system availability* (high availability), the critical points in an SAP system are the message, enqueue, and ATP services and the database instance (called *single points of failure,* or SPOFs). In general, these services cannot be distributed over several servers. If a server with one of these services goes down, then the entire SAP system goes down. Therefore, mainly for reasons of availability, the database and central SAP instances (with message, enqueue, and ATP services) should be operated on the same computer and should be specifically protected by a *failover solution,* which almost all hardware providers offer. For very large installations, however, for performance reasons you should configure the database and central SAP instances on separate servers.

[+] If you use the *ATP server* or *locking with quantity* in the availability check, you should configure at least five dialog work processes on the enqueue server, even if no dialog users are working on this server. You can find more detailed information on locking with quantities and the ATP server in Chapter 10, Section 10.4, ATP Server.

6.2.2 Distributing Dialog, Background, and Spool Work Processes

In a distributed SAP system, *dialog, background,* and *spool services* are distributed to the application server. In practice, an error is frequently made: Although the dialog work processes are configured on separate application servers, the background work processes are kept on the database server. The following observations explain why you should not run background work processes on the database server:

▶ The load generated by background programs can fluctuate greatly at different times, for example, because of background programs that run on particular days or at the end of the month. This may result in a temporary CPU bottleneck on the database server if several background programs are started at the same time. By distributing the background work processes on the application server, you can control these high load peaks more easily.

▶ Dialog and background load often complement each other; for example, dialog workload occurs during the day, whereas background load is scheduled to run overnight. If in this situation all background work processes are configured on the central server; the application servers (on which dialog work processes are configured) remain unused at night, while at the same time, there may be a CPU bottleneck caused by parallel-running background programs on the central server.

▶ System administrators sometimes find that background programs run much faster on the database server than on the application server (sometimes reported to be only half as fast or less). However, this is not a valid argument for leaving background work processes on the database server. Rather, it points to a network problem between the database and application servers, which must be resolved. (For example, SAP Notes 72638 and 31514 describe these kinds of problems with the TCP/IP connection between SAP instances and an Oracle database.)

6.2.3 Distributing Users and Work Processes over CPU Resources

How many work processes should be configured in an SAP system, and how should they be distributed over the application servers? Two ratios are relevant here:

▶ Number of users to number of dialog work processes

▶ Number of work processes to number of processors

The first ratio is calculated from the think time and the response time:

Number of users:number of dialog work processes =
(think time + response time) ÷ response time

291

The *response time* is the average time that the SAP system requires to process a user request. The *think time* is the time one user takes to enter data into the presentation server and interpret it; pauses by the user are included. It is difficult to provide a general rule for these activities. They depend on the user's activities, the SAP applications and modules installed, the SAP release, and the CPU type (that is, the amount of processor power installed), which all vary from one SAP system to another.

Please note that in this formula, the response time to the presentation server is included. In the workload monitor, however, we measure the response time of the application server. The difference between these is the network time needed to transfer data between the application server and the presentation server. This network time should be low: <10% of the response time of the application server.

The optimal ratio of number of work processes to number of processors should be individually determined for each SAP system. There is no one valid guideline value for all SAP systems. The ratio of the number of work processesto the number of processors is determined from the response time and the CPU time:

Number of work processes:number of processors = response time ÷ CPU time

[Ex] So, if we assume that the CPU time should be at least 20% (or one-fifth) of the response time, then a maximum of five work processes should be configured per CPU.

Dispatcher wait time When should we configure more or fewer work processes? The argument for a high number of work processes is obvious: If users have to wait in the SAP dispatcher queue for work processes, then the temptation to make more work processes available is strong so that more users can work at the same time. This is the case if work processes are being blocked by wait situations, which actually incur no CPU load, for example, when work processes are running in PRIV-Mode (explained in detail in Chapter 8) or are often blocked by lock situations on the database. On the other hand, "pumping up" the number of work processes may not help much if resources are scarce at a lower level. Adding more work processes only eases the symptoms, but it generally does not resolve the performance problem.

Having too few SAP work processes leads to *dispatcher wait times,* which are indicated in the workload monitor. However, the reverse does not apply; a dispatcher wait time does not automatically mean there are too few work processes. You must first carry out a comprehensive bottleneck analysis to find out if other performance problems are blocking the work processes.

A high number of SAP work processes makes it possible to process many user requests at the same time. If the number of simultaneous processes is significantly higher than the number of processors, then this causes wait situations in the operating system queue. Because work processes receive CPU time more or less concurrently (or, to be more precise, in time slices), the number of context switches on the operating-system level increases with the number of work processes. (*Note:* Here we are talking about the rotation of process contexts in the processor from one SAP work process to the next. This should not be confused with SAP context switching, that is, the roll-in and roll-out of user contexts in SAP work processes.) Each context switch increases the load on the operating system by consuming processor time and memory for context information. However, waiting in the SAP dispatcher queue does not use CPU resources. Taking all of this into consideration, we can see that if all available CPU resources are in use, it is better to tolerate dispatcher wait times and allow fewer work processes, than to burden the operating system with too many work processes and the numerous context switches involved. Benchmark measurements, in fact, show that if all available CPU resources are in use, reducing the number of work processes actually improves performance.

CPU wait time

The CPU wait time is not explicitly indicated in the workload monitor. However, high CPU wait time leads to increased processing time. By comparing processing time and CPU time, you can determine if there are wait situations on the CPU. You can find a more detailed description in Chapter 3, Section 3.3, Workload Analysis.

Other situations that suggest reducing the ratio of work processes to CPU processors include the following:

▶ In contrast to UNIX, with Windows, the context switch puts considerable load on the operating system. Therefore (and particularly for

Windows NT), we recommend having a small number of work processes per CPU processor. (See also SAP Note 68544.)

▶ Reducing the number of work processes also reduces the number of database processes and the need for main memory. This is of particular advantage for databases in which each SAP work process has only one database process assigned to it.

[!] Therefore, you should only increase the number of SAP work processes if neither the CPU nor the server memory are being fully utilized. If a CPU or main memory bottleneck already exists, as well as high processing time on an application server, reducing the number of work processes can improve performance.

6.2.4 Dynamic User Distribution: Configuring Logon Groups

Logon groups are used to dynamically distribute the load being processed by the dialog work processes. These include:

▶ Online requests via SAP GUI (dialog request)

▶ Online Web requests that are directly intended for the ABAP part of the SAP NetWeaver AS (HTTP and HTTPS requests)

▶ Online Web requests that are first processed by the external ITS or the SAP J2EE Engine, and in turn log on to the ABAP server via RFC to implement the business logic

▶ RFC request of external systems (RFC load that is internally generated in the system and not controlled via logon groups)

Previously in this chapter, we discussed the difference between user distribution in the SAP GUI and Web logons. Once a user has logged on to an SAP system via the SAP GUI, he works on a particular ABAP instance until logging off. There is no feature to enable a dynamic, load-related switch to another ABAP instance during a user session. Only by logging off and logging on again can the user switch the application instance in the SAP GUI. When you log on via a web browser, each request is freshly distributed, whereas requests belonging to a transaction are re-sent to the same instance.

To achieve a dynamic distribution of dialog users on the ABAP instances, you can set up logon groups (or work groups), to which one or more ABAP instances can be allocated. The user chooses a particular logon group when logging on to the SAP system, or a Web request is distributed via these groups. From among the allocated SAP instances, the system automatically selects the one with the best performance statistics or the least users.

Use the following transaction to set logon groups (Transaction SMLG): TOOLS • CCMS • CONFIGURATION • LOGON GROUPS. Additional information on this transaction is available in SAP Online Help.

The simplest variant is to set one logon group over all SAP instances, thereby achieving a uniform distribution of users. Alternatively, users can be distributed according to the following criteria:

▶ **Logon groups according to SAP application**
You can set logon groups such as FI/CO, HR, SD/MM, and so on. The advantage of this method is that, for example, only the programs of the assigned SAP applications are loaded in the program buffer of a particular instance. As a result, the program buffer requires less memory, and this helps avoid displacements.

▶ **Logon groups according to language, country, or company division**
If you operate an SAP system for several countries or languages, you can set up the logon groups accordingly, for example, Austria, Poland, and Czech Republic. This way, only text and data relating to the specific country are loaded into the buffers of the corresponding SAP instances, and less memory is required for the table buffer.

▶ **Logon groups for certain user groups**
You can set up a special logon group for, say, employees in telesales, because their work is particularly performance-critical. The corresponding SAP instances should operate with a particularly high level of performance (for example, with no background or update work processes, few users per server, very fast processors, or a dedicated network). Another example of a user-specific logon group is one for employees in controlling, who draw up time-consuming reports in dialog mode. For this group, you should assign an SAP instance for

which the SAP profile parameter `rdisp/max_wprun_time` (which limits the runtime of an ABAP program in dialog mode) is set particularly high. In addition, setting a low value for this parameter on all other instances means these lengthy reports will not be run on those instances, where they could cause performance problems for other users. In this way, you can separate performance-critical applications (such as order entry in telesales) from less critical (albeit resource-intensive) applications such as controlling.

▶ **Logon groups for SAP Internet Transaction Server or for the SAP J2EE Engine**
SAP ITS or the SAP J2EE Engine can be logged on to the application level using either a dedicated SAP application instance (with data on the application server and the instance number) or with a logon group (data on the message server and a logon group). For optimal availability and workload distribution, you should use a logon group. It makes sense to set up a separate logon group for logons via SAP ITS or the SAP J2EE Engine.

▶ **Logon groups for the SAP Web Dispatcher**
You can set up one or more logon groups that the SAP Web Dispatcher can use for direct ABAP Web service requests. If you don't configure logon groups for the SAP Web Dispatcher, the load is distributed to all ABAP instances on which ICM is configured. You can also determine that certain groups of requests are distributed to dedicated logon groups based on their URLs.

▶ **Logon groups for ALE/RFC**
Asynchronous RFCs (aRFCs) are used to run applications in parallel. If the degree of parallelizing is not limited, however, it can result in a snowballing of RFCs, which can bring the application level to a standstill for the user (all work processes are busy). To avoid these situations, it is useful to define specific SAP instances with a special logon group for incoming RFC load, so work processes for RFCs are kept separate from work processes for online users, and users are not restricted in their work.

Guidelines When setting up logon groups, you should bear the following guidelines in mind:

▶ After assigning instances to logon groups, check to see if the instances are evenly distributed or if any group has too many or too few resources assigned to it.

▶ If there are temporary load peaks, for example, increased activity in the FI/CO group toward the end of the month or financial year, bottlenecks might occur on the corresponding instances. On the other hand, this can be useful for ensuring that resources will be available for other users such as those in telesales.

▶ If an application server hangs, or if you temporarily disconnect an application server, the users must be redistributed.

▶ Bearing all of the above in mind, at least two SAP instances should be assigned to each logon group.

To sum up, setting up logon groups involves extra administration and monitoring work. You should therefore not set up unnecessarily large numbers of logon groups.

[+]

6.2.5   Limiting Resources per User

Using SAP profile parameters, you can limit the resources available to users on the SAP application instances. These include:

▶ Automatic logoff of inactive users. The time after which an inactive user is logged off should be at least one to two hours; otherwise the frequent logging on can, itself, generate unnecessary load.

▶ Limiting the runtime of programs. This should not be less than the default value of 300 seconds; it should also be possible to execute longer-running programs on some instances.

▶ Apportioning memory consumption. A more detailed description can be found in Chapter 8, Memory Management. If you want to put strict limits on memory use for some instances, configure individual instances so that programs with a high memory use can also be finished on them.

▶ Limiting multiple logons and the use of parallel sessions. Normally, this should not be done.

You will find profile parameters for entering the corresponding settings in Appendix C.

[+] The resources available to users should only be limited to a useful extent. The main focus of your work should be on optimizing programs, tuning instances, and training users in the correct use of programs. An intense limiting of resources obstructs users' work and is often perceived by them as spoon-feeding, which can lead to user dissatisfaction.

6.2.6 Planning Operation Modes

The demands made on an SAP system vary over the course of 24 hours. During the day, for example, many dialog users are working with the system, whereas the demands made on the system by background programs usually increase at night. To adapt the number of SAP work processes to changing demands, the SAP system allows you to define different operation modes for daytime and nighttime operation. A certain number and type of work processes are assigned to an operation mode. The SAP system automatically adjusts the operation mode according to the time.

You can define operation modes using the following transaction: TOOLS • CCMS • CONFIGURATION • OP MODES AND SERVERS. You can set the times for changing the operation mode by using the following transaction: TOOLS • CCMS • CONFIGURATION • OP MODES TIMETABLE.

You can find more detailed information on setting and monitoring operation modes in SAP Online Help.

6.2.7 Update

If you need to make changes to a database table in an SAP transaction, they are first collected in the main memory, and when the transaction is completed, they are bundled and asynchronously updated. Figure 6.2 shows the steps involved in an update.

In our example, the characteristics of a material need to be changed. For this, a change is necessary in the table MARA, among other things. In the dialog part of the transaction, however, the MARA table is not directly changed in the database; rather, the information to change is temporarily stored in special database tables known as *update tables*. This is shown in Figure 6.2, step ❶, which shows an Insert operation (Insert) in the update table VBMOD and represents other update tables, such as VBHDR and VBDATA. On completion of the dialog part of the transaction, the dialog work process selects an application server with update work processes and sends a message to the message server (❷). This in turn forwards the update request to the corresponding dispatcher of the application server (❸). The latter allocates the request to an update work process (❹). The update work process reads the information from the update tables (Select in step ❺) and finally changes the application table with an update operation — the MARA table in Figure 6.2 (UPDATE in step ❻). This process is known as an *asynchronous update*.

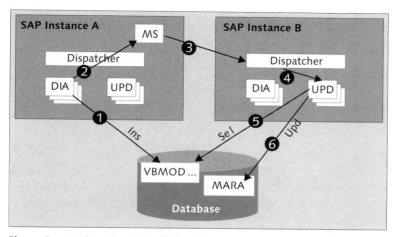

Figure 6.2 Update Step Cycle (DIA, dialog work process; UPD, update work process; MS, message service)

In an SQL trace, you can identify the end of a transaction's dialog part with the help of `Insert` statements on the VBMOD, VBHDR, and VBDATA tables. The start of an update step is indicated by `Select` statements on this table.

Monitoring Update Requests

If update processing is terminated (status `Err`), you must manually restart or delete the request. If you cannot start the processing of an update request, for example, because the update process was deactivated or because of an error, there is no application server with update work processes; the request status remains as `Init`. If the SAP profile parameter `rdisp/vbstart` is set to the default of 1 (one) when the SAP system is restarted, the update request will be tried again. Each application instance only updates the update requests that were assigned to it when it stopped. If `rdisp/vbstart < > 1` or if the repeat fails to update the request, you must manually restart or delete the update.

[!] Interrupted or unexecuted updates lead to a situation where documents entered or changed by users are not saved in the corresponding application table and are therefore "nonexistent" for the user. The daily check of updating tasks is therefore an important task for the SAP system administrator. If interrupted updates are not investigated immediately, there is little chance of finding the cause of the error after a few days have passed.

A monitor is available for controlling update records via TOOLS • ADMINISTRATION • MONITOR • UPDATE. Alternatively, you can enter Transaction SM13.

If an update request is correctly completed, the corresponding entries in the update tables are deleted. The update tables should therefore be empty (including erroneous requests and requests currently being processed). If the update tables grow considerably because of erroneous, incorrectly processed requests, this will soon lead to massive performance problems.

VBMOD, VBHDR, VBDATA The update tables VBMOD, VBHDR, and VBDATA are among the most frequently modified tables in the SAP system. If bottlenecks arise with hard drive access to these tables, it may be helpful to partition or distribute these tables over several hard drives. For some database systems, it can be useful to change the order of the key fields in these tables. However, this should only be carried out by a specialist with knowledge of database and SAP tuning or based on recommendations from SAP. You can find further information in the documentation on the SAP profile parameter `rdisp/vb_key_comp` or in SAP Notes on this parameter.

Distributing Update Work Processes

In small SAP installations, the update work processes, along with database instances and message, enqueue, and ATP services, are all configured on a single machine. In medium and large SAP installations, updates should not be configured centrally on the database server. There is some debate as to whether or not a central update server should be set up in this case (an SAP instance dedicated solely to updates) or if the update tasks should be distributed symmetrically over all application servers. Here are some good reasons why you should use a distributed arrangement:

▸ The failure of a central update server would cause system activity to come to a standstill. With distributed update work processes, this problem would not occur.

▸ A symmetrical configuration of application servers enables you to add or remove application servers to or from the SAP system without needing to readjust the workload distribution.

▸ Distributed update work processes can handle temporary load peaks better than a single server.

Therefore, for a large SAP installation, there are good arguments for distributing not only background work processes, but also update work processes equally over the application servers.

You activate the dispatching of update requests by setting the SAP profile parameter `rdisp/vb_dispatching` to 1 (one) in the default profile. The SAP system ensures that all instances receive update requests that are proportional to the number of update work processes configured on them. This normally guarantees a balanced workload distribution. However, the system does not actually check the load distribution. If, for example, an SAP instance has only one update work process, which entails a very long-running update request, the dialog work process continues to send update requests to this instance despite the free update work processes available on other instances. We recommend, therefore, that you never configure just one update work process on an instance. You should configure at least two.

Dispatching update requests

As described here, update dispatching is the standard solution for all applications. Only in special cases and with the specific recommendation

[+]

of SAP should you use the local update method or update multiplexing, which we do not explain in this book.

As a rule of thumb, you can configure update work processes at a ratio of 1 to 4 for dialog work processes, based on the total of all SAP instances.

Selecting Types of Update

To enable the prioritization of update requests (and in so doing, distribution of workload over time), there are different types of updates. We differentiate between the asynchronous V1, V2, and V3 updates and the synchronous and local updates. In general, SAP sets the update type when your software is delivered. You only have to decide on the update type yourself in certain individual cases and or when there are customer developments.

V1, V2, and V3 updates

To enable you to distribute or prioritize update requests, the update function modules are classified as V1, V2, and V3. A V1 update is the "normal" type of update, as was previously described.

V2 function modules differ from the V1 type in two aspects: First, they are processed without enqueue locks (for more information on locks, see Chapter 10, Locks), and second, they are given lower priority. The following rules apply for priority decisions between V1 and V2 updates:

▶ The standard update work processes (task type Upd) process V1 modules with complete priority, which means no V2 module will be processed as long as there are V1 modules waiting to be processed (if V2 update work processes have been configured).

▶ This workload distribution rule can mean that in extreme situations, absolutely no V2 functions are being processed. This obstructs V2-type update work processes, which are processed as V2 functions. To ensure that V2 functions are also processed during times of high workload, you should also always configure V2 update work processes. As a rule, allow a ratio of one V2 update work process for every four V1 update processes.

Modules that are absolutely necessary for operation are classified as V1. Modules can be classified as V2 if they can be processed during times of lower workload and without the protection of enqueue locks (such as updating statistics).

Interfaces for the maintenance of statistic systems, such as the *SAP Logistics Information System* (LIS), are generally carried out by V2 function modules (however, in customizing , you can select between V1, V2, and V3).

V3 function modules are also processed without enqueue locks. As with V1 and V2 modules, at the end of the dialog part of the transaction, entries are written to the update tables; however, the update is not started. The update requests remain in the update tables until a background job explicitly processes them. This background job is application-specific. It may contain its own application logic, which could be, for example, to accumulate update requests in the main memory and only write the prepared data to the database afterward. For tables with frequently changing values, this can mean a considerable reduction in database changes. The information about whether a business processes can be updated in V3 can be found in the corresponding documentation or in customizing.

With V3 updates, you can separate the update workload from the dialog workload when it comes to processing time, by starting updates during times of low dialog activity. Yet, because no locks are held with V3 updates, their use is limited. One case where V3 updates can be used is in maintaining the SAP NetWeaver Business Warehouse interface.

You can see the update type in the Function Builder (Transaction SE37) on the Attributes screen. Under PROCESSING TYPE • UPDATE MODULE, the entry Start Immediately or Immediate Start, No Restart (or: V1 update), Start Delayed (V2) or Collective Run (V3) is activated. A change to this characteristic is considered an object modification.

As previously described, updates in update work processes are usually asynchronous, which means the dialog work process does not wait until the update task has concluded its work. Rather, once the data has been temporarily stored in the update tables, the users are informed that the transaction has been completed so that they can continue with their work, although the update task is still running. However, synchronous updating is also possible; here, the dialog work process waits for the

Synchronous update

update work to finish. (In the work process monitor, Transaction SM50 or SM66, this situation is displayed with the status Stopped and reason Upd). Synchronous updating is activated with the AND WAIT clause for the ABAP statement COMMIT WORK.

However, *synchronous updating* has hardly any advantages and is therefore practically never used. Rather, in cases where immediate updating is necessary, local updating is used, as described below.

Local update | The third type of updating is to carry out the update directly in the dialog or background work process, which means no update work process is enlisted. This method is known as *local update*. With this method, the update data is not stored in update tables in the database; rather, it is stored in the main memory of the application server. The update is executed directly after completion of the dialog part of the transaction in the dialog work process (or in the background work process if it is a background process). Local updating is activated in the program using the ABAP statement SET UPDATE TASK LOCAL.

What are the advantages of local updates? The concept behind asynchronous updates is that the total response time for processing a transaction is divided into a dialog response time (which the user sees directly) and an update time (which runs without the user being aware of it). To achieve this, additional work is involved, that is, writing and reading the update tables. With local updates, both parts of the transaction occur one after the other, but the additional work of writing to the update tables is avoided. Local updates are mainly used for background processes with mass updates and for interface programming with massive parallel asynchronous RFCs. In both cases, the advantage lies in the fact that entries do not have to be written to the update table. This is preferred with mass updates because bottlenecks can occur in I/O channels to the update tables. Furthermore, the updates are started immediately, and as a result, they are not affected by potential overloading of the update work processes.

Table 6.3 provides an overview of update types and their most important properties.

Update Type	Method	With Enqueue	Advantages	Limitations	Example of Use
Asynchronous V1	Asynchronous in update WP	Yes			Standard
Asynchronous V2	Asynchronous in V2 update WP	No	Prioritizing, because V2 WPs are configured	No locks	Statistical data (can be selected for LIS interfaces)
Asynchronous V3	Started by background job, then asynchronous in V2 update WP	No	Prioritizing, because V2 WPs are configured; load distributed over time because of update planning; performance advantage because of accumulation of changes in background program	No locks	Statistical data (can be selected for LIS interfaces, standard for BW interfaces)
Synchronous	Synchronous in update WP (dialog or background WP stops)	Yes	Reliable confirmation to user	Longer dialog response time	None
Local	Directly in dialog or background WP	Yes	Reliable confirmation to user; no entries in VB tables, resulting in lower database workload	Longer dialog response time	Background processing, tRFC, and qRFC processing
Abbreviations: WP, work process; LIS, SAP Logistics Information System; BW, SAP NetWeaver Business Warehouse					

Table 6.3 Overview of Update Types

6.3   Remote Function Calls (RFCs)

Remote function calls (RFCs) allows one program to execute another program remotely, that is, from a different location.

6.3.1   Concepts

RFCs are used for the following purposes:

▸ Communication between different systems, such as between two SAP systems or between an SAP system and an external system.

▸ Within an SAP system:

 ▸ Communication between application instances or between the application level and the presentation level (GUI communication).

Parallelization
 ▸ Parallelizing processes: Because one program after another can start several RFCs asynchronously without waiting for processing to finish, RFCs are used to parallelize processes and dynamically distribute workload over the different servers within an SAP system.

With RFCs, SAP systems (for instance, SAP ERP, SAP APO, and SAP NetWeaver BW) of different versions can be linked, or SAP systems can be linked with external systems, for example, an SAP ERP system with an external warehouse management system, where the SAP ERP system creates the transfer orders for stock movements and sends them to an external system via RFC. When the warehouse management system has carried out a transfer order, it executes a transaction using RFC to inform the SAP ERP system of the movement of goods.

How the business processes of an enterprise are distributed over different SAP components is of critical importance for the subsequent administration of the system. An advantage of a distributed, linked system landscape is that the individual parts of the system can be handled more flexibly in all contexts (for example, build, upgrade, administration, organization, and so on). With interfaces, which have to be built and operated, the total expense for building and administration (and hardware requirements) is greater than in a large, integrated system.

Coupling types
With RFCs, the system can be linked in two ways. We differentiate between types of coupling:

▶ *Hard coupling*, in which one system relies on the partner system being available. If communication is interrupted, for example, as the result of a network malfunction or because the partner system is not working, the other system can continue working. However, the functions that use the RFCs will be terminated with an error.

▶ *Soft coupling* does not require this reciprocal availability of the systems. Rather, the systems exchange data periodically. If one system is temporarily unavailable, the other system can continue to work without any problems. An example of soft coupling is ALE (*application link enabling*) coupling.

The process that starts the RFC is called the sender or client, and the process in which the RFC is executed is the recipient or server. We differentiate between four types of RFCs: synchronous, asynchronous, transactional, and queued.

RFC types

▶ A *synchronous RFC* is characterized by the sender waiting while the RFC runs in the recipient process.

▶ With an *asynchronous RFC*, the sender does not wait until the RFC recipient process has been completed. Rather, when the RFC has started, the sender can continue working. Therefore, a sender can start several asynchronous RFCs at the same time. (With a synchronous call, on the other hand, only one RFC can run at a time, because the sender has to wait until processing has finished.)

▶ A *transactional RFC* is an asynchronous RFC that runs under special security conditions. We'll discuss details on this later in this chapter.

▶ A *queued RFC* (qRFC) is a transactional RFC for which the processing sequence in the destination system complies with the call sequence in the source system (for all qRFCs in a particular queue).

You can recognize an RFC in an ABAP program by the syntax `CALL FUNC-TION <function name> DESTINATION <connection name> ....` The variable `<connection name>` contains the name of the RFC connection, also called the destination.

ABAP coding

If the function call contains the clause `STARTING NEW TASK`, it is an asynchronous RFC; the clause `IN BACKGROUND TASK` indicates a transactional RFC. If the call only contains the clause `DESTINATION`, but neither `START-`

ING NEW TASK nor IN BACKGROUND TASK, then the RFC is started as a synchronous RFC.

The following code starts the functional module Z_BC315_RFC synchronously, asynchronously, and transactionally. (DESTINATION 'NONE' here means that the destination and source systems are identical.)

```
* Synchronous RFC
CALL FUNCTION 'Z_BC315_RFC'
     DESTINATION 'NONE'
     EXCEPTIONS
          argument_error = 1
          send_error     = 2
          OTHERS         = 3.


 * Asynchronous RFC
CALL FUNCTION 'Z_BC315_RFC'
     STARTING NEW TASK task
     DESTINATION 'NONE'
     EXCEPTIONS
          communication_failure = 1
          system_failure        = 2
          RESOURCE_FAILURE      = 3.


* Transactional RFC
CALL FUNCTION 'Z_BC315_RFC'
          IN BACKGROUND TASK
          DESTINATION 'NONE'.
COMMIT WORK.
```

All RFCs, whether synchronous, asynchronous, or transactional, are started in dialog work processes. Therefore, you should not be deceived by the syntax IN BACKGROUND TASK; this has nothing to do with background work processes. Transactional RFCs are also executed in dialog work processes. You can find a detailed introduction to the programming of RFCs online in ABAP Help under the statement CALL FUNCTION.

6.3.2   RFC Cycle

When you execute an RFC, the following process is launched:

1. First, the sender (the work process that wants to start the RFC) creates a connection with the recipient system. This connection is made

using the gateway services of the two systems involved (initializing phase). The dispatcher on the recipient system looks for a free dialog work process that can execute the RFC. In the work process overview (Transaction SM50 or SM66), the sender work process is in Stopped status during this time, with CPIC as the reason. The Action/Reason for waiting column shows the entry CMINIT.

2. When the connection between the sender work process and the recipient work process has been set up, the data necessary for executing the RFC is transferred. Now, in the work process overview for both the sender work process and the recipient work process, the status Stopped is displayed, with CPIC as the reason, and Action/Reason for Waiting is CMSEND. After the entry CMSEND, there is a number. This is known as the communication ID.

3. After this point, synchronous and asynchronous RFCs are treated differently. Once all necessary data has been transferred, and the RFC has been started on the recipient side, with asynchronous RFCs the connection is broken, and the program on the sender side continues working without waiting for the end of the RFC. This type of processing means, for example, that another RFC can now be started, which will then run parallel to the first.

4. With synchronous RFCs, the sender side waits until the RFC has finished processing. During the wait time, the user context on the sender side is rolled out of the work process so that it is available to other users. In the work process overview on the sender side, there is nothing to be seen of the running RFC and the waiting program. On the sender side, the waiting program can only be seen as a session in the user monitor (Transaction SM04) and as an open communication connection in the gateway monitor (Transaction SMGW). On the recipient side, the running RFC creates a status entry of Running in the work process overview. In the user monitor (Transaction SM04), the incoming RFC can be identified by the terminal entry APPC-TM. Beginning with SAP Basis 4.6, there is a special column in the user monitor for user type (Type). For an RFC connection, you will see the entry RFC.

5. Once the recipient side has closed the processing of the synchronous RFC, the waiting context on the sender side has to be "awakened,"

that is, rolled in to a work process. During the subsequent data transfer from recipient to sender, in the work process overview, both work processes display the status Stopped, with CPIC as the reason and CMRECEIVE as Action/Reason for Waiting.

6. Finally, the connection is closed. The recipient work process is free again, and the sender work process continues with its work.

Duration In this procedure, creating the connection (the CMINIT phase) should only take a few milliseconds. If you find this status often in the work process overview, there may be an overload in the recipient system. (We'll cover further details on this in the next section.) The duration of the CMSEND and CMRECEIVE phases depends mainly on the amount of data to be transferred and the speed of the network. No time data can be given for these phases.

Figure 6.3 illustrates the course and measured times of a synchronous RFC, which are displayed in the single-record statistics (Transaction STAD or STAT), and in the workload monitor (Transaction ST03 or ST03N).

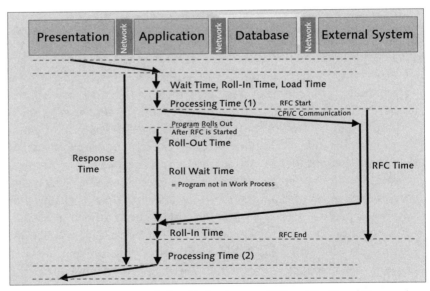

Figure 6.3 Transaction Step Cycle with Synchronous RFC and the Times Measured

While the sending program is waiting for the response to the synchronous RFC, the user context is rolled out of the work process to make it available for other users. When the RFC has ended in the recipient system, there is a roll-in to a work process, and the transaction step is continued. During an RFC call, the response time for the calling program is still growing. In an analysis of the lost time (see Chapter 3, Section 3.3, Workload Analysis) the roll wait time has to be subtracted from the total response time, because during this time, the calling system does not require any CPU resources. In a single statistical record for a transaction step with a synchronous RFC, a roll wait time is also listed. (However, for very short RFCs with a response time of less than 500 ms, there is no roll-out.) You will find no roll wait time for an asynchronous RFC, because the program is not rolled out; rather, it continues working.

Roll wait time

The total time for the RFC appears in the RFC+CPIC Time field of the single statistical record and the workload monitor. For asynchronous RFCs, this includes phases 1 to 3 of the previous list. As a rule of thumb, the RFC time here should not be longer than 50 ms per call. For synchronous RFCs, the RFC time includes phases 1 to 6. It is clear that the RFC time here must be greater than the roll wait time.

RFC time

6.3.3 Configuring and Testing RFC Destinations

RFC connections (also called destinations) can be set in the transaction Display and Maintenance of RFC Destinations (Transaction SM59). You can access this transaction via the menu path TOOLS • ADMINISTRATION • ADMINISTRATION • NETWORK • RFC DESTINATIONS.

Setting up destinations

In this transaction, all available RFC destinations are first presented in a tree structure. Table 6.4 describes the four possible types of RFC destinations.

Double-click a destination to select it, and you are taken to a screen with details on that destination. The layout of this screen will differ according to the destination type. Figure 6.4 shows one example.

Destination Type	Description
Internal destination	RFC connections to all SAP application instances are on the same SAP system. These connections are automatically generated when you install the SAP system in the form <server name>_<SAP system name>_<instance number>. Here, you will also find the destination NONE, which always indicates the current instance.
R/3 destinations	RFC connections are to other SAP systems, such as connections in the form TMSADM@<System 1>DOMAIN_<System 2>. These are needed by the Transport Management System (TMS) and are generated during the build.
TCP/IP destinations	These are connections to non-SAP systems. Many standard destinations are already preconfigured here.
Destinations via ABAP drivers	Not of interest here.

Table 6.4 RFC Destination Types

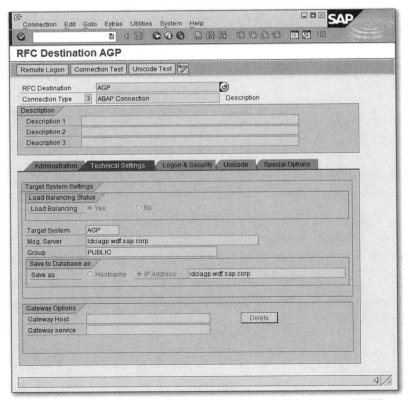

Figure 6.4 Configuration of an External RFC Connection (Transaction SM59)

In addition to details on the configuration of the RFC destination, in the list of buttons, you will find the function Test Connection. Execute this function now if you anticipate problems with a connection. It logs on to the recipient system and transfers some test data. Then it shows the response time for the data transfer or an error message if the logon was not successful.

Testing

The response time for the transfer of test data depends on the network used. Ideally, the response time should be between 10 and 100 milliseconds. If you execute the connection test at times of both high and low system load, you can determine whether the connection has a capacity overload when there is high workload.

Response time

High response times can be due to three things:

▶ The network connection is generally slow or overloaded.

▶ The recipient system is physically overloaded.

▶ Too few processes are configured in the recipient system to receive RFCs.

Table 6.5 provides a list of possible sources of problems when setting up connections.

Destination Type	Connection Test Result	Measures To Be Taken
R/3	Error message "TCP/IP Timeout"	The recipient system cannot be contacted. Check the availability of the recipient system and the network connection.
	High response times (>100 ms) for a connection to an SAP system	▶ Check the network connection to the external system with the help of the ping command or using the network provider's tools. Optimal ping response times are within hundredths of a second. ▶ Log on and performance-test the recipient system. Are all work processes busy?
TCP/IP	Error message "Partner program not registered"	Begin the corresponding recipient process.

Table 6.5 Sources of Problems When Setting Up Connections

Destination Type	Connection Test Result	Measures To Be Taken
	Error message "TCP/IP Timeout"	Check the network connection between the SAP gateway process in question and the other side. If the gateway needs to be maintained, view information on it by clicking the Gateway button. If this is not the case, the local gateway of the SAP application server will always be used. If you still want to change subsequent gateway settings, do so via the menu DESTINATION • GATEWAY OPTIONS. (This is always done on both sides.)
	High response times (>100 ms) for a connection to an external system	▸ Check the network connection to the external system with the help of the ping command or using the network provider's tools. Optimal ping response times are within hundredths of a second. ▸ Check to see how many parallel recipient processes are started on the other side to receive the IDocs. If high load develops on the recipient side, it can be useful to increase the number of processes. ▸ Please refer to SAP Notes 63930 and 44844 on RFC connections with SAP Gateway registration.

Table 6.5 Sources of Problems When Setting Up Connections (Cont.)

SAP system as recipient

Depending on the recipient system, you can configure different parameters for the connection. If the recipient is an SAP system, first decide if logon should be done via logon groups or directly via a set application server. You can make this choice by setting the Load Distribution option. If the load distribution is activated, the message server and the corresponding logon group have to be reported to the recipient system. If the connection is made without load distribution, the data on the application server (Target Machine field) and instance number (System Number field) are requested.

[+] You should log on using a logon group. This procedure has two advantages over direct logon to a dedicated application server:

▸ Several application servers can be assigned to a logon group. If one server is down, another server can process the incoming RFCs (high availability aspect).

▶ There is logon balancing; that is, the workload is distributed among the instances, which averts a capacity overload (performance optimization aspect).

You can continuously monitor the availability of important RFC connections with the central CCMS monitor (Transaction RZ20). For more detailed information on how to activate this monitoring, see the document "Monitoring RFC Destinations and Services," which you will find in the SAP Service Marketplace under System Monitoring and Alert Management, Media Library.

Continuous monitoring of RFC connections

6.3.4 Monitoring Inbound and Outbound Loads

You can monitor the inbound and outbound workloads created by RFCs in the RFC profile in the workload monitor. You will find this in SAP Basis 4.6 (from Basis support package 22) in the new workload monitor (Transaction ST03N) or in the old workload monitor (Transaction ST03) by following the menu path GOTO • PROFILES • RFC PROFILE.

The profiles under the menu options Clients and Client Destinations correspond to the outbound RFCs (the local system is the sender or client). Under Server or Server Destinations, you can see the load created by inbound RFCs (the local system is the recipient or server). Tables 6.6, 6.7, and 6.8 show the different RFC profiles (Client Destinations, Server Destinations, Clients, and Server) of the performance indicators and the different views specified in the RFC profiles.

Profile	Description
Client Destinations and Server Destinations	The single-record statistics write total statistics records to each transaction step, with data on everything that has been executed for each RFC destination. In these profiles, you will find the total workload generated by RFCs.
	Warning: Data on the function module name and the corresponding view (see Table 6.8) is of no significance (and is no longer displayed in the new workload monitor).
Clients and Server	The single-record statistics write the function module name of the five most expensive function modules (this can be changed using the parameter stat/rfcrec) in a transaction step to the statistical record. In these profiles, you will find the workload of these five expensive function modules. These statistics are particularly useful for an introduction to application analysis, because with them, you can see which functions create the highest workloads.

Table 6.6 RFC Profiles

Field	Explanation
Quantity	Number of remote function calls (RFCs).
Call Time	Response time for the RFCs, measured in the sender system. The difference between call time and execution time is the time it takes to make the connection and transfer data between the sender and recipient systems. As a rule of thumb, this time should not be more than 20% of the call time. If this value is exceeded, look for a bottleneck in the connection between sender and recipient.
Execution Time	Response time for the RFCs, measured in the recipient system. The execution time is the net time for the execution of the RFCs in the recipient system.
Sent Data	Quantity of data sent.
Received Data	Quantity of data received.

Table 6.7 Fields in the RFC Profile in the Workload Monitor (Transaction ST03/ ST03N)

View	Button	Remarks
Transaction codes	Transaction Code	
User names	User Names	This view is useful if a user name is associated with a particular transfer channel. For example, you can set up your RFC connection so that sales orders are sent in your system under a user RFC_SALES.
RFC function modules	Function Modules	This view is suitable mainly for application analysis, because it enables you to identify the functions that create the highest workload. This view is of no consequence in the profiles Client Destinations and Server Destinations.
External RFC destinations	Remote Destinations	You can enter remote SAP instances as remote destinations, for example, or as names of servers that run programs with which the local SAP system communicates via RFC.
Local RFC destinations	Local Destinations	Distribution of the RFC load over the instances in the local SAP system.

Table 6.8 Views in the RFC Profile of the Workload Monitor

Evaluating profiles   To evaluate the RFC profile, proceed as follows:

1. Sort the RFC profile according to the Call Time column. The functions or destinations with the longest processing times are at the top of the list. Note: In some SAP kernel versions, for software imports (program

tp) incorrect times are calculated for call time, so extremely high times are given for the server from which the software import was started. However, in the profile, these can be recognized immediately.

2. Compare the values given for Call Time and Execution Time. As a rule of thumb, the difference between them should not be greater than 20%. If you do this comparison in the different views, you can identify destinations, function modules, or users for which there may be a problem with communication between the sender and recipient. Analyze the connection and data transfer by testing the relevant connection, and generate an RFC trace for the corresponding program.

3. You can then sort the RFC profile according to Execution Time, Sent Data, and Received Data to identify the function modules with the highest workloads.

In the Interface Load section of the SAP EarlyWatch Alert report, you can get a weekly overview of the most important destinations and function modules called as RFCs. The tables in the SAP EarlyWatch Alert report are a compressed version of the RFC statistics.

SAP EarlyWatch Alert

To correctly interpret the statistical information on RFCs included in the workload monitor (Transaction ST03N) and in the single-record statistics (Transaction STAD), you need to understand how these statistics are generated. Otherwise, it is easy to draw the wrong conclusions. We'll now describe how RFC statistics are generated and what you should bear in mind when interpreting them.

How are RFC statistics generated?

Let's assume that in a transaction step, RFCs are sent to several destinations — destinations A, B, C, and so on. The RFCs sent to destination A will be called A1, A2, A3,... and those sent to B will be B1, B2, and so on. For performance reasons, it is not possible to write statistics for all RFCs. The statistics are created as follows:

▶ On the sender (client) side, detailed statistical information is saved for the five most expensive RFCs (in one transaction step). The information saved includes user, destination, sender and recipient instances, name of the function module, time called, time executed, and volume of data transferred. These statistics are referred to as the client statistics records. The RFC client profile is generated from these statistics.

▶ Also on the sender side, detailed statistical information is saved on the five most expensive destinations, which in turn contains the total of all RFCs sent to these destinations. The information saved includes user, destination, sender and recipient instances, call number, time called, time executed, and volume of data transferred. The name of the function module is not included here, because these statistics are the total for all RFCs to a destination, so all function modules are combined. These statistics are referred to as the *client destination statistics records*. The RFC client destination profile is generated from these statistics.

▶ On the recipient (server) side, similar statistics are generated and are known as the *server statistics records* and the *server destination statistics records*.

Changing the profile parameters stat/rfcrec

From the rules described thus far, we can see that the RFC profile in the workload monitor does not cover the entire RFC load, because statistics are only collected for the five most expensive destinations and the five most expensive calls (per transaction step). You can, however, change the limit for how many destinations and calls should be included, using the profile parameter stat/rfcrec. If you do not change these parameters, the default value is five. In practice, this standard setting covers 50 to 90% of the RFC load (depending on the size of the system). Raising the stat/rfcrec parameter causes a greater load for the statistics collector and may lead to performance problems. In general, therefore, you should not change the default setting.

Interpreting the RFC server statistics

When analyzing RFC statistics on the recipient or server system, in the workload monitor (Transaction ST03N), or in the single-record analysis (Transaction STAD), select task type RFC to analyze the load generated by inbound RFCs. Further analyses related to shares of CPU time, database response time, and so on can then take place, just as with transaction steps in the dialog task. Be careful, however, of two special situations that can sometimes lead to confusion:

1. The first occurs when an RFC calls another RFC. In this case, the time taken for the execution of the second RFC is not added to that of the first, so the response time for the first RFC only takes into account the time that it is actually in the work process. The roll wait time (that is,

the time it spends waiting for the second RFC to finish its work) is not included in the response time. This provision was set to avoid "multiple counting" of RFC times. (Note: The calculation is different for transaction steps in the dialog task. If an RFC is started from the dialog task, the response time does include the time for the RFC execution, even if the work process is rolled out. It has been set in this way because response time in a dialog task should reflect the time that a user spends waiting in front of the screen.)

2. The second situation arises when the sender does not close the connection to the recipient. Here is an example: Assume that a sender executes an RFC in a recipient system (an SAP system) and for performance reasons, does not close the connection after execution. This procedure is often followed when several RFCs are sent one after the other, because performance suffers each time a connection is set up. Also assume that each RFC is very fast — that each execution takes, for example, 20 ms. How does the recipient system respond in this case?

After execution of the first RFC, the RFC server work process waits 500 ms. If the sender calls the recipient system again before the end of this wait time, then the RFC is executed in the same work process. As a result, the user context does not have to be rolled in and rolled out. If no other RFC is executed within the 500 ms, then the user context is rolled out of the work process, which is then available for requests from other users. (The user context and the CPIC connection still exist; they are just rolled out of the work process.) A statistics record is created at roll-out. The response time shown in this statistics record is the time during which the work process was occupied. Let's say, for example, that four RFCs were executed in close succession, with a response time of 20 ms each. Then the work process waits another 500 ms. The response time for the RFC call would show as about 600 ms. You can find the response times for the four RFCs in the details of the statistics records.

To summarize, we can say that the response time in the dialog task reflects the time that a user spends waiting for a response. This includes both the time it takes for the request to be processed in the work process and the time the request has to wait for any external RFCs. The response time in the RFC task, on the other hand, reflects the time that an RFC has been in a work process.

6.3.5 Configuring Parallel Processes with Asynchronous RFCs

As we have already seen, *asynchronous RFCs* are used to parallelize applications, because the sender side does not have to wait for an RFC to be finished; it can send other RFCs immediately. If the degree of parallelizing is not limited, however, it can result in a snowballing of RFCs, which can bring the application level to a standstill for the user (all work processes are busy).

Limiting RFC resources

There are two ways to avoid this situation: You can create your own SAP instances with a dedicated logon group, as explained in Section 6.2.4, Dynamic User Distribution: Configuring Logon Groups. In addition, the resources for RFC processing can be limited for each SAP instance. In this way, a certain share of the resources can be reserved for dialog applications. For asynchronous RFCs (ABAP keyword STARTING NEW TASK <Task Name> DESTINATION IN GROUP <Group>), the load information is evaluated on the recipient side. As many aRFCs are sent to each application instance as there are resources available. If an application instance has no more free resources available, then no more aRFCs are sent to it. The request for resources is repeated until all aRFCs have been processed.

Resources available for aRFC processing are set in profile parameters. With the help of the program RSARFCLD the quotas can be configured dynamically. You can find further information on profile parameters in Appendix C, Performance-Relevant Configuration Parameters and Key Figures, and in SAP Note 74141.

[+] Quotas are only effective for aRFCs using RFC server groups and for qRFCs, but not for synchronous RFCs and aRFCs without using RFC server groups.

6.3.6 Monitoring Data Transfer with Transactional RFCs

A transactional RFC is an asynchronous RFC that runs under special security conditions. Transactional RFCs (tRFCs) are not executed immediately; rather, the calls are first gathered in an internal table. On the next COMMIT WORK statement, all calls are processed in order of sequence. If update records are also generated before the COMMIT WORK statement, then the transactional RFCs are only executed if the update modules can be processed without error. The transactional RFCs of a transaction form a *logical unit of work* (LUW) for each destination.

All tRFCs are displayed on the sender side in the tables ARFCSSTATE and ARFCSDATA. Each LUW is identified with a universally unique ID. On COMMIT WORK, the call bearing this ID is executed on the corresponding target system. If a call error occurs, all executed database operations from the previous calls are revoked (ROLLBACK), and a relevant error message is written to the ARFCSSTATE table. If an LUW is successfully executed on the target system, this is confirmed in the target system. The corresponding entries in the ARFCSSTATE and ARFCSDATA tables are deleted on the sender side. You can evaluate error messages regarding tRFCs with the help of Transaction SM58.

Interrupted or unexecuted tRFCs lead to inconsistencies between systems and considerably impair the business process. The daily checking of errors in interface processing (Transaction SM58) is therefore an important task of the SAP system administrator. **[!]**

If the target system cannot be reached because, for example, the connection is currently not active, by default, a background job is planned for each failed tRFC so that the tRFC will be started again at regular intervals (report RSARFCSE with the ID of the tRFC as a parameter).

Dealing with tRFC errors

If a lot of tRFCs are transferred for a particular connection, which is then interrupted, the sending SAP system might be inundated with background jobs that will continue trying to send tRFCs to the unavailable system, with no success. This can lead to considerable performance problems in the sender system if the recipient system is not available over a certain period of time. We therefore recommend that for connections in which more than 50 tRFCs have to be transferred each day, you deactivate the scheduling of background jobs in the event of error. To do this, select the destination in question in Transaction SM59: DESTINATION • TRFC OPTIONS. In the next screen, activate the option Suppress Batch Job in the Event of Communication Error and confirm your entry with the function Continue. Now, in the event of error, no background jobs will be created and processed for the tRFC. Instead of these individual jobs, you must now schedule the report RSARFCEX to run regularly (about every 30 minutes) with the destinations in question and with the current date as the variant (explicit parameter for variants). The program now searches the ARFCSSTATE table sequentially for tRFCs that have not yet been sent and tries to send them. This adjustment should only be carried out and tested by an experienced system consultant.

Reorganization of tRFC tables

If errors occur when you're sending tRFCs, the corresponding entries in ARFCSSTATE and ARFCSDATA tables are not deleted. As a result, these tables have to be reorganized at regular intervals. For this purpose, you should schedule RSARFC01 to run at least once a week as a background job. Otherwise, performance problems might occur with the ARFCSSTATE and ARFCSDATA tables. You can find additional notes on undeleted tRFC protocol entries in SAP Note 375566, Many Entries in the tRFC and qRFC Tables.

6.4 SAP Virtual Machine Container

SAP Basis 7.00 provides two different Java runtime environments: the J2EE Engine and the Virtual Machine Container (VMC). Whereas the J2EE Engine can be operated with Java Virtual Machines (JVM) by Sun, IBM, HP, and (as of SAP Basis 7.10) the SAP JVM, the VMC exclusively runs on the JVM by SAP. The performance analysis of the J2EE Engine has already been discussed in other chapters; therefore, we'll now take a closer look at the performance analysis of the VMC.

VMC technology

The VMC component enables the operation of a Java Virtual Machine (JVM) within the classical SAP work processes, along with the ABAP runtime environment. For this purpose, a pool of JVMs is created in the shared memory of the ABAP instance, and (if required) a JVM is taken from this pool and displayed in the address space of the ABAP work process. When a transaction step is complete, the JVM is hidden from the address space and returned to the pool. The user data accumulated in the Java part of the application (*session*) is also stored in the shared memory; however, they are copied to another part of the shared memory. Therefore, in the next transaction step, the user data can be processed in another work process by another JVM (by copying the user data from the shared memory). At the end of the transaction, the user data is released. Memory management of the VMC is basically identical to memory management of the ABAP runtime environment and is no longer similar to a "normal" Java runtime environment in which the user data is maintained in the local memory of the JVM and cannot be moved easily from one JVM to another. The benefit of the VMC is higher stability due to the processing of only one transaction step and one work process at a time in the JVM. However, this stability has a considerably high price within Java development, because the Java-side user data must meet specific requirements so it can be copied by the VMC to *shared closures* of the shared memory at the end of a transaction step.

Java applications based on the VMC include pricing, tax calculation, and configuration, that is, applications known as *Internet Pricing and Configuration* (IPC). IPC was ported in SAP Basis 7.00, for example, by means of SAP CRM 5.0 to the VMC.

VMC applications

Why do these applications use a "special" technology? Initially during the development of SAP CRM, the need arose to provide functions such as pricing, tax calculation, and configuration both as applications for PCs (*mobile clients*) and as server applications. Therefore, Java was selected as the programming language. Debates over performance reasons argue against implementation based on the SAP J2EE Engine; therefore, the first SAP CRM versions included a separate IPC application with its own software logistics and administration. As of SAP Basis 7.10, it was integrated into the ABAP runtime environment.

You can find most of the critical performance key figures of the VMC in the workload monitor (Transaction ST03N) and in the single-record statistics (Transaction STAD). Table 6.9 shows the most critical key figures.

Performance analysis

If you determine that there is a problem in the VMC, based on the performance key figures, you can monitor it using the VMC monitors (Transactions SM52 and SM53) and via central CCMS monitoring (Transaction RZ20).

Field	Explanation
VMC Time	The time the work process required in the VMC. This time is part of the processing time in the statistical main record. If the processing time is high, it is worth checking whether it was caused by high VMC times.
VMC CPU Time	CPU time required by the VMC. This time is part of the CPU time in the statistical main record.
Garbage Collection Time	Time that was used by the VMC for garbage collection. This time is part of the VMC time. As a rule of thumb, this time should not exceed 5% of the VMC time.
Memory Allocated	The memory used by the VMC.
Memory Transferred to Shared Memory	The memory copied to the shared memory by the VMC. This typically includes the amount of user data that has been copied to the user area of the shared memory at the end of the transaction step after garbage collection.

Table 6.9 VMC Statistic Fields in the Workload Monitor (Transaction ST03N) and in the Single-Record Statistics (Transaction STAD)

6.5 Summary

The most important method for optimizing workload distribution in an SAP system is the *configuration of work processes*. The number of work processes to be set up depends on the demands made on the SAP system and the CPU resources available. Important considerations are: Is the system to be used mainly for OLTP (online transaction processing) or for OLAP (online analytical processing) applications? Will there be more dialog processing or more background processing?

You should take the following guidelines into account:

► About 10 to 30% of CPU requirements for the entire system is normally consumed by the *database service*. Ensure that any SAP instances residing on the database server do not consume too much CPU capacity. Too many work processes on a database server can lead to CPU bottlenecks, which in turn lead to higher database times and inconvenience for all users.

▶ About 10 to 20% of CPU requirements for the entire SAP system is normally consumed by the *SAP update service.*

▶ In comparison to SAP GUI scenarios, the use of a web browser as the presentation server requires an additional CPU capacity of approximately 10 to 30% for preparing the screen pages in HTML. Depending on the technology used, this preparation is performed by the ABAP application instances, the Java application instances, or the external ITS (see also Chapter 7, SAP GUI and Internet Connection).

The SAP Web Dispatcher is used for distributing Web requests to Java or ABAP application instances. The message server is deployed for distributing SAP GUI, background, and update requests.

We recommend the following procedure for distributing work processes on the ABAP instances:

▶ Message, enqueue, and ATP services should be on one ABAP instance (known as the *central SAP instance*). There should be at least five dialog work processes on this instance. For small and medium installations, this central SAP instance is configured on the database server. For large installations, it is located on a separate application server.

▶ Dialog, background, update, and spool work processes should be equally distributed on the remaining application servers in a symmetrical manner. You must take into account the CPU capacity of individual servers when configuring the work processes. If you configure the update service on one instance, at least two update work processes should be configured there.

Additional techniques for system load management include:

▶ Central update server and background server

▶ Update types (V1/V2/V3 and local update), dedicated updates, and update multiplexing

▶ Logon groups for dynamic user distribution

▶ System parameters for automatic logoff, prohibiting double logons, and restricting the runtime of programs (time-out)

However, please note that these techniques involve higher administration and monitoring effort. The rule of thumb is that the system should be configured as symmetrically as possible and as asymmetrically as necessary.

There is no rule for how many SAP work processes per processor can be configured. A guideline value is 5 to 10 work processes per processor. Often, SAP administrators and consultants make the mistake of increasing the number of work processes to solve any type of performance problem. This can lead to problems that are as serious asthe initial problem and in some cases even worse.

Interfaces are a core element of the SAP technology. Remote function calls (RFCs) constitute the most important interface technology.

You can proactively eliminate RFC interface performance problems with appropriate configurations of the RFC connection and recipient instance. If performance problems still occur, there are some good analysis tools that you can use, such as the work process overview, the RFC profile in the workload monitor, single-record statistics, performance trace (RFC trace), and the transaction for configuring RFC connections.

Communication between ABAP work processes and the Virtual Machine Container is also done via RFC. The VMC runtimes can be found in the single-record statistics and the workload monitor and therefore are the starting points for performance analysis.

Important Concepts in this Chapter

After reading this chapter, you should be familiar with the following concepts:

- ▶ Load distribution
- ▶ SAP Web Dispatcher, message server
- ▶ Logon groups
- ▶ Update dispatching
- ▶ Update: V1, V2, V3, and local updates
- ▶ Remote function calls: RFC, aRFC, tRFC, and qRFC

▶ Roll wait time and RFC time

▶ RFC profile in the workload monitor

▶ Virtual Machine Container

Questions

1. Where should background work processes be configured?

   a) Background work processes should always be configured on the database server. Otherwise, the runtime of background programs will be negatively affected by network problems between the database server and the application server.

   b) If background work processes are not located on the database server, they must all be set up on a dedicated application server, known as the background server.

   c) Background work processes can be distributed evenly over all of the application servers.

2. How should you configure and monitor the dynamic user distribution?

   a) By setting the appropriate SAP profile parameter, for example `rdisp/wp_no_dia`

   b) By using Transaction User Overview (SM04)

   c) By using Transaction Maintain Logon Groups (SMLG).

You will find questions on the RFC topic at the end of Chapter 7, SAP GUI and Internet Connection.

7   SAP GUI and Internet Connection

There are two access options for working with an SAP solution: Users are now using the classical SAP GUI for Windows or Java environment or a web browser to log onto SAP systems; the advantage is that no special GUI programs need to be installed on their desktop computers.

The first section of this chapter discusses the performance monitoring of programs where users use SAP GUI to interact with the SAP system, particularly with SAP GUI *controls*.

The following sections then introduce performance monitoring for Web-based user interfaces (Web UIs). Communication between the web browser and the SAP application level is effected by one of the following:

► Web applications based on the SAP Internet Transaction Server (SAP ITS)

► Business Server Pages (BSPs), Web Dynpro for ABAP, and Integrated Internet Transaction Server (ITS)

► JavaServer Pages, Java servlets, and Web Dynpro for Java applications based on the J2EE runtime environment of SAP NetWeaver Application Server (SAP J2EE Engine)

When Should You Read this Chapter?

This chapter introduces administrators and developers to the configuration and monitoring of SAP GUI interfaces and Web interfaces of the SAP Internet Transaction Server, SAP J2EE Engine, and ABAP server. Before reading this chapter, you should read Chapter 4, Identifying Performance Problems in ABAP and Java Programs, and Chapter 6, Section 6.3, Remote Function Calls (RFCs).

7.1   SAP GUI

For the implementation of the graphical user interface using SAP GUI, the application developer can access *SAP GUI controls*. They enable the developer to design interfaces with user-focused interaction design and personalization of functionality.

7.1.1 Interaction Model and Measuring Performance

SAP GUI controls

Controls are interface elements that allow application developers to more precisely adapt their user interfaces to the needs of users and allow them to integrate a greater number of different elements into one screen. Typical controls include:

▶ ABAP List Viewer Control (ALV Control)

▶ Textedit Control

▶ HTML Control

[Ex]

You will find examples of controls in your SAP system under TOOLS • ABAP WORKBENCH • DEVELOPMENT • ABAP EDITOR • ENVIRONMENT • CONTROL EXAMPLES (Transaction DWDM).

Controls are not screen elements in the traditional sense; rather, they are software components that run independently in the SAP GUI program. They have their own functions that operate at the GUI level and require no communication with the application level.

In a traditional list or a traditional tree structure (prior to SAP Basis 4.6), for example, each scroll operation or each collapse or expansion of a branch in the tree represented a communication step between the GUI and application levels. When the new List Viewer Control or Tree Control is used, a larger volume of data is transferred the first time the list or tree is constructed. Consequently, you can navigate the list or tree independently in the GUI without referring back to the application level. Other actions that can be processed directly in the GUI with some controls include functions such as Find and Replace.

Fewer communication steps

Therefore, the new interaction model results in fewer communication steps (on average) between the presentation and application levels. This is a distinct advantage for users who call up a screen once and then navigate it frequently. On the other hand, the network load is greater when the screen page is being constructed for the first time. The new interaction model is therefore a disadvantage if you only call up a complex screen once and then immediately exit it. In general, tests show that the average network load since Release 4.6 has been higher in comparison with previous versions (SAP Note 164102).

It is not possible to determine which actions require a communication step with the application level if you are not familiar with the actual programming. Application developers are required to transfer data to the GUI in logical batches. Lists or trees that are only a few pages long are transferred intact, whereas very long ones are transferred in batches (for trees, a fixed number of nodes in advance). The new interaction model clearly imposes extra responsibility on application developers, because they can now decide how much data in their programs is to be sent to the GUI and in how many batches.

In one transaction step, several interactions between the application level and the GUI may be necessary to construct a screen. This interaction is referred to as a *roundtrip*. Data is transferred in a roundtrip on the basis of a synchronous RFC from the application level to the GUI. The entire duration of all communication with the GUI within a transaction step is referred to in statistics records as *GUI time*. The program is rolled out of the work process as it waits at the application level for the GUI to respond. This wait time is referred to in the statistics as the *roll wait time*. In general, in a statistics record for a transaction step in which controls are constructed and no RFC to an external system is issued, the roll wait time and the GUI time are approximately the same. If controls are constructed and external RFCs are started in a transaction step, the roll wait time will be greater than the GUI time, because the roll wait time includes the time for issuing the RFCs to the GUI and the time for the external RFCs.

Roundtrip, roll wait time, and GUI time

The volume of data transferred between the application level and the GUI can be calculated from the statistics records for the fields Terminal Out-Message (application level to GUI) or Terminal In-Message.

Transferred data volume

The first and the last interaction between the SAP GUI and the application level is recorded not only in the GUI time, but also in a separate time — the *frontend time* (FE Net Time or Net Time). This time is relevant for every type of SAP GUI interaction and in cases in which no controls

Frontend time

are used. The entire time that is required for the network traffic between the SAP GUI and the application level and for the display of the user interface via the SAP GUI therefore results as the total of the frontend time and the GUI time. The GUI time is part of the response time unlike the frontend time; that is, the overall response time in the SAP GUI results as the total of response time and frontend time.

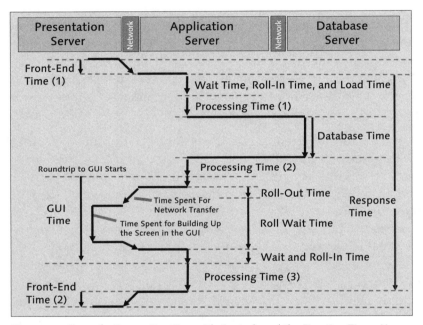

Figure 7.1 Flow of a Transaction Step with Controls and the Duration Times Measured

One specific detail must be considered for measuring the frontend time. The frontend time is calculated as the difference between the total response time, which is measured by the SAP GUI, and the response time, which is determined by the application instance. Because the transaction in the SAP GUI is not completed until the application instance has rolled out the program from the work process, the frontend time cannot be stored in the actual statistics record on the transaction step that is written at roll-out. Instead, the SAP GUI doesn't send the frontend time until the next interaction with the application layer so that the frontend time can be stored in the next statistics record. Therefore, a statistics record always includes the frontend time of the previous transaction step. The display transaction on the single-record statistics (STAD) takes this effect into account so that the frontend time is displayed correctly, with the exception of those cases where the assignment cannot be ensured due to technical reasons, for example, because there has been no subsequent interaction with the SAP GUI.

Figure 7.1 illustrates the times measured in a transaction step with controls.

7.1.2 Analyzing and Optimizing the Performance of GUI Communication

If you suspect that your system is having problems with GUI communication when constructing controls, first call up the single-record statistics (Transaction STAD; see Chapter 4, Section 4.1, Single-Record Statistics):

Single-record statistics

1. In the selection screen, you can restrict your search, for example, to the user who reported the problem or to a transaction or program name and a certain period of time.

2. You then access the overview screen. Use the Select Fields function to choose the fields that primarily indicate problems with GUI communication: GUI Time, FE Net Time, No. of Roundtrips, Terminal In-Message, and Terminal Out-Message.

   Now scroll the list and search for transaction steps with high GUI times or a high data transfer volume (Terminal Out-Message). The following guidelines can be followed here.

You should aim for an average rate of 1KB per 100 ms for transferring data to the GUI. One second for 1KB would be the slowest acceptable rate. If these guidelines are exceeded frequently, it can only be assumed that there is either a problem in the network or a hardware bottleneck on the presentation server.

It is also possible that the transfer rate is acceptable and the GUI time is still high because too much data is being transferred. As a guideline value, a transaction step should not transfer more than 5 to 8KB, on average. Even a complex screen layout should not require more than 50KB of data. If these values are frequently exceeded, the problem lies in the program or in the way it is being used.

Performance Trace

The *Performance Trace tool* (Transaction ST05) is another important tool you can use to analyze performance problems with the GUI:

1. Activate the Performance Trace (SQL trace, enqueue trace, and RFC trace) for the user activity being investigated and then list the trace result.

2. Search the trace for RFC modules that are intended for your presentation server. To do this, look for the name of your presentation server in the Object column. Typical function modules for transferring data to the GUI include SAPGUI_PROGRESS_INDICATOR and OLE_FLUSH_CALL (see also Figure 4.3 in Chapter 4, Identifying Performance Problems in ABAP and Java Programs).

3. Add up the response times for these function modules and check whether this accounts for a significant portion of the overall response time.

4. Compare the response time and the volume of data transferred for each function module. The response time (in microseconds) for an RFC is shown in the Duration field in the basic trace list. To work out the volume of data transferred, double-click the relevant line in the trace list and take the value from the Bytes sent field. Compare the values with the guideline values specified.

The Automation Queue Trace is a developer tool for analyzing the performance of controls. You can activate it via the SAP GUI. You will find further information on this in SAP Note 158985.

High GUI time despite a moderate volume of data

If you discover that the GUI time is high despite a relatively small volume of data, this can be for two reasons: There may be a hardware bottleneck on the presentation server, or on the other hand, there may be a network bottleneck. Often the simplest way to analyze this further is to filter out the users who typically experience these problems from the single-record statistics.

The fields Terminal Out-Message (in the single-record statistics) and Bytes Sent (in the Performance Trace) indicate the uncompressed volume of data for the screen layout or RFC. This data is compressed before being sent over the network so that, in effect, a much smaller volume of data is sent.

Figure 7.2 shows an example of a statistics record with extremely slow **[Ex]** GUI communication. Of the 27.5 seconds the transaction step takes, 22.5 seconds can be attributed to GUI time. In this case, the volume of data transferred (Terminal Out-Message field, not shown in the figure) is 17KB. At 1.5 seconds per kilobyte, the transfer rate does not meet our expectations.

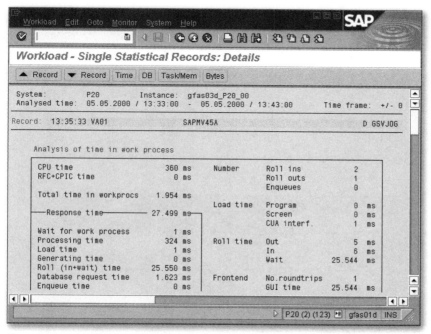

Figure 7.2 Example of a Statistics Record (Transaction STAD) with Extremely Slow GUI Communication

In a subsequent analysis step, we'll look closely at the network between the presentation and application levels. To do so, you can use the Check LAN by Ping function in the operating system monitor:

1. In the operating system monitor (Transaction ST06), select OTHER FUNCTIONS • LAN CHECK BY PING. Then select the Presentation Server function.

2. You will see a list of all of the logged-on presentation servers. Mark the presentation server you want to analyze (or choose 10 presenta-

tion servers at random) and select it using the Pick function. Then start the network analysis with the 10 x Ping function.

3. Figure 7.3 shows an example of the analysis result. Ten presentation servers were selected in this example; their names and IP addresses are shown in the Server Name and Server IP columns, respectively. The minimum, average, and maximum runtimes for a ping command (Min/ms, Avg/ms, and Max/ms columns, respectively) are shown on the screen for each of these servers, as well as the number of pings that were not answered (in the Loss column). Typical response times for a ping with a packet size of 4KB are as follows:

- In a local area network (LAN): <20 milliseconds

- In a wide area network (WAN): <50 milliseconds

- With a modem connection (for example, 56KB): <250 milliseconds

- There should be no loss of data packages (losses)

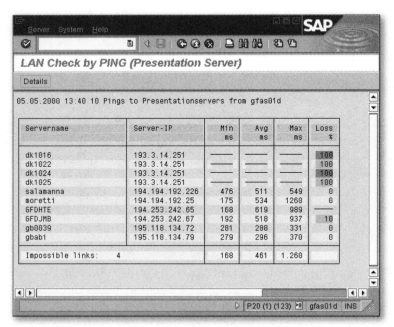

Figure 7.3 Example of a Network Analysis Between Application and Presentation Levels (Transaction ST06)

The screen image shown in Figure 7.3 is taken from the same SAP system as Figure 7.2. The analysis shows a completely corrupt network with major communication problems. Connections can't be set up to some of the presentation servers, whereas others respond with a turnaround of 300 to 500 ms. This explains the poor GUI times witnessed in the statistics record in Figure 7.2. For the moment, nothing more can be done here from the point of view of the SAP system. In the next steps, the network must be analyzed using appropriate vendors' tools, and the network must be repaired.

The second case that was described occurs if the transfer rate is good (on average 100 ms/KB or better), but problems arise because too much data is transferred in a transaction step. This problem can only be resolved by transferring less data in each step, which can be done by simplifying the screen. Often, standard SAP-supplied screens contain more information than individual users need for their work. Transaction variants allow the screens to be adapted to the actual needs of users and at the same time enable an improvement in performance. For a description of how to use transaction variants to optimize performance, refer to SAP Note 332210 and the example Transaction VA01 (Create Sales Order). If the problem still cannot be resolved, the transaction's developer must perform a detailed analysis.

Large volume of data

You should be able to solve the problem easily if the SAP_GUI_PROGRESS_INDICATOR module accounts for a considerable proportion of the overall response time in the Performance Trace. The module simply updates the status message in the footer of your GUI during a dialog step. For example, the module sends messages, such as Data Being Loaded, and updates the small clock in the lower-left corner of the screen, which displays the progress of an operation. You can easily disable this status display at the user level by setting the value of the parameter SIN to zero (0).

Other Optimization Options

We recommend that network communication between the GUI and application level be switched to Low Speed Connection in WAN (wide area network) environments. This will reduce the volume of data transferred per dialog step (see SAP Note 164102). You can activate the low-speed

Low-speed connection

connection in the SAP logon window by selecting the entry for an SAP system and selecting the menu option Low Speed Connection under the menu option Properties Advanced.

SAP Easy Access menu

Beginning with SAP Basis 4.6, the entry point for users is the *SAP Easy Access menu*, as opposed to the old SAP default menu. Users are presented with personalized menus that have been assigned to them based on their roles. The personalized menu only contains transactions users actually need. As an alternative, you can use the global SAP menu. Ensure that the SAP Easy Access menu works efficiently, because there is nothing more frustrating for users than having to wait for their initial screens after logon. The most important recommendations are to avoid unwieldy background images in the SAP Easy Access menu (which should be no larger than 20KB) and to restrict the number of transactions in a role (ideally, 1,000 or fewer). SAP Note 203924 provides information needed to efficiently customize the menu.

7.2   SAP NetWeaver Application Server

These days, every child (and we do mean *child* literally, here) knows the protocol language of the Internet. For example, if you enter the command *http://www.sesameworkshop.org/* in the address field of the web browser, a user-readable screen page of a well-known public TV children's show appears.

Here, the *Hypertext Transfer Protocol* (HTTP) is used, and *http://www.sesameworkshop.org/* is what is referred to as a *Unified Resource Locator* (URL), because it identifies a specific page on the Internet. The result of the request is displayed in *Hypertext Markup Language* (HTML).

Web applications

The SAP NetWeaver Application Server is the basis, among others, for SAP ERP, SAP NetWeaver BW, and SAP CRM. (Basis releases 6.10 through 6.40 were called SAP Web Application Server.) With the SAP NetWeaver Application Server (SAP NetWeaver AS), three techniques are available for working with Web applications (see also Figures 1.3 and 1.4 in Chapter 1, Performance Management, for further explanation of this information):

▶ **Web applications based on SAP Internet Transaction Server (ITS)**
This technique is available beginning with SAP R/3 3.1. SAP no longer recognizes applications based on the ITS as of SAP R/3 4.6C. Given that SAP and their customers have made substantial investments in ITS applications, SAP still maintains ITS and integrates has integrated it into the SAP NetWeaver Application Server. It is available in two versions: external ITS, an independent installation, and ITS integrated into the kernel of the ABAP server.

▶ **Web applications based on Business Server Pages and Web Dynpro for ABAP**
With SAP Web Application Server 6.10, Web applications can be developed directly in the ABAP development environment and executed in the ABAP runtime environment. These applications are called *Business Server Pages* (BSPs). To execute these Web applications, it is not necessary to install any additional software components (or a separate Web server). This technology is developed further in *Web Dynpro for ABAP*.

▶ **Web applications based on JavaServer Pages, Java servlets, and Web Dynpro for Java**
With the SAP J2EE Engine, the SAP Web Application Server contains a complete development and runtime environment for Java Web applications (JavaServer Pages and Java servlets) and for backend Java applications (Enterprise Java Beans). A particularly simple development environment for UIs is *Web Dynpro for Java* technology.

Web technology is not only used for creating user interfaces, but also increasingly for standardizing interfaces between systems. Here, we differentiate between Web services for communication between applications within an enterprise *(application to application,* A2A) and communication between enterprises *(business to business,* B2B). Both types of Web services use HTTP as the protocol language. XML *(eXtended Markup Language)* is used as the data-transfer language in Web services for system interfaces.

Web Services

The Internet Communication Manager (ICM) acts as the manager for the Web requests addressed to the SAP NetWeaver Application Server. It receives all requests from Web clients and distributes them to the ITS, SAP Dispatcher, or J2EE server.

Internet Communication Manager (ICM)

In the following section, we'll detail the options for analyzing the behavior of Web applications on the presentation server. The subsequent three sections are dedicated to analyzing server-related Web applications that run on the ITS, ABAP server, and SAP J2EE Engine. First, we want to conclude this section by providing some basic considerations for using Web UIs and ICM trace, which is used for all three SAP Web technologies.

7.2.1 Planning the Use of Web UI and the SAP GUI

All but a few SAP applications are Web-enabled, which means a company can strategically opt for a Web UI as their single UI solution. The alternative would be to implement a double-track solution and deploy the Web UI for specific users and applications and the classical SAP GUI for other users. In this section, we'll clarify the details that should guide you in this respect.

Pure Web applications

First, some SAP applications will only run with the Web UI. These include all solutions for the Internet or intranet, for example, SAP Employee Self-Service (SAP ESS), SAP CRM, and Enterprise Buyer Professional (E-Procurement). Here, the decision is already made. These Web applications are optimized for the requirements of the Internet.

The situation is somewhat different for many transactions in SAP ERP or SAP APO. These will run with the Web UI as well as the SAP GUI, but you should keep performance in mind.

Performance of the Web UI and the SAP GUI

Essentially, additional work is required to use the Web UIs (CPU time and data transfer), which can mean delays when compared to the SAP GUI. You should consider the following aspects:

▸ The CPU time required by the server for converting the SAP screens to HTML pages

▸ The higher data transfer between the server and browser (in comparison to data transfer between the application level and the SAP GUI)

▸ The generation time of the Web browser: higher than the processing time in the SAP GUI

The extent to which the response time is faster for a user using the Web UI as opposed to the SAP GUI depends ultimately on the functions used and the hardware. You can assume around one extra second for the CPU time on the ITS and the frontend. With respect to a higher volume of traffic, SAP rightly refers to its SAP GUI as an *ultra-thin client*, because the data traffic between the application level and the GUI is very low, about 3 to 5KB per screen switch for transactions with controls. In SAP NetWeaver Application Server Web transactions, 10 to 40KB are transferred. Therefore, SAP products are at the lower end of the Internet standard in terms of data traffic; typical web pages transfer up to 200KB. This increased data traffic is barely noticeable in terms of turnaround in high-bandwidth LANs. However, this difference can seriously impair the performance of the Web UI when compared to the SAP GUI in a WAN with low bandwidth and high latency time. We therefore recommend that you perform evaluation measurements as described in the following sections.

Similar considerations apply for using SAP NetWeaver BW. Here you must decide on the use of SAP Business Explorer (BEx) Web analyzer, a Microsoft Excel-based frontend with an SAP add-in for communication with the SAP NetWeaver BW server, and Web-based reporting.

7.2.2 HTTP Trace in the Internet Communication Manager

At the beginning of this chapter, we mentioned that all Web requests to the SAP NetWeaver Application Server are run via the Internet Communication Manager (ICM). Chapter 2, Monitoring Hardware, Databases, and SAP Basis, presented a bottleneck analysis for these components.

You can activate a trace on the ICM. Call the ICM monitor (Transaction SMICM) and navigate to GOTO • HTTP PLUGIN • SERVER LOGS. Under the Loghandler menu option, you can find the functions Display Entries, Activate, and Deactivate. In the default display, the HTTP trace displays the IP address of the Web server, the time stamp, the HTTP command, and the return value, for example, 200 for a successful processing, the size of the request in bytes, and the duration of the request.

ICM Monitor

The configuration of the parameter `icm/HTTP/logging_0` determines which data is traced. With parameter maintenance (Transaction RZ11), you can find detailed documentation that describes the standard log file formats.

Logging in the
end-to-end trace

For an end-to-end (E2E) trace using SAP Solution Manager, HTTP logging is activated in a target-oriented manner to measure the server times. You can configure the ICM so that an HTTP log entry is only written if the E2E trace plug-in is used. The ICM checks whether the request includes the field X-CorrelationID and then writes a log entry. For this purpose, the parameter `icm/HTTP/logging_0` is set to `PREFIX=/, LOGFORMAT=SAPSMD, LOGFILE=icmhttp.log, MAXSIZEKB= 10240, SWITCHTF=day, FILEWRAP=on` .

7.3   Analyses on the Presentation Server

All server components can possibly be technically flawless, yet users still complain of poor performance. This section will describe a procedure to use in this situation. For the most part, this solution is independent of the server used, which means it can be used for an ABAP server, ITS, J2EE Engine, or any other server technology. You can also use this method to analyze the HTTP flow of Web applications in your online bank.

Parallel queries

Figure 7.4 shows the cycle of a Web application transaction step from the presentation server view. Whereas in the previously described SAP GUI scenario the interactions between the presentation and application servers run sequentially, here the web browser can start multiple requests to the Web server at the same time and build the data parallel to the running requests. For a request to the Web server, there are four decisive times, which are denoted A, B, C, and D in the figure:

▶ **Time A (beforeNavigate2)**
The web browser receives the message that a request is to be started either via user interaction or during the preparation of a previously started request. At this time, the preparation time starts.

▶ **Time B**
The preparation time ends and the web browser sends the request to the Web server.

▶ **Time C**
The web browser has received all information from the Web server, and communication is completed with a return value, for example, 200 for a successful transfer. Now the rendering phase starts.

▶ **Time D (documentComplete)**
The rendering of the request is completed.

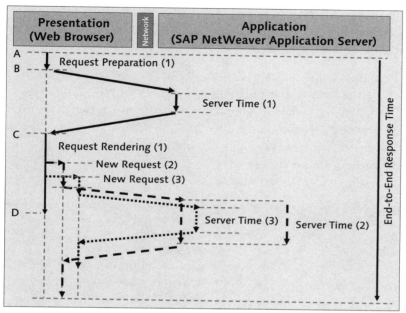

Figure 7.4 Transaction Step of a Web Application Between the Presentation Server (Web Browser) and the Application Server (Web Server)

7.3.1 Presentation Server Trace for Web Applications

The presentation server trace is created using the *SAP HTTP plug-in* of the SAP Solution Manager. The practical handling of trace plug-ins has already been described in detail in Chapter 4, Identifying Performance Problems in ABAP and Java Programs (for instance, Figure 4.4). | SAP HTTP plug-in

Some data collected by the trace plug-in on the presentation server is displayed directly in the trace plug-in. These values are the transferred data volume (Sent Bytes, Received Bytes), requests and responses, and the maximum and current number of connections to the SAP NetWeaver Application Server.

In practice, SAP Solution Manager carries out the trace preparation and displays the requests on the time axis. However, you can take critical key figures from the trace file without requiring SAP Solution Manager (which will be described in this section for didactical reasons). For this purpose, analyze the trace file, which you can find on the presentation server in the *BusinessTransaction.xml* file, under the creation date and name in the *logs* subdirectory. You can view the data file, for example, in a spreadsheet program or another suitable program for displaying XML files.

Transaction step At the transaction step level, that is, the time between two Next Step clicks, you determine the CPU times for the user CPU and the system CPU (ucpu and kcpu fields). As previously mentioned, a transaction step usually involves several requests to the Web server. For each request, the parameters described in Table 7.1 and the time of the web browser event, such as beforeNavigate2 (time A in our description) and documentComplete (time D), are recorded.

Field	Explanation
dsrGuid	Universally unique identifier (UUID) for the distributed statistic record. Based on this identifier, you can identify all subsequent statistic records created in the SAP NetWeaver Application Server for this request and for all traces (performance, SQL, and functional).
x-timestamp	Send time of the request (time B in our description).
Duration	Response time of a request in milliseconds. The time measurement starts with the sending of the first byte and ends with the receipt of the last byte (time period between B and C).
ReturnCode	Return value of the request, for example, 200 (successful transfer) or 401 (no authorization), or the cache entry if the request can be answered from the browser buffer.
Sent	Data volume sent in bytes, uncompressed.
Rcvd	Data volume received in bytes, uncompressed.
RequestLine	Line information of the request.
RequestHeader	Header information of the request.
ResponseHeader	Header information of the response.

Table 7.1 Presentation Server Trace Fields

Using these values, you determine the following critical key figures for each transaction step:

Key Figures

▶ **Total runtime of the request**
Corresponds to the time required on the server and network (`duration`)

▶ **Transferred data volume (uncompressed)**
Total of the transferred data volume of all requests to the Web server (Sent, Rcvd)

▶ **Browser CPU time**
Total user and system CPU time (`ucpu`, `kcpu`)

▶ **Total response time**
Difference between the first `beforeNavigate2` time and the last `documentComplete`.

Because several requests and the CPU-consuming preparation of the server requests run in parallel, a total of the CPU times and the request times is not the total response time; it is usually larger.

[+]

The total of request runtime and browser CPU time are good key figures for determining at which point performance problems occur and how you need to proceed:

▶ **The browser CPU time is high**
You have to consider whether the PC being used is perhaps not powerful enough. If this accounts for a significant part of the runtime, you can assume that an investment in new hardware will ensure additional performance.

▶ **The requests' runtime total is high**
There is a problem in either the network or the server.

For network connections with low throughput (for example, a WAN), you can check the relation of the transferred data volume to the response time for a request to clarify the situation. If this relation approximately corresponds to your network capacity, for example, 64KB/second for an ISDN connection, you can assume that the network connection causes the bottleneck; however, this is only an indication, because you can't predict the compression rate. In Windows, you can only measure the compressed data volume using operating system tools such as the PER-

FMON program (described in the next section). Conversely, you can't automatically assume that the server is responsible if the relation of the transferred data volume to the response time is considerably smaller than the network capacity, because there are also numerous other performance pitfalls in the network, such as large latencies. To solve this question, you need to find the server time required, which SAP Solution Manager determines via an end-to-end trace.

In all cases, you can improve performance by optimizing the application, that is, by transferring less data or reducing the number of requests to the Web server to avoid unnecessary routing of Web requests.

[+] Instead of the SAP HTTP plug-in described here, you can use third-party tools.

7.3.2 Operating System Performance Tools

PERFMON On Windows platforms, you can use the presentation server trace or the PERFMON program to view the behavior of your presentation server on the time axis:

1. Start PERFMON on your Windows presentation server. Select START RUN • PERFMON. (If PERFMON is not there, you can install it by selecting START SETTINGS • CONTROL PANEL • ADD/REMOVE PROGRAMS.)

2. Set up PERFMON:

    ▶ First, measure the CPU utilization on your presentation server. In the PERFMON menu, select EDIT • ADD TO CHART. Select the value Processor for Object and the value %Processor Time for Counter.

    ▶ You will also need the transferred data volume for your analysis. Select the value Network Interface for Object and the value Bytes Received/sec for Counter. Note: Depending on the type of network connection, the Category and Item name may differ from these examples. You may have to start processes at the Windows level to monitor network traffic.

3. Start your analysis: To do this, call the Web application you want to test. In the PERFMON screen, observe how quickly the network and CPU utilization increase on the presentation server after the application is started.

An evaluation of the analysis provides information that relates to:

Evaluation

▶ **The browser CPU time (also referred to as the rendering time)**
This is the time during which your browser is busy generating the HTML page. You will recognize this if the CPU utilization is close to 100%.

▶ **The network transfer time**
This is the time it takes for data to be transferred to the browser. You can identify it by the high network transfer rate. For example, if you use an ISDN line, you can see that the bandwidth of the ISDN line is at 8KB/sec.

▶ **The residual time**
If neither the CPU activity on your presentation server nor the network activity are being measured, although the hourglass appears in the browser, you can assume that the time can be found on the SAP NetWeaver Application Server.

7.3.3 Continuously Monitoring Web Applications

With the Alert Monitor in the CCMS, you can monitor sequences of web pages with periodic test requests. In a Web store, for example, you can use this tool to check requests at intervals of 10 minutes, such as if catalog access to selected products is still possible or if the product configurator, pricing, or availability check are still working. CCMS offers a special environment for this: the *Generic Request and Message Generator* (GRMG), in which you can define and run your own test applications.

Generic Request and Message Generator

In a typical Web scenario (for example, Internet sales in SAP CRM), this type of test would run as follows: Periodically at defined intervals, the CCMS monitoring infrastructure sends a test request to the GRMG test application. This application is a JSP servlet or an SAP ABAP object class supplied by SAP, or it can be written specifically for the customer's application. This test application tests the availability of components needed for the correct functioning of the Internet application. The result of the test is transferred to the CCMS monitoring infrastructure. From there, the corresponding alerts can, for example, be sent to the graphic alert manager in SAP Solution Manager or to an email or telephone server via SAPConnect.

Monitoring test applications is an ideal complement to the internal monitoring of the SAP NetWeaver Application Server. It not only tests the technical availability of the application, but can also provide details on the result of an application (for instance, has a reasonable price been calculated?). However, if an alarm is set off (possibly indicating the failure of a Web application), no further insight is provided for analyzing the cause of the error. Furthermore, it is not proactive; in other words, it only reports reactive errors, whereas monitoring work processes could trigger an alarm if a certain utilization level is exceeded, although the end user has not yet detected problems.

You will find technical documentation in the SAP Service Marketplace under *http://service.sap.com/systemmanagement* • SYSTEM MONITORING.

Non-SAP Tools Many vendors now offer tools for monitoring URLs. Appendix G refers to an web page that summarizes information on such monitoring products.

These tools enable central monitoring of strategically important web pages, regardless of which server supplies the pages. They also offer content check; in other words, it is possible to check whether the correct contents are displayed. You can also define other URL transactions, that is, sequences of HTML pages, which should be run periodically. (You have to ensure here that no real documents are created.)

7.4   Internet Transaction Server

Since SAP R/3 3.1, it has been possible to directly access the SAP application layer via the Internet Transaction Server (ITS) and a Web server from a web browser. Microsoft Internet Information Server and Netscape Enterprise Server are examples of suitable Web servers in this context.

7.4.1   ITS Fundamentals

AGate and WGate The ITS comprises two components: the *WGate* and the *AGate*. The WGate sets up the connection to the Web server. Its task is to recognize and forward Web server requests that are addressed to the ITS. On the NT platform, the WGate is a dynamic link library (DLL) that is incorporated into the Web server. The AGate is the portal to the SAP application level and handles the main work on the ITS. It reads input data from the Internet/intranet HTTP query and sends it to the SAP application level. The incoming SAP screens then convert it to HTML pages.

Various techniques are available to application developers for implementing Web applications for their SAP solutions. The most important of these are:

▶ In the *SAP GUI for HTML*, the AGate generically converts the SAP transaction screen to HTML. As a result, every SAP transaction can be executed in the browser (with a few minor restrictions). HTML-specific programming is not necessary.

▶ *Easy Web Transactions* (EWTs) replace the earlier Internet Application Components (IACs). An EWT comprises a transaction in the SAP system and HTML templates on the ITS AGate. If an EWT is called from the browser, the AGate starts the transaction in the SAP system. The AGate logs on here via the DIAG protocol and appears like a Windows GUI to the application server. The AGate reads the contents from the screen returned by the application server, including the fields, table, buttons, and so on and inserts these into the HTML template at the appropriate places.

▶ In the case of Easy Web Transactions (EWTs) with flow logic, the dialog flow is exported to the ITS; in other words, program text in the ITS (so-called flow logic files) determine which screen will be processed next. In this way, only the data retrieval takes place at the application and database level, generally via RFCs.

▶ With a WebRFC, HTML preparation takes place at the application level. If a WebRFC query is executed in the browser, the WGate and AGate forward this query directly as an RFC to the application level. The data is then retrieved at this level, and the complete HTML page is generated and transferred via the RFC interface. The AGate and WGate send the completed HTML page to the browser.

Web application techniques can be classified according to which part of the transaction is executed at the application level and which part on the ITS. Table 7.2 provides a detailed list of the steps executed by different Web applications.

Programming models

	EWT Without Flow Logic	EWT with Flow Logic	SAP GUI for HTML	WebRFC
Logon at SAP application level	DIAG protocol	RFC protocol	DIAG protocol	RFC protocol
Business logic (data retrieval, updating, and calculation)	Application and database level			
Generating HTML pages	AGate (from HTML template and SAP screen)	AGate (generic from SAP screen)	Application level	
Flow logic (dialog flow)	Application level	AGate (with flow logic file)	Application level	

Table 7.2 Programming Modules for Web Applications with the SAP ITS

Before we discuss configuration and tuning options for the ITS, let's examine in detail how a dialog step is executed in a Web application.

Logging on to the application server

If you want to call an Easy Web Transaction via the Internet, you will typically enter a URL such as this: *http://<sapwebserver>.<company.com>/ scripts/wgate/<tcode>/!*

This URL can be interpreted as follows: *<company.com>* stands for your Internet address and *<sapwebserver>* for the name of the Web server belonging to your SAP system. The */scripts/wgate* suffix indicates to the web server that this query is being forwarded to the WGate. The WGate then forwards the query directly to the ITS AGate. Figure 7.5 shows these steps as steps ❶ and ❷.

The AGate interprets *<tcode>* as the name of a service file, *<tcode>.srvc,* and searches for it from the directory of its service files (step ❸ in Figure 7.5). Among other things, the AGate finds the name of the SAP transaction being called in this file. According to naming conventions, the name of the service file should comply with the transaction code.

[Ex] Typical Web transactions include those from the SAP Online Store (Transaction VW01 or WW10) or from the human resources department: employee self-services such as time recording on the Web (Transaction CATW) or travel accounting on the Web (Transaction PRWW). In accordance with naming conventions, the associated service files would then be *vw01.srvc*, *ww10.srvc*, and so on.

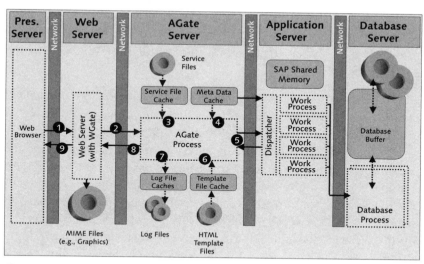

Figure 7.5 Transaction Steps in the SAP ITS

With the information from the service file, the AGate logs on to the application level ❺. This is done via the DIAG protocol for EWTs without flow logic and the SAP GUI for HTML, and via the RFC protocol for EWTs with flow logic and WebRFC (see Table 7.2).

Data retrieval for the transaction reads the data from the database and calculates the defined dependencies. If necessary, the data is checked and changed in the database. Data retrieval, update, and calculation are performed essentially at the application and database levels.

The AGate now generates the HTML page from the SAP screen returned to the AGate from the application level. For an EWT, the AGate searches in its templates directory for an HTML template that belongs to the relevant service and fills this with the data from the SAP screen ❻. The generated HTML page is sent to the WGate ❼, which supplements the HTML page with integrated multipurpose Internet mail extensions (MIME) files (for instance, graphics and audio files) and sends it to the browser ❾.

Generating HTML pages

351

SAP GUI for HTML You can call up the SAP GUI for HTML as follows: *http://<sapwebserver>* *.<company.com>/scripts/WGate/webgui/!*. This activates the *webgui.srvc* service in the AGate. When you enter this URL, you are presented with a logon screen. When you have logged on to the application level, the *webgui* service translates all transactions to HTML, enabling you to work through your browser just like with the SAP GUI for Windows or the SAP GUI for Java.

WebRFC The following syntax starts a *WebRFC query*: *http://<sapwebserver>.<company.* *com>/scripts/WGate/webrfc/!?_function =<function module> &<_variable1>=* *<value>....* The first thing to notice from the address is that the *webrfc.srvc* service is called. This is followed by the name of the RFC module and the variables (separated by question marks) to be passed to the module. An example in which the WWW_GET_REPORT module is called with the variable REPORT = RSCONN01 reads as follows: *http://<sapwebserver>.<company.* *com>/scripts/WGate/webrfc/!?_function=www_get_report&_report=rsconn01*. For the WebRFC, the entire HTML page is already generated at the application level. The AGate and WGate then simply forward this to the browser.

Each of these transactions has advantages and disadvantages. When you start a Web development project, you have to decide which technique best meets the functional requirements of the project. Different techniques impact the sizing, configuration, and performance of the ITS. We'll discuss these in the next sections.

7.4.2 Configuring ITS

Thanks to its architecture, the ITS can be scaled almost arbitrarily. In this section, we'll show you how to optimally adapt the ITS to load requirements.

For a development, test, or small production system without special high-availability requirements, it is possible to install all levels of the SAP technology (presentation level, Internet level, application level, database level) on one computer.

If availability and throughput requirements are greater, it makes sense to distribute the individual levels over several computers. (Security also plays a role here, as we'll explain.)

The first step in scaling is to provide separate computers for the Internet level (ITS and Web servers), thereby separating these from the SAP application level and the database level.

Configuring ITS Instances

The ITS, like the application level, is organized in instances, which means several *ITS instances* can be installed on one computer and managed separately. Theoretically, it is possible for the different ITS instance services to point to different SAP systems. However, for administration reasons, this is not recommended for production operations. You should set up your system landscape so that one ITS instance always points to one SAP system.

ITS instances

The ITS instance can be logged on to the application level using either a dedicated instance (and specifying the application server and instance number) or via a *logon group* (specifying the message server and a logon group). For optimal availability and workload distribution, you should use a logon group. This setting is made in the service files on the AGate.

Logon via a logon group

Depending on throughput requirements, you can run several ITS instances (possibly pointing to different SAP systems) on one computer. You can also run several ITS instances for one SAP system and distribute these to different computers. To ensure optimally high availability, at least two computers are needed for the Internet level, each of which runs one ITS instance. Each ITS instance points to at least two SAP instances via a logon group, which in turn are configured on different computers.

Scalable ITS instances

For security reasons, access to the AGate file system must always be protected, because anyone who has access to the AGate can define a service and execute all function modules released for Internet usage on the application server. The best way to protect the AGate is to set up a *firewall* between the AGate and the WGate, because the data flow is then the responsibility of SAP and can be properly monitored according to proprietary protocols. Security experts report that a firewall around

Firewall between AGate and WGate

the Web server (WGate) is much less reliable. The best configuration is to operate the Web server (with WGate) and the AGate on different computers and to separate these via a firewall. This configuration is mandatory if the ITS connects your SAP system with the Internet. It is up to you to decide whether this high degree of security is also appropriate for intranet projects.

An ITS configuration that is optimized in terms of availability, performance, and security therefore comprises a dual Web server configuration (with WGate), ITS Agate, and SAP instance; if one computer fails, the remaining computer can take over the load. The database and the application levels should be protected in parallel with the enqueue server using a suitable, high-availability solution at the operating system level (switch-over solution).

Configuration of Work Processes, Sessions, and Caches

Work processes and sessions
Queries from the dispatcher (mapping manager process) are assigned within an ITS instance to an ITS work process (work thread). The ITS work process copies the query data to a specific memory area — the user session. You can define the number of ITS work processes and sessions on the ITS. You will find an overview of performance-related ITS parameters in Appendix C.

The ITS architecture is therefore similar to an SAP application instance, which also has a dispatcher and several work processes that access global user contexts (sessions). However, the ITS does not have a dispatcher queue. If all ITS work processes are reserved, the dispatcher sends back an error message to the browser (while an application instance "parks" the query, in this case in the dispatcher queue).

Cache mechanisms
The ITS uses *cache mechanisms* to optimize performance, which means service files, interfaces from SAP function modules invoked by the ITS, HTML templates, module calls (when using flow logic), and log entries are stored in the main memory. These cache mechanisms can be enabled and disabled via parameters (see Appendix C).

To reduce the volume of data transferred, you should activate compression in the ITS service file. You will find a description of the parameters and the corresponding SAP Note in Appendix C. You can only compress data with ITS if the web browser allows it.

Data compression

The following factors can limit the performance of the ITS:

Performance-limiting factors

► **Hardware bottlenecks**
A CPU or main memory bottleneck (high paging activity).

► **The number of work processes and user sessions**
If too few are configured, error messages are issued, because the ITS can no longer edit the queries being sent to it.

► **Restriction on the addressable memory**
The addressable memory is restricted to 2GB per AGate process because of the current Windows architecture. If the AGate process requests additional memory during runtime, error messages are issued that can be monitored in the AGate and operating system log files.

► **Restrictions caused by network connections**
The AGate process can set up a maximum of 4,096 user sessions on the application level. This restricts the maximum number of logged-on users per AGate and SAP application instance. Therefore, you may have to configure several AGate and SAP application instances.

► **Incorrect configuration of the cache mechanisms**
If the cache mechanisms are not activated correctly, too much file traffic will be needlessly generated.

To avoid hardware bottlenecks before an installation, you should have your hardware partner draw up a sizing proposal before production operation starts. You will find information on ITS sizing in the SAP Service Marketplace under *http://service.sap.com/sizing*. Recommended settings for work processes, sessions, and cache mechanisms are available in Appendix C.

Sizing

If bottlenecks arise at runtime, you can localize them using analysis tools. You will find a description of the tools and associated methods in the next sections.

7.4.3   ITS Administration Tools

Administration
instance

You can manage and monitor an ITS instance in the administration instance of ITS; moreover, you can also monitor the ITS using the central CCMS monitor (see Appendix C). Start the administration instance in a browser, using the following URL: *http://<sapwebserver>.<company.com>:<portnumber>/scripts/wgate/ admin/!,* where *<company.com>* stands for your Internet address, *<sapwebserver>* is the ITS Web server, and *<portnumber>* stands for the TCP port to which the administration instance "listens."

You can use the administration instance to perform the following:

▶ Start and stop ITS instances

▶ Change ITS parameters

▶ Evaluate the ITS log files (error and performance logs)

▶ Establish current performance and capacity utilization

Log files

The log files you can monitor are the AGate log (*AGate.trc*), dispatch log (*Mmanager.trc*), performance log (*PERFORMANCE.LOG*), workload distribution log (*LOADSTAT.LOG*), and access log (*ACCESS.LOG*).

7.4.4   Performing a Bottleneck Analysis for the ITS

Problem: All ITS
work processes
are busy

If the number of free ITS work processes is close to zero, error messages are issued, because the ITS can no longer process the queries sent to it. Check whether the problem can be resolved by increasing the number of ITS work processes. Essentially, the same rule applies here as for the application level: The number of ITS work processes should only be increased if hardware resources are still free. However, the problem of work processes being occupied can also be caused by a programming error, which means the program on either the AGate (business HTML or flow logic) or application server (ABAP) was configured inefficiently and requires an unnecessary volume of resources (or in extreme cases, gets caught in an endless loop).

Problem:
Insufficient
addressable
memory

You can check the display of freely addressable (virtual) memory to see whether this will cause a bottleneck. Overall, on Windows, 2GB can be addressed per AGate process. If this limit is reached, you can resolve the problem by starting several AGate processes for each ITS instance. A bottleneck in the addressable memory also causes an error entry to be written to the AGate log (*AGate.trc*).

You will recognize a *hardware bottleneck* by a high level of CPU utilization and a high paging rate (see also next section).

Problem: Hardware bottleneck

The ITS hangs if no more drive space is available. This can happen, for example, if log files are not reorganized as recommended over a long period or if you forget to reduce the trace level after preparing a detailed runtime analysis.

Problem: Standstill due to a lack of drive space

7.5 Business Server Pages (BSPs), Web Dynpro for ABAP, and Integrated ITS

This section will present the architectures behind Business Server Pages (BSPs), Web Dynpro for ABAP, and integrated ITS, as well as methods for monitoring their performance.

7.5.1 Fundamentals of Business Server Pages and Web Dynpro for ABAP

Business Server Pages and *Web Dynpro for ABAP* applications offer one possible way to write SAP Web applications. BSPs consist of individual web pages written in HTML and ABAP or JavaScript as scripting languages. Provided with the same technological basis, Web Dynpro for ABAP is a further development of a declarative, model-oriented development environment. The programming model of Web Dynpro for ABAP is based on the *Model View Controller (MVC) design pattern*. Originally developed in the Smalltalk-80 environment, it is the de facto standard for the development of user interfaces today. It allows for a strict separation of data models (Model), presentation of data on the interface (View), and processing control (Controller). As far as performance analysis methods are concerned, it makes no difference whether you use the simple BSP programming model or Web Dynpro for ABAP as the development environment. In the following sections, we'll present a performance analysis based on the static BSP development model.

BSPs and Web Dynpro for ABAP applications are developed entirely in the SAP Development Workbench, which means no BSP elements are stored in file systems outside the SAP system database, as happens with external SAP ITS or SAP J2EE Engine. An SAP work process generates the HTML pages at runtime. In SAP Basis 6.10, the SAP Development Workbench and the SAP runtime environment were enhanced with Internet Communication Framework (ICF) and Internet Communication Manager (ICM). Both are delivered and installed with SAP NetWeaver Application Server.

Logging on to the application server You can call a BSP application in an SAP system by entering the following URL in your web browser: *http://<sapserver>: <port>/sap/bc/bsp/ sap/<bsp_application>/<page>*, where *<sapserver>* stands for the name of an application server on which the SAP system is running. This must always be given in full, for example, *sapapp1.city.company.com,* and not just *sapapp1.* *<port>* is the TCP/IP port to which the application server answers. In SAP Web AS 6.10, the default value is 8080. As of SAP Web AS 6.20, the default value is zero for security reasons; the administrator must set it to the preferred value. *<bsp_application>* is the name of the BSP application, and *<page>* is the name of the page within the application.

[Ex] Each SAP NetWeaver Application Server is delivered with a few test applications and tutorials. To execute a BSP example, enter the following URL in your Internet browser: *http://<sapserver>:<port>/sap/bc/bsp/ sap/tutorial_2/default.htm,* where, *<sapserver>* stands for the name of the server on which the SAP Web Application Server is running. A window will then appear and ask you for your user name and password. When you have entered these correctly, a small Web application, Welcome to Our Online Book Catalog!, will appear in your browser.

A range of BSP test applications are supplied with each SAP NetWeaver Application Server, including those whose names begin with "IT" and training applications with names that begin with "tutorial."

[+] In SAP Web AS 6.10, the included BSP applications are automatically active. Beginning with SAP Web AS 6.20, for security reasons, BSP applications are not functional when delivered and must be explicitly activated (SAP Note 517484).

Figure 7.6 shows the development of a BSP application. On the left-hand side of the illustration is the HTML page Your Book Search Results as presented in a browser. On the right-hand side is the corresponding coding. A BSP application is initially made up of the actual web page, written in HTML, into which the ABAP coding for preparing data is embedded in tags, for example, ABAP loops for filling tables. The programming model is therefore similar to JavaServer Pages (JSPs), with which Java applications are integrated into HTML text.

Development environment for BSPs

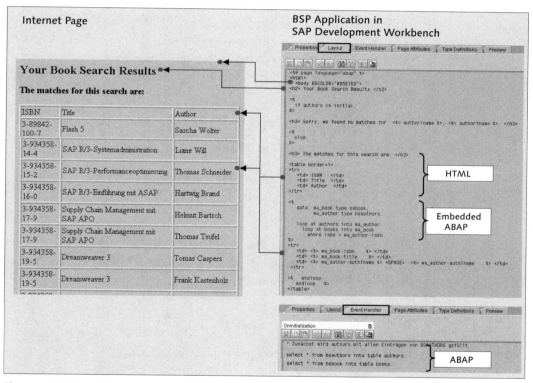

Figure 7.6 HTML Page "Your Book Search Results" (left) and the Corresponding Program Text in HTML and ABAP (right)

A BSP application also includes *events*, which are program segments written in ABAP that are processed at a particular point in time, such as when the web page is initialized or after data has been entered. These events enable the control of images on the page and the acquisition of data (for

Events

example, access to the database). A complete BSP application can be made up of several such web pages.

The SAP development environment (ABAP Workbench, Transaction SE80) has been enhanced with appropriate functions for BSP development. To display a BSP in an SAP system, proceed as follows in the Development Workbench:

1. Click the Repository Browser button.

2. In the box under the button, select BSP Application, and in the input field under it, enter "TUTORIAL_"2"," and confirm your entry.

3. In the Pages subtree of the tree that appears, look for the HTML pages that belong to the preferred BSP application. Select, for example, default.htm. You will now find yourself in the development environment for a specific BSP.

To see a preview of the web page, select the Preview tab.

To display the program code of the web page, select the Layout tab.

To display the events belonging to a BSP (that is, the program code executed when, for example, a page is called or when an entry is made), select the Events tab.

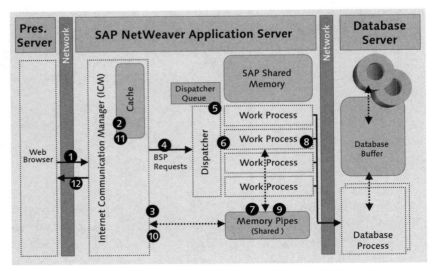

Figure 7.7 Transaction Step Cycle in SAP NetWeaver AS when a BSP Is Called

When a BSP is called, the steps shown in Figure 7.7 are executed to generate an HTML page. The web browser first sends its request to the Internet Communication Manager (ICM) ❶, which checks to see if the browser request can be answered using the information stored in its cache ❷. If not, it passes the request on to the SAP dispatcher ❹ after having stored the data in memory pipes ❸. Memory pipes form part of the shared memory of the SAP instance and are used in communication between the ICM and the SAP work processes. If a dialog work process is available for processing, and the dispatcher does not have to park the request in the queue ❺, the dispatcher passes the request on to a work process ❻, which reads the necessary data from the memory pipes ❼ and processes the request ❽. When the work process has processed the BSP and created the web page, it puts the data in the memory pipes ❾ and passes control back to the ICM. This, in turn, sends the prepared HTML page to the web browser ❿–⓬.

Generating HTML pages

7.5.2 Fundamentals of the Integrated ITS

The integrated ITS is implemented as the HTTP request handler in the Internet Communication Framework (ICF). The corresponding ITS request (that is, the ABAP program logic and creation of the HTML page) is processed in an ABAP work process. ITS templates and MIME files are stored directly in the database. You activate the integrated ITS using the profile parameter `itsp/enable = 1`. The programming models are supported by the integrated ITS SAP GUI for HTML and Easy Web Transactions (EWT), without flow logic.

You can log on to the SAP GUI for HTML via the URL *http://<sapserver>. <company.com>:<port>/sap/bc/gui/sap/its/webgui?*. Start a typical Easy Web Transaction, the SRM eShop, by entering *http://<sapserver>:<port>/sap/ bc/gui/sap/its/bbpstart/!*

Compared to the old, external ITS, the integrated version provides major total cost of ownership (TCO) wins that can be allocated to the following architecture changes:

Architecture changes

▶ The ICM assumes the role of web Server so that the integrated ITS does not require a separate Web server.

▶ The integrated ITS is implemented as the HTTP request handler in the Internet Communication Framework (ICF); a separate installation (of the AGate) is not required.

▶ Software logistics, monitoring, and administration can be used as in any other ABAP program.

Migration

Provided you use an external ITS and change the version, we recommend the integrated ITS. Services written for the external ITS, however, don't automatically run in the integrated version, but you must implement a migration to the Internet Communication Framework (ICF). In SAP Online Help, you can find a migration guide for this purpose.

Main memory consumption

The integrated ITS uses the global extended memory (*SAP EG Memory*) for storing the runtime versions of HTML business templates, also referred to as *preparsed templates*. Here, a separate runtime template is stored for every browser type (for example, Internet Explorer or Firefox) and language, so that the size of the memory area can be derived from the total of the number of different applications, number of browser types, number of languages, and an average memory requirement per application. You can assume an average memory requirement per application of 10MB for an SAP GUI for HTML applications. This is supplemented with approximately 3MB per session in extended memory. The size of SAP EG memory is configured using the `em/global_area_MB` parameter. For a large number of planned sessions, there might be configuration problems in computers with 32-bit operating systems. You can solve these problems by switching to 64-bit hardware or distributing the load to multiple computers.

Objects stored in the shared memory only include HTML business templates. Graphics files (*MIME files*) are stored in the local ICM memory.

Monitoring and configuration parameter

You use the ITS status monitor (Transaction SITSPMON) to monitor required memory. You will find an overview of the configuration parameters in Appendix C.

7.5.3 Fundamentals of ABAP Web Services

You can use ABAP Web services to communicate between applications and the HTTP protocol.

A very simple Web service is *http://<server>:<port>/sap/bc/ping*. It tries [Ex] to log on to the ABAP server and returns a simple message if logon was successful: Server Successfully Reached. ABAP Web services are defined in the service maintenance (Transaction SICF), and our example can be found under default_host, sap, bc, ping. If you open the service definition and then navigate to the Handler List table, you can find the implementing class, in our example, CL_HTTP_EXT_PING. Double-click the class to navigate there. A simple reply document is created with the logon message.

The performance analysis of ABAP Web services for communication between systems does not differ from BSPs, Web Dynpro for ABAP, or internal ITS. Therefore, it will be included in the sections that follow.

7.5.4 Implementing the Performance Analysis of ABAP Web Services (BSPs, Web Dynpro for ABAP, and ITS Applications)

When analyzing the performance of ABAP Web services, you can use all of the procedures and tools you have previously used for performance analyses on SAP GUI applications. However, there are some special characteristics to in mind, which we'll discuss here.

If users complain about poor performance, and if there actually is a performance problem, start the work process monitor (Transaction SM50 or SM66). If all work processes are occupied, you should carry out a bottleneck analysis, as described in Chapter 2, Monitoring Hardware, Databases, and SAP Basis, to isolate the cause of the bottleneck and identify the user or program at the root of the problem.

General performance analysis

If you cannot see any long-running processes in the work process monitor, but users still notice a problem with performance, start the ICM monitor (Transaction SMICM). If all ICM threads are occupied, then the problem might be resolved by increasing the number of ICM threads.

If you use integrated ITS and a problem with high memory allocation exists in the extended memory, refer to the notes on integrated ITS in Section 7.52 Fundamentals of the Integrated ITS.

To evaluate past performance, call up the workload monitor (Transaction ST03N). Along with the familiar task types (for instance, Dialog, Background, Update, and so on), the monitor now displays the new task types HTTP, HTTPS, and SMTP (only where the requests in question are processed by the system). Based on these task types, you can easily evaluate the activity and response times of specific requests.

Activating the performance statistics

To analyze performance with the workload monitor, you must activate the writing of performance statistics. By default, the SAP kernel does not write statistics records for HTTP, HTTPS, or SMTP requests. To activate the statistics, set the value of SAP profile parameter `rdisp/no_statistic` to blank. (In other words, in the profile parameter file, add the row `rdisp/no_statistic =`. The standard kernel value is PLUGIN.) You can change this SAP profile parameter in a running system. To do so, proceed as follows:

1. First, in the system load monitor (Transaction ST03N), select the Expert role (button in the upper-left corner).

2. Then in the tree, follow the menu path COLLECTOR & PERF. DATABASE • STATISTICS RECORDS AND FILES • ONLINE PARAMETERS, DIALOG STEP STATISTICS.

3. The Runtime Parameters of Statistics Collection table is displayed. In the `rdisp/no_statistic` column, delete the value PLUGIN. (As long as the value PLUGIN remains in the `rdisp/no_statistic` column, no statistics records will be written. If the column is empty, then statistics writing is activated.)

4. Activate the changes you have made by clicking the Activate Values button.

In addition to the familiar task types Dialog, Background, Update, and so on, you will now find the task types HTTP, HTTPS, and SMTP in the workload monitor (where the system processes the requests in question). Online changes are only activated when you next start the corresponding SAP instance. To activate the statistics permanently, you have to change the parameter in the configuration file, as previously described.

Detailed analysis

In the transaction profile of the workload monitor, you can carry out a detailed analysis of the requested Web applications and select the granularity of the web page performance statistics to be displayed in the transaction profile. To do so, proceed as follows:

1. In the system load monitor (Transaction ST03N), select the Expert role (button in the upper-left corner).

2. In the tree, follow the path COLLECTOR & PERF. DATABASE • SYSTEM LOAD COLLECTOR • STATISTICS TO BE GENERATED • DIALOG STEP STATISTICS.

3. Select one of the following options:

   ▶ Complete Breakdown According to Application and Page: The performance statistics are created per web page, which means there will be an entry in the transaction profile for each web page processed.

   ▶ Break Down According to Application: As was mentioned, a BSP or Web Dynpro for ABAP application can comprise several web pages. With this setting, a performance statistic will be created in the transaction profile for each BSP application, but not broken down for each individual page.

   ▶ Accumulate Under Report SAPMHTTP: There is no breakdown according to ABAP application, which means all Web requests are brought together in the transaction profile under the entry SAPMHTTP.

From SAP NetWeaver 7.0 on (see SAP Note 992474), instead of the activation option, you can use the report `SWNC_CONFIG_URL` to configure this setting.

Activating statistics causes only a slight loss in performance, so it is almost always recommended. Only in systems with very heavy loads should you check to see if performance can be markedly improved by deactivating statistics for BSP applications.

If you want to analyze the performance of a particular ABAP Web service in detail, you can use single-record statistics (Transaction STAD). Given that ABAP Web services are mainly applications programmed in ABAP, tools available for detailed analysis include the Performance Trace, ABAP runtime analysis, and the debugger. (You can find an introduction to these tools in Chapter 4, Identifying Performance Problems in ABAP and Java Programs.)

Special
performance
analysis

To analyze the single-record statistics (Transaction STAD) for ABAP Web services, in the single-record selection screen, in the Task Type field, select the value H for HTTP requests or T for HTTPS requests. Writing of the single-record statistics must be activated in the SAP kernel, as previously described.

You can activate the ABAP runtime analysis (Transaction SE30) in service maintenance (Transaction SICF). In the object tree on the left-hand side of the screen, select an ABAP Web service. Then in the menu, select the function EDIT • RUNTIME ANALYSIS • ACTIVATE. A dialog window is displayed, into which you enter the name of the BSP and the period for which the runtime analysis should be active. Select the checkbox Only Calls from SAPGUI-IP, and select the function Activate.

For the evaluation, select the menu function SYSTEM • RESOURCES • RUNTIME ANALYSIS • EXECUTE, or enter Transaction SE30. You will then find yourself in the maintenance transaction for the ABAP runtime analysis, which is presented in detail in Chapter 4, Identifying Performance Problems in ABAP and Java Programs. To display the runtime analysis of an ABAP Web service, click the Other File button. A dialog window is displayed in which you can select the performance file by indicating which user executed the ABAP Web service. The analysis is carried out as described in Chapter 4.

7.5.5 Monitoring Web Service Calls

If an ABAP server calls Web services, these calls are recorded in the statistics record. You can find the details of outbound HTTP calls in the single-records statistics under HTTP RECORDS • AS CLIENT. There you can find the time for the calls as Calling Time and data on the call targets and the quantity of data transferred.

Because the process of an HTTP call is very similar to a synchronous RFC, Figure 6.3 in Chapter 6, Workload Distribution and Interfaces, can help you gain a better understanding. For an HTTP call, the Calling Time in the HTTP Records section assumes the role of the RFC time. So for a transaction step with an HTTP call without an RFC call and SAP GUI control, the rule applies that the HTTP calling time must be greater than the roll wait time. If you detect a high roll wait time in the main part of the statistics record and cannot attribute this to either the RFC time or the GUI time, you should consider whether a time-intensive HTTP call could be the cause.

7.6   JavaServer Pages and Web Dynpro for Java

With the SAP J2EE Engine, the SAP NetWeaver Application Server has a full-fledged J2EE application server, making it possible to develop and operate Java applications on the basis of JavaServer Pages (JSPs), Java servlets, and Enterprise Java Beans.

You can install and operate the SAP J2EE Engine either as a freestanding component (for example, with SAP NetWeaver Portal) or as part of the SAP NetWeaver AS (such as with SAP ERP). When you install SAP NetWeaver AS, the SAP J2EE Engine is automatically (but optionally) installed.

7.6.1   Fundamentals of the SAP J2EE Engine, Portal, and Web Dynpro for Java

JavaServer Pages (JSPs) and Java servlets are programs that can be executed by a user via the HTTP protocol. In JSPs, the applications are made up of HTML pages with embedded Java code. Java servlets are Java programs that generate HTML pages. Along with JSPs, they represent the presentation and control logic of a business application. Enterprise Java Beans, on the other hand, are Java programs in which the application logic of a business application is programmed.

With the SAP NetWeaver Application Server, it is possible to develop Web applications in which presentation and control logic is represented in the Java runtime environment and application logic is represented in the ABAP runtime environment. There are numerous advantages to this approach, including the fact that investments already made in ABAP applications are protected and the access to experienced developers and processes in the ABAP area. It is possible to create applications completely in Java, however.

Distributing logic to ABAP and Java

Logging on to the
application server

You can use the following URL to log on to a Java application called Hello, which is delivered with the SAP J2EE Engine as an example: *http://<sapserver>:<port>/Hello.*

In general, you can access a Java Web application via the URL *http://<server>:<port>/<alias>*, where *<sapserver>* stands for the name of an application server on which the dispatcher of the J2EE clusters is running, and *<port>* is the TCP/IP port to which the dispatcher answers. You can find the port in the configuration file *cluster/dispatcher/cfg/services/http.properties*. For an installation of the J2EE Engine without SAP NetWeaver AS (a stand-alone installation), this will be port 3011. For an installation that is part of SAP NetWeaver AS, the port is 5xx00, where xx is the two-figure system number of the SAP instance. Finally, *<alias>* is the user-defined name of the application.

SAP NetWeaver
Portal

The *SAP NetWeaver Portal* is used in combination with the Java-based user management and is based on the *User Management Engine* (UME) to structure user web pages. Logon to SAP NetWeaver Portal is done via the URL *http://<sapserver>:<port>/portal/irj*. One or more roles can be assigned to a user. A role comprises one or more work areas (for instance, work set or work center) and is therefore the least granular unit in the hierarchy of portal units. Work areas, in turn, are combined in portal pages. Portal pages, in turn, consist of iViews, which are the smallest units, that is, the atoms of the user's portal application. The actual applications run in the iViews. Many preconfigured iView templates are available, which you can activate using simple configurations, for example, to integrate any SAP transaction in the SAP GUI for HTML, a web page selectable via an URL, or content of the knowledge management system in the portal. Other essential iView types are Java or Web Dynpro for ABAP applications. In addition, the portal offers more functions for navigating between applications, such as *object-based navigation* and *drag-and-relate* functionality.

Web Dynpro
for Java

Web Dynpro for Java is a descriptive development environment for the development of user interfaces in business applications and has been a strategic technology for SAP and the development of user interfaces since 2004. The user interfaces run in the web browser, and the development model is based on the Model View Controller concept (MVC).

You start a Web Dynpro for Java application using the following URL: *http://<sapserver>:<port>/webdynpro/dispatcher/<WebDynpro-Name>*. An example would be the very useful Web service navigator, which you can user to test the Web services (comparable to Test Transaction SM37 for ABAP function modules). Start it with the URL *http://<sapserver>:<port>/ webdynpro/dispatcher/sap.com/tc~esi~esp~wsnav~ui/WSNavigator*. You can find the */webdynpro/dispatcher/* schema in the presentation server trace and the statistics records so that you can easily identify a Web Dynpro application.

To process the request, the server must usually also obtain and process data. This can be done either with direct database access or indirectly via the ABAP server. Access to the ABAP server is via the Java Connector (JCo). From a technical point of view, this is Enterprise Java Beans in the Java runtime environment and BAPI in the ABAP runtime environment. Alternatively, you can access the database directly from a Java application via the following interfaces: Native JDBC (dynamic SQL, DB-platform dependent, and past SAP extensions, such as table buffering of Java data dictionary), Open SQL for Java (dynamic SQL, DB platform-independent, with table buffering), SQLJ (static SQL, as in ABAP), and EJB-CMP (Container-Managed Persistence). For more information on these interfaces, see the technical documentation on the SAP J2EE Engine.

Let's look at an example of an application you want to develop on the basis of SAP ERP. You have decided that a Web interface for a logistics application should be set up using the SAP J2EE Engine. Access should be made to tables in the SAP component Sales and Distribution (SD). The question you and the development team now face is whether it is better to access the SAP logistics tables directly from the Java Web application or if this should be done via the interfaces (BAPIs) of the ABAP server. If you use the BAPIs, access is also automatically made to the SAP Basis services, such as SAP table buffering, enqueue management, and unique document number assignment. Direct access to the database tables from the Java environment without using these services could lead to data inconsistencies in the application. Basic logistic functions such as availability check or pricing must also be done in Java, which can lead to problems of inconsistency, too. In this case, you should opt for "mixed" development, that is, using ABAP-BAPIs. An example of an application

[Ex]

of this type in the SAP ERP system is Employee Self-Services (ESS) and Manager Self-Services (MSS).

With SAP Web AS 6.30, enqueue management in Java is available. You can set locks via the enqueue server of the ABAP runtime environment. Here, inconsistency problems regarding locks can at least be avoided.

7.6.2 Analyzing Java Applications

In previous chapters, we presented tools for analyzing Java applications. We want to summarize them again here.

SAP Solution Manager Diagnostics provides lists, including the most expensive portal objects. The Top iView list provides all portal applications, regardless of where they are implemented. Top Servlets, Top Web Dynpro Applications, and Top KM Methods show you the most critical applications running on the SAP J2EE Engine, and the lists Top SQL Statements and Top JCo Call indicate the most expensive requests to the database and ABAP server (see Chapter 3, Workload Analysis).

With an overview of the programs to be analyzed, you can use the end-to-end trace of SAP Solution Manager, including the presentation server trace (this chapter), the statistics records, and the Introscope trace (see Chapter 4, Identifying Performance Problems in ABAP and Java Programs).

7.7 Summary

Basically, there are two sure-fire ways to create a performance problem in the area of frontend communication. The first is to transfer large volumes of data to the frontend client. The second is to program a high number of roundtrips (that is, communication steps between the frontend client and the server).

Applications based on the SAP GUI can often react to nonoptimal programming in a half-tolerant way, because the protocol between the SAP GUI and SAP NetWeaver Application Server is an SAP DIAG protocol, with which data transfer is kept to a minimum. For Web applications that use the HTTP protocol, on the other hand, even when programming is optimal, more data is usually transferred than with SAP GUI applications. With this type of application, substandard programming will almost certainly lead to performance problems.

Nonoptimal programming can mean that an application works fine in the LAN (local area network), such as in the developer's work center, but on the WAN (wide area network), such as at the work station of a company field sales employee, there may be catastrophic performance problems.

In this section we'll describe the performance aspects of four important techniques for SAP frontend programming.

In SAP GUI applications, RFCs have been used for communication between the SAP application level and the SAP presentation level to set up screen elements known as controls. Tools such as single-record statistics, Performance Trace (RFC trace), and network check are available in the operating system monitor for analyzing possible performance problems (for example, in the network-to-presentation servers).

There are several relevant points relating to the performance of the Web connection to the SAP Internet Transaction Server. First, there is the selection of the correct GUI: The SAP GUI for HTML is not the obvious choice for some user groups. In some cases, it makes sense to continue using the SAP GUI for Windows (or Java). ITS configuration involves the redundant installation of WGate and AGate; the configuration of the ITS work processes (threads), sessions, and caches; and the creation of SAP system logon groups. Finally, you should be familiar with ITS performance monitoring and analysis. The central CCMS Alert Monitor provides constant monitoring, whereas analyses with the ITS administration tool are helpful in the event of performance problems.

When operating Web applications based on Business Server Pages (BSPs) and Web Dynpro for ABAP, web pages are generated by the "classic" SAP work processes. Familiar tools such as the workload monitor and Performance Trace have been extended as necessary for performance analysis.

With the SAP J2EE Engine, you can develop and operate Web applications using JavaServer pages, Web Dynpro for Java, Java servlets, and Enterprise Java Beans. The SAP J2EE Engine is integrated into the SAP monitoring concept, that is, in the central CCMS control monitor.

The method described in this chapter for analyzing the performance of HTML pages on the presentation server (for instance, with the E2E trace plug-in of SAP Solution Manager and operating system tools such as PERFMON) is generic and can be used not only for HTML pages that have been generated by the SAP NetWeaver AS, but also for those generated by other servers.

Important Concepts in this Chapter

After reading this chapter, you should be familiar with the following concepts:

▶ Roll wait time, RFC time, and GUI time

▶ Controls and frontend communication

▶ Choosing the correct GUI: SAP GUI for Windows, SAP GUI for HTML, or SAP GUI for Java Environment

▶ Performance analysis using the SAP HTTP plug-in for Microsoft Internet Explorer and using PERFMON

▶ SAP Internet Transaction Server: WGate, AGate, thread and session concepts, and caching on the ITS

▶ Integrated ITS, Business Server Pages, and Web Dynpro for ABAP

▶ JavaServer Pages, Java servlets, Web Dynpro for Java, and Enterprise Java Beans

Questions

1. What is a high roll wait time?

   a) A unique indication of a GUI communication problem, for example, in the network between the presentation server and the application server.

   b) A unique indication of an RFC communication problem with SAP or non-SAP systems.

   c) A clear indication of a problem with GUI, RFC, or HTTP communication.

   d) A problem caused by an ineffective network between the application and the database level.

2. In a transaction step, a transaction is processed and controls are used, but neither an external RFC nor an HTTP target is called. Which of the following statements are correct?

a) The GUI time is greater than the roll wait time.

b) The RFC time is greater than the roll wait time.

c) The roll wait time is always greater than zero.

d) The roll wait time is normally greater than zero, although it can also be zero.

e) The roll wait time is always zero.

3. In a transaction step, a transaction that uses no controls and no synchronous RFCs is processed, although asynchronous RFCs are called. Which of the following statements are correct?

a) The GUI time is greater than the roll wait time.

b) The RFC time is greater than the roll wait time.

c) The roll wait time is always greater than zero.

d) The roll wait time is normally greater than zero, although it can also be zero.

e) The roll wait time is always zero.

4. A Web application that uses ITS and an SAP system is running "too slowly." What analyses do you perform?

a) Use the ITS administration and monitoring tool or the central CCMS monitor to check if all work processes (threads) or sessions are running on the ITS, or if the CPU is constantly running.

b) In the work process overview for the connected SAP system, check if all work processes are running.

c) Using a performance trace and the single record statistics, analyze the response time of the connected SAP system, and compare it with the user-measured response time for the presentation server.

d) Using an analysis tool on the presentation server (for example, E2E trace plug-in of SAP Solution Manager), check the data transfer volume to the browser and the compilation time for an HTML page, and compare the required time with the total response time.

8 Memory Management

This chapter describes the SAP memory areas that you must configure for an SAP instance: the SAP buffer, SAP roll memory, SAP extended memory, SAP heap memory (variable local memory of SAP work processes), SAP paging memory, and the fixed local memory of SAP work processes.

The chapter is divided into two sections: The first section explains the concepts and functions of the individual memory areas and their influence on SAP system performance. The second section contains important implementation information for various operating systems and gives concrete recommendations on configuration.

Key factors influencing configuration are as follows:

- **Physical main memory (RAM)**
  Are the physically available main memory and virtually allocated memory in a proper ratio to one another? Which memory areas most urgently need attention when resources are low?

- **Operating system options and restrictions**
  Do these permit the desired configuration? What do you have to look out for on systems with 32-bit and 64-bit architectures?

When Should You Read this Chapter?

Read this chapter if you want to reconfigure SAP memory management following a reinstallation, an upgrade, or a system expansion or if you discover performance problems in memory management.

8.1 Memory Management Fundamentals

Before we explain the memory areas of an SAP instance, we'll introduce some key terms in this section.

8.1.1 Basic Terms

More memory can be allocated virtually in all operating systems than is physically available. The term *memory* always refers to *virtual memory*, which the operating system manages either in the *physical main memory* or in the *swap space*. The maximum amount of virtual memory that can be allocated is limited by two variables:

▶ All processes, together, cannot allocate more memory than the sum of the physical main memory and the available swap space. This limit is due to physical hardware restrictions.

▶ Each individual process cannot allocate more memory than the maximum addressable memory area *(address space)* permitted by the operating system. This logical limit is imposed by the architecture of the operating systems. The address space is theoretically 4GB (2^{32}) for 32-bit architecture, but the memory that can be addressed is far less than this (between 2.0 and 3.8GB, depending on the operating system). This is a serious restriction in terms of the practical configuration. The address space restriction is not relevant (in practical terms) anymore in the case of 64-bit operating systems.

The operating system manages two types of memory: local memory and shared memory. Local memory is always allocated to just one operating system process; in other words, only this one process can write or read from this memory area. Shared memory, on the other hand, is accessible to multiple operating system processes. For example, all SAP buffers reside in shared memory, because all SAP work processes of an SAP instance have to write to and read from the SAP buffer. In addition, local memory is created for every SAP work process. (The local memory of an SAP work process includes, for example, the SAP cursor cache and I/O buffer for transferring data to and from the database, as described in Chapter 4, Section 4.3.2, Evaluating an SQL Trace.) The virtually allocated memory is the sum of the local memory and the shared memory.

If there are several SAP instances or one SAP instance and one database instance on a computer, the processes of one instance can always only access the shared memory of "its own" instance, but not the shared objects of other instances.

In the *32-bit technology* used until now, a process can theoretically address a maximum of 4GB memory. In practice, a large percentage of memory cannot be used because of fragmentation, so the memory actually available to an SAP work process is much less. SAP Note 146528 outlines restrictions for the different operating systems.

32-bit and 64-bit technology

These problems have been solved with *64-bit technology*. An address space of several terabytes is available to the work process in this case. To use 64-bit technology, your hardware, operating system, database software, and SAP kernel all must be 64-bit (-ready). The 64-bit SAP kernel has no new functions compared with the 32-bit version. The 64-bit SAP kernel has the same functionality as the 32-bit version, and there is no difference in handling, either for users or for administrators, but memory management in the 64-bit SAP kernel is simplified considerably compared to the 32-bit version. You will find details in SAP Note 146289.

Currently, 64-bit SAP kernels have been released for all operating systems. Beyond that, since 2007 SAP has supported new versions of its products only as 64-bit and Unicode versions. You will find information on released 64-bit products in SAP Notes for the component XX-SER-SWREL or in the SAP Service Marketplace under *http://service.sap.com/platforms* and in the product availability matrix under *http://service.sap.com/pam*. For Linux, you can find the relevant information under *http://www.sap.com/linux* • PLATFORMS • HARDWARE LIST; for Windows, under *http://www.saponwin.com*.

Language is a source of misunderstanding, and this definitely applies in the case of SAP memory management. For example, the same terms are used at the operating and SAP system levels to describe different things: We distinguish between operating system paging and SAP paging, context switching at the operating system level and context switching at the SAP level, and so on. Even the term *heap* has multiple meanings. At the operating system level, it is used to refer to the local memory allocated by an operating system process. At the SAP level, on the other hand, *heap* describes a special local memory area; that is, the SAP heap memory is only a small part of the heap referred to at the operating system level.

[!]

To limit confusion, we prefix the SAP terms explicitly in this book with "SAP," for example, SAP heap memory or SAP paging memory, to distinguish them from other operating system terms. If you are reading secondary literature or information in the SAP Service Marketplace, use the term's context to clarify whether the author is referring to the SAP term or the operating system term.

8.1.2 SAP Roll Memory, SAP Extended Memory, and SAP Heap Memory

This section will introduce the terms *user context, SAP roll memory, SAP extended memory*, and *SAP heap memory*.

User context

An SAP transaction generally extends over several transaction steps or screen switches. Data (such as variables, internal tables, and screen lists) is generated during these steps and stored in the application server memory. This data is referred to as *user context*.

Session

When you open a new session by selecting SYSTEM • CREATE SESSION, a new user context is also created. The data from the transactions executed in the two sessions is stored independently in different memory areas. Sessions that are explicitly opened by users in this way are called *external sessions*. An ABAP program can also open a new session implicitly from another program, for which a new user context is then likewise created. The ABAP commands in this case are SUBMIT, CALL TRANSACTION, CALL DIALOG, CALL SCREEN, CALL FUNCTION IN UPDATE TASK, CALL FUNCTION IN BACKGROUND TASK, and CALL FUNCTION STARTING NEW TASK. Sessions opened implicitly by the program are called *internal sessions*.

User contexts are stored in *SAP roll memory, SAP extended memory*, or *SAP heap memory*. You can set parameters to influence which memory area will be used.

SAP roll memory

The initial part of the user context is stored in the *local SAP roll area of the work process*. Because this is local memory, each SAP work process can only access its own roll area. Figure 8.1 illustrates two SAP work processes and their local roll areas.

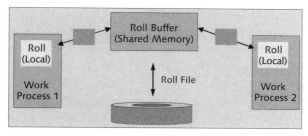

Figure 8.1 Roll Memory

At the end of the transaction step, the user exits the work process so that another user can use this work process. The content of the user's local work process roll area has to be backed up, so the local roll area is copied to the *shared SAP roll area*. The shared roll area is either a memory area in the shared memory of the application server (the *SAP roll buffer*) or a file on the application server's hard drive (the *SAP roll file*), or a combination of the two. The shared roll area is accessible to all of an instance's work processes. The process of copying the local roll memory to the shared roll area is called *roll-out* (see also Chapter 3, Section 3.3.1, Transaction Step Cycle). If the user is assigned a different work process in the next transaction step, the user context is copied from the shared roll area to the local roll area of the new work process. The user can then continue working with the old data. This procedure is called *roll-in*. Figure 8.1 shows the roll buffer and the roll file. The two arrows in the diagram symbolize the copy process for a roll-in and roll-out.

Use the following SAP profile parameters to configure the size of SAP roll memory:

> ztta/roll_area, rdisp/roll_SHM, rdisp/roll_MAXFS

- ▶ ztta/roll_area establishes the size of the local SAP roll area in the work process and applies equally to all work process types.

- ▶ The SAP profile parameter rdisp/ROLL_SHM establishes the size of the SAP roll buffer.

- ▶ The rdisp/ROLL_MAXFS parameter defines the size of the entire shared SAP roll area (that is, roll buffer plus roll file).

User contexts are generally stored in the *SAP extended memory*. The SAP extended memory is allocated as shared memory: Consequently, all SAP instance work processes can edit the stored user contexts directly.

> SAP extended memory

Therefore, the entire user context is not copied when rolled in to the local memory of the work process; rather, only the addresses indicating where the user context is located in the SAP extended memory are copied, in other words, the *pointers*. The volume of data copied in a roll-in or roll-out is reduced considerably by using SAP extended memory, which makes the roll process much faster overall. The SAP system is generally configured so most user context data is stored in SAP extended memory.

em/initial_
size_MB, em/
block_size_KB,
ztta/roll_extension

SAP extended memory is allocated as shared memory.

▸ The size of SAP extended memory allocated when the SAP instance starts up is defined by the SAP profile parameter `em/initial_size_MB`.

▸ SAP extended memory is split internally into blocks of size `em/block-size_KB`. The default block size is 1,024KB and must not be changed unless explicitly recommended by SAP.

▸ The SAP profile parameter `ztta/roll_extension` defines the maximum size of a user context in SAP extended memory. This measure prevents an individual user from occupying the entire SAP extended memory with a very memory-intensive transaction, leaving no memory for other users.

SAP heap memory

The third memory area where user contexts can be stored is the *SAP heap memory*. Whereas the roll area allocation is already fixed as local memory by a work process at startup, the SAP heap memory is variably allocated as local memory as required, that is, when the user context exceeds a certain size. The memory is released when the transaction has ended.

abap/heap_area...

▸ The SAP profile parameters `abap/heap_area_dia` and `abap/heap_area_nondia` define the quotas of SAP heap memory that a dialog work process or a nondialog work process can allocate.

▸ `abap/heap_area_total` specifies the total SAP heap memory that can be allocated by all work processes.

▸ The maximum possible value for the `abap/heap_area...` parameter is 2,000,000,000, or more precisely, $2^{31}-1$ (which is approximately 2GB).

When a transaction is complete, an SAP work process that has allo- cated SAP heap memory must release this memory. This is achieved (in technical terms) by the work process restarting as soon as the allocated memory exceeds the value `abap/heaplimit`. If the work process allocates less SAP heap memory, the memory is released in the ABAP — that is, it can be used again by the next transaction — but not at the operating system level. It is therefore highly preferred in this case for the work processes to be restarted. The corresponding entry in the SAP SysLog (Transaction SM21) should not be understood as an error message, but simply as information.

abap/heaplimit

Figure 8.2 shows the memory areas and the related configuration parameters.

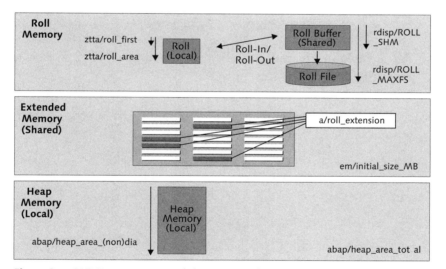

Figure 8.2   SAP Memory Areas and the Associated SAP Profile Parameters

Sequence in Which Memory Is Allocated

Dialog work processes store user context data in the following order:

1. When a transaction starts, the user context is stored in the local roll area of the work process up to a size of `ztta/roll_first`, which should be set to 1 (1 byte). This means that absolutely no SAP roll memory should be reserved initially. (However, administrative data

ztta/roll_first

up to 100KB is always stored in the local roll area of the work process for technical reasons, even if `ztta/roll_first` = 1.)

2. If the size of the user context exceeds the value of `ztta/roll_first`, the data is stored in SAP extended memory.

3. If SAP extended memory is used up, or if the user context reaches the `ztta/roll_extension` quota, the remainder of the local roll area is used, up to the size of `ztta/roll_area`.

4. If the context continues to grow, and if the memory requirement also exceeds this value, the work process allocates SAP heap memory as required. The disadvantage of using the SAP heap memory is that this memory is local and cannot be copied (rolled; as with the SAP roll memory) to a shared memory area. If a process allocates SAP heap memory, the context can no longer be transferred to another work process. The work process remains assigned exclusively to one user. This state is referred to as *PRIV mode (private mode)*, and the status is documented in the work process overview in the Status and Reason columns by the values Stopped and PRIV.

5. If the value `abap/heap_area_dia` is reached for one work process or reaches the value `abap/heap_area_total` for all work processes, the program will terminate.

Figure 8.3 shows the memory areas that a dialog work process accesses. Initially, these are memory areas for user-independent objects, for example, the SAP buffer. Work processes store user-dependent objects (user contexts) in SAP roll memory, SAP extended memory, or SAP heap memory.

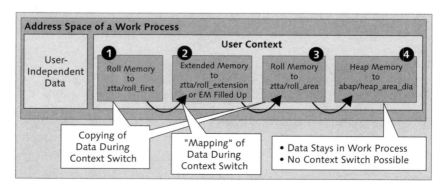

Figure 8.3   Order in Which Memory Is Allocated for SAP Work Processes

Performance Aspects

To ensure optimal performance, data copying during a context switch should be kept to a minimum; in other words, as little SAP roll memory as possible should be used. We therefore recommend that operating systems set `ztta/roll_first = 1`.

SAP extended memory full

What happens if the *SAP extended memory* is fully occupied? Two scenarios are possible here, neither of which is optimal in terms of performance:

► Because SAP extended memory is fully occupied, user contexts up to the size of `ztta/roll_area` are stored in the local roll area (see Figure 8.3 and Table 8.1). It may therefore be necessary with every context switch to repeatedly copy (roll) data of several megabytes. This typically leads to wait times in roll management, particularly if the roll buffer is full and data has to be written to the roll file. If this happens with large application servers with more than 100 users, performance abruptly collapses with catastrophic effects. An example is described in Chapter 2, Section 2.5, Analyzing SAP Work Processes.

► The local roll area (`ztta/roll_area`) can be reduced to help remedy this situation. If SAP extended memory is fully occupied, only a small amount of roll memory is used, and the volume of data to be copied with a context switch is reduced. Instead, the context data is stored in SAP heap memory, which means the work processes cease rolling and switch to PRIV mode, in other words, they remain assigned exclusively to one user between transaction steps. If too many work processes are in PRIV mode at the same time, there will not be enough free work processes available to the dispatcher. This can lead to high dispatcher wait times and a collapse in performance.

It is particularly important to ensure that SAP extended memory is large enough and can be enlarged further if necessary. In an ideal scenario, SAP extended memory would be infinitely extendable, and SAP roll and heap memories would be unnecessary. However, this has not been possible to date because operating system restrictions limit the size of SAP extended memory. Therefore, you can use mechanisms in the SAP system to reduce the need for SAP extended memory.

For example, memory is requested in the following sequence for UNIX *nondialog work processes:*

Nondialog work processes

1. The user context is stored initially in the local roll memory of the work process until it reaches a size of `ztta/roll_area`.

2. If additional memory is required, the work process allocates SAP heap memory as required until a value of `abap/heap_area_nondia` is reached or until the entire SAP heap memory (`abap/heap_area_total`) is used up.

3. If one of these limits is exceeded, the work process reserves SAP extended memory until the `ztta/roll_extension` quota is reached or until SAP extended memory is used up.

4. If these limits are also exceeded, the program terminates.

Dialog work processes essentially use shared SAP extended memory (as previously described), but nondialog work processes should primarily use local heap memory. The sequence in which memory is allocated by dialog and nondialog work processes, as summarized in Table 8.1, is hence quite complementary. The reason for the different implementations is that nondialog work processes do not have to exchange their user contexts, because background, update, and spool requests are always executed fully by one work process; in other words, there is no user-switching in nondialog work processes. Therefore, nondialog work processes essentially use local SAP heap memory to reserve shared SAP extended memory for dialog work processes.

Windows This behavior is valid for UNIX. For Windows operating systems, the memory allocation for nondialog work processes is identical to dialog work processes.

	Dialog Work Processes	Nondialog Work Processes (UNIX)
1	Local SAP roll memory up to `ztta/roll_first`	Local SAP roll memory up to `ztta/roll_area`
2	SAP extended memory until `ztta/roll_extension` is reached or until SAP extended memory is used up	SAP heap memory until `abap/heap_area_nondia` is reached or until SAP heap memory is used up

Table 8.1 Memory Allocation Sequence for Dialog and Nondialog Work Processes Under UNIX

	Dialog Work Processes	Nondialog Work Processes (UNIX)
3	Local SAP roll memory up to `ztta/roll_area`	—
4	SAP heap memory until `abap/heap_area_dia` is reached or until SAP heap memory is used up	SAP extended memory until `ztta/roll_extension` is reached or until SAP extended memory is used up
5	Program termination	Program termination

Table 8.1 Memory Allocation Sequence for Dialog and Nondialog Work Processes Under UNIX (Cont.)

Zero Administration Memory Management

SAP has included Zero Administration Memory Management since SAP Basis 4.0 for Windows. The goal is to reduce the number of SAP profile parameters and to considerably simplify administration. Zero Administration Memory Management does not require any manual settings and adjusts dynamically to the user's memory requirements. Even hardware changes (for example, memory extension) are recognized, and the parameters set accordingly.

The SAP profile parameter `PHYS_MEMSIZE` defines how much of a computer's total physical main memory should be used for the SAP instance. The default value for `PHYS_MEMSIZE` is the size of the physical main memory. All other memory area configuration parameters are calculated on the basis of the `PHYS_MEMSIZE` parameter.

PHYS_MEMSIZE

The dynamically extensible SAP extended memory forms the basis for Zero Administration Memory Management. The memory extends until the limit set by the SAP profile parameter `em/max_size_MB` is reached or until the address space in the Windows paging file is full. Because the default value of `em/max_size_MB` is 20,000MB, only the size of the Windows paging file represents the actual limit for extending the SAP extended memory.

SAP heap memory has become less important beginning with SAP Basis 4.0 (Windows), because nondialog work processes, like dialog work processes, allocate SAP extended memory first, and this memory is available

385

without limit. The SAP profile parameter abap/heap_area... is therefore now superfluous and is set to 2,000,000,000 (bytes).

The SAP profile parameter ztta/roll_extension is likewise obsolete and is set to 2,000,000,000. The quota of SAP extended memory that an individual user context can reserve is defined by the em/address_space_MB parameter. The default value of the parameter is 512 (MB).

[+]   You will find up-to-date information on Zero Administration Memory Management in SAP Note 88416.

Memory Management for IBM i

The implementation of *memory management on IBM i* can use a special feature of this platform — the concept of single-level storage. That is, every memory address has a physical representation in an auxiliary storage pool (ASP) in memory on the installed hard drive. The main memory of the machine can be regarded in principle as a large data cache. There is no swap space with a defined size.

Memory management on the IBM i has changed considerably since SAP Basis 4.6 compared with the previous versions, in which the benefits offered by the availability of Teraspace were used. Teraspace avoids the 16MB limit for shared memory segments at the operating system level, and therefore very large address spaces can be used.

In general, since SAP Basis 4.6, the configuration of memory management for an SAP system on the IBM i is not all that different from a UNIX system. Only the ztta/roll_area parameter is still subject to the 16MB limit; in other words, this parameter must not be set to a value greater than 16MB (which in practice is not done anyway on UNIX systems). SAP Notes 121625 and 139326 list the current restrictions for the various SAP profile parameters.

Because IBM i uses the single-level storage concept, no dedicated SAP page or roll file is required. You do not need to specify the rdisp/ROLL_SHM and rdisp/ROLL_MAXFS parameters. From SAP Basis 4.6 on, the size of SAP extended memory is defined via the em/initial_size_MB parameter, as on other platforms (maximum value is 8GB). This type of memory was requested dynamically by the system in older versions, up to a maximum of 8GB.

8.1.3   SAP EG Memory and SAP Paging Memory

As previously noted, user contexts are stored in extended, roll, and heap memory. However, memory areas are also required in which data can be stored globally between user contexts. SAP extended global memory (SAP EG memory) and SAP paging memory are available for this purpose.

SAP EG memory is used to store data across user contexts. Its use is only relevant since SAP Kernel 4.6D. (This data was previously stored in subareas of SAP roll memory and had to be tediously copied with each context switch.) SAP EG memory enables fast and copy-free switching based on mapping, as was already implemented for actual user contexts in SAP extended memory.

Extended global memory (SAP EG memory)

The size of SAP EG memory is configured using the `em/global_area_MB` parameter. The recommended size for SAP Kernel as of version 4.6D is 10% of SAP extended memory. (The standard delivery size of 32KB generally suffices for older versions.) If you use the ITS integrated in the kernel as of SAP Basis 6.40, SAP EG memory needs to be set higher, depending on the number of users and the ITS applications; you can find sizing rules in Chapter 7, SAP GUI and Internet Connection. Don't forget, however, that the size of SAP EG memory has to be subtracted from the size of SAP extended memory to calculate the remaining storage space for the user contexts.

One memory area we haven't discussed yet is *SAP paging memory*. Under no circumstances should SAP paging memory be confused with the paging memory of the operating system. The objects that are stored in SAP paging memory can be divided into three groups:

SAP paging memory

▶ **ABAP data clusters stored temporarily with the ABAP statement IMPORT/EXPORT FROM/TO MEMORY**
This data is stored in SAP paging memory because it is not tied to a user context. The `IMPORT/EXPORT FROM/TO MEMORY` statement exports the data from a user context via the paging memory and then imports it into another context.

> ▶ **Parameters transferred when programs and transactions are called**
> A new user context is created when an ABAP program calls another
> program or transaction. The variables and lists transferred when the
> relevant program is called or ended are likewise stored in SAP paging
> memory.

> ▶ **Data extracts created by the ABAP statement EXTRACT**
> Beginning with SAP Basis 4.5, extracts are no longer stored in SAP
> paging memory; rather, they are stored in a storage buffer for smaller
> extract volumes or in local files for large extract volumes.

Table 8.2 summarizes the data objects and associated ABAP statements.

ABAP Object	Associated ABAP Statement	SAP Basis
Data extracts	EXTRACT	Up to 4.0B
Data cluster	IMPORT/EXPORT FROM/TO MEMORY	Independent
Parameter for calling programs, transactions, and so on	SUBMIT REPORT, CALL TRANSACTION, CALL DIALOG, CALL SCREEN, CALL FUNCTION IN UPDATE TASK, CALL FUNCTION IN BACKGROUND TASK, CALL FUNCTION STARTING NEW TASK	Independent

Table 8.2 ABAP Objects and Statements Using SAP Paging Memory

rdisp/pg_MAXFS,
rdisp/pg_SHM

SAP paging memory, like the roll area, comprises a memory area in the
shared memory of the application server (the SAP paging buffer) and
an SAP paging file on one of the application server's hard drives. The
SAP profile parameters rdisp/PG_MAXFS and rdisp/PG_SHM determine
the size of SAP paging memory and the SAP paging buffer, respectively.
SAP paging memory is less critical to performance than other memory
areas. However, you should set rdisp/PG_MAXFS to a sufficiently large
value to prevent program terminations with the errors TSV_TNEW_PG_
CREATE_FAILED or SYSTEM_NO_MORE_PAGING. A value of 32,000
(256MB) should suffice for all normal requirements. If the SAP profile
parameter is set to 32,000, and if a program still terminates, there is
likely a fault in the program itself (see the relevant Notes in the SAP
Service Marketplace).

8.2   Configuring and Monitoring SAP Memory Areas

We'll pursue two main objectives when optimizing memory area configurations:

▶ **Performance**
As many users as possible should be able to work efficiently.

▶ **Stability**
Programs should not terminate because of a memory bottleneck (particularly background programs with very high memory requirements).

Achieving these objectives would not be difficult if all SAP memory areas could be set to whatever size is needed to prevent both terminations and bottlenecks. Unfortunately, two main factors stand in the way of implementing this simple strategy:

▶ **Physical main memory (RAM))**
The ratio between available physical main memory and used memory should be sensible so that main memory bottlenecks do not arise and server performance does not deteriorate because of excessive paging.

▶ **Operating system swap space or paging file**
The swap space must be large enough to create the desired memory areas. However, less importance is attached to this factor, because the swap space does not play a role in terms of price and can therefore be made whatever size you want.

▶ **Operating system restrictions**
The 32-bit architecture still used restricts the memory that can be addressed by processes. This restriction must be taken seriously, particularly for computers with a 2GB main memory or higher, because the memory areas cannot be made large enough to ensure optimal performance.

Where computers have a small main memory, the different memory areas of the SAP system (and those of the database instance, if available on the same computer) compete for the scarce main memory resources. Where computers have a large main memory, the key issue is how large a memory area can be configured without terminations being triggered because of address space restrictions in the operating system. In the past, both issues made it almost imperative to customize the SAP memory management of individual SAP systems for optimal hardware performance. Now, however, thanks to Zero Administration Memory Management, an initial step has been taken to radically simplify memory management configuration. The problem of address space restrictions has been all but eliminated with the use of 64-bit architecture. Memory management configuration has been simplified considerably, thanks to these two techniques.

Table 8.3 and Figure 8.4 summarize the different memory areas and their properties.

Memory Area	Implementation	Size (MB)	Contents
SAP roll memory	Shared memory (roll buffer), roll file	$n \times 10$	User contexts: temporary transaction-based data assigned to a user session
SAP extended memory	Shared memory	$n \times 100$ to $n \times 1,000$	For example, screen lists, internal tables, variables, administrative data
SAP heap memory	Local memory	$n \times 100$ to $n \times 1,000$	
SAP buffer	Shared memory	$n \times 100$	Global data that can be accessed by all users, for example, program codes, table and field definitions, and so on
SAP EG memory	Shared memory (part of SAP extended memory)	$n \times 10$	Temporary data exchanged between user contexts
SAP paging memory	Shared memory (paging buffer), SAP paging file	$n \times 100$	Temporary data exchanged between user contexts, data extracts (up to SAP Basis 4.0)
SAP work processes	Local memory	$n \times 10$ per WP	Executable programs, local data, local roll (ztta/roll_area), and local paging memory (rdisp/PG_local); SAP cursor cache and so on

Table 8.3 Memory Areas and Contents of an SAP Instance

Memory Area	Implementation	Size (MB)	Contents
Compare:			
Database instance	Shared memory, local memory	$n \times 100$ to $n \times 1.000$	Database buffer and database processes

Table 8.3 Memory Areas and Contents of an SAP Instance (Cont.)

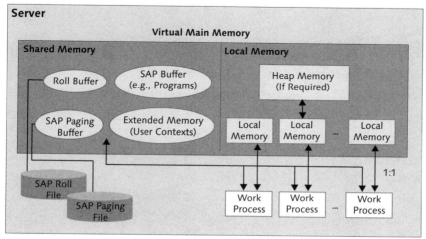

Figure 8.4 Memory Areas in the SAP System

8.2.1 Monitoring Swap Space

The recommendations in this book assume that sufficient swap space is available. "Sufficient" means the swap space is at least three times the size of the physical memory, or at least 3.5GB, overall.

You can use the following procedure to check whether the swap space is large enough and whether the SAP profile parameter `abap/heap_area_total` is set correctly.

Step 1: Calculate the Available Memory

Add together the physical main memory of the computer and the available swap space. You will find both values in the operating system monitor (Transaction ST06) in the fields Physical Memory and Swap Space.

Available Memory = Physical Memory + Swap Space

On the Windows platform, available memory is also referred to as *commit charge limit*.

Step 2: Calculate the Virtual Memory Required

Call the SAP memory configuration monitor (Transaction ST02) and select DETAIL ANALYSIS MENU • STORAGE.

Add up the following values:

▶ Virtual Memory Allocated (the memory allocated by the relevant SAP instance at startup).

▶ Maximum Heap Area for All Work Processes (the memory that can be allocated temporarily as needed by this SAP instance; this value is equal to `abap/heap_area_total`).

▶ Add an extra 100MB for the operating system as a safety margin.

▶ If there are several SAP instances on the computer, repeat this calculation for each SAP instance.

▶ If there is a database instance on the computer, add its memory requirement to this. You will find guidelines in Chapter 2, Section 2.3.1, Analyzing the Database Buffer, or in Appendix B.

▶ If other programs are running on the computer, calculate their memory allocations and add them, too.

Step 3: Compare the Available Memory with the Virtual Memory Required

The following must apply:

Virtual Memory Required < Available Memory

If this condition is not fulfilled, you have two options:

▶ Reduce the memory required by, for example, reducing the `abap/heap_area_total`. We recommend, however, that the `abap/heap_area_total` value be greater than 600,000,000 (600MB).

▶ Extend the swap space.

If the available memory is much greater than the virtual memory required, you can increase `abap/heap_area_total` accordingly. The maximum value for `abap/heap_area_total` is 2,000,000,000 (2GB) for SAP Basis 4.0.

This is a good starting point for calculating the size of the swap space, **[!]** but it does not cover all eventualities or domains of operating systems (for example, fragmented memory areas, which can become considerable over time). We therefore strongly advise that you monitor the free swap space.

You should in any case avoid computer bottlenecks in memory due to a too-small swap space. *All* processes are simultaneously affected by these bottlenecks, so it is hard to tell which process will terminate first. Perhaps an important operating system or database process will terminate because of a general memory bottleneck. If the swap space is too small, uncontrolled errors and terminations may occur, or the operating system itself may terminate. (See also SAP Note 38052, "System Panic, Termination Because of Swap Space Bottleneck.")

8.2.2 Address Space Restrictions (32-Bit and 64-Bit Architecture)

To recap, the virtual memory allocated must first be in a sensible ratio to the physical main memory and, second, fit into available memory (that is, the sum of physical main memory and swap space). There is now a third restriction: It must be possible to *address* the memory from a work process.

Address Space

Address space is the number of memory addresses a process has at its disposal. The size of addressable memory is between 1.8 and 3.8GB ($\leq 2^{32}$ = 4GB) for 32-bit versions of the SAP kernel. All memory areas that a work process has to access must fit into the addressable memory: the local work process memory, the SAP buffer, including SAP roll and SAP paging buffer (about 100MB), SAP extended memory (100 to 1,000MB), and SAP heap memory (100 to 1,000MB). From this, it is clear that if memory area allocation is too large, less address space is available for other memory areas; the memory areas have a reciprocal relationship with one another (see Figure 8.5).

Let's again summarize the difference between available memory and available address space. The memory areas of *one* work process (the shared memory of *one* instance and the local memory of *one* work process) must fit in the *available address space*, whereas the areas of *all* work processes (that is, the shared memory of *all* instances and the local memory of *all* work processes) must fit in the *available memory*. If several SAP instances or one SAP and one database instance are installed on one computer, the address space only includes the memory areas of one instance (because a work process only has to address the areas of its instance), whereas the available memory must offer sufficient space for the shared memory areas of all instances.

UNIX Operating Systems

Figure 8.5 shows the standard implementation of SAP extended memory on UNIX operating systems. The work process must address the entire SAP extended memory.

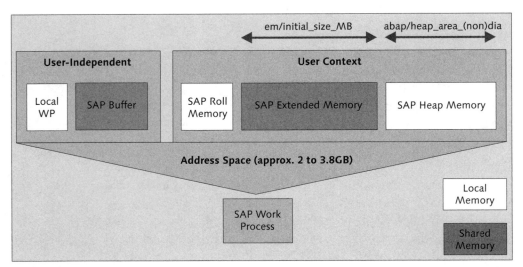

Figure 8.5 Work Process Address Space Allocation in a Standard Implementation for UNIX Operating Systems

If SAP extended memory is too large, a work process will not be able to address any SAP heap memory. We therefore recommend that SAP extended memory (em/initial_size_MB) be no larger than 2GB. The maximum possible size of SAP extended memory is considerably smaller than this on some operating systems. This recommendation only applies for 32-bit architectures.

32-bit architecture

Therefore, the address space of the operating system restricts the size of the memory areas, particularly SAP extended memory, and directly affects the number of users who can work on an SAP instance. One particular problem that arises on computers with a physical main memory of more than 2GB is that the main memory cannot be used effectively by an SAP instance, because instance processes cannot address this memory. Installing more than one SAP instance on a computer can circumvent the problem of restricted address space.

64-bit technology solves these problems and is now available in all operating platforms. An address space of several terabytes is available to the work process in this case. To use 64-bit technology, your hardware, operating system, database software, and SAP kernel all must be 64-bit (-ready). The 64-bit SAP kernel has no new functions compared with the 32-bit version; The 64-bit SAP kernel has the same functionality as the 32-bit version, and there is no difference in handling, either for users or for administrators, but memory management in the 64-bit SAP kernel is simplified considerably compared to the 32-bit version. You will find details in SAP Note 146289.

64-bit architecture

We recommend using 64-bit implementation for your platform and version if possible, particularly when using computers with a physical main memory in excess of 2GB. With SAP NetWeaver 2004s (SAP Basis 7.00), SAP explicitly recommends in its product availability matrix not using 32-bit technology for production (SAP Note 996600). The use of Unicode and the Internet Pricing and Configuration Engine (IPC) and Internet Transaction Server (ITS) (which used to be independent processes) have been integrated into the SAP kernel and consequently occupy memory in the same address space. You also obtain more information, along with recommendations on the limits on the use of 32-bit technology for the independent ITS (SAP Note 959781) and for SAP liveCache (SAP Note 622709).

Windows Operating Systems Below 32-Bit

To work around this restriction on the size of SAP extended memory in 32-bit Windows operating systems (which are still being used), the implementation is different on Windows. Figure 8.6 illustrates the implementation using Windows as an example: Only one part of SAP extended memory (em/address_space_MB) is addressed by the work process. This implementation has the advantage that the entire SAP extended memory can be larger than the address space of the work process. The overall size of SAP extended memory is therefore only limited by the size of the swap space.

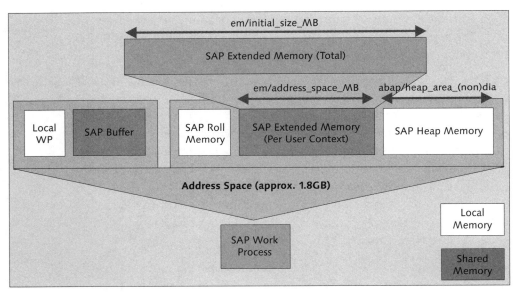

Figure 8.6 Address Space Allocation of a Work Process in a Windows Implementation

Note that each work process can, in principle, access all objects stored in SAP extended memory, whereas a transaction step can only access an area the size of em/address_space_MB. The SAP profile parameter em/address_space_MB defines the maximum size that a user context can reserve in SAP extended memory. The default size of the user quota em/address_space_MB is 512MB. The SAP profile parameter ztta/roll_extension is no longer used by default as of SAP Basis 4.0; `ztta/roll_extension` is set to 2,000,000,000.

[+] A comparable implementation of SAP extended memory in Windows also currently exists for the AIX operating system. See SAP Note 95454 for more information.

The maximum amount of *SAP heap memory* that a work process can address is calculated from the size of the address space minus the shared memory areas addressed by the SAP work process and the local work process memory (about 10MB). If a work process tries to allocate more SAP heap memory than there is address space available, the program will terminate with the error STORAGE_PARAMETERS_WRONG_SET. The next section describes how to deal with this error.

SAP heap memory

Other Restrictions

[!] Operating system restrictions can keep the SAP instance from starting or cause it to only start with errors if the memory areas are too large or can also trigger ABAP errors at runtime (e.g., STORAGE_PARAMETERS_ WRONG_SET). You will find more detailed information on diagnostics and troubleshooting in the next section. Appendix C contains notes for the individual operating systems, which describe restrictions, possible errors, and potential solutions. You can also contact your hardware partner or SAP for information on the latest restrictions.

memlimits Utility

The `memlimits` utility tests the limits of the memory that can be allocated on your operating system. Start the `memlimits` program at the operating system level.

The following output (excerpt) is shown on UNIX systems:

UNIX

```
+-------------------------------------------------------+
|                    Result (UNIX)                      |
+-------------------------------------------------------+
Maximum heap size per process........:   640 MB
Maximum protectable size (mprotect)..:   996 MB
    em/initial_size_MB > 996 MB will not work
Maximum address space per process....:  1252 MB
```

```
Total available swap space...........:   1300 MB
```

▸ **Maximum heap size per process**
This value indicates how much memory can be allocated locally by a process and limits the sum of fixed local memory for SAP work processes and SAP heap memory:

Fixed Local Work Process Memory + Variable Local Work Process Memory (SAP Heap Memory) < Operating System Heap (UNIX)

▸ **Maximum protectable size (mprotect)**
This value limits the SAP extended memory.

The `memlimits` program issues the following warning in this case: `em/initial_size_MB > 996 MB will not work`. This warning has only limited applicability. On the one hand, it does not guarantee that this size of SAP extended memory can actually be allocated. On the other hand, there are special solutions for large installations in some operating systems that allow more memory to be allocated. You will find further information (SAP Notes) on this in Appendix C. Your hardware partner will also be able to supply information on special solutions.

▸ **Maximum address space per work process**
This value limits the sum of all memory areas that a process can allocate
(for instance, SAP buffer, SAP extended memory em/initial_size_MB, SAP heap memory, and so on).

Windows The following result output (excerpt) is shown on Windows operating systems:

```
+-------------------------------------------------------+
|                    Result (Windows)                   |
+-------------------------------------------------------+
Maximum heap size per process........:   1988 MB
Total available swap space...........:   1988 MB
```

▸ **Maximum heap size per process**
Maximum memory that can be allocated per process. Because there are no other restrictions in Windows relating to shared or local memory, this value restricts the sum of all memory areas that can be

allocated by a process (for instance, SAP buffer, SAP extended memory `em/address_space_MB`, SAP heap memory, and so on).

The `Maximum heap size per process` represents an upper limit in terms of the memory that can actually be allocated. However, because part of the address space can be lost as a result of fragmentation, the real addressable memory is less than this.

Ensure that the SAP system is stopped when you execute the `memlimits` program. You can access a description of this program, along with possible options, by running the command `memlimits -h` at either a UNIX console or the Windows command prompt (cmd.exe).

8.2.3 Configuring and Monitoring SAP Memory Areas

How do you configure SAP memory management? In this section, a list of points will assist you with your configuration (as much as possible; some special cases might not be covered):

▶ **Total main memory requirement**
Your hardware partners can establish the main memory requirements for your SAP system, based on information you provide about system requirements. For small and medium installations, you can perform the sizing yourself using Quick Sizer (SAP Service Marketplace).

▶ **Number of computers**
First, establish the number of computers. This is generally done in cooperation with your hardware partner, because deciding how many computers should be distributed over your SAP system depends essentially on the hardware platform.

▶ **Several SAP instances per computer**
The decision as to whether several SAP instances are configured per computer is also made in conjunction with your hardware partner. The following reasons support configuring several SAP instances on one server with more than four processors and 2GB of main memory.

The physical main memory cannot be used effectively with an SAP instance because of operating system–specific restrictions (for example, address space, shared memory, and so on), but with the inclusion of 64-bit architecture, this reason is obsolete.

Performance problems (wait situations) can arise in the dispatcher and in the roll and buffer administration on computers with more than four processors and a corresponding number of SAP work processes. These can be reduced if several SAP instances are configured.

Basically, the trend is to create a large instance on each computer with many work processes and a large SAP extended memory. We do not recommend creating an unnecessary number of instances, because each instance involves administration and monitoring effort.

▶ **SAP buffer**
The memory requirement of the SAP buffer basically depends on the SAP components that are operated on relevant SAP instances. Overall, there is a typical memory requirement of 500MB to 3GB for all SAP buffers, which depends (among other things) on whether Unicode is used. The largest are the SAP program buffers, at 400MB or more, and the SAP table buffer (for generic and single-record buffering), at 100MB or more. The SAP buffer memory area is allocated for each SAP instance. If the SAP system is distributed over multiple instances, each with a few users and work processes, the memory requirement of the overall system will be greater than if the system is distributed over relatively few instances with more users and work processes each per instance. Chapter 2, Section 2.4, Analyzing SAP Memory Configuration describes the monitoring of the SAP buffer following production startup.

▶ **SAP extended memory and roll buffer**
Zero Administration Memory Management sets the SAP extended memory and roll buffer automatically, based on the SAP profile parameter PHYS_MEMSIZE. For SAP systems in which Zero Administration Memory Management is not yet active, you will find information on configuring and monitoring SAP extended memory and the roll buffer at the end of this section.

▶ **Memory for SAP work processes**
The memory requirement for an SAP work process can be estimated at around 7.5MB. You will find more detailed information on the

number of required work processes and their distribution in Chapter 6, Workload Distribution and Interfaces.

▶ **Database instance**
The Quick Sizer program can also provide you with recommendations on the main memory requirement of the database instance. As a guide, you can assume about 20 to 30% of the overall main memory for the database instance, in other words, the sum of the main memory sizes for all computers. You will find further details on the memory areas of the individual database systems and their monitoring in production operation in Chapter 2, Section 2.3.1, Analyzing the Database Buffer, and in Appendix B.

SAP Extended Memory

The SAP extended memory requirement (em/initial_size_MB) depends on the number and activities of users and is difficult to calculate before actually going live. When setting this SAP profile parameter initially in a nonproduction system, you can pragmatically base your estimate on the size of the physical main memory. Configure about 70 to 100% of the physical main memory that is available for the SAP instance as SAP extended memory.

Let's say, for example, that you want to configure a database instance and an SAP instance on a computer with 1,500MB of physical main memory. You estimate a main memory requirement of 500MB for the database instance. This leaves 1,000MB for the SAP instance. Therefore, you should set the SAP extended memory to an initial size of between 700 and 1,000MB.

[Ex]

As explained in Section 8.2.2, Address Space Restrictions, you cannot exceed 2,000MB for the SAP extended memory for 32-bit operating systems. The maximum size of the SAP extended memory per SAP instance is even less than this on some operating systems.

In a production SAP system, adapt the size of the SAP extended memory to the actual requirement. Monitoring the SAP extended memory in the SAP memory configuration monitor (Transaction ST02) is described in Chapter 2, Monitoring Hardware, Databases, and SAP Basis. If you find that the SAP extended memory is frequently 100% occupied, proceed as follows:

▶ Extend the SAP extended memory. On the one hand, you are restricted here by the limits of your operating system; on the other hand, however, the size of SAP extended memory should not greatly exceed the size of physical main memory (although this is not a strict limit).

▶ Check to see which users are taking up an above-average amount of space in SAP extended memory by calling the *mode list.* In the SAP memory configuration monitor (Transaction ST02), select: DETAIL ANALYSIS MENU • SAP MEMORY • MODE LIST.

A screen opens that shows you a list of logged-on users (Name column) and their sessions. If a user has opened several external sessions, his name will appear several times in the list. The Ext Mem [kB] and Heap [kB] columns indicate how much memory the users are occupying in SAP extended memory or SAP heap memory. The lower part of the list contains a history of the users with the highest memory allocations.

You can use this list to identify users with above-average memory allocations. Establish which programs these users are currently executing and check whether these programs can be optimized.

▶ If you cannot extend SAP extended memory because of the previously listed restrictions, and if you establish from the mode list that only a few users have a large share of extended memory, you can reduce the user quota (ztta/roll_extension). As a result, individual user sessions take up less memory in SAP extended memory and use SAP heap memory instead. This approach has two disadvantages, however:

  ▶ Work processes are more likely to switch to PRIV mode. The number of dialog work processes may have to be increased in this case.

  ▶ Less memory is available overall to the individual user. In the worst case scenario, this can cause programs with a very high memory requirements to terminate.

8.2.4 Assistance with Troubleshooting

An optimal memory area configuration should not just guarantee good performance, but should also prevent program termination due to memory bottlenecks.

The following errors can arise because of an incorrect memory area configuration:

▶ The SAP instance does not start because the operating system cannot provide the requested memory areas.

▶ Session terminations: A dialog window appears on the user's screen with the error message Roll-Out Failure. The session then disappears, and the user is logged off.

▶ ABAP program terminations: You will find the logs for these errors (dumps) in Transaction ST22: TOOLS • ADMINISTRATION • MONITOR • DUMP ANALYSIS.

Four factors come into play with this error:

▶ There is a program error (for example, an endless loop), or the program has been used incorrectly. As a result, an unnecessary amount of memory is requested.

▶ The SAP profile parameters are set incorrectly.

▶ The swap space on the operating system is not large enough.

▶ The configuration parameters of the operating system are set incorrectly, or operating system limits have been reached (for example, the maximum addressable memory).

ABAP Program Terminations

You can view the logs of ABAP program terminations with Transaction ST22. The following error messages related to memory area configuration may come up:

▶ **STORAGE_PARAMETERS_WRONG_SET, SYSTEM_ROLL_IN_ERROR, TSV_TNEW_BLOCKS_NO_ROLL_MEMORY, TSV_TNEW_PAGE_ALLOC_ FAILED, TSV_TNEW_INDEX_NO_ROLL_MEMORY**
The memory for user contexts is used up.

▶ **PXA_NO_SHARED_MEMORY**

Or the message System Not Ready (PXA_NO_SHARED_MEMORY) appears when the user logs on to the SAP system.

The program buffer is the last object the SAP system creates in shared memory. If sufficient shared memory is not available at this time, the system cannot create the program buffer. The system is then simply started as an "emergency system" with a minimal program buffer. In general, this is caused by allocated areas in the shared memory (particularly SAP extended memory and program buffer) that violate the operating system–specific restrictions.

▶ **DBIF_RTAB_NO_MEMORY, DBIF_RSQL_NO_MEMORY**

The program encounters a memory bottleneck during an operation in the database interface.

▶ **EXSORT_NOT_ENOUGH_MEMORY**

The program encounters a memory bottleneck during sorting.

▶ **RABAX_CALLING_RABAX**

This error occurs if the attempt to create an error log also fails after a program has been terminated due to lack of memory. This error is also a follow-on error.

▶ **SYSTEM_NO_MORE_PAGING, TSV_TNEW_PAGE_ALLOC_FAILED**

SAP paging memory is used up (see Section 8.1.3, SAP EG Memory and SAP Paging Memory).

▶ **SET_PARAMETER_MEMORY_OVERFLOW**

Memory for the SET/GET parameter (SPA/GPA memory) is used up. This termination is particularly likely with a file transfer to the presentation server (download/upload) and a local execute (SAPLGRAP program). Extend the memory area with the SAP profile parameter ztta/parameter_area.

▶ **SYSTEM_NO_ROLL**

SAP Basis uses the profile parameter ztta/max_memreq_MB to limit the volume of memory that can be allocated with a single call. If the parameter is set too low, this error can occur. You will find details in SAP Note 353579.

▶ **EXPORT_NO_SHARED_MEMORY**

The memory of the export/import SHM buffer is full. For more information on this buffer, refer to Chapter 9, Section 9.5, Monitoring Object-Oriented Application Buffers. This buffer doesn't allow any displacements. The error message described should actually be caught by the program. Before you increase the buffer using the configuration parameters listed in Appendix C, you should check in the main memory configuration monitor (Transaction ST02) to see which objects occupy the buffer and search for SAP notes on these objects or the program that triggers the error.

You will find detailed information on how much memory was requested **[Ex]** at the time of termination in the error message logs. To do this, compare the following two lines in the error log:

```
Extended memory area (EM) 52 431 655
fixed allocated memory (HEAP) 80 004 928
```

These values are critical for analyzing the error:

▶ **Extended memory area (EM)**
Amount of SAP extended memory that was occupied at the time of termination.

▶ **Fixed allocated memory (HEAP)**
Amount of SAP heap memory that was occupied at the time of termination.

Therefore, the memory requested for the user context in this example is 52,431,655 bytes + 80,004,928 bytes = 132.5MB. (SAP roll memory of size `ztta/roll_area` is added to this, which is less than 10MB by default.)

To continue the analysis, proceed as follows:

▶ First, check for cases of unnecessary memory consumption that may   Application error
have been caused by a nonoptimal or inefficient use of a program. We assume as a reference that a program executed in dialog mode by a number of users should not allocate more than 100MB. Background programs (for example, billing runs at night on a dedicated application server) should not require more than 1GB. Depending on the

operating system, 1 to 3GB is regarded as "conclusive" for 32-bit versions.

If a program terminates with a memory consumption level above this reference value, consult the user on whether the program was used inappropriately or whether the work list can possibly be split into smaller portions to allow repeated executions with lower memory consumption.

If this is not possible, contact the developer if the program is user-defined, or search the SAP Service Marketplace for information on optimizing the program.

Quotas reached
▶ While searching for application errors, you should also check whether the program has reached the limits defined by the SAP profile parameter. The memory available for a user context is derived from the sum of ztta/roll_extension (quota in SAP extended memory) and abap/heap_area_dia or abap/heap_area_nondia (quotas in SAP heap memory). SAP roll memory is added to this with a size of less than 10MB per context (ztta/roll_area). The program aborts in the previous example, because these quotas are reached. The parameters in this example amount to ztta/roll_extension = 52,428,800 (bytes) or abap/heap_area_dia = 80,000,000 (bytes). A comparison with the values Extended Memory (EM) and Fixed Allocated Memory (HEAP) from the log at the time of termination shows that the program was terminated because it had reached its quotas for SAP extended memory and SAP heap memory. In this case, you should extend these SAP profile parameters.

Roll , extended, or SAP heap memory occupied
▶ If the problem was not caused by ztta/roll_extension and abap/heap_area_(non)dia quotas being reached, use the SAP memory configuration monitor (Transaction ST02) to check whether SAP extended memory or SAP heap memory was 100% occupied at the time roll memory terminated. If so, extend the relevant memory areas if possible. The relevant SAP profile parameters in this case are rdisp/ROLL_MAXFS, em/initial_size_MB, and abap/heap_area_total.

Operating system limits reached
▶ Finally, it is possible that the SAP kernel requests memory from the operating system, but the operating system cannot provide this memory. For example, the STORAGE_PARAMETERS_WRONG_SET error

log contains an entry like "The program had already requested 109,890,288 bytes from the operating system via 'malloc' when the operating system reported, on receiving a new request for memory, that it had no more memory available." This could be caused by incorrectly set operating system parameters or limits imposed by the operating system architecture or by a too-small swap space. Operating system restrictions can also keep the SAP instance from starting if incorrect SAP profile parameters are selected.

▶ To avoid possible errors in the *SAP kernel*, ensure that you are using an up-to-date SAP kernel.

Error in SAP kernel

You will find further information on memory management errors in the *developer logs (dev traces)* for the work processes. To view this information, first call the work process overview (Transaction SM50). Select a work process and the menu path PROCESS • TRACE • DISPLAY FILE.

Developer logs ("dev traces")

If the SAP instance does not start with a profile, you will find the files in the directory *\usr\sap\<SID>\<Instance_name><Instance_number>\work*. These files must always be backed up for subsequent analysis, because they will be overwritten when the work process restarts, and without them, an error analysis is practically impossible.

Checking Profile Parameter Settings

SAP Note 103747 provides recommendations on setting the *profile parameters* that configure memory. If problems arise despite these recommendations and contrary to expectations, you should check the settings.

An outline of an ABAP report is listed below, which you can use to establish the maximum amount of memory that can be allocated on your system. Use this ABAP report to test your system's parameter settings.

```
report zusemem.
* Report for checking the limits of the allocable memory
* parameters mb type I.
data itab(1024) type c occurs 0.
data str(1024).
do mb times.
```

```
      do 1024 times. append str to itab. enddo.
    enddo.
    skip.
    write: / 'At the moment', mb,
              'MB of this program are being used.'.
```

The ZUSEMEN report enables you to reserve a certain amount of memory. To do this, execute the report in the ABAP editor (Transaction SE38). A selection screen opens with the input parameter MB, which prompts for input of the memory size to be allocated by the report. In the ABAP editor menu, select PROGRAM • RUN to start the report and allocate the preferred amount of memory. Extend the MB parameter gradually to establish the limit at which the report terminates.

To check how much memory can be allocated by background programs, create a variant for this report and execute it in the background.

Monitor the memory allocation of the report in a second mode in the SAP memory configuration monitor or in the previously described mode list.

abap/heap_
area_dia

If the report is running interactively, you will notice that the program first allocates SAP extended memory to a quota of ztta/roll_extension and then SAP heap memory up to a quota of abap/heap_area_dia. If the requested memory exceeds the sum of both quotas, the program terminates with the error TSV_TNEW_PAGE_ALLOC_FAILED. We can assume here that the size of abap/heap_area_dia was set to such a low value that the SAP extended memory, SAP heap memory, and all other memory areas that the work process must address do not exceed the address space of the work process. (Refer also to Figures 8.5 and 8.6 in Section 8.2.2, Address Space Restrictions.) If, on the other hand, abap/heap_area_dia is set to such a high value that the requested SAP heap memory exceeds the address space, the report terminates with the error STORAGE_PARAMETERS_WRONG_SET. In Figure 8.5 and Figure 8.6, this would be the equivalent of the rectangle that symbolizes the SAP heap memory extending over the rectangle that represents the address space. With UNIX, you should set abap/heap_area_dia so that the STORAGE_PARAMETERS_WRONG_SET error does not arise.

If you start the report in the background, whether the report first occupies SAP extended memory or SAP heap memory depends on your operating system and your SAP kernel version. If the report occupies SAP extended memory first (as is the case, for example, in SAP Basis 4.0B and Windows), the same parameterization applies as for dialog work processes.

abap/heap_area_nondia

If the report allocates SAP heap memory first, note how the allocated SAP heap memory extends until it reaches the quota of abap/heap_area_nondia before the report starts to reserve SAP extended memory. If the abap/heap_area_nondia parameter is set too high, that is, larger than the maximum permitted by the operating system for the SAP heap memory, the report terminates with the error STORAGE_PARAMETERS_WRONG_SET before switching to SAP extended memory. In this case, reduce the value of abap/heap_area_nondia until the STORAGE_PARAMETERS_WRONG_SET error no longer occurs. As a rule, abap/heap_area_dia and abap/heap_area_nondia should be set to the same value; that is, to be safe, set both values to the smaller of the two values calculated. Errors such as DBIF_RSQL_NO_MEMORY, DBIF_RTAB_NO_MEMORY, or EXSORT_NOT_ENOUGH_MEMORY can arise in some cases. These errors occur if the database interface or the sort algorithm in SAP Basis requests additional heap memory from the operating system, and the system cannot provide it because SAP heap memory has already used up the available heap memory in the operating system. (*Note:* It is important at this point to distinguish between heap memory at the operating system level and SAP heap memory.) You can generally resolve this problem by reducing the abap/heap_area_dia and abap/heap_area_nondia parameters by increments of 50MB until the error no longer occurs. Therefore, less SAP heap memory is allocated, and more memory is available for the database interface or the sort algorithm.

8.3   Summary

You must configure six memory areas for an SAP instance:

▶ SAP buffer

▶ SAP roll memory

- SAP extended memory

- SAP heap memory

- SAP paging memory

- Local SAP work process memory

The goals of configuring SAP memory are *stability* (avoiding program terminations because of memory bottlenecks) and *performance* (fast access to the data and fast context switching).

The following factors affect configuration:

- **Physical main memory (RAM)**
  When configuring memory, you can allocate more virtual memory than available physical memory. An optimal main memory configuration would be a ratio of virtual main memory to physical main memory ≤ 150%. The *Quick Sizer* in the *SAP Service Marketplace* is a tool you can use to estimate the physical main memory requirement for small and average-size installations.

- **Swap space or paging file of the operating system**
  The basis for all recommendations assumes that sufficient swap space is available (about 3 to 4 RAM, but at least 3.5GB).

- **Operating system restrictions**
  If 32-bit architecture is still being used, you should identify if the operating system restrictions (for instance, the maximum address space) permit the configuration you want.

Zero Administration Memory Management considerably simplifies the administration of memory management, and *64-bit architecture* allows computers with large main memories to be configured more easily and used more effectively.

The following SAP profile parameters are relevant primarily for stability (that is, for avoiding program terminations):

```
em/initial_size_MB, em/address_space_MB, ztta/roll_exten-
sion, rdisp/roll_area, rdisp/ROLL_MAXFS, abap/heap_area_(non)
dia, abap/heap_area_total, rdisp/PG_MAXFS, abap/buffersize, ztta/
max_memreq_MB
```

The following SAP profile parameters are relevant primarily for performance:

em/initial_size_MB, ztta/roll_first, rdisp/ROLL_SHM, rdisp/PG_SHM, and all parameters for configuring the SAP buffer.

Important Concepts in this Chapter

After reading this chapter, you should be familiar with the following concepts:

▶ Physical main memory, swap space, and virtual allocated memory

▶ Local memory and shared memory

▶ User context

▶ SAP roll memory, SAP extended memory, and SAP heap memory

▶ Address space, 32-bit architecture, and 64-bit architecture

Questions

1. Which SAP profile parameters determine the parts of (a) extended memory and (b) heap memory that will be held in the physical main memory or in the swap space?

   a) SAP extended memory is always kept completely in the physical main memory, and the heap memory is created in the swap space.

   b) None. The distribution of memory areas to the physical main memory and swap space (that is, the page out and page in) is performed automatically by the operating system. An application program (such as an SAP or database program) cannot influence this distribution.

   c) The SAP profile parameter ztta/roll_extension determines which part of extended memory will be held in physical main memory, whereas similarly, the abap/heap_area_(non)dia parameter determines this for heap memory.

2. Under what circumstances might an SAP instance not start (or only start with error messages) after you have changed SAP memory management parameters?

a) The program buffer (`abap/buffer_size`) cannot be created in the preferred size because of address space restrictions.

b) The physical memory is not sufficient for the new settings.

c) The swap space is not sufficient for the new settings.

d) The extended memory (`em/initial_size_MB`) cannot be created in the preferred size because of address space restrictions.

9 SAP Buffering

Every SAP instance has various buffers in which data to be accessed by users is stored. When data is in the buffer, the database does not have to be accessed, because buffers enable direct reads from the main memory of the application server. There are two advantages to this:

► Accesses to SAP buffers are normally 10 to 100 times faster than accesses to the database.

► Database load is reduced. This is increasingly important as your system size grows.

A distinction is made between table buffers, object-oriented application buffers, and system buffers.

Types of buffers

For each table defined in the ABAP or Java dictionary, you can decide if and how the table should be buffered. Each ABAP instance has two buffers to enable table buffering: the *single-record table buffer* (also known as the *partial table buffer, TABLP*) and the *generic table buffer (TABL)*. Each J2EE instance has one table buffer. Figure 9.1 shows SAP table buffers and applies to both the ABAP server and SAP J2EE Engine. When an SAP system is delivered, the default settings determine whether a table should be buffered. However, it may be necessary to change these settings to optimize runtime. The developer of customer-developed tables must always establish these settings.

Application programs can use *object-oriented application buffers* to store data for all users and provide it to other users for reuse. On the ABAP server, these are the *export/import buffer*, the *export/import SHM buffer*, and the buffering of *shared objects*.

System buffers are used by the ABAP server or the SAP J2EE Engine for performance optimization and cannot be influenced explicitly by application programs. Examples are the *program buffer* and the *number range buffer*.

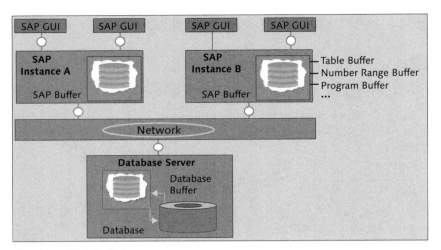

Figure 9.1 SAP Buffering

[+] This chapter deals with table buffering at the SAP application level. Chapter 11, Optimizing SQL Statements, covers table buffering at the database level.

When Should You Read this Chapter?

You should read this chapter to help you:

▶ Get detailed information on the options for SAP buffering

▶ Monitor and optimize the efficiency of buffering SAP tables at regular intervals

▶ Decide whether customer-created database tables should be buffered

▶ Decide whether to buffer the condition tables created during customizing for central SAP functions such as price determination or output determination

▶ Decide whether you as the ABAP developer want to use the object-oriented application buffers

To better understand this chapter, you should have some familiarity with ABAP programming and SQL programming.

9.1 Preliminary Remarks Concerning Chapters 9, 10, and 11

The following remarks concern the tuning measures dealt with in Chapters 9 through 11: setting buffering for tables and number ranges and creating, changing, or deleting database indexes. These measures, when correctly implemented, are important techniques for optimizing performance. However, if not implemented correctly, they can lead to massive performance problems and in some cases to data inconsistencies. Changing the buffer mode for tables and number ranges, or creating, changing, or deleting database indices involves changes to the SAP system and should only be carried out by experienced developers or consultants.

The main goal of the following chapters is to help you *identify* performance problems in these areas, that is, find the program or table causing the problem; then you can deal with it. However, before making any concrete changes to solve the problem, you should perform a *technical analysis* and a *logical analysis*. This book explains the procedure for a technical analysis. A system or database administrator can carry out this type of analysis. Only the developer can execute a logical analysis. Bear in mind the following recommendations:

Technical analysis –
logical analysis

- For customer-developed objects (for example, program, table, index, number range, and so on), changes to the buffering status or database indices should be performed only after careful consultation between the developer and system or database administrator.

- If the objects identified are from the SAP standard, the buffering status and database indices of SAP tables are already preset when the SAP system is delivered. In some cases, it may be necessary to change these standard settings. Before you perform a change, look in the SAP Service Marketplace for notes on the program name, table, or number name, which will confirm whether or not you can change the object in question. These notes reflect the SAP developer's input for the logical analysis. Changes performed without the proper expertise can lead to unexpected performance problems and data inconsistencies. Note the warnings and recommendations provided in the various sections of this book.

Important performance optimization steps are to *verify* the success of changes that have been carried out and then *document* the analysis, the changes made, and their verification.

9.2 Table Buffering Fundamentals

The following sections deal with the fundamentals of table buffering. These include the types of buffering, how to access buffers, synchronizing buffers, and activating buffers. Finally, we'll deal with the question of which tables should be buffered.

9.2.1 Buffering Types

We differentiate between three types of table buffering: single-record buffering, generic buffering, and full buffering.

Single-record buffering is suitable for accesses that are executed using all table keys, in other words, all fields of the primary index. With single-record buffering, each record (a row in a table) that is read from the database for the first time is archived in the buffer. Whenever the record needs to be read again, it can be read directly from the buffer.

[Ex] Take, for example, a table <tab_sngl> with the key fields <key1>, <key2>, and <key3>. A record is read from the table with the following SQL statement:

```
SELECT SINGLE * FROM <tab_sngl> WHERE <key1> = a1 AND
<key2> = a2 AND <key3> = a3
```

Assuming that single-record buffering is activated for table <tab_sngl>, the single-record buffer will be accessed for this SQL statement and not the database.

[+] To access the buffer, the ABAP keyword SINGLE *must* be contained in the SQL statement. SQL statements in which not all key fields are specified in the Where clause cannot be processed from single-record buffers; instead, the database will be accessed.

When you first attempt to access a table for which single-record buffering is activated, if the required record is not in the database, information

Single-record buffering

is stored in the buffer to indicate that the record does not exist. In other words, information on a failed retrieval is also buffered. On a second attempt to access this record, the buffer search recognizes that the record does not exist and makes no attempt to access the database. Therefore, the number of entries for a specific table in the single-record buffer may be larger than the number of actual records in that table in the database.

Full buffering is another way of buffering tables. With fully buffered tables, when a table record is first read, the entire table is loaded into the buffer. This type of buffering is mainly used for small tables.

Full buffering

Figure 9.2 contrasts the different types of buffering. The buffered records of a table are shown in dark gray. A fully buffered table is shown on the left. Because the table is either completely contained in the buffer or not at all, all entries will be dark gray or there will be none at all. The right-hand table in Figure 9.2 shows a single-record buffered table. Some individual records are buffered and others are not.

The third form of buffering is *generic buffering with <n> key fields*. On the first read access of a record in a generically <n> buffered table, all records with the same <n> key field values as the target records are loaded into the buffer. In Figure 9.2, the second table from the left is activated for generic buffering and *n* = 1. For this table, all records with the first key value 002 are stored in the buffer. These records make up a *generic region*. Similarly, in the third column from the left, under Generic Buffering, Using Two Key Fields, the buffer contains generic regions with the first two key fields being the same.

Generic buffering

For table <tab_gen2>, generic-2 buffering has been set. The first two primary key fields are the client (MANDT) and the company code (BUKRS). The table also contains the primary key fields <key3> and <key4>. Let's also assume that the table contains data on the company codes Poland, Czech Republic, and Slovakia. The table is now accessed with the following SQL statement:

[Ex]

```
SELECT * FROM <tab_gen2> WHERE mandt = '100' AND bukrs =
'Poland' AND <key3> = a3
```

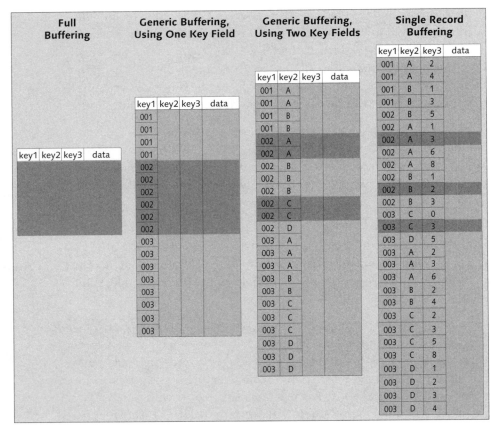

Figure 9.2 Generic Regions of a Table

This statement causes the buffering of all records in table <tab_gen2> that correspond to client 100 and company code Poland. If your SAP system has users corresponding to the different company codes working on different application servers, only the data relevant to the company code used on a particular application is loaded in the buffers of that server.

The database interface in the SAP work process carries out buffer management. Single-record buffered tables are stored in the SAP single-record buffer (TABLP); generic and fully buffered tables are stored in the generic SAP table buffer (TABL). The tables in the buffer are sorted according to the primary key.

9.2.2 Buffer Accessing

Even after a table is stored in the buffer, the database interface does not automatically access the table buffers. As previously explained, to access a single-record buffered table, all of a table's primary key fields must be specified in the Where clause of the SQL statement with an EQUALS condition. Similarly, for a generic-*n* buffered table, the first *n* primary key fields in the Where clause must be specified with an EQUALS condition. Examine the following examples:

For table <tab_gen3>, generic-3 buffering has been set. The fields <key1>, <key2>, <key3>, and <key4> are the key fields of the table. **[Ex]**

The following SQL statements access the SAP buffer:

▶ SELECT * FROM <tab_gen3> WHERE <key1> = a1 AND <key2> = a2 AND <key3> = a3

▶ SELECT * FROM <tab_gen3> WHERE <key1> = a1 AND <key2> = a2 AND <key3> = a3 and <key4> > a4

The following SQL statements cannot be processed with the help of the SAP buffer and require access to the database:

▶ SELECT * FROM <tab_gen3> WHERE <key1> = a1

▶ SELECT * FROM <tab_gen3> WHERE <key3> = a3

The buffer for the generic-3 buffered table is not accessed, because the fields <key1>, <key2>, and <key3> are not all specified.

With a fully buffered table, the buffer is always accessed, provided the table in question has been loaded into the buffer.

Table <tab_ful> has full buffering. The fields <key1>, <key2>, <key3>, and <key4> are the key fields of the table. **[Ex]**

The following SQL statements access the SAP buffer:

▶ SELECT * FROM <tab_ful> WHERE <key1> = a1 AND <key2> = a2 AND <key3> = a3

▶ SELECT * FROM <tab_ful> WHERE <key3> = a3

Because the second statement does not specify the fields <key1> and <key2>, and the table in the buffer is sorted according to these key fields, all of the data in the table must be read sequentially. If the table is relatively large (for example, has more than 100 records) it will be more effective to optimize table access by not buffering the table, but by creating a secondary index on the database using the field <key3>.

As this example shows, access to a database can in some cases be more optimal than accessing a buffer. We'll look at this in greater detail at a later stage in the book.

Other exceptions The following SQL statements do *not* access the SAP buffer:

- ▶ SQL statements with the clause BYPASSING BUFFER. This clause is used to indicate statements that should definitely not access the buffer.
- ▶ SELECT FOR UPDATE statements. These statements set a database lock; as a result, they involve database access.
- ▶ SQL statements using the aggregate functions SUM, AVG, MIN, and MAX.
- ▶ SQL statements with SELECT DISTINCT.
- ▶ SQL statements containing the operator IS NULL or IS NOT NULL.
- ▶ SQL statements that trigger sorts (except sorts by primary key) or that contain the GROUP BY operator.
- ▶ SQL statements that access views (except projection views), joins, and statements with subqueries.
- ▶ Native SQL statements.

These checks are also included in the Code Inspector; that is, if an SQL statement on a buffered table meets these exception conditions, the Code Inspector informs you about it. You should then check whether it would be better to change the statement so that it can be processed in the buffer.

9.2.3 Buffer Synchronization

If an entry to a buffered table is changed, the corresponding entries in the table buffers of all SAP instances must be updated. This process is referred to as *buffer synchronization*.

First, we'll look at changes to tables executed with an ABAP statement without a Where clause, that is, with the ABAP statements (instructions)

UPDATE dbtab, INSERT dbtab, MODIFY dbtab, and DELETE dbtab. Only one row in the table is changed in this case.

Buffer synchronization involves four steps, as illustrated in Figure 9.3. For example, assume that one record is changed in the buffered table T001:

Synchronization cycle

1. The buffered table T001 is changed by the ABAP statement UPDATE T001 for SAP instance A. The database interface modifies table T001 on the database and the buffer entry for instance A at the same time. Therefore, the buffer of the local SAP instance A is *updated synchronously*. At this time, the buffers of all SAP instances (except for A) are not up-to-date.

2. After table T001 has been changed in the database, the database interface (DBIF) for SAP instance A logs the change by writing an entry to database table DDLOG.

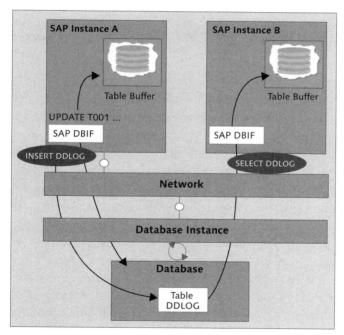

Figure 9.3 Buffer Synchronization

3. Table DDLOG is periodically read by all SAP instances. On the basis of the DDLOG entry, the buffer entry for table T001 is *invalidated*. The buffers of the SAP instances are still not updated, but the content of table T001 in the buffer is marked as being invalid.

4. If table T001 is read again on an SAP instance other than A, the database interface can recognize that the data in the buffer is no longer valid. The data is reloaded from the database into the buffer. In this way, the buffers of all SAP instances other than instance A are *asynchronously* updated.

Pending period

After an invalidation, the contents of a table are not immediately loaded into the buffer at the next read access. Rather, a certain waiting or *pending period* is observed. The next *n* accesses are redirected to the database. The buffer is only reloaded after the pending period. This protects the buffer from frequent successive invalidation and reload operations. You can find profile parameters for parameterizing the pending period in Appendix C. They should not be changed.

[+]

The synchronization mechanism described here applies not only to table buffers, but also to numerous SAP system buffers such as the program buffer.

rdisp/bufrefmode, rdisp/bufreftime

The SAP profile parameters `rdisp/bufrefmode` and `rdisp/bufreftime` control buffer synchronization. The parameter `rdisp/bufrefmode` should be set for an SAP system with only one SAP instance to "sendoff, exeauto." The sendoff entry means that no DDLOG entries can be written (because there is no other SAP instance to be synchronized), and exeauto means table DDLOG is read periodically. This is necessary for buffer synchronization after an import using the transport programs `tp` or `R3trans`. (The Change and Transport System [CTS] writes entries to the DDLOG table to enable buffer synchronization after the import of buffered objects, for example, table contents and programs.) In an SAP system with multiple SAP instances, `rdisp/bufrefmode` must contain the value "sendon, exeauto." You should not change the default value of 60 (seconds) for `rdisp/bufreftime`, which specifies the frequency of buffer synchronization; this means table DDLOG is read every 60 seconds.

Table entries are *invalidated* as follows:

▸ If a record is changed in a table with single-record buffering, then just this record is invalidated. All other buffered table entries remain valid.

▸ If a record in a fully buffered table is changed, then the entire contents of the table are invalidated.

▸ If a record in a generically buffered table is changed, then the generic area in which this record is located is invalidated.

Therefore, table contents are invalidated in the same units that they are filled.

A somewhat different buffer synchronization procedure is used when a buffered table is changed by an ABAP statement that uses a Where clause, for example, with UPDATE <dbtab> WHERE..., DELETE FROM <dbtab> WHERE.... You can use this type of ABAP statement to change several records in a table. And as a result, the entire <dbtab> table in question is invalidated in the buffer of the local SAP instance (for example, our instance A) and on all other servers. Therefore, changes using Where clauses can increase buffer management workload much more than change operations that do not use Where.

When program or customizing settings are transported, invalidations also occur. Therefore, imports should not be carried out in a production system at times of high workload. We recommend that imports be scheduled once or twice per week at times of low workload.

[+]

Invalidations should not be confused with *displacements*, which are displayed in the SAP memory configuration monitor (Transaction ST02) in the Swaps column. When there is not enough space in the buffer to store new data, data that has not been accessed for the longest time is displaced. Displacement occurs asynchronously (determined by accesses to the buffer) when the space available in the buffer falls below a certain level or when access quality falls below a certain point.

9.2.4 Activating Buffering

1. To activate or deactivate table buffering, call the ABAP dictionary function by selecting: TOOLS • ABAP WORKBENCH • DICTIONARY.

2. Enter the table name, click the Display button, and then select Technical Settings. Figure 9.4 shows a screenshot of the user inferface.

3. To activate buffering, select Buffering Switched On. Finally, enter the buffering type (full, generic, or single record) and in the case of generic buffering, the number of key fields.

4. Save the new settings.

5. Once you have saved the settings, you can activate the changes. The settings should then show the status Active, Saved.

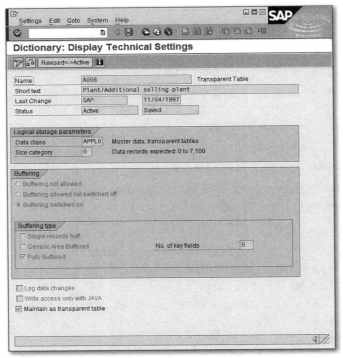

Figure 9.4 Technical Settings of a Table

[+] Because a table's technical settings are linked to the Change and Transport System (CTS), to change the buffering for a table, you need a change request. You can activate or deactivate buffering while the SAP system is running.

There are three options for setting buffering:

▸ **Buffering not allowed**
This setting deactivates buffering for a table. Use it if a table should not be buffered under any circumstances, for example, if it contains transaction data that is frequently changed.

▸ **Buffering allowed but switched off**
This setting also deactivates buffering for a table. It means that it is possible to buffer this table, but for performance reasons in this particular system, buffering has been deactivated, for example, because the table is too large. Whether a table with this characteristic should in fact be buffered can be ascertained from the analyses described later in this chapter.

▸ **Buffering switched on**
This setting activates the buffering for the table.

If you try to activate buffering for a table that was delivered with the setting Buffering Not Allowed, this is considered a modification of the SAP system and must be registered in the SAP Service Marketplace. You should activate buffering for these tables only if SAP explicitly advises you to do so.

[!]

If you set the buffering type for a client-dependent table to Full, the table will automatically be buffered as generic 1.

[+]

9.2.5   Which Tables Should Be Buffered?

If tables will be buffered, they must satisfy the following *technical prerequisites*:

Technical prerequisites

▸ Buffered data will be stored redundantly on all SAP instances. As a result, buffering is only suitable for small tables that are read frequently.

▸ Buffer synchronization causes a considerable loss in performance when accessing buffered tables. Therefore, only tables that are not changed often should be buffered.

▶ Buffered tables are sorted and stored according to key fields. Table buffering is therefore optimal for statements that access the table through the key fields. Table buffers do not support searches using secondary indexes.

▶ Buffer synchronization occurs after a certain delay. Therefore, you should only buffer tables for which short-term inconsistencies are acceptable.

In SAP systems, we differentiate between three types of data: transaction data, master data, and customizing data.

Never buffer transaction data!

Transaction data includes items such as sales orders, deliveries, material movements, and material reservations. This data might be stored in the tables VBAK, LIKP, MKPF, and RESB, which grow over time and can reach several megabytes or even gigabytes in size. In principle, transaction data should not be buffered.

As a rule, do not buffer master data!

Typical *master data* includes, for example, materials, customers, and suppliers and is stored in the tables MARA, KNA1, and LFA1. Tables with master data grow slowly over time and can reach a size of several hundred megabytes. Therefore, master data is generally not buffered. Another argument against buffering master data tables is that master data is normally accessed with many different selections and not necessarily via the primary key. You can optimize accesses to these tables by using secondary indices, rather than buffering.

Customizing data is normally buffered!

Customizing data maps, among other things, the business processes of your enterprise in the SAP system. Examples of customizing data include the definition of clients, company codes, and plant and sales organizations. This information is stored in tables T000, T001, T001W, and TVKO. Customizing tables are generally small and seldom changed once the system has gone live. Therefore, customizing data is well suited to table buffering.

[Ex]

Table TCURR, for example, contains exchange rates for foreign currencies. The key fields in this table are MANDT (client), KURST (type of exchange rate), FCURR (source currency), TCURR (target currency), and GDATU (start of validity period). In most customer systems this table is small; it is rarely changed and meets all of the conditions for buffering. Therefore, it is delivered by SAP with the status Full Buffering set.

In some SAP systems, however, this table may grow quickly because many exchange rates are required and rates frequently change. Because the table is fully buffered, older entries (with validity periods that have long since expired) are loaded into the buffer, although they are no longer necessary for normal operation. As a result, when the table reaches a certain size, table buffering is no longer effective. If the table is changed during daily operation, invalidations and displacements reduce performance.

In this case, you should remove the table from buffering and try to achieve a long-term application-specific solution: Are all table entries really necessary? Can old entries be removed, for example, by archiving? We'll look at this example again in greater detail in Section 9.3.4, Detailed Table Analysis.

Condition tables contain the customizing data for central logical functions that determine information such as pricing, output determination, partner determination, account determination, and so on. These functions are used in the logistics chain and for incoming sales orders, goods issue, billing, and so on. These transactions are extremely critical for performance in many SAP systems, so optimized buffering of condition tables should receive special priority.

Condition tables

Condition tables are A*<nnn>*, B*<nnn>*, C*<nnn>*, D*<nnn>*, KOTE*<nnn>*, KOTF*<nnn>*, KOTG*<nnn>*, and KOTH*<nnn>*, where *<nnn>* = 000–999. Tables with *nnn* = 000–499 are part of the SAP standard and, with a few exceptions, are delivered with the attribute Buffering Switched On. Tables with *nnn* = 500–999 are generated in customizing as required and are not initially buffered.

Table A005 contains customer- and material-specific price conditions. In other words, you can maintain a price condition in this table for every combination of customer and material. In addition, you can set a validity period for the price condition. If customer-specific prices are used intensively in an SAP system, and these prices are frequently changed, this table would grow very quickly. A problem similar to what was described in the TCURR table example would occur. In this case, the table would

[Ex]

have to be removed from buffering. Other condition tables that also grow quickly include A017 and A018 (prices for suppliers and material numbers).

9.3 Monitoring Table Buffering on the ABAP Server

Three problems can occur in the area of SAP table buffering, and they should be monitored:

▶ If table buffers are designed too small, *displacements (swaps) can* occur. Chapter 2, Section 2.4, Analyzing SAP Memory Configuration, describes displacement monitoring. Before continuing with a detailed analysis, ensure that the table buffer has at least 10% free space and at least 20% free directory entries.

▶ Tables may have been buffered that, for performance reasons, should not have been buffered, because they are changed *(invalidated)* too often or because they are too large.

▶ Tables that should be buffered for performance reasons are not buffered. This applies mainly to tables that are created in the customer system, whether explicitly in the ABAP dictionary or implicitly in customizing (for example, condition tables).

Monitoring table buffering is not a task that you need to carry out periodically. Some examples of when table buffers should be examined include:

▶ Users complain about occasional long response times in a transaction that normally runs quickly.

▶ When analyzing the SQL statistics or an SQL trace, you find expensive SQL statements related to buffered tables, which would indicate reload processes caused by incorrect buffering.

▶ When analyzing the single-record statistics (Transaction STAT), you frequently find the entry "Note: Tables were saved in the table buffer" (see also Chapter 4, Section 4.1, Single-Record Statistics).

The monitors and strategies that follow can help you identify problems with incorrectly buffered tables.

9.3.1 Table Access Statistics

SAP table access statistics (also called *table call statistics*) is the most important monitor for analyzing SAP table buffering.

1. The monitor can be started as follows: TOOLS • ADMINISTRATION • MONITOR • PERFORMANCE • SETTINGS/BUFFER • BUFFER.

2. A selection screen appears where you can select the time period, the SAP instance, and the type of table to be analyzed. For this analysis, select All Tables, Since Startup, and This Server.

3. A screen is displayed that lists details of ABAP and database accesses and buffer status for all tables in the SAP system. You can navigate between different lists by using the arrow buttons. By double-clicking a row, you can view all of the information available for that table.

Table 9.1 describes the most important fields.

Field	Explanation
Table	Name of the table: If it is a pooled table, the name of the table pool is given first, —for example, KAPOL A004.
Buffer State	The status of the table in the buffer (if this table can be buffered). See Table 9.2 for more information.
Buf Key Opt	Buffering type: Ful indicates full buffering, Gen indicates generic buffering, and Sng indicates single-record buffering.
Buffer Size (Bytes)	Space occupied by the table in the SAP table buffer.
Maximum Size (Bytes)	Maximum size of the table in the SAP table buffer since system startup.
Invalidations	Number of invalidations.
ABAP/IV Processor Requests	Number of ABAP table access requests received by the database interface, subdivided into direct reads, sequential reads, updates, inserts, and deletes.
DB Activity	Number of database operations (Prepare, Open, Reopen, Fetch, or Exec) that the database interface has forwarded to the database, subdivided according to direct reads, sequential reads, updates, inserts, deletes.
DB Activity— Rows Affected	Number of rows transferred between the database and the SAP instance.

Table 9.1 Fields in SAP Table Access Statistics

Table access in an ABAP program is called a *request*. We differentiate between five types of requests: direct reads, sequential reads, inserts, updates, and deletes. Direct reads are SELECT SINGLE statements that specify all of the primary key fields in the Where clause with an EQUALS condition. All other Select statements are known as sequential reads. Inserts, updates, and deletes are referred to as *changes*.

In a request, the ABAP program calls up the database interface of the SAP work process. The database interface checks to see if the SAP instance's table buffer can provide the data needed for the query. If not, the database interface passes the SQL statement on to the database. An SQL statement performing a read is made up of an OPEN operation that transfers the SQL statement to the database and one or more fetches that transfer the resulting data from the database to the SAP work process. An SQL statement that is performing a change is similarly made up of an OPEN operation and an EXEC operation. For more detailed explanations of the Prepare, Open, Reopen, Fetch, and Exec operations, see Section 4.3.2, Evaluating an SQL Trace.

For tables that cannot be buffered, the database interface automatically passes each request on to the database. For direct reads, inserts, updates, and deletes, each request corresponds to exactly one OPEN and one FETCH. For sequential reads, the situation is more complex, because there can be more than one OPEN or FETCH for each request.

For tables that can be buffered, requests encounter one of three possible situations:

▸ The content of the table is located in the buffer with a Valid status. The required data can be read from the buffer. As a result, this request requires no database activity.

▸ The content of the table is located in the valid buffer, but the SQL statement does not specify the correct fields, or it contains the clause BYPASSING BUFFER to prevent reading from the SAP buffer. You can find a complete list of SQL statements that do not read from the SAP buffer in Section 9.2.2, Buffer Accessing. In this situation, database activity is required to satisfy the request.

▸ The table content is not yet located in the buffer or is not valid. In this situation, the data needed for the request cannot be read from the buffer. The database interface loads the buffer (if the table is not Pending).

During the initial buffer load process, the Database Activity: Rows Affected field is not increased. If a table has been loaded only once into the buffer, and all subsequent requests are read from the buffer, the value in Database Activity: Rows Affected remains zero in the table access statistics. If the table is invalidated or displaced and then reloaded into the buffer from the database, or if the buffer is bypassed, the Database Activity: Rows Affected field is increased by the number of table rows that are read.

The Buffer State field shows the *buffer status* of a table. Table 9.2 lists the various statuses.

Buffer status

Status	Explanation
Valid	The table (or parts of it) is valid in the buffer, which means the next access can be read from the buffer.
Invalid	The table has been invalidated. It cannot be reloaded into the buffer yet, because the operation that changed the table has not been completed with `Commit`.
Pending	The table has been invalidated. It cannot be loaded at the next access, because the pending period is still running.
Loadable	The table has been invalidated. The pending period has expired, and the table will be reloaded at the next access.
Loading	The table is currently being loaded.
Absent, Displaced	The table is not in the buffer (because, for example, it was never loaded or it has been displaced).
Multiple	Can occur for tables with generic buffering: Some generic areas are valid; others have been invalidated because of changes.
Error	An error occurred while the table was being loaded. This table cannot be buffered.

Table 9.2 Buffering Statuses

Figure 9.5 shows a screenshot of a table access statistic in an SAP system. **[Ex]** The list is sorted according to the DB Activity – Rows Affected column, which indicates the number of records read from the database. You will find buffered tables at the top of the list, such as the condition tables A004, A005, and A952. The entry KAPOL preceding the name indicates that these tables are located in the KAPOL table pool. We'll return to the evaluation of this example in the next section.

9.3.2 Analyzing Buffered Tables

We'll now identify buffered tables for which buffering reduces rather than increases performance. To do so, proceed as follows:

1. Start the SAP table call statistics: TOOLS • ADMINISTRATION • MONITOR • PERFORMANCE • SETUP/BUFFERS • CALLS.

2. In the screen that appears, select All Tables, Since Startup, and This Server.

3. The screen that appears next should resemble the one shown in Figure 9.5.

Step 1: Determining Number of Database Accesses

Rows affected First, sort the table call statistics according to the DB Activity – Rows Affected column. The number of rows affected is an indication of the database load caused by accesses to the table. The tables with high database activity will appear at the top of the list. These should be transaction data tables or large master data tables, for example, the tables VBAK, S508, and MDVM in Figure 9.5. For many of these tables, the number of requests is approximately the same as the number of rows affected.

For buffered tables, the number of rows affected should be low, because data accesses to these tables should be read from the buffer and not from the database. Therefore, these tables should not appear toward the top of the list. If, as in Figure 9.5, you find buffered tables with a high number of rows affected, there are two possible causes:

▶ The table is relatively large and has been changed or displaced. Reloading processes and database read accesses during the pending period reflect a high number of rows affected. Check to see if buffering should be deactivated for these tables.

▶ The type of buffering does not match the Where clause in the read accesses, so the database interface cannot use the buffer.

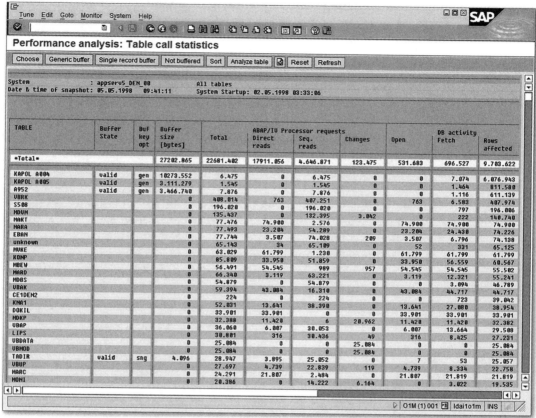

Figure 9.5 Table Call Statistics (First Example)

If buffered tables appear among the top entries in the table call statistics, **[+]** sorted according to rows affected, this is a sure sign that buffering these tables is counterproductive. These tables should be analyzed in greater detail.

Step 2: Analyzing the Rate of Changes and Invalidations

Next, determine the rate of change for the buffered tables (Changes/ Requests in the table calls statistics) and the number of invalidations. To do this, sort according to the Invalidations or Changes column. Using the guideline values presented earlier, check to see if buffering should be deactivated for the tables with the highest rates of change and the most invalidations.

Step 3: Determining Table Size

Sort the table call statistics according to table size (the Buffer Size column). First, you should check the buffering status of the largest table. It should be Valid. By comparing the values for Buffer Size and Size maximum, you can see if generic areas of the table have been displaced or invalidated. Also check, using the following guideline values, if buffering should be deactivated for the largest table.

The following counters may be useful when deciding whether a table should be buffered or not: Tables that are smaller than 1MB and with an invalidation rate less than 1% do not generally present any technical problems and can be buffered. Tables between 1 and 5MB should have an invalidation rate of less than 0.1%. For tables that are larger than 5MB, the developer must decide whether table buffering is worthwhile on an individual basis. (Note: These guideline values reflect users' practical experiences at the time of this book's writing.)

Step 4: Logical Analysis

Before deactivating table buffering, you should consider the following recommendations:

▶ **For customer-developed tables**
You should only make changes to the table buffering status after the joint consideration of the developer and system administrator.

▶ **For tables created by SAP**
Occasionally, you may need to deactivate buffering for a table that had buffering activated in the standard delivery. An example could be the previously mentioned TCURR table or SAP condition tables (such as Annn). However, never deactivate buffering unless you have analyzed the table functions closely. This applies in particular to SAP Basis tables such as DDFTX and USR*. If you find an SAP table for which you want to deactivate buffering, first look for related notes in the SAP Service Marketplace.

Verifying the Effects of Changes

When the buffering mode of a table has been changed, you should verify its success.

Ideally, you should know the programs and transactions that access the table in question and directly observe how the changes affect runtime.

In the table call statistics, you can verify the success of your changes by comparing the number of requests to rows affected. The purpose of a table buffer is to reduce the number of database accesses. This should be reflected in the ratio of requests to rows affected. If by changing the buffering for a table you have not managed to increase this ratio, reanalyze the buffer and, if in doubt, undo the changes made to buffering.

Figures 9.5 and 9.6 show screenshots of table call statistics from two real SAP systems. Both lists are sorted according to the DB Activity – Rows Affected column.

[Ex]

We will first look at Figure 9.5. As previously mentioned, we expect that tables with transaction data or a large volume of master data would be at the top of the list, such as VBRK, S508, and MDVM. However, at the top of the list, we see the buffered condition tables A004, A005, and A952. The buffering status of these tables is Valid, which means these tables are located in the buffer. When comparing the columns Abap/iv Processor Requests – Total and DB Activity – Rows Affected, you will see that per request (that is, per ABAP access), an average of 1,000 rows are read from the table. For these three tables, a total of about 7.5 million rows were read. This represents approximately 75% of the records read for all of the tables, together (9.7 million). It is likely that the very high number of reads for these three tables is caused by frequent buffer load processes.

To verify this suspicion, examine the number of invalidations and the size of the table in the buffer: Double-click the row containing the table you want to analyze. This takes you to a screen summarizing all of the available information on this table. In our example, you will see that tables A004, A005, and A952 are frequently invalidated, which means they have an invalidation rate of more than 1% of the total requests. The size of the tables in the buffer (Buffer Size [Bytes] field in Figure 9.5) is between 3 and 10MB. According to our guidelines for table buffering, these tables should not be buffered. By analyzing table call statistics in this case, we come to the conclusion that buffering should be deactivated for tables A004, A005, and A952.

When looking at the Changes column in Figure 9.5, you might at first be surprised to see that tables A004, A005, and A952 are invalidated, although no changes are indicated in the Changes column. This is because the Changes column only displays changes that are performed on the local SAP instance (here, appserv5_DEN_00). Modifications are not shown in the Changes field if they are executed on other SAP instances or if the changes to the customizing tables are carried out in another SAP system (such as the development system) and then transferred to the SAP system being examined. Nevertheless, these changes from other SAP systems do cause invalidations of buffer entries and start local buffer reloading.

An analysis similar to the one just carried out on the table call statistics shown in Figure 9.5 can also be carried out for Figure 9.6. In this example, the list is also sorted according to DB Activity – Rows Affected, and we also have several buffered tables at the top of the list. The entry Displcd in the Buffer State column shows that table A005 was not invalidated because of a change; rather, it was displaced because of a lack of space in the buffer. Therefore, two factors come together in this example: On the one hand, tables were buffered that were possibly too large and changed too often for buffering, and on the other hand, the table buffer is too small, and this caused displacements. You can see if displacements occur in the table buffer by checking the Swaps column in the SAP memory configuration monitor (Transaction ST02).

Because the example in Figure 9.6 reveals two problems, the corresponding solution strategy is more complex. First, the size of the table buffers should be increased. You should examine the size and number of invalidations in tables A005, A004, A006, and A017 in more detail, and (using the previously listed guideline values) you should decide whether buffering should be deactivated for these tables. For example, if you find that table A005 is larger than 1MB, and the number of invalidations is greater than 0.1%, you should deactivate buffering for this table. After this first optimization step, carry out a second analysis on the table call statistics to see if the number of database accesses to the buffered tables is noticeably reduced. If not, analyze the table statistics further to determine whether you need to enlarge the table buffer size or deactivate buffering for other tables.

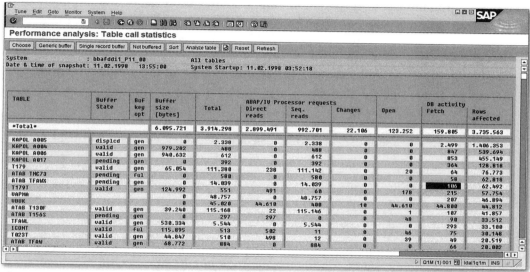

Figure 9.6 Table Call Statistics (Second Example)

For computers with a large main memory, it is not unusual for the generic buffer table to be configured with as much as 100MB and single-record buffers configured for 40MB.

[+]

9.3.3 Analyzing Tables that Are Currently Not Buffered

In this section, we'll describe an analysis that will help you decide if you should activate buffering for tables that are currently not buffered. To perform the analysis, call up the table call statistics and proceed as follows:

Step 1: Access Statistics

To identify tables that are currently not buffered and may potentially benefit from buffering, first, sort the table call statistics monitor according to the abap/iv Processor Requests – Total column. You will normally find the tables DDNTF and DDNTT at the top of the list. These are ABAP

Requests

dictionary tables that are stored in the NTAB buffers — the field description buffer and the table definition buffer. The next tables in the list will be as follows:

▶ Tables with transaction data or large master data tables, such as MARA, MARC, VBAK, and MKPF from SAP logistics modules, and SAP update tables VBHDR, VBMOD, and VBDATA. These tables cannot be buffered.

▶ Buffered tables with customizing data. Ensure that buffered tables with a high number of requests show the Valid status.

If there are nonbuffered customizing tables at the top of the list, sorted by requests, you should consider activating buffering for them.

Pay particular attention to customer-developed tables. These include tables explicitly created in the ABAP dictionary (for example, tables with names that begin with Y or Z) and condition tables generated during customizing (for example, with A*nnn, nnn* ≥ 500).

The result of our first step is a list of tables that could potentially be buffered, because they receive a high number of requests.

Step 2: Technical Analysis

Determine the invalidation rate and size of the table with a technical analysis.

Changes

One criterion for deciding if a table should be buffered is the change rate, which can be calculated from the ratio of changes to requests. Note that the Changes column only displays the changes on the selected SAP instance, but not changes performed on other SAP instances or those imported as table content.

Table size

You should also determine the size of the table (see also Section 9.3.4, Detailed Table Analysis).

Step 3: Logical Analysis

Check to see if the logical prerequisites for buffering are met (see also Section 9.2.5, Which Tables Should Be Buffered?):

▶ **For customer-developed tables**

To determine if the technical prerequisites for buffering are met, contact the table's developer to find out the purpose of the table and determine whether or not the it should be buffered, from a logical point of view. For example, condition tables are usually suited to buffering. The developer sets the type of table buffering. Note that single-record buffering and generic buffering are only useful if the key fields are specified in the Where clause of the access requests.

Changes to table buffering status should only be made after joint deliberation between the developer and system administrator.

▶ **For tables created by SAP**

The buffering status of SAP tables was preset when the SAP system was delivered. Usually, most of the tables that can be buffered are buffered. If you find an SAP table that you think should be buffered, check for relevant notes in the SAP Service Marketplace. Never activate buffering for tables with the characteristic Buffering Not Allowed unless you have explicit instructions to do so from SAP.

Activating buffering can lead to logical inconsistencies because of asyn- **[!]** chronous buffer synchronization. You should therefore never activate buffering if you are not sure how the table functions or what types of accesses are made to the table. Activating buffering can also cause performance problems if the table is too big and/or is changed too frequently.

9.3.4 Detailed Table Analysis

With detailed table analysis, you can determine the size of a table, the number of table entries, and the distribution of the generic regions in a table:

1. To start the detailed table analysis, mark a table in the table call statistics monitor and click the Analyze button, or enter Transaction DB05. For older SAP versions, start the report RSTUNE59.

2. Enter a table name and select Analysis for Primary Key. Start the analysis. (*Note:* This may take some time for large tables.) The results of the analysis are then shown.

3. Use this list to check the size of the table. In the upper part of the list you will find, among other things, the number of table entries and the size that the table would be if fully buffered. This size can be smaller or larger than the space needed for the table on the database. For example, database fragmentation can cause the table to consume unnecessary database space. In addition, unlike some databases, the table buffer does not compress empty fields to minimize the need for storage space.

4. Check the distribution of generic areas of the table. You will find the necessary information in the lower part of the analysis screen.

[Ex] Table 9.3 shows an example of the possible distribution of generic regions in table TCURR. (See also Section 9.2.5, Which Tables Should Be Buffered?) The distribution displayed is for production client 100.

Rows per Generic Key	Distinct Values	1–10	11–100	101–1,000	1,001–10,000	10,000–100,000	>100,000
MANDT	The following distribution applies to client 100						
1. KURST	41	10	14	11	0	6	
2. FCURR	1,311	877	209	175	50		
3. TCURR	5,188	1,921	2,920	347			
4. GDATU	169,795	169,795					

Table 9.3 Example of a Detailed Analysis of Generic Regions for Table TCURR

This distribution analysis is interpreted as follows:

▶ **KURST row**
The Distinct Values column shows the number of generic regions, which in this example is the number of different types of currency exchange (KURST field). Table TCURR contains 41 types of currency exchange. Of these, 10 types have between 1 and 10 entries in the table (1–10 column), 14 types have between 11 and 100 entries, and so on. Finally there are six exchange rates with between 10,000 and 100,000 entries. No exchange rate type has more than 100,000 entries.

▶ **FCURR row**
There are 1,311 different combinations of exchange rate types (KURST

field) and source currencies (FCURR). No combination has more than 10,000 entries. (The 10,000–100,000 row is empty.)

▶ **Last row; GDATU**

There are 169,795 different entries with the combination MANDT, KURST, FCURR, TCURR, and GDATU. This is also the total number of entries in client 100, because MANDT, KURST, FCURR, TCURR, and GDATU make up the complete primary key for table TCURR.

Ultimately, one row of this distribution analysis shows the average number of rows read when one, two, or n fields of the primary key are specified.

How does this distribution analysis help you decide how table TCURR should be buffered?

Evaluating the analysis

▶ First, you can see that table TCURR has 169,795 entries in the live client. If TCURR has full or generic-1 buffering, a change operation always invalidates the client entirely. Therefore, after a change operation, 169,795 records must be reloaded into the buffer. In other words, the buffer loading process is justified only if users need to make over 100,000 read accesses. The invalidation rate for this table must be very low to ensure that buffering the table does not cause too great a reduction in performance.

▶ If you decide to set generic-3 buffering for table TCURR, a maximum of 1,311 generic regions would be buffered, as shown in the FCURR row of the Distinct Values column. The largest regions (50 in total) contain between 1,001 and 10,000 records. If a record in the table TCURR is changed, then a maximum of 10,000 records would be invalidated and reloaded.

▶ It would also be possible to set generic-4 buffering. Up to 5,188 generic regions would then be buffered.

From this analysis, it is clear that full buffering for table TCURR is out of the question. Depending on the invalidation rate, this table should be set to generic-3 buffering or not buffered at all.

The larger the table, the more you should favor generic buffering.

[+]

In the initial screen of the detailed table analysis, you have the option of selecting the Analysis for Fields function. This enables you to start analyses for any combination of table fields, which are specified in Field1, Field2, and so on. With this analysis, you can determine the selectivity of a secondary index. (See also Chapter 11, Section 11.2, Optimizing SQL Statements Through Secondary Indexes.)

9.3.5 Monitoring Buffer Synchronization (DDLOG Entries)

The buffer synchronization monitor displays the remaining, undeleted entries in the DDLOG table.

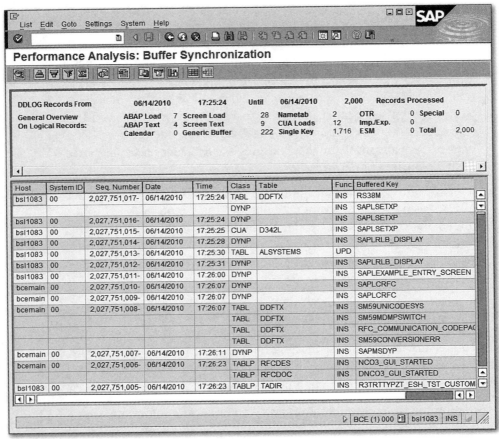

Figure 9.7 Buffer Synchronization Monitor

1. You can start the monitor via the menu path TOOLS • ADMINISTRA-
   TION • MONITOR • PERFORMANCE • SETUP/BUFFERS • BUFFERS • DETAIL
   ANALYSIS MENU • BUFFER SYNCHRON.

2. In the selection screen, you can specify the buffer for which you want
   to view the synchronization activities. You can select all buffers with
   the Select all button.

3. Then select Read DDLOG. A list appears that displays the synchronization operations according to the selection criteria entered.

Figure 9.7 shows an example of the output of this monitor. Table 9.4
explains the various fields.

Field	Explanation
Hostname	Name of the application server that has written the synchronization entry. If the referral originates from an import, this column shows the entry "tp" or "R3trans."
ID and SEQ. No.	Unique identification (for internal use).
Date and Time	Time stamp.
Class	Name of the buffer: NTAB, ABAP, TABLP, TABL, etc.
Tablename	Name of the synchronized table.
Func	Database operation: INS, DEL, UPD.
Object Key	Relevant key if the invalidated area is a generic region.

Table 9.4 Fields in the Buffer Synchronization Monitor

9.3.6 SQL Statistics and SQL Trace

Normally, buffered tables should not cause any database accesses, except
for the initial loading of the buffer. After the SAP system has been in
production operation for some time, no SQL statements used for loading
the buffer should appear in the *SQL statistics* or in *SQL trace*. However,
if these statements appear among the expensive statements in the SQL
statistics or in SQL trace, it means they are not being buffered properly.

You can recognize an SQL statement that was used to load a buffer as
follows:

▶ The Where clause for the generic-*n* buffered tables specifies the first *n* fields with an equals sign. For a table with full buffering or generic-1 buffering, this is the client (if the table is client-dependent).

▶ The SQL statement contains an ORDER-BY condition, which contains all of the fields of the table key.

[Ex] The following SQL statement loads the buffer for table TMODU, a generic-1 buffered table:

```
SELECT * FROM "TMODU" WHERE "FAUNA" = :A0 ORDER BY "FAUNA",
"MODIF", "TABNM", "FELDN", "KOART", "UMSKS"
```

If the table to be buffered is a pooled table, there is a database access during buffer loading to the table pool in which the table is located.

[Ex] Pooled table A002 is fully buffered and located in the KAPOL table pool. The SQL statement for loading the buffer is:

```
SELECT "TABNAME", "VARKEY", "DATALN", "VARDATA" FROM "KAPOL"
WHERE "TABNAME" = :A0 ORDER BY "TABNAME", "VARKEY"
```

ATAB and KAPOL are important table pools. ATAB contains many SAP Basis buffered tables (such as T<*nnn*>); KAPOL contains many condition tables (such as A<*nnn*>).

9.4   Monitoring the Table Buffering on the SAP J2EE Engine

Programming the table buffer on the SAP J2EE Engine is similar to buffering the ABAP server. The buffering properties of a table are set in the table editor of the Java dictionary, which is also like the ABAP tables. It is possible to set the buffer properties Fully Buffered, Generic Buffered, and Single Record Buffered. The table buffer also stores the negative search results; that is, a fully buffered table is stored if the entire table is empty, generic buffered tables are stored whether a generic region has no entries in the database, and single records (for which no data exists in the database table) in single-record buffered tables are stored. The same rules apply as for the statements in which no buffer is used (see Section 9.2.2, Buffer Accessing).

You use the catalog buffer to buffer metadata from the tables and access it via Open SQL. It is identical to the NTAB and FTAB buffer of the ABAP server. Use this monitor to check the buffer quality. You can start the monitor in the local SAP NetWeaver Administrator by selecting PROB-LEM MANAGEMENT • DATABASE • OPEN SQL MONITORS • CATALOG BUFFER MONITOR.

Catalog buffer

The following information is displayed:

▶ **Buffer ID**
Identifier for the buffer instance within a J2EE instance consisting of a combination of database computer, database name, and database schema

▶ **References**
Number of current read accesses to the buffer instance

▶ **Max**
Maximum number of entries in the buffer

▶ **Current**
Current number of entries in the buffer

▶ **Free:**
Number of free entries in the buffer

▶ **Displacements**
Number of displacements in the buffer

The Buffered Catalog Tables and Catalog Table Columns subscreens display the tables and table columns for which metadata has been buffered.

You use the table buffer to buffer the content of tables that are accessed via Open SQL. You can start the monitor in the local SAP NetWeaver Administrator by selecting PROBLEM MANAGEMENT • DATABASE • OPEN SQL MONITORS • TABLE BUFFER MONITOR.

Table buffer

For each buffer (there is one buffer for each J2EE instance), the Administration and Displacement tables provide administrative information such as the start time and reset time of the buffer, buffer size, and information about the stored objects and accesses.

The list of buffered objects is in the Buffered Objects table. Table 9.5 displays the information provided for each buffered object, which you can use to determine whether buffering in the table is efficient and useful.

Field	Explanation
Table Name	Name of the buffered table
Status	Status of the table in the buffer
Buffering	Buffering type: full, generic, or single record
Generic Key	Number of key fields that make up generic buffer regions
Count	Number of table records in the buffer for which values are available in the database table
Not Founds	Number of records in the buffer for which no values are available in the database table
Size (B)	Space occupied by the table in the table buffer of the SAP J2EE Engine
Invalidations	Number of invalidations
Transactions	Number of transactions that currently change the buffer entries in the table
Reloads	Current size of the reload counter
Successful Reads	Number of read operations that have been successfully processed by the buffer since the last table reset
Missed Reads	Number of read operations that have not been successfully processed by the buffer since the last table reset
Successful Modifications	Number of modifications that have been successfully implemented by the buffer since the last table reset
Missed Modifications	Number of modifications that have not been successfully implemented by the buffer since the last table reset
Data Size (B)	Size of the buffer entries in bytes

Table 9.5 Table Call Statistics Fields in the SAP J2EE Engine Table Buffer

Buffer synchronization Because every J2EE instance has its own buffer, the data must be synchronized. You do this via the entries in table BC_SYNCLOG, the same as with table DDLOG on the ABAP server. You can find the entries in this table in the local SAP NetWeaver Administrator monitor: PROBLEM MAN-AGEMENT • DATABASE • OPEN SQL MONITORS • SYNC LOG MONITOR.

9.5 Monitoring Object-Oriented Application Buffers

The term *object-oriented application buffer* refers to buffers or memory areas where objects can be stored to be reused by other users. In this context, the term *objects* doesn't refer only to objects in the sense of the *ABAP Objects* programming language, but generally also to data structures that are defined in the ABAP dictionary. The following buffers are available:

▶ Export/import buffer

▶ Export/import SHM buffer

▶ Shared objects

Table 9.6 shows an overview of the most important properties of these three buffering types.

Property	Export/Import Buffer	Export/Import SHM Buffer	Shared Object
Command for writing the buffer entry	EXPORT TO SHARED BUFFER	EXPORT TO SHARED MEMORY	Methods of the generated area class
Command for reading the buffer entry	IMPORT FROM SHARED BUFFER	IMPORT FROM SHARED MEMORY	Methods of the generated area class
Command for deleting the buffer entry	DELETE FROM SHARED BUFFER	DELETE FROM SHARED MEMORY	Methods of the generated area class
Buffered objects	ABAP structures, internal tables	ABAP structures, internal tables	Instances of ABAP objects
Copy or reference?	Copy	Copy	Reference
Displacement	Yes	No	Can be configured at class level
Invalidation across application servers?	No	No	Can be triggered by the program

Table 9.6 Comparison of Object-Oriented Application Buffers of the ABAP Server

Property	Export/Import Buffer	Export/Import SHM Buffer	Shared Object
Display of the memory consumption in the SAP memory configuration monitor (ST02) in row	Export/Import	Export/Import SHM	Shared Objects (as of Version 7.10) For more details, refer to Transaction SHMM
Availability	As of 4.0	As of 6.10	As of 6.40

Table 9.6 Comparison of Object-Oriented Application Buffers of the ABAP Server (Cont.)

Export/import
buffer and export/
import SHM buffer

The first three rows of Table 9.6 list the ABAP commands for writing, reading, and deleting a buffer entry. The command syntax and the objects that can be buffered are very similar for export/import buffers and for export/import SHM buffers. Refer to the ABAP help to learn more about these commands. The two buffers have the same memory usage behavior. They both copy the data during the read and write process; that is, data exists redundantly in the writing program, in the buffer, and in the reading program. There is no automatic synchronization between the SAP application instances for the two buffers; in other words, at one point in time, application programs may run on an instance and write a buffer entry in this instance, and do so at a later point in time on another instance where no buffer entry exists.

The displacement behavior is the essential differentiation criterion between these two buffers. If there's a lack of space, objects are displaced from the export/import buffer using a least recently used (LRU) mechanism; this doesn't apply to the export/import SHM buffer. Programs must respond to this difference as follows:

▶ If the export/import buffer is supposed to be used, a program cannot be sure that an already written buffer entry still exists in the buffer; that is, the program must be able to restore the data from the database at any time.

▶ If the export/import SHM buffer is supposed to be used, a program cannot be sure that there's still sufficient space in the buffer if an entry is to be written. If the buffer is full, the `EXPORT_NO_SHARED_MEM-`

ORY runtime error is triggered, which must be caught in the program as follows:

```
TRY.
EXPORT ... TO SHARED MEMORY.
CATCH cx_sy_export_no_shared_memory.
ENDTRY.
```

If the export/import SHM buffer is used, the program must ensure that it deletes obsolete data because otherwise the buffer "overflows." This must also be ensured in case of error, for example, using a background program that determines and deletes application data that is no longer required. If the buffer is full, users can no longer write to this buffer and must omit buffering.

The two buffers are monitored in the SAP memory configuration monitor (Transaction ST02). There you can navigate to the buffer details from the Detail Analysis Menu or by double-clicking the row that belongs to the buffer in the main screen. These details include, among other things, the appropriate configuration parameters and the buffered contents. For more information refer to Chapter 2, Section 2.4, Analyzing SAP Memory Configuration, and Chapter 8, Memory Management; Appendix C includes the configuration parameters for the buffers.

An example of using the export/import buffer is the availability check (ATP check) in SAP ERP, which is presented in Chapter 10, Locks; an example of using the export/import SHM buffer is the OLAP cache of SAP NetWeaver BW, which is the subject of Chapter 12, Optimizing Queries to SAP NetWeaver Business Warehouse.

ABAP objects — in the sense of the *ABAP Objects* programming language — can be buffered as so-called shared objects. The benefit of this buffering is that you access buffered ("shared") objects via a reference; that is, they are not copied to and from a buffer, but exist only once in the writing and the reading program. This reduces the cost for the main memory and the CPU.

Shared Objects

You can use shared objects in two different usage scenarios: First, for use as a shared buffer; that is, infrequently changed data is written to the shared memory by a user and read by a potentially high number of users. Second, for buffering within a transaction or user session; that is, a user writes to the shared memory and then reads from this memory. If it is used as a shared buffer, the buffering takes place at the application instance level.

The ABAP help provides further information on programming using shared objects. You can find the help, for example, if you open the documentation on the CL_SHM_AREA class in the ABAP Class Builder (Transaction SM24).

Shared objects instances can have multiple versions; that is, you can create a new version of a user session; the previous one is thus set to *obsolete*. Other sessions that have already set a shared lock for the previous version can still work on the previous version. New read accesses, however, access the new version. If the last shared lock is removed from an obsolete version, it enters the *expired* status and is then deleted from the memory. For a change, an invalidation can be across all application instances; for this purpose, the application program must call the invalidated method of the generated area class. Like for the invalidation in the table buffer, you write an entry in the DDLOG table that asynchronously triggers the invalidation on other instances.

Creating areas

You create areas for the shared objects in the shared objects area configuration (Transaction SHMA). In this transaction, you can select an area for a shared objects class and display and change the properties. The basic properties, the fixed properties, and the dynamic properties are determined in development and can only be changed via a modification. For the runtime settings, however, in the transaction you only maintain default values that you can overwrite in Transaction SHMM.

The dynamic properties include, among other things, information on whether the instances of a class may be displaced from the memory area (*displacement type*). Provided that the memory for Shared Objects is completely filled, instances of objects that allow displacement are deleted from the main memory.

The runtime settings comprise the parameters for a maximum size of a version and a maximum number of versions. Moreover, the lifetime parameter can be used to control the instances' lifetime. With this parameter you can specify that an instance will automatically expire after a specific period of time after its creation (entry: Until Expiration) or if it hasn't been read or changed for a specific period of time (entry: Without Read Access); or you can specify that it is built after a specific period of time (entry: Until Build).

To monitor the shared objects areas and to change the runtime behavior, you use the shared objects area monitor (Transaction SHMM). When you call this monitor, in the Areas tab you can find a list of shared object areas that are currently maintained in the main memory, including information on the number of instances and the memory requirement. In the Shared Objects Memory tab, you can find the following information:

▶ **Occupied Size**
The (net) size occupied by shared objects

▶ **Free Memory**
The memory that can still be allocated for shared objects

▶ **Allocated Size**
The (gross) memory already occupied by shared objects

The data is interpreted as follows: The main memory allocated for shared objects is determined by the `abap/shared_objects_size_MB` parameter. A specific share of this value is reserved for administration. The remaining part that is available for user data results from the value: Allocated Size plus Free Memory. Within the allocated size, a specific share of the memory is not used because the fixed splitting of the main memory into blocks results in fragmentation effects. The fragmentation is defined by the value Allocated Size minus Occupied Size.

As of Basis Version 7.10, you can find the memory occupied by the shared objects in the memory configuration monitor (Transaction ST02) in the Shared Objects row. In this row in the CurUse[KB] column, you can find the value Allocated Size (from Transaction SHMM), and in the In Mem[KB] column the value Allocated Size plus Free Memory.

Finally, the three buffering options are supposed to be distinguished from two programming techniques that are used for transferring data between a user's sessions. One of these techniques includes the command combination `EXPORT TO MEMORY` and `IMPORT FROM MEMORY`. With these commands, you can write data to the SAP paging memory or read it. This data, however, is only available for the exchange between inter-

SAP paging memory

nal sessions and cannot be read by programs of other users or programs of another external session of the same user. This command is suitable to exchange small to medium-sized data quantities between programs at short notice, for instance, in case of a SUBMIT or CALL TRANSACTION command. After the external session has been completed, this memory is automatically cleared. Copying data between the program and SAP paging memory can — depending on the system settings — be done either in the main memory or, for larger data quantities, using a file access. Chapter 8, Memory Management, particularly Section 8.1.3, SAP EG Memory and SAP Paging Memory, provides details on SAP paging memory and on external and internal sessions.

If you need to exchange data between external sessions, you can use the SET PARAMETER and GET PARAMETER statements. However, this exchange may only include very small data quantities, for example, user parameters. Chapter 8, Section 8.2.4, Assistance with Troubleshooting, provides details on ABAP error messages and the configuration of the relevant memory area.

9.6   Summary

Buffering tables in the main memory of the SAP application server is an important instrument for optimizing performance. Table buffering is only effective if the following conditions are met:

- The table must be relatively small.
- The table must be accessed relatively often.
- The invalidation rate for the table must be low.
- Short-term inconsistency between application servers, brought about by asynchronous buffer synchronization, can be tolerated.
- Access to the table must use the first n fields of the primary key, where n is less than the total number of key fields.

The synchronization and loading processes of incorrectly buffered tables can cause a reduction in performance that far outweighs any gains in performance provided by buffering. Users will sporadically notice long response times in a transaction that normally runs quickly.

The table call statistics monitor is the central tool for monitoring SAP table buffering. Using these statistics, you can decide whether buffering a particular table is effective or not. The main statistics to look at are the number of ABAP requests (ABAP/IV Processor requests), the size of tables (Buffer Size [Bytes]), the number of invalidations, and the database activity (DB activity – Rows affected). Figure 9.8 shows the corresponding procedure roadmap for analyzing table buffering.

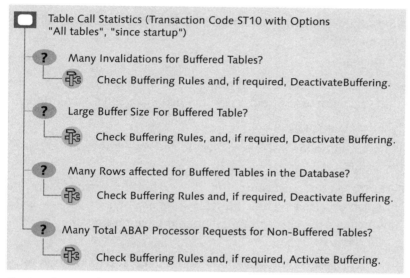

Figure 9.8 Procedure Roadmap for Analyzing the Efficiency of Table Buffering

Moreover, you can use object-oriented application buffers to reuse data between programs of the various users. Three buffering types are available for this purpose: buffering in the *export/import buffer*, in the *export/import SHM buffer*, or as *shared objects*, which differentiate in the details described in this chapter. If a buffering of objects is supposed to be used, you must decide in each situation which buffering type covers the requirements of the application best.

Important Concepts in this Chapter

After reading this chapter, you should be familiar with the following concepts:

▶ Generic regions of a table

▶ Single-record buffering and generic buffering

▶ Buffer synchronization

▶ Invalidation and displacement

▶ Buffering of objects

Questions

1. Which of the following factors are reasons for not activating full buffering on a table?

   a) The table is very large.

   b) In the SQL statement most frequently used to access the table, the first two of five key fields are contained in an equals condition.

   c) The table is changed often.

2. Which of the following statements are correct with regard to buffer synchronization?

   a) During buffer synchronization, the application server where the change occurred sends a message through the message server to implement the change in the buffered table on the other application servers.

   b) After a transaction changes a buffered table, the transaction must first be completed with a database commit before the table can be reloaded into the buffer.

   c) In a central system, the SAP profile parameter `rdisp/bufrefmode` must be set to "sendoff, exeoff."

   d) In a central SAP system, the entries in the table buffer are never invalidated, because the table buffer is changed synchronously after a database change operation.

10 Locks

In an SAP system, many users can simultaneously read the contents of database tables. However, for changes to the dataset, you must ensure that only one user can change a particular table's content at a time. For this purpose, table content is locked during a change operation. The first section of this chapter introduces you to the concept of locking for SAP and database systems.

If locks remain in place for a long time, wait situations can occur, which limit the throughput of the SAP system. The second part of the chapter deals with the general performance aspects of using locks.

The SAP system uses special buffering techniques for availability checking with ATP logic, and for document number assignment. These techniques (discussed in Sections 10.3 and 10.4) reduce lock time and can maximize throughput.

When Should You Read this Chapter?

You should read this chapter to help you:

▶ Find out more about database locks and SAP enqueues

▶ Analyze system problems that are caused by database locks or enqueues

This chapter does not offer instruction on programming SAP transactions. Use ABAP textbooks or SAP Online Help for this.

10.1 Database Locks and SAP Enqueues

To book a vacation, you must check that all necessary components are available: flights, hotels, bus or boat transfers, and so on. The "all or nothing" principle applies: If no flights are available, you will not need a hotel room and so on. Since you usually check the availability of the vari- [Ex]

455

ous components one after the other, you want to be certain that another user doesn't change any of the items in the sequence before the entire booking is completed.

You can use locks to do this, which preserve data consistency. The locking concepts of SAP and database systems have the same ultimate purpose of preserving data consistency, but they are based on different technologies and used in different situations. Locks that the database system manages are known as *database locks*, and locks that the SAP system manages are known as SAP enqueues.

10.1.1 Exclusive Lock Waits

The lock handler of a database instance manages database locks. The locked entity is typically a row in a database table (special exceptions are detailed later). Database locks are set by all data-changing SQL statements (UPDATE, INSERT, DELETE) and by the statement SELECT FOR UPDATE. Locks are held until the SQL statement COMMIT (database commit) finalizes all changes and then removes the corresponding database locks. The time interval between two commits is called a *database transaction*. A program can undo the effects of all modifying SQL statements by executing a database rollback with the SQL statement ROLLBACK. In this case, all database locks are also removed.

[Ex] A program that uses database locks to make a travel booking, for example, would use the SQL statement SELECT FOR UPDATE. A particular item of travel data is read and locked with this statement. When each relevant data item has been read and the booking is ready to be made, the data is changed in the table rows with the command UPDATE, and then the COMMIT command is used to finalize changes and release all locks. Once a lock has been set, other users can still read the affected data (a simple SELECT is still possible), but they cannot lock it. Therefore, they cannot perform an UPDATE or SELECT FOR UPDATE, which means the original lock is *exclusive*.

[Ex] After a transaction step, the SAP work process automatically triggers a database commit (or a database rollback). This removes all locks and means a database lock does not last through multiple transaction steps (through multiple input screens in the SAP system).

10.1.2   SAP Enqueues

To lock through several SAP transaction steps, use SAP enqueue administration. Work processes in the enqueue table, located in the main memory, manage SAP enqueues. To retain these enqueues even when an SAP instance is shut down, they are also saved in a local file on the enqueue server.

An SAP enqueue locks a logical object. Therefore, an enqueue can lock rows from several different database tables if these rows form the basis of a single business document. An SAP enqueue can also lock one or more complete tables. SAP enqueue objects are defined and modified in the ABAP dictionary (dictionary section Lock Objects. They are closely related to the concepts *SAP transaction* and *logical unit of work* (SAP LUW). Both of these are described extensively in the ABAP literature for dialog programming. Therefore, this chapter will not discuss the functions and uses of these techniques as part of ABAP programs. Rather, we will focus on aspects related to performance analysis. If you discover performance problems caused by the incorrect use of SAP enqueues, consult the responsible ABAP developer.

SAP enqueue objects

An SAP enqueue is a logical lock that acts within the SAP system. If a row in a database table is locked by an SAP enqueue, it can still be changed by an SQL statement executed from the database or by a customer-developed ABAP program that does not conform to SAP enqueue conventions. Therefore, SAP enqueues are only valid within the SAP system. Database locks, in contrast, resist all change attempts. They lock a table row "tight" for all database users and prevent changes by users outside the SAP system.

For each object that can be held by an enqueue, there are two function modules: an enqueue module and a dequeue module. To set an enqueue, an ABAP program must explicitly call the enqueue module; to remove it, the program must call the corresponding dequeue module. As a result, SAP enqueues can be held in place through multiple transaction steps. When an SAP transaction is completed, all SAP enqueues are automatically removed.

Function modules

Let's discuss how SAP enqueue administration works, using our vacation example. The trip includes several components, such as flight, hotel

[+]

457

reservations, and bus transfers. The individual components of the trip are processed on different input screens, with several transaction steps, and are locked using SAP enqueues. After determining the availability of each component, you can confirm the booking for the entire trip. This concludes the dialog part of the transaction. Under the protection of the enqueues, an update work process then transfers the changes to the database tables. When the update has been completed, the SAP LUW is finished, and the enqueues are unlocked.

An SAP LUW can also contain program modules that require a V2 update. An SAP enqueue is not used for this. You should not use modules that use this V2 update to process data that requires the protection of enqueues.

Table 10.1 compares the main features of database locks and enqueues.

	DB Locks	SAP Locks (Enqueues)
Locked object	Individual rows of a database table	Logical object, such as a document defined in the ABAP dictionary
How object is locked	Implicitly using modifying SQL statements (such as UPDATE and SELECT FOR UPDATE)	Explicitly by the ABAP program calling an enqueue module
How lock is removed	Implicitly with the SQL statement COMMIT or ROLLBACK Usually at the end of a transaction step	Explicitly by calling a dequeue module Usually at the end of an SAP transaction
Maximum duration	One transaction step	Over multiple transaction steps
Result of lock conflicts	Wait situation, referred to as exclusive lock wait	Program-specific, for example, the error message "Material X is locked"
How to monitor	Transaction DB01, Exclusive Lock Waits	Transaction SM12, Enqueue Monitor

Table 10.1 Features of Database Locks and SAP Enqueues

10.2 Monitoring Locks

In this section, you will find information on how to monitor database locks and SAP enqueues.

10.2.1 Exclusive Lock Waits

What happens in the event of a lock conflict, when a work process wants to lock an object that is already locked? With database locks, the second process waits until the lock has been removed. This wait situation is known as an *exclusive lock wait*. Most databases do not place a time limit on these locks. If a program fails to remove a lock, the wait situation can continue indefinitely.

This could become a major problem if the program fails to release a lock on critical SAP system data such as the number range table NRIV. There is a danger that one work process after another will be waiting for this lock. If all work processes are waiting, no work process is available to allow you to intervene from within the SAP system. If you can identify the program holding the problem lock, you can terminate it through the operating system as a last alternative.

To monitor current lock wait situations, call the database lock monitor (Transaction DB01), which you can start from the DBA Cockpit (Transaction DBACOCKPIT by selecting PERFORMANCE • WAIT SITUATIONS ON LOCKS AND DEADLOCKS or from the system-wide work process overview (Transaction SM66) by selecting GOTO • DB LOCKS.

For a description of this monitor and information on how to troubleshoot lock wait situations, see Chapter 2, Section 2.3.4, Other Database Checks. Lock wait situations increase database time and result in high database times in workload monitor statistics. Some database systems explicitly monitor lock wait times, which you can view in the database performance monitor.

With the following sample program you can provoke a lock situation on the database:

```
REPORT zts_lock.
DATA: lv_text type natxt.
```

Exclusive lock waits

[Ex]

```
SELECT SINGLE FOR UPDATE text FROM T100 INTO lv_text WHERE
sprsl = 'DE' AND ARBGB = '00' AND msgnr = '001' .
BREAK-POINT.
```

To do so, proceed as follows:

1. Start the program in the ABAP Workbench (for instance, via Transaction SE38). After a few seconds, the debugger opens, and the program stops at the BREAK-POINT command. Before that, the program has set a database lock using the SELECT SINGLE FOR UPDATE command. Because the program waits in the debug mode, this database lock is not undone.

2. Now open a second session and restart the program. An hourglass is displayed in the second session.

3. Again, you can restart the program in a third session, and the system again displays an hourglass.

4. Open another session and start the database lock monitor as previously described. The lock situation is displayed, and you can see which work process holds the lock and which one waits. Based on the work process overview (Transaction SM50) and the database process monitor, you can now analyze what happens in the process that holds the lock. In this example, the process overview displays the Stopped status gives and Debug as the reason.

5. Now go to the debugger, where you continue the execution of the program in the first session. The program is terminated, and the database lock is undone due to an implicit commit or rollback of the database interface. As a result, the program can continue in the second session, which had to wait at the SELECT SINGLE FOR UPDATE command up to now. So within a very short period of time, it will reach the BREAK-POINT command and start the debugger.

6. Continue the program in the debugger for the second session, and, if you started the program in further sessions, in these sessions to release the locks.

Typical problems Basically, you should set programs to request locks as late as possible. It is preferable for a program to read and process data from the database before setting locks or making changes in the database. This is illustrated in Figure 10.1. The top part of the diagram shows how several changes are made during a database transaction and how, as a result, database locks are held for too long. The lower part of the diagram shows a more appropriate programming method: The transaction is programmed so that it collects the changes in an internal table and then transfers these changes to the database as a group at the end of the transaction. This reduces the lock time in a database.

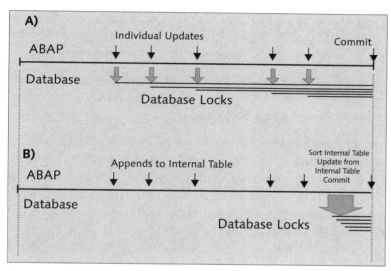

Figure 10.1 Locks Should Be Set as Late as Possible.

Performance problems due to delays in releasing locks frequently occur when customers modify the programming of update modules. The separation of update modules from dialog modules is an attempt to reduce the number of locks needed in the dialog part of a transaction, because changes to the database and the associated locks are mainly the task of the update modules. However, sometimes the update module is modified, for example, to supply a customer-developed interface with data. This modification may cause problems if the update module has already set locks and, for example, the modification generates expensive SQL statements. The locks cannot be released until the SQL statements are fully processed, and lengthy lock waits may result.

Causes

Another source of problems with locks is background programs that set locks and then run for several hours without initiating a database commit. If dialog transactions need to process the locked objects, they will be forced to wait until the background program finishes or initiates a database commit. To solve this problem, you should either ensure that the background program initiates a database commit at regular intervals (without sacrificing data consistency) or that it runs only when it will not interfere with dialog processing. Similar problems may occur when background jobs are run in parallel, that is, when a program is started several times simultaneously. Parallel processing is recommended only when the selection conditions of the programs do not lock the same data.

While you are working in the ABAP debugger, database commits are generally not initiated, and all locks stay in place until you are finished. You should therefore avoid using the debugger in a production SAP system.

Deadlocks We'll now present an example of a situation known as a *deadlock*. Assume that work process one and work process two both want to lock a list of materials. Work process one locks material A, and work process two locks material B. Then, work process one tries to lock material B, and work process two tries to lock material A. Neither work process is successful because the materials already have locks on them. The work processes block each other. A deadlock is identified by the database instance and solved by sending an error message to one of the work processes. The corresponding ABAP program is terminated, and the error is logged in the SAP syslog.

You can avoid deadlocks with correct programming. In our example, the program should be changed so that its internal material list is sorted before any locks are set. Then the lock on material A will always be set before the lock on material B. Therefore, programs requiring the same materials are serialized and not deadlocked.

Deadlocks should occur very rarely. Frequent deadlocks indicate incorrect programming or configuration of the database instance.

Table locks In some database systems such as DB2 and MaxDB, if a work process places single-row locks on more than 10% of the single rows in a table, the locks are automatically replaced by table locks. Here, the database decides that it is more efficient to lock the entire table for a work process than to maintain several locks on individual rows. Table locking has consequences for parallel processing in background jobs, where each program is intended to update a different part of the same table at the same time. It is not possible to schedule background jobs so that one updates the first half of the table and the other updates the second half, because the database may decide to lock the table exclusively for one of the jobs. One program that is particularly affected by this is the period closing program in materials management.

There are database parameters you can use to specify when the database should convert single-row locks to a table lock. **[+]**

Sometimes the database locks entire tables for administrative reasons. This happens when indexes are created or when particular tables and indexes are analyzed, for example, during the Oracle analysis VALIDATE STRUCTURE. If these actions are performed during production operation, substantial performance problems may result. **[!]**

10.2.2 SAP Enqueues

SAP enqueues are managed in the enqueue table located in the global main memory of the enqueue server. The work processes in the enqueue server directly access the enqueue table; the enqueue server also carries out lock operations for work processes from other application servers, which are communicated via the message service. The following abbreviations are used in Figure 10.2: DIA, dialog work process; ENQ, enqueue work process; MS, message service; DP, dispatcher; ENQ tab, enqueue table.

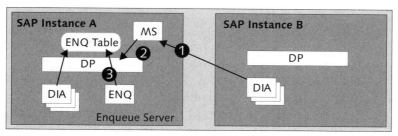

Figure 10.2 Communication for Setting and Removing SAP Enqueues

For work processes in the enqueue server, setting and releasing locks takes less than 1 millisecond; for work processes in other application servers, it takes less than 100 milliseconds.

If an SAP enqueue is requested but is already held by another user, the attempt to set a lock is rejected, and an error message is sent back to the ABAP program. The application developer has to decide how to deal with this error message with suitable programming. For programs in dialog mode, the error message is normally forwarded to the user, for example, with the message "Material X is locked by user Y." For background programs, you will normally attempt to set the lock again later. After a certain number of unsuccessful attempts, as error message is written to the program log.

If SAP enqueues are held for too long, performance problems can arise because after a failed attempt, the user will repeat the entry. Take, for example, a user who needs to process a material list, and to do so needs to set 100 SAP enqueues. If the attempt to set lock number 99 fails, the program is interrupted with the message "Material number 99 is locked," and all of the previous system work is in vain and must be repeated. Therefore, rejected enqueue requests lead to higher system workload and restrict the throughput of transactions.

You can get an overview of all currently active SAP enqueues by using Transaction SM12: TOOLS • ADMINISTRATION • MONITOR • LOCK ENTRIES.

Start the test programs to diagnose errors: EXTRAS • DIAGNOSE, or EXTRAS • DIAGNOSE IN VB.

If errors are identified, check the SAP Service Marketplace for notes or contact SAP directly.

You can view statistics on the activity of the enqueue server with the menu option EXTRAS • STATISTICS.

The first three values show the number of enqueue requests, the number of rejected requests (unsuccessful because the lock requested was already held by another), and the number of errors that occurred during the processing of enqueue requests. The number of unsuccessful requests should not be more than 1% of the total number of enqueue requests. There should be no errors.

10.3 Number Range Buffering

With many database structures, it is necessary to be able to directly access individual database records. You do this with a unique key. *Number ranges* assign a serial number that forms the main part of this key. Examples of these numbers include order numbers and material master numbers. SAP number-range management monitors the number status so that previously assigned numbers are not reissued.

10.3.1 Fundamentals of Number Range Buffering

A business object for which a key must be created using the number range is defined in the SAP system as a *number range object*. A number range contains a *number range interval* with a set of permitted characters. The number range interval is made up of numerical or alphanumeric characters and is limited by the From-Number and To-Number fields. You can assign one or more intervals to a number range.

The current number level of a range, which is the number that is to be assigned next, is stored in the database table NRIV. If a program needs a number (for example, from the number range MATBELEG), it goes through the following steps:

Technical implementation

1. The program reads the current number level from the NRIV table and, at the same time, locks the MATBELEG number range. To set the lock, the SQL statement `SELECT FOR UPDATE` is applied to the row of the NRIV table that corresponds to the MATBELEG number range.

2. The program increases the number range level by one by updating the table NRIV.

3. The number range in the database remains locked until the program completes its DB LUW by performing a database commit or database rollback. If an error occurs before the lock is released, the document cannot be created, and the change in table NRIV is rolled back; that is, the previous number level is returned. This ensures that numbers are assigned *chronologically* and *without gaps*.

Bottlenecks can occur when many numbers are requested from a particular number range within a short period of time. Because the number range is locked in the database from the time of the initial reading of the current number level to the time of the database commit, all business processes competing for number assignment must wait their turn, and this limits transaction throughput.

Buffering the corresponding number range solves this lock problem. SAP offers two ways of doing this: *main memory buffering* and buffering each SAP instance in an additional database table (NRIV_LOKAL).

Main memory buffering

By buffering number ranges in main memory, the database table NRIV does not have to be accessed for each number assignment; rather, the number is read from the buffer. The number range interval buffer is located in the main memory of SAP instances. A certain amount of new numbers is stored in each buffer. When these numbers have been used up, a new set of numbers is obtained from the database. The number range level in the database table NRIV is increased by the range of numbers transferred to the buffer. When a number is taken from the buffer and assigned to a document, the number range level in the database remains unchanged.

Entering the number range buffer

Entering a set of new numbers in a buffer involves several technical steps, as follows:

1. For example, a program needs a number from the MATBELEG number range, which is buffered in the main memory. It discovers that the number range buffer in its SAP instance is empty.

2. The program starts an asynchronous RFC to fill the number range buffer. This RFC is processed in a second dialog work process. Table NRIV is read and locked, the number range buffer is filled, table NRIV is updated, and the action is concluded with a database commit. The first work process (in which the original program is running) remains stopped while this takes place. In the work process overview, the Action field shows Stopped and Reason displays NUM.

3. When the number range buffer has been filled, the original program can resume work.

During this process, the program that checked the buffer for a number and the program that refills the number range buffer must run in separate database LUWs. This is the only way to ensure that the commit of the second program can finalize the changes in table NRIV and release the lock without performing a commit for the first program's LUW database. To accomplish this, the two programs are run in separate work processes.

To guarantee that work processes are available for refilling the buffer with new numbers, the work process dispatcher program gives preferential treatment to requests for new number sets.

Main memory buffering of number ranges has the following consequences:

▶ When an SAP instance is shut down, the remaining numbers in the buffer, that is, the numbers that have yet to be assigned, are lost. This causes a gap in number assignment.

▶ Due to the separate buffering of numbers in various SAP instances, the chronological sequence in which numbers are assigned is not reflected in the sequence of the numbers themselves, which means a document with a higher number may have been created before a document with a lower number.

You should not buffer this object in main memory if you prefer to prevent gaps in the number assignment for a particular document type or number range object or if sequential numbering of documents is required by law.

[!]

In this case, you can use another buffering technique: Instead of managing the number range for a particular type of document centrally in a single row of table NRIV, number intervals are selected by the system for each SAP instance and managed in a separate database table (NRIV_LOKAL). In this table, the name of the SAP instance forms part of the primary key. Database locks associated with number assignments for new documents will then appear only in those areas of table NRIV_LOKAL that correspond to a particular SAP instance.

Buffering in NRIV_LOKAL

With extended local number-range buffering (SAP Note 179224), you can buffer number range intervals for each SAP instance *and* buffer work processes locally. (The name of the SAP instance and the logical number of the work process form part of the primary key of the local number range.) With this buffering technique, one lock problem is conclusively ruled out.

Keep in mind the following points:

▶ Buffering in table NIRV_LOKAL is useful only when the user is working simultaneously on several SAP instances. For very high throughput (for example, processing point-of-sale entries in SAP for Retail), local buffering on the instance and work process levels (or if possible, main memory buffering) is recommended.

▶ Numbers are not assigned to documents in numerical order. Therefore, a document with a higher number may have been created before a document with a lower number.

▶ Some of the numbers in a particular interval may not be assigned, for example, at the end of a financial year or during the renaming of an instance. The program RSSNR0A1 shows details on the numbers that have not been assigned.

To enter a new set of document numbers in table NRIV_LOKAL, a new interval is *synchronously* read from table NRIV, and the affected row of table NRIV remains locked until the commit occurs. If the interval of numbers read from table NRIV is too small, frequent accesses to table NRIV to obtain new numbers during mass processing may cause lock waits. Therefore, when large quantities of similar documents are being created across several instances, ensure that the selected interval is sufficiently large.

Table 10.2 provides a summary of the buffer types for number ranges.

Buffering Type	Method	Advantages	Limitations	Example of Use
No buffering	N/A	No gaps in number allocation, chronological order	Lock waits with parallel processing	Only if it is essential to have no gaps in number allocation, if numbers must be in sequence, and only a low throughput is needed

Table 10.2 Types of Buffering for Number Ranges

Buffering Type	Method	Advantages	Limitations	Example of Use
Main memory	In the main memory	No lock wait problems, fast access (main memory instead of database)	No gaps in number allocation, no chronological order	Standard for most number ranges
Local, on instance level	Temporarily stored on the database table NRIV_ LOKAL, with number range and SAP instance forming part of the key	Lock wait problems reduced, number allocation almost gap-free	Sequence not chronological, locks occur within an instance, many instances necessary if throughput is high	Largely replaced by the method described in the following line in this table
Local, on instance and work process level	Temporarily stored on the database table NRIV_ LOKAL, with number range, SAP instance, and work process number forming the key	No lock wait problems, number allocation practically gap-free	Sequence not chronological	Processing point-of-sale entries in SAP for Retail

Table 10.2 Types of Buffering for Number Ranges (Cont.)

10.3.2 Activating Number Range Buffering

To activate or deactivate number range buffering, proceed as follows:

1. Call the Number Range Maintenance transaction: TOOLS • ABAP WORKBENCH • DEVELOPMENT • OTHER TOOLS • NUMBER RANGES or enter Transaction SNRO.

2. Enter an object name and select Change.

3. To activate the main memory buffering, from the menu, select EDIT • SET UP BUFFERING • MAIN MEMORY.

   Enter the quantity of numbers to be held in the buffer in the No. of Numbers in Buffer field and save the change. The specified amount of numbers from table NRIV will thereby be buffered.

To activate buffering in table NRIV_LOKAL, in the menu of the number range maintenance transaction, select EDIT • SET UP BUFFERING • LOCAL FILE. To deactivate the buffering, from the menu, select EDIT • SET UP BUFFERING • NO BUFFERING.

[+] Please note that these changes will be overwritten if the number range object is replaced with, for example, a new release. After every update, check whether number range buffering has been affected.

Finding out the current number range level

To view the current *number range level*, use Transaction SNRO. For buffered number range objects, the level indicated here is the next available number that has not yet been transferred to a buffer in an application server. The level indicated is higher than the last number assigned.

You can check the current number level of the buffer for each SAP instance with Transaction SM56.

1. Call Transaction SM56, and in the menu select GOTO • ITEMS.
2. In the dialog box, enter the client, the relevant number range object, and if required, the relevant subobject.

10.3.3 Monitoring Number Range Buffering

To identify performance problems related to number assignment, call the exclusive database lock monitor (Transaction DB01). At peak processing times, lock waits of several minutes for table NRIV are too long. If this occurs, from the initial screen of the database lock monitor, proceed as follows:

1. Identify the number range involved:
   ► If you are using an Oracle database, double-click the row showing the lock on table NRIV. This brings you to a screen with detailed information on the locked row. The name of the number range is indicated in the Object column (for example, RF_BELEG).
   ► For other databases, start an SQL trace for a user who is waiting for the database lock to be removed. With this SQL trace, you can identify the number affected by the lock in the SQL statement.

2. Find out the buffering status of the number range.

- ▸ If buffering is not currently activated, check to see if the corresponding object can be buffered.

- ▸ If the number range is already buffered, check whether the quantity of numbers in the buffer can be increased. Table NRIV will then be accessed less frequently.

Only experienced SAP developers or consultants should change the buffering mode for number ranges for the following reasons:

[!]

- ▸ Activating buffering may cause gaps in number assignment, which could be a problem if gap-free number assignment is mandatory or if it is assumed that numbering will be gap-free.

- ▸ Having too few numbers in the buffer can cause performance problems by requiring the buffer to be refilled too often. The disadvantage in having a range that is too large is that too many numbers are lost if the SAP instance is shut down.

SAP Notes on many number ranges are available in the SAP Service Marketplace and contain details on buffering status and recommendations for how many numbers should be loaded into a number range buffer. You should never change the buffering mode for an SAP default number range without first looking for relevant notes on the object. Some notes are listed in Appendix G.

10.4 ATP Server

The availability check establishes the availability of materials in the SAP logistics modules, for example, for sales orders or production orders. The availability check discussed in this book is based on ATP logic (available to promise) .

Either of two factors can reduce performance during an availability check:

- ▸ **Locks**
  The material being checked for availability must be locked with an SAP enqueue. When the lock is in place, it may block other users who need to work with the material, especially if the lock remains for a

long time or the material is frequently worked on. As a result, locks limit the throughput of the availability check.

▶ **Read accesses for tables RESB and VBBE**
An availability check is used to ensure that a material will be available at a specific time in the future. As part of the check, incoming movements planned before that time are added to the current stock, whereas planned outward movements are subtracted. In this context, totaling material reservations and secondary requirements for production orders is critical to performance, as is the totaling of customer requirements for sales orders, which are stored in tables RESB and VBBE, respectively. Reading and calculating these reservations and requirements can lead to a high availability check runtime.

[+] Table RESB may be as large as 1GB or even larger. Depending on customizations, the current date through the date on which the material should be available must be read for the availability check on all RESB records for a material.

The availability check is carried out on a dedicated SAP instance — the *ATP server*. The ATP server has a buffer in shared memory in which ATP-relevant information is stored. This significantly reduces accesses to the database tables RESB and VBBE. The ATP server is not a separate installation. It is a logical service running on an SAP instance, and as such it forms part of the SAP system.

10.4.1 ATP Server Fundamentals

ATP server functionality

Figure 10.3 shows how an ATP server works in the system landscape. If an SAP work process on SAP instance B has to check the availability of a material, it uses a remote function call (RFC) to communicate the request through the network to the server where the ATP server resides. In Figure 10.3 the ATP server is configured on SAP instance A (❶). This call is sent between the gateway services of the two SAP instances (❷). A dialog work process on the ATP server (❸) processes the availability check. The following abbreviations are used in Figure 10.3: DIA, dialog work process; GW, gateway service; DP, dispatcher; ENQ tab, enqueue table; E/I buffer, export/import buffer.

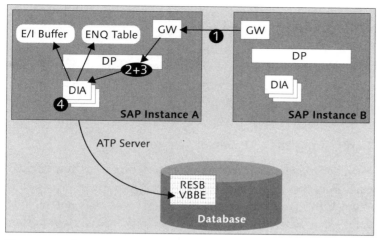

Figure 10.3 Communication During an Availability Check Using the ATP Server

The SAP work process on the ATP server uses subtotals for calculating the availability of a material, which have already been calculated for other availability checks and are stored in the main memory of the ATP server in the *export/import buffer*. These subtotals consist of a calculation for each day's material reservations (from table RESB) or sales requirements (from table VBBE) for every possible combination of material, plant, storage location, and batch. Daily totals per combination of material, plant, storage location, and batch are compressed and stored in the export/import buffer. The export/import buffer therefore contains two groups of entries: one for RESB data and one for VBBE data. The size of the entries depends on the number of days for which subtotals exist.

When checking the availability of a material, the work process does not read RESB and VBBE data from the database; rather, it reads from the export/import buffer (see Figure 10.3). This method considerably improves performs. Special delta processing guarantees consistency between the buffer and database.

While checking availability, the SAP work process sets and removes SAP enqueues that are necessary to guarantee data consistency. To set and remove enqueues with only minimal performance loss, the ATP and enqueue servers should run on the same SAP instance.

A special SAP technique is used in the ATP server availability check: *locking with quantities*. Instead of relying on exclusive SAP enqueues, which allow only one user to lock a material, this technique uses *shared enqueues*. Shared enqueues can be used by several users on the same object at the same time, which means several users can check the availability of a material at the same time.

10.4.2 Configuring the ATP Server

[!] Correctly configuring the ATP server is a technical procedure that resolves two specific problems with the availability check: frequent accesses to the RESB and VBBE tables. However, the ATP server does not solve all the problems associated with the availability check. It is very important to optimize application-related aspects of the availability check during customizing. For example:

▸ Set sensible reorder times and planned horizons for materials.

▸ Deactivate individual checking of materials that are used in bulk, such as screws or nails.

▸ Regularly archive reservations.

The SAP Empowering Workshop, "Technical Optimization of the Availability Check," provides application-related optimization measures.

[+] Tables RESB and VBBE are accessed by database views during the availability check. An availability check with SQL trace will give you access to the views ATP_RESB or ATP_VBBE.

Activate To activate the ATP server, set the SAP profile parameter rdisp/atp_server to the name of the SAP instance that provides the ATP server (for example, enqhost_PRD_00). The value of this parameter must be identical for all SAP instances and should therefore be set in the default profile. The ATP server and the enqueue server should run on the same SAP instance.

Sizing The SAP profile parameters rsdb/obj/buffersize and rsdb/obj/max_objects configure the size and maximum number of entries in the export/import buffer. The size of an entry in the export/import buffer depends on the number of days for which subtotals exist. For each additional day, the size of the entry increases by around 50 bytes. If reservations are calculated for a combination of material, plant, storage location, and batch for 20 days, the size of the entry would be around 1KB. If your company expects a maximum of 10,000 combinations, and for each combination there are an average of 20 days of daily reservation or sales requirement subtotals, you would set the size of the export/import buffer to 20,000KB (parameter `rsdb/obj/buffersize`) and the maximum number of entries at 20,000 (parameter `rsdb/obj/max_objects`).

You should activate *locking with quantities* for all materials to be checked for availability using the ATP server. This is done using the checking group of each material. To activate locking with quantities for a checking group, proceed as follows:

Activating locking with quantities

1. Call up customizing: Tools • Business Engineer • Customizing • Continue.

2. Select Implement projects • Display SAP Reference IMG.

3. Select: Sales and distribution • Basic functions • Availability check and transfer of requirements • Availability check • Availability check with ATP logic and against planning • Define checking groups. A screen appears in which you can set the characteristics of the checking groups for the availability check.

4. To set locking with quantities for a particular checking group, select the checkbox in the Block QtRq column.

Many availability checks are carried out simultaneously on large installations, and as a result, some parameters on the enqueue or ATP server may limit the number of RFC connections and must be set to values that are sufficiently large. Table 10.3 lists these parameters.

Other resources

To ensure that sufficient dialog work processes are available for the availability check, you require at least five dialog work processes on the enqueue/ATP server, even if no users are working on this server. The enqueue server also requires sufficient SAP extended memory. Monitor the use of extended memory at regular intervals.

Parameter Name	Description	Minimum Size for Locking with Quantities
rdisp/tm_max_no	Maximum number of frontend connections in table tm_adm.	≥500
rdisp/max_comm_ entries	Number of maximum possible CPIC/RFC connections (table comm_adm)	≥500
gw/max_conn	Number of maximum possible gateway connections (table conn_tbl)	≥500
rdisp/wp_no_dia	Number of dialog work processes	≥5
em/initial_size_MB	Size of extended memory	≥250
rdisp/ROLL_SHM	Size of roll buffer in 8KB blocks	≥4,000 (32MB)

Table 10.3 Parameter Settings for the ATP Server or Enqueue Server When Using Locking with Quantities

[+] For the most recent information on sizing for the export/import buffer, see SAP Notes 24762 and 99999.

You can also use locking with quantities independently of the ATP server. Note the recommendations provided in the "Other Resources" section above if you set locking with quantities without the ATP server.

10.4.3 Monitoring the ATP Server

Transaction ACBD offers monitoring and administration functions for the export/import buffer in the ATP server, such as:

▶ Complete or partial deletion of the export/import buffer (with regard to ATP data)

▶ Adjusting the export/import buffer to the database

This transaction allows data from the database to be preloaded into the export/import buffer. Otherwise, data loading does not occur until the first availability check is made for each combination of material, plant, and table.

You can monitor the contents of the export/import buffer (from a technical point of view) in the SAP memory configuration monitor (Transaction ST02) by selecting DETAIL ANALYSIS MENU • IMPORT/EXPORT BUFFER • BUFFERED OBJECTS. The most important fields in this monitor are Table

Name (ATPSB for ATP server objects), Object Name (this field contains the clients, the information, whether it is an RESB entry [RE] or a VBBE entry [VB], the plant, and the material number), Size (size of an entry), and Used (number of accesses to this entry).

You can monitor the shared enqueues that are used when locking with quantities in the SAP enqueue monitor (Transaction SM12). They are indicated by the entry ATPENQ in the Table field and are marked with a cross in the Shared field.

Monitoring SAP enqueues is one of the regular system administration **[+]** tasks. SAP enqueues that are held over several hours are an indication of an error in a program or that a program is being used incorrectly.

10.5   Summary

The database and SAP systems both offer their own lock concepts (database locks and SAP enqueues). Locks held for a long time can lead to performance problems and can even bring the system to a standstill. You can monitor exclusive database lock wait situations with the help of Transaction DB01 and wait situations caused by SAP enqueues with the help of Transaction SM12.

Give special attention to locks associated with both number ranges (used to generate, for example, order numbers or document numbers) and availability checks. Sections 10.3, Number Range Buffering, and 10.4, ATP Server, show ways to identify bottlenecks in these areas and how to avoid them. Key topics in this respect are the ATP server (for the availability check) and number range buffering (for number assignment).

Important Concepts in this Chapter

After reading this chapter, you should be familiar with the following concepts:

▶ Database locks and SAP enqueues

▶ Locking with quantities

▶ ATP server

▶ Reset or check the number range buffer

Questions

1. Which of the following statements are correct?

   a) When you set an SAP enqueue, you lock one or more tables in the database.

   b) After an SAP enqueue has been placed, the corresponding database table can still be changed by an `Update` request from programs such as customer-developed ABAP reports.

   c) A database lock is usually released at the end of a transaction step, whereas an SAP enqueue is usually released at the end of an SAP transaction.

   d) A database lock that lasts too long can cause an SAP system *standstill*.

2. Which of the following statements are correct with regard to the ATP server?

   a) The ATP server should always be configured on the database server.

   b) The ATP server is an independent SAP installation with its own database on a separate computer.

   c) The ATP server reduces the number of accesses to tables RESB and VBBE.

3. When buffering number range objects in main memory, which of the following considerations should you bear in mind?

   a) Because buffering occurs in all SAP instances, buffer synchronization may cause some numbers to be assigned twice.

   b) Gaps occur in the number assignment when you are using buffered number ranges. You must check whether these gaps are permitted by law and are acceptable from a business point of view.

   c) If the quantity of numbers in the buffer is too small, performance problems will result (particularly during mass data entry using batch or fast input).

   d) Sufficient physical memory must be available, because number range buffering consumes a lot of memory.

11   Optimizing SQL Statements

During application programming, SQL statements are often written without sufficient regard to their subsequent performance. Expensive (long-running) SQL statements slow performance during production operation. They result in slow response times for individual programs and place excessive loads on the database server. Frequently, you will find that 50% of the database load can be traced to a few individual SQL statements. This chapter does not begin with the design of database applications; rather, it describes how you can identify, analyze, and optimize expensive SQL statements in a production system. In other words, What can be done if a problem has already occurred?

As the database and the number of users grow, so do the number of requests to the database and the search effort required for each database request. This is why expensive or inefficient SQL statements constitute one of the most significant causes of performance problems in large installations. The more a system grows, the more important it becomes to optimize SQL statements.

This chapter starts with a detailed instruction to analyze SQL statements that refer to the introductory sections in Chapter 2 on SQL statistics (Section 2.3.2, Identifying and Analyzing Expensive SQL Statements) and in Chapter 4 on the SQL trace (Section 4.3.2, Evaluating an SQL Trace).

You can optimize the runtime using database indexes if the selection conditions for the database access are designed in such a way that only a small quantity of data is returned to the application program. To understand the mode of action of indexes and be able to evaluate their significance for performance, you require a brief theoretical introduction to tables, indexes, and the database optimizer. This is followed by a section that describes the practical administration of indexes and table statistics that are required for the database optimizer to decide on the appropriate index. The section on database indexes concludes with a description of the rules for good index design.

If a large quantity of data is transferred from the database to the application server, you can only achieve an optimization by rewriting the program or changing the users' approach to work. The third section of this chapter deals with these measures; this section is primarily aimed at ABAP developers. You'll first get an overview of the *five golden rules of SQL programming,* which are followed by examples, for instance, of database views, the FOR ALL ENTRIES clause, and the design of input screens to avoid performance problems.

Business warehouse applications are a special case, which frequently evaluate thousands to millions of data records. The next chapter describes the optimization options for these applications.

When Should You Read this Chapter?

You should read this chapter if you have identified expensive SQL statements in your SAP system and want to analyze and optimize them. You can read the first and second sections of this chapter without previous knowledge of ABAP programming, whereas the third section assumes a basic familiarity.

This chapter is not an introduction to developing SQL applications. For this, refer to ABAP textbooks, SQL textbooks, or SAP Online Help.

11.1 Identifying and Analyzing Expensive SQL Statements

[+] The following sections describe how to identify and analyze expensive SQL statements.

11.1.1 Preliminary Analysis

The preliminary step in identifying and analyzing expensive SQL statements is to identify SQL statements for which optimization would be genuinely worthwhile. The preliminary analysis prevents you from wasting time with SQL statement optimizations that cannot produce more than trivial gains in performance.

For the preliminary analysis, there are two main techniques: an SQL trace or the SQL statistics. An SQL trace is useful if the program containing the expensive SQL statement has already been identified, for example, through the workload monitor, work process overview, or users' observations. You don't require any initial information to analyze the SQL statistics. Using the SQL statistics enables you to order statements according to the system-wide load they are generating. For both analysis techniques, the sections that follow describe individual analysis steps.

The flowchart in Figure 11.1 shows techniques for identifying expensive SQL statements that are worth optimizing. The following shapes are used in the diagram:

▶ A round-cornered rectangle indicates where a specific SAP performance monitor is started.

▶ A diamond shape indicates a decision point.

▶ The parallelogram indicates the point at which you have successfully identified expensive SQL statements that are worth optimizing.

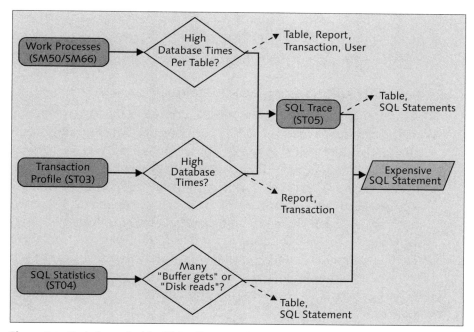

Figure 11.1 Techniques for Identifying Expensive SQL Statements

Preliminary Analysis Using the SQL Trace

Create an SQL trace using Transaction ST05 as described in Chapter 4. Display the SQL trace results in one user session by selecting List Trace. The Basic SQL Trace List screen appears. Call Transaction ST05 in another user session and display the compressed summary of the results, as follows: GOTO • SUMMARY • COMPRESS.

If you sort the data in the compressed summary according to elapsed database time, you can find the tables that were accessed for the longest times. Use these tables in the Basic SQL Trace List screen to look up the corresponding SQL statements. You should consider only these statements for further analysis.

List of identical accesses

In a third user session, get a list of all identical accesses from the Basic SQL Trace List screen by selecting GOTO • IDENTICAL SELECTS. Compare these identical selects with the trace and the compressed summary. By totaling these durations, you can estimate roughly how much database time could be saved by avoiding multiple database accesses. Unless your savings in database time is sufficiently large, there is no need to perform optimization.

As a result of this preliminary analysis, you will have made a list of any statements you want to optimize.

Preliminary Analysis Using the SQL Statistics

Monitor the SQL statistics from the main screen in the database performance monitor (Transaction ST04) by selecting the Detail Analysis menu. Look under the heading Resource Consumption By. Then (for Oracle), select SQL Request; for Informix, select SQL Statement. In the dialog box that appears, select Enter. The screen Database Performance: Shared SQL appears. For an explanation of the screen, see Chapter 2. Expensive SQL statements are characterized by a large number of logical or physical database accesses. To create a prioritized list of statements in which the top-listed statements are potentially worth optimizing, sort the SQL statistics according to logical accesses (indicated, for example, by buffer gets), physical accesses (shown as disk reads), or runtime of the SQL statements.

Further Preliminary Analysis

Regardless of whether you begin your analysis from an SQL trace or the SQL statistics, before you proceed to a detailed analysis, perform the following checks:

▶ Create several SQL traces for different times and computers to verify the database times noted in the initial SQL trace. Determine whether there is a network problem or a temporary database overload.

▶ If the expensive SQL statement is accessing a buffered table, use the criteria presented in Chapter 9, SAP Buffering, to determine whether table buffering should be deactivated, that is, whether the respective buffer is too small or contains tables that should not be buffered because they are too large or too frequently changed.

▶ Check whether there are any applicable SAP Notes in the SAP Service Marketplace by using combinations of search terms, such as performance and the name of the respective table.

11.1.2 Detailed Analysis

After listing the SQL statements that are worth optimizing, perform a detailed analysis to decide on the optimization strategy. Optimization can take one of two forms: optimizing the ABAP program code related to an SQL statement or optimizing the database, for example, by creating indexes.

Whether to optimize the code or the index

SQL statements that attempt to operate on a great number of data records in the database can only be optimized by making changes to the ABAP programming. The left-hand part of Figure 11.2 shows the activities of a statement that requires this kind of optimization. The stacked, horizontal black bars depict data. Look at the amount of data records depicted both in the database process and in the application server; this shows that the statement has transferred a lot of data to the application server. Therefore, a large number of data blocks (the pale rectangles containing the data bars) were read from the database buffer or the hard drive. For a statement like this, the statement's developer should check whether the program actually needs all of this data or whether a significant amount of the data is unnecessary. The amount of data that constitutes a significant amount varies. For a dialog transaction with an expected response time

High transfer load

of around one second, 500 records transferred by an SQL statement is a significant number. For a reporting transaction, 10,000 records would normally be considered a significant number. For programs running background jobs (for example, in the SAP application module CO), the number of records that constitutes a significant number may be considerably larger.

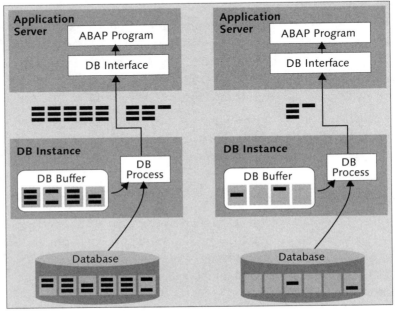

Figure 11.2 Expensive SQL Statements (Left: The Statement Tries to Transfer Too Much Data. Right: The Statement Unnecessarily Reads Too Many Data Blocks.)

High read load   In contrast, an expensive SQL statement of the type requiring database optimization is shown in the right-hand part of Figure 11.2. Although the SQL statement transferred only a few data records (represented by the horizontal black bars) to the application server, the selection criteria has forced the database process to read many data blocks (the pale rectangles, some of which contain the data bars). Many of these data blocks do not contain any sought-after data; therefore, the search strategy is clearly inefficient. To simplify the search and optimize runtime, it may be helpful to create a new secondary index — or a suitable index may already exist, but is not being used.

In this chapter, we'll analyze the two types of expensive SQL statements.

A third type of expensive SQL statement is those with aggregate functions (Count, Sum, Max, Min, Avg), which can be found in BW applications, for example. Here as well, a large number of data records is read on the database and a small number is transferred. They are therefore similar to expensive SQL statements of type II; however, the background is different. For statements that are identified as expensive SQL statements of type II, a large number of data records is read on the database due to an inefficient search strategy; for SQL statements with aggregate functions, many data records are read to form aggregates. This type of evaluation is discussed in the next chapter.

Detailed Analysis Using an SQL Trace

For each line in the results of an SQL trace (Transaction ST05), looking at the corresponding database times enables you to determine whether you can optimize a statement by using database techniques such as creating new indexes. Divide the figure in the Duration column by the entry in the Rec (records) column. If the result is an average response time of less than 5,000 microseconds for each record, this can be considered optimal. Each FETCH should require less than about 100,000 microseconds. If the average response time is optimal, but the runtime for the SQL statement is still high due to the large volume of data being transferred, only the ABAP program itself can be optimized. For an expensive SQL statement in which a FETCH requires more than 250,000 microseconds but that targets only a few records, a new index may improve the runtime.

To do this, from the Basic SQL Trace List screen, select ABAP Display to go to the ABAP code of the traced transaction and continue your analysis, as follows.

Detailed Analysis Using the SQL Statistics

The evaluation of the optimization potential due to data of the SQL statistics depends on the statistics that the database or the database interface provides for this database system. Many database systems indicate the average response time for a statement, and you can calculate the average number of records read per statement (see Section 2.3.2, Identifying and Analyzing Expensive SQL Statements). You can anticipate a threshold value of 2 ms per record as a criterion for good performance. Statements that fall below this threshold value cannot be optimized using database means; here you can only check whether you can reduce the number of calls by changing the application coding. For statements whose average execution times clearly exceed this value, you can check whether you can improve performance with database means, for instance, indexing.

Another criterion for evaluating an SQL statement's optimization potential is the number of logical read accesses for each execution (indicated as Gets/Execution for Oracle) and the number of logical read accesses for each transferred record (indicated as Bufgets/Records for Oracle; see Appendix B, which includes information on the different databases).

However, statements that read an average of less than 10 blocks or pages for each execution and appear at the top of the sorted SQL statistics list due to high execution frequency cannot be optimized by using database techniques such as new indexes. Instead, consider improving the ABAP program code or using the program in a different way to reduce the execution frequency.

Good examples of SQL statements that can be optimized by database techniques (for example, creating or modifying new indexes) include SQL statements that require many logical read accesses to transfer a few records. These are SQL statements for which the SQL statistics shows a value of 10 or higher for Bufgets/Records.

Determining
programs

For SQL statements that need a change to the ABAP code, identify the various programs that use the SQL statement and improve the coding in each program. You can go directly from the SQL statistics to ABAP coding (ABAP Coding button).

Further Detailed Analysis

After determining whether the SQL statement can be optimized via a new index or changes to the program code, you will need more detailed information about the relevant ABAP program. The following information is required for optimizing the SQL statements:

► The purpose of the program

► The tables that are involved and their contents, for example, transaction data, master data, or customizing data, and the size of the tables and whether the current size matches the size originally expected for the table

► The users of the program and the developer responsible for a customer-developed program

After getting this information, you can begin tuning the SQL statement as described in the following sections.

11.2   Optimizing SQL Statements Through Secondary Indexes

To optimize SQL statements using database techniques (such as creating new indexes), you must have a basic understanding of how data is organized in a relational database.

11.2.1   Database Organization Fundamentals

The fundamentals of relational database organization can be explained via a simple analogy based on a database table: the Yellow Pages telephone book.

When you look up businesses in a Yellow Pages telephone book, you probably never consider reading the entire telephone book from cover to cover. You more likely open the book somewhere in the middle and zero in on the required business by searching back and forth a few times, using the fact that the names are sorted alphabetically. If a relational database, however, tried reading the same kind of Yellow Pages data in a database table, it would find that the data is generally not sorted; instead, it is stored in a type of linked list. New data is added (unsorted) to the end of the table or entered in empty spaces (where records were deleted from the table). This unsorted, telephone book version of a database table is laid out in Table 11.1.

[Ex]

Exceptions are the database systems SAP MaxDB and Microsoft SQL Server, which store tables in a sorted manner. Appendix B deals with their specific characteristics.

Page	Column	Position	Business Type	Business Name	City	Street	Telephone No.
			...				
15	2	54	Video rentals	Video Depot	Boston	Commonwealth Ave.	(617) 555-5252
			...				
46	1	23	Florist	Boston Blossoms	Boston	Oxford Street	(617) 555-1212
46	1	24	Video rentals	Beacon Hill Video	Boston	Cambridge Street	(617) 555-3232
			...				

Table 11.1 Example of an Unsorted Database Table

One way for the database to deal with an unsorted table is by using a time-consuming sequential read — record by record. To save the database from having to perform a sequential read for every SQL statement query, each database table has a corresponding primary index. In this example, the primary index might be a list that is sorted alphabetically by business type and name and includes the location of each entry in the telephone book (see Table 11.2).

Business Type	Business Name	Page	Column	Position
...				
Florist	Boston Blossoms	46	1	23
...				
Video rentals	Beacon Hill Video	46	1	24
Video rentals	Video Depot	15	2	54
...				

Table 11.2 Primary Index Corresponding to the Sample Table

Because this list is sorted, you (or the database) do not need to read the entire list sequentially. Instead, you can expedite your search by first searching this index for the business type and name, for example, video rentals and Video Depot, and then using the corresponding page, column, and position to locate the entry in the Yellow Pages telephone book (or corresponding database table). In a database, the position data consists of the file number, block number, position in the block, and so on. This type of data about the position in a database is called the *row ID*. The Business Type and Business Name columns in the phone book correspond to the primary index fields.

Search mechanisms

A primary index is always *unique;* that is, for each combination of index fields, there is only one table entry. If our telephone book example was an actual database index, there could be no two businesses with the same name. In reality, this might not be true; a phone book might, for example, list two separate outlets for a florist in the same area and with the same name.

In our example, the primary index helps you only if you already know the type and name of the business you are looking for. However, if you only have a telephone number and want to look up the business that corresponds to it, the primary index is not useful, because it does not contain the field Telephone No. You would have to read the entire telephone book, entry by entry. To simplify this kind of search query, you can define a *secondary index* that contains the field Telephone No. and the corresponding row IDs or the primary key. Similarly, to look up all of the businesses on a street in a particular city, you can create a sorted secondary index with the City and Street fields, and the corresponding row IDs or the primary key. Unlike the primary index, secondary indexes are as a rule not unique; that is, there can be multiple similar entries in the secondary index. For example, "Boston, Cambridge Street" will occur several times in the index if there are several businesses on that street. The secondary index based on telephone numbers, however, would be unique, because telephone numbers are unique.

Secondary indexes

Execution Plan

If you are looking up all video rental stores in Boston, the corresponding SQL statement would be as follows:

Optimizer and execution plan

```
SELECT * FROM telephone book WHERE business type = 'Video
rentals' AND city = 'Boston'.
```

In this case, the database has three possible search strategies:

1. Search the entire table.

2. Use the primary index for the search.

3. Use a secondary index based on the field City.

The decision as to which strategy to use is made by the *database opti-mizer* program, which considers each access path and formulates an *execution plan* for the SQL statement. The optimizer is a part of the data-base program. To create the execution plan, the optimizer *parses* the SQL statement. To look at the execution plan (also called the explain plan) in the SAP system, use one of the following: SQL trace (Transaction ST05), the database process monitor (accessed from the Detail Analysis menu of Transaction ST04), or the Explain function in the SQL statistics (also accessed from the Detail Analysis menu of Transaction ST04).

[+] The examples presented here are limited to SQL statements that access a table and do not require joins between multiple tables. In addition, the examples are presented using Oracle access types, which include index unique scan, index range scan, and full table scan. Appendix B explains corresponding access types for other database systems.

Index unique scan An index unique scan is performed when the SQL statement's Where clause specifies all primary index fields through an EQUALS condition. For example:

```
SELECT * FROM telephone book WHERE business type =
'Video rentals' AND business name = 'Beacon Hill Video'.
```

The database responds to an index unique scan by locating a maximum of one record — hence the name *unique*. The execution plan is as follows:

```
TABLE ACCESS BY ROWID telephone book
    INDEX UNIQUE SCAN telephone book___0
```

The database begins by reading the row in the execution plan that is indented farthest to the right — here, INDEX UNIQUE SCAN tele-phone book___0. This row indicates that the search will use the primary index telephone book___0. After finding an appropriate entry in the primary index, the database then uses the row ID indicated in the primary index to access the table telephone book. The index unique scan is the most efficient type of table access; it reads the fewest data blocks in the database.

For the following SQL statement, a full table scan is performed if there is no index based on street names:

Full table scan

```
SELECT * FROM telephone book WHERE street = 'Cambridge Street'
```

In this case, the execution plan contains the row `TABLE ACCESS FULL telephone`. The full table scan is a very expensive search strategy for tables greater than 1MB and causes a high database load.

An index range scan is performed if there is an index for the search, but the results are not unique; that is, multiple rows of the index satisfy the search criteria. An index range scan using the primary index is performed when the `Where` clause does not specify all of the fields of the primary index. For example:

Index range scan

```
SELECT * FROM telephone book WHERE business type= 'Florist'
```

This SQL statement automatically results in a search using the primary index. Because the `Where` clause specifies not a single record but an area of the primary index, the table area for business type Florist is read record by record. Therefore, this search strategy is called an index range scan. The results of the search are not unique, and zero to *<n>* records may be found. An index range scan is also performed via a secondary index that is not unique, even if all of the fields in the secondary index are specified. Such a search would result from the following SQL statement, which mentions both index fields of the secondary index:

```
SELECT * FROM telephone book WHERE city = 'Boston' AND street=
'Cambridge Street'
```

The execution plan is as follows:

```
TABLE ACCESS BY ROWID telephone book
    INDEX RANGE SCAN telephone book___B
```

The database first accesses the secondary index `telephone book___B`. Using the records found in the index, the database then directly accesses each relevant record in the table.

Without more information, it is difficult to determine whether an index range scan is effective. The following SQL statement also requires an index range scan: SELECT * FROM telephone book WHERE Name LIKE 'B%'. This access is very expensive, because only the first byte of data in the index key field is used for the search.

[Ex] Consider the following SQL statement (Listing 11.1):

```
SQL Statement
    SELECT * FROM mara WHERE mandt = :A0 AND bismt = :A1
Execution plan
TABLE ACCESS BY ROWID mara
    INDEX RANGE SCAN mara____0
```

Listing 11.1 Index Range Scan

The primary index MARA____0 contains the MANDT and MATNR fields. Because MATNR is not mentioned in the Where clause, MANDT is the only field available to help the database limit its search in the index. MANDT is the field for the client. If there is only one production client in this particular SAP system, the Where clause with MANDT = :A0 will cause the entire table to be searched. In this case, a full table scan would be more effective than an index search; a full table scan reads only the whole table, but an index search reads both the index and the table. You can therefore determine which of the strategies is more cost-effective only if you have additional information, such as selectivity (see the following discussion on optimization). In this example, you need to know that there is only one client in the SAP system. (For more on this example, see the end of the next section.)

Methodology for Database Optimization

Exactly how an optimizer program functions is a well-guarded secret among database manufacturers. However, broadly speaking, there are two types of optimizers: *rule-based optimizers* (RBOs) and *cost-based optimizers* (CBOs).

[+] All database systems used in conjunction with an SAP system use a cost-based optimizer.

An RBO bases its execution plan for a given SQL statement on the Where clause and the available indexes. The most important criteria in the Where clause are the fields specified with an EQUALS condition and that appear in an index, as follows:

Rule-based optimizer (RBO)

```
SELECT * FROM telephone book WHERE business type= 'Pizzeria'
AND business name = 'Blue Hill House of Pizza' AND city =
'Roxbury'
```

In this example, the optimizer decides on the primary index rather than the secondary index, because two primary index fields are specified (business type and business name), whereas only one secondary index field is specified (city). One limit to index use is that a field can be used for an index search only if all of the fields to the left of that field in the index are also specified in the Where clause with an equals condition. Consider two sample SQL statements:

```
SELECT * FROM telephone book
 WHERE business type like 'P%' AND business name = 'Blue Hill
of Pizza'
```

and

```
SELECT * FROM telephone book WHERE business name = 'Blue Hill
of Pizza'
```

For either of these statements, the condition business name = 'Blue Hill House of Pizza' is of no use to an index search. For the first example, all business types beginning with P in the index will be read. For the second example, all entries in the index are read, because the business type field is missing from the Where clause. Whereas an index search is therefore greatly influenced by the position of a field in the index (in relation to the leftmost field), the order in which fields are mentioned in the Where clause is random.

To create the execution plan for an SQL statement, the CBO considers the same criteria as described for the RBO, plus the following criteria:

Cost-based optimizer (CBO)

▶ **Table size**
For small tables, the CBO avoids indexes in favor of a more efficient, full-table scan. Large tables are more likely to be accessed through the index.

▶ **Selectivity of the index fields**
The selectivity of a given index field is the average size of the portion of a table that is read when an SQL statement searches for a particular, distinct value in that field. For example, if there are 200 business types and 10,000 actual businesses listed in the telephone book, then the selectivity of the field Business Type is 10,000 divided by 200, which is 50 (or 2% of 10,000). The larger the number of distinct values in a field, the higher the selectivity and the more likely the optimizer will use the index based on that field. Tests with various database systems have shown that an index is used only if the CBO estimates that, on average, less than 5 to 10% of the entire table has to be read. Otherwise, the optimizer will decide on the full-table scan.

Therefore, the number of different values per field should be considerably high.

▶ **Physical storage**
The optimizer considers how many index data blocks or pages must be read physically on the hard drive. The more physical memory there is that needs to be read, the less likely it is that an index is used. The amount of physical memory that needs to be read may be increased by database fragmentation (that is, a low fill level in the individual index blocks).

▶ **Distribution of field values**
Most database systems also consider the distribution of field values within a table column, that is, whether each distinct value is represented in an equivalent number of data records or if some values dominate. The optimizer's decision is based on the evaluation of data statistics, such as with a histogram or spot checks to determine the distribution of values across a column.

▶ **Spot checks at time of execution**
Some database systems (for example, MaxDB and SQL Server) decide which access strategy is used at the time of execution, not during parsing. During parsing, the values satisfying the Where clause are still unknown to the database. At the time of execution, however, an

uneven distribution of values in a particular field can be taken into account by a spot check.

To determine the number of distinct values per field in a database table, use the following SQL statement: **[+]**

`SELECT COUNT (DISTINCT <dbfield>) FROM <dbtable>`.

To find the number of distinct values for each field of a database table, use Transaction DB02, and (for Oracle):

1. Select Detailed analysis.

2. In the dialog box under the Object field, enter the name of the table and select OK.

3. Then select Table Columns. The new screen lists each field of the selected table (under the Database column). The corresponding number of distinct values is indicated under Distinct Values. The corresponding menu path for other database systems is explained in SAP Online Help.

To make the right decision on optimal access, the CBO requires statistics on the sizes of tables and indexes. These statistics must be periodically generated to bring them up-to-date. To ensure that this occurs, schedule the relevant generating program using the DBA Planning Calendar (Transaction DB13). If the table access statistics are missing or obsolete, the optimizer may suggest inefficient access paths, which can cause significant performance problems.

Table statistics

An advantage to using the RBO is that you do not need to generate table access statistics. Generating these statistics requires administrative work and places a load on the system. The program that generates the statistics must run several times a week at periods of low system load.

RBO or CBO? (advantages and disadvantages)

The advantage of the CBO is its greater flexibility, because it considers the selectivity of specified fields. Recall Listing 1.1 with table MARA. The SQL statement was as follows: `SELECT * FROM mara WHERE mandt = :A0 AND bismt = :A1`. Here, the CBO, which knows that MANDT contains only one distinct value, would decide on a full table scan, whereas the

RBO (automatically preferring an index) would choose the less effective index range scan.

[Ex] To see how indexes can improve performance for the execution of SQL statements, reconsider the previous example (Listing 11.1) of an SQL statement affecting table MARA:

```
SELECT * FROM mara WHERE mandt = :A0 AND bismt = :A1
```

In the SAP system, table MARA contains material master data. The primary index MARA___0 contains the following fields: MANDT (which identifies the client system) and MATNR (the material number). Another field in table MARA is BISMT, which indicates the old material number. This field is used when new material numbers are introduced because of internal company reorganization, but the old, familiar material numbers must remain available to make searches easier for users. Therefore, the SQL statement in the previous listing searches for material using an old material number.

If there is no secondary index with the field BISMT, the database optimizer has two possible access paths: the full table scan or an index range scan through the primary index MARA___0. If there are no table access statistics, the optimizer cannot recognize that the field MANDT is very unselective. After locating the field MANDT in both the Where clause and the index, the optimizer decides on an index range scan through the primary index MARA___0. Because the optimizer is not provided with any statistics, it again cannot recognize that the field MANDT is very unselective.

If statistics on table MARA are available, the optimizer decides on a full table scan. Table 11.3 compares the runtimes of accessing table MARA in various situations, using a MARA with 50,000 entries. The full table scan has a runtime of 500,000 microseconds. This is clearly more effective than the index range scan through the unfavorable primary index MARA___0 (using the MANDT and MATNR fields), which requires 3,500,000 microseconds. The runtime decreases dramatically to 3,000 microseconds after the creation of a secondary index based on the field BISMT. Using this secondary index therefore represents a thousand-fold improvement over using the primary index.

	Access Path	With Index Based on Fields	Runtime in Microseconds
Without table access statistics Without secondary index based on the field BISMT	Index range scan	MANDT, MATNR	3,500,000
With table access statistics Without secondary index based on the field BISMT	Full table scan	N/A	500,000
With table access statistics With secondary index based on the field BISMT	Index range scan	BISMT	3,000

Table 11.3 Comparison of Runtimes for an SQL Statement Affecting Table MARA Using Different Search Strategies

Background: Sequential Read or Record-by-Record (Statistical) Read

Comparing the first and the second sample access shows that a full table scan has a higher performance than an access via an "inefficient" index. Why? Let's discuss this in a short example. In a full table scan, the database instance can sequentially read and browse the data blocks. File systems often support such accesses via anticipatory reading of blocks. In an index range scan for an inefficient index, the database instance initially reads the index, also sequentially. But because the database could not attain any fundamental limitations on the index, it now reads the table record by record, that is, it toggles between the blocks that include the records. This difference is particularly fatal if the blocks are not located in the main memory but must be read from the hard disk. In a sequential read, the read head is positioned once and can then read the blocks one after the other. It can be possible that the table is not located in one single section of the hard disk, but you still assume a small number of positioning operations. But if you need to read the table record by record, the read operation of every record entails a new positioning operation, unless two records that are adjacent in the index are located right next to each other on the hard disk. Such a positioning operation alone takes 6 ms in current hard disks.

There is a second reason why you should use a full table scan instead of an index range scan, which reads large parts of a large table: In a full table scan, some databases don't fill the data buffer, but directly transfer the data to the application. Therefore, no displacement occurs in the data buffer in this case.

Result
This example shows that it is important to create the right secondary indexes for frequently used SQL statements. In addition, up-to-date table statistics are required for the database optimizer to determine the best access path.

11.2.2 Administration for Indexes and Table Access Statistics

Creating and Maintaining Indexes

You create and maintain indexes in ABAP Dictionary Maintenance, which you can access by using Transaction SE11 or, from the SAP initial screen, by selecting TOOLS • ABAP WORKBENCH • DICTIONARY. To see the table fields of an existing index, after entering a table name, select Display. The primary index fields of a table are marked in the Key column. To see the associated secondary indexes, select Indexes. The primary index is not included in the list of indexes, because it was shown on the preceding screen.

To create a new secondary index for a table:

1. Select TOOLS • ABAP WORKBENCH • DEVELOPMENT • DICTIONARY.

2. Enter the table name and select Display. Then select GOTO • INDEXES • CREATE.

3. In the new screen, enter a short description, name the index fields, and select Save. The index now exists in the ABAP Dictionary but has not yet been activated in the database.

4. To activate the index in the database, select INDEX • ACTIVATE.

5. After the index has been activated in the database, the screen displays the message "Index MARA~T exists in database system Oracle."

[!]
Activating an index for a large table in the database is especially time-consuming. During this process, INSERT, UPDATE, and DELETE operations that affect the corresponding table are blocked. Therefore, avoid creating new indexes for large tables during company business hours. To activate indexes with an appropriate background job, use Utilities for ABAP Dictionary Tables (Transaction SE14).

After activating a new index, you may need to generate new table access **[+]** statistics so the optimizer can consider the new index when calculating the execution plan.

Optional indexes are indexes that SAP delivers as database-dependent or deactivated. In ABAP Dictionary Maintenance (Transaction SE11), an index of this type is indicated by selecting the fields for selected database systems. These indexes are activated on specific database systems only or activated if required.

Although an index may be defined as a database index in the ABAP Dictionary, it can be (or become) missing in the database, for example, due to not being activated or due to being deleted and not re-created during database reorganization. This type of index is called a missing index. To determine whether a database index is missing, in the DBA Cockpit (Transaction DBACOCKPIT) select DIAGNOSIS • MISSING TABLES AND INDICES. Alternatively, use Transaction DB02 and select Missing Indices.

Indexes missing on the database

The display of missing indexes is divided into primary and secondary indexes.

If a primary index is missing, the consistency of the data is no longer **[!]** ensured. There is a danger that duplicate keys can be written. If a primary index is missing, duplicate keys may also be written, and therefore the consistency of the data is no longer guaranteed. This status is critical for the system and requires immediate intervention by the database administrator.

To solve the problem of a missing primary index that is known to the ABAP Dictionary but does not yet exist (or no longer exists) in the database, re-create the index in ABAP Dictionary Maintenance:

Optional indexes

1. Use Transaction SE11 or, from the SAP initial screen, select TOOLS • ABAP WORKBENCH • DEVELOPMENT • DICTIONARY.

2. Enter the table name and select Display. Then select DISPLAY • UTILITIES • DATABASE UTILITY • INDEXES • PRIMARY INDEX • CREATE DATABASE INDEX.

If no errors occur, the index has been created on the database. If errors do occur (for example, due to duplicate keys), contact SAP.

Missing secondary
indexes
Missing *secondary indexes* can cause performance problems if the index belongs to a table that is larger than about 1MB. To create the missing index:

1. Use Transaction SE11 or, from the SAP initial screen, select: TOOLS • ABAP WORKBENCH • DEVELOPMENT • DICTIONARY.

2. Enter the table name and select DISPLAY • INDEXES.

3. Select the missing index and then select ACTIVATE.

Alternatively, you can create missing indexes directly from the DBA Cockpit. For this purpose, select an index in the list of missing database objects and select Create in DB. Using this function, you can create the index directly, in the background, or via mass processing.

Consistency check
fundamentals
For the consistency check between the ABAP repository and the database catalog, the check program accesses table DBDIFF, where you store exceptional cases for the check. In other words, in this table you can specify that a table is not supposed to have any primary index, which may be possible for BW tables, for example. Another exception is temporary objects that exist in the database but not in the ABAP repository. To maintain table DBDIFF, you can use the SAP_UPDATE_DBDIFF report, which updates the table and enters temporary objects in the table. Or you can use the DBDIFFVIEW maintenance view, which you can call via the table maintenance (Transaction SM30). Via these views, you can also enter exceptions manually.

Generating Table Access Statistics

Usually, you can schedule the program that generates table access statistics to run as a periodic background job using the DBA planning calendar, which you can find in the DBA Cockpit (Transaction DBACOCKPIT) in the Jobs area; in older versions use Transaction DB13 or DB13C.

The statistics-generation programs that are indicated in the calendar are database-dependent, for example, AnalyzeTab for Oracle, Update sta0 for Informix, and Update Statistics for SQL Server.

[+] To find out which programs need to be scheduled to run periodically and how to schedule them for a specific brand of database, see SAP Online Help, the SAP Notes in Appendix C, and the book *SAP NetWeaver AS*

ABAP System Administration (Frank Föse, Sigrid Hagemann, and Liane Will; SAP PRESS, 2008).

Updating or creating new table access statistics is a resource-intensive process with runtimes of several hours for an entire database. Most database systems use a two-step process:

1. **Requirements analysis:** Finds the tables for which statistics should be created

2. **Statistics generation:** Generates the statistics

Table DBSTATC controls statistics generation. To view the contents of this table, use Transaction DB21, or from the SAP initial screen, select TOOLS • CCMS • DB ADMINISTRATION • COST BASED OPTIMIZER • CONTROL ALL STATISTICS.

The resulting screen lists SAP tables whose cost-based optimizer statistics are to be checked and updated and provides several columns of relevant information, such as:

▸ **Database field**
If this field is empty, the entry applies to all database types. If a value is entered in this field, it applies only to a specified database type.

▸ **Usage Type field**
The O entry means the statistics are only used by the optimizer; the A entry indicates that extended statistics are supposed to be calculated for the application monitor, which can be very time-consuming.

▸ **Active column**
The default setting is A; that is, the table is supposed to be analyzed if the check run revealed that new statistics are necessary. U means the statistics are always updated, that is, independent of the check, which prolongs the runtime of the statistics run. The analysis excludes tables with the entries N (no statistics are created, existing ones are deleted) or R (statistics are generated temporarily for the application monitor and then deleted).

▸ **To Do column**
In this column, the control table DBSTATC sets an X if statistics for a given table are to be generated when the generation program runs next.

▶ **Method field**

This field is only relevant for the Oracle database system. It describes the statistics creation method.

[Ex] For the database administration of Oracle databases, you can also use the SAPDBA utility or the BRCONNECT program as of SAP Basis Version 6.10. For each run of the statistics generation program, you can monitor the logs created:

1. To monitor these logs after a run of the statistics generation program SAPDBA for an Oracle database, select TOOLS • CCMS • DB ADMINISTRATION • DBA LOGS.

2. Then select DB Optimizer.

   The resulting screen might show, for example, the following information:

   ```
   Beginning of Action  End of Action       Fct Object    RC
   24.04.1998 17:10:12  24.04.1998 17:35:01 opt PSAP%     0000
   24.04.1998 17:36:30  24.04.1998 18:26:25 aly DBSTATCO  0000
   ```

   In the first row, the value opt in the column Fct indicates that a requirement analysis was performed. The value PSAP% in the column Object indicates that the requirement analysis was performed for all tables in the database. Compare the beginning and ending times in the first row, and you can see that the requirement analysis took 25 minutes.

   In the second row, the value aly in the column Fct indicates that a table analysis run was performed. The value DBSTATCO in the column Object indicates that the table analysis was performed for all relevant tables. (These are all tables listed in the control table DBSTATC — usually only a small percentage of the total database tables.) Comparing the beginning and ending times in the second row, you can see that the table analysis took almost an hour. The operations in both rows ended successfully, as indicated by the value 0000 in the column RC.

SAP tools for generating table access statistics are specifically adapted to the requirements of the SAP system. Certain tables are excluded from the creation of statistics, because generating statistics for those tables would be superfluous or would reduce performance. Ensure that the table access statistics are generated only by the generation program released specifically for SAP.

When an SAP system is used in conjunction with Oracle databases, no statistics are created for pooled and clustered tables, such as the update tables VBMOD, VBHDR, and VBDATA. For these tables, the Active field in Transaction DB21 displays the entry R.

[Ex]

Therefore, you must make sure to generate the table access statistics only using SAP tools. For further information, refer to the SAP database administration online Help.

[!]

To check whether statistics were generated for a particular table, you can use Transaction DB20. This transaction indicates whether the statistics are current, that is, the deviation between the number of entries in the database and the last check, and when the last update run took place. The system also displays the settings for the table from table DBSTATC. With this function you can re-create statistics.

Whenever you create new tables or indexes, you should then use Transaction DB20 to update the statistics manually, so that the optimizer has a sound evaluation basis for calculating the executing plans.

In the DBA Cockpit, you can find enhanced, database-specific information for some database systems. Examples include the following:

▶ For Oracle, in the Space area: <CHOOSE A TABLE> • TABLE COLUMNS

▶ For Microsoft SQL Server, in the Space area: <CHOOSE A TABLE> • SHOW STATISTICS

Depending on the database system, the new screen indicates the following information: the date of the last analysis, the accuracy of the analysis, the number of occupied database blocks or pages, the number of table rows, and the number of different entries per column (distinct values).

11.2.3 Reorganizing Tables and Indexes

If an SQL statement has a high database time even though the index and the application coding is optimally designed for the access, you should examine whether the index is fragmented. An index is referred to as fragmented if the ratio of memory space and content is extremely poor. Let's

Fragmentation of indexes

consider the following example: A table is filled with 1 million records, and 99% of the records are deleted again, that is, the space of 99 deleted entries still exists next to one remaining index entry. Usually, the database instance doesn't automatically merge the remaining entries; that is, the blocks or pages that used to be occupied are not released again. Now the problem is that the remaining information is distributed across many blocks so that an index range scan must read a relatively high number of index blocks (with reference to the data records returned). This status is referred to as *fragmentation*. The reorganization of the index, that is, the deletion and re-creation, is a corrective measure here. Index RESB__M (SAP Note 70513) is a typical example of an index with a reorganization requirement. Table RESB contains the material reservations in production planning, so it is a table that is changed extremely often.

[+] Problems in fragmenting indexes don't occur in all database systems. Refer to the literature that is available for your database system to get information on whether this problem may be relevant to you. In principle, you should be cautious about reorganizing indexes proactively. Reorganization is resource-intensive and results in a poor performance during the reorganization because, on the one hand, resources are required for the rebuild and, on the other hand, the index is missing during this time and the table may be locked for changes. You should reorganize indexes only after a thorough analysis.

Checking the index quality

The following details the index quality check based on an Oracle database:

1. In the DBA Cockpit, select SPACE • SEGMENTS • DETAILED ANALYSIS.

2. The Segments Specific Selection Window dialog window opens. In the Segment field, enter the name of the table followed by "*" (placeholder) to select the table and the associated indexes. Alternatively, you can enter the database name of the index directly.

3. The Detailed Analysis screen is displayed again, where you can see a list of the selected tables and indexes. Select the index to be examined, and go to the Main Data tab to continue the analysis. In this tab, you can find information on the last analysis of the index (Last Analysis). Moreover, this screen includes buttons to start a current analysis (Validate) and to rebuild an index (Rebuild).

4. Now go to the STORAGE • STORAGE QUALITY tab. The list displayed in this tab provides key figures on the memory quality that was determined in the last analysis run. If you don't find any information here, start the RSORATAD program, and enter the relevant index as the segment to manually start the analysis. The result is displayed in the screen of the RSORATAD program or in the Storage Quality screen in the DBA Cockpit.

5. The index memory analysis calculates the space that is required in theory for an index (Number of Blocks (Calc) key figure) and compares it with the space actually used (Number of Blocks (Used) KEY FIGURE); both are indicated in blocks. The ratio of the two values is the memory quality of the index (Index Storage Quality (%) key figure). Low memory quality means more blocks need to be read than are theoretically required to store the information. A value below 70% is considered poor memory quality.

If an index turns out to be fragmented, you can re-create it on the database as described in the section Creating and Maintaining Indexes. Then you need to use an SQL trace to check whether the SQL statement has actually become faster. Furthermore, you should check how fast the index degenerates again.

11.2.4 Rules for Creating or Changing Secondary Indexes

Preliminary Checks

Creating or changing a secondary index changes the SAP system and can improve or worsen the performance of SQL statements. Therefore, only experienced developers or consultants should make changes to indexes. Before creating or changing an index, proceed as follows:

▶ If the SQL statement for the new index originates from a standard SAP program:

  ▶ Check the relevant SAP Notes in the SAP Service Marketplace that describe ways of optimizing SQL statement performance. If there are no relevant SAP Notes, submit a problem message at the SAP Service Marketplace.

▸ When optimizing customer-developed SQL statements, try to avoid creating secondary indexes on SAP transaction data tables. As a rule, transaction data tables grow linearly over time and cause a corresponding growth in the size of related secondary indexes. Therefore, searching via a secondary index will eventually result in an SQL statement that runs increasingly slowly. Therefore, SAP uses special search techniques for transaction data, such as match-code tables and SAP business index tables (for example, the delivery due index).

▸ If the SQL statement originates from a customer-developed program, rather than create a new index, you may be able to do one of the following:

  ▸ Rewrite the ABAP program in such a way that an available index can be used.

  ▸ Adapt an available index in such a way that it can be used.

▸ Never create a secondary index on SAP Basis tables without an explicit recommendation from SAP. Examples of these tables include NAST and tables beginning with D010, D020, and DD.

Rules for Creating Secondary Indexes

The following basic rules govern secondary index design. For primary indexes, in addition to these rules, there are other considerations related to the principles of table construction:

Rule 1: Include only selective fields in the index

▸ An index is useful only if each corresponding SQL statement selects just a small part of a table. If the SQL statement that searches according to a particular index field causes more than 5 to 10% of the entire index to be read, the cost-based optimizer will not consider the index useful and will choose the full table scan as the most-effective access method. (The value of 5% should only be considered as an estimate value.)

Examples of selective fields include document numbers, material numbers, and customer numbers. Examples of nonselective fields include SAP client IDs, company codes or plant IDs, and account status.

▶ As a rule, an index should contain no more than four fields. Too many fields in the index will lead to the following effects:

Rule 2: Include only a few fields in the index

  ▶ Change operations to tables take longer, because the index must be changed accordingly.

  ▶ More storage space is used in the database. The large volume of data in the index reduces the chance that the optimizer will regard using the index as economical.

  ▶ The parsing time for an SQL statement increases significantly, especially if the statement accesses multiple tables with numerous indexes, and the tables must be linked with a join operation.

▶ To speed up accesses through an index based on several fields, the most selective fields should be positioned farthest toward the left in the index.

Rule 3: Position selective fields to the left in an index

▶ To support the optimizer in choosing an index, it is sometimes necessary to use nonselective fields in the index in a way that contradicts rules 1 to 3. Examples of such fields typically include the fields for client ID (Mandt field) and company code (Bukrs field).

Rule 4: Exceptions to Rules 1, 2, and 3

▶ Avoid creating nondisjunct indexes, that is, two or more indexes with generally the same fields.

Rule 5: Indexes should be disjunct

▶ Despite the fact that the ABAP Dictionary defines a maximum of 16 indexes for each table, as a rule, you should not create more than 5 indexes. One exception is for a table that is used mainly for reading, such as a table containing master data. Having too many indexes causes problems similar to those resulting from an index with too many fields. There is also an increased risk that the optimizer will choose the wrong index.

Rule 6: Create only a few indexes per table

Keep in mind that every rule has exceptions. Sometimes you can find the optimal index combination only by trial and error. Generally, experimenting with indexes is considered safe, as long as you keep the following points in mind:

[+]

▶ Never change indexes for tables larger than 10MB during company business hours. Creating or changing an index can take from several minutes to several hours and blocks the entire table. This can cause serious performance problems during production operation.

▶ After creating or changing an index, always check whether the optimizer program uses this index in the manner intended. Ensure that the new index does not result in poor choices for other SQL statements (discussed later on).

Optimizing SQL Statements (Where Clause)

Before creating a new index, you should carefully check whether it would be possible to rewrite the SQL statement so that an available index can be efficiently used. The following example will demonstrate this point.

Example: Missing Unselective Field in the Where Clause

While analyzing expensive SQL statements in client-specific code, you notice the following statement:

```
SELECT * FROM bkpf WHERE mandt = :A0 AND belnr = :A1
```

Table BKPF contains FI invoice headers and thus can be quite large. The Belnr field is the invoice number. Therefore, access appears to be very selective. Detailed analysis reveals that there is just one (primary) index with the Mandt (client), Bukrs (booking account), and Belnr (document number) fields. Because the Bukrs field is not in the SQL statement, the database cannot use all the fields that follow in the index for the search. In our example, the highly selective Belnr field cannot be used for the index search, and the entire table must be searched sequentially.

These programming errors occur frequently when the unselective field (the booking account in this case) in a system is not used (because there is only one booking account in the client system). The remedy is simple: An Equal or In condition can be added to the unselective field of the Where clause. The efficient SQL statement would be:

```
SELECT * FROM bkpf WHERE mandt = :A0 AND bukrs = :A1 AND
belnr = :A2.
```

Alternatively, when the booking account is not known to the program at the time of execution, but the developer is sure that only a certain number of booking accounts exist in the system, then the statement would be:

```
SELECT * FROM bkpf WHERE mandt = :A0 AND belnr = :A2 AND
bukrs IN (:A3, :A4, :A5, ...).
```

The sequence of AND-linked partial clauses within the Where clause does not matter. The programming example WITH Index-Support can be found in Transaction SE30 under Tips and Tricks.

Example: Missing Client in the Where Clause

A similar situation leads to performance problems when you add CLIENT SPECIFIED to the ABAP SQL statement and forget to specify the client in the Where clause. Most SAP indexes begin with the client; therefore, for this SQL statement, the client field is not available for an efficient index search.

Although these may appear to be trivial errors, they are unfortunately frequent in client-specific code. Table 11.4 lists the most important SAP tables in which this problem can occur. When you're choosing the selective fields, you must also give the unselective fields in every case.

SAP Functionality	Table	Unselective Fields (Must be Specified in the SQL Statement)	Selective Fields
FI	BKPF (document headers)	BUKRS (booking account)	BELNR (document number)
FI	BSEG (document headers, part of the cluster table RFBLG)	BUKRS (booking account)	BELNR (document number)
Comprehensive	NAST (message status)	KAPPL (application key)	OBJKY (object number)
WM	LTAK/LTAP (transfer order headers and items)	LGNUM (warehouse number)	TANUM (transfer order-number)
MM	MAKT (material-description)	SPRAS (language key)	MAKTG (material description in capital letters)

Table 11.4 Examples of Tables with Leading Unselective Fields in the Primary Index

Example: Alternative Access

Occasionally, you can optimize an unselective access for which there is no index by first taking data from a different table. With the dummy data, you then use an index search to efficiently search for the data you want. Consider the following SQL statement:

```
SELECT * FROM vbak WHERE mandt = :A0 AND kunnr = :A1
```

This SQL statement from a client-specific program selects sales documentation (table VBAK) for a particular client (Kunnr field). Because there is no suitable index in the standard program version, this statement requires the entire VBAK table (perhaps many gigabytes in size) to be read sequentially. This access is not efficient.

You can solve this problem by creating a suitable secondary index (along with the disadvantages already discussed), although a developer with some understanding of the SD data model would find a different way. Instead of directly reading from table VBAK, table VAKPA would first be accessed. The optimal access would be:

```
SELECT * FROM vakpa WHERE mandt = :A1 AND kunde = :A2,
```

and then

```
SELECT * FROM vbak WHERE mandt = :A1 AND vbeln = vakpa-vbeln.
```

In this access sequence, table VAKPA (partner role sales orders) would be accessed first. Because there is an index with the Mandt and KUNDE fields, and the Kunnr field is selective, this access is efficient. (Over time, if a large number of orders accumulates for a client, access will begin to take longer.) Table VAKPA contains the Vbeln field (sales order number), which can be used to efficiently access table VBAK via the primary index. You can optimize access by replacing one inefficient access with two efficient ones, although you have to know the data model for the application to be able to do this. SAP Notes 185530, 187906, and 191492 catalog the most frequent client code performance errors in the SAP ERP logistics modules.

These examples show that it is possible to considerably improve the performance of the relevant SQL statement without creating a new secondary index. This kind of optimization is preferable. Every new index requires space in the database; increases the time required for backup, recovery, and other maintenance tasks; and affects performance when you're updating.

What To Do if the Optimizer Ignores the Index

If you find that the cost-based optimizer program refuses to include a particular secondary index in its execution plan, even though this index would simplify data access, the most likely reason is that the table access statistics are missing or not up-to-date. Check the analysis strategy and determine why the table has not yet been analyzed. (See SAP Online Help on database administration.) You can use Transaction DB20 to manually create up-to-date statistics, and then check whether the optimizer then makes the correct decision.

In rare cases it is necessary to include *hints* in the database interface or the database optimizer so that the correct access path can be found. Let's take a look at an example.

Hints

The ZVBAK sample table is supposed to include a ZVBAK-STATUS status field. In this example, assume that the table has 1 million entries, of which 100 have the status O for open, and 999,900 entries have the status C for closed. An index is created via the STATUS field, and the statistics is newly created. Now it is specified that the optimizer doesn't use the index via the status for executing the following SQL statement:

[Ex]

```
SELECT * FROM zvbak WHERE status = "O"
```

The general problem with this application is that the STATUS field is filled asymmetrically and the database must recognize this. Because if you select with STATUS = O, the database should take the index via the STATUS because the index is selective in this case; but if you select with the limitation STATUS = C, the index is not supposed to be used because it would lead to a record-by-record read of 999,900 records of the ZVBAK table, which, as you learned earlier in this chapter, has a lower performance than a full table scan. To make this distinction, first, you must ensure that the database recognizes the asymmetrical distribution of the STATUS field and doesn't just determine that the STATUS field has two different entries. For this purpose, you must create statistics with histograms that take into account the distribution of entries. For Oracle databases you must explicitly specify which statistics are created;

other database systems consider this automatically. Second, you must explicitly inform the database about the type of limitation to the STATUS field. Usually, the database interface converts literals and constants in SQL statements into variables so that the following SQL statement is sent to the database:

```
SELECT * FROM zvbak WHERE status = :A0
```

The reason for this substitution is that the database optimizer can reuse an access path that has already been calculated and doesn't need to determine a new access path for every statement.

In this example, this substitution has a negative impact. The database optimizer cannot decide from the variabilized statement whether the selection is made based on the selective value O or the nonselective value C and will presumably decide against the index on the STATUS field.

In this case it is possible to give the database interface a hint to transfer constants and literals not as variables, but as concrete values. The hint is &SUBSTITUTE LITERALS&. Using the &SUBSTITUTE VALUES& hint also ensures that ABAP variables are transferred to the database not as variables but as concrete values.

In general, hints in Open SQL start with the %_HINTS keyword at the end of an SQL statement. This is followed by the database type and the hint text.

In Native SQL, you must take into account the syntax of the corresponding database. For example, for an Oracle database you can use the statement

```
SELECT /*+ FULL likp */ * FROM likp WHERE ...
```

to force a full table scan.

[!] Hints often turn out to be "time bombs," because after an SAP or database upgrade (or even after a database patch) hints become superfluous and result in accesses with low performance. Therefore, you must analyze and test all hints after an upgrade. In the standard SAP system, hints are used only in exceptional cases.

The appendix provides a list of notes on database hints for the various database systems.

Other reasons why the optimizer cannot find the appropriate index and solutions can be the following:

▶ If the Where clause is too complex and the optimizer cannot interpret it correctly, you may have to consider changing the programming. Examples are provided in the next section.

▶ Sometimes deleting the table access statistics, or even appropriately modifying the statistics, will cause the optimizer to use a particular index. (Therefore, the generation program released specifically for R/3 chooses not to generate statistics for some tables, so ensure that you create table access statistics with the tools provided by SAP.)

▶ In either of these cases, the solution requires extensive knowledge of SQL optimization. If the problem originates from the standard R/3 software, consult SAP or your database partner.

Monitoring Indexes in the SQL Statistics

Before and after creating or changing an index, monitor the effect of the index on the SQL statistics. To monitor the SQL statistics in R/3, from the main screen in the database performance monitor (Transaction ST04), select the Detail Analysis menu, and under the header Resource Consumption By:

1. For ORACLE, select SQL Request. In the dialog box that appears, change the default selection values to zero and click OK.

2. Choose Select Table.

    Specify the table you want to create or change the index for, and select Enter.

    The resulting screen displays the SQL statements that correspond to this table.

3. Save this screen, along with the execution plan for all SQL statements, in a file.

4. Two days after creating or changing the index, repeat steps 1 to 3, and compare the results with those obtained earlier to ensure that no

SQL statement has had a loss in performance due to poor optimizer decisions. In particular, compare the number of logical or physical accesses per execution (these are indicated, for example, in the Reads/ Execution column), and check the execution plans to ensure that the new index is used only where appropriate.

[+] To check the index design using the SQL statistics in a development/test system, ensure that the business data in the system is representative, because the data determines the table sizes and field selectivity considered by the cost-based optimizer. Before testing, update the table access statistics so they reflect the current data.

11.3 Optimizing SQL Statements in the ABAP Program

Database indexes can be used to optimize a program only if the selection criteria for the database access are chosen so that just a small amount of data is returned to the ABAP program. If this is not the case, then the program can only be optimized by rewriting it or by changing the user's work habits.

11.3.1 Rules for Efficient SQL Programming

This section explains the five basic rules for efficient SQL programming. It does not replace an ABAP tuning manual and is limited to a few important cases.

[+] Related programming techniques are explained with examples at the end of this section and in the following sections. For a quick guide to efficient SQL programming, go to the ABAP Runtime Analysis (Transaction SE30) and select Tips and Tricks: SYSTEM • UTILITIES • ABAP RUNTIME ANALYSIS • TIPS AND TRICKS.

The new screen lets you display numerous examples of good and bad programming.

Rule 1

SQL statements must have a Where clause that transfers only a minimal amount of data from the database to the application server, or vice versa. This is especially important for SQL statements that affect tables larger than 1MB. For all programs that transfer data to or from the database:

▶ If the program contains CHECK statements for table fields in SELECT ... ENDSELECT loops, then replace the CHECK statement with a suitable Where clause.

▶ SQL statements without Where clauses must not access tables that are constantly growing, for example, transaction data tables such as BSEG, MKPF, and VBAK. If you find these SQL statements, rewrite the program.

▶ Avoid identical accesses, that is, the same data being read repeatedly. To identify SQL statements that cause identical accesses, trace the program with an SQL trace (Transaction ST05), view the results, and select GOTO • IDENTICAL SELECTS. Note the identical selects and return to the trace results screen to see how much time these selects required. This tells you how much time you would save if the identical selects could be avoided. You can find an example of this situation in the next section.

Transfer few records

Rule 2

To ensure that the volume of transferred data is as small as possible, examine your programs as follows:

Keep the volume of transferred data small

▶ SQL statements with the clause SELECT * transfer all of the columns of a table. If all of this data is not really needed, you may be able to convert the SELECT * clause to a SELECT list (SELECT <column 1> <column 2>) or use a projection view.

▶ There is both an economical and an expensive way of calculating sums, maximums, or mean values in relation to an individual table column:

First, you can perform these calculations on the database using the SQL aggregate functions (SUM, MAX, AVG, etc.) and then transfer only the results, which is a small data volume. Second, you can initially transfer all of the data in the column from the database into the ABAP program and perform the calculations on the application server. This transfers a lot more data than the first method and creates more database load.

► A Where clause that searches for a single record often looks as follows:

```
CLEAR found.
SELECT * FROM dbtable WHERE field1 = x1.
    found = 'X'. EXIT.
ENDSELECT.
```

The disadvantage of this code is that it triggers a FETCH on the database. For example, after 100 records are read into the input/output buffer of the work processes, the ABAP program reads the first record in the buffer, and loop processing is interrupted. Therefore, 99 records were transferred needlessly. The following code is more efficient:

```
CLEAR found.
SELECT * FROM dbtable UP TO 1 ROWS WHERE field1 = x1.
ENDSELECT.
IF sy-subrc = 0. found = 'X'. ENDIF.
```

This code informs the database that only one record should be returned.

Rule 3

Use array select
instead of
single select

The number of fetches must remain small. Using array select instead of single select creates fewer, more lengthy database accesses instead of many short accesses. Many short accesses cause more administrative overhead and network traffic than fewer, more lengthy database accesses. Therefore, avoid the following types of code:

```
LOOP AT itab.
    SELECT FROM dbtable WHERE field1 = itab-field1.
    <further processing>
ENDLOOP.
```

and:

```
SELECT * FROM dbtable1 WHERE field1 = x1.
    SELECT * FROM dbtable2 WHERE field2 =
        dbtable1-field2.
```

```
            <further processing>
        ENDSELECT.
    ENDSELECT.
```

Both examples make many short accesses that read only a few records. You can group many short accesses to make a few longer accesses by using either the FOR ALL ENTRIES clause or a database view. Both options will be described in the example in the following section.

Rule 4

The Where clauses must be simple; otherwise, the optimizer may decide on the wrong index or not use an index at all. A Where clause is simple if it specifies each field of the index using AND and an equals condition.

Keep the Where clauses simple

Virtually all optimizers have problems when confronted with a large number of OR conditions. Therefore, you should use the disjunct normal form (DNF) whenever possible, as described in the following example on avoiding OR clauses.

Instead of the following code:

[Ex]

```
SELECT * FROM sflight WHERE (carrid = 'LH' or carrid = 'UA')
    AND (connid = '0012' OR connid = '0013')
```

it is better to use:

```
SELECT * FROM SFLIGHT
    WHERE ( CARRID = 'LH' AND CONNID = '0012')
       OR ( CARRID = 'LH' AND CONNID = '0013')
       OR ( CARRID = 'UH' AND CONNID = '0012')
       OR ( CARRID = 'UH' AND CONNID = '0013').
```

The other way of avoiding problems with OR clauses is to divide complex SQL statements into simple ones, and store the selected data in an internal table. To divide complex SQL statements, use the FOR ALL ENTRIES clause (see More About FOR ALL ENTRIES Clauses, below).

Sometimes you can use an IN instead of an OR. For example, instead of field1 = x1 AND (field2 = y1 OR field2 = y2 OR field2 = y3), use field1 = x1 and field2 IN (y1, y2, y3). Try to avoid using NOT conditions in the Where clause. These cannot be processed through an index. You can often replace a NOT condition by a positive IN or OR, which can be processed using an index.

Rule 5

Some operations, such as sorting tables, can be performed by the database instance and the SAP instance. In general, you should try to transfer any tasks that create system load to the application servers, which can be configured with more SAP instances if the system load increases. The capacity of the database instance cannot be increased as easily. The following measures help avoid database load:

▸ SAP buffering is the most efficient tool for reducing load on the database instance caused by accesses to database data. You should buffer tables on application servers as much as possible to avoid database accesses (see Chapter 9, SAP Buffering).

▸ If a program requires sorted data, either the database or the SAP instance must sort the data. The database should perform the sort only if the same index can be used for sorting as for satisfying the Where clause, because this type of sort is inexpensive.

[Ex] Consider the table <DBTABLE> with the fields <FIELD1>, <FIELD2>, <FIELD3>, and <FIELD4>. The key fields are <FIELD1>, <FIELD2>, and <FIELD3>, and these comprise the primary index <TABLE__0>. To sort the data by the database, you can use the following statement:

```
SELECT * FROM <dbtable> INTO TABLE itab
       WHERE <field1> = x1 and <field2> = x2
       ORDER BY <field1> <field2> <field3>.
```

Here, a database sort is appropriate, because the primary index TABLE__0 can be used both to satisfy the Where clause and to sort the data. A sort by the fields <FIELD2> and <FIELD4> cannot be performed using the primary index TABLE__0, because the ORDER_BY clause does not contain the first primary index field. Therefore, to reduce database load, this sort should be not be performed by the database, but by the ABAP program. You can use ABAP statements such as:

```
SELECT * FROM <dbtable> INTO itab
```

```
          WHERE <field1> = x1 and <field2> = x2.
SORT itab BY <field2> <field4>.
```

Similar (sorting) considerations apply when you use the GROUP BY clause or aggregate functions. If the database instance performs a GROUP BY, this increases the consumption of database instance resources. However, this must be weighed against the gain in performance due to the fact that the GROUP BY calculation transfers fewer results to the application server. (For more information on aggregate functions, see Rule 2 earlier in this section.)

11.3.2 Example of Optimizing an SQL Statement in an ABAP Program

This section uses an example to demonstrate each step in optimizing an SQL statement.

Preliminary Analysis

In this example, a customer-developed ABAP program is having performance problems. As an initial attempt to remedy this, run an SQL trace (Transaction ST05) on a second run of the program when the database buffer has been loaded. The results of the trace show the information in Listing 11.2.

[Ex]

```
Duration Object   Oper     Rec    RC  Statement
   1,692 MSEG     PREPARE          0  SELECT WHERE MANDT ..
     182 MSEG     OPEN             0
  86,502 MSEG     FETCH     32     0
     326 MKPF     PREPARE          0  SELECT WHERE MANDT ..
      60 MKPF     OPEN             0
  12,540 MKPF     FETCH      1  1403
      59 MKPF     REOPEN           0  SELECT WHERE MANDT ..
   2,208 MKPF     FETCH      1  1403
      60 MKPF     REOPEN           0  SELECT WHERE MANDT ..
   2,234 MKPF     FETCH      1  1403
      61 MKPF     REOPEN           0  SELECT WHERE MANDT ..
   2,340 MKPF     FETCH      1  1403
...  (32 more indiv. FETCHES)
  43,790 MSEG     FETCH     32     0
      61 MKPF     REOPEN           0  SELECT WHERE MANDT ..
```

```
2,346 MKPF     FETCH     1     1403
   60 MKPF     REOPEN          0   SELECT WHERE MANDT ..
2,455 MKPF     FETCH     1     1403
 . . .
```

Listing 11.2 Example of an SQL Trace

The trace begins with a FETCH operation on table MSEG, which reads 32 records, as indicated by the 32 in the Rec column. Next, 32 separate FETCH operations are performed on table MKPF, each returning one record, as indicated by the 1 in the column Rec column. This process is repeated with another FETCH operation that reads 32 records from table MSEG and 32 more single-record FETCH operations on table MKPF, and so on until all records are found.

Now view the compressed summary. To do this from the SQL trace results screen, select GOTO • SUMMARY • COMPRESS. Table 11.5 lists the results.

TCode/ Program	Table	SQL-Op	Accesses	Records	Time in Microseconds	Percent
SE38	MKPF	SEL	112	112	319,040	61.7
SE38	MSEG	SEL	1	112	197,638	38.3
Total					516,678	100.0

Table 11.5 Compressed Summary of an SQL Trace

The compressed summary shows that almost two-thirds (61.7%) of the database time is used for the individual FETCH operations on table MKPF, and more than one-third (38.3%) is used for the FETCH operations on table MSEG.

Detailed Analysis

In the detailed analysis step prior to tuning, you find the tables, fields, and processes that are important for tuning the SQL statements you identified in the preliminary analysis. To increase the performance of specific SQL statements, you can either improve the performance of the database instance or reduce the volume of data transferred from the database to the application server. In Table 11.5, the SQL trace results show that the response times per record are approximately 3,000 microseconds for accesses to table MKPF and approximately 1,800 microseconds for accesses to table MSEG. Because these response times are good, you can conclude that database performance is also good. The only remaining way to increase the performance of SQL statements in the ABAP program is to reduce the amount of data transferred.

View the identical selects: From the SQL trace (Transaction ST05) results screen, select GOTO • IDENTICAL SELECTS. In our example, the resulting list shows 72 identical SQL statements on table MKPF. This is around 60% of the total of 112 accesses to table MKPF, as indicated in the compressed summary. Therefore, eliminating the identical accesses would result in about 60% fewer accesses and correspondingly less access time.

To access the code from the SQL trace results screen, position the cursor on the appropriate program in the Object column and click ABAP Display. In this example, accessing the code reveals that the following ABAP statements caused the database accesses analyzed in the SQL trace:

Accessing the code

```
SELECT * FROM mseg INTO CORRESPONDING FIELDS OF imatdocs
        WHERE matnr LIKE s_matnr.
  SELECT * FROM mkpf WHERE mblnr = imatdocs-mblnr
          AND mjahr = imatdocs-mjahr.
      imatdocs-budat = mkpf-budat.
      APPEND imatdocs.
      ENDSELECT.
ENDSELECT.
```

Listing 11.3 Program Context for SQL Trace

You now need to know from which tables the data is being selected. This is indicated in ABAP Dictionary Maintenance (Transaction SE11). In this example, the two affected tables, MKPF and MSEG, store materials documents for goods issue and receipt. MKPF contains the document heads for the materials documents, and MSEG contains the line items. The program reads the specific materials documents from the database and transfers them to the internal table IMATDOCS. The materials are listed in the internal table S_MATNR.

Table information

Table fields that you need to know in this example are:

- Table MKPF:
  - MANDT: Client (primary key)
  - MBLNR: Number of the material document (primary key)
  - MJAHR: Material document year (primary key)
  - BUDAT: Posting date in the document
- Table MSEG:
  - MANDT: Client (primary key)
  - MBLNR: Number of the material document (primary key)
  - MJAHR: Material document year (primary key)
  - ZEILE: Position in the material document (primary key)
  - MATNR: Material number
  - WERKS: Plant

This program excerpt selects the materials documents corresponding to the materials in the internal table S_MATNR and transfers the document-related fields MANDT, MBLNR, MJAHR, ZEILE, MATNR, WERKS, and BUDAT to the ABAP program. In the SQL statement, S_MATNR limits the data volume transferred to the ABAP program from table MSEG. Because the MATNR field is in table MSEG, data selection begins in table MSEG rather than in MKPF. For each of the records selected in MSEG, the data for the field BUDAT is read from table MKPF and transferred to internal table IMATDOCS.

Nested SELECT loop

The program in this example resolves these tasks with a nested SELECT loop. As you will see in the excerpt, the external loop executes a FETCH operation that returns 32 records. Then each record is processed individually in the ABAP program, and a relevant record from table MKPF is requested 32 times. The program resumes the external loop, collecting another 32 records from the database, and then returns to the internal loop, and so on until all requested documents are processed.

When you have identified the SQL statements that must be optimized (in the preliminary analysis), and the related tables, fields, and processes (in the detailed analysis), you can start to tune these statements, as follows.

Tuning the SQL Code

Comparing the excerpted programming with the rules for efficient SQL programming reveals three areas where these rules contradict the current example:

▶ **Contradiction to rule 1**
Identical information is read multiple times from the database.

Contradiction to rules

▶ **Contradiction to rule 2**
SELECT * statements are used, which read all of the columns in the table. These statements are, however, few in number.

▶ **Contradiction to rule 3**
Instead of a small number of FETCH operations that read many records from table MKPF, the program uses many FETCH operations that read only one record. This creates an unnecessary administrative burden in terms of REOPEN operations and network traffic.

The following subsections provide two tuning solutions for this example of poor data accesses.

Solution 1

Identical database accesses occur because of the nested SQL statements. In the example, the first SQL statement accesses table MSEG to obtain the following data: MANDT=100, MBLNR=00005001, and MJAHR=1998, and the ZEILE field specifies the 10 rows from 0000 to 0010. The second SQL statement searches table MKPF based on the keys MANDT=100, MBLNR=00005001, and MJAHR=1998 and reads identical heading data 10 times. Using nested SQL statements always poses the risk of identical accesses, because the program does not recognize which data has already been read. To avoid identical accesses, read all of the data from table MSEG, and then read the heading data from table MKPF only once, as indicated in the rewritten version of the program in Listing 11.4.

Identical SQL statements

To reduce the amount of data transferred for each table record, convert the SELECT * clause to a SELECT list.

SELECT * clause

To convert the numerous single record accesses to table MKPF into larger FETCH operations, you can use the FOR ALL ENTRIES clause.

Bundling Fetch operations

The optimized program now looks as follows:

```
SELECT mblnr mjahr zeile matnr werks FROM mseg
                INTO TABLE imatdocs
                WHERE matnr LIKE s_matnr.
If sy-subrc = 0.
    SORT imatdocs BY mblnr mjahr.
    imatdocs_help1[] = imatdocs[]
    DELETE ADJACENT DUPLICATES FROM imatdocs_help1
                COMPARING mblnr mjahr.
    SELECT mblnr mjahr budat FROM mkpf
                INTO TABLE imatdocs_help2
                FOR ALL ENTRIES IN imatdocs_help1
                WHERE mblnr = imatdocs_help1-mblnr
                    AND mjahr = imatdocs_help1-mjahr.
    SORT imatdocs_help2 BY mblnr mjahr.
    LOOP AT imatdocs.
        READ TABLE imatdocs_help2 WITH KEY mblnr = imat
                                            docs-mblnr
                mjahr = imatdocs-mjahr BINARY SEARCH.
        imatdocs-budat = imatdocs_help2-budat.
        MODIFY imatdocs.
    ENDLOOP.
ENDIF.
```

Listing 11.4 Optimized ABAP Code

Here are some comments on the optimized program:

1. The required data is read from table MSEG. The SELECT * clause has been replaced with a SELECT list, and the SELECT ... ENDSELECT construction has been replaced with a SELECT ... INTO TABLE ....

2. The statement IF sy-subrc = 0 checks whether records have been read from the database. In the following steps, the internal table IMATDOCS_HELP1 is filled. To avoid double accesses to table MKPF, table IMATDOCS is sorted by the command SORT imatdocs, and the duplicate entries in MBLNR and MJAHR are deleted by the command DELETE ADJACENT DUPLICATES. Finally, the data that was read from table MSEG and stored in table IMATDOCS and the data that was read from MKPF and stored in the table IMATDOCS_HELP2 are combined and transferred to the ABAP program. To optimize the search in internal table IMATDOCS_HELP2, it is important to sort the table and include a BINARY SEARCH in the READ TABLE statement.

After performing these changes, repeat the SQL trace to verify an improvement in performance. Now the SQL trace results look as follows.

```
Duration Object    Oper       Rec    RC
    1,417 MSEG      PREPARE           0
       65 MSEG      OPEN              0
   57,628 MSEG      FETCH      112 1403
    6,871 MKPF      PREPARE           0
      693 MKPF      OPEN              0
  177,983 MKPF      FETCH       40 1403
```

Listing 11.5 SQL Trace of Optimized Code

Observe the following access improvements over the previous version of the program:

▶ Using a SELECT list to access table MSEG now allows all 112 records to be transferred in a single FETCH operation. Using SELECT * enabled only 32 records per FETCH operation. The time for MSEG access is reduced from 197,638 microseconds to 57,628 microseconds.

▶ By avoiding identical accesses to table MKPF, and using the SELECT list and the FOR ALL ENTRIES clauses, you have reduced MKPF access from 319,040 microseconds to 177,983 microseconds.

The database access time is reduced by half.

More About FOR ALL ENTRIES Clauses

The FOR ALL ENTRIES clause is used to convert many short SQL statements into a few longer SQL statements, especially for LOOP ... ENDLOOP constructions or (as in the previous example) for nested SELECT loops.

When you use the FOR ALL ENTRIES clause, the database interface creates, for example, a Where clause that translates the entries of the internal driver table (in this example, IMATDOCS_HELP1) into separate conditions, which are then combined with each other through a disjunct normal OR. In this example, the database interface creates the following SQL statement:

```
SELECT
    "MBLNR" , "MJAHR" , "BUDAT"
FROM
```

```
        "MKPF"
WHERE
      ( "MANDT" = :A0 AND "MBLNR" = :A1 AND "MJAHR" = :A2 )
  OR ( "MANDT" = :A3 AND "MBLNR" = :A4 AND "MJAHR" = :A5 )
  OR ( "MANDT" = :A6 AND "MBLNR" = :A7 AND "MJAHR" = :A8 )
              <n times>
  OR ( "MANDT" = :A117 AND "MBLNR" = :A118 AND "MJAHR"
          = :A119)
```

Listing 11.6 Generated Statement when Using the FOR ALL ENTRIES Clause

To calculate *<n>*, the SAP work process takes the smaller of the following numbers: the number of entries in the internal driver table (here, IMATDOCS_HELP1) and the SAP profile parameter `rsdb/max_blocking_factor`. If the number of entries in the internal driver table is larger than `rsdb/max_blocking_factor`, the work process executes several similar SQL statements on the database to limit the length of the `Where` clause. The SAP work process joins the partial results, excluding duplications.

The execution plan for the above statement is as follows:

```
Execution Plan
SELECT STATEMENT
      CONCATENATION
          TABLE ACCESS BY INDEX ROWID MKPF
              INDEX UNIQUE SCAN MKPF_____0
          TABLE ACCESS BY INDEX ROWID MKPF
              INDEX UNIQUE SCAN MKPF_____0
                  <n times>
          TABLE ACCESS BY INDEX ROWID MKPF
              INDEX UNIQUE SCAN MKPF_____0
```

Listing 11.7 Execution Plan for the Generated Statement

When using the FOR ALL ENTRIES clause, observe the following prerequisites.

Avoid empty driver tables
The driver table (here, IMATDOCS) must not be empty. If the driver table is empty of data, the FOR ALL ENTRIES clause reads the entire database table. In our example, the driver table contains the header information for the materials documents. If it is empty, line item data is not required, and the second, expensive SQL statement need not be executed. To avoid executing the second statement, the program should check that

the driver table is empty by using the ABAP statement `IF sy-subrc = 0`. This ensures that the SQL statement with the `FOR ALL ENTRIES` clause is processed only if table IMATDOCS was previously filled.

The driver table (here, IMATDOCS) must contain no duplicate entries. If the driver table contains duplicate entries, the corresponding data is read twice from the database. Therefore, there should be no duplicate entries in the driver table. In the above code example, duplicate entries are avoided by sorting the driver table and then deleting the duplicates.

No duplicate entries

Depending on the database system, the database interface translates a `FOR ALL ENTRIES` clause into various SQL statements. In our example, the database interface uses the `FOR ALL ENTRIES` clause to generate equivalent conditions based on `OR`. Alternatively, the database interface can also translate the clause into SQL statements using an `IN` or `UNION` operator. This is controlled through SAP profile parameters, which you should not change without explicit instructions from SAP.

[+]

Solution 2

The second way to optimize the program requires creating a database view on tables MSEG and MKPF. In our example, this would be the view Z_MSEG_MKPF with the following properties:

- Tables: MKPF and MSEG
- Join conditions:
  - MSEG-MANDT = MKPF-MANDT
  - MSEG-MBLNR = MKPF-MBLNR
  - MSEG-MJAHR = MKPF-MJAHR
- View fields:
  - MSEG-MANDT
  - MSEG-MBLNR
  - MSEG-MJAHR
  - MSEG-ZEILE
  - MSEG-WERKS
  - MKPF-BUDAT
  - MSEG-MATNR

[+] To create a database view, use ABAP Dictionary Maintenance (Transaction SE11).

With this view, the ABAP program can be formulated as follows:

```
SELECT mblnr mjahr zeile matnr werks budat FROM z_mseg_mkpf
            INTO TABLE imatdocs
            WHERE matnr LIKE s_matnr.
```

The SQL trace then displays the following information:

```
Duration Object       Oper      Rec   RC
   1,176 Z_MSEG_MKP  REOPEN            0
  49,707 Z_MSEG_MKP  FETCH       112 1403
```

Compare this with the optimized version in solution 1. The database time has again been reduced by half.

The execution plan is as follows:

```
Execution Plan
SELECT STATEMENT
    NESTED LOOP
          TABLE ACCESS BY INDEX ROWID MSEG
              INDEX RANGE SCAN MSEG~M
          TABLE ACCESS BY INDEX ROWID MKPF
              INDEX UNIQUE SCAN MKPF~0
```

Listing 11.8 Execution Plan with Database View

The database optimizer decides

Checking for identical accesses and joining data in the ABAP program is no longer necessary. When you compare the two solutions — the first with the FOR ALL ENTRIES clause and the second with the database view — a clear argument favors converting nested SELECT loops into database views. However, using a database view means that, in addition to selecting the right indexes, the database optimizer must make correct choices on the following issues:

► **The sequence of accessing the tables**
In our example, the optimizer should decide to first read table MSEG and then table MKPF.

► **The type of table join**
The optimizer should decide on a *nested loop join* to join the data from

both tables. The available join methods vary according to the database system (see the manufacturer's documentation).

You should monitor the performance associated with using a view. During the corresponding join operation, partial sort operations occur on the database, during which performance problems may occur. If the database has problems choosing the appropriate execution plan for the SQL statement that accesses the view, it may be wiser to explicitly program the table-accessing sequence and joining of the ABAP program data.

11.3.3 Presetting Field Values in Report Transactions

Often when display transactions are called, a screen appears with up to 10 or more selection fields. By entering appropriate selection criteria, the user can limit the number of hits. If precise, focused selection criteria can be specified, then the database can more quickly find the information by using an index. If no criteria whatsoever is entered, a full table scan may be performed on the corresponding database table.

This means that poor user habits create performance problems, which can be prevented in the following ways:

Countermeasures

▶ **End-user education**
You can broadcast user messages to educate users about unproductive selections and their consequences (that is, How do I make the right selection?). Selection screens should be filled with criteria that are as specific as possible. If at all possible, a value should always be entered into the first field (document number, requirement tracking number, material number, etc.) along with other entries (purchasing group, purchasing organization, plant, etc.). When the user is selecting from supplier orders, the supplier should be specified, as well as a time interval for the order date that is as short as possible. Users should be made aware that a selection result containing several hundred entries is not optimal.

▶ **Changing field attributes on selection screens**
For example, you can change field attributes and designate certain very selective fields as required fields. Although this restrictive method effectively limits selection possibilities, it must be adjusted to the special requirements of the users. Also, default values for fields can be

prespecified. The user can then overwrite any necessary default entries (for example, if the user is filling in for a coworker who is on sick leave).

To change field attributes and specify user default values, you must make changes to the ABAP code for all previously listed transactions.

[Ex] For example, if you call Transaction ME57 to select purchase requisitions, a window with more than 20 input fields is displayed. If no other values are entered into fields in this window, a full table scan of table EBAN (purchase requisitions) will be performed. A discussion with the users responsible for the transaction and business process would probably result in the following types of suggestions for improvement:

▶ Users could be required to enter a purchasing group (required field).

▶ Users are usually only interested in orders with the status N (not closed). If the processing status N is given in addition to other selection criteria, like a date range, then the statement is more efficient, because far fewer records will be read. Unfortunately, users often forget to enter the N. Organizational methods cannot be expected to control this problem, because some 2,000 users execute the transaction. Instead, a simple solution would be to preset this field with the default value N.

▶ To further limit selections, the date range should be as narrow as possible; that is, the default date should be the current calendar date.

The following section describes the method for implementing these improvements.

Defining
required fields

First, determine the report name and the name of the field that will be made a *required field*:

1. To call the transaction for optimization (in our example, Transaction ME57), from the SAP initial screen, select SYSTEM • STATUS.

2. In the Report field, you will find the associated report (RM06BZ00).

3. Leave the Status window (click Continue).

4. Using the cursor, select the field to be made a required field — in this example, Purchasing Group. Then, press F1, which brings up context-sensitive Help for the Purchasing Group field.

5. Click Technical Info and, under Field name, find EKGRP, the name of the field to be changed.

Next, determine the place to change in the report code to make this a required field. The field definition is either in the report or in a logical database. To find out whether the field definition is in the report itself:

Determining codes

1. Exit the context-sensitive Help and Transaction ME57, and call the ABAP editor (Transaction SE38).

2. In the Program field, enter the report name (RM06BZ00) and select SOURCE CODE • DISPLAY.

3. Select Search (glasses icon).

4. In the Search field of the new dialog box, enter the name of the field (EKGRP). In the Search Range section, select the Global in Program field.

5. If the search finds the field, then you have found where the coding must be modified.

If the field is not found, then search in the logical database to which this report is associated:

1. Call the ABAP editor (Transaction SE38).

2. In the Program field, enter the report name (RM06BZ00) and select ATTRIBUTES • DISPLAY.

3. In the Logical Database field, you will find the report associated with this logical database (for example, BAM).

4. Double-click the database name (BAM) to open a window with the definition of the logical database.

5. Use the arrow keys to go to the Logical Databases: Editor Display Program DB<db>SEL screen; <db> is the name of the logical database. This screen contains the definition of the EKGRP field.

After you have identified where to change the code, make EKGRP a required field by adding the ABAP keyword OBLIGATORY to the corresponding line.

To do this, change the line ba_ekgrp FOR eban-ekgrp MEMORY ID ekg to ba_ekgrp FOR eban-ekgrp MEMORY ID ekg OBLIGATORY. The next time you

Changes

531

call Transaction ME57, the Purchasing Group field will be a required field, and a question mark will appear on the screen.

This field will also be required in all reports that use the same logical database. You can find the effected programs using the where-used list.

Presetting default values   Our second improvement involved entering default values in fields. To do this, first find the place in the code where the field is defined, as previously described. For example, find the definition of Processing Status (in our example, in Include `FM06BCS1` of the report `RM06BZ00`). Then change the line `s_statu FOR eban-statu` to `s_statu FOR eban-statu DEFAULT 'N'`. The next time you call Transaction ME57, the field Processing Status will already contain the value N. You can set the default value for the date the same way.

Other possible definition variations (besides `DEFAULT` and `OBLIGATORY`) can include:

▶ `NO-DISPLAY`
The selection does not appear on the screen but can be preset with default values.

▶ `NO-EXTENSION`
The selection allows only one input line; that is, you cannot access the Multiple Selection screen, because its button does not appear on the selection screen.

▶ `NO INTERVALS`
The `SELECT` option appears without an Until field on the selection screen. The button for selecting the Multiple Selection screen appears immediately after the From field. This produces a simplified selection screen, which is especially helpful for a `SELECT` option in which no interval is normally used. For further information, see the context-sensitive Help F1 for the `SELECT-OPTIONS` ABAP statement.

Transaction variants   As an alternative to modifying the coding, you can assign a default variant to a transaction. To do this, you must assign a system variant to the report (`RM06BZ00` in this example):

1. Call the ABAP editor (Transaction SE38).

2. In the Program field, enter the report name (`RM06BZ00`) and select Variant, Display.

3. In the Variants field, enter the name "CUS&DEFAULT" and select Create.

4. You can now create a variant, preset default values, hide fields, and configure other specifications. For additional help in creating variants, please refer to Chapter 11 in the book *Discover ABAP* by Karl-Heinz Kühnhauser (2nd edition, SAP PRESS, 2008).

The variant created must be a system variant, which means it must begin with CUS&. To create a system variant, you need a correction order and a modification key from the SAP Service Marketplace.

You must ensure that the system variant created is automatically used at the transaction start:

1. Call the ABAP Repository Browser (Transaction SEU) and select OTHER OBJECTS • EDIT, which will take you to the Other Development Objects screen.

2. Select Transaction, enter Transaction ME57, and select Display.

3. Select DISPLAY • CHANGE.

4. In the Start with Variant field, enter the name of the newly defined system variant (CUS&DEFAULT). Save the change; entering the system variant is considered a modification.

Now, when you start Transaction ME57, the fields will reflect your changes.

The user interface will have been modified to look like this: **[Ex]**

▶ Purchasing Group is now a required field (as a result of the ABAP code modification).

▶ The default value N has been set for the Processing Status field, so it is no longer available for entries (as a result of system variant customization).

▶ The Delivery Date field is automatically preset to the current calendar date and to a date far in the future.

In addition to the default variant, you can also create other variants, such as those with different preset processing status indications. You can view these variants by selecting GOTO • VARIANTS • GET. You may want to authorize some users to create new variants and restrict other users to using only those variants already created.

11.4 Expensive SQL Statements Due to Incorrect Buffer Settings and Administration Tools

Incorrect buffer settings

Expensive SQL statements may also be due to incorrect settings for SAP buffering, such as a too-small buffer or buffering for tables that should not be buffered because they are too large or too often changed. Examine the tables accessed by the expensive SQL statements in the SQL statistics monitor (Transaction ST04) or SQL trace (Transaction ST05). If the tables accessed are the kinds of tables in Table 11.6, an incorrect buffer setting may be indicated. SQL statements that access these tables do not originate directly from an ABAP program; they are triggered on behalf of an ABAP program by SAP Basis to obtain background information, for example, load ABAP programs, ABAP Dictionary objects, or buffered tables.

SAP Buffer	Related SAP Basis Table
Table definitions (TTAB)	DDNTT
Field definitions (FTAB)	DDNTF
Program (PXA)	D010*
Screen	D020*
Table buffer	ATAB, KAPOL

Table 11.6 SAP Buffers and Related SAP Basis Tables

[Ex] The following SQL statement is an example from SAP Basis that reads table D010S to load an ABAP program into the program buffer:

```
SELECT
    "BLOCKLG" , "BLOCK"
FROM
    "D010S"
WHERE
 "PROG" = :A0 AND "R3STATE" = :A1 AND "R3MODE" = :A2 AND
"R3VERSION" = :A3 AND "BLOCKNR" = 1
```

The SQL statistics monitor (Transaction ST04) may indicate expensive SQL statements (with many buffer gets) that do originate not from an SAP application transaction, but from database monitoring programs such as the analysis program RSORATDB, the auxiliary program SAPDBA (for example, with the SAPDBA options -next, -check, and -analyze), and non-SAP database monitoring tools. To avoid disrupting production operation, you should run these programs only during times of low workload. For example, the default setting for running RSORATDB causes it to run at 7:00 a.m. and 7:00 p.m. as part of the background job SAP_COLLECTOR_FOR_PERFORMANCE.

DB administrations tools

You can identify SQL statements that are used for monitoring the database by table names such as DBA_SEGMENTS, DBA_INDEXES, and USER_INDEXES (for Oracle), or SYSTABLES and SYSFRAGMENTS (for Informix). To find out if an SQL statement belongs to the SAP system or to one of these database administration and monitoring tools, check whether the corresponding table exists in the ABAP Dictionary (Transaction SE11). If the table is not listed, the SQL statement is from a database administration and monitoring tool.

The following is an example of an SQL statement that the SAP administration and monitoring tool SAPDBA for Oracle executes:

[Ex]

```
SELECT
 OWNER,SEGMENT_NAME,SEGMENT_TYPE,NEXT_EXTENT/:b1,PCT_INCREASE
FROM SYS.DBA_SEGMENTS
WHERE TABLESPACE_NAME=:b2 AND(SEGMENT_TYPE='TABLE'
    OR SEGMENT_TYPE='INDEX' OR SEGMENT_TYPE='CLUSTER')
    AND NEXT_EXTENT/:b1*DECODE(PCT_INCREASE,0,:b4,
    ((POWER(1+PCT_INCREASE/100,:b4)-1)/(PCT_INCREASE/100)))>:b6
```

If administration programs like this cause expensive statements in a production system (as indicated in the SQL statistics monitor, Transaction ST04) and are executed during times of high workload, they should be run infrequently.

11.5 Summary

The options available for optimizing execution performance for SQL statements include creating or changing indexes, creating table access statistics, and optimizing ABAP code. Figure 11.3 shows a procedure roadmap covering these optimization techniques.

In addition, it can be helpful to investigate connections between expensive SQL statements and their use in associated programs. For example, users should:

► Limit the kinds of selection data they enter in SAP screens so that few records must be read.

► Use match codes when searching for business data.

► Use SAP information systems (for example, EIS, VIS, LIS, etc.) or SAP NetWeaver BW instead of writing one-off programs to obtain ad hoc reports.

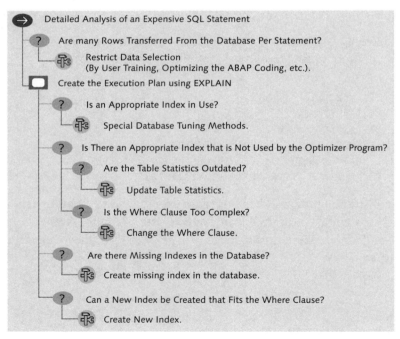

Figure 11.3 Procedure Roadmap for Optimizing Expensive SQL Statements

Users may not be aware that they are contributing to the long runtime of an SQL statement by not using appropriate limiting conditions when searching the database.

In the cases described in this section it is possible to significantly improve the performance of the corresponding SQL statement without creating a new secondary index. Of course, this type of optimization is preferred because every new index occupies space in the database and prolongs the times necessary for backup, recovery, and other maintenance work and consumes performance during the update.

Additional tuning measures exist that you can use when the volume of data records transferred by an SQL statement cannot be further reduced, and you are sure that the optimal index is being used.

Important Concepts

After reading this chapter, you should be familiar with the following concepts:

▶ Logical and physical read accesses (buffer gets, disk reads)

▶ Primary and secondary indexes

▶ Selectivity

▶ Database optimizer and execution plan

▶ Table access statistics

Questions

1. Which of the following statements is correct with regard to expensive SQL statements?

a) They can lead to hardware bottlenecks (a CPU or I/O bottleneck) and negatively affect the runtimes of other SQL statements.

b) They can occupy a lot of space in the data buffer of the database, displace objects that are needed by other SQL statements, and negatively affect the runtimes of other SQL statements.

c) They can occupy a lot of space in the SAP table buffer and displace objects, which causes unnecessary reload operations.

537

d) If they are performed after database locks were set by the same program, this can cause exclusive lock wait situations in the database, which can cause a brief system standstill.

e) Expensive SQL statements in programs for reporting or in background programs are not normally a problem for the database.

2. In the results of an SQL trace, you find an SQL statement that has a runtime of one second and selects only 10 records. Which of the following could be the reason for the long runtime?

a) There is a (CPU or I/O) hardware bottleneck on the database server.

b) There is a network problem between the application server and the database server.

c) The database optimizer has created an inefficient execution plan, for example, by choosing an inefficient index.

d) There is no appropriate index for the SQL statement.

e) There are exclusive lock waits in the database.

3. In the SQL statistics, you find an SQL statement with 10,000 logical read accesses per execution (indicated as Gets/Execution). Which of the following could be the reason for this high number of read accesses?

a) There is a (CPU or I/O) hardware bottleneck on the database server.

b) There is a network problem between the application server and the database server.

c) The database optimizer has created an inefficient execution plan, for example, by choosing an inefficient index.

d) There is no appropriate index for the SQL statement.

e) There are exclusive lock waits in the database.

f) A large number of records are being transferred from the database to the ABAP program.

4. Which access is faster if you don't want an SQL statement to read the entire table: a full table scan or an index range scan?

   a) The full table scan is always faster; an index is only useful for a fully qualified access (index unique scan)

   b) The index range scan is always faster because less data needs to be read than in a full table scan

   c) If more than approximately 10 to 20% (rule of thumb) of the data in a table is supposed to be read, a full table scan is faster, because the table can be accessed sequentially, whereas an index range scan must access the database record by record.

12 Optimizing Queries to SAP NetWeaver Business Warehouse

The form of data store, as it exists for the transactional handling of business documents, is not suitable for analytical applications (reporting). Both the flexibility and the performance suffer when reporting is carried out on transactional data. The data for analytical applications is therefore transferred to appropriate database tables. These tables can reside in the same database as the original data, or they can reside in a separate database. The concept of separating data for analytical applications from the transactional data has already been traced in SAP R/3 in applications such as the *Logistic Information System* (LIS) and in the *Executive Information System* (EIS). You can find its consistent further development in *SAP NetWeaver Business Warehouse* (SAP NetWeaver BW).

SAP NetWeaver BW considers two processes with regard to performance: the load performance, namely, the performance when extracting, transferring, and loading transactional original data in SAP NetWeaver BW, and the query performance, namely, the performance of data queries in SAP NetWeaver BW.

When Should You Read this Chapter?

You should read this chapter if you have identified expensive, long-running SAP NetWeaver Business Warehouse queries in your SAP system and want to analyze and optimize them in detail. The previous chapter on SQL statements is a prerequisite for understanding this chapter.

This chapter isn't an introduction to SAP NetWeaver Business Warehouse architecture and administration; it can only offer an initial insight into the performance analysis and optimization of SAP NetWeaver BW.

12.1 Fundamentals of SAP NetWeaver Business Warehouse

Analytical applications

When we discuss the subject of SQL statements in the environment of SAP NetWeaver Business Warehouse, referred to as *BW queries*, it is helpful to first show what differentiates transactional applications (OLTP), which were the focus of the previous chapter, and analytical applications (OLAP), which we'll discuss in this chapter, from one another.

We can divide analytical applications into three groups. First are *reports*. These are summarizing reports on important key figures such as turnover, costs, and margin in the form of tables, graphics, maps (geographical distribution of key figures), formatted reports (corporate balance sheet), or dashboards (interactive graphics with an evaluation of key figures, for example, in the form of traffic light icons for decision makers). *Simulation and planning applications* form the second group. These are characterized by their use of analytical data to make forecasts on future behavior. Their technical special feature is that they also return data to the database. *Data mining procedures*, that is, statistical procedures such as correlation and cluster analyses, form the third group used for the creation or verification of hypotheses.

Regardless of their type, analytical applications always access data in a specific way. They select individual key figures of business documents and access either all or at least a large number of business documents. The data store used for transactional applications for business documents, which has been optimized for rapidly storing data and for working with small data quantities, is not suitable for analytical applications: The data store is oriented ("normalized") by documents. Many data blocks must therefore be read from the database via joins to determine the key figures. Furthermore, the number of indexes must be restricted on transactional tables. Many reporting queries therefore cannot be supported via an index. The solution to these problems is a separate data store in a data warehouse

12.1.1 Overview of the Most Important Concepts in SAP NetWeaver BW

InfoObjects

The smallest modeling units of SAP NetWeaver BW are the *InfoObjects*. These are the data elements from which the reporting is compiled. Modeling information such as data type, field names, texts, and other specific properties are specified in the InfoObjects. InfoObjects are divided into *key figures* on the one hand, and into *characteristics* and *attributes*, on the other. Key figures are the parameters on which are reported, for example, turnover, costs, and material stock. Characteristics and attributes are specific features according to which key figures are reported on, for example, time characteristics such as year and month and characteristics such as customer, customer group, region, employee, and department. Key figures are aggregated via the characteristics according to the following methods and depending on their type:

- ▶ **Type flow**
  Can be totaled across all characteristics (examples: turnover, costs)

- ▶ **Type stock**
  Can be totaled, but according to chronological characteristics (examples: material stock, number of employees)

- ▶ **Type value per unit**
  No totaling is possible — only MAX, MIN, AVG (example: exchange rate)

InfoProviders are made up of InfoObjects. InfoProviders containing data and those not containing any data are differentiated from one another. Data-containing InfoProviders are InfoCubes, DataStore objects (DSOs), and InfoObjects (master data objects, which you can report on). InfoProviders that do not contain any data but refer to other data sources are InfoSets, virtual providers, MultiProviders, and HybridProviders. We'll focus on InfoCubes in this section and deal with DataStore objects to some extent.

InfoProvider

From the reporting point of view, an *InfoCube* is essentially a complete data quantity for an application (self-contained). From the technical point of view, an InfoCube is formed by a set of database tables arranged in the star schema. We'll now discuss the star schema in detail.

InfoCube

Imagine that the data you're reporting on is stored in many small cubes that in turn form a large cube. Imagine a large Rubik's Cube. The classic textbook example is a cube with the dimensions time, product, and customer. The key figures are stored as a function of the dimensions inside the small cubes. In the simple example, the key figures could be the

[Ex]

quantity of the product sold, the gross and net turnover, and the margin. The finest query granularity in our example would therefore be the question regarding quantity, turnover, and margin for one specific customer and a product on a specific day. In reality, with reporting objects we are generally dealing with more than three dimensions, and the objects are not cubes (which have the same length of side in all dimensions). However, the concept of an InfoCube has simply prevailed because human beings think in three spatial dimensions

Different set operations are now possible based on this build, for example, transposing dimension axes (pivoting), aggregating along specific dimensions (rollup), drilling down dimensions (drilldown), segmenting using specific filter criteria (slice and dice), to name only the most basic operations.

DataStore object

A *DataStore object* (DSO) is a data quantity prepared for reporting via a business document, for example, sales orders. DataStore objects are flat database tables, the columns of which consist of the key of the associated business document, (for example, the sales order number or item), the characteristics, and the key figures of the document.

Direct reporting is possible via InfoCubes and DataStore objects. The fundamental difference (apart from data quantity and performance) between InfoCubes and DataStore objects is that the InfoCube does not contain any information on the actual object; that is, you cannot navigate from the report to the individual document. InfoCubes therefore have a considerably better performance optimization potential and smaller data growth. There are only a few options for performance optimization for DataStore objects.

Data is frequently stored in DataStore objects first (that is, with a document key), and then it is compressed into InfoCubes.

HybridProviders and MultiProviders

Combined reporting is possible via *HybridProviders,* for example, via an InfoCube and a logically associated DataStore object or via an InfoCube and a virtual provider that reads current data directly from the source system. If you cleverly apply this technology, it is possible to compromise between modest data growth and good performance on the one hand, and up-to-date data and document reference (for more recent documents) on the other.

544

For performance reasons or functional reasons, an InfoCube can be divided so that only the MultiProvider defined on the individual InfoCubes comprises the complete data quantity for the reporting. Homogeneous and heterogeneous complex MultiProviders are distinguished from one another. A homogeneous MultiProvider is based on several InfoProviders of equal structure that contain different data. One example would be a MultiProvider based on InfoProviders of equal structure that each contain the data of a business year. For example, BasicCube A could contain the data from 2007, Cube B the data from 2008, Cube C the data from 2009, and so on. A query that compares the data of the current year with that of the previous year can be parallelized via the individual cubes. Heterogeneous MultiProviders are made up of InfoProviders with a different structure. The BasicCubes only partly conform in characteristics and key figures.

BW queries are generated programs that run on one or several InfoProviders and correspond to a specific report purpose. *Reports* are the graphical preparation of these, for example, in the form of a table or graph.

Queries and reports

BW queries are modeled and generated in the Query Designer. They would be displayed as a sequence of SQL statements in the database.

BW queries are displayed as reports on the presentation server in the SAP NetWeaver BW Standards *BEx Web analyzer* or *web reporting*. In addition, the products of *SAP BusinessObjects™* are based on BW queries, and there are a large number of third-party presentation tools. The SAP BEx Web analyzer is a Microsoft Excel add-in extended by SAP. It is installed like SAP GUI (since 1999 as optional component) on the presentation server. The hardware prerequisites for the presentation server are the same as those for the respective SAP GUI (see SAP Note 26417). With Web reporting, the report is displayed in the web browser. We won't discuss the differences that exist functionally between the SAP BEx Web analyzer and Web reporting. We'll deal with the performance aspects of both display tools in this chapter.

SAP NetWeaver BW frontend

SAP BusinessObjects, an SAP subsidiary company, is the leading software manufacturer for BW applications, including:

SAP Business-Objects

- ▸ SAP BusinessObjects Enterprise, a flexible BW application platform
- ▸ Crystal Reports®, among other things, a reporting solution for formatted reports, for example, company balance sheets

▶ SAP BusinessObjects Web Intelligence, a solution for ad hoc reporting

▶ SAP BusinessObjects Voyager, a special solution for business analysts via which current business figures can be accessed

▶ SAP BusinessObjects Xcelsius Enterprise, a solution for creating dashboards via which it is possible to display company key figures mainly in small and mid-sized companies on an overview page

▶ SAP BusinessObjects Polestar, a solution for searching for business concepts

These products can be based on different levels of SAP NetWeaver BW, queries, InfoProviders, or even on tables; that is, the performance optimization technologies presented in this chapter are also applied to products of SAP BusinessObjects. However, we won't discuss the individual products here.

ETL process   The process of *extracting* data from the source systems, *transforming* and processing data in a unique reporting format, and *loading* it in the data stores in SAP NetWeaver BW is referred to as the *ETL process*. The process accounts for a significant proportion of the load in the SAP NetWeaver BW system. The processes are mapped by default in SAP NetWeaver BW via background processes that run within process chains. Besides the business steps, the ETL process can also contain administrative steps that are carried out to optimize performance. This can be, for example, the deletion and re-creation of indexes during the load process or the automatic compression of data after loading. SAP NetWeaver BW has an appropriate functionality to maintain process chains.

12.1.2   InfoCube and Extended Star Schema

Fact table and Dimension table   As already mentioned, InfoCubes are converted in SAP NetWeaver BW into a relational database as arranged tables in the *extended star schema*. At the focus of the star schema is a table, namely, the *fact table*. The key fields of the fact table are the dimensions of the InfoCube — the *dimension ID*.

Dimensions are generally mapped via several characteristics and attributes. The dimension IDs in the characteristics are converted in the dimension tables that are grouped around the fact table in the shape of a star. The key field of the dimension tables is the dimension ID. Other fields of the table are the characteristics constituting the dimension. The upper half of Figure 12.1 illustrates this and shows the "core" of the star schema, the fact table, and the dimension tables and the key correlations between these. In the lower part of the figure, the extended table structure is, for example, displayed for a characteristic. The type of table that will be more precisely explained in the text is specified in parentheses. You can also see this later in Table 12.1.

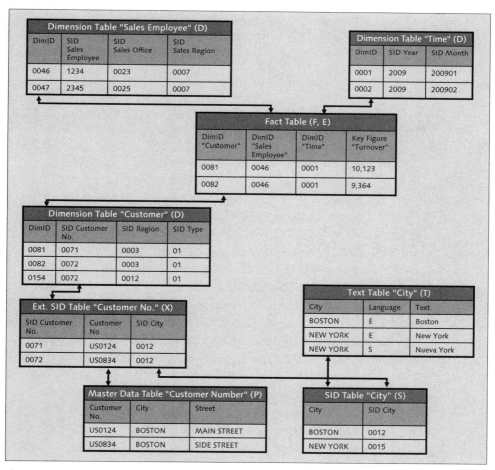

Figure 12.1 Example of an InfoCube in the Extended Star Schema

[Ex] Let's consider a report displaying the turnover of the first quarter of 2009 for a specific sales representative as an example. The period (first quarter of 2009) and the ID of the sales employee (1234) are available as restrictive characteristics. The grouping takes places according to the month and the customer region. The query should then be mapped as follows as a database join via the fact table (FSALESREV; alias in the SQL statement: F) and the dimension tables for time (DSALESREVT; alias: DT), sales employees (DSALESREV1; alias D1), and customer (DSALESREV2; alias D2):

```
SELECT
      DT.SID_OCALMONTH D2.S_REGCODE, SUM ( F.GROSSAMOUNT),
      SUM ( F.NETAMOUNT ), SUM ( F.UNITS ), COUNT (*)
FROM
      FSALESREV F
      JOIN DSALESREVT DT ON F.KEY_SALESREVT = DT.DIMID
      JOIN DSALESREV1 D1 ON F.KEY_SALESREV1 = D1.DIMID
      JOIN DSALESREV2 D2 ON F.KEY_SALESREV2 = D2.DIMID
WHERE
      ( DT.SID_OCALMONTH BETWEEN 200901 AND 200904 )
      AND D1.S_EMPLOYEE = 1234
GROUP BY
      DT.SID_OCALMONTH, D2.S_REGCODE
```

We can closely study the properties of InfoCube accesses using this example. In the SELECT clause, you can find characteristics from dimension tables and aggregates (total, mean value, maximum or minimum) via the stored key figures (gross amount, net amount, and quantity sold) in the fact table. The FROM clause contains the JOIN clauses via the fact table and the dimension tables involved. The WHERE clause contains the restrictive clauses in the characteristics. The GROUP BY clause forms the conclusion, and specifies via which characteristics aggregation groups should be formed. The example given uses the naming conventions of SAP NetWeaver BW, where some simplifications have been made to improve legibility. Among other things, the prefixes of the tables have been omitted, and the joins in the unit and package dimension that SAP NetWeaver BW also generates automatically in each query, and which we will deal with later, are missing.

In the example given, FSALESREV displays the fact table of the Info-Cube SALESREV. DSALESREVT, DSALESREV1, and DSALESREV2 are the dimension tables of the dimensions time, sales employee, and customer. The InfoCube could contain further dimensions, for example, product. However, these aren't important in this query. As you can see from the above query, the fact table has the KEY_SALESREVT, KEY_SALESREV1, and KEY_SALESREV2 key fields that represent the individual dimensions. With the help of these key fields, the joins are formed in the dimension tables — the key field of which is DIMID. Besides the key field, the dimension tables contain the dimension characteristics in other fields. In the case given, the time dimension is accessed via the characteristic month. Access could also be carried out via other time characteristics like the calendar week, the quarter, the year, the weekday (Mon, Tue...), and so on. The characteristic sales employee is restricted to the sales dimension (S_EMPLOYEE). This dimension could also contain the characteristics sales office or sales organization. Grouping is ultimately carried out via the customer region (S_REGIONCODE) in the customer dimension. The dimension customer could, for example, be mapped via other characteristics and attributes such as customer number, customer type, country, city, ZIP code, and so on.

Facts and dimension tables belong to the core of an InfoCube; that is, they are individually formed for each InfoCube. The master data tables that we'll now discuss can, however, be reused in different InfoCubes.

After having explained the core aspects of the InfoCube access, we must now deal with detailed questions that arise when handling characteristics. These are, for example, questions concerning the time dependency of characteristics, characteristic hierarchies, and language-dependent texts. All of these details can significantly impact performance.

Master data – characteristics and attributes

We use the following nomenclature for characteristics and attributes:

▶ **Characteristics**
  InfoObjects are referred to as *characteristics* that are directly mapped in a dimension table. In the example given in Figure 12.1, these are the customer in the customer dimension (that is, the customer number), the customer region, and the customer type, (for example, business or private customer).

▶ **Navigation attributes**

These are InfoObjects that you can use in the report for navigation purposes and that are not independent elements of the dimension but instead are assigned as attributes characteristics. The example in Figure 12.1 is Street.

▶ **Display attributes**

These are only displayed in reports. Operations such as filtering, navigating, and so on, are not possible via these attributes. Examples of display attributes are texts describing characteristics.

Navigation and display attributes are closely linked with a characteristic. However, the link can be time-dependent. Dependency is maintained in the master data tables, the X tables, and Y tables with time-dependent attributes.

During the data modeling, the project team must decide which master data is to be a characteristic, a navigation attribute, or a display attribute.

SIDs   To understand the modeling of characteristics and attributes displayed in the lower part of Figure 12.1, it is still important to know that SAP NetWeaver BW uses internal keys to identify characteristics and navigation attributes, namely, the 4-byte *SIDs*. In other words, the actual IDs of the master data in the dimension tables (for example, the customer number) are not used, but instead the internal SIDs are used. SIDs are converted into actual IDs in the SID tables. There are three types of SID tables: the simple SID table (also referred to as the S table in Figure 12.1 for the attribute city), the extended SID table (also X table in Figure 12.1 for the attribute customer number) that which in addition to the SID/ID conversion still contains the SIDs of the assigned navigation attributes, and the extended SID table for time dependent navigation attributes that also still contains a validity area for the attribute assignment (Y table).

Figure 12.1 presents the modeling options already discussed and their specification in tables as an example of the customer dimension. In this dimension, the information on the customer region is formed as an appropriate characteristic; that is, it appears as a field in the dimension table. The city navigation attribute and the street display attribute exist for the customer number characteristic. This dependency is stored in the master data table (P). An extended SID table (X) exists for the customer number characteristic, and a simple SID table (S) for the city navigation attribute. Ultimately, the correlation to the text table (T) is still displayed for the city.

The mapping of the time dependency presents a special challenge — also with respect to performance. Let's assume that customer X moves on a specific date. The question arises whether the turnover of customer X is to be assigned to the old or the new region. Three alternatives are possible:

Time dependency

- The turnover — also backdated — is always assigned to the current region. In this case, the assignment of the customer to the region must only be centrally changed once it's in SAP NetWeaver BW, and the reporting assigns the total turnover to the new region after the change. No additional master data entries may be generated that describe the time dependency.

- The turnover is to be assigned before the move to the old region and after the move to the new region. In this case, two dimension IDs with the customer and old region as well as customer and new region key figures must be created in the dimension table. In the fact table, the turnover is assigned to the dimension ID that belongs to the combination customer and old region before the move and to the dimension ID that belongs to the combination customer and new region after the move. Figure 12.1 shows this in the Dimension Table "Customer" (DSALESREV2): Two entries in the dimension table exist for the customer with SID 0072.

- The third alternative is key date–related reporting. If the report is generated on a key date before the move, the total turnover is assigned to the old ZIP code area and to the new ZIP code area with a key date after the move. In this case, a validity is maintained to the assignment of the customer's ZIP code (valid from and valid to) that is evaluated for the runtime of the query so that the correct assignment can be determined. This option is not displayed in Figure 12.1. This can, however, be implemented in SAP NetWeaver BW when you use time-dependent Y and Q tables instead of the X and Q tables displayed.

As already seen in the examples, time dependencies in SAP NetWeaver BW are always linked with additional table entries, higher data quantities, and potentially poorer performance. You must always carefully check the time dependency of the individual characteristics regarding the performance analysis.

Hierarchies Characteristics frequently form within a dimension of hierarchies. One option of dealing with simple "fixed" hierarchies consists in including these as characteristics in the dimension. One example is the hierarchy levels sales employee, sales office, and sales region that are integrated as characteristics in the sales dimension in Figure 12.1. The advantage of this modeling method is that the hierarchy levels can be directly accessed without other detailed joins.

With more complex hierarchy requirements, for instance, if the number of hierarchy levels is to be flexibly formed, this modeling option reaches its limits. In this case, hierarchies are mapped in appropriate master data tables that are evaluated for the runtime (H, K, I, and J tables in Table 12.1).

Time, unit, and package dimension in SAP NetWeaver BW Three dimensions in SAP NetWeaver BW are already specified: time dimension (DT), package dimension (DP), and unit dimension (DU). The information on time and on the units of the key figures is managed in the time dimension and in the unit dimension.

The package dimension manages in which load package the data is loaded in SAP NetWeaver BW. This dimension has a purely administrative significance. We'll discuss the impact of this dimension on performance in more detail in Section 12.3.3, Compressing the Fact Table.

All necessary fact and dimension tables and indexes are created automatically in the database when an InfoCube is implemented in SAP NetWeaver BW. Table 12.1 lists the naming conventions. You can find further details on the first four columns later in this section. We'll discuss the differences between the uncompressed and compressed fact table and the last column of Table 12.1, the indexing of tables, in detail in Section 12.3.

Function	Name of Database	Key Fields	Other Fields	Indexing
Fact table (uncompressed)	/<PF>/ F<InfoCube>	Dimension IDs of the InfoCube, including package dimension (KEY_ <InfoCube><X>), <X>: P, T, U, 1, 2, ...	Key figures	Index on each dimension ID field
Fact table (uncompressed)	/<PF>/ E<InfoCube>	Dimension IDs of the InfoCube, without package dimension	Key figures	Index via each dimension ID field, a B* index on all dimension ID fields
Dimension table	/<PF>/ D<InfoCube> <X>, <X>: P, T, U, 1, 2, ...	Dimension ID of the InfoCube (DIMID)	SID (4-byte integer) of the InfoObjects involved in the dimension	Primary index via dimension ID, indexes on each SID field, an index on all SID fields
Standard SID table	/<PF>/ S<InfoObject>	Master data ID, (for example, material number)	SID (4-byte integer)	Primary index via master data ID, index on SID field
SID table with time-constant navigation attribute	/<PF>/ X<InfoObject>	SID (4-byte integer)	Key fields of the master data, and time-constant navigation attributes	Primary index via SID; further indexes can be created manually
SID table with time-dependent navigation attribute	/<PF>/ Y<InfoObject>	SID (4-byte integer), validity area (VALIDFROM, VALIDTO)	Key fields of the master data and time-dependent navigation attributes	Primary index via SID; other indexes can be created manually
Master data view (view of the P and Q table)	/<PF>/ M<InfoObject>		view of the P and Q table	None, because view

Table 12.1 Overview of the Tables of an InfoCube in SAP NetWeaver BW

Function	Name of Database	Key Fields	Other Fields	Indexing
Master data table with time-constant attribute	/<PF>/ P<InfoObject>	Master data ID, (for example, material number)	Other time-constant attributes on the master data, (for example, material group)	Primary index via key field
Master data table with time-dependent attribute	/<PF>/ Q<InfoObject>	Master data ID, validity area (VALIDFROM, VALIDTO)	Other attributes on the master data	Primary index via key fields
Text table	/<PF>/ T<InfoObject>	Master data ID, language code, possible validity area (VALIDFROM, VALIDTO)	Language-dependent description in different lengths	Primary index via key fields
Hierarchy table (hierarchical relationship of the characteristic values)	/<PF>/ H<InfoObject>	Hierarchy node ID	Parent node ID, hierarchy level, and so on	Primary index via key fields, index on parent nodes
Hierarchy SID table (translation of the characteristic values in SID key)	/<PF>/ K<InfoObject>	SID hierarchy node	SID	Primary index via key fields, index, via SID
SID structure of the hierarchy nodes	/<PF>/ I<InfoObject>	SID hierarchy node, master data ID		Primary index via key fields
Hierarchy intervals	/<PF>/ J<InfoObject>	Hierarchy node ID, node ID	Interval: from and to	Primary index via key fields

<PF> stands for the namespace prefix that separates SAP objects from customer objects, (for example, BI0 or BIC), <InfoCube> stands for the name of the InfoCube, and <InfoObject> for the name of an InfoObject.

Table 12.1 Overview of the Tables of an InfoCube in SAP NetWeaver BW (Cont.)

12.1.3   Overview of the Options for Performance Optimization

As previously mentioned, this chapter is unable to offer a comprehensive introduction to SAP NetWeaver BW design. Therefore, we'll discuss only the most important points to be considered here under performance aspects in design.

As you can see from the descriptions of this section, good performance and data quantity, both of which you can report on, are in natural conflict. That is, as part of the design, you should take into consideration that no unnecessary data is entered and loaded in SAP NetWeaver BW.

Performance and data quantity

However, data modeling itself also plays an extremely big role in the performance. Keep in mind the following points:

- Under performance aspects, the InfoCube should generally be preferred over other InfoProviders such as DataStore objects and virtual providers. An InfoCube stores the data for reporting purposes more efficiently than a DataStore object. Aggregates, which we'll discuss in Section 12.3, Technical Optimization Options in Detail, can only be formed in InfoCubes for performance optimization, and only InfoCubes can be indexed in SAP NetWeaver BW Accelerator.

- When designing InfoCubes, you must ensure that you carefully select the characteristics and attributes. It may make sense to replace a large InfoCube with several smaller InfoCubes and then merge these virtually in a MultiProvider. The advantage of this approach is that the OLAP processor parallelizes queries on the individual cubes.

- In a BW query, navigation attributes require additional join operations compared to characteristics that are an element of a dimension. Dimension characteristics therefore generally have a performance advantage over navigation attributes.

- Time dependencies, hierarchies, and multilinguism increase the data quantity in the master data tables and lead to more complex joins when calculating the data. They therefore contribute to an increase in query runtimes. If possible, you should map simple hierarchies as characteristics in a dimension (as in the earlier example: sales region, sales office, sales employee).

▶ According to a rule of thumb, the number of entries in a dimension table should not be greater than 10% of the entries in the fact table. You should model dimensions exceeding this guideline value as *line item dimensions*. With this type of modeling, the SID key of the characteristic is directly stored in the fact table; that is, access to the dimension table can become obsolete. The disadvantage of this option is that the dimension may only precisely contain this one characteristic. Application cases are, for example, large material or customer dimensions. A typical optimization in this context is moving characteristics between the dimension tables of the InfoCube. It may therefore make sense to move characteristics between dimensions to obtain a line item dimension.

▶ You can specify a size category for each table in the SAP NetWeaver BW system. This setting impacts the physical storage in the database and should be correctly specified with regard to the modeling.

Performance and being up-to-date

Another rival of good performance is the preference for the most up-to-date data in SAP NetWeaver BW. You can be up-to-date using two methods: the frequent loading of data in SAP NetWeaver BW or the use of virtual InfoProviders that via RFC directly access the source system to the reporting. Both methods impact performance. Frequent loading generates an additional load both in the source system and in the SAP NetWeaver BW system itself. A second factor that negatively impacts performance is that the OLAP cache, which we'll present among other topics in Section 12.3, Technical Optimization Options in Detail, is invalidated by the data loading so that the results stored there are lost. The disadvantage of using virtual InfoProviders is that besides access to the InfoCube, which is by far the most efficient way to implement BW queries, the source system can be directly further accessed to prepare current data.

Figure 12.2 provides a summary of the options for how a query can be processed from the OLAP processor. Synchronous access paths while executing a BW query are marked by continuous arrows; data load processes are marked by dashed arrows. The OLAP processor checks first whether the query has already been executed and whether the results are already in the OLAP cache ❶. In this case, the OLAP processor must not access deeper layers. The OLAP cache can also be actively prefilled via the reporting agent.

The following options are available if the query cannot be answered from the OLAP cache:

▶ The query is processed in the associated database tables and indexes for a DataStore object (DSO ❷). In this case, there are no further optimizations.

▶ The data in InfoCubes ❸ is stored in a form optimized for reporting and provided with indexes to optimize the search. InfoCubes should be regularly compressed to reduce the data quantity.

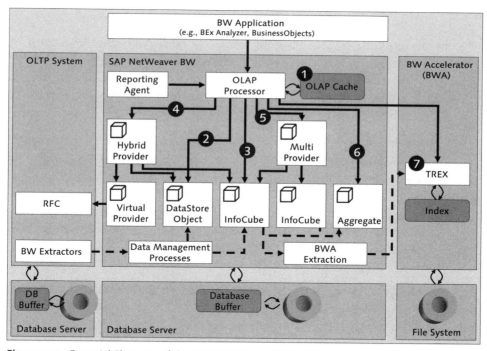

Figure 12.2 Essential Elements of the SAP NetWeaver BW Architecture and Performance Optimization Options

▶ HybridProviders ❹ consist of an InfoCube in which older data is found and a DataStore object (DSO) or RemoteProvider that allows access to more recent data. The HybridProvider allows joint reporting on both data sources. With a HybridProvider, the advantages of the InfoCube regarding data compression and performance optimization for large data quantities are linked with the advantages of the up-to-date state of the reporting via DSOs or RemoteProviders.

▶ If the data has been distributed via a MultiProvider ❺ to several Info-Cubes, SAP NetWeaver BW parallelizes the query automatically, and therefore reduces the runtime of the query. However, it requires more resources if the query results are not already buffered in the OLAP cache.

▶ Aggregates ❻ that can be created for InfoCubes help reduce the runtime of queries that must aggregate many data records. If there is a suitable aggregate, the OLAP processor accesses the aggregate and not the InfoCube.

▶ InfoCubes can also be indexed in SAP NetWeaver BW Accelerator ❼. In this case, the query is executed in SAP NetWeaver BW Accelerator, which compresses and partitions the data and parallelizes the queries and therefore allows a considerably faster execution of the query than in the InfoCube.

In Section 12.3, Technical Optimization Options in Detail, the technical optimization options via correct indexing, compression, OLAP cache, and aggregates are displayed in detail. We'll deal with SAP NetWeaver BW Accelerator in the next chapter. We'll conclude this section with an overview of the administration tools in SAP NetWeaver BW, and Section 12.2, Analysis of Expensive BW Queries, will be dedicated to the techniques of performance analysis in the SAP NetWeaver BW environment.

12.1.4 Overview of the SAP NetWeaver BW Administration Tools

SAP NetWeaver BW Administrator Workbench

The central SAP NetWeaver BW administration tool is the Administrator Workbench (Transaction RSA1), via which the properties of SAP NetWeaver BW objects are specified and via which SAP NetWeaver BW objects are managed. The most important function required in relation to performance optimization is the administration of InfoCubes. You do this via the Manage Data Targets detailed view that you open by selecting an InfoCube and by selecting the Manage option in the context menu (right-click). On the screen you will find the Performance and Rollup tabs and so on, with detailed administration functions that we'll discuss in more detail later in this chapter (see also Figure 12.3). You can also open the Maintenance For Aggregate screen from SAP NetWeaver BW Administrator Workbench by selecting the Aggregates option in the context menu on an InfoCube. Alternatively, using the Transaction RSDDV, you can directly jump to the aggregate maintenance. We'll deal with further detailed functions of SAP NetWeaver BW Administrator Workbench that are important for the performance of queries and InfoCubes and for the creation of statistics later on.

With the test environment, you can debug queries and analyze statistics and execution plans in detail, among other things.

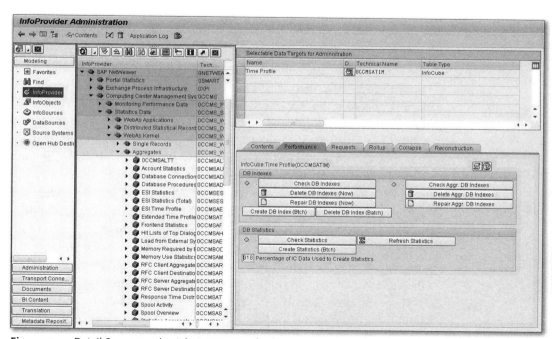

Figure 12.3 Detail Screen on the Administration of InfoCubes in the SAP NetWeaver BW Administrator Workbench (Transaction RSA1)

You will find the SAP NetWeaver BW workload statistics in the workload monitor (Transaction ST03N) in a separate branch that we'll present in detail in the following section of this chapter.

SAP NetWeaver BW workload statistics

To analyze the performance of a specific query, use the test environment for BW queries (Transaction RSRT). Transaction LISTCUBE is a helpful tool for displaying the detailed technical structure and the content of InfoProviders. Finally, Transaction RSRV provides a range of useful checks.

12.2   Analysis of Expensive BW Queries

Like in Chapter 11, Optimizing SQL Statements, we'll deal with the analysis methods first, before discussing the optimization options. Also like in Chapter 11, we'll start with the question of which queries are worth optimizing.

BW queries in the workload monitor and in the single-record statistics For BW queries, you will find the entry BI_CLIENT_RUNTIME in the display in the workload monitor and in the single-record statistics in the Transaction Code column — regardless of whether the queries come from the SAP BEx Web analyzer or from Web reporting. You can therefore simply identify BW queries by this entry. The task type is generally RFC because both the SAP BEx Web analyzer and Web reporting are connected via RFC to the ABAP server. You can use the workload monitor and the single-record statistics, for example, to identify the load generated from SAP NetWeaver BW and distinguish between other components that run on the same system. What is problematic with the analysis is that a navigation step in the SAP NetWeaver BW presentation server does not correspond to a statistics record in the ABAP server, but instead several accesses required by a navigation step can be distributed to several statistics records. You cannot use the average response time of the statistics records in the SAP NetWeaver BW context to indicate the average response time in the presentation server. Therefore, and because important information for SAP NetWeaver BW in the statistics record is missing, the single-record statistics and series profiles in the workload monitor are not sufficient for a differentiated internal analysis.

SAP NetWeaver BW detailed statistics Detailed statistics for BW queries offer additional options for the workload analysis in SAP NetWeaver BW. You can generate them two ways: in the test environment for BW queries or by default for each execution of a BW query.

If you already know the BW query for which a performance analysis is to be carried out, the test environment lends itself as a tool for further analysis for BW queries (Transaction RSRT):

Test environment for BW queries

1. To execute a BW query in the SAP NetWeaver BW test environment, enter the query name directly in the Query field or select a query using the input help. When you choose a display mode with the Query Display selection box, the HTML display mode is the most convenient. Then select Execute + Debug.

2. To open the display of detailed statistics on the query, select the OTHER • DISPLAY STATISTICS DATA and the Do Not Use Cache option in the opening Debug Options dialog box.

3. The BW query is now executed, and the result is displayed. If you leave the display by clicking the green back arrow, the Statistcs Data On The Query Runtime screen displays detailed runtime statistics.

4. The statistics are spread over two tabs: Frontend/Calculation Layer and Aggregation Layer. Table 12.2 lists and describes the most important fields of the statistics.

The logging of the performance statistics can also be activated while the system is in operation. This is possible in the SAP NetWeaver BW Administrator Workbench (Transaction RSA1) under TOOLS • BI STATISTICS SETTINGS (prior to Version 7.0: TOOLS • BI STATISTICS FOR INFOPROVIDERS). The statistics for the query performance that the OLAP processor generates and for the load procedures of warehouse management can be activated separately for each provider and for each BW query. When you use MultiProviders and HybridProviders, you must also activate this logging. The activation at the level of the individual underlying providers is not sufficient.

Activating SAP NetWeaver BW statistics

When the logging is activated, the OLAP processor logs statistical data if a query is executed. This data is stored in database tables beginning with RSDDSTAT. You can display the statistics in the workload monitor (Transaction ST03N) or directly in the table browser (Transaction SE16) via the table view SDDSTAT_OLAP (prior to Version 7.0 in the table RSDDSTAT). Table 12.2 shows the most important fields of the SAP NetWeaver BW statistics. The technical field names in the database in the RSDDSTAT_OLAP database view and RSDDSTATDM are indicated in parentheses.

Field	Explanation
Session UUID (SESSIONUUID)	Unique identification of the session on the presentation server
Step UID (STEPUID)	Unique identification of the navigation step
Step type	Type of presentation software, for example, Java for presentation in Web Dynpro Java, BEx for presentation in the SAP BEx Web analyzer
User name (UNAME)	User name
Start time (STARTTIME)	Time at which the step was started
Handle type (HANDLETP)	SAP NetWeaver BW components to be executed, for example, OLAP for the OLAP processor
InfoProvider (INFOPROV)	Name of the InfoProvider
Object name (OBJNAME)	Name of the object to be processed, for example, BW query, data element, routine
Event ID (EVENTID) and text	Identification and description of the running result
Duration (EVTIME)	Runtime for a result, in seconds
Counters and event counters (EVCOUNT and EVENTIDCNT)	Counters that are specifically set for an event
Basis provider (PARTPROV)	Name of the Basis provider that distinguishes itself from the InfoProvider when the latter is, for example, a HybridProvider
Aggregate (AGGREGATE)	Name of the aggregate that has been accessed. (For an access to SAP NetWeaver BW Accelerator, you'll find the name of the InfoCube with an attached $X indicator in this field.)
Table type (TABLTP)	Type of table that has been accessed, for example, E, and F for E and F fact table
Read time (TIMEREAD)	Runtime for the reading in the database, in seconds
Records, selected (DBSEL)	Number of data records read in the database
Records, transferred (DBTRANS)	Number of data records transferred from the database to the application server

Table 12.2 Most Important Fields of the SAP NetWeaver BW Statistics

SAP NetWeaver BW Statistics in the Workload Monitor

To analyze the runtime of BW queries in the workload monitor, select the BW Server Workload option under Workload Monitors (Transaction ST03N) in the expert mode in the left navigation window. You'll find below this point the periods (days, weeks, months) for which you can select the SAP NetWeaver BW statistics, as shown in Figure 12.4. There is no option for selection by instance as there is with the other workload statistics.

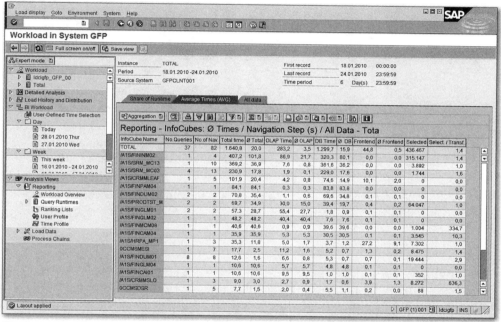

Figure 12.4 Performance Statistics on BW Queries in the Workload Monitor (Transaction ST03(N))

After you have loaded the performance statistics, you have access to the load profiles in the lower-left window of the workload monitor under the option Analysis Views. Table 12.3 describes these in more detail.

High database response times are considered to be the most significant performance problem to handle in the SAP NetWeaver BW environment. We'll now describe how to proceed when database response times make up the essential part of the response time.

Analyzing high database response times

563

Profile	Description
Reporting workload overview	Shows the response times and the number of queries at the level of the presentation techniques, for example, Java for queries from the portal or BEx for SAP BEx Web analyzer queries.
Reporting query runtimes	Shows the response times and the data quantities processed at the level of queries or InfoCubes (switchable via the Aggregation button).
Reporting—hit lists	Shows the hit list of the most expensive queries that have been executed.
Reporting—user profile	Shows the response times and the number of queries at the user level. By clicking the Aggregation button, you can determine whether the list of users or user types is reported on.
Reporting—time profile	Shows the response times and the number of queries over time. You can select the time interval via the Interval button.
Load data—DTP	Shows runtimes and processed data quantities for load procedures at the data-source and source-system level.
Process chains	Shows runtimes and processed data quantities for load procedures at the process-chain level.

Table 12.3 Load Profiles for SAP NetWeaver BW

In an initial step, you establish whether the time the database needs to read a record is satisfactory. You determine the ratio from database response time (read time in the SAP NetWeaver BW statistics) and the data records selected in the database. Keep in mind that the ratio cannot simply be formed here from database response time and data records read from the single-record statistics because only the number transferred to the application server is logged in the single-record statistics. However, because it is characteristic for SAP NetWeaver BW to aggregate data via many data records, you require the data records read prior to aggregation to be able to make a sound statement. Only the SAP NetWeaver BW statistics provides this. A guideline value for an optimal rate of data read is 0.1 milliseconds per data record. You should check the defined ratio against this guideline value.

If you see that the data read time in the database is not optimal, you should check the indexing (including the correct parameterization of the database and the optimizer statistics) of the tables or the SQL statements involved in a subsequent step. You will find the SQL statements involved in a BW query either via the performance trace (Transaction ST05) or by executing the BW query in an SAP NetWeaver BW test environment (Transaction RSRT) in the debug mode and selecting DATABASE • DISPLAY EXECUTION PLAN followed by OTHER • DO NOT USE CACHE in the Debug Options dialog box. The execution of the BW query for each SQL statement that the OLAP processor carries out is stopped, and the SQL statement is displayed with the execution plan. To further analyze the indexing, continue with Section 12.3.1, Managing Indexing. If you cannot identify any problems in the area of indexing, the next thing to check is whether there is a general database problem (I/O bottleneck, CPU bottleneck, bottleneck in the file system, network problem, and so on).

Nonoptimal data read time

As the next parameter, you should take a look at the ratio of records selected (read) in the database to transferred records. If this is high (>10) and the database response time makes up more than 30% of the total response time, you have the option to support BW queries using precalculated aggregates (see Section 12.3.6, Aggregates).

High number of selected records

If the number of records selected (read) from the database is high, another reason could be the read mode of the BW query (see Section 12.3.2, Settings on Data Selection).

A third point that you should analyze based on the statistics is the behavior of identical queries. The second and all subsequent identical calls of a query should be read from the OLAP cache, that is, the database response time, and the records selected from the database should be zero or close to zero. If you suspect that subsequent queries are not being carried out from the OLAP cache, you should continue with the analysis in Section 12.3.4, Monitoring the OLAP Cache.

Identical calls from BW queries

It is now assumed as a result of the analysis that you know the BW query as well as the SQL statement within the BW query that has the longest runtime. Furthermore, you should know which users require the data in which up-to-date form and how frequently they start the query. Using this information, you can now go into the details of the technical optimization options.

12.3   Technical Optimization Options in Detail

With regard to technical options for performance optimization, the degree of the performance improvement and flexibility, costs, and complexity compete with one another. Table 12.4 shows an overview of the technical optimizations that we'll present in detail in this section. We'll discuss SAP NetWeaver BW Accelerator in the next chapter.

Measure	Performance Optimization Potential	Restrictions	Costs
Use of the correct database parameterization (see notes in Appendix G)	Partly deals with factors concerning better query response times in comparison to less optimal database parameters	Possible conflicts regarding the parameterization if SAP NetWeaver BW is run in conjunction with the OLTP system in a database	Very low
Use of the correct indexes	Partly deals with factors concerning better query response times in comparison to nonindexed tables	Greater space requirement, poorer load performance	Low; administration of the indices by SAP NetWeaver BW largely automated
Settings on the data selection	Data required for the compilation of the report is only read when the setting is correct; this results in improved response times for individual steps	None	None
Compression of the fact table	Improved (in the single- to double-digit percentage area) query response times as a result of additional data compression	Load procedures in SAP NetWeaver BW can no longer be selectively repeated	Low; can be largely automated

Table 12.4   Overview of Technical Options for Performance Optimization for InfoCubes in SAP NetWeaver BW

Measure	Performance Optimization Potential	Restrictions	Costs
Use of the SAP NetWeaver BW-(OLAP) cache	Consistently good response times for buffered queries	Reading from the cache works only on the second call; cache is invalidated during loading	low; occasional monitoring of the cache size, possible optimization of the query settings is necessary so that the cache can be optimally used
Precalculation of reports	Consistently good response times for reports calculated in advance	Only possible for a few reports	Costs for the definition of the reports to be calculated
Aggregates	Partly dealing with factors concerning better query response times as a result of use of stored intermediate results (aggregates)	Aggregates can only be formed for selected accesses, restrictions with the use of aggregates, greater space requirement, poorer load performance	Costs relating to the definition and maintenance of aggregates
SAP NetWeaver BW Accelerator	Dealing with factors concerning better query response times as a result of full indexing of attributes in TREX	None	Own system, own hardware necessary, costs regarding administration, however, reduced as a result of appliance solution
Clearing of dimension and master data tables	Improved query response times as a result of smaller data quantities	None	Costs for the drawing up and implementation of criteria, according to which data is cleared/cleaned (obsolete data, duplicate data, and so on)

Table 12.4 Overview of Technical Options for Performance Optimization for InfoCubes in SAP NetWeaver BW (Cont.)

12.3.1 Managing Indexing

As already described, SAP NetWeaver BW creates the tables and indexes listed in Table 12.1 in the database based on the modeling of the Info-Cube. That is, no manual administration costs are initially incurred for identifying and creating the correct indexes. However, manual interventions may be necessary with large InfoCubes with over a million data records in the fact table. Therefore, we'll now discuss in greater detail the topic of indexing and the database optimizer.

Star join execution plan

First we'll focus on the execution plan for the BW query presented in Section 12.1.2, InfoCube and Extended Star Schema. The query that determines the turnover for a specific sales employee reads:

```
SELECT
    DT.SID_0CALMONTH D2.S_REGCODE, SUM ( F.GROSSAMOUNT),
    SUM ( F.NETAMOUNT ), SUM ( F.UNITS ), COUNT (*)
FROM
        FSALESREV F
        JOIN DSALESREVT DT ON F.KEY_SALESREVT = DT.DIMID
        JOIN DSALESREV1 D1 ON F.KEY_SALESREV1 = D1.DIMID
        JOIN DSALESREV2 D2 ON F.KEY_SALESREV2 = D2.DIMID
WHERE
        ( DT.SID_0CALMONTH BETWEEN 200901 AND 200904 )
        AND D1.S_EMPLOYEE = 1234
GROUP BY
        DT.SID_0CALMONTH, D2.S_REGCODE
```

The associated execution plan in a MaxDB database could read as follows:

```
TABLENAME     COLUMN OR INDEX     STRATEGY
D1                                TABLE SCAN
F             FSALESREV~7         JOIN VIA INDEXED COLUMN
              KEY_SALESREV1           (USED INDEX COLUMN)
DT            DIMID               JOIN VIA KEY COLUMN
                                          TABLE HASHED
D2            DIMID               JOIN VIA KEY COLUMN
                                          TABLE HASHED
```

The execution plan of a MaxDB database has the advantage that it can be read from top to bottom — unlike, for example, the execution plan of an Oracle database that must be read from the inside out. You can find a more accurate description of the execution plans of the various databases in Appendix B.

The execution of the SQL statement starts with a full table scan on the table with the alias D1 (Table DSALESREV1, dimension table in the sales employee dimension). The field D1.S_EMPLOYEE is specified in the WHERE clause, so it is no surprise that the database opts for this table as an entry point. However, the type of access cannot be understood immediately because a full table scan is usually only expected with non-qualified accesses.But a full table scan can definitely be the fastest access with small tables because you avoid making any "detour" via the index. With larger tables, you should check at this point whether the index that should exist according to Table 12.1 is missing in the S_EMPLOYEE field in the DSALESREV1 table.

As a second operation, the database accesses the fact table via the index using the DIMID keys determined from table DSALESREV1.

In other steps, the join is formed via the dimension tables of the time and customer dimensions, each with accesses via the DIMID key.

The execution plans are similar for the SQL accesses in the core of the star schema. The optimizer generally opts for the access to one or several dimension tables, with small dimension tables with a full table scan, and for dimension tables with many entries via an index scan. The fact table is then accessed via a suitable index, and the joins are formed via the missing dimension tables. As join methods, other methods are applied besides the nested loop join that you learned about in Chapter 11, Optimizing SQL Statements, for example, the hash join.

You cannot practically impact the optimizer's decision regarding in which sequence and with which methods it executes the join. Only the following points remain to be checked:

▶ SAP makes recommendations relating to the database parameter settings. These parameters can impact which operations are available to the optimizer. For example, with the Oracle parameter HASH_JOIN_ENABLED, you can specify whether a hash join is allowed to be executed or not. We cannot discuss the recommendations in detail because they depend on the database and the version. You will find the recommendations in the SAP Notes in Appendix G or in the SAP GoingLive report.

▶ The indexes listed in Table 12.1 must be available.

▶ The associated statistics must be available (see Chapter 11, Optimizing SQL Statements).

▶ If you're in doubt, you must check the fragmentation level of the indexes (see also Chapter 11).

Background: Bitmap Index

In a brief example (refer to the literature on SAP NetWeaver BW performance listed in Appendix G for a more detailed presentation) we'll discuss a special feature in the SAP NetWeaver BW environment: the bitmap index. You generally create indexes in the database in the form of *B* trees*. The B* tree is a hierarchical store form, in which the actual index entries, that is, the references of the indexed fields, are on the exact position of the entry in the table (row ID) on the lowest level (*leafs*) and in which a hierarchical *tree* including references is built. You can find the leafs in a binary search based on these references.

You use a bitmap index to create an index on a field with low cardinality. A bit is created for each specification of a field in a bitmap index that contains the value 1 if the indexed field contains a particular value. Otherwise, it contains a 0. An example would be the Gender field, which can have the specifications male and female. In this case, two binary fields are created in the index. The first is filled when the specification is given as male, and the second when it is given as female.

Bitmap indexes have the advantage over B* tree indexes in that the space requirement is lower in fields with a lower cardinality, which leads to improved read performance. Another advantage is that bitmap indexes can be combined on several fields. The bitmap index has disadvantages concerning modifying accesses. It is considerably worse here than the B* tree index. Moreover, it loses its read performance advantage with high cardinality.

With Oracle databases, SAP NetWeaver BW uses bitmap indexes by default for the indexes in the dimension IDs in the fact tables. You can, however, change this in a B* tree index. You select the High Cardinality indicator in the modeling of the InfoCube (in the Define Dimensions dialog box). We do not recommend this, because Oracle can only use bitmap indexes when executing the star join (see SAP Note 1013912).

Transactional InfoCubes that, for example, are used in SAP Strategic Enterprise Management (SAP SEM) are another exception. These InfoCubes are used in planning applications and are therefore described frequently. As already mentioned, bitmap indexes show poor performance with modifying operations; that is, B* tree indexes are used in the dimension IDs of the fact tables for this type of InfoCube.

With regard to the fundamentals of index administration and its tools, we refer to the administration activities presented in the previous chapter such as the monitoring of missing indexes, optimizer statistics, and index fragmentation. There are, however, some special features in the SAP NetWeaver BW environment that we'll presented next.

Indexes in the fact and dimension tablesn

You can manage the indexes of the fact and dimension tables of an Info-Cube in the SAP NetWeaver BW Administrator Workbench (Transaction RSA1). Select an InfoCube, and select Manage in the context menu. In the following Manage Data Targets detailed view, select the Performance tab. Here you will find the following options:

- **Check DB Indices**
  Checks the existence of the indexes for fact and dimension tables according to the indexing schema displayed in Table 12.1, the result is displayed as a green, yellow, or red traffic light icon next to the button.

- **Delete DB Indices (immediately)**
  Deletes all of the indexes on the InfoCube.

- **Repair DB Indices (immediately)**
  Rebuilds missing indexes and corrects faulty indexes on the Info-Cube.

- **Build DB Indexes (batch)**
  Rebuilds all of the indexes on the InfoCube in the background.

- **Delete DB Index (batch)**
  Deletes all of the indexes on the InfoCube in the background.

- **Check Statistics**
  Checks the existence and actuality of the statistics ofthe fact and dimension tables, the result is displayed as a green, yellow, or red traffic light icon next to the button.

▶ **Recalculate Statistics**
Calculates the statistics on the InfoCube.

▶ **Compilation of Statistics (batch)**
Calculates the statistics on the InfoCube in the background.

Analog functions are provided for the administration of indexes in the aggregates.

When no indexes are found on an InfoCube, you should check first whether they have been deleted as a result of the data loading.

Properties on the InfoProvider
The properties on the InfoProvider control how the system should behave with respect to indexes and statistics during data load. You can access the properties on the InfoProvider from the SAP NetWeaver BW Administrator Workbench (Transaction RSA1) by double-clicking the InfoProvider and following the menu path ADDITIONS • INFOPROVIDER PROPERTIES • DISPLAY or CHANGE. Select the DB Performance tab in this detailed view. You can select the following options:

▶ Delete index prior to each data load and then rebuild

▶ Delete index prior to each delta load and then rebuild

▶ Recalculate DB statistics after each loading

▶ Recalculate statistics also after delta upload

We particularly recommend deleting and re-creating indexes with large data load procedures. This is the case when the amount of data to be newly loaded is on the same scale as the data already available in SAP NetWeaver BW. You should then select the automatic recalculation of statistics if, based on the analysis, you determine that the database optimizer chooses a nonoptimal access path because of obsolete statistics after loading or, proactively, if it is clear that the distribution of data or its cardinalities will change significantly as a result of loading. The standard process described in Chapter 11, Optimizing SQL Statements, for updating the statistics should generally suffice.

Indexing master data tables (X and Y tables)
The master data tables of the navigation attributes (X and Y tables) are indexed by default only via the primary index. If navigation attributes are used in BW queries, this takes place via an additional join. With large master data tables, another secondary index in these tables can improve

the performance. A rule also applies here that you should choose a bit-map index in the case of a lower cardinality of the characteristic and a B* tree index in the case of higher cardinality. It is important to bear in mind that an additional index can negatively impact the load performance. You should therefore check whether a new index essentially improves the query runtime and whether the load performance suffers as a result.

A DataStore object is a redundant data quantity prepared for reporting via a business document, for example, sales orders. DataStore objects are flat database tables, the columns of which consist of the key of the associated business document (for example, the sales order number or order item), characteristics, and the key figures of the document.

Indexing of DataStore objects

We'll refer to the example from the previous section. If the turnover figures are stored in a DataStore object, the access that determines the turnover in the first quarter for a sales employee is as follows:

```
SELECT
  O1.CALMONTH, O1.REGCODE,
  SUM ( O1.GROSSAMOUNT), SUM ( O1.NETAMOUNT ),
  SUM ( O1.UNITS ), COUNT (*)
FROM
  B0000124000 O1
  JOIN SEMPLOYEE S1 ON O1.S_EMPLOYEE = S1.S_EMPLOYEE
  JOIN SREGIONCODE S2 ON O1.S_REGCODE = S2.S_REGCODE   JOIN
SCALMONTH S4 ON O1.CALMONTH = S4.CALMONTH
WHERE
  S3.SID = 1234
  AND ( D4.SID BETWEEN 200901 AND 200904 )
GROUP BY
  O1.CALMONTH, O1.REGCODE
```

No indexes are generated by default for the tables of the DataStore objects. You must determine the most frequent accesses for these objects and create the necessary indexes for these accesses. You should create the indexes in the maintenance interface for DataStore objects in the Indexes branch, not directly in the index maintenance for the table (Transaction SE11).

12.3.2 Settings on Data Selection

You can specify at the InfoProvider and BW query level whether a query exclusively reads data that is necessary for the current display or whether data is read in advance. Reading data in advance means for the performance of the report that the runtime is longer during the first call. However, other navigation steps without accesses to the database are carried out. You have the following options:

- **A: Query is supposed to read all data simultaneously**
  With this option, all data in the user context is loaded during the first call of the query. Further navigation steps can be carried out without access to the database.

- **X: Query is supposed to read during navigation**
  The query during the first call reads only the data that is necessary for the initial report. The data is read if you navigate in the report.

- **H: Query is supposed to read during expansion of navigation/hierarchy**
  This option reads the most selective data. If you navigate in a hierarchy, this option reads only the part of the hierarchy tree that is being drilled down, whereas option X reads the entire tree in advance.

Default setting
You should choose option H as the default setting because users perceive few, long system interaction steps as being more disruptive than very short runtimes are helpful. Only in exceptional situations, for example, with very small InfoCubes, should you deviate from this.

You open the settings on the data selection via the SAP NetWeaver BW Administrator Workbench (Transaction RSA1). Double-click to select an InfoProvider, and follow the menu path ADDITIONS • INFOPROVIDER PROPERTIES • DISPLAY or CHANGE. In this detailed view, select the Query/Cache tab. Check or change the Read Mode entry there. A change applies to all queries created in the future. For existing queries or queries where the read mode deviates from the default version of the InfoProvider, you can override the properties in the test environment for BW queries (Transaction RSRT) in the Properties dialog box.

12.3.3 Compressing the Fact Table

The package dimension includes information about in which load package the data is loaded in SAP NetWeaver BW. That is, assume information on the turnover for customer X, for product Y on day T, is loaded in load package P1. Then, assume that information on the turnover for customer X, for product Y on day T, is again loaded in a second load package, P2. In this case, this second value is not written as an update in the existing row in the fact table; instead, a new row with a new package number, P2, and with otherwise identical key fields, is inserted in the fact table. Entries with a different package ID and an otherwise identical key are not important to the reporting. The key figures of these entries are aggregated with the reporting. They have a purely administrative function. If there is a problem, you can retrace, via the package ID, when the data was stored in SAP NetWeaver BW. In case of errors, you can also selectively delete and reload data.

Additional entries with a different package ID and otherwise identical key fields naturally have an impact on data volume and performance. Therefore, you can merge entries with a different package ID and otherwise identical key fields (this consequently means these can no longer be selectively deleted). SAP NetWeaver BW has two fact tables for each InfoCube: the F table that contains the package dimension and the E table that no longer contains the package dimension. When the InfoCube is compressed, the entries from the F table are deleted and written via the package IDs aggregated as an entry in the E table.

Merging entries

One initial indicator for compressing an InfoCube is a long access to the F table, for example, in SAP NetWeaver BW statistics or in SQL trace.

Continue with the analysis in the SAP NetWeaver BW Administrator Workbench (Transaction RSA1), select the InfoCube in question, and then select Manage in the context menu. In the following Manage Data Targets detailed view, first select the Requests tab, which shows the list of data packages that have been loaded in the InfoCube. The Compression Status of the InfoCube column displays via a green checkmark whether a package has already been compressed. If you see that packages have not been compressed, then compressing the InfoCube can considerably improve performance.

Select the Compression tab, where you will find the necessary functions for compressing data packages.

You should be able to trace the success of the compression using the size of the E and F table. The F table should be reduced by considerably more data records than the E table has grown.

Table partitioning

Another improvement in performance occurs when you use table partitioning at the database level. Whereas the F table is partitioned according to the package ID to enable an efficient request management, the E table is partitioned according to a time characteristic because it is assumed that filtering is performed according to a time characteristic. You can improve the database performance of the queries via this partitioning. This, however, depends on the database system used.

12.3.4 Monitoring the OLAP Cache

The OLAP cache stores the results of BW queries in the main memory and supplies the subsequent executions of the same query with this data so that the database no longer has to be accessed. The OLAP cache can always then supply a subsequent detailed query if either the selection is identical or a subset of the original query is queried. We'll illustrate this with the following example: The sales key figures for a specific employee are selected and then grouped according to regions like in the query in Section 12.1.2, InfoCube and Extended Star Schema. If the key figures for the same employee are selected only for one region, then this query is supplied from the buffer.

Invalidation of buffered data

As soon as data in the InfoCube is changed, a query based on this Info-Provider can no longer be supplied from the OLAP cache. The OLAP processor checks this by adjusting the time stamp of the buffer entry with the change time stamp of the InfoCube (in the RSDINFOPROV-DATA table). A frequent data load therefore results in the buffer being able to be used less frequently. It is possible to counteract this to a certain extent by automatically preloading queries. We'll discuss this in the next section.

The OLAP cache is also no longer used when the query definition is changed and newly generated or if master data in the query or hierarchies used as a selection or presentation hierarchy is activated. SAP Notes 688085 and 1138864 describe technical details of the buffer invalidation.

Virtual characteristics or key figures that are determined by a customer exit are not buffered by default. The Cache Use Despite Virtual Characteristics/Key Figures option in the Properties dialog box (Transaction RSRT) explicitly specifies that the data after it has been read from the database and has passed the customer exit and is to be written in the cache. The buffered data is then accessed. However you must consider that this data is subsequently not invalidated in the cache if the underlying data has been changed. You should therefore only activate this option after a thorough check.

Virtual data

A similar case exists with specific InfoProviders where data changes are not subject to the control of the SAP NetWeaver BW system (for example, RemoteCubes). The results of the queries in these objects are also not buffered by default. You can define the cache validity period in the customizing settings on the InfoProvider (SAP Note 822302).

Another problem while using the OLAP cache occurs when the setting for variables on a query is Mandatory During Query Navigation. In this case, the variable becomes an element of the key in the cache entry. To be able to use such an entry again, you must precisely select the same variable selection because this specifies the key. If, however, you select the Modifiable During Query Navigation variable setting for a query, the variables are no longer part of the key of the cache entry, but instead also assume the selection conditions that are one hierarchy level lower in the cache and that are flexibly evaluated during subsequent queries. The setting for variables should be Modifiable During Query Navigation for greater applicability. You'll find a detailed display of this effect in SAP Note 751402. We'll describe the analysis tool for this effect later in this section (OLAP Cache Monitor).

Changeability of variables during navigation

The OLAP cache uses four memory areas: the cross-session export/import buffer of the ABAP application instance for global memory, the cross-session main memory buffer, the file system of the ABAP application instance and the database as persistent buffers, and the process-local memory of the session (roll and extended memory). You can set the use

Configuration of the OLAP cache

of these memory areas via configurations globally for the entire system or individually for individual InfoProviders and queries. To change the global settings, go to SAP IMPLEMENTATION GUIDE • SAP NETWEAVER • BUSINESS WAREHOUSE • PERFORMANCE • GLOBAL CACHE SETTINGS (IMG, Transaction SPRO) or call Transaction RSCUSTV14. Here you can configure whether the cross-session buffer should be used. You can specify the persistence mode (file, database, or no persistence), the sizes of process-local and cross-session main memory buffers, and the name of the swap file.

It is important to keep in mind that the global buffer is active. Assume 200MB as a guideline value for its size. You must then choose the size of the export/import buffer of the ABAP application instance accordingly. You can monitor the buffer via the memory configuration monitor (Transaction ST02; see Section 2.4, Analyzing SAP Memory Configuration) and configure it via the parameters `rsdb/esm/buffersize_kb` and `rsdb/esm/max_objects`. A size of 200MB (`rsdb/esm/buffersize_kb = 200000`), and 10,000 objects (`rsdb/esm/max_objects = 10000`) is recommended for an SAP NetWeaver BW system (see also SAP Note 656060).

Buffer properties for InfoCubes and BW queries

Besides the buffer settings available to the entire system, you can set the buffering mode individually for each InfoProvider. This happens in the InfoProvider Edit Properties dialog box that you call from the SAP NetWeaver BW Administrator Workbench (Transaction RSA1) by double-clicking the InfoProvider and following the menu path ADDITIONS • INFOPROVIDER PROPERTIES • DISPLAY or CHANGE. Select the Query/Cache tab in this detailed view. Here you can set the Cache Mode and the Persistence Mode to establish whether and how the queries are buffered on an InfoProvider.

You can override InfoProvider properties for a BW query in the test environment for BW queries (Transaction RSRT) in the Properties dialog box. There you can also set the cache mode (but not the persistence mode).

OLAP cache monitor

You monitor the OLAP cache in the OLAP cache monitor (Transaction RSRCACHE). OLAP Cache Monitor screen (Figure 12.5) is structured as follows: In the first line, you can find navigation functions that are useful in the SAP NetWeaver BW monitoring environment, for example, the list of application instances, the maintenance dialog for the configuration parameters of the OLAP cache, and a navigation to the memory configuration monitor (see Chapter 2, Monitoring Hardware, Databases, and SAP Basis). The functions of the OLAP cache monitor start in the second row, where you will find the Cache Parameter (that is also the initial screen), Main Memory, Shared Objects, and Query Aggregate functions. The Main Memory function, which is divided into the Technical Info, Buffer Objects in Hierarchical Display, and Buffer Objects in List Display subfunctions will be presented in this section. The Technical Info function provides you with information on the size of the global, cross-session main memory buffer of the OLAP cache and its use.

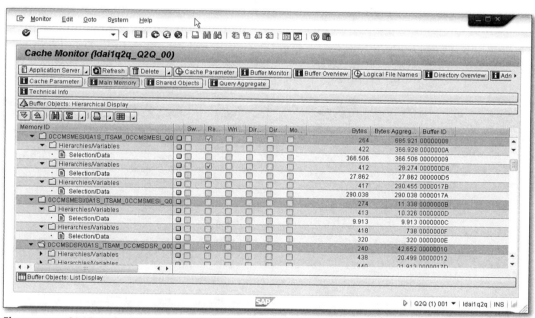

Figure 12.5 OLAP Cache Monitor with the Hierarchical Display of the Objects Buffered in the Main Memory

The Buffer Objects in Hierarchical Display subfunctions and Buffer Objects in List Display list the buffer entries in hierarchical or table form. Figure 12.5 shows a screenshot of the hierarchical display. At the highest level under the Query Directory master directory is the name of the BW query for which the buffer entries have been generated. One level down, you will find the Hierarchies/Variables entries that specify for the buffer entry which fixed characteristics and hierarchies have been used by the BW query. At the lowest level, you will find entries of the Selection/Data type that contain the concrete selection conditions. You will find the Detail function in the context menu. If you select these, detailed data is displayed showing the user who created the entry, the time it was created, and how frequently it has been read. This also applies to entries of the Hierarchies/Variables type and the variables and hierarchies.

The Hierarchies/Variables level is particularly interesting for performance analysis. A buffer entry can only be reused when the entries in a subsequent query precisely match at this level. If the buffer is not used, you can determine the reason here.

In addition, you can find the function for deleting buffer entries in the context menu.

Table 12.5 describes in detail the significance of the monitor columns.

Field	Explanation
Swapped	Displays whether an entry has been swapped from the main memory
Read	Displays whether an entry has been used by a subsequent query
Write	Displays that the entry has been persisted when the cache mode is persistent
Dirty	Displays that an entry has been persisted prior to displacement
Directory	Indicator for the master directory
Changed	Displays that the query has been changed
Bytes	Size of the entry in bytes
Bytes Aggregated	Size of the entry and all the underlying entries in bytes

Table 12.5 Fields of the OLAP Cache Monitor in the Display of the Objects Buffered in the Main Memory

12.3.5 Precalculation of Reports

SAP NetWeaver BW allows certain reports to be calculated in the background. That is, they are available via a user in the OLAP cache during the first call. This is also known as the "warm up" of the OLAP cache. There are two functions that you use for precalculation: the background print of queries and the precalculation of Web templates.

Background Print of Queries

1. To print a query in the background , in the SAP NetWeaver BW Administrator Workbench (Transaction RSA1), select the Print submenu in the Reporting Agent menu.

2. Then select an InfoProvider and a query, and select the New Setting option in the context menu (right-click). You are redirected to the New Reporting Agent Settings screen. You can specify the printing configuration in the Print Settings tab. These settings can remain empty if the reporting agent is only going to be used to preload a query in the OLAP cache.

3. Next, you create a variant. Again select the InfoProvider and the query, and select the Maintaining Variants option in the context menu. By creating the variant, you specify the entries for the query that is to be calculated.

4. You must now create a scheduling package. Select the InfoProvider and the query, and click the New button (leaf icon) in the Scheduling Packages tab on the right side of the screen.

5. Now assign the previously created reporting agent setting to the newly created scheduling package. To open this, drag and drop the reporting agent setting in the scheduling package. You can assign several reporting agent settings to a scheduling package. These are then carried out simultaneously in a background job.

6. The scheduling package must then be scheduled as a background job. Select the scheduling package, and then select the Schedule option from the context menu. You are redirected to the Start Times dialog box, in which you can specify the start time for the background job.

Precalculation of Web Templates

1. To precalculate a Web template, select Reporting Agent in the menu in the SAP NetWeaver BW Administrator Workbench (Transaction RSA1), and then select the Web Templates submenu.

2. Click the New button (leaf icon) to create a Web template for the preferred query.

3. Select the Web template, and select the New Setting option in the context menu (right-click).

4. In the Parameter tab, specify what is to be precisely calculated. For the pure precalculation of queries, the select the DATA option under CALCULATE.

5. If the query has input parameters, you must create a variant using the input parameters analogous to printing.

6. You must now create a scheduling package that is also analogous to printing, link it with the reporting agent settings, and schedule it as a background job.

If you use the precalculation intensively, this can result in conflicts that have a counterproductive impact on performance because, for example, the results generated by the precalculation displace the cache entries of the dialog user or it results in performance problems as a result of locking conflicts between the background processes and dialog processes. There therefore exists a series of notes that address this subject in the SAP Note system. As highlights for dealing more with this topic, see Notes 807967, 859456, and 1006905.

12.3.6 Aggregates

Aggregates allow you to calculate data in advance and store it, and then make it available to users. Aggregates emerge from a Basis InfoCube in which individual characteristics of the InfoCubes are omitted, and the facts are aggregated along these characteristics.

[Ex] Figure 12.6 goes back to the previously described example of the InfoCube with the dimensions customer, sales employee, and time. In this example, two aggregates have been formed on this InfoCube, one on the characteristics sales employee and time, and one on the characteristic customer.

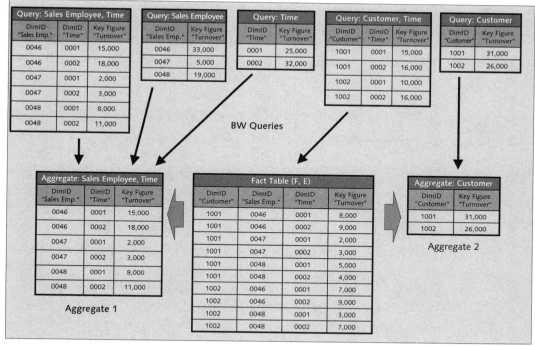

| Query: Sales Employee, Time | | |
DimID "Sales Emp."	DimID "Time"	Key Figure "Turnover"
0046	0001	15,000
0046	0002	18,000
0047	0001	2,000
0047	0002	3,000
0048	0001	8,000
0048	0002	11,000

| Query: Sales Employee | | |
DimID "Sales Emp."	Key Figure "Turnover"
0046	33,000
0047	5,000
0048	19,000

| Query: Time | |
DimID "Time"	Key Figure "Turnover"
0001	25,000
0002	32,000

| Query: Customer, Time | | |
DimID "Customer"	DimID "Time"	Key Figure "Turnover"
1001	0001	15,000
1001	0002	16,000
1002	0001	10,000
1002	0002	16,000

| Query: Customer | |
DimID "Customer"	Key Figure "Turnover"
1001	31,000
1002	26,000

BW Queries

| Aggregate: Sales Employee, Time | | |
DimID "Sales Emp."	DimID "Time"	Key Figure "Turnover"
0046	0001	15,000
0046	0002	18,000
0047	0001	2,000
0047	0002	3,000
0048	0001	8,000
0048	0002	11,000

Aggregate 1

| Fact Table (F, E) | | | |
DimID "Customer"	DimID "Sales Emp."	DimID "Time"	Key Figure "Turnover"
1001	0046	0001	8,000
1001	0046	0002	9,000
1001	0047	0001	2,000
1001	0047	0002	3,000
1001	0048	0001	5,000
1001	0048	0002	4,000
1002	0046	0001	7,000
1002	0046	0002	9,000
1002	0048	0001	3,000
1002	0048	0002	7,000

| Aggregate: Customer | |
DimID "Customer"	Key Figure "Turnover"
1001	31,000
1002	26,000

Aggregate 2

Figure 12.6 Principle of Performance Optimization via Aggregates Using Two Aggregates and Five BW Queries.

The first aggregate has emerged by omitting the customer characteristic, and the second aggregate by omitting the sales employee and time characteristics. The key figures are aggregated away via "omitted" characteristics. That is, in the example already given, the total has been simply formed for the turnover key figure. Let's now consider the five example queries displayed in the figure to see how the aggregates impact their performance. The first query, via the characteristics sales employee and time, can be directly answered from the identical aggregate, and instead of ten records in the fact table, only six records must be read from the aggregate. The same applies to the queries via sales employee and time. They can be answered by further aggregating the aggregate via sales employee and time, and they benefit from the preprocessing of data. The query via the characteristic customer can be answered from the aggregate of the same name. Here, instead of ten records from the fact table, only two records must be read from the aggregate. That is, the improvement in performance is greatest here. Ultimately, for the last query that presents a drill-down of data according to customer and time, none of the existing aggregates can be used because the drill-down according to the customer characteristic is missing in the first aggregate, and in the second the layout according to the time characteristic is missing. The fact table must be accessed to process this query. No improvement in performance can therefore be achieved with the defined aggregates.

Comparison: aggregates and indices

Aggregates function similarly to indexes. Indexes are — as we have seen — always effective when the data to be read in the WHERE clause is already heavily restricted. That is, if a table contains 1 million entries, and you want to read only 100 of these, an index helps you find these entries quickly. If, however, you are interested in the total, maximum, or minimum of these 1 million records, an index doesn't help you. In this case, you need an aggregate for performance optimization.

Aggregates — like indexes — are physically stored in the database and therefore require memory space. Like indexes, a developer or administrator must decide on which fields (i.e., characteristics) aggregates are to be created. Like indexes, it is not possible to create aggregates on all combinations of characteristics. The number of possible combinations for which aggregates can be created grows exponentially with the number of characteristics in the InfoCube. A choice must therefore be made. The use of aggregates is transparent for the user. That is, apart from an improved performance, he doesn't perceive anything from the use of an aggregate. The OLAP processor automatically decides which aggregate to use. It assumes the role that the database optimizer assumes when using indexes.

Aggregates are in turn implemented as InfoCubes. Just like the Basis InfoCubes, they have an E and an F fact table. They either have their own dimension tables or, if possible, also use respective dimension tables of the Basis InfoCube. Table 12.6 lists the naming conventions for the tables used for aggregates.

You must keep in mind the following properties of aggregates with regard to creation and maintenance:

▶ Aggregates can only be created for Basis InfoCubes. There is no aggregate support for Operational Data Source (ODS) objects, InfoSets, RemoteCubes, or InfoObjects that are declared as InfoProviders. Therefore, when designing your reporting, you should consider keeping data in InfoCubes so you can use performance optimization via aggregates.

▶ Queries that are defined on MultiProviders can use the aggregates of the underlying Basis InfoCubes. Aggregates are therefore always defined on the Basis InfoCubes, but not on MultiProviders.

▶ Aggregates support the display of totals and minimum and maximum, but not the mean values.

With the rebuild of an aggregate, data from the Basis InfoCube is compressed according to the definition of the aggregate. The aggregates are then also updated (rollup) with each data loading after filling the Basis InfoCube. Aggregates must also be adapted when changes are made to the master data or hierarchy. SAP NetWeaver BW provides administration tools for the data management of aggregates. For the database, aggregates are only tables without any further semantics, unlike indexes, where the database software is responsible for data management.

Function	Name of Database
Fact table (uncompressed)	/<PF>/F1XXXXX
Fact table (compressed)	/<PF>/E1XXXXX
Dimension table	/<PF>/D1XXXXX<Y>, <Y>: P, T, U, 1, 2, ...
<PF> stands for the namespace prefix that separates SAP objects from customer objects, (for example, BI0 or BIC), 1XXXXX stands for a six-digit sequential combination allocated by SAP NetWeaver BW for the aggregates, which begins with a 1.	

Table 12.6 Overview of the Tables for Aggregates in SAP NetWeaver BW

In Section 12.2, Analysis of Expensive BW Queries, we addressed the criteria for aggregates to contribute to the improvement in performance of queries. We'll summarize those criteria here:

Criteria for the creation of aggregates

▸ High database response times relative to both the entire response time (>30%) and absolute time (>3 seconds)

▸ High number of selected records (>10,000) and a high ratio of selected to transferred records (>10)

Creating Aggregates

You open the aggregate maintenance on an InfoCube as follows:

1. Double-click the InfoProvider you want in the SAP NetWeaver BW Administrator Workbench (Transaction RSA1), and select the Maintain Aggregates menu option in the context menu (right-click). Alternatively, use the Transaction RSDDV.

2. You are redirected to the Maintenance of Aggregates screen. You will find on the left-hand side of this screen the configuration of the InfoCube as a template for the definition of the aggregates. On the right-hand side, you'll find the aggregates already created and their properties, which we'll describe in detail later.

3. You can create an aggregate via the New button (leaf icon). to which you assign by clicking and dragging the mouse from the left-hand characteristics and/or attributes screen area. The sequence is not relevant — unlike with indexes.

4. Then save the aggregate. A six-digit number that begins with a 1 is assigned internally to the aggregate, and it cannot be changed. The name you give the aggregate is displayed.

5. In the lower-right screen area, you will find messages that help you create the aggregate and warn you in case the aggregate is inconsistently defined.

6. The aggregate must then be created in the database and filled with data. You do this by using the Activate function in the application toolbar.

In the Maintenance of the Aggregates screen, several columns in the list of aggregates in the upper-right screen area give information on the current properties of the aggregates. Table 12.7 describes these columns in detail.

Field	Explanation
Aggregates	Name of the aggregate.
Technical Name	Technical name specified by SAP NetWeaver BW, which cannot be changed.
Save	Displays whether an aggregate has been saved (disk icon).
Suggested Action	If you allow SAP NetWeaver BW to make a suggestion for the optimization of aggregates, suggestions for action are displayed in this field, if required: for example, the suggestion to activate this aggregate.
Status	Status traffic light icon that displays whether the aggregate is active (green traffic light icon), has not yet been activated (red traffic light icon) or is active and has been changed (yellow traffic light icon).
Filled/Deactivated	Status traffic light icon that displays whether the aggregate is filled with data (green traffic light icon), not filled (red traffic light icon) or is deactivated for the reporting (gray traffic light icon)
Evaluation	SAP NetWeaver BW calculates an evaluation of an aggregate, consisting of the following source systems: ▶ Ratio of records in the InfoCube to the number of records in the aggregate (a large ratio results in a good evaluation) ▶ Use (frequent use results in a good evaluation) The result of the evaluation is displayed in the form of a plus or minus sign and ranges from five plus signs to five minus signs.
Records	Number of records in the aggregate.
Records Compressed	Average number of records that have been read in the InfoCube or in a superordinate aggregate to determine a record in the aggregate. The greater this value is, the more suitable the aggregate is to improve performance. A value greater than 10 (guideline value) is considered to be a good compression.
Use	Frequency of use of the aggregate. The use count is reset with each rebuild.
Last Use	Date of last use of the aggregate.

Table 12.7 Selected Fields of the Aggregate Maintenance (Properties of the Aggregates)

Creating Aggregates on Suggestion of SAP NetWeaver BW

You'll find a function in the aggregate maintenance that allows suggestions to be made for aggregates. This function uses the following methods:

▶ SAP NetWeaver BW analyzes the queries that have been defined on an InfoProvider and can deduce from this which aggregates are required to optimize this query.

▶ SAP NetWeaver BW knows the user's behavior as a result of the BW statistics and can take into consideration which navigation steps the user frequently carries out and include this in the calculation of the aggregate suggestions. This procedure only comes into consideration when there is meaningful usage data.

If there is usage data, then proceed as follows:

1. Double-click the InfoProvider in the SAP NetWeaver BW Administrator Workbench (Transaction RSA1), and select the Maintain Aggregates menu option in the context menu (right-click). Alternatively, use Transaction RSDDV.

2. Select the SUGGEST • SUGGEST (STATISTICS, OTHERWISE QUERY) menu option. You are redirected to the Specify Evaluation of Statistics Data dialog box. In this screen, you can restrict the period for which the SAP NetWeaver BW statistics should be used for the aggregate suggestion (you should specify a period with the most representative usage possible), and you can specify that only navigation steps with a particular runtime should be included in the analysis. Close the dialog box by clicking the green checkmark.

3. You are redirected back to the aggregate maintenance. You will now find a list of aggregates in the right-hand screen area that are named STAT 1, STAT 2, and so on. In the Evaluation column, you will find an evaluation of the aggregates conducted by the system (see also Table 12.7). The aggregates are not yet activated at this time.

4. You can now save the aggregate suggestions with or without activating. You can also rename the aggregates. The six-digit number remains internally intact as a technical name.

5. Alternatively, you can allow the aggregate suggestions to be further optimized. Use the SUGGEST • OPTIMIZE function in the menu. The system then merges the assumed weakest aggregates with others and therefore reduces the size of the suggestion list. The emerging aggregates will optimize the runtime less heavily than the original ones. Disk space and loading resources and the administration costs are

therefore reduced. The optimization function is iterative; that is, is can be repeated.

If there is no usage data, an aggregate suggestion can be generated for individual queries. You open this via the SUGGEST • SUGGEST FROM QUERY function in the of the aggregate maintenance menu. Instead of the dialog box being used to specify the statistics data, a selection list of queries (Select Queries for Analysis dialog box) is offered, from which you specify one or several queries for the calculation of the aggregate suggestion. The system creates two aggregate suggestions for each selected query: a minimal aggregate that the query optimally supports with a minimal drill-down and a maximal aggregate that the query optimizes with a maximal drill-down. The latter can be almost as large as the InfoCube. You can also use the optimization function again for this suggestion.

Checking, Merging, and Switching Off Aggregates

The efficiency of aggregates should be checked regularly. The criteria for the good quality of aggregates are high compression and high usage. You'll find these key figures together with an overall evaluation that SAP NetWeaver BW carries out in the list of aggregates in aggregate maintenance. Table 12.7 describes in detail the fields in the aggregate list.

Weak aggregates can possibly be merged with others. You can either carry out this optimization manually or use the previously described optimization function in the aggregate maintenance while the system is in operation.

On the other hand, you can also temporarily switch off an aggregate to observe the emerging performance changes. Use the Switch On/Off function in the application toolbar of the aggregate maintenance. The definition and the database tables of the aggregate remain intact, and data is supplied but no longer used to execute queries. This is displayed in the Filled/Deactivated column in the aggregate list via a grey icon.

Switching off temporarily

Checking Indexing on the Aggregates

The indexing of the aggregates follows the indexing schema for Info-Cubes. SAP NetWeaver BW offers a buffer function for the indexes and statistics of aggregates like it does for InfoCubes. You can find these in the

Performance tab of the Maintenance of Data Targets screen that you open by selecting an InfoCube from the SAP NetWeaver BW Administrator Workbench (Transaction RSA1) and then selecting the Manage function in the context menu. There the Check Aggregates Indices, Delete Aggregates Indices, and Repair Aggregates Indices functions are available. The functionality corresponds to the one for InfoCubes described in Section 12.3.1, Managing Indexing.

Maintaining Aggregates

The continuous maintenance of aggregates comprises three tasks:

▶ The supply of aggregates after the data load in the InfoCube (rollup)

▶ The compression of the aggregates

▶ The up-to-date condition of the aggregates after changes to the master data or the hierarchy

Supply of the aggregates

After the data load takes place in the InfoCubes, the associated active aggregates must be supplied with data. Until the aggregates are supplied with data, only the old data is available for the reporting.

Data is supplied either automatically or manually. You define the automatic supply of data in the aggregates in the Maintenance of Data Targets screen that you open by selecting an InfoCube from the SAP NetWeaver BW Administrator Workbench (Transaction RSA1) and then selecting the Manage function in the context menu. There you select ENVIRONMENT • AUTOMATIC REQUEST PROCESSING in the menu. You are redirected to the Maintenance of the Automatisms screen, where you activate the Rollup of Data in the Aggregates function under Automatic Processing.

With the manual supply of aggregates, you can specifically roll up individual load requests. This function can also be found in the Maintenance of Data Targets screen in the Rollup tab.

If several aggregates exist on an InfoCube, SAP NetWeaver BW checks whether highly aggregated aggregates can be filled from slightly weaker aggregated aggregates to avoid a fact table having to be accessed for the supply of each aggregate. SAP NetWeaver BW carries out this optimization automatically. In individual cases, it can make sense to analyze this supply hierarchy and to even create aggregates that optimize the supply of other aggregates. We won't discuss this optimization option here. Bear in mind, however, that the deactivation of an aggregate, even if it does not negatively impact the query performance, can lead to performance problems with the rollup.

The runtime for filling aggregates can be monitored in two ways. On the one hand, you can specifically search for background jobs for the supply of aggregates in the job overview of SAP Basis (Transaction SM37) by entering the search item "BI_SAGGR*" in the Jobname field, via which all jobs that supply aggregates begin. On the other hand, statistics on the aggregate filling of SAP NetWeaver BW are stored in the RSDDSTAT-AGGR table, provided that the statistics have been activated for the InfoProvider (see Section 12.2, Analysis of Expensive BW Queries). You can evaluate the table using the table browser (Transaction SE16).

Like InfoCubes, aggregates also have a fact table for uncompressed data (F table) and one for compressed data (E table). An automatic compression is initially defined for all aggregates. That is, the data is automatically moved under compression via the request ID from the F table to the E table after supply takes place. Data packages can therefore no longer be selectively deleted. If a data package must be deleted from an InfoCube, the aggregates must be deactivated and rebuilt.

Compression of the aggregates

You can deactivate the automatic compression if data packages frequently must be deleted. The associated Compress after RollUp function can be found in the Maintenance of the Data Targets screen in the Rollup tab. You can also trigger the manual compression there.

When the master data or hierarchies are changed in the InfoCube, the changes are adapted in the database by the *change run*. These changes must also be made in the aggregates. A list of the characteristics, hierarchies, and aggregates impacted by the change must be created first with the RSDDS_CHANGERUN_MONITOR report or Transaction RSATTR. Then the change run can be started in the SAP NetWeaver BW Administrator Workbench (Transaction RSA1), via the Tools • Hierarchy/Attribute Changes menu option or via the report RSDDS_AGGREGATES_MAINTAIN.

Change run

The change run can be a time-consuming process that can even be optimized again. You can learn more about this in the special literature listed in Appendix G.

12.4 Summary

In SAP NetWeaver BW, data for reporting purposes is redundantly stored on transactional original data. You should keep performance quality in mind during the design of InfoProviders, particularly regarding:

▶ keeping unnecessary data from collecting in SAP NetWeaver BW,

▶ storing data in InfoCubes because this has the highest performance optimization potential,

▶ and using logical partitioning of data in suitable Basis InfoCubes.

SAP NetWeaver BW has standard tools for performance analysis via detailed SAP NetWeaver BW internal statistics and numerous check programs that, for example, check indexing and statistics. You can use these for an extended performance analysis.

Performance can be further improved via suitable administration, for example, via the regular compression of InfoCubes, the monitoring of the OLAP cache and its prefilling, and ultimately via the creation and monitoring of aggregates.

Figure 12.7 shows the most important elements of performance analysis for a BW query in a roadmap.

Important Concepts

You should be familiar with the following concepts after studying this chapter:

▶ InfoProviders, InfoCubes, InfoObjects, and BW query

▶ Star schema, fact tables, dimension tables, and master data tables

▶ OLAP cache and precalculation of queries

▶ Compression of InfoCubes

▶ Aggregates

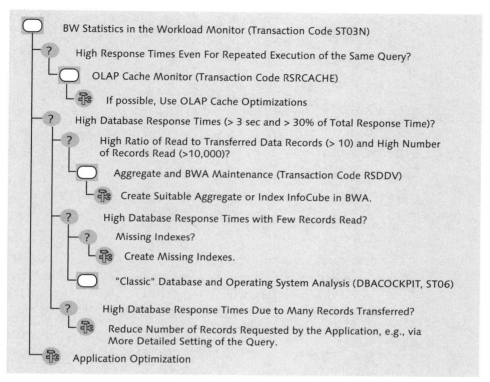

Figure 12.7 Roadmap of the Performance Analysis of BW Queries

Questions

1. Which optimization potential do you see when the SAP NetWeaver BW statistics displays a high ratio of selected data records in the database to transferred data records for a query?

   a) The OLAP cache has not been filled or invalidated, because otherwise the selected records of the database could have been read from the OLAP cache. You should check whether the cache can be enlarged or the query can be precalculated.

   b) A suitable index on the fact table can help reduce the number of records selected from the database.

   c) A suitable index on the SID table can help reduce the number of records selected from the database.

d) A suitable aggregate can help reduce the number of records selected from the database.

2. Which tables can be compressed?

   a) Fact tables of InfoCubes

   b) Fact tables of aggregates

   c) Dimension tables

   d) Master data tables

   e) Tables of DataStore objects

3. Which statements on aggregates and indexes are correct?

   a) Indexes are almost completely replaced by aggregates in the SAP NetWeaver BW environment.

   b) Indexes and aggregates are complementary. That is, indexes are there to improve performance where the selection has been heavily restricted in a query, whereas aggregates improve performance when a large number of data records must be totaled and a minimum or a maximum must be formed.

   c) Both indexes and aggregates require memory space and resources when filling data in SAP NetWeaver BW.

   d) Aggregates are logical constructs that apart from low administrative overheads do not require any memory space or resources.

   e) The use of indexes and aggregates in queries is specified by the database optimizer. That is, he decides whether and which index or which aggregate is used to execute the query.

13 Optimizing Search Queries Using TREX

The previous chapters dealt with the optimization of SQL queries in general and in the SAP NetWeaver BW environment in particular. In this context, you've repeatedly come across indexing as a critical means of performance optimization. This chapter will present a highly specialized and highly efficient indexing software, *TREX*, which you can use as a supplement to the optimization methods presented so far.

Originally, SAP developed TREX as a text search engine, and its name derives from the original application, *Text Retrieval and Information Extraction*. Texts that can be searched can include, for example, documents that were stored in the knowledge management component of an SAP system and documents on Web or file servers, but also descriptive texts and appendixes of master data such as business partners (customers, suppliers, employees) and products, as well as transaction data, for instance, sales and service documents. Additionally, you can manage structured attributes, for instance, the author or the title of a document, in separate indexes. This way, you can collect the entire knowledge of an enterprise with a holistic search; this application is therefore traded under the name *SAP NetWeaver Enterprise Search* in SAP's product portfolio.

Text Retrieval and Information Extraction

In the meantime, besides the text and attribute search, TREX has also been used for optimizing BW queries — known as SAP NetWeaver BW Accelerator. In SAP Business ByDesign™, SAP's new on-demand solution, the usage of TREX goes even further; here, TREX is used for the optimization of queries in almost all areas. However, we don't discuss this usage here because the focus is on SAP Business Suite applications.

When Should You Read this Chapter?

You should read this chapter if you want to use TREX either as a search engine within the scope of text searches or the enterprise search scenario or for the optimization of BW queries within the scope of SAP NetWeaver BW Accelerator.

This chapter is not an introduction to TREX; that is, the functionality provided by TREX is only discussed in excerpts. The focus is on topics that are significant for performance behavior.

13.1 Fundamentals and Architecture of TREX Considering Performance Aspects

Initially, this section answers the question of how the optimization of search queries using TREX differs from the methods previously discussed. The essential characteristics of TREX searches include the following:

▶ **High level of data compression**
Typically, compression factors ranging between 10 and 100 are reached compared to classical indexing with indexes in the form of B* trees.

▶ **Column-based data storage**
In TREX, the indexed data is stored in columns, not in rows as is the case in a database. The row-based storage in the database means you must always load all data of a row into the main memory of the database buffer because it is located on the same page (also referred to as "block" in the database language) even if only one column in a table or an index must be searched. In the extreme case, this means you must load data for every access to the main memory even though this data is never read.

▶ **Indexes in the main memory**
The compression of data and the column-based data storage enables you to keep indexes completely in the main memory and thus utilize the performance benefit that in-memory computing has in comparison to the classical database processing with the displacing data buffer.

▶ **Parallelization of search queries**
You can easily distribute TREX indexes to different servers to parallelize search queries.

A TREX index must not be confused with a database index. A TREX index **[+]** corresponds to a database table. Indexes in the sense of a database don't exist in TREX, with the exception of delta indexes.

The following subsections discuss some compression techniques of TREX, the TREX search techniques, and its architecture.

13.1.1 Data Compression in TREX

For the practical work using TREX you don't need to understand how TREX compresses its data. Nevertheless, it's not a waste of time to get some insight into these techniques. TREX uses many alternative compression techniques that are not perceivable for the users assuming that one of the techniques implemented will "get a hit." The following brief introduction is by no means complete. Rather, the goal is to present important concepts for the discussion.

Dictionary coding is the first compression technique used by TREX. Every TREX index has a dictionary in which all values, be they numerical or alphanumerical, are converted into integer IDs. If different values are supposed to be indexed in index n, then you must select the length for the integer ID as the logarithm of n for basis 2. Internally, TREX can use the short integer IDs for calculation instead of the long values that are specified externally.

Dictionary coding

For example, with two bytes you can map a period of approximately 180 years at the day level; in other words, instead of eight bytes, which a date field requires in a relational database table, the internal calculation can be done with two bytes. For other values, the compression may be even higher.

You've already came across the procedure of dictionary coding in the star schema of SAP NetWeaver BW. Instead of master data, you only store integer IDs (Dim-ID, SID) in the fact and dimension tables.

Difference coding is the second fundamental compression technique used by TREX. Assume that TREX is used for indexing texts and is supposed to remember that the word *performance* appears at the following positions in the document in this book:

Difference coding

3, 16, 56, 90, 120, 234, 256, 270, 345, …

In this case, you require considerably less space if you only store the differences:

3, 13, 40, 34, 30, 114, 12, 14, 75, ...

The higher the number, the more efficient the difference coding.

Take a look at a second example of difference coding: The system is supposed to index the occurrence of the attribute 2009 (i.e., the year 2009) in a table (for instance, a fact table in SAP NetWeaver BW). The first occurrence of the attribute 2009 in the table is to be at position 934,234, the next at position 934,235, and then 934,236, 934,237, and so on up to 935,449. As difference coding, this indexing can be written as follows: 934,235, 1, 1, and so on — a total sequence of 1,214 1s after the first occurrence. Such a "run" can be written more efficiently as follows: 934,235 x 1,214.

The last example of difference coding comes from the lexical area: The following words are supposed to be stored in a text dictionary: burger, burglar, burgundy, burner, burnish, burnisher, burnside. Difference coding utilizes the similarity of these words and stores them as follows:

6BURGER43LAR44UNDY33NER43ISH72ER44SIDE

This coding is to be read as follows: The block starts with a word consisting of six letters: burger. The next word uses the first four letters and adds three new ones: BURG+LAR. The next word uses the first four letters and adds four new ones: BURG+UNDY.

To build a text dictionary, you split the word list to be indexed into blocks with *m* words each. You code each block according to the difference procedure described previously. If you now want to know the ID for a specific word, you first consider the first words in a block to search for a block that must contain a word; you then search for the position of the searched word in this block. The ID comprises the number of the block multiplied by *m* plus the position of the word in the block. The reverse procedure applies if a search query provides the ID and you now want to know which word is behind this ID. This way, you can very efficiently compress a text dictionary.

However, the very efficient compression comes at a price. Once an index has been created, changes are only possible with a great deal of effort;

that is, you cannot insert new words easily. To reduce the effort of the index update, you can split a TREX index into a main index and a smaller *delta index*, where you can insert new words. Every query is run in parallel in the main and in the delta index. If the delta index has reached a specific size, the two indexes must be combined, which de facto corresponds to a rebuild of the index.

Other compression techniques worth mentioning here include golomb and gamma coding for compressing large integers and bit vectors for compressing scarcely occupied columns.

13.1.2 Search Techniques

TREX is used in various applications and can be applied in custom developments of SAP partners and customers. The currently most important applications are:

TREX applications

▶ **Text search in the portal and knowledge management (KM)**

▶ **Search Engine Service (SES)**
TREX-based indexing and search for business documents in the SAP Business Suite. This technology has been available as of SAP NetWeaver 7.0 and is primarily used in SAP ERP 6.0, for instance, to search for business partners and products, usually in the input help.

▶ **Enterprise File Search (EFS)**
TREX-based indexing and search for text documents from file servers and Web servers and via WebDAV. This technology has also been available as of SAP NetWeaver 7.0.

▶ **SAP NetWeaver Enterprise Search (ESH)**
This product combines the previous indexing and search scenarios in one solution. You can distinguish between the *embedded scenario*, which enables you to search documents in exactly one system (SAP Note 1254901) and is the direct successor of the search engine service, and the *hub scenario*, which enables a search across multiple systems. This search is used in SAP Business Suite 7 (SAP ERP 6.04, SAP PLM 7.00, SAP CRM 7.00, and so on). The hub scenario runs on a separate SAP NetWeaver system.

Refer to the SAP Service Marketplace at *http://service.sap.com/nwes70* to obtain detailed information on adapters that you can use to connect TREX with the various data sources.

SAP NetWeaver BW Accelerator is another usage area of TREX.

Search functions TREX provides the following functions that are rendered by the individual servers (note that this list is not complete):

▶ Simple (exact) search, search for phrases, search for combinations (Boolean search), fuzzy search

▶ Query search and join engine

▶ Linguistic analysis and search

▶ Attribute analysis and search

▶ Concordance search and ranking

▶ Categorization and text mining

Linguistic analysis and search For indexing, you convert text documents from different file formats such as HTML, Adobe PDF, or Microsoft Office, remove the formatting, and then analyze them. The goal of the text analysis is to restore the principal part of concepts. This process is referred to as *stemming* and includes the following:

▶ Verbs return to their indicative; for instance, *goes* and *went* become *go*.

▶ Substantives return to their nominative; for instance, *houses* and *house's* become *house*.

▶ Compounds are split, for instance, *housewife* or *lawsuit*.

▶ Derived adjectives and adverbs return to their basic form; for instance, *drinkable* and *drinking* become *drink*.

For this purpose, two procedures are used: the rule-based root recognition, which is based on rules only, and lexicon-based root recognition, which uses a lexicon.

These analyses depend on the language. Before TREX can run the analysis, it automatically identifies the language on the basis of typical letter combinations such as *ght* (English) or *sch* (German). SAP Note 631390 identifies the languages that TREX supports.

In the text search, TREX creates concordances and ranking lists; that is, it not only provides a hit list — as would be the case in an SQL database — but it also assesses documents found according to their concordance. This function is based on statistical data about how often the searched terms occur in the documents found and in all other documents. The index server creates this ranking during the search.

Concordance search and ranking lists

13.1.3 Architecture of TREX

Figure 13.1 shows the architecture of TREX. TREX has an ABAP and a Java interface (API). These interfaces are used, for example, by SAP NetWeaver Portal (Java) or SAP NetWeaver BW Accelerator (ABAP), but also by many other components. SAP provides adapters that you can use to connect TREX with an SAP R/3 system, SAP ERP, KM, and so on. The interfaces connect via one of the following servers, which form the communication layer of TREX:

► Web server for HTTP-based communication

► RFC server for RFC-based communication with the ABAP server

► Internet Communication Manager (ICM) also for HTTP-based communication with the ABAP server. With this protocol you can transfer larger quantities of data with a higher performance than via RFC.

Java-based applications such as SAP NetWeaver Portal and KM connect via the Web server; ABAP-based applications connect via RFC or ICM.

Moreover, TREX includes a Python API, which is deployed for administration purposes and is used by the TREX administration tool and for test programs.

The other TREX servers divide the work as follows:

► The name server is responsible for distributing the load. It manages the status information of all available components.

► The index server manages the search indexes; that is, it performs the indexing work and the actual processing of the search query.

► The preprocessor preprocesses documents and queries; that is, for indexing, it converts the documents to be indexed from specific formats, for instance, HTML, Adobe PDF, Microsoft Office, and so on, and extracts the words from the user-defined text that are supposed to be indexed. In doing so, it implements the linguistic conversions mentioned above.

▶ The queue server manages the queue of queries to be processed in case of asynchronous indexing queries.

▶ The alert server regularly checks the consistency of the TREX installation, for instance, the consistency of the indexes, and sends alerts to the administrator in case of errors or problems.

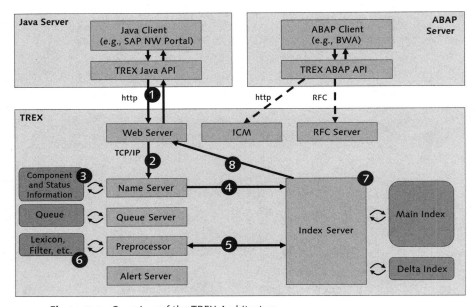

Figure 13.1 Overview of the TREX Architecture

Process flow of a search query Based on Figure 13.1, you can retrace the process flow for processing a search query. The following example presents a text search query from SAP NetWeaver Portal that is directed to TREX via the Java interface. The Java interface connects to the Web server of the TREX installation ❶. This Web server in turn forwards the query to the name server ❷. The name server uses the available component and status information ❸ to determine which index server is supposed to implement the processing and forwards the query to the selected index server ❹. The index server determines that the query is a text search that must be processed linguistically. For this purpose, it passes the query to the preprocessor to implement the linguistic analysis ❺. (We'll discuss the task of the preprocessor later.) After the processed query has been returned to the index server, it runs the actual search in the index ❼. After the search has been completed, it returns the result to the Web server ❽. The Web server then passes the result to the client via the Java interface.

An indexing query is processed by TREX as follows: Here as well, a Java client is the starting point, for example, the indexing of text documents in SAP NetWeaver Portal. In this case as well, the Web server directs the query to the name server. If the indexing is supposed to be synchronous, the name server returns the name and port of the index server that is supposed to perform the indexing. In asynchronous indexing, the name server returns the name of a queue server.

Process flow of an indexing query

The queue server transfers the documents to the preprocessor. The preprocessor performs the following steps:

Preprocessor

1. The preprocessor loads the document. The application controls whether it sends a document directly or only a reference to the storage location of the document (URI). The application can tie this to the size of the document, for example. If the application has transferred a URI, the preprocessor loads the document from the storage location that the URI references.

2. The preprocessor extracts the content and converts it to the Unicode format UTF-8.

3. The preprocessor performs a linguistic analysis and extracts the terms to be indexed.

4. Finally, the preprocessor returns the result to the queue server.

The queue server manages one queue per index; in this queue, the server collects the documents sent by the application. The queue server holds the indexing query in the queue until free resources are available or the configured time has been reached when the indexing is supposed to take place. Because the updating process of an index can be time-consuming, you can specify that it is only run at specific times or depending on the number of documents collected. If the start condition is met, the queue server sends the documents to the index server, where it triggers the optimization. As previously mentioned, this means the main index is written completely anew or, if configured, the delta index is updated.

Index types   TREX differentiates between logical and physical indexes. A physical index is the smallest index unit and contains the indexed data. A physical index is always managed by one index server. A logical index doesn't contain data, but refers to other indexes. For example, an index can be divided into multiple physical indexes that are located on different index servers and kept together by a logical index. The reason for this division can be, on the one hand, that an index server cannot keep the entire index in the main memory due to its size. (This reason is no longer applicable with the implementation of the 64-bit version of TREX.) On the other hand, the division can occur because the queries on the index are supposed to be run in parallel on multiple index servers. An application accesses the logical index, and the division is not perceivable for this application — except that the performance improves when subqueries are run in parallel.

The text indexing, the attribute indexing, and the data for the text mining are located in separate storage areas in the index itself. Depending on the application scenario, these areas can be filled or empty. Other index types are indexes where you store the links between business document types (join indexes, which are used in the enterprise search scenario, among others) and a special type for the use in the SAP NetWeaver BW Accelerator scenario, which is modeled on the basis of the SAP NetWeaver BW InfoCube's star schema.

Besides these indexes, TREX includes the delta indexes that have already been presented.

Sizing and configuration   For recommendations on sizing, configuration, and released platforms for TREX for text search, refer to the SAP website on sizing at *http://service.sap.com/sizing*.

TREX is available on Windows and Linux operating systems. Up to Version 7.0, TREX can be operated in 32-bit operating systems; as of Version 7.1 it is only released for 64-bit platforms. If possible, you should operate TREX on a 64-bit operating system platform to not be subject to the address space restrictions described in Chapter 8, Memory Management.

You can operate TREX in combination with other software components on a computer. However, you must remember that it holds the indexes in the main memory. You should avoid paging (see Chapter 2, Section 2.2, Hardware Monitoring) by all means.

13.1.4 Specific Characteristics of SAP NetWeaver BW Accelerator

You can use SAP NetWeaver BW Accelerator for SAP NetWeaver BW versions as of 7.0. Figure 12.2 in the previous chapter illustrates the basic architecture for connecting TREX in the SAP NetWeaver BW Accelerator scenario with SAP NetWeaver BW. For search queries, the communication is from the OLAP processor via the ABAP interface and the RFC server of TREX. For indexing queries, the communication is via the Internet Communication Manager of TREX.

Even if an InfoCube was indexed in SAP NetWeaver BW Accelerator, the OLAP cache is still used with priority.

[+]

The Web server, the preprocessor, and the queue server are not used with SAP NetWeaver BW Accelerator. Additional internal services have been implemented in the index server for use by SAP NetWeaver BW Accelerator. The use of these services is not perceivable to the user except for the improved performance. In principle, in SAP NetWeaver BW Accelerator TREX must not be used in parallel for text searches, even if this would be possible from the technical perspective.

After you've connected SAP NetWeaver BW Accelerator with an SAP NetWeaver BW system, you can activate indexing via SAP NetWeaver BW Accelerator at the InfoCube level. Upon activation, SAP NetWeaver BW Accelerator creates a fact index for the fact tables and a characteristics index for the X, Y, and S tables. These indexes have been specially developed for use in SAP NetWeaver BW Accelerator. Indexes in X, Y, and S tables can be reused beyond InfoCubes boundaries.

Decomposition and partitioning

SAP NetWeaver BW Accelerator stores the indexed data per column — in contrast to a database that stores the data on a row basis. This procedure, which is also referred to as *vertical decomposition*, has the benefit that only columns specified in the WHERE condition of the query must be stored and read in the main memory, instead of having to read all columns implicitly because they were stored in the same block. In combination with the compression methods described at the beginning of this chapter, you can compress the data of an InfoCube by a factor of at least five and keep it in the main memory.

For further optimization, SAP NetWeaver BW Accelerator partitions the indexes horizontally and assigns them to different physical index servers so that the queries can be parallelized. SAP NetWeaver BW Accelerator derives the degree of parallelization from the number of available processors.

SAP NetWeaver BW Accelerator derives the vertical decomposition, the necessary compression algorithms, and the horizontal *partitioning* completely from the metadata of the SAP NetWeaver BW InfoCube model; that is, the administrator doesn't have to make any manual specifications. The same applies to the execution of queries. SAP NetWeaver BW Accelerator has its own optimization service, which calculates the execution plan for a query in SAP NetWeaver BW Accelerator. This service requires no intervention from the administrator.

Background: Appliance

SAP supports SAP NetWeaver BW Accelerator only as an appliance solution. This means SAP NetWeaver BW Accelerator software is already installed on a computer at the hardware partner. This computer consists of a memory system with a capacity in the terabyte range and a blade server. Computers with three blades (two production blades and one reserve) and up to 100 (or even more) blades are available. TREX runs on every blade; the scaling takes place only by adding additional blades. Currently, hardware partners for SAP NetWeaver BW Accelerator include Hewlett-Packard, IBM, Fujitsu-Siemens, and Sun Microsystems. 64-bit SUSE-Linux is used as the operating system. A 64-bit platform was selected to avoid the address space restrictions described in Chapter 8, Memory Management. The SAP NetWeaver BW system, to which SAP NetWeaver BW Accelerator is connected, is not subject to any other platform restrictions. The network connection between SAP NetWeaver BW and SAP NetWeaver BW Accelerator must perform at least one gigabit per second.

The following consequences result from the fact that SAP NetWeaver BW Accelerator is released only as an appliance solution:

► The platform combinations of operating systems, CPU types, and memory systems are restricted. This restriction is necessary because TREX has been optimized specifically for the SAP NetWeaver BW Accelerator scenario on the platforms used.

► In the SAP NetWeaver BW Accelerator scenario, TREX generally runs alone on a computer (blade server). As previously mentioned, the benefit of TREX is that the indexes can be held in the main memory. This prevents paging to the hard disk swap space due to the coexistence with other software components.

This reduces administration costs because many administration tasks concerning the installation, configuration, installation of monitoring and the security concept, and so on have already been performed by SAP and hardware partners and because other tasks, such as the creation of sizing, have become considerably easier.

SAP Note 917803 provides sizing information for SAP NetWeaver BW Accelerator. Sizing is easiest if you already use SAP NetWeaver BW. You can then use a program that is specified in the SAP note to calculate the main memory requirement of SAP NetWeaver BW Accelerator from the existing SAP NetWeaver BW data. If you implement SAP NetWeaver BW Accelerator at the same time as SAP NetWeaver BW, you must use a T-shirt sizing, which is also described in SAP Note 917803.

Sizing

13.1.5 Overview of TREX Administration Tools

If the TREX tool that you operate is connected to an ABAP system, you can manage it via an ABAP-based administration tool (Transaction TREXADMIN). After you've called the transaction, you select the corresponding RFC connection to TREX to access the most essential administration functions.

TREXADMIN

These and other administration functions are also available in a separate administration tool, which is based on the Python API of TREX. You start the Python API directly on the computer where TREX is installed. In UNIX, you require an environment with a graphical interface (for instance, *X server*) to be able to start the administration tool; a row-based terminal program like *telnet* is not sufficient for this purpose. To log on, you require a suitable administration user, for instance, *<sapsid>adm*. With this user, you go to the TREX directory and start the administra-

Python API

tion tool using the command TREXAdmin.sh (Bourne shell) or TREXAdmin. csh (C-shell).

In Windows, select START • PROGRAMS or ALL PROGRAMS • SAP TREX • INSTANCE <INSTANCE NUMBER> • TOOLS • TREX ADMINISTRATION. Alternatively, in Windows Explorer you can start the *TREXAdmin.bat* file in the TREX directory.

The third option for managing TREX is to use commands in the operating system. However, we don't further discuss this option in this book.

The following sections use the menu paths and names of the administration functions in the ABAP-based administration tool. You won't have any problems finding the corresponding functions in the Python-based administration tool if required. If important functions are not available in the ABAP tool, reference is made to the Python-based administration tool.

TREX alert server TREX includes its own alert server — a process that continuously analyzes the TREX installation with regard to possible errors and problems. The result of the checks is displayed in the Alerts tab in the TREX administration tools (Transaction TREXADMIN and the separate administration tool) and in the central monitoring tool of CCMS. Alternatively, you can specify in the alert server that emails be sent in case of problems.

The alert server is automatically started on every computer with TREX services when TREX is started. You can view the status of the alert server in the service overview of TREX.

The checks that are run include the availability, performance, and consistency of the TREX installation. The checks are bundled in check sets. The Standard and HPA check sets (HPA stands for *High Performance Analytics* and refers to SAP NetWeaver BW Accelerator in this case) are included in the standard version. The following sections describe individual checks, which are particularly important in the context of performance analysis.

The presentation of the check results in the TREX administration tools comprises three areas: The Summary area, which provides a summary of the check results, the Current area, which summarizes the check results of the last check, and the History area, which displays the results of the previous checks.

If you operate TREX within the scope of a SAP NetWeaver BW Accelerator scenario, SAP NetWeaver BW provides Transaction RSDDBWAMON, which should be sufficient for the administration of TREX within SAP NetWeaver BW Accelerator.

SAP NetWeaver BW Accelerator–specific tools

The SAP NetWeaver BW Accelerator indexing is created in SAP NetWeaver BW in Transaction RSDDV, which can also be used for maintaining aggregates.

You can use the test environment for queries (Transaction RSRT) for examining the performance of queries that are run in SAP NetWeaver BW Accelerator. Some additional analysis options are available for this purpose.

SAP NetWeaver BW Check Transaction RSRV provides additional checks in the SAP NetWeaver BW Accelerator environment.

13.2 Implementing the Performance Analysis on TREX

The goal of the TREX performance analysis is to determine whether TREX has any performance issues and how any issues must be classified. In this context, consider the questions that came up in Chapter 3, Workload Analysis, and apply these specifically to TREX:

- ▶ Is there a general performance problem in TREX?
  - ▶ Are there overload situations in TREX?
  - ▶ Are the overload situations temporary or permanent?
  - ▶ Is there a hardware bottleneck?
  - ▶ Is there a performance problem due to a nonoptimal workload distribution between computers?
  - ▶ Is there a performance problem due to a nonoptimal temporal distribution of search queries and indexing queries; that is, does the performance problem arise because indexing queries are processed at times with high loads that are attributable to search queries?
  - ▶ Is there a performance problem due to a nonoptimal configuration?

609

▶ Is there a special performance problem in TREX, that is, a problem that emerges in very specific searches?

13.2.1 Monitoring the Utilization of the TREX Servers

Creating the Hardware Analysis

The hardware analysis examines whether a hardware bottleneck exists with regard to CPU, main memory, I/O, or network in one or more computers. Besides the tools provided by the hardware partners, you can implement the analysis using the operating system monitor of the ABAP server, which you can also use to monitor computers on which no ABAP instance runs. Chapter 2, Section 2.2, Hardware Monitoring, provides the relevant description of the analysis.

[+] If you determine that there's a bottleneck in the CPU, main memory, I/O, or network, this doesn't indicate that your TREX installation doesn't have sufficient hardware resources. Initially, you should run the other checks to see whether the hardware requirement can be reduced with optimization options.

In the TREX alert server, the following checks are implemented that send alerts in case of high hardware utilization:

▶ **CPU_usage**
Generates a warning in case of CPU usage of 70% and an error in case of usage of 90%.

▶ **Memory_usage**
Generates a warning in case of main memory usage of 70% and an error in case of usage of 90%.

▶ **Shared_memory**
Generates a warning in case of shared memory usage of 75% and an error in case of usage of 85%.

▶ **Disk_usage**
Checks the free disk space and generates a warning if less than 50GB is available and an error if the free space is less than 10GB. If this check sends an alert, you should first check if a high trace level was set and if the disk space is occupied by trace files.

Monitoring the Current Utilization of the TREX Servers

To monitor the utilization of the TREX server (or services), navigate to Transaction TREXADMIN in the Services tab (see Figure 13.2). There you can find a table of the TREX services with the information listed in Table 13.1.

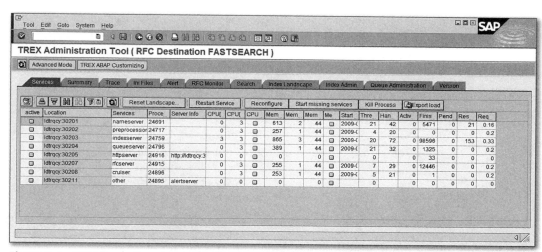

Figure 13.2 TREX Server Overview in the ABAP-Based Administration Tool (Transaction TREXADMIN)

Field	Explanation
Active	A green traffic light indicates that a service is active.
Location	Name of the computer and port to which the server answers.
Services	Type of service that runs the process: name server, index server, and so on.
Process-ID	Process identification: The process ID is important if you've identified an expensive process using the operating system monitor and now search for the corresponding application process.

Table 13.1 Fields of the TREX Server Overview

Field	Explanation
CPU – Process CPU in %	The process' CPU utilization in % since the last refresh of the monitor. You can refresh the values of the monitor by clicking the Refresh button above the server list.
CPU – Total CPU in %	CPU utilization of all processes on the corresponding computer, including the processes that don't belong to TREX.
CPU Usage	CPU workload caused by the process, displayed as a traffic light. The traffic light is green for a CPU workload of 0–70%, yellow for 71–85%, and red for more than 85%. In the Python TREX administration tool, this information is presented in a bar chart.
Memory Usage of this Process (in MB und in %)	Main memory that is allocated by the process, in MB and in %. The value includes both the memory that is held in the physical main memory and the paged memory.
Memory Usage of all Processes	Utilization of the physical main memory by all processes in the relevant computer.
Memory Usage	Main memory workload caused by the process, displayed as a traffic light. For the traffic light colors, the same threshold values apply as for the CPU.
Requests/Sec	Average number of requests per second.
Finished Request	Total number of requests since start.
Response Time	Average response time of the last requests in seconds.
Active Requests	Number of currently active requests.
Pending Requests	Number of pending requests.
Server Info	Additional details on the server.

Table 13.1 Fields of the TREX Server Overview (Cont.)

In combination with the data of the operating system monitor, you can now assess whether the services of TREX or other processes on the same computer cause a high CPU utilization or a high main memory utilization (paging).

You can determine the CPU utilization of TREX by simply adding up the values of the CPU – Process CPU in % column. You cannot determine the memory that is actually required by TREX simply by adding up the values of the Memory Usage of this Process column. Because the processes share memory areas, this value is an upper estimate of the memory actually required. You obtain the lower estimate through the value for the index server.

The Memory Usage of this Process value for the index server comprises the memory required for the procedures of the index server and the indexes that are currently held in the main memory. You can find the concrete value for the size of the indexes if you navigate to the Index Admin tab in the TREX administration tool and select the Index Info Summary function there. A dialog window opens where you can view the values for all indexes, the number of indexed documents, and the memory requirement on the hard disk and the estimated main memory requirement if all columns are loaded. In the screen below the Index Administration tab, you can also monitor the data on the size of the individual indexes. For this purpose, open the input help in the screen. The system displays a list of all indexes available. In the input help, select one, several, or all indexes (using the key combination Ctrl + A), and exit the input help by clicking the Continue button. The system now displays the status of the indexes, the estimated size in the main memory, the size in the hard disk, and further details for the indexes selected.

TREX collects the key performance key figures described in Table 13.1 and additional performance key figures in one-minute intervals for a period of one week. You can export this history of key figures to a local file in CSV format by clicking the Export load button in the TREX server overview and further analyze it in a spreadsheet program. Alternatively, you can visualize the data directly as graphics in the Python-based administration tool. There you can also find a description of the values. Table 13.2 describes the most critical values in the file.

Further performance key figures and history

Field (Display in the Python Tool)	Field (Column Name in the CSV File)	Explanation
Host	Host	Computer name.
Time	Time	Time stamp in one-minute intervals.
CPU	cpuUsed	CPU utilization in % (all processes).
Memory Used	memoryUsed	Size of the physical main memory used in KB (all processes).
Memory Size	memorySize	Size of the physical main memory in KB.
Disk Used	diskUsed	Size of the hard disk memory used in MB.
Disk Size	diskSize	Size of the hard disk memory in MB.
Swap In	swapIn	Swap-in rate in KB per minute.
Swap Out	swapOut	Swap-out rate in KB per minute.
Index Read Requests	searchCount	Internal number of search requests within one minute. A search request of a client can result in multiple internal search requests if multiple indexes are integrated in the search.
Index Read Time	searchTime	Runtime of the search requests within one minute in milliseconds. The average runtime in milliseconds for the search request results from the searchTime/searchCount ratio.
Index Write Requests	indexingCount	Number of indexing requests.
Index Write Time	indexingTime	Runtime of the indexing requests in milliseconds.
Index Merge Requests	mergeCount	Number of requests for the integration of the delta index with the main index.
Index Merge Time	countTime	Runtime of requests for the integration of the delta index with the main index.
Index Server Memory	indexserverMemory	Allocated main memory of the index server in KB.
Queue Server Memory	queueserverMemory	Allocated main memory of the queue server in KB.
RFC Server Memory	RFCserverMemory	Allocated main memory of the RFC server in KB.

Table 13.2 Fields of the TREX Workload Overview File

Based on these key figures, you can answer the following questions:

▶ If you observe a CPU or main memory bottleneck: Does this bottleneck lead to increased response times, or is the workload still tolerable?

▶ If you observe increased response times for search queries at specific times: Do increased response times occur in periods in which the number of indexing queries or queries for integrating the delta index with the main index is high? In this case you can consider finding a better distribution solution for the workload for indexing or integration. Section 13.3.5, Configuring Queue Servers, discusses this subject in detail.

In the administration tool, the screen in the Summary tab provides an overview of the most important key figures of TREX at a glance. There you can find, among other things, information on open alerts, memory utilization, and activity. This screen also indicates instantly whether traces have been activated. Normally, they should be deactivated.

[+]

13.2.2 Creating and Evaluating the Python Trace

You can use a Python trace to measure the time of individual queries on TREX. For use in the SAP NetWeaver BW Accelerator scenario, Transaction RSRV is available in the SAP NetWeaver BW system, which is discussed in Section 13.4, Indexing InfoCubes in SAP NetWeaver BW Accelerator.

To activate the Python trace, in the TREX administration tool navigate to the Trace tab, where you click the Set Python Trace button and then Add Trace. A dialog window opens where you specify the server, the user to which the trace is supposed to refer, and the scope of the trace. To log the search queries, select the index server. Enter the name of the trace file in the File Name input field. After you've completed your entries, click the Next button to exit the dialog window. The trace is now activated.

You can find the trace file under the name you specified in the trace list in the Trace tab. You can open the trace file and analyze it by double-clicking the file name. A recorded TREX search query starts with the following entry in the trace file:

```
# tracing searchTable call (thread 1233201472) at 2009-07-13
08:14:14.660
# ccms user 'SCHNEIDERT'
```

In this entry, you can determine the time stamp and the user. This is followed by the content of the actual search query. The entry in the trace file is concluded as follows:

```
# tracing searchTable result (thread 1233201472) at 2009-07-13
08:14:14.665
# found 200 of 1925 documents after 5ms (0ms)
```

This entry includes the number of documents found, the total number of documents in the index, and the TREX runtime.

Once a Python trace has been created, you can "replay" it. The Python-based administration tool provides a function for this purpose. It enables you to transfer the trace file and the indexes concerned to a test system where you can analyze the problem independent of the live operation. This procedure is particularly suitable if the SAP support team must analyze the problem.

[+] The screen in the Search tab of the TREX administration tool is provided to test individual search queries. In this screen, you can directly run a search for a TREX index. This function is of particular importance in combination with the trace.

13.3 Technical Optimization Options in Detail

This section presents the technical optimization options for TREX. These include:

▶ **Divide indexes**
Distribute a large index across multiple servers (in a distributed TREX installation).

▶ **Landscape reorganization**
By redistributing the index files to index servers, you can improve performance, particularly after you've added or deactivated index servers. This option is also relevant for SAP NetWeaver BW Accelerator.

▶ **Delta indexes**

Using delta indexes you can reduce the update time for indexing. Delta indexes are also used for SAP NetWeaver BW Accelerator; that is, the principles presented in this section also apply to SAP NetWeaver BW Accelerator. The SAP NetWeaver BW Accelerator administration offers its own maintenance functions that you should use instead of the ones presented in this section.

▶ **Master and slave index server**

The use of master and slave index servers enables you to separate the workload resulting from the index update from the workload resulting from the search queries.

▶ **Configure the queue server**

An appropriate parameterization enables you to distribute the workload for updating and optimizing indexes adequately. In SAP NetWeaver BW Accelerator, the queue server is not used; that is, this option is not relevant for SAP NetWeaver BW Accelerator. The indexing is completely controlled from SAP NetWeaver BW via the InfoProvider administration.

▶ **Distribution of preprocessing**

The appropriate configuration of the preprocessors enables you to specify how the workload is distributed in preprocessing.

Section 13.4, Indexing InfoCubes in SAP NetWeaver BW Accelerator, discusses SAP NetWeaver BW Accelerator–specific optimizations.

13.3.1 Dividing Indexes

If you operate TREX on multiple computers, it can be useful to divide large indexes and distribute them to several computers; that is, several index servers. For division, you create multiple physical indexes and one logical index that encloses the physical indexes.

To divide an index, select the Index Landscape tab in the TREX administration tool. Select an index, and then click the Divide/Merge Index button. A dialog window opens where you can specify the number of parts and the attribute based on which the division is supposed to be made. On the basis of the current utilization status, TREX decides how the index parts are to be distributed across the existing servers.

[**!**] Whether a manual division of an index makes sense depends on the scenario used. First, you should gather information about whether the manual division of indexes of a specific index type is allowed and useful for the application that you use. In the SAP NetWeaver BW Accelerator scenario, for example, the division is controlled automatically; that is, you should avoid any manual intervention in this case. Another example of a restriction is that a document index cannot be divided if you use text mining. Furthermore, prior to a manual division you should specify whether the size of the index causes any performance problem (for instance, due to corresponding traces). You should first test the division in a test system with regard to functionality and performance.

13.3.2 Reorganizing TREX

TREX assigns index files to index servers that load these files to the main memory of the relevant computer. This assignment is not changed automatically in the running operation. So in time, when indexes grow irregularly or if computers are added to or removed from the TREX system landscape, it may be possible that the CPU and main memory of individual computers are not used optimally. In this case, the assignment of index files to index servers can be optimized by reorganizing TREX.

The TREX alert server automatically checks whether reorganization is necessary; the alert details contain information about to what degree the required memory would be distributed more evenly.

TREX also creates an optimization plan. The only manual interaction of the administrator is to determine the appropriate time. During the reorganization, TREX doesn't recalculate the indexes, but only changes the distribution of the existing index files to the servers, which means index files are loaded from the hard disk to the main memory and temporary wait times occur for search queries. Indexing is interrupted; the indexes concerned are indicated with a yellow traffic light in the Index Landscape window.

In Transaction TREXADMIN in the expert mode (Advanced Mode button) you can find the result of the check of whether reorganization is necessary in the Target State/Next Reorg TABLE in the Reorg tab. With the Start Reorg button, you can start the reorganization immediately or at a specific time. For SAP NetWeaver BW Accelerator, you can also start a reorganization process from the SAP NetWeaver BW Accelerator monitor.

In the Python-based TREX administration tool under the Reorg function in the Summary, Plan, Usage by Service, and Usage by Index tabs, you can find more detailed information on the utilization and the suggested reorganization steps. In the Interactive Reorg and Options tabs, you can find parameters that impact the reorganization. For more information on this topic refer to the SAP help.

13.3.3 Using Delta Indexes

Initially, let's briefly discuss the difference between the terms *delta indexing* and *delta index*. Delta indexing means the periodic indexing of documents in TREX. The delta indexing is triggered by the corresponding application and can be performed with or without a delta index. The delta index is a technical utility to accelerate the delta indexing if the main index is too large and the index update takes too long.

Delta indexing

As mentioned previously, the index update is a very time-consuming process due to the high compression. To accelerate the update, you can create a delta index that includes the newly added data. The fact that the data is not compressed in a time-consuming process in the delta index has the result that the memory requirement per entry is considerably larger than in the main index. There are different implementations of the delta index: an older implementation as a simple list and a newer implementation as a B* tree index in the main memory. For a TREX restart, the delta indexes in the main memory are lost; they are rebuilt based on the delta log information that is stored in the hard disk.

Delta index

In a search query, the two indexes are searched in parallel. After a specific period of time, the delta index must be merged with the main index. In this merge process ("merge"), the system generates a copy of the main index and a new delta index that includes updates that occur during the merge so that TREX can constantly process both search and update queries — except for the short period of time when it needs to switch from one delta index to another.

Merge

Delta indexing is deactivated by default. The following rules apply to its activation:

▸ During the initial build of the index, or if a large quantity of data (compared to the data already indexed) is supposed to be indexed, a delta index doesn't make any sense.

▸ Delta indexing is recommended if the main index has reached a specific size. If the delta index is activated too early, this doesn't result in any performance gain. The threshold value for activation that SAP indicates in its online help is 100,000 to 1,000,000 documents or 500MB of data in the main index.

▸ In a distributed TREX system, the delta indexing not only accelerates the update of the main index, but it also enables a fast index replication with a low network load because only the delta index needs to be replicated.

▸ Only a small delta index accelerates the update. As of a specific size, the delta index must therefore be merged with the main index. In the integration process, TREX automatically creates a new delta index.

Activating the delta index

The delta index is deactivated by default. You can activate it for each index. Proceed as follows:

1. Start the TREX administration tool, and navigate to the Index Administration window.

2. Select the index for which you want to activate the delta index, and select Delta On.

[!] The use of delta indexes depends on the application used and its version. So before you activate the delta index, you should check whether the use makes sense for your scenario. SAP Note 1345777 provides further information and restrictions on the search enterprise service scenario.

[+] In the SAP NetWeaver BW Accelerator application scenario, you use the SAP NetWeaver BW Accelerator administration tool (Transaction RSD-DBWAMON) to activate delta indexes. For the search in the portal and KM, you can activate the delta index using the Python-based administration tool.

In the process for merging the delta index with the main index, TREX rewrites all files of the main index. The duration of the merge process depends on the size of the main index and can take a couple of minutes to several hours.

The merge process can be implemented manually or be time-controlled, either via the queue server or a TREX-internal scheduler (Python scheduler). The threshold value recommended by SAP to trigger an integration is 500MB. The Index Administration screen in the TREX administration tool indicates the size of the delta index. In the same screen, you can trigger the merge manually. For this purpose, select the index and then select Merge Index.

Alternatively, the queue server can trigger the integration periodically. For this purpose, set the Merge Time for Delta Index parameter for the corresponding queue. Section 13.3.5, Configuring Queue Servers, provides details on this topic. For more information on the Python scheduler refer to the SAP help.

13.3.4 Using Master and Slave Index Servers

So far, you've gotten to know two methods that are suitable to reduce the workload on the index server: the distribution of physical indexes across multiple index servers and the use of delta indexes. A third method is to use master and slave index servers to separate the workload caused by a change to the indexes from the workload caused by the search. In this scenario, the master index server only handles the update of indexes, whereas the search on copies of the indexes runs on the slave index server. You can create one or more slave index servers for each master index server.

To ensure a high availability design of TREX, you can also create a third type of index server — the backup index server. It assumes the job of one or more master index servers in case of failure.

You can link the master/slave scenario with decentralized or central data retention. For decentralized data retention, the master and the slave index server have separate file systems, and the replication of the index data from the master to the slave index server is performed via the network. For central data retention, however, the master and the slave index server access the same file system; that is, the master and the slave index are located on the same file system, there is no network traffic, and the replication is easier, as is outlined in the following. For central data retention, the central file system typically involves a Network Attached Storage Server (NAS Server) or a Storage Area Network (SAN) that must also ensure the high availability of data. A backup index server can only be set up in central data retention.

Replication In central data retention, the replication of the master index server to the slave index servers is as follows:

1. In the first replication, the master index server generates a snapshot of the index. The name server notifies the slave index servers, which request the snapshot of the index.

2. After the snapshot has been distributed across the slave index servers, they integrate the snapshot with their index. During this phase, the index is in the inactive status and is not available for the search.

3. For every subsequent replication, the master index server compares the current master index with the snapshot, determines the difference information, and updates the snapshot. The name server notifies the slave index servers, which now request the difference data.

4. Once the difference data has been distributed across the slave index servers, they integrate the difference data with their index. During this phase, the index is again in the inactive status and is not available for the search.

In decentralized data retention, the replication of the master index server to the slave index servers is as follows:

1. In the first replication, the master index server generates a snapshot of the index. The slave index server connects to the snapshot and uses it as the slave index.

2. In the second replication, the master index server generates a second snapshot to which the slave index server switches.

3. For every subsequent replication, the master index server compares the current master index with the snapshot that is not used by slave index servers at this time, determines the difference data, and updates

the snapshot. Then the slave index servers switch to the updated snapshot.

These two process descriptions indicate that the replication is considerably more time-consuming for the decentralized data retention and leads to a longer interruption of the search service.

In both cases, the time consumed for the replication is reduced because a delta index is used.

You can find the following administration functions in a separate TREX **[+]** administration tool. In the ABAP-based administration tool (Transaction TREXADMIN) in the advanced mode in the Landscape tab, you can find a display function for the existing configuration.

The replication can be triggered manually or automatically. We recommend starting the first replication manually and then configuring an automatic replication.

Triggering the replication

You can trigger the manual replication as follows:

1. In the TREX administration tool navigate to the Index Landscape window.

2. Then select Replicate All to replicate all indexes, or select only one index and select Replicate Index in the context menu.

There are various options to configure an automatic replication. If you want to ensure that an index is replicated immediately after an update, you can configure this process as follows:

1. In the TREX administration tool navigate to the LANDSCAPE • CONFIGURATION • INDEX window.

2. Select the Autoreplication checkbox to activate the automatic replication.

Additional options to trigger the replication include the following:

▶ You can set the queue parameter Replicate after Optimization. Section 13.3.5, Configuring Queue Servers, provides details on the configuration of the queue server. This parameter causes a replication, but only for index changes that were initiated by the queue server.

▶ You can set the queue parameter Replication Time (time control). This option is only suitable if the replication is not time-critical and is supposed to be run when the workload on TREX is low.

▶ You can use the Python scheduler. Details are available in the SAP documentation.

Finally, let's get to know two configuration parameters that you can use to control the replication load and the search behavior during the replication.

With the configuration parameter Replication Threads, you can determine how many indexes can be replicated in parallel. You can set this parameter in the TREX administration tool in the Landscape Configuration window.

With the parameter Search Version, you can control how fast the system switches to the updated version of the index in the replication process. If you select Majority, the system switches when the current version is available on at least half of the slave index servers. This is the default setting. If you select latest, the system switches as soon as a more current version is available on the master index server. As long as no slave index server has the current version, search queries are sent to the master index server even if it is not responsible for search queries. This setting ensures that search queries always run on the latest version of the index, but it can lead to performance problems because search queries must be answered temporarily by the master index server alone. You can set the Search Version parameter for all future master indexes in the Landscape Configuration window. For existing indexes, this parameter is available in the Index Landscape window. Select an index there, and then select Landscape Configuration IN THE CONTEXT MENU.

13.3.5 Configuring Queue Servers

The queue parameters specify when the queue server triggers the indexing of documents and their incorporation into the index. Moreover, they specify the modalities of automatic index replication and the automatic integration of the delta index with the main index. Using an optimizing configuration of the queue parameters, you can avoid overload situations in TREX.

When an index is created, the application determines whether a queue is supposed to be created or not. It uses the default settings for the queue parameter that apply to all queues. You can change the parameters for individual queues in the TREX administration tool under QUEUE ADMINISTRATION • SET QUEUE PARAMETER.

Table 13.3 provides a list of the queue parameters (the SAP help provides the exact Syntax of the entries allowed). To better understand the parameters, let's first define the terms *indexing* and *optimization,* which are associated with the index update. *Indexing* means the transfer of data from the queue server to the index server. Initially, the data is temporarily stored in the index server and is not contained in the index. The complexity increases linearly with the quantity of data. *Optimization* is the incorporation of data in the index so that it becomes visible and searchable there. If a data quantity x is sent in n packages to the index server, and every package is immediately optimized there, the complexity increases quadratically with the number of packages. So you should ensure that only a few and rather large packages are sent and that as many packages as possible are optimized jointly and not individually, unless the package would be very large anyway. Thus, the time effort is more in the optimization and less in the indexing.

Queue parameters

Parameter	Explanation
Schedule Type	Start condition for indexing. The following values are possible: ▶ Time: The indexing is supposed to be run time-controlled. The queue server is supposed to trigger indexing at specific times or at specific intervals. You define the schedule using the Schedule Time parameter. ▶ Count: The indexing is supposed to be run quantity-controlled. The queue server is supposed to trigger indexing as soon as a specific number of documents has been collected in the queue. You define the number using the Schedule Max Docs parameter. ▶ Both: The indexing is supposed to be run controlled by time or quantity, depending on which start condition is met first.

Table 13.3 Parameters for Controlling the Index Update and Optimization

Parameter	Explanation
Schedule Time	Schedule according to which the queue server triggers indexing. You have two options. You can either specify points in time, for instance, All(0:00): Indexing is executed every day at midnight; or Mon(0,6:15,20): Indexing is executed every Monday at 6:15 a.m. and at 8:00 p.m. Alternatively, you can specify time intervals, such as All-0:30: Indexing is run every 30 minutes. This parameter is only evaluated if Schedule Type is set to Time or Both.
Schedule Max Documents	Number of documents the queue server collects before it triggers indexing. This parameter is only evaluated if Schedule Type is set to Count or Both.
Transmit Bulk Size	Maximum number of documents that are indexed at once. If more documents are queued for indexing, the queue server distributes them to subsequent indexing runs.
Max Size of Index Bulk	Maximum quantity of data (in bytes) that is indexed at once. The duration of indexing depends on the documents' size. If documents have a size of several MB, the indexing takes longer. Therefore, the parameter specifies an upper limit for the data quantity. If the documents exceed this limit, the queue server distributes them accordingly.
Optimize Bulk Size	Specifies after how many indexing runs the queue server triggers optimization. In the optimization phase, the index server rebuilds the index. It adds new documents to the index, removes deleted documents from the index, and optimizes the index structure so that the search queries can be processed as fast as possible. As long as the optimization runs, the queue server doesn't trigger any other indexing. It waits until optimization is completed.
Initial Indexing Mode	Specifies the optimization behavior for large data quantities to be indexed. The setting On ensures that the index server doesn't optimize until a larger amount of documents has been indexed. If you choose Off, the index server may also optimize smaller document quantities.
Merge Time for Delta Index	Schedule according to which the queue server triggers the requests for integrating the delta index with the main index. The same syntax as for the Schedule Time parameter is used.
Replication Time	Schedule according to which the queue server triggers the index replication. The same syntax as for the Schedule Time parameter is used.
Replicate After Synchronize	Specifies whether the master index server replicates directly after an update (as an alternative to setting the Replication Time parameter).

Table 13.3 Parameters for Controlling the Index Update and Optimization (Cont.)

Parameter	Explanation
Max Retry Count	Number of retries in case of failed processing steps before the queue server ultimately classifies a step as failed. A retry of processing can be useful, for example, for the indexing of external websites that are temporarily not available due to an overload of the Web server.
Trace Level	Information about which type of message is supposed to be written to the trace file. The following values are possible: ▶ FATAL: Only log serious errors that may jeopardize the system ▶ ERROR: Log all errors additionally ▶ WARNING: Log warnings additionally ▶ INFO: Log current activities additionally ▶ DEBUG: Log further debug information additionally Increasing the trace level may lead to a significant growth of the trace file and space issues in the file system. Simultaneously, the logging of data reduces the performance of TREX.

Table 13.3 Parameters for Controlling the Index Update and Optimization (Cont.)

13.3.6 Distributing the Preprocessing (Configuring the Preprocessor)

Up to now, we've paid special attention to the optimization of the workload on the index server through distributed index servers, master and slave index servers, delta indexes, and the time control of the index update by the queue server. The main focus of performance monitoring must be on the index server.

However, in specific usage scenarios the preprocessing of the documents to be indexed by the preprocessor can be a resource-intensive activity, so the preprocessing can be distributed in such cases.

As discussed in Section 13.1.3, Architecture of TREX, the preprocessor in the text search environment is involved both in indexing and in search queries. For a preprocessor, you can initially specify which type of queries are supposed to be processed. In Search mode it is supposed to be involved only in search queries; the Index mode defines the responsibility for indexing queries, and the Any mode indicates that

Preprocessor modes

the preprocessor may process both types of queries. Note that the system ignores these configuration parameters if no suitable preprocessor is available for the type of query selected. Then a search query is assigned to a preprocessor with the Index configuration and vice versa.

Preprocessor capacity

The preprocessor capacity is defined by the number of preprocessors per computer and the number of threads per preprocessor. SAP help recommends configuring a maximum of one preprocessor per CPU and a maximum of three threads per preprocessor on one computer. In this case, you can utilize the full computer performance for preprocessing if required. If other services run on this server, the capacity must be reduced accordingly.

Every preprocessor has its own main memory area. The more preprocessors you start, the higher the main memory requirement is.

To enable a queue server to exploit the full capacity of the preprocessors, you must configure the *pool size* there. This specifies how many preprocessor threads a queue server can address in parallel, so the pool size must be set to the same value as the number of preprocessor threads.

The assignment of a document to a preprocessor is as follows:

1. The queue server starts a quantity of preprocessor clients; the number is defined by the pool size. If a document is queued for preprocessing, the queue server transfers it to a preprocessor client.

2. The preprocessor client requests a preprocessor from the name server. The name server returns the name of the preprocessor with the lowest number of accesses.

3. The preprocessor client transfers the document to the preprocessor. While it waits, it doesn't receive any other documents from the queue server.

4. As soon as the document is processed, the preprocessor sends a confirmation to the preprocessor client and to the queue server. The queue server can now distribute the documents to the preprocessor client.

13.4 Indexing InfoCubes in SAP NetWeaver BW Accelerator

The criteria according to which the indexing of an InfoCube in SAP NetWeaver BW Accelerator can achieve a decisive performance improvement for the queries are based on the query performance analysis key figures presented in Chapter 12, Section 12.2, Analysis of Expensive BW Queries. They correspond closely to the criteria for creating aggregates:

Criteria for indexing in SAP NetWeaver BW Accelerator

▶ High database response times relative to both the entire response time (>30%), and the absolute response time (>3 seconds)

▶ High number of selected records (>10,000) and a high ratio of selected to transferred records (>10)

Take into account that SAP NetWeaver BW replaces the database access; that is, it can only optimize this part. SAP NetWeaver BW Accelerator won't achieve any improvement if the majority of the response time occurs in the SAP NetWeaver BW server itself, for instance, as CPU time or even in the frontend application, because complex calculations are made, for example. SAP NetWeaver BW Accelerator won't ensure any significant runtime reduction if the database time is high because a large number of data records are transferred to the SAP NetWeaver BW server. In these cases, you must start with the optimization in the SAP NetWeaver BW server or the corresponding application. As an example, Chapter 12, Optimizing Queries to SAP NetWeaver Business Warehouse, discussed the case that a query reads all data in the first call.

Thanks to the optimizations described, the execution of a query in SAP NetWeaver BW Accelerator is 10 to 100 times faster than in an InfoCube and frequently faster than in an aggregate. It is important to understand that SAP NetWeaver BW Accelerator doesn't store any aggregates but calculates the aggregation at runtime. So in comparison to aggregates, SAP NetWeaver BW Accelerator has the following benefits:

SAP NetWeaver BW Accelerator versus aggregates

▶ SAP NetWeaver BW Accelerator can accelerate all possible accesses to the InfoCube with only one indexing. Aggregates, by contrast, only optimize individual navigation steps of queries. You can therefore achieve higher user satisfaction.

▶ The SAP NetWeaver BW Accelerator indexing of an InfoCube requires — just like aggregates — memory space in the hard disk and space in the main memory of TREX or in the main memory of the database server to execute the query. However, the space requirement of the SAP NetWeaver BW Accelerator indexing is small compared to the size of the InfoCube. You've already learned that the number of possible aggregates grows exponentially with the number of characteristics. Therefore, the space requirement for aggregates will usually exceed the space requirement for SAP NetWeaver BW Accelerator indexing.

▶ Selecting and monitoring the appropriate aggregates is a time-consuming administration process that requires valuable resources. The administration of SAP NetWeaver BW Accelerator is considerably easier.

So SAP NetWeaver BW Accelerator is particularly suitable if the optimization cannot be achieved using a few specific aggregates or if the utilization of InfoCubes fluctuates greatly so that no reliable statement can be made about which navigation steps the users perform.

If an InfoCube has been indexed in SAP NetWeaver BW Accelerator, the OLAP processor doesn't use aggregates in parallel in SAP NetWeaver BW.

Creating an SAP NetWeaver BW Accelerator Index

To open the SAP NetWeaver BW Accelerator index administration of an InfoCube, proceed as follows:

1. From the SAP NetWeaver BW Administrator Workbench (Transaction RSA1), double-click the InfoProvider and select the Maintain BW Accelerator menu option in the context menu (right-click). Alternatively, select an InfoCube in Transaction RSDDV, and start the wizard by clicking the BWA Index button.

2. If no SAP NetWeaver BW Accelerator index has been created for the InfoCube, the wizard asks whether you want to create an index. For an affirmative answer, click the Continue button. The wizard creates the index in SAP NetWeaver BW Accelerator.

3. In the second step of the wizard, you can fill the index. Whereas the creation of the (empty) index in the first step is done immediately, the filling process can consume a lot of time (several minutes to hours). This action is therefore executed by a background program. If you click Continue, the system opens a dialog window where you specify the start condition of the job. When you save your entry, you return to the wizard, which now displays the message that the job has been scheduled successfully.

4. After you've successfully completed the filling process, the traffic light color in the Index Info tab switches to green. The OLAP processor can now use the SAP NetWeaver BW Accelerator index.

5. To exit the wizard, click the End Maintenance button.

6. You can find an overview of all SAP NetWeaver BW Accelerator indexes in Transaction RSDDV via the BWA Indexes button. This list includes, among other things, the technical name of the index in TREX, the activation and fill status, and the number of entries in the index.

The maintenance wizard also provides the following additional functions:

Other functions

▶ **Delete Index**
Provided that an index has already been defined and filled for an Info-Cube, you can use the wizard to delete the index.

▶ **Fill Index**
Provided that an index has already been defined for an InfoCube but hasn't been filled yet, you can use the wizard to fill the index.

▶ **Logs**
Via the Application Logs button, you can have the system display the logs of the administration processes. Logs are provided for initial filling, update (roll-up), compression, deletion, change run, and checks, provided that these processes have been executed.

▶ **Properties**
As soon as you've defined an index for an InfoCube, you can click the Index Properties button to display and change the properties of the index.

SAP NetWeaver
BW Accelerator
indexes for
Polestar
To generate SAP NetWeaver BW Accelerator indexes that are optimized for use by the SAP BusinessObjects Polestar program, you are provided with a separate wizard in Transaction RSDDV.

Checking and Switching Off the SAP NetWeaver BW Accelerator Indexing

The test environment for SAP NetWeaver BW queries (Transaction RSRT) provides some options for checking the efficiency of SAP NetWeaver BW Accelerator indexing:

▶ You also use the OTHERS • DISPLAY STATISTICS DATA and DO NOT USE CACHE OPTIONS for performance analysis of SAP NetWeaver BW Accelerator indexing because a query is preferably answered from the OLAP cache in the case of SAP NetWeaver BW Accelerator indexing.

▶ You use the SAP NetWeaver BW Accelerator SERVER • DO NOT USE BWA INDEX option to create comparable performance measurements for the execution of a query with or without SAP NetWeaver BW Accelerator indexing.

▶ The Performance Measurement (TREX Times) option enables you to have TREX create advanced performance statistics.

After you've activated SAP NetWeaver BW Accelerator indexing, you can determine in the single-record statistics and in the workload monitor that the database response times drastically decrease for the relevant InfoCubes. You can find RFC response times instead that represent the runtime of the query in TREX.

If SAP NetWeaver BW Accelerator has processed a query, you can find the name of the InfoCube with an appended $X indicator in the SAP NetWeaver BW statistics tables in the AGGREGATES field of the RSDDSTAT_DM view.

Switching off
To switch off an SAP NetWeaver BW Accelerator index for use in the query execution to determine, for example, the resulting performance changes, select the BW ACCELERATOR • INDEX SETTING • SWITCH ON/OFF BWA INDEXES FOR QUERIES function in the SAP NetWeaver BW Accelerator administration (Transaction RSDDBWAMON).

Maintaining SAP NetWeaver BW Accelerator Indexes

After each delta load of data into the SAP NetWeaver BW system, you must update the SAP NetWeaver BW Accelerator index. In this process, SAP NetWeaver BW Accelerator behaves like an aggregate toward the SAP NetWeaver BW system; that is, the administration functions described in the Maintaining Aggregates subsection of Chapter 12, Section 12.3.6, Aggregates, are also used in the SAP NetWeaver BW Accelerator case.

SAP NetWeaver BW stores separate statistics on the performance of roll-up in SAP NetWeaver BW Accelerator in the tables RSDDSTSTTREX and RSDDSTSTTREXSERV if the Sap NetWeaver BW statistics are activated (see Chapter 12, Section 12.2, Analysis of Expensive BW Queries).

If the index update takes too long, you can optimize it using two options:

▶ If the update on TREX takes a long time and the index is large, you can reduce the update time by creating a delta index.

▶ If the data retrieval in SAP NetWeaver BW takes a long time, you can further parallelize the update run. The corresponding parameters are available in the SAP NetWeaver BW Accelerator administration (Transaction RSDDBWAMON) in the BW ACCELERATOR • INDEX SETTING • CHANGE GLOBAL PARAMETERS function.

For SAP NetWeaver BW Accelerator you don't create delta indexes via the TREX administration tools (as previously described). Instead, proceed as follows:

Creating and monitoring a delta index in SAP NetWeaver BW Accelerator

1. Select the BW ACCELERATOR • INDEX SETTING • SET DELTA INDEX function in the SAP NetWeaver BW Accelerator administration (Transaction RSDDBWAMON).

2. A dialog window opens where you set the activation indicator in the Delta Index column. As a result, a delta index is created and filled with the next index update.

If you've created a delta index, you must periodically check whether the delta index is supposed to be integrated with the main index. For this case as well, SAP NetWeaver BW provides a separate check as an alternative to the TREX administration already presented:

1. In the check transaction of SAP NetWeaver BW (Transaction RSRV) under BW ACCELERATOR • BW ACCELERATOR PERFORMANCE, select the Size of Delta Index check.

2. To integrate the delta index with the main index, select Correct Error TO SWITCH TO THE CHANGE MODE. You can then implement the integration.

Alternatively, you can use the RSDDTREX_DELTAINDEX_MERGE program.

Compressing the fact table

The SAP NetWeaver BW Accelerator index, unlike the fact tables of the InfoCube and the fact tables of aggregates, is not compressed by merging the load requests. So if the InfoCube is greatly compressed, the number of entries in the fact table is lower than the number of fact entries in the SAP NetWeaver BW Accelerator index. If this difference becomes large, you can achieve the compression in the SAP NetWeaver BW Accelerator index only by building the index completely anew. A corresponding check exists in the TREX alert server. This check compares the number of entries in the fact table with the number of fact entries in the SAP NetWeaver BW Accelerator index.

Change run

Changes to the master data and hierarchies must be applied in the SAP NetWeaver BW Accelerator index.

13.5 Summary

To optimize search queries, TREX offers the following strengths:

▶ Strong compression so the indexed data can be read quickly

▶ In the attribute search and in the SAP NetWeaver BW Accelerator scenario: storage of data in columns so that only those columns that are actually searched for need to be read — in contrast to row-based storage in databases, where the system must read entire rows in the main memory (database buffer)

▶ Partitioning of indexes, distribution of the parts to different servers, and parallelization of queries

In the TREX performance analysis, you must initially ensure that no main memory or CPU bottleneck occurs. The TREX architecture is designed in such a way that it always completely loads the index parts required into the main memory and doesn't displace them flexibly from the main memory like a database. For the analysis, you use the operating system monitor and the TREX server overview.

In the event of an unfavorable distribution of indexes to the index servers in a distributed TREX installation, TREX proactively creates reorganization suggestions, which you should implement in due time.

You can optimize performance during the data loading process by either of two measures: using the delta indexes or configuring the queue server that controls the update. However, the queue server and the delta indexes are not used or supported in some application scenarios.

You can separate the workload that accumulates due to the index update from the workload that is generated by the search queries. For this purpose, you can configure master and slave index servers that process update or search queries separately.

In the SAP NetWeaver BW Accelerator scenario, you can conduct indexing in TREX for each InfoCube. Comparable to aggregates — or, in other words, as an alternative — you must then integrate the TREX indexes with the data load process.

Background: The Future of Databases

Scientists from the Hasso Plattner Institute in Potsdam, Germany, and from SAP have continuously developed the idea of SAP NetWeaver BW Accelerator and examined the option to store business documents directly in a column-based database (TREX) and thus omit the traditional redundant data stores for OLTP and OLAP purposes. Additional core concepts of this approach include the following:

▶ Data is stored on a column basis using "lightweight" compression algorithms.

▶ Data is retained in the main memory (in-memory computing). In this context, the concept relies on the continued price decline of main memories.

> ▶ Indexes and materialized aggregates are omitted. Search queries and aggregates are always calculated at runtime. The corresponding procedures are available in the database (TREX), are optimized for the processor technology used, and are run in parallel. Here, the concept is based on the availability of computers with parallel processors (multicore, multithread architectures, see Chapter 2, Monitoring Hardware, Databases, and SAP Basis).
>
> ▶ The concept makes a virtue of the necessity that changes are performance-critical in the column-based, compressed storage of data: Changes to data are only implemented via the insert process (insert-only approach). For data records that have already been inserted, you can only change the status retroactively. With this concept, the database has a complete change history; that is, explicit change histories like the ones provided by many business documents become superfluous. At runtime, users can access any status of data in the past that taps completely new application fields.
>
> If you're interested in this concept, you can obtain additional information from the Hasso Plattner Institute website at *http://epic.hpi.uni-potsdam.de/Home/MemoryBasedDataMgmt.*

Important Concepts

After studying this chapter, you should be familiar with the following concepts:

▶ Compression techniques: dictionary coding and difference coding

▶ Vertical decomposition and partitioning

▶ Delta indexing and delta index (difference!)

▶ TREX services: name server, index server, preprocessor, and queue server

▶ Master index server, slave index server, and backup index server

Questions

1. Which activities are important to obtaining good performance for TREX queries?

   a) You must ensure that no CPU bottleneck or main memory bottleneck (paging) exists.

b) The TREX data buffer should achieve a read quality of at least 98%, or at least 99% in the SAP NetWeaver BW Accelerator scenario.

c) In a distributed TREX installation, the distribution of indexes to the index servers may not be optimal; in this case, you should promptly initiate a redistribution of indexes to index servers (reorganization).

d) In the SAP NetWeaver BW Accelerator scenario you must make sure that the SAP NetWeaver BW statistics for InfoCubes that are indexed in SAP NetWeaver BW Accelerator are activated so that TREX calculates the correct aggregates in the SAP NetWeaver BW Accelerator scenario.

Appendices

A Performance Analysis Roadmaps and Checklists

Appendix A contains the most important procedure roadmaps and checklists for performance analysis of SAP-based software components.

The prerequisites for performing an analysis are as follows:

- The component starts without error.

- Sufficient work processes are still available to run the performance analysis.

- If there are no available work processes, you can call the SAP auxiliary program dpmon. This program is called on the operating system level and enables you to access basically the same information as is found in the work process overview.

The checklists for performance analysis contain references to other sections in this book that explain available optimization options. Please ensure that you carefully consider the explanatory and cautionary notes in these sections before making any changes to your system.

[+]

A.1 Roadmaps

The roadmaps in this section explain how to proceed through the most important performance monitors. The following key explains the icons that appear in the procedure roadmaps (see Figures A.1 through A.12):

- **Rectangular monitor icon**
  Tells you to start a particular performance monitor.

- **Question mark icon**
  Indicates that you are at a decision point. If you can answer the question beside this icon with "Yes," then you may proceed as described in the next line of the roadmap.

▶ **Exclamation mark icon**
   Indicates the intermediate status of the analysis. Proceed to the next point on the roadmap.

▶ **Horizontal arrow icon**
   Indicates another procedure roadmap. Continue the analysis in the roadmap indicated.

▶ **Tools icon**
   Indicates possible solutions for performance problems. (See also the checklists for performance analysis in the next section.)

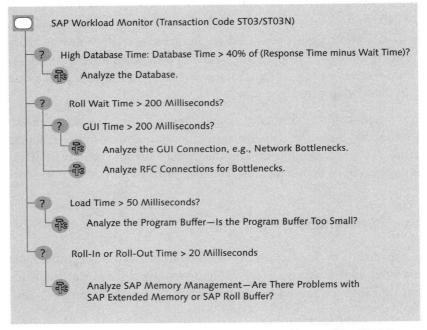

Figure A.1 Workload Analysis I: General Performance Problems on the ABAP Server

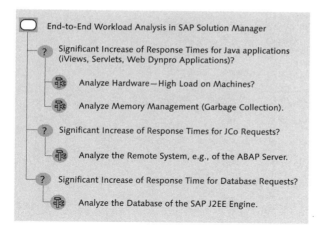

Figure A.2   Workload Analysis II: General Performance Problems on the SAP J2EE Engine

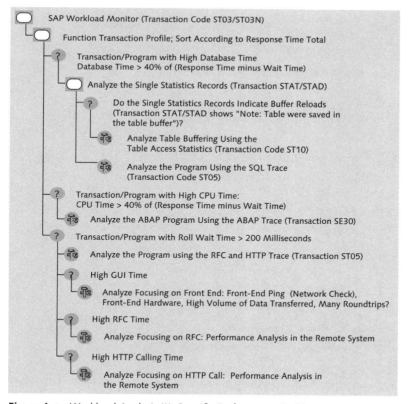

Figure A.3   Workload Analysis III: Specific Performance Problems (ABAP)

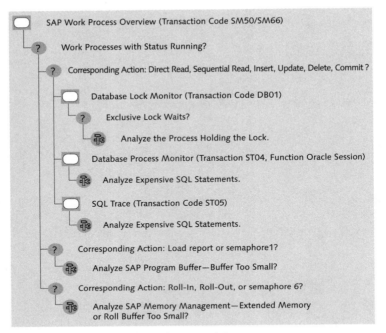

Figure A.4   Detailed Analysis of SAP Work Processes

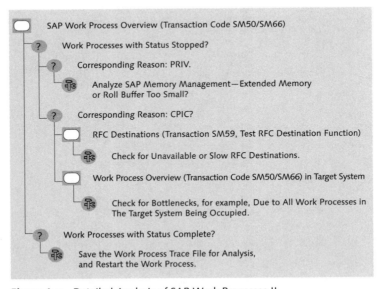

Figure A.5   Detailed Analysis of SAP Work Processes II

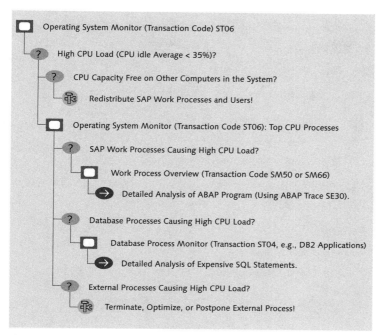

Figure A.6 Detailed Analysis of a Hardware Bottleneck (CPU)

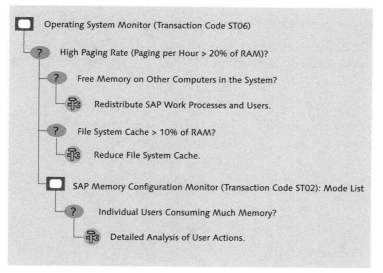

Figure A.7 Detailed Analysis of a Hardware Bottleneck (Main Memory)

645

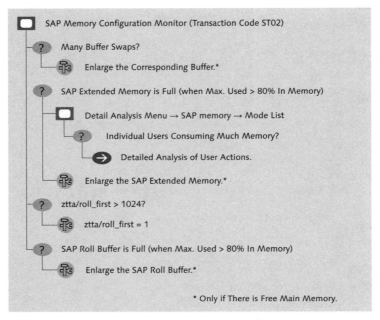

Figure A.8   Detailed Analysis of SAP Memory Configuration

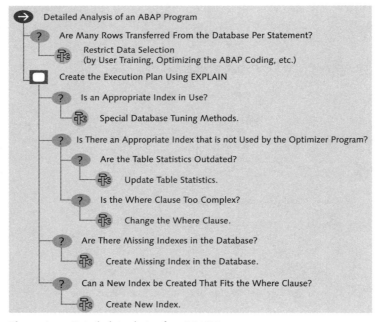

Figure A.9   Detailed Analysis of an ABAP Program

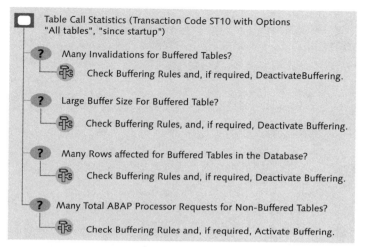

Figure A.10 Optimization of Table Buffering

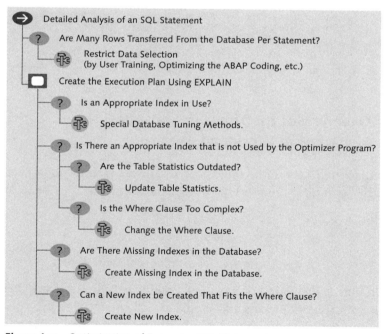

Figure A.11 Optimization of Expensive SQL Statements

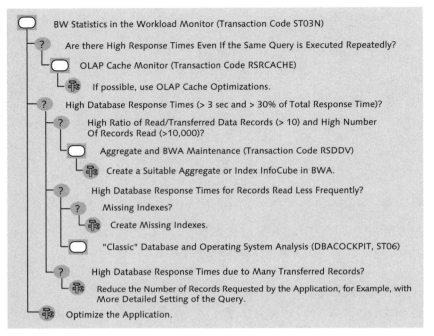

Figure A.12 Optimization of Expensive SAP NetWeaver BW Statements (BW Queries)

A.2 Overview of the Times in Statistics Records and Workload Monitor

For the times indicated in the single-record statistics (Transaction STAD) and in the workload monitor (ST03N), the following relationships apply:

The time in the work process is calculated as follows:

Time in work process = response time – wait time – roll wait time

The wait time is the period of time that a query waits in the dispatcher queue for a free work process and should actually be referred to as dispatcher wait time because there are many more wait situations in the system. The roll wait time occurs if a running program is rolled out from the work process because it waits for the response of a communication partner for an RFC or HTTP communication.

The processing time is defined as follows:

Processing time = response time – wait time – roll wait time – roll-in time – load and generation time – database time – DB procedure time

The processing time therefore excludes all times when the program waits for the work process, is rolled-in to the work process, is loaded or generated, and waits for the database, an RFC, or an HTTP call. In other words, this is the time in which the work process executes the program (excluding the SQL statements contained in the program, stored procedures, RFCs, and HTTP calls).

Usually, this relation applies:

Processing time > CPU time

This rule can be violated in individual cases because CPU is required in the work process during the roll-in, loading, and generation and during the database call, and the CPU time therefore runs in these times as well.

Another rule is that a large difference between processing time and CPU time should result in a detailed analysis (see Chapter 3, Section 3.3.2, Interpreting Response Times).

For the roll wait time, this relation applies:

RFC time + GUI time + HTTP time > roll wait time

RFC time, GUI time, and HTTP time (calling time in the HTTP area) are gross times for an RFC, an RFC to GUI, or an HTTP call. They comprise the setup of communication, data transfer, and the roll-out and roll-in, respectively. The roll wait time, however, is the net time that the system waited for the communication partner. Note that a role wait time can occur in an RFC but doesn't have to (Chapter 6, Section 6.3, Remote Function Calls (RFCs), and Chapter 7, Section 7.1, SAP GUI).

The response time that a user actually perceives in SAP GUI results from the following formula:

SAP GUI response time = response time + frontend time

The SAP GUI response time is not explicitly indicated in the single-record statistics and workload monitor. Also note that the frontend time (FE net time) cannot always be determined and can therefore equal zero in individual cases (SAP Note 679918).

The entire time for communication with the SAP GUI results from:

Frontend time + GUI time

The GUI time is part of the response time; the frontend time is not part of it (Chapter 7, Section 7.1, SAP GUI).

Only in transactions in the SAP GUI, a time for the communication with the frontend can be indicated in the single-record statistics and the workload monitor. Other UI technologies, such as Web UI or the Excel-based SAP BEx Web analyzer, use other analysis methods (Chapter 7, Section 7.3, Analyses on the Presentation Server, and Chapter 12, Section 12.2, Analysis of Expensive BW Queries).

One specific detail occurs when an RFC calls another RFC. To avoid double counts, the roll wait time is subtracted from the response time in the calling remote function.

A.3   Checklists

This section contains problem checklists, that is, short summaries for individual problems that are frequently identified in performance analysis. Each checklist identifies the priority of the problem, provides indications and procedures for finding and analyzing the problem, gives applicable solutions and references to portions of this book relevant to the problem, points out essential reading before attempting to solve the problem, and furnishes a boxed reminder.

The checklists suggest the following priorities:

▸ **Very high**
Reserved for when there is a danger that performance problems will soon cause a system standstill and there are no longer sufficient free work processes available to analyze or solve the problem. The only alternative is to stop the software component.

▸ **High**

Problems that are likely to drastically reduce system-wide performance.

▸ **Medium**

Problems that are likely to drastically reduce the performance of individual programs or application servers. Do not underestimate the impact of these problems on critical business processes or the possibility of the problem escalating.

▸ **Low**

Do not list performance problems with a low priority in the checklists.

Detailed Analysis of Hardware Resources (Transaction ST06)

Problem: CPU Bottleneck Due to High Resource Consumption from Individual Processes	
Priority	Medium to high.
Indications and procedures	A computer has less than 20% CPU capacity available. Check this using the Top CPU Processes function in the operating system monitor. To access this function, use Transaction ST06 and select DETAIL ANALYSIS MENU • TOP CPU PROCESSES. The new screen shows individual processes that consume considerable CPU resources over long periods of time.
Solution	▸ Use the work process overview (Transaction SM50 or SM66) to identify the SAP work process, the program, and the user; then analyze the program or reschedule it.
	▸ Identify the Java process in the process overview in the SAP Management Console; then analyze the program.
	▸ Identify the database processes in the database process monitor (for example, ST04, Detailed Analysis menu, Oracle Session [for an Oracle database]), and optimize the corresponding SQL statement.
	▸ For external processes with high CPU utilization, optimize or terminate them.
See	Chapter 2, Section 2.2, Hardware Monitoring.

Problem: CPU Bottleneck Due to Nonoptimal Load Distribution	
Priority	Medium: This problem can lead to high response times on specific computers.
Indications and procedures	In a distributed system with multiple computers, you detect a hardware bottleneck on at least one computer, whereas other computers still have available, unused resources.
Solution	Redistribute the SAP work processes, after which you may need to reset the associated virtual memory areas, buffers, and user distribution.
See	Chapter 2, Section 2.2, Hardware Monitoring, and Chapter 6, Workload Distribution and Interfaces.

Problem: Main Memory Bottleneck	
Priority	Medium to high: This problem can lead to high response times on specific computers.
Indications and procedures	A computer displays high paging rates, which are especially critical for increased CPU usage. Calculate the main memory allocated by SAP instances and the database, and compare it with the physically available main memory on the individual computers. If the allocated memory exceeds the physically available main memory by more than 50%, and there are high paging rates, you have a main memory bottleneck.
See	Chapter 2, Section 2.2, Hardware Monitoring.

Detailed Analysis of SAP Work Processes (Transactions SM50, SM66)

Problem: Terminated Work Processes	
Indications and procedures	In the local work process overview (Transaction SM50), if you detect numerous terminated work processes (indicated as complete in the Status column) and find that you cannot restart them, it is likely that there is a problem with the R/3 kernel or with logging on to the database.

Problem: Terminated Work Processes	
Solution	Check whether the SAP kernel version is up-to-date by calling Transaction SM51 and selecting Release Info. Refer to the SAP Service Marketplace for relevant SAP Notes or contact SAP Support.
See	Chapter 2, Section 2.5, Analyzing SAP Work Processes.

Problem: Work Processes Stuck in Private Mode or in Roll-In/Roll-Out	
Priority	Medium to high: This problem can lead to high response times on specific computers.
Indications and procedures	More than 20% of the work processes are indicated in the work process overview (Transaction SM50 or SM66) as being in PRIV mode or in roll-in or roll-out.
Solution	The problem is in SAP memory management. Correctly set the parameters of SAP memory management, for example, em/initial_size_MB, rdisp/ROLL_SHM, ztta/roll_extension. See also the checklist Extended Memory Is Too Small in this section.
See	Chapter 2, Section 2.5, Analyzing SAP Work Processes, and Section 2.4, Analyzing SAP Memory Configuration.

Problem: Deactivated Update Service	
Priority	Very high: This problem can cause a standstill in the SAP system.
Indications and procedures	All update work processes (indicated as UPD in the work process overview) are occupied. Transaction SM13 indicates that the update has been deactivated.
Solution	The system log contains an entry for the time, user, and reason for the deactivation. Resolve the reported problem (for example, a database error). Then reactivate the update service with Transaction SM13.
See	Chapter 2, Section 2.5, Analyzing SAP Work Processes, and Section 2.3, Database Monitoring.

Problem: High Database Response Times	
Priority	Medium to very high.
Indications and procedures	The Action column in the work process overview (Transaction SM50 or SM66) indicates sequential read, direct read, waiting for DB lock, or other database activities for various work processes.
Solution	The problem is related to the database. Therefore, rather than increasing the number of SAP work processes, examine the database more closely (see Detailed Analysis of the Database, below).
See	Chapter 2, Section 2.5, Analyzing SAP Work Processes, and Section 2.3, Database Monitoring.

Problem: Long Runtimes for Individual Programs	
Priority	Medium: This problem can lead to high response times for specific programs.
Indications and procedures	Programs with long runtimes block work processes.
Solution	Determine whether the related ABAP program is still running properly. Analyze the affected programs and optimize or terminate them as appropriate.
See	Chapter 2, Section 2.5, Analyzing SAP Work Processes, and Chapter 4, Identifying Performance Problems in ABAP and Java Programs.

Problem: Non-Optimal Load Distribution	
Priority	Medium: This problem can lead to high response times on specific computers.
Indications and procedures	In a distributed system with multiple computers, you detect a work process bottleneck on at least one computer, whereas other computers still have free work processes.
Solution	Call Transaction SMLG and check whether all of the servers are available for load distribution with logon groups or whether logon errors have been reported. Use Transaction SMLG to optimize the logon groups.
See	Chapter 2, Section 2.5, Analyzing SAP Work Processes, and Chapter 6, Workload Distribution and Interfaces.

Problem: Insufficient Work Processes	
Priority	Medium: This problem can lead to high response times on specific computers.
Indications and procedures	None of the previously listed problems apply, but there is still a problem with work processes.
Solution	If the computer has sufficient reserves of CPU and main memory, increase the number of SAP work processes.
See	Chapter 2, Section 2.5, Analyzing SAP Work Processes, and Chapter 6, Workload Distribution and Interfaces.

Detailed Analysis of the J2EE Engine

Problem: Frequent Full Garbage Collection	
Priority	High: This problem can cause temporary standstills of several seconds in the SAP J2EE Engine.
Indications and procedures	Frequent full garbage collections: The time required for garbage collections is greater than 5%. The growth rate of old memory space (OGR) does not decrease significantly at times of low load.
Solution	Check whether the load distribution is unfavorable and analyze the Java programs.
See	Chapter 2, Section 2.6, Analyzing Java Virtual Machine (JVM) Memory Management and Work Processes

Problem: High Number of Occupied Java Threads	
Priority	High: This problem can cause temporary standstills of several seconds in the SAP J2EE Engine.
Indications and procedures	Run a Java thread dump; it lists all Java programs that are active.
Solution	Check whether the load distribution is unfavorable and analyze the Java programs.
See	Chapter 2, Section 2.6, Analyzing Java Virtual Machine (JVM) Memory Management and Work Processes

Detailed Analysis of the Database (Transaction DBACOCKPIT)

Problem: Long Database Locks	
Priority	Medium to very high: This problem can cause a standstill in the SAP system.
Indications and procedures	In the database monitor select PERFORMANCE • WAIT EVENT ANALYSIS • LOCK MONITOR (Oracle) (or DB01). Refresh this monitor several times within a short time frame and check whether long-lasting wait situations occur because of database locks. With the help of the fields Client Host and Client PID in the work process overview, you can determine which programs and users hold locks. Determine whether the related ABAP program is still running properly.
Solution	Terminate a program or process manually if required after consulting the affected users.
See	Chapter 2, Section 2.3, Database Monitoring.

Problem: CPU Bottleneck on the Database Server	
Priority	High: This problem can lead to high database response times.
Indications and procedures	Call the operating system monitor (Transaction ST06) on the database server and see whether it shows a CPU bottleneck.
Solution	Check whether the CPU bottleneck originates from expensive SQL statements, incorrectly set database buffers, or an I/O bottleneck. You may need to reduce the load on the database server or increase its CPU capacity.
See	Chapter 2, Section 2.3, Database Monitoring, Section 2.2, Hardware Monitoring, and Chapter 6, Workload Distribution and Interfaces.

Problem: Number of Logical Processors for the Database Instance	
Priority	High: This problem can lead to high database response times.
Indications and procedures	There are profile parameters that specify the maximum number of processors that are physically available to the database instance. These parameters include `MAXCPU` (for MaxDB) and `NUMCPUVPS` (for Informix). Check whether this parameter is optimally configured.
Solution	If necessary, adjust this parameter.
See	Chapter 2, Section 2.3, Database Monitoring, and Chapter 6, Workload Distribution and Interfaces.

Problem: Database Buffer Too Small	
Priority	Medium to high: This problem can lead to high database response times.
Indications and procedures	Call the database performance monitor in the Performance Overview screen (Oracle), and check whether the buffer quality and other key figures match recommended values.
Solution	Increase the size of the buffer once by 25%, and then check whether the quality improves.
See	Chapter 2, Section 2.3, Database Monitoring.

Problem: Expensive SQL Statements	
Priority	Medium to high: This problem can lead to high database response times.
Indications and procedures	Call the database monitor and select PERFORMANCE • SQL STATEMENT ANALYSIS • SHARED CURSOR CACHE (Oracle). For other database examples, see Appendix B. In the database process monitor, check whether there are any expensive SQL statements, that is, statements with disk drive reads that amount to more than 10% of the total physical reads or buffer gets that amount to more than 10% of the total reads.
See	Chapter 2, Section 2.3, Database Monitoring, and Chapter 11, Optimizing SQL Statements.

Problem: Database I/O Bottleneck

Priority	Medium to high: This problem can lead to high database response times.
Indications and procedures	► Call the database monitor and select PERFORMANCE • WAIT EVENT ANALYSIS • FILESYSTEM REQUESTS (ORACLE). In the OS monitor of the database server (ST06): DETAIL ANALYSIS MENU • DISK
	► If the value in the Util column is greater than 50%, this indicates an I/O bottleneck. Check whether data files that are heavily written reside on these disks.
Solution	Resolve the read/write (I/O) bottleneck by improving table distribution in the file system. Ensure that heavily accessed files do not reside on the same drive. These include files for the swap space, redo log, and transaction log.
See	Chapter 2, Section 2.2, Hardware Monitoring, and Section 2.3, Database Monitoring.

Problem: Statistics for the Database Optimizer Are Obsolete or Not Available

Priority	Medium to high: This problem can lead to high database response times.
Indications and procedures	To check whether optimizer statistics are created regularly, call the DBA Planning Calendar.
Solution	Schedule the program for updating statistics.
See	Chapter 2, Section 2.3, Database Monitoring, Chapter 11, Optimizing SQL Statements, and SAP Online Help for topics on database administration.

Problem: Missing Database Indexes

Priority	Very high if a primary index is missing: This can cause data inconsistencies.
	Medium if a secondary index is missing: This can cause high response times for individual programs.

Problem: Missing Database Indexes

Indications and procedures	Check whether there are any missing database indexes by calling the monitor for analyzing tables and indexes (Oracle), and selecting DETAIL ANALYSIS MENU • STATE ON DISK: MISSING INDICES.
Solution	Re-create the missing indexes.
See	Chapter 2, Section 2.3, Database Monitoring, and Chapter 11, Optimizing SQL Statements.

Problem: Large Differences in Database Times Caused by Buffer Load Process

Priority	Medium to high: This problem can lead to high response times for specific programs.
Indications and procedures	To view occasional, long database accesses to buffered tables, use one of the following: the local work process overview (Transaction SM50), an SQL trace (Transaction ST05), or the single-record statistics (Transaction STAD).
Solution	Call the table access statistics (Transaction ST10) and verify the efficiency of table buffering.
See	Chapter 9, SAP Buffering.

Problem: Network Problems

Priority	Medium to high: This problem can lead to high response times on specific computers.
Indications and procedures	Determine whether there is a network problem between the database server and the application server by comparing SQL trace results on these two servers.
Solution	Resolve the network problem between the two servers.
See	Chapter 2, Section 2.3, Database Monitoring, and Chapter 4, Section 4.3.2, Evaluating an SQL Trace.

Detailed Analysis of Memory Management and Buffers) (Transaction ST02)

Problem: Extended Memory Is Too Small	
Priority	High.
Indications and procedures	To determine whether either the extended memory or roll buffer is too small, use the SAP memory configuration monitor (Transaction ST02). See also in this appendix, Work Processes Stuck in Private Mode or in Roll-in/Roll-out.
Solution	Correct the SAP memory configuration parameters such as `em/initial_size_MB`, `rdisp/ROLL_SHM`, and `ztta/roll_extension`. If you have sufficient main memory on the server, you can increase the memory size by 20 to 50%. Check to see if this improves the situation.
See	Chapter 2, Section 2.4, Analyzing SAP Memory Configuration, and Chapter 8, Memory Management.

Problem: Displacements in SAP Buffers	
Priority	Medium.
Indications and procedures	Look for displacements in the SAP buffers in the Swaps column in the SAP memory configuration monitor (Transaction ST02). Displacements mean the buffers are configured too small.
Solution	Increase the maximum number of buffer entries or increase the size of the respective, provided the computer still has sufficient main memory reserves.
See	Chapter 2, Section 2.4, Analyzing SAP MemoryConfiguration.

Detailed Analysis of Internet Transaction Server

Problem: All ITS Work Processes (Work Threads) or All Sessions Are Occupied	
Priority	High.
Indications and procedures	The ITS administration and monitoring tool indicates that all ITS work processes or all sessions are occupied.

Problem: All ITS Work Processes (Work Threads) or All Sessions Are Occupied	
Solution	Short term: Restart the ITS. Medium term: Increase the number of processes or optimize the load distribution.
See	Chapter 7, Section 7.4.4, Performing a Bottleneck Analysis for the ITS.

Problem: Insufficient Addressable (Virtual) Memory	
Priority	High.
Indications and procedures	Enter the problem in the AGate log (AGate.trc).
Solution	Start more AGate processes per ITS instance.
See	Chapter 7, Section 7.4.4, Performing a Bottleneck Analysis for the ITS.

Problem: Standstill Due to a Lack of Disk Drive Space	
Priority	Very high.
Indications and procedures	Enter the problem in the AGate log and the operating system monitor.
Solution	Determine the cause of the rapid growth in data, for example, reorganized log files. Also, the trace level may have been reduced after the generation of a detailed runtime analysis.
See	Chapter 7, Section 7.4.4, Performing a Bottleneck Analysis for the ITS.

B   Database Monitors, Buffers, and SQL Execution Plans

SAP Basis (that is, the ABAP server and SAP J2EE Engine) currently supports seven relational database management systems, each with its own architecture:

▶ SAP MaxDB

▶ IBM DB2 for Linux, UNIX, and Windows; IBM DB2 for IBM i; IBM DB2 for zSeries

▶ IBM Informix Dynamic Server (up to SAP Basis Version 6.40)

▶ Oracle

▶ Microsoft SQL Server

However, SAP Basis has database monitors that cover basic database functioning, regardless of the database system. To help customers analyze and tune their databases, SAP Basis has a custom-developed database performance monitor with basic functions that work independently of the database system used.

The database monitor has been completely revised for SAP Basis Version 7.0 and is now referred to as the *Database Administrator Cockpit* (DBA Cockpit). It replaces the old transaction codes for database performance (ST04), database locks (DB01), data management (DB02), and planning calendar and database jobs (DB12, DB13, DB13C, and DB24). In an SAP system of Version 7.0 and later, you can use the old transaction codes (ST04, DB01, and so on) to directly go to the appropriate page in the DBA Cockpit. SAP Note 1027146, Database Administration and Monitoring in the DBA Cockpit, provides an overview of the DBA Cockpit availability.

Changes in Version 7.0

From the DBA Cockpit, you can manage multiple databases of systems, that is, multiple databases of ABAP-based systems, on the basis of the SAP J2EE Engine, and liveCache installations.

You can start the DBA Cockpit with Transaction DBACOCKPIT or via the SAP menu path ADMINISTRATION • CCMS • DB ADMINISTRATION • DBA COCKPIT.

The system takes you to the screen DBA Cockpit: System Configuration Maintenance. The DBA Cockpit screen is divided into three areas. The upper-left area includes buttons to navigate to the system configuration and to select databases for monitoring. The lower-left area includes a navigation tree that takes you to the individual monitoring and administration functions. Besides the performance-relevant monitors in the Performance branch, you can find further database administration functions, for instance, for data management. The area on the right comprises the actual monitor that you've selected via the navigation tree.

[+] Before you read the sections on the individual databases in this appendix, you should have read Chapter 2, Section 2.3, Database Analysis, to understand the basic strategies of the database performance analysis in the SAP environment.

[!] The guideline values provided in the following for each database system are simply rules of thumb for good performance. A database instance may still be able to run well even if the buffer quality is poor. Therefore, to avoid unnecessary investment in time and energy in optimizing the buffer quality, check the database response times using the workload analysis. See Chapter 2, Section 2.3.1, Analyzing the Database Buffer, on how to proceed in the case of poor buffer quality.

This book uses the path names and names of the DBA Cockpit. In an SAP system with a version prior to 7.0, you can find the database performance monitors in the SAP menu under TOOLS • ADMINISTRATION • MONITOR • PERFORMANCE • DATABASE • ACTIVITY. Or you can enter Transaction ST04. The screen Database Performance Analysis: Database Overview is displayed. Under Detail Analysis Menu, you can find the detail monitors on database processes, database locks, SQL statistics, file system statistics, and so on.

Execution plans for SQL statements
The description of the database monitors for the individual databases is followed by a comparison overview of SQL execution plans.

SAP J2EE Engine
The SAP J2EE Engine provides local database monitors that you can use, for example, in a Java-only installation. You can find these monitors and the SQL trace for the SAP J2EE Engine in the local SAP NetWeaver Administrator; they are presented in Section B.9.

B.1   IBM DB2 for Linux, UNIX, and Windows

Memory allocated by a DB2 database installation is made up of two parts: the *database global memory*, allocated in the shared memory of the database server, and the *agent private memory*, the memory for the individual database processes, which in DB2 are referred to as *agents*. For every SAP work process (at least) one agent is started, and the total memory requirement is calculated as follows:

DB2 database buffer

Total memory = database global memory + agent private memory × number of SAP work processes

The most important elements of the database global memory are (see also Table B.1):

Database global memory

▶ The *buffer pool*, which buffers tables and index pages

▶ The *database heap*, a memory area for internal control structures

▶ The *lock list*, an area of the memory in which database locks are administered

▶ The *package cache*, which buffers the run schedules for already-executed SQL statements

▶ The *catalog cache*, which buffers the database's data dictionary information

The agent private memory includes, for example, the *application support layer* and the memory area for sorting result quantities of SQL statements *(sort heap)*. Note that most memory areas are only allocated when they are actually used. Exceptions include the buffer pool, the lock list, and the application support layer, which are allocated when the database instance is started.

You can create several *buffer pools* for a single DB2 database instance. Allocating specific data to be contained in selected buffers occurs at the table spaces level. The block size of data pools and the associated table spaces is identical. Blocks can be between 2KB and 32KB in size. As of SAP Basis Version 7.0, the database is created with the UNIFORM block size. For new installations with DB2, only a block size of 16KB and a 16KB buffer pool are used. So variable block and buffer pool sizes can only be found in systems that have been installed prior to Version 7.0.

Data buffer

The size of DB2 buffer pools is set using the parameter `buffpage` or with the command `Alter Bufferpool` individually for each buffer pool. Logical read accesses to the buffer pool are executed in the database performance monitor and are separated according to table and index pages. Under PERFORMANCE • DATABASE IN THE DBA COCKPIT, you can find a global overview, and the same information, separated according to buffer pool, is shown under PERFORMANCE • BUFFERPOOLS. You can find logical accesses to table pages in the DATA • LOGICAL READS field, and logical accesses to index pages in the INDEX • LOGICAL READS field. Similarly, the physical read accesses can be found in the DATA • PHYSICAL READS and INDEX • PHYSICAL READS fields.

Database System	Name of Buffer	Key Figure and Assessment	Parameter
DB2 for LUW	Buffer pool	Hit ratio for all buffers ≥96% for OLTP systems, ≥94% for SAP NetWeaver BW (OLAP) systems	`buffpage, dbheap`
	Package cache	Hit ratio ≥98%	`pckcachesz`
	Catalog cache	Hit ratio: not relevant Overflows	`catalogcache_sz`
	Locks	Lock escalations ~0	`locklist`

Table B.1 Guideline Values for Evaluating the Performance of Database Buffers (DB2 for LUW)

Database process monitor

To identify expensive SQL statements, proceed as follows in a DB2 for LUW database:

1. In the DBA Cockpit, select PERFORMANCE • APPLICATIONS. The Application Snapshot screen is displayed. This monitor shows all database processes, which are referred to as *agents* in DB2.

2. The Application Status column shows the status of an agent. The most important statuses are:

   ► **UOW Waiting**
   An agent currently has no task; that is, it waits. When you select

the Active only filter, the system hides these database processes, and the list is limited to the currently active processes.

▶ **UOW Executing**

An agent executes an SQL statement.

▶ **Lock Wait**

An agent cannot execute an SQL statement because the information required is locked by another agent.

3. The Name of Application column indicates whether the running application is an SAP work process (disp+work) or a "foreign" process. The Application PID column specifies the SAP work process ID, and the Host Name column gives the name of the SAP application server or, for foreign processes, the PID and computer name of the corresponding application.

Select the Statement Text tab to display the SQL statement that is currently being executed.

To analyze the SQL statistics for a DB2 database, select PERFORMANCE • SQL CACHE in the DBA Cockpit. In the dialog box that appears, change the default selection values to zero and click OK. A list appears that contains all SQL statements for which the database has statistics. These are all statements that have been executed since the database start, provided that they have not been displaced due to the limitation of the memory area intended for this purpose. The initial part of the SQL statement is located in the SQL Text column. To view the complete SQL statement and the *access plan*, double-click the appropriate row. For each SQL statement, the list includes the details shown in Table B.2.

SQL statistics

Field	Explanation
Executions	Number of times the statement has been executed since the start of the database or since the monitor reset
Total Execution Time (ms)	Total execution time for the statement, across all executions in milliseconds
Total Execution Time (%)	Total execution time for the statement, in percentage across all executions of all statements

Table B.2 *Most Important Fields of the SQL Statistics (SQL Cache) for DB2 for LUW*

Field	Explanation
Average Execution Time (ms)	Average execution time for a statement, in milliseconds
Hit Ratio for Buffers (%)	Hit quality in the database buffer for the statement
Rows Read	Number of rows read for a statement
Rows Read (%)	Number of rows read for a statement in percentage of all rows read
Rows Written	Number of rows written for a statement
Rows Written (%)	Number of rows written for a statement in percentage of all rows read
SQL Sorts	Number of sorts in the database
Sort Overflows	Number of sort overflows
Total Sort Time (ms)	Time for sorting at the DB level, for instance, DB-internal sorting for the join formation or the ORDER BY clause in the SQL statement

Table B.2 Most Important Fields of the SQL Statistics (SQL Cache) for DB2 for LUW (Cont.)

Expensive SQL statements are indicated by a high execution time. Therefore sort the list by the numbers in the Total Execution Time column. This organizes expensive SQL statements in the order of required analysis and possible optimization. You should also take the number of executions into account here.

Database locks All database systems have a monitor for displaying exclusive lock waits. In DB2 for LUW, you can find this monitor in the DBA Cockpit under PERFORMANCE • WAIT SITUATIONS ON LOCKS AND DEADLOCKS.

I/O performance To achieve optimal database performance, I/O activity (read/write accesses) should be evenly distributed on the database's hard disks.

In the DBA Cockpit under PERFORMANCE • DATABASE • AVERAGE TIME you can find critical key figures about the I/O performance at the table area level. If the average read and write times (depending on the underlying storage subsystem) are above the performance-critical threshold value of 5 ms for read times and 1 ms for write times, you should examine the table areas in detail. To control this, there are monitors that display the I/O workload distribution at the file system level. For this purpose, start the PERFORMANCE • TABLE AREAS or TABLES MONITOR FROM THE DBA Cockpit.

The number of write and read operations and the associated file IDs are displayed for each table or table area. Using this monitor, you can identify frequently used data files and ensure that they are located on different data media. This prevents the I/O requests for these objects from directly competing with each other.

Database error or message files contain important information on errors and the general condition of the database. You should check the logs regularly. For the DB2 for LUW example, you can find the log in the DBA Cockpit under DIAGNOSIS • DB2 LOGS. For more detailed information about the error messages, refer to the manuals for your specific database.

Database error log file

Notes on DB2 for LUW usually have the *DB6* abbreviation in the SAP note system to distinguish them from the other two DB2 databases: DB2 for iSeries (*DB4*) and DB2 for zSeries (*DB2*) (Table B.3).

SAP notes

Note Number	Title
1027336	DB6: New Functions in the DBA Cockpit
1086130	DB6: Standard Parameter Settings for DB2 V9.5
899322	DB6: Standard Parameter Settings for DB2 V9.1
584952	DB6: Standard Parameter Settings for DB2 UDB
150037	Database Hints in Open SQL for DB6 (DB2 for LUW)
868888	DB6: Optimization Guidelines
1292796	DB6: Indirect Hints in Open SQL (DB2 for LUW)
860724	DB6: Configuration of the Planning Calendar
434495	DB6: Maintenance of the Table Statistics via DB13
1312006	DB6: Database Performance Warehouse—Main Note
1269697	DB6: Performance During Backup
150037	Database Hints DB2 for LUW

Table B.3 SAP Notes on Performance Topics for DB2 for Linux, UNIX, and Windows

B.2   IBM DB2 for IBM i

Because the database and the operating system are very closely linked in IBM i, an analysis of performance problems should always start with the operating system monitor (Transaction ST06). Memory pool paging, drive utilization, and the IBM i system values are critical for system performance, as is CPU utilization.

The main memory is partitioned into memory pools that applications can utilize as needed. You can find an overview of the main memory configuration by selecting DETAILED ANALYSIS MENU • POOL in the operating system monitor (ST06), or by using the command WRKSYSSTS on the operating system level.

Compared with Transaction ST06, the command WRKSYSSTS has the advantage that you can determine the data in less than one hour; therefore, high short-term loads can be identified.

The paging rate (DB Fault + Non-DB Fault) should be clearly kept below the value of 10 page faults per second for the MACHINE pool. You can use the formula below to find out whether the paging rate is acceptable in the BASE pool:

$$Max \ (DB \ Faults + Non\text{-}DB \ Faults) \leq Number \ of \ CPU \times CPU \ Load \ (\%)$$

[Ex]   Example: For three CPUs, the average utilization of which is 70%, it is acceptable if the total of DB faults and non-DB faults per second is less than 210. A high paging rate usually indicates a memory bottleneck.

The main memory configuration output contains a right-hand column with the heading Paging Option. In this column, the value *CALC should be set for the memory pool associated with the SAP system. *CALC activates the expert cache, which contains data for frequently processed SQL queries in the main memory, thereby reducing the need for hard drive access.

Hard drives   With iSeries, the hard drives play an important part in determining system performance. The percent-busy rate (operating system command WRKDSKSTS) should be less than 30% per drive. Values that exceed this have a major impact on total system performance. High percent-busy rate values are often caused by poor data distribution on the hard drive.

You can resolve this problem on the operating system level by using the tools TRCASPBAL and STRASPBAL.

Furthermore, you should check the IBM i system value settings; suggested values are available in SAP Note 428855.

The DBA Cockpit (Transaction DBACOCKPIT) is available as of SAP Basis Version 7.0 for monitoring and managing the database DB2 for IBM I — like for the other databases. This cockpit enables you to monitor databases of several systems (ABAP, Java). You can still use the traditional Transaction ST04 to go to the DBA Cockpit. Version 6.40 also provides Transaction DB4COCKPIT, which is standardized via the DBA Cockpit for Version 7.0. This section describes the menu paths in the DBA Cockpit as of Version 7.0. In older versions, you can find the same information as in the DBA Cockpit; however, the menu paths and names may vary.

DBA Cockpit for DB2 for IBM i

The *database process monitor* displays the currently active database processes. The monitor displays the SQL statements that are being processed and can indicate the SAP work processes to which a database process is allocated. You can find the database process monitor for DB2 for IBM i in the DBA Cockpit under DIAGNOSIS • LOCK MONITOR; select a process from the list and click Display Job Log/Display Spool Files. Under the same menu path, you can also find information on *exclusive lock waits on the database*.

Database process monitor, database locks

Depending on the version, the DB2 for IBM i database offers two options to analyze time-consuming SQL statements. A memory-resistant database monitor is available for older database versions. Data for SQL statements executed on the system are first stored in main memory and are then copied at regular intervals by SAP jobs to corresponding tables. As of Version V5R4M0, you have the option to evaluate the plan cache of the SQL Query Engine instead of the memory-resistant database monitors; as of DB2 for IBM i 6.1, this is the standard procedure. You activate the database evaluation using the SAP profile parameter as4/dbmon/enable=1; you can switch to the plan cache dump via the SAP profile parameter as4/dbmon/classic=0 (see SAP Note 1083218).

SQL statistics

In the DBA Cockpit, you can display a list of the most expensive SQL statements, which are also referred to as *SQL Query Engine Plan Cache* (for short: SQE Plan Cache) in DB2 for IBM i. For this purpose, select

SQL Statements in the Performance tree. In both cases, you can view details on implementing the statement by clicking a line within the list (Explain). Then the entire statement text is displayed, as well as statistical details on the frequency of executions, the host variable for the most expensive execution (in hexadecimal values), and details on the implementation. These details enable you to check whether you might improve the implementation of the SQL statement by using an additional index.

In addition to reviewing the list of 50 (for ST04) or 300 (for DB4COCKPIT and DBACOCKPIT) slowest statements, it can also be useful to check the lists contained in the following menus: DETAILED ANALYSIS MENU • INDEX ADVISED and DETAILED ANALYSIS MENU • INDEX CREATED, or DETAILED ANALYSIS MENU • TABLE SCANS. You can use the suggestions provided by Index Advised immediately, whereas for the Table Scans category, you should check the sizes of the tables and result sets. For small tables or large result sets, it may be faster to read the table as entirely blocked instead of accessing it via an index. However, if you create an index or read a few records from a large table via a table scan, an index can substantially improve performance. In this case, you must find out whether the increased performance for this request justifies the additional effort involved in updating an index when the table content changes. If the slow request isn't executed very often, but the table is modified frequently, an additional index can have drawbacks.

The display contains the name of the SQL packet and various execution times. The SQL packet is usually used to determine the table name or ABAP report in which the statement in question was executed. Furthermore, you can click the SQL packet name to show the SQL execution plan, which provides information about the implementation of the SQL query.

Related tuning measures Because the database optimizer generates an SQL packet that persistently stores access information when an SQL statement is first run, the first execution (*prepare phase*) takes a relatively long time (shown in the SQL trace). If there is already an SQL packet, the database optimizer can use its contents when the statement is executed again, without having to redetermine the optimal access path (see CHECK PREPARED statement). The command sequence ODP CLEANUP in the SQL trace represents another special requirement. When an SQL query is executed, a portion of the information is stored in open data paths (ODPs). For performance reasons, only the most recent 800 ODPs per SAP work process are used. If more ODPs are needed, the least used ones are deleted by means of an algorithm. This process usually occurs via a `Commit` statement and is shown in the SQL trace. The time needed for this depends on the system workload; it can be very long in systems with memory bottlenecks (several hundreds of milliseconds). In the SAP statistics (ST03, STAD), these times are part of the commit times.

You can obtain patches for the operating system and IBM i database software in the form of cumulative PTF packages (CUM packages), DB fix packs, and individual PTFs. When the corrections have been implemented, the SQL packet may have to be deleted to get rid of the problem, or the database optimizer may have to be invoked to redetermine the execution plan. A note in the PTF readme file will indicate if this is necessary. For CUM packages and DB fix packs, the SQL packets should be deleted as a preventative measure. System performance may suffer until the SQL packets are rebuilt. For IBM i, a background update of optimizer statistics is not necessary, because the statistics are managed by the system and are always up to date.

Table B.4 lists the most essential notes on performance monitors and on database performance.

SAP Notes

Note Number	Title
531337	Performance for Open SQL ""FOR ALL ENTRIES"
517589	Client Copy Performance
450351	Performance Problems in 3-Tier or Virtual Host Systems
898203	"ALL I/O" and "UPTO <n> ROWS" Performance
497608	Display the Last Executed SQL Statement
1083218	Evaluation of the Plan Cache for DB2 on i5/OS
1109771	Conditional Statement Hints
541508	Check of the System Parameters for BW
485420	Database Hints DB2 for IBM i
1028173	DBA Cockpit for DB2 for IBM i (with Detailed Documentation Attached)

Table B.4 SAP Notes on DB2 for IBM i Performance Topics

B.3   IBM DB2 for z/OS

DB2 data buffer

DB2 for z/OS allocates various buffers in the main memory on the database server (see also Table B.5):

▶ The data buffer contains several (virtual) buffer pools and a buffer table and index pages.

▶ The record identifier (RID) pool buffers index pages are accessed with `List Prefetch`.

▶ The sort pool buffer data is used to control the sorting of data.

▶ The dynamic statement cache buffers SQL statement execution plans. It consists of the system-wide Environment Descriptor Manager (EDM) pool (EDM DSC Cache as of DB2 version 8) and local database thread caches.

Data buffer

Buffer pools can be created in units of 4KB pages, 8KB pages, 16KB pages, and 32KB pages. The number of possible buffer pools depends on the DB2 version. You can change the size of a buffer pool with the command `ALTER BUFFERPOOL`. The *read random hit ratio* in a buffer pool measures the quality of the buffer; that is, for random read accesses, the number of successful accesses to data in the buffer is compared to the total number of random data accesses. If all table spaces are buffered by only one buffer pool, then the tables will compete for table spaces on this buffer. To achieve the best possible data buffering, table spaces that are frequently accessed should be assigned buffer pools of their own (buffer pool tuning). You can set the attributes of these buffer pools to take into account the access mode (random or sequential) and properties (size, number of changes) of the buffered tables.

Dynamic statement cache

The SAP Basis database interface uses dynamic SQL statements, which are executed in two phases (stages): The first phase is the prepare phase, in which the database optimizer determines the optimal access path. The second phase is the execution phase; this optimal access path is used to access data. During the prepare phase, a *skeleton* is created for each SQL statement. A skeleton consists of the executable (*prepared*) statement and the *statement string* (the statement written in a character set). Skeletons are first buffered locally in the local cache of the respective thread. The

DB2 parameter CACHEDYN = YES ensures that a skeleton for each dynamic SQL statement is also stored in the EDM pool (as of DB2 version 8 in the EDM DSC cache). The EDM pool also contains skeleton cursor tables, skeleton package tables, cursor tables, and package tables, as well as database descriptors.

Because SAP programs run with the bind option KEEPDYNAMIC(YES), statement skeletons (in addition to COMMIT time points) remain in the local thread caches. When a statement is executed, the local cache (as of DB2 version 8, the EDM DSC cache) and the EDM pool are searched for a prepared statement. If one is found, the prepare and execution phases are avoided or shortened.

The *global cache hit ratio* measures how well the EDM pool (as of DB2 version 8, the EDM DSC cache) acts as a system-wide buffer for SQL statement skeletons.

Global cache hit ratio

Name of Buffer	Key Figure and Assessment	Parameter
Buffer pool	Read random hit ratio ≥95%	
RID pool	RID list limit reached: a high value indicates expensive SQL statements.	MAXRBLK
EDM pool	EDM pool full failures = 0	EDMPOOL
EDM statement cache	Statement cache global hit ratio ≥95%	EDMPOOL EDMSTMTC CACHEDYN

Table B.5 Guideline Values for Evaluating the Performance of Database Buffers (DB2 for z/OS)

The *database process monitor* displays the currently active database processes. You can find the database monitor for DB2 for z/OS in the DBA Cockpit under PERFORMANCE • THREAD ACTIVITY.

Database process monitor

You can find the monitor for displaying *exclusive lock waits* in the database for DB2 for z/OS in the DBA Cockpit under PERFORMANCE • DB2 SUBSYSTEM ACTIVITY, or you can enter Transaction DB01.

Database locks

SQL statistics The SQL statistics are available in the DBA Cockpit under PERFORMANCE •
STATEMENT CACHE.

SAP Notes Table B.6 lists the most essential notes on performance monitors and
database performance.

Note Number	Title
1027452	DB2 z/OS CCMS: DBACOCKPIT
496904	Performance Notes Database Parameter FS-AM for DB2
122599	DB2/390: Update Performance
1008334	DB2-z/OS: Performance Problems with DB2 V8/V9
1062976	DB2-z/OS: Fast Load
162034, 724614	Database Hints DB2 for zSeries
1149824	DB2-z/OS: BI 7.x: DB Settings and Performance

Table B.6 SAP Notes on DB2 for z/OS Performance Topics

B.4 IBM Informix Dynamic Server

Because the support for Informix ends with SAP Basis Version 6.40, the
DBA Cockpit is not available for Informix. Therefore, you must use the
old database performance monitor (Transaction ST04) for the performance analysis of an Informix database.

Data buffer In the initial screen of the SAP database performance monitor (Transaction ST04) under the header Data Buffers, you will find the most
important information about the size and performance of the Informix
data buffer. Since Version 10.00, Informix supports different page sizes
for Dbspaces. This involves several data buffers for the various page
sizes. Since then, their size is no longer determined via the BUFFERS
parameter, but via one or multiple entries of the BUFFERPOOL parameter
in the *ONCONFIG* file.

To evaluate the read quality of the database buffer, you can apply the
general rule that the read quality should be higher than 95%, and the

write quality should be higher than 82%. The write quality only plays a minor role for performance, particularly in systems with only a few database modifications, because it can drop below the defined value without affecting the overall performance.

In an Informix database system, *allocated memory* is divided into three areas, whose respective sizes are shown under the header Shared Memory in the database performance monitor (Transaction ST04) (see also Table B.7):

Database memory areas

▶ The *resident portion* of the shared memory contains, among other things, the data buffer and the buffer for the database locks. When the database is started, the resident portion is allocated and is mainly taken up by the data buffer and the number of database locks configured.

▶ The *virtual portion* of the shared memory covers, among other things, the memory for database processes, called "session pools." Their sizes are defined by the parameter SHMVIRTSIZE at database startup.

▶ The *message portion* is small and of no importance for tuning. It is used for communicating with the application (that is, an SAP work process) via a shared memory connection. This is implemented only for UNIX operating systems. Consequently, the message portion only exists in UNIX systems.

The virtual portion of the shared memory has the special feature that it can enlarge itself while the database is running. However, the enlargement process is resource-intensive. If you set the initial size of the virtual portion parameter SHMVIRTSIZE too small, you will get continual enlargements during production operation, which negatively impacts database performance. Therefore, ensure that the database instance allocates sufficient memory to the virtual portion at startup. To verify the initial size of the virtual portion, before you stop the database, compare the current size of the virtual portion displayed in the database performance monitor with the parameter SHMVIRTSIZE. If the current size of the virtual portion exceeds the size in SHMVIRTSIZE, you must increase the parameter accordingly. Specific actions as they occur in period-end closings also can result in an increased memory requirement for the database.

Virtual portion

Therefore, you should ensure that sufficient memory is available in your system beyond what is needed for normal operation.

If the operating system cannot provide sufficient memory, errors will occur when the virtual portion automatically enlarges. In this case, the Informix database instance terminates with a corresponding error message, and all open transactions are canceled. Because this usually leads to data loss and a temporary system standstill, observing the memory consumption of the Informix database instance is important for system stability. SAP Notes containing explanations and solutions for the errors are listed in at the end of this section.

Name of Buffer	Key Figure and Assessment	Parameter
Data buffer	Read quality >95%	BUFFERS, BUFFERPOOL
	Write quality >82%	BUFFERS, BUFFERPOOL
Virtual portion	Virtual portion = SHMVIRTSIZE	SHMVIRTSIZE

Table B.7 Guideline Values for Evaluating the Performance of Informix Database Buffers

Database process monitor

The *database process monitor* displays the currently active database processes, which are called *threads* for Informix. The monitor displays the SQL statements that are being processed and can indicate the SAP work processes to which a database process is allocated. You can reach the database process monitor for Informix in the database performance monitor (Transaction ST04) via the menu path DETAIL ANALYSIS MENU • INFORMIX SESSION.

Database locks

You can find the monitor for displaying *exclusive lock waits* in the database in the database performance monitor (Transaction ST04) under DETAIL ANALYSIS MENU • EXCLUSIVE LOCKWAITS or via Transaction DB01.

SQL statistics

You can find the SQL statistics in the database performance monitor (Transaction ST04) under DETAIL ANALYSIS MENU • SQL STATEMENT. For Informix, the statistics includes, among others, the key figures listed in Table B.8.

Field	Explanation
Total Execution	Number of times the statement has been executed since the start of the database
Page/Disk Reads	Number of physical read accesses required for all of the executions of the statement
Pg Reads/ Execution	Number of physical read accesses required, on average, for one execution of the statement
Buffer Reads	Number of logical read accesses required for all of the executions of the statement
Buf. Read/ Execution	Number of logical read accesses required, on average, for one execution of the statement
Estimated Costs	Estimated cost for the execution of the statement
Estimated Rows	Estimated number of rows read for the execution of the statement

Table B.8 Fields of the SQL Statistics (Informix)

The monitor you can use to monitor the distribution of accesses to files and hard disks and identify *hot spots* is available in the database performance monitor (Transaction ST04) under DETAIL ANALYSIS MENU • CHUNK I/O ACTIVITY.

Hard disk monitor

Table B.9 lists the most essential notes on performance monitors and on database performance.

SAP Notes

Note Number	Title
520402	New Version of Informix Database Monitor
29873	Informix: Performance Analysis of SELECT-Statements
181945	Performance Guide: BW on Informix
334224	Important Notes on Index Creation
152913	Database Hints Informix
79191	Create "detached Index"

Table B.9 SAP Notes on Informix Performance Topics

B.5   SAP MaxDB

As of SAP Basis Version 7.0, the DBA Cockpit (Transaction DBACOCKPIT) is available to monitor and manage the SAP MaxDB database. For older versions, you use the administration transaction with Transaction DB50. The screen of Transaction DB50 is split into two parts: the left-hand pane contains the menu with the various monitoring and managing functions, and the right-hand pane displays the corresponding data. Transaction DB50 must be set up prior to its use. You will find further information on this in SAP Note 588515. This section describes the menu paths in the DBA Cockpit. In Transaction DB50, you can find the same information as in the DBA Cockpit; however, the menu paths and names may vary.

MaxDB database
buffer

The following buffers in the database server's virtual memory are essential for accelerating the database accesses (see also Table B.10):

▶ The *data cache*, where table and index pages are buffered.

▶ The *catalog cache*, which stores the SQL command context, especially the execution plans for SQL statements.

Name of Buffer	Key Figure and Assessment	Parameter
Data cache	Hit ratio ≥98%	DATA_CACHE
Catalog cache	Hit ratio ≥86%	CAT_CACHE_SUPPLY

Table B.10   Guideline Values for Evaluating the Performance of Database Buffers (SAP MaxDB)

At the operating system level, MaxDB uses threads, which means that in the OS monitor, you can only see a process (called kernel). In UNIX, you can still find an additional watchdog process in the process list, which starts the actually working kernel process. A user task is assigned to an SAP work process as soon as it is connected to MaxDB. This user task in turn is executed in user kernel threads (UKT). The number of parallel UKTs is determined by the MAXCPU parameter, whereas the number of user tasks is controlled via the MAXUSERTASKS parameter. This parameter is configured according to the following rules:

► For hosts with only one CPU, select `MAXCPU = 1`.

► For hosts with several CPUs, select the following values for `MAXCPU`:

  ► Between 30 and 50% of the CPUs if an SAP instance also runs on this host.

  ► Up to the full number of existing CPUs minus 1 if only the MaxDB runs on this host; one CPU should be reserved for the operating system requirements.

The necessary user tasks (`MAXUSERTASKS`) are configured based on all connecting work processes, whereas two user tasks are accepted per work process. In theory, controlled by the application, up to 16 user tasks can be assigned to a work process before the database interface prevents any further additions. Usually, such special application properties are explicitly indicated in the installation guide.

The database process monitor, which is also referred to as the Task Manager in MaxDB and which you can find in the DBA Cockpit under PERFORMANCE • KERNEL THREADS • TASK MANAGER, displays a list of database tasks sorted by different criteria (active tasks, user tasks, and so on). The Application Server column displays the name of the computer on which the SAP work process runs, and Application PID displays the process ID. Combining these with the work process overview (Transaction SM50 or SM66), you can identify the user and the ABAP program that is responsible for a long-lasting database task.

Database process monitor

Active tasks can have the following statuses:

► **Running**
The task is running and utilizes CPU.

► **Runnable, Vsleep**
The task is waiting for a free slot in the thread (UKT).

► **LogIoWait**
The task is waiting for its log request to be processed by the log writer.

► **IOWait (R) or IOWait (W)**
The task is waiting for a read or write operation.

▶ **Vbegexcl or Vsuspend**
The task is waiting for a MaxDB lock to be allocated.

▶ **Vwait**
The task is waiting for the release of a different application's lock (after a commit or rollback of the other application).

Log writer activity is decisive regarding performance. You can also monitor the throughput of the log writer in the database process monitor. You can find information on the log writer in the database process monitor in the System Tasks tab under the Logwr task type. Select this type, and click the Display Task Details button. A dialog window opens, where you select the I/O Operations tab. The times in this window are indicated in seconds. Read/write times of more than two milliseconds can indicate a performance problem, especially if change operations are frequently carried out.

For user tasks, read times of more than 10 milliseconds indicate a performance problem. The pager tasks perform the write process asynchronously during the savepoints; therefore, higher write times can occur, which doesn't necessarily have to result in a performance problem.

You can switch the time measurement for database tasks switched on and off using the clock icons in the toolbar of the database process monitor.

SQL statistics

Several types of performance problems can occur with SQL statements:

▶ Single SQL statements take a long time, whereas the basic performance is good. The reason for this lies in the SQL statements themselves. To analyze the long-running statements and to test custom applications, you should use the command monitor.

▶ The overall database performance is bad, and almost every SQL statement takes longer than expected. You should use the resource monitor to analyze this kind of problem.

The command monitor records data on the performance of individual SQL statements that meet certain conditions. The monitor must be switched on prior to the analysis. You can set the selection criteria for storing SQL statements in the DBA Cockpit under the option PERFORMANCE • SQL PERFORMANCE • COMMAND MONITOR by selecting the pencil icon. You can use the following selection criteria:

- Number of page accesses
- Statement runtime
- Selectivity (ratio of qualified records over total retrieved records)

When the monitor has been activated, the data listed in Table B.11 is displayed for the recorded statements. You display the recorded data by clicking the Refresh Monitor Status BUTTON (clock icon with checkmark).

Field	Explanation
Operation	Type of database operation, for instance, SELECT, UPDATE, and so on.
Tables	Tables in the SQL statement.
Executions	Number of executions, only in the resource monitor; in the command monitor, every execution of a statement is listed separately.
Runtime (in Seconds)	Time required for all of the executions of the statement(s).
Average, Minimum and Maximum Runtime (in Seconds)	Average, minimum, and maximum runtime (in seconds), in the resource monitor only.
#P Accesses:	Number of database pages accessed (in the buffer or on the hard drive).
#P/R:	Number of database pages accessed per qualified row.
#R Read	Number of rows accessed to process the request.
#R Qualified	Number of rows that have been selected by the WHERE clause. For joins, this also includes rows selected to implement the merge procedure.
#R Retrieved	Number of rows that have been returned to the SAP work process.
#Disk I/O	Number of accesses to the hard drive.

Table B.11 Fields of the Command Monitor or the Resource Monitor (SAP MaxDB)

You can view additional parameters by selecting an SQL statement. Additional functions involve the display of the execution plan and the call point in the ABAP program. (For more details, see SAP Note 216208.)

The resource monitor displays aggregated information on SQL statements; that is, it enables you to identify statements that don't use many resources but that are executed frequently. You can call this monitor as follows: PERFORMANCE • SQL PERFORMANCE • RESOURCE MONITOR. The resource monitor collects and aggregates data for all SQL statements, so it is very resource-intensive in operation and should therefore not be activated permanently. You activate and deactivate the monitor using the icons displaying a lit or a dead match, respectively. The resource monitor aggregates SQL statements that originate from the same application call locations. The overall load caused by an SQL statement is reflected in the total number of rows read or in the total runtime value.

Database locks   To analyze the database locks, for MaxDB select PERFORMANCE • SQL LOCKS • WAIT SITUATIONS in the DBA Cockpit. Locks can only exist at the row level. However, if a transaction requests locks amounting to 10% of the maximum number of possible lock list entries, the row locks in the table will be converted to a table lock. This process is referred to as *lock escalation*; the entire table is locked until the transaction triggers a commit or rollback. The alternative of the unlimited growth of the lock list per transaction — like other database systems — puts considerable load on the entire database because for every lock request, the system repeatedly searches the entire list of locks to determine whether a lock already exists for the object to be locked. You can find further information on lock escalations via the menupath PERFORMANCE • SQL LOCKS • OVERVIEW. This list also contains information on the number of available lock entries and the current and maximum number of locks. You should particularly avoid lock escalations in OLTP systems, for instance, by increasing the MAXLOCKS parameter. The maximum number of database locks is determined by the MAXLOCKS parameter. However, don't forget that a lock entry requires 200 bytes of memory. You can find further information in SAP Note 1243937.

Hard disk monitor   In the DBA Cockpit under PERFORMANCE • I/O OPERATIONS • OVERVIEW, you can find a list of configured data files, also referred to as *data volumes*, which include information on the data volume read and written. To achieve optimal database performance, I/O activity (read/write accesses) should be evenly distributed on the database's volumes.

SAP recommends creating multiple data volumes with the same size for a MaxDB database. The number of data volumes and the size of an individual volume, respectively, calculates as the square root of the entire database size. For a database with 100GB, you would create 10 volumes with a size of 10GB each. This recommendation is based on the finding that neither too many nor too few volumes should be created to achieve an optimal distribution.

You should pay particular attention to the log area (log volume) because the system writes to this file at particularly short notice and synchronously. Here the latency during the write access on the system side should be kept as low as possible to be able to obtain up to two milliseconds per log page written, as previously discussed.

The I/O times — as mentioned earlier — are available in the database process monitor or in the operating system monitor.

DB Analyzer is a separate program that runs periodically at the operating system level and analyzes various aspects of stability and performance. You can find the results of Database Analyzer in the SAP system in the DBA Cockpit under PERFORMANCE • DATABASE ANALYZER. **DB Analyzer**

Among other aspects, DB Analyzer analyzes the following:

▶ Low cache rates

▶ Nonoptimal access strategies of SQL statements

▶ Overflow of the log queue

▶ Long lock times (tasks in status vwait/vsuspend)

▶ Long command times (receive/reply)

▶ High I/O activity

▶ Nonoptimal write times of the log writer or read times of the user tasks

Table B.12 lists the most essential notes on performance monitors and database performance. **SAP Notes**

Note Number	Title
819641	FAQ: SAP MaxDB Performance (This note refers to other FAQ notes on performance topics.)
1111426	Parameter Check for liveCache/MaxDB Instances
1243937	FAQ: MaxDB SQL Locks
652096	Database Hints MaxDB
1028751	DBA Cockpit for MaxDB

Table B.12 SAP Notes on MaxDB Performance Topics

B.6 Oracle

SAP Notes

Chapter 2, Section 2.3, Database Monitoring, provides extensive information on the DBA Cockpit for Oracle. Table B.13 lists the most essential notes on performance monitors and on database performance.

Note Number	Title
618868	FAQ: Oracle Performance
1027146	Database Administration and Monitoring using the DBA Cockpit
1028624	Overview of the DBA Cockpit for Oracle
601157	Oracle 9i: Server Parameter File
592393	FAQ: Oracle
619188	FAQ: Oracle Wait Events
130480	Database Hints Oracle

Table B.13 SAP Notes on Oracle Performance Topics

B.7 Microsoft SQL Server

SQL Server
database buffer

SQL Server allocates memory in three areas:

▶ *Data cache*, for buffering table pages and index pages (in 8KB blocks) (see also Table B.14).

▶ The SQL Server database instance buffers information on SQL statements and their execution plans in the procedure cache. The procedure cache is about 50 to 500MB in size and adjusts dynamically. For Basis versions older than 7.0, the SAP database interface converts almost all SQL statements into *stored procedures,* which are stored at runtime in the procedure cache including the associated execution plans. With Basis Version 7.0, this behavior has changed. In SQL Server 2005/2008, a real *statement cache* is now available that stores the parameterized SQL statements and their execution plans.

▶ A *fixed portion of memory* totaling 20 to 100MB, depending on the size of the system, is dynamically allocated, for example, for connections between the R/3 work processes and the database (around 400KB of memory for each work process), database locks (around 60 bytes of memory for each lock), and open objects (around 240 bytes of memory for each open object). The SQL Server database offers you a choice between three strategies when it comes to total memory allocation.

Either you assign the database a fixed memory size or you have SQL Server allocate memory freely or within certain limits. The setting for this strategy is displayed in the Memory Setting field Auto, Fixed, or Range).

Memory allocation strategies

The size of the memory actually allocated by SQL Server at a specific time is displayed in the database monitor in the Current memory field. As of Version 6.40, only the Current memory value is displayed, whereas in Version 6.20, you can find the additional parameters Minimum and Maximum, which restrict the memory size.

On 32-bit Windows platforms, the maximum value that can be allocated is 16GB (theoretically up to 64GB), whereas on 64-bit Windows platforms, this value can be as high as 512GB.

If an SAP instance is located on the database server, we recommend that you assign a fixed memory size for the SQL server database, rather than allow the size of the allocated memory to vary dynamically.

The database performance monitor (Transaction ST04) indicates the size of the SQL Server data cache as the data cache. The performance of the

Data cache

data cache is reflected in the buffer quality, indicated as the hit ratio (Table B.14).

Procedure cache
In the database performance monitor (Transaction ST04), the size and utilization of the *procedure cache* are indicated as Procedure Cache and Hit Ratio %.

Name of Buffer	Key Figure and Assessment	Parameter
Data cache	Cache hit ratio >97%. (See SAP Note 515376 for interpreting the value.)	MIN SERVER MEMORY, MAX SERVER MEMORY

Table B.14 Guideline Values for Evaluating the Performance of SQL Server Database Buffers

SQL Server dynamically adjusts the sizes of the procedure cache and the fixed portion of database memory. The remaining portion is used for the data cache. Therefore, the size of the data cache is determined indirectly by the total memory allocated to the SQL Server database.

Database process monitor
The *database process monitor* displays the currently active database processes. The monitor displays the SQL statements that are being processed and can indicate the SAP work processes to which a database process is allocated. You can find the database monitor for SQL Server in the DBA Cockpit under PERFORMANCE • DATABASE PROCESSES.

Database locks
You can find the monitor for displaying *exclusive lock waits* in the database in the DBA Cockpit under PERFORMANCE • LOCKS, or you enter Transaction DB01.

With SQL Server, you can display a history of all lock wait situations that last more than one minute by enabling the Turn Collector Job On option in the Blocking Lockstats monitor.

SQL statistics
The SQL statistics, which is referred to as *procedure cache* in SQL Server, is available in the DBA Cockpit via PERFORMANCE • ADDITIONAL FUNCTIONS • SAP SQL STATISTICS. In SQL Server, the SQL statistics is held by the SAP database interface.

Hard disk monitor
To achieve optimal database performance, I/O activity (read/write accesses) should be evenly distributed on the database's hard disks. The monitor you can use to monitor the distribution of accesses to files and

hard disks and identify *hot spots* is available for SQL Server in the DBA Cockpit under PERFORMANCE • I/O PERFORMANCE. In this context, refer to SAP Note 521750 for SQL Server 2000 and SAP Note 987961 for SQL Server 2005.

Table B.15 lists the most essential notes on performance monitors and database performance.

SAP Notes

Note Number	Title
555223	FAQ: Microsoft SQL Server
1152848	FAQ: Wait Events in SQL Server
1085937	Wait Event Analysis for SQL Server
521750, 987961	FAQ: SQL Server 2000/2005 I/O Performance
1027512	MSSQL: DBA Cockpit for Basis Release 7.00 and Higher
327494, 879941, 1237682	Configuration Parameters for SQL Server 2000/2005/2008
111291	FAQ: SQL Server—Analysis and Prevention of Deadlocks
133381	Database Hints SQL Server
SDN article	The SAP DBA Cockpit for Microsoft SQL Server

Table B.15 SAP Notes on Microsoft SQL Server Performance Topics

B.8 Execution Plans for SQL Statements

When an SQL statement is executed, there are often several possible access paths for locating the relevant data. The access path adopted is called the *execution plan* (also referred to as the *access plan*) and is determined by the Database Optimizer program.

This appendix provides examples of execution plans for various database systems. Additionally, it focuses on the following three questions:

▶ How do you recognize whether an index is being used for a search?

▶ How do you recognize which index is being used?

▶ How do you identify the index fields being used for the search?

For each database, the following five types of accesses to the table MONI are illustrated: All of the examples involve searches on the table MONI. The table MONI has the key fields RELID, SRTFD, and SRTF2. These form the primary index MONI~0. In the SAP systems on which the sample execution plans were created, the table MONI consists of approximately 2,000 to 2,500 rows. A fifth sample statement selects data from a database view via the tables TADIR, DD010L, and DD010T.

For each database, the following types of accesses to the table MONI are illustrated:

Sequential read using a full table scan
1. In this type of access, no WHERE clause is specified:

```
SELECT * FROM "MONI"
```

Because the SQL statement contains no information on how to limit the search, the database table is read sequentially with a full table scan. A full table scan is also executed if the limiting information provided does not match the available indexes.

Direct read
2. In this type of access, all three of the key fields in MONI's primary index are specified with an EQUALS condition. This is known as a fully qualified access or a direct read:

```
SELECT * FROM "MONI" WHERE "RELID" = :A0 AND "SRTFD" =
:A1 AND "SRTF2" = :A2
```

The SQL statement contains all of the information required to directly access data through the primary index.

Sequential read using the first key field
3. In this type of access, the first key field of the primary index is specified with an EQUALS condition:

```
SELECT * FROM "MONI" WHERE "RELID" = :A0
```

The database instance reads the database rows that fulfill the specified WHERE clause through the primary index MONI~0.

Sequential read using the second key field
4. In this type of access, the second key field of the primary index is specified with an EQUALS condition:

```
SELECT * FROM "MONI" WHERE "SRTFD" = :A0
```

This type of access does not result in a binary search.

[Ex]
To show what is meant by binary and sequential searches, consider a telephone book, which is sorted by surname (first primary key field)

and then by first name (second primary key field). If you are searching for the surname, you begin by entering the list at a more or less random point and try to get closer to the correct name in jumps, doing as little name-by-name scanning as possible. For a computer, this is known as a binary search, because a computer's jumps decrease by a factor of two with each jump. However, if you are searching by first name only, you must sequentially search the entire telephone book. A sequential search is equivalent to a full table scan.

Instead of using a binary search, a sequential read using the second primary key field uses one of two database access strategies:

▸ Indexes are not used at all, or the first field in an index may be missing. In this case, the access must use a full table scan.

▸ Indexes are read sequentially to access the appropriate table row through a direct read. This strategy is advantageous if the index in the database occupies far fewer blocks or pages than the table, and only a small number of table fields are being sought.

5. A fifth example examines the access to a database view. The database view INFO_DOMAT is defined via the tables TADIR, DD010L, and DD010T. The conditions are:

Access to a database view

```
DD01L.DOMNAME = TADIR .OBJ_NAME
DD01L.DOMNAME = DD01T .DOMNAME
DD01L.AS4LOCAL = DD01T .AS4LOCAL
```

The OBJ_NAME field is the key field of the TADIR table, and the DOMNAME field is the key field of the DD010L and DD010T tables. Moreover, the following restrictions are defined in the view definition:

```
TADIR.PGMID =   'R3TR',
TADIR.OBJECT    =    'DOMA'
```

The examined SQL statement is:

```
SELECT * FROM "INFO_DOMAT" WHERE "DEVCLASS" = :A0
```

A secondary index is defined for the DEVCLASS field that belongs to the TADIR table; it is relatively selective. It can be expected that the database optimizer decides to first access the TADIR table via the secondary index and then read the missing data line by line from the D010L and D010T tables (*nested loop join*).

B.8.1 Oracle

[+]

Chapter 11, Optimizing SQL Statements, explains the Oracle execution plans, but we include them here to enable you to compare them with the execution plans of other database systems:

Sequential read using a full table scan

1. Execution plan:

```
Execution Plan
SELECT STATEMENT ( Estimated Costs = 9.082 ,
                   Estimated #Rows = 20.321 )
  1 TABLE ACCESS FULL MONI
  ( Estim. Costs = 9.082 , Estim. #Rows = 20.321 )
  Estim. CPU-Costs = 236.940.094 Estim. IO-Costs = 7.260 )
```

In this case, the optimizer estimates the access cost at 9,082, which is indicated by the entry Estimated Costs = 9.082. For an Oracle database, the cost of an access is indicated as blocks. From Oracle version 9i onward, the following additional information is provided regarding access costs: The number of rows to be read is estimated to be 20,321 (Estimated #Rows = 20.321). In addition, for each access the estimated CPU cost (Estim. CPU-Costs) and estimated I/O cost (Estim. IO-Costs) are indicated.

Direct read (index unique scan)

2. Execution plan:

```
Execution Plan
SELECT STATEMENT ( Estimated Costs = 4 ,
                   Estimated #Rows = 1 )
  2 TABLE ACCESS BY INDEX ROWID MONI
    ( Estim. Costs = 4 , Estim. #Rows = 1 )
    Estim. CPU-Costs = 28.936 Estim. IO-Costs = 3
    1 INDEX UNIQUE SCAN MONI~0
      ( Estim. Costs = 3 , Estim. #Rows = 20.321 )
      Search Columns: 3
      Estim. CPU-Costs = 21.565 Estim. IO-Costs = 2
      Access Predicates: "RELID"=:A0 AND
        "SRTFD"=:A1 AND "SRTF2"=:A2
```

The line INDEX UNIQUE SCAN MONI~0 indicates which index has been used. The search strategy INDEX UNIQUE SCAN shows that all fields of the key have been specified, and therefore accesses are carried out via the primary index. The cost of the index access is listed in the area below the index. In addition to the cost, the number of columns that can be used to meet the search criterion in the index is also indicated when you use an index (Search Columns). The total costs of the table and index access are listed in the area below the table. For example, for the index unique scan, three blocks are read in the index. After that, the block must be read from the table to fulfill the request. From this information, the total costs are derived: Estim. Costs = 4. In the SAP system screen, click the Access Predicates entry to receive detailed information on the search fields used; in this presentation of the execution plans, this information has been inserted directly for the sake of simplicity.

3. Execution plan, index range scan via the MONI~0 index:

Sequential read using the first key field

```
Execution Plan
SELECT STATEMENT (Estimated Costs = 1.763 ,
                Estimated #Rows = 2.032)
      2 TABLE ACCESS BY INDEX ROWID MONI
       ( Estim. Costs = 1.763 , Estim. #Rows = 2.032 )
        Estim. CPU-Costs = 12.963.547
        Estim. IO-Costs = 1.663
         1 INDEX RANGE SCAN MONI~0
          ( Estim. Costs = 62 , Estim. #Rows = 2.032 )
            Search Columns: 1
            Estim. CPU-Costs = 889.721
            Estim. IO-Costs = 55
            Access Predicates "RELID"=:A0
```

4. Execution plan: In the fourth example, the access plan depends on the Oracle version. For Oracle 8, the optimizer decides that the specified field is useless for restricting the blocks to be read, because no index exists for this field. The optimizer therefore decides to perform a full table scan, meaning the database process must check for the WHERE clause in all blocks of the table. The execution plan is the same as in the first example. For Oracle 9, the optimizer determines that a field located before the specified field in the index has not been specified (here, RELID). The index is then split up logically into smaller subindexes for the various values of the unspecified field. The number of subindexes depends on the number of values of the unspecified field. No longer is the entire index searched for the specified field (here, SRTFD); only each individual subindex is searched. We recommend

Sequential read using the second key field

this type of access if the index contains few values for the unspecified field and many values for the specified field.

```
Execution Plan
SELECT STATEMENT ( Estimated Costs = 42 ,
                   Estimated #Rows = 18 )
        2 TABLE ACCESS BY INDEX ROWID MONI
        ( Estim. Costs = 42 , Estim. #Rows = 18 )
        Estim. CPU-Costs = 288.575 Estim. IO-Costs = 39
            1 INDEX SKIP SCAN MONI~0
                ( Estim. Costs = 26 , Estim. #Rows = 18 )
                Search Columns: 1
                Estim. CPU-Costs = 175.160
                Estim. IO-Costs = 24
                Access Predicates "SRTFD"=:A0
                Filter Predicates "SRTFD"=:A0
```

5. Execution plan:

```
Execution Plan
SELECT STATEMENT ( Estimated Costs = 5 , Estimated #Rows = 4
)
   8 TABLE ACCESS BY INDEX ROWID DD01T
     Estim. CPU-Costs = 3.061 Estim. IO-Costs = 0
     7 NESTED LOOPS
       ( Estim. Costs = 4 , Estim. #Rows = 4 )
       Estim. CPU-Costs = 34.260 Estim. IO-Costs = 4

        5 NESTED LOOPS
          ( Estim. Costs = 3 , Estim. #Rows = 3 )
          Estim. CPU-Costs = 25.078 Estim. IO-Costs = 3

           2 TABLE ACCESS BY INDEX ROWID TADIR
             ( Estim. Costs = 2 , Estim. #Rows = 3 )
             Estim. CPU-Costs = 15.465 Estim. IO-Costs = 2
                1 INDEX RANGE SCAN TADIR~DEV
                  ( Estim. Costs = 1 , Estim. #Rows = 28 )
                  Search Columns: 3
                  Estim. CPU-Costs = 5.353 Estim.
                    IO-Costs = 1
                  Access Predicates: "T2"."DEVCLASS"=:A0
                  AND "T2"."PGMID"='R3TR' AND
                  T2"."OBJECT"='DOMA'

           4 TABLE ACCESS BY INDEX ROWID DD01L
             Estim. CPU-Costs = 3.205 Estim. IO-Costs = 0
```

```
      3 INDEX RANGE SCAN DD01L~0
        Search Columns: 1
        Estim. CPU-Costs = 1.504 Estim.
          IO-Costs = 0
        Access Predicates:
         "T1"."DOMNAME"="T2"."OBJ_NAME"
  6 INDEX RANGE SCAN DD01T~0
     Search Columns: 2
     Estim. CPU-Costs = 1.544 Estim. IO-Costs = 0
     Access Predicates "T1"."DOMNAME"=
     "T3"."DOMNAME"
     AND "T1"."AS4LOCAL"="T3"."AS4LOCAL"
     Filter Predicates
         "T1"."AS4LOCAL"="T3"."AS4LOCAL"
```

The database begins by reading the row in the execution plan that is indented the furthest to the right (1), the INDEX RANGE SCAN TADIR~DEV entry. This shows that the access starts via the TADIR~DEV index and that three fields of the index are used for the search. Under Access Predicates, you can find the details of the search conditions. In the SAP system screen, click the Access Predicates entry to see the values that have already been entered in the execution plan for the sake of simplicity. The data on the index is then used to access the TADIR table, entry (2), and then nested loop joins to the DD01L and DD01T tables, which are accessed via the primary index, whose DOMNAME field is filled from the join condition.

B.8.2   SAP MaxDB

1. Execution plan:

Sequential read using a full table scan

TABLENAME	COLUMN OR INDEX	STRATEGY	PAGECOUNT
MONI		TABLE SCAN	65
	RESULT IS NOT COPIED , COSTVALUE IS		65

Because this is a full table scan, no index is used. In all execution plans, the Owner column, which specifies the database user of the SAP system and is identical in all execution plans of a system, was omitted for the sake of clarity.

Direct read

2. Execution plan:

```
TABLENAME    COLUMN OR INDEX    STRATEGY              PAGECOUNT
MONI                            EQUAL CONDITION            79
                               FOR KEY COLUMN
             RELID             (USED KEY COLUMN)
             SRTFD             (USED KEY COLUMN)
             SRTF2             (USED KEY COLUMN)
                    RESULT IS NOT COPIED , COSTVALUE IS   1
```

The search strategy identifies the fields RELID, SRTFD, and SRTF2 as relevant for the search. The strategy EQUAL CONDITION FOR KEY COLUMN shows that all of the fields of the primary index are specified. This enables a direct read of the table.

Sequential read using the first key field

3. Execution plan:

```
TABLENAME    COLUMN OR INDEX    STRATEGY              PAGECOUNT
MONI                            RANGE CONDITION           65
                               FOR KEY COLUMN
             RELID             (USED KEY COLUMN)
                    RESULT IS NOT COPIED , COSTVALUE IS   1
```

MaxDB stores tables sorted by key fields so that a table and its primary index constitute one database object. Here, with the field RELID as the first key field, the table is accessed without an index using the strategy RANGE CONDITION FOR KEY COLUMN.

Sequential read using the second key field

4. Because only the field SRTFD is specified for the fourth example, MaxDB also performs a full table scan. Therefore, this execution plan is identical to the first example.

In contrast to many other database systems, MaxDB differentiates between accesses through the primary index and the secondary index. For primary index access, it uses the access strategy RANGE CONDITION FOR KEY COLUMN.

Access to a database view

5. Execution plan:

```
TABLENAME    COLUMN OR INDEX    STRATEGY                  PAGECOUNT
TADIR        TADIR~DEV          EQUAL CONDITION FOR INDEX 25338
                               ONLY INDEX ACCESSED
             DEVCLASS          (USED INDEX COLUMN)
             PGMID             (USED INDEX COLUMN)
```

```
          OBJECT           (USED INDEX COLUMN)
          PGMID            (USED KEY COLUMN)
          OBJECT           (USED KEY COLUMN)
DD01L     DOMNAME          JOIN VIA KEY RANGE        1038
DD01T     DOMNAME          JOIN VIA KEY RANGE        1075
                 NO TEMPORARY RESULTS CREATED
                 RESULT IS COPIED   , COSTVALUE IS    135
```

The execution plan, which must be read from top to bottom, shows that the database optimizer decides to first access the TADIR~DEV index — as expected. Here, it fills the DEVCLASS field from the WHERE condition and PGMID and OBJECT from the restricting condition. The database optimizer subsequently uses the DOMNAME key field, which is filled from the join condition, to access the DD01L and DD01T tables line by line.

B.8.3   IBM DB2 for Linux, UNIX, and Windows

1. Execution plan:

Sequential read using a full table scan

```
AccessPlan ( Opt Level = 5 ; Parallelism =  None )
0 SELECT STATEMENT ( Estimated Costs =  6,724E+04 [timerons] )
     1 RETURN
          2 TBSCAN MONI
```

2. Execution plan:

```
Access Plan    ( Opt Level = 5 ; Parallelism =  None )
0 SELECT STATEMENT ( Estimated Costs =  5,249E+01 [timerons]
     1 RETURN
          2 FETCH MONI
               3 IXSCAN MONI~0 #key columns:  3
```

The search strategy IXSCAN MONI~0 #key columns: 3 indicates that all three fields of the index MONI~0 are relevant for the search; all three fields are referred to as predicates.

3. Execution plan:

Sequential read using the first key field

```
Access Plan    ( Opt Level = 5 ; Parallelism =  None )
0 SELECT STATEMENT ( Estimated Costs =  1,755E+03 [timerons]
1 RETURN
          2 FETCH MONI
               3 IXSCAN MONI~0 #key columns:  1
```

The line `IXSCAN MONI~0` indicates that the table is accessed via the index MONI~0. The number of `key columns` indicates how many index fields are used as predicates for the search: one field in this example.

Sequential read using the second key field

4. Execution plan:

```
Access Plan     ( Opt Level = 5 ; Parallelism =  None )
0 SELECT STATEMENT ( Estimated Costs =  2,972E+02 [timerons]

        1 RETURN
            2 FETCH MONI
                3 IXSCAN MONI~0 #key columns:  0
```

In our fourth example, the access results in a sequential index scan of the index `MONI~0`. Like a DB2 UDB for zSeries, DB2/UDB for UNIX and Windows also decides to read the index MONI 0 first to locate the appropriate pages of the table. Because the field SRTFD specified in the `WHERE` clause is the second field in the index, and the first field hasn't been specified, the index can only be used to a limited extent for the search. Therefore, the #key columns used is 0 in this example. The second field in the index is used as a *sargable predicate*.

You can retrieve detailed information on the access plans by clicking the Details button: Place the cursor on the step (FETCH, IXSCAN, ...) and click the Details button, or select GOTO • DISPLAY DETAILS. The display contains an analysis of the predicates used and enables you to determine which index fields the optimizer includes during an access operation.

Access to a database view

5. Execution plan:

```
Access Plan     Opt Level = 5 ; Parallelism = None
0 SELECT STATEMENT ( Estimated Costs =  1,977E+02 [timerons] )
    1 RETURN
        2 NLJOIN
            3 [O] NLJOIN
                4 [O] FETCH TADIR
                    5 IXSCAN TADIR~DEV #key columns:  3
                6 [I] FETCH DD01T
                    7 IXSCAN DD01T~0 #key columns:  2
            8 [I] FETCH DD01L
                9 IXSCAN DD01L~0 #key columns:  2
```

As expected, in step 5, `IXSCAN TADIR~DEV`, the database optimizer first accesses the TADIR table via the TADIR~DEV index to then read the missing data line by line from the DO10L and DO10T tables (*nested loop join*).

B.8.4 IBM DB2 for IBM i

1. Execution plan:

```
MAIN LEVEL 1
    SUBSELECT LEVEL 1
        File R3B46DATA/MONI   processed in join position 1
                              using arrival sequence.
        Arrival sequence used to perform record selection
            Reason code:         T1 No indexes exist.
```

Sequential read using a full table scan

2. Execution plan:

```
MAIN LEVEL 1
    SUBSELECT LEVEL 1
        File R3B46DATA/MONI   processed in join position 1
                              using access path "MONI+0".
        Index R3B46DATA/"MONI+0"    was used to acces
                                    records from file
R3B46DATA/MONI
            Reason code: I1 record selection
            Key fields of the access path used:
                RELID
                SRTFD
                SRTF2
            Key row positioning using 3 key field(s).
```

Direct read

The search strategy `Key row positioning using 3 key field(s)` indicates that all three fields of the index MONI+0 will be used for the search.

3. Execution plan:

```
MAIN LEVEL 1
    SUBSELECT LEVEL 1
        File R3B46DATA/MONI processed in join position 1
                            using access path "MONI+0".
        Index R3B46DATA/"MONI+0"   was used to access
                                   records from file R3B46DATA/
                                   MONI
```

Sequential read using the first key field

```
Reason code: I1 record selection
Key fields of the access path used:
   RELID
   SRTFD
   SRTF2
Key row positioning using 1 key field(s).
```

The database optimizer chooses the index MONI~0. The search strategy Key row positioning using 1 key field(s) indicates that the first field, RELID, will be used for the search.

Sequential read using the second key field

4. Execution plan:

```
MAIN LEVEL 1
   SUBSELECT LEVEL 1
      File R3B46DATA/MONI  processed in join position 1
                           using arrival sequence.
      Arrival sequence used to perform record
      selection
            Reason code:  T3 Query optimizer chose
                          table scan over available
                          indexes.
```

The database optimizer will decide on the full table scan because this will be more efficient than access through an index. The reason code, T3 Query optimizer chose table scan over available indexes, explains this.

Access to a database view

5. Execution plan:

```
Details iSeries-EXPLAIN
Execution Time (ms)
      OPEN                    29

      HARD CLOSE               0
      CLOSE                    6
ODP Implementation         R Query implemented as reusable ODP
Host Variable Implementation  I (Interface Supplied Values)

MAIN LEVEL
   SUBSELECT 1
      JOIN POSITION 1
      Join Position 1 for       R3CHBDATA/TADIR
```

```
        Index R3CHBDATA/TADIR+DEV was used by Query on
R3CHBDATA/TADIR
      JOIN POSITION 2
        Join Position 2 for          R3CHBDATA/DD01L
        Index R3CHBDATA/"DD01L+0" was used by Query on
R3CHBDATA/DD01L
      JOIN POSITION 3
        Join Position 3 for          R3CHBDATA/DD01T
        Index R3CHBDATA/"DD01T+0" was used by Query on
R3CHBDATA/DD01T
      Index Scan-key Selection
      All Indexes Considered for     R3CHBDATA/TADIR
      All Indexes Considered for     R3CHBDATA/DD01L
      All Indexes Considered for     R3CHBDATA/DD01T
```

In DB for IBM i — like in all other databases — the database optimizer first accesses the TADIR table via the TADIR~DEV index to then read the missing data line by line from the D010L and D010T tables using a *nested loop join*.

B.8.5 IBM DB2 for z/OS

1. Execution plan:

Sequential read using a full table scan

```
Explanation of query block number: 1    step: 1
Query block type is SELECT
Performance appears to be  good.
Index is used. Index scan by non-matching index.
Method:
        access new table.
        unknown or no prefetch is used
        new table:
                SAPR3.MONI
                table space locked in mode:  N
        Accesstype: by index.
                Index: SAPR3.MONI~0 (non-matching index)
                Index columns (ordered): RELID SRTFD SRTF2
                DB2 can at least use the index to pick out
                those pages from the table space that
                contain data of the table: MONI
```

The MONI table is created on a DB2 for z/OS database as a cluster table (*VOLATILE* table attribute), so the DB2 optimizer always chooses the access via the index. In a full table scan via a noncluster table (SELECT * FROM T100), the access plan is as follows:

```
Explanation of query block number: 1    step: 1
Query block type is SELECT
Performance appears to be bad
No index is used. Sequential tablespace scan
Method:
            access new table.
            data pages are read in advance
            pure sequential prefetch is used
            new table:
                        SAPR3.T100
                        table space locked in mode:   N
            Accesstype: sequential tablespace scan.
```

Direct read   2. Execution plan:

```
Explanation of query block number: 1    step: 1
Performance appears to be optimal.
Index is used. Index Scan by matching Index.
Method:
            access new table.
            unknown or no prefetch is used
            new Table:
                SAPR3.MONI
                table space locked in mode:   N
            Accesstype: by index.
                Index: SAPR3.MONI~0 (matching Index)
                Index columns (ordered): RELID SRTFD SRTF2
                with 3 matching columns of 3 Index-Columns.
```

The search strategy with 3 matching columns of 3 Index-Columns indicates that all three fields of the index MONI~0 will be used for the search.

Sequential read using the first key field   3. Execution plan:

```
Explanation of query block number: 1    step: 1
Query block type is SELECT
Performance appears to be good.
Index is used. Index Scan by matching Index.
Method:
```

```
access new table.
unknown or no prefetch is used
new Table:
       SAPR3.MONI
       table space locked in mode:  N
Accesstype: by index.
       Index: SAPR3.MONI~0 (matching Index)
       Index columns (ordered): RELID SRTFD SRTF2
       with 1 matching columns of 3 Index-Columns.
```

The database optimizer chooses the index MONI~0. The search strategy `with 1 matching columns of 3 Index-Columns` indicates that the first field of the index `MONI~0` will be used for the search.

4. Execution plan:

Sequential read
using the second
key field

```
Explanation of query block number: 1    step: 1
Query block type is SELECT
Performance appears to be good.
Index is used. Index Scan by nonmatching Index.
Method:
        access new table.
          new Table:
               SAPR3.MONI
               table space locked in mode:  N
        Accesstype: by index.
            Index: SAPR3.MONI~0 (nonmatching Index)
            Index columns (ordered): RELID SRTFD SRTF2
     DB2 can at least use the index to pick out those
     pages from the table space, that contain data of
     the table: MONI
```

The database optimizer chooses to use the index MONI~0 for the search. Because the field SRTFD specified in the SQL statement is the second field, and the first field, RELID, is missing from the WHERE clause, the index must be read sequentially. This is indicated by the access strategy `Index Scan by nonmatching Index`.

5. Execution plan:

Access to a
database view

```
Explanation of query block number: 1    step: 1
Query block type is SELECT
Performance appears to be optimal
Index is used. Index scan by matching index.
Method:
```

703

access new table.
unknown or no prefetch is used
new table:

    SAPR3.TADIR
    table space locked in mode: N
Accesstype: by index.
    Index: SAPR3.TADIR~DEV (matching index)
    Index columns (ordered): DEVCLASS PGMID OBJECT
    with 3 matching columns of 3 index columns.
Explanation of query block number: 1   step: 2
Query block type is SELECT
Performance appears to be good
Index is used. Index scan by matching index.
Method:

    join each row of composite table, with matching rows
    of new table (nested loop Join).
    unknown or no prefetch is used
    new table:

    SAPR3.DD01L
    table space locked in mode: N
Accesstype: by index.
    Index: SAPR3.DD01L~0 (matching index)
    Index columns (ordered): DOMNAME AS4LOCAL AS4VERS
    with 1 matching columns of 3 index columns.
Explanation of query block number: 1   step: 3
Query block type is SELECT
Performance appears to be good
Index is used. Index scan by matching index.
Method:

    join each row of composite table, with matching rows
    of new table (nested loop Join).
    unknown or no prefetch is used
    new table:

    SAPR3.DD01T
    table space locked in mode: N
Accesstype: by index.
    Index: SAPR3.DD01T~0 (matching index)
    Index columns (ordered): DOMNAME DDLANGUAGE ...
    with 1   matching columns of 4 index columns.

As expected, the database optimizer first accesses the TADIR table via the TADIR~DEV index to then read the missing data line by line from the D010L and D010T tables (*nested loop join*).

The comments on performance visible in the DB2 for z/OS execution plans are automatically displayed, depending on the access type. For a sequential tablespace scan (a full table scan), the automatic text is "performance appears to be bad"; for an index range scan, the text is "performance appears to be good"; for an index unique scan, the text is "performance is optimal." However, they should not be understood as valid descriptions of the current performance situation. A full table scan on a small table does not cause a performance problem, whereas an index range scan on a large table with selection conditions that do not strictly limit the data volume can considerably reduce performance.

B.8.6 IBM Informix Dynamic Server

1. Execution plan:

Sequential read using a full table scan

```
Estimated Cost: 59
Estimated # of Rows Returned: 1478
  1) sapr3.moni: SEQUENTIAL SCAN(Serial, fragments: ALL)
Query statistics:
  Table map :
  Internal name      Table name
  t1                 moni
  type   table  rows_prod   est_rows   rows_scan  time       est_cost
  scan   t1     1458        1478       1458       00:00.00   59
```

The *estimated costs* of the access are a numerical value that the database optimizer of the Informix database instance provides to compare different access paths of an SQL statement. This value cannot be converted directly in time and is not suitable for comparing different SQL statements. However, it is an indicator to compare different execution plans for tuning a statement.

Informix prepends the time of optimization to every execution plan. This time of optimization is left out in all execution plans for clarity reasons. It can be particularly beneficial if, for example, the indexing or statistics have changed.

705

Direct read   2. Execution plan:

```
Estimated Cost: 1
Estimated # of Rows Returned: 1
  1) sapr3.moni: INDEX PATH
     (1) Index Keys: relid srtfd srtf2 (Serial, fragments:
ALL)
          Lower Index Filter: ((sapr3.moni.srtfd = ... AND
                                sapr3.moni.relid = ... ) AND
                                sapr3.moni.srtf2 = ... )
Query statistics:
  Table map :
  Internal name     Table name
  t1                moni
  type    table   rows_prod   est_rows   rows_
scan   time          est_cost

  scan    t1      1           1          1          00:00.00  1
```

The third line, sapr3.moni: INDEX PATH, indicates that Informix accesses the table through an index. The next line lists the fields in the index: relid, srtfd, and srtf2. To determine the name of the index used from the listed fields, check the fields as listed in the ABAP Dictionary (Transaction SE11). The lines below indicate which index fields will be used for the search. Here they are relid, srtfd, and srtf2.

Sequential read using the first key field   3. Execution plan:

```
Estimated Cost: 20
Estimated # of Rows Returned: 412
  1) sapr3.moni: INDEX PATH
     (1) Index Keys: relid srtfd srtf2 (Serial, fragments:
ALL)
          Lower Index Filter: sapr3.moni.relid = '...'
Query statistics:
  Table map :
  Internal name     Table name
  t1                moni
  type    table   rows_prod   est_rows   rows_scan   time
est_cost

  scan    t1      394         413        394         00:00.00  20
```

The line `sapr3.moni: INDEX PATH` signifies that Informix accesses the tables through the index. The line `Index Keys: relid srtfd srtf2` indicates which index keys are in the index. The line `Lower Index Filter: sapr3.moni.relid = '...'` indicates which index field will be used for the search. In this execution plan, it is the field `relid`.

4. Execution plan:

Sequential read using the second key field

```
Estimated Cost: 48
Estimated # of Rows Returned: 63
  1) sapr3.moni: INDEX PATH
    (1) Index Keys: relid srtfd srtf2   (Serial, fragments:
ALL)
        Index Self Join Keys (relid )
        Lower Index Filter: sapr3.moni.relid = sapr3.moni.
relid AND
                            sapr3.moni.srtfd = '...'
Query statistics:
  Table map :
  Internal name     Table name
  t1                moni
  type    table  rows_prod  est_rows  rows_
scan   time        est_cost

  scan   t1     72          63        72         00:00.00   48
```

The execution plan shows that Informix accesses the tables through the index using the RELID, SRTFD, and SRTF2 fields. But because the leading index field is not specified in the `WHERE` condition, the optimizer decides on the index self join. As a result, the entire index is searched, but a table scan is avoided. The estimated costs are somewhat lower than in the sequential scan of the first example.

5. Execution plan:

Access to a database view

```
Estimated Cost: 111
Estimated # of Rows Returned: 2
  1) sapr3.tadir: INDEX PATH
    (1) Index Keys: devclass pgmid object
        Lower Index Filter: ((sapr3.tadir.devclass = 'SDIC'
AND
                            sapr3.tadir.object = 'DOMA' )
```

```
                  AND
                                          sapr3.tadir.pgmid = 'R3TR' )
        2) sapr3.dd011: INDEX PATH
          (1) Index Keys: domname as4local as4vers
              Lower Index Filter: sapr3.dd011.domname =
                                  sapr3.tadir.obj_name
    NESTED LOOP JOIN
        3) sapr3.dd01t: INDEX PATH
              Filters: sapr3.dd011.as4local = sapr3.dd01t.as4local
          (1) Index Keys: domname ddlanguage as4local as4vers
              Lower Index Filter: sapr3.tadir.obj_name =
                                  sapr3.dd01t.domname
    NESTED LOOP JOIN
    Query statistics:
      Table map :
      Internal name       Table name
      t1                  tadir
      t2                  dd011
      t3                  dd01t
      type      table   rows_prod   est_rows   rows_
    scan  time        est_cost
       scan    t1      305          154         305              00:00.00
    17
      type      table   rows_prod   est_rows   rows_
    scan  time        est_cost
       scan    t2      305          10023       305              00:00.00  1
       type     rows_prod  est_rows  time       est_cost
       nljoin   305         14        00:00.00   103
       type     table   rows_prod   est_rows   rows_
    scan  time        est_cost
       scan    t3      610          19229       610              00:00.00  1
       type     rows_prod  est_rows  time       est_cost

       nljoin   610         3         00:00.01   111
```

The execution plan shows that the system first selects from the TADIR table. Here, the access is via the index with the DEVCLASS, PGMID, and OBJECT fields. The `devclass = 'SDIC'` condition comes from the WHERE clause; the other two are specified in the definition of the INFO_DOMAT view. With every line from TADIR found here, appropriate lines are now searched for in the DD01L table. The procedure is called nested loop join because two search loops are nested in one another. Here again, the access is via an index. The result of the search performed up to this point is used in the last step to retrieve the still missing data from the DD01T table via a nested loop join and add it to the overall result.

B.8.7 Microsoft SQL Server

1. Execution plan:

```
Clustered Index Scan(OBJECT:([PAL].[pal].[MONI].[MONI~0]))
```

Sequential read using a full table scan

In SAP systems that run on an SQL Server database, all tables are stored according to the key. The primary index is a *clustered index*. That's why the table data is located at the lowest level of the clustered index MONI~0. The key word Scan indicates that all data pages in the index MONI~0 are read. PAL is the name of the SAP system or the database.

2. The execution plan for the fully qualified access is as follows:

```
Clustered Index Seek(OBJECT:([PAL].[pal].[MONI].[MONI~0]),
      SEEK:([PAL].[pal].[MONI].[RELID]=[@1] AND
            [PAL].[pal].[MONI].[SRTFD]=[@2] AND
            [PAL].[pal].[MONI].[SRTF2]=CONVERT_
IMPLICIT(int,[@3],0))
                        ORDERED FORWARD)
```

Direct read

The search strategy is indicated in the parentheses after Seek and shows that the fields RELID, SRTFD, and SRTF2 will be used for the search.

3. Execution plan:

```
Clustered Index Seek(OBJECT:([PAL].[pal].[MONI].[MONI~0]),
      SEEK:([PAL].[pal].[MONI].[RELID]=[@1]) ORDERED FORWARD)
```

Sequential read using the first key field

The search strategy Clustered Index Seek indicates that the index MONI~0 and the field RELID will be used for the search.

4. Execution plan:

```
Clustered Index Scan(OBJECT:([PAL].[pal].[MONI].[MONI~0]),
      WHERE:([PAL].[pal].[MONI].[SRTFD]=[@1]))
```

Sequential read using the second key field

SQL Server uses the clustered index for the fourth example also. Because the field SRTFD specified in the SQL statement is the second field, and the first field, RELID, is missing from the WHERE clause, the index must be read sequentially. This is indicated in the WHERE search function instead of SEEK, which was used in the previous example.

In contrast to many other database systems, SQL Server differentiates between accesses through the primary index and the secondary index. For primary index access, it uses the access strategy Clustered Index Seek.

Access to a database view

5. Execution plan:

```
|--Nested Loops(Inner Join, OUTER REFERENCES:([T1].[AS4LOCAL],
      [T2].[OBJ_NAME], [Expr1007]) OPTIMIZED WITH UNORDERED PREFETCH)
    |--Nested Loops(Inner Join, OUTER REFERENCES:([T2].[OBJ_NAME],
       [Expr1006]) OPTIMIZED WITH UNORDERED PREFETCH)
    |   |--Index Seek(OBJECT:([TADIR].[TADIR~DEV] AS [T2]),
    |          SEEK:([T2].[DEVCLASS]='/ASU/MAIN_DDIC' AND
    |              [T2].[PGMID]='R3TR' AND
    |              [T2].[OBJECT]='DOMA') ORDERED FORWARD)
    |   |--Clustered Index Seek(OBJECT:([DD01L].[DD01L~0]
    |                                   AS [T1]),
    |       SEEK:([T1].[DOMNAME]= [TADIR].[OBJ_NAME]
    |         as [T2].[OBJ_NAME]) ORDERED FORWARD)
    |--Clustered Index Seek(OBJECT:([DD01T].[DD01T~0] AS [T3]),
    |       SEEK:([T3].[DOMNAME]=[TADIR].[OBJ_NAME]
    |         as [T2].[OBJ_NAME]),
    |       WHERE:([DD01L].[AS4LOCAL] as [T1].[AS4LOCAL]=
    |              [DD01T].[AS4LOCAL] as [T3].[AS4LOCAL])
    |          ORDERED FORWARD)
```

The access starts with an index seek in the index for the DEVCLASS field. Then the database instance reads the missing data from the D010L and D010T tables using a nested loop join, that is, line by line.

B.9   Local Database Monitors and SQL Trace in the SAP J2EE Engine

On the SAP J2EE Engine, the database process monitor is in the local SAP NetWeaver Administrator: *http://<server>:<port>/nwa*, where *<server>* stands for the name of an application server on which the dispatcher of the J2EE clusters is running, and *<port>* is the TCP/IP port to which the dispatcher answers. Select PROBLEM MANAGEMENT • DATABASE • OPEN SQL MONITORS • NATIVE DB MONITORS • SHOW DATABASE ACTIVITY.

Database process monitor

You can find the monitor for database locks in the local SAP NetWeaver Administrator by selecting PROBLEM MANAGEMENT • DATABASE • OPEN SQL MONITORS • NATIVE DB MONITORS • SHOW CURRENT EXCLUSIVE LOCK WAIT SITUATIONS.

Database locks

The statistics on table accesses in general and on SQL statements is available in the local SAP NetWeaver Administrator under PROBLEM MANAGEMENT • DATABASE • OPEN SQL MONITORS • TABLE STATISTICS MONITOR OR PROBLEM MANAGEMENT • DATABASE • OPEN SQL MONITORS • OPEN SQL STATISTICS.

Table and SQL statistics

The functions for starting, stopping, and analyzing an SQL trace on the SAP J2EE Engine are in the local SAP NetWeaver Administrator: PROBLEM MANAGEMENT • DATABASE • OPEN SQL MONITORS • SQL TRACE ADMINISTRATION. This opens a list of J2EE instances.

SQL trace

You start the trace by selecting one or several instances and the function Switch Trace On for the Selected Nodes. In the Trace Option subscreen, you can specify whether the call stack should be recorded for every SQL statement.

Starting and stopping the trace

Use the Switch Trace Off for the Selected Nodes function to stop the trace.

By default, new files are created for a new trace, which means you can review old traces until you delete them.

SQL trace on the SAP J2EE Engine is also activated and analyzed within the scope of an end-to-end trace in SAP Solution Manager.

[+]

Analyzing the trace To finally analyze the trace, call the SQL Trace Evaluation function in the Open SQL Monitor. This opens a list of the created traces. Select the trace you want to analyze and select Display Selected Trace.

In the Toggle Advanced Selection Criteria subscreen, you can define which accesses will be viewed in the trace analysis. It also enables you to restrict the trace according to user. Table B.16 lists which data the system displays when you want to view the details of an access. It only presents fields with values.

Field	Explanation
Time	Start time of the JDBC call
Duration	Duration of the JDBC call in microseconds
Method Name	Name of the JDBC method
JDBC Method Input Parameters	Input parameters of the JDBC method
DB Error Code	Error code if there's a database error
DB Error SQL State	Status of the database statement if there's an error
Statement	SQL statement or JDBC method call
SQL Statement Bind Parameters	Parameters of the SQL statement
Result	Result of the JDBC method call
Database ID	Identifier of the database connection, combination of the name of the DataSource and database user, linked by "&"
Number of Calls	Number of subsequent calls with identical results (for totals records)
Minimum Duration of a Single Call in Microseconds	Minimum duration of a JDBC method call (for totals records)
Maximum Duration of a Single Call in Microseconds	Maximum duration of a JDBC method call (for totals records)

Table B.16 SQL Trace Fields

Field	Explanation
Average Duration of a Single Call in Microseconds	Average duration of a JDBC method call (for totals records)
J2EE Application	Name of the J2EE application
J2EE User	Name of the J2EE user
J2EE Transaction	Identifies the J2EE transaction
J2EE Session	Identifies the J2EE session
Result Set ID	Identifies the result set (for internal purposes)
Table Names	All involved tables (only for Open SQL statements)
Thread	Identifies the thread that executed the SQL statement
DB Session ID	Identifies the database session
Vendor SQL Connection ID	Identifies the vendor SQL connection
Vendor SQL Statement ID	Identifies the vendor SQL statement
Stack Trace	Call stack (if recording is activated)
DSR Transaction ID	Identifies the distributed statistics record; used to clearly identify the trace in the end-to-end analysis when the trace is enabled via SAP Solution Manager
Unique Log Record Number	Identifies the logging API

Table B.16 SQL Trace Fields (Cont.)

C   Performance-Relevant Configuration Parameters and Key Figures

This appendix lists performance-relevant configuration parameters and performance key figures in the central CCMS monitor. We've tried to summarize the most essential details from the large amount of information; however, we cannot guarantee the list's completeness.

The most essential performance key figures enable you to monitor system performance in the central CCMS Alert Monitor (Transaction RZ20). Chapter 2, Section 2.8, Continuous Monitoring Using CCMS, introduces this monitor.

C.1   ABAP Server

Configuration Parameters

This appendix lists configuration parameters that are relevant to performance. Please note the following:

▶ To display the list of current parameter settings for a given SAP instance, call the SAP memory configuration monitor (Transaction ST02), and then select Current Parameters.

▶ Because exact configuration suggestions only make sense for concrete SAP systems and become obsolete rather quickly, there are no direct suggestions for them in this book.

▶ You can change parameters either directly in the profile files or by using Transaction RZ10.

▶ Operating system limits affect memory management for your SAP release. Ensure that the operating system can administer the memory size you want to configure. For information on operating system limits, see Chapter 8, Memory Management.

▶ When changing memory management parameters, always keep a backup of the old instance profiles. This backup will enable you to revert to the former parameter values if required. Before restarting the instance, test the new instance profiles using the auxiliary program `sappfpar` on the operating system level. After instance restart, verify that the instance is running without error. To obtain a description of the program `sappfpar`, execute the operating system command `sappfpar ?`.

[!] When you are trying to change particular parameters, warnings may appear indicating that changes should not be made without express instructions from SAP. Heed these warnings. Instructions from SAP on changing the parameters can be provided by SAP employees or hardware or database partners who have analyzed your system or through recommendations in an SAP Note. You can find SAP Notes in the SAP Service Marketplace. Ensure that the SAP Note applies to your SAP version, database system, database version, operating system, and operating system version.

Documentation For help on SAP Basis profile parameters, use Transaction RZ11:

1. Enter Transaction RZ11.
2. Enter the SAP profile parameter for which you require more information.
3. Select Documentation.

Buffers The group in Table C.1 contains a listing for each SAP buffer, describing the buffer and related SAP profile parameters.

Buffer Name: Table Definition (TTAB)	
Parameter	**Description**
`rsdb/ntab/ entrycount`	This parameter specifies the maximum number of buffer entries.
	The size of the TTAB buffer is approximately equivalent to the maximum number of entries multiplied by 100 bytes.
Buffer Name: Field Description (FTAB)	
Parameter	**Description**
`rsdb/ntab/ftabsize`	Buffer size allocated at instance startup in kilobytes.
`rsdb/ntab/ entrycount`	The maximum number of buffer entries divided by two.

Table C.1 Parameters for SAP Buffers (See SAP Note 103747)

Buffer Name: Field Description (FTAB)	
Parameter	**Description**
rsdb/ntab/ftabsize	Buffer size allocated at instance startup in kilobytes.
rsdb/ntab/ entrycount	The maximum number of buffer entries divided by two.

Buffer Name: Initial Record (IRDB)	
Parameter	**Description**
rsdb/ntab/irbdsize	Buffer size allocated at instance startup in kilobytes.
rsdb/ntab/ entrycount	The maximum number of buffer entries divided by two.

Buffer Name: Short Nametab (SNTAB)	
Parameter	**Description**
rsdb/ntab/sntabsize	Buffer size allocated at instance startup in kilobytes.
rsdb/ntab/ entrycount	The maximum number of buffer entries divided by two.

Buffer Name: Program (PXA)	
Parameter	**Description**
abap/buffersize	Buffer size allocated at instance startup in kilobytes.

Buffer Name: CUA	
Parameter	**Description**
rsdb/cua/buffersize	Buffer size allocated at instance startup in kilobytes.
The maximum number of buffer entries in the CUA buffer equals half the value of the buffer size.	

Buffer Name: Screen	
Parameter	**Description**
zcsa/presentation_ buffer_area	The buffer size allocated at instance startup (in bytes) equals half the value of this parameter.
sap/bufdir_entries	This parameter specifies the maximum number of buffer entries.

Table C.1 Parameters for SAP Buffers (See SAP Note 103747) (Cont.)

Buffer Name: Export/Import	
Parameter	**Description**
`rsdb/obj/buffersize`	Buffer size allocated at instance startup in kilobytes.
`rsdb/obj/max_objects`	This parameter specifies the maximum number of buffer entries.
`rsdb/obj/large_object_size`	Typical size of the largest objects, in bytes.

Buffer Name: Export/Import SHM	
Parameter	**Description**
`rsdb/esm/buffersize_kb`	Buffer size allocated at instance startup in kilobytes.
`rsdb/esm/max_objects`	This parameter specifies the maximum number of buffer entries.
`rsdb/esm/large_object_size`	Typical size of the largest objects, in bytes.

Buffer Name: Generic Key Table	
Parameter	**Description**
`zcsa/table_buffer_area`	Buffer size allocated at instance startup in bytes.
`zcsa/db_max_buftab`	This parameter specifies the maximum number of buffer entries.

Buffer Name: Single Record Table	
Parameter	**Description**
`Rtbb/buffer_length`	Buffer size allocated at instance startup in kilobytes.
`Rtbb/max_tables`	This parameter specifies the maximum number of buffer entries.

Buffer Name: Calendar	
Parameter	**Description**
`zcsa/calendar_area`	Buffer size allocated at instance startup in bytes.
`zcsa/calendar_ids`	This parameter specifies the maximum number of buffer entries.

Table C.1 Parameters for SAP Buffers (See SAP Note 103747) (Cont.)

Main Memory for Shared Objects	
Parameter	**Description**
abap/shared_objects_size_MB	Allocated main memory for shared o(including administration information, in megabytes)

Table C.1 Parameters for SAP Buffers (See SAP Note 103747) (Cont.)

SAP currently supports a number of operating systems for the implementation of the SAP application level:

Memory Management

▶ UNIX dialects such as AIX, HP-UX, Linux, and Solaris

▶ Windows

▶ IBM i, IBM zSeries

You can find detailed information about available platforms in the SAP Service Marketplace under *www.service.sap.com/platforms*.

Table C.2 lists SAP profile parameters for SAP memory management.

With Zero Administration Memory Management, the parameters marked with an asterisk (*) in Table C.2 are automatically set at instance startup. These automatic settings are overwritten if there are different values for these parameters in the instance profile. If your system uses Zero Administration Memory Management, SAP recommends that you delete the parameters listed in Table C.2 from the instance profile and configure only the parameter PHYS_MEMSIZE. See also Chapter 8, Memory Management, and SAP Note 88416.

The following classifications are shown in the Type column in Table C.2: P denotes parameters that directly affect the performance of the SAP system. S denotes parameters that ensure the secure operation of the SAP system under high load.

Parameter	Description	Type
ztta/roll_area*	Total local SAP roll area for all work processes.	S/P

Parameter	Description	Type
ztta/roll_first*	Portion of the local SAP roll area allocated to a dialog work process before SAP extended memory is allocated.	P
Rdisp/ROLL_SHM*	Size of the SAP roll buffer in shared memory.	P
Rdisp/PG_SHM*	Size of the ABAP paging buffer in shared memory. (For SAP Version 4.0 and later, this has little effect on performance.)	P
Rdisp/ROLL_MAXFS*	Size of the global SAP roll area, which comprises the SAP roll buffer plus the SAP roll file.	S
rdisp/PG_MAXFS*	Size of the ABAP paging area, which comprises the ABAP paging buffer plus the ABAP paging file.	S
em/initial_size_MB*	Initial size of SAP extended memory.	S/P
em/max_size_MB*	Maximum size of SAP extended memory. Some operating system limits keep the size of SAP extended memory smaller than this value.	S/P
em/blocksize_KB*	Size of a block in SAP extended memory. Default value 1024. Warning: Do not modify this parameter without prior recommendation by SAP.	P
em/address_space_MB*	The address space reserved for SAP extended memory (currently applies only under Windows NT).	S/P
ztta/roll_extension*	Maximum amount of SAP extended memory that can be allocated for each user context.	S/P

Table C.2 Parameters for SAP Memory Management (See SAP Notes 103747 and 88416)

abap/heap_area_dia*	Maximum SAP heap memory for each dialog work process.	S

Parameter	Description	Type
abap/heap_area_nondia*	Maximum SAP heap memory for each nondialog work process.	S
abap/heap_area_total*	Maximum SAP heap memory for all work processes.	S
abap/heaplimit*	Limit in the SAP heap memory that flags work processes so they are restarted after the end of the current transaction and can therefore release the heap memory.	S
em/global_area_MB	Size of global extended memory (SAP EG Memory) for SAP Basis 4.6D and later.	S

Table C.2 Parameters for SAP Memory Management (See SAP Notes 103747 and 88416) (Cont.)

Parameter	Description
rdisp/mshost	Name of the computer where the message server is running.
rdisp/msserv	Name of the message service.
rdisp/enqname	Name of the SAP instance where the enqueue server is running.
rdisp/atp_server	Name of the SAP instance where the ATP server is running.
rdisp/wp_no_dia	Number of dialog work processes (per SAP instance).
rdisp/wp_no_btc	Number of background work processes.
rdisp/wp_no_enq	Number of enqueue work processes.
rdisp/wp_no_spo	Number of spool work processes.
rdisp/wp_no_vb	Number of update work processes.
rdisp/wp_no_vb2	Number of work processes for V2 updates.

Table C.3 SAP Profile Parameters for Load Distribution

Parameter	Description
rdisp/vb_dispatching	Activates or deactivates update dispatching. If the parameter is set to 1 (the default setting), update dispatching is activated. If the parameter is set to 0, update dispatching is not activated.
rdisp/vbstart	This parameter controls the behavior of the update service at SAP system startup. At startup, the update service checks its queue to see whether there are any update requests that have not yet been processed. Such requests are marked and then processed. If the parameter is set to 1 (the default setting), the update service processes update requests that have not yet been processed. If the parameter is set to 0, waiting update requests are not automatically processed.
rdisp/max_wprun_time	This parameter limits the maximum runtime of a transaction step in a dialog work process (in seconds). When this time has expired, the user request is terminated with the error message "TIME_OUT." The default setting is 300.
	Warning: If a Commit Work command is executed in a program, this runtime starts again. While an SQL statement is being processed on the database, the program is *not* terminated, even when this runtime expires.
rdisp/gui_auto_logout	If there is no GUI activity for rdisp/gui_auto_logout seconds, the frontend is automatically logged off. If the parameter has the value 0, there is no automatic logoff.
login/disable_multi_gui_login	If this parameter is set to 1, multiple dialog logon connections (for the same client with the same user name) are blocked by the system. This parameter works for SAP GUI logon connections. This parameter has no effect on someone logging on using the Internet Transaction Server (ITS) or remote function call (RFC).

Table C.3 SAP Profile Parameters for Load Distribution (Cont.)

Parameter	Description
login/multi_login_users	This list contains the names of users who are authorized for multiple logon connections. Commas separate the user names (without client entry).
rdisp/max_alt_modes	This parameter specifies the number of parallel modes per logon session that a user is authorized to open. This should only be done for specific reasons (e.g., acute memory bottleneck). Depending on the situation, the system may, itself, automatically create invisible parallel modes. As of Basis Version 6.10 a maximum of 16 sessions is possible; 6 sessions for older versions. The default setting is 6 sessions.

Table C.3 SAP Profile Parameters for Load Distribution (Cont.)

Parameter	Description
rsdb/max_blocking_factor	See Chapter 9, Section 9.3.2, Analyzing Buffered Tables. Warning: Do not modify this parameter without prior recommendation by SAP.
dbs/io_buf_size	Size of the data area in an SAP work process, through which data is transferred to or copied from the database by an SQL statement (in bytes). Warning: Do not modify this parameter without prior recommendation by SAP.

Table C.4 SAP Profile Parameters for the Database Instance

Parameter	Description
rdisp/bufrefmode	Defines the type of buffer synchronization. Possible settings: Sendon or Exeauto (for a distributed system) and Sendoff or Exeauto (for a central system).
rdisp/bufreftime	Time interval between two buffer synchronizations (in seconds).

Table C.5 SAP Profile Parameters for Buffer Synchronization

723

Parameter	Description
zcsa/inval_reload_c	Number of accesses the systems waits before it reloads an entry into the buffer after an invalidation; applies to individual buffer entries. Warning: Do not modify this parameter without prior recommendation by SAP.
zcsa/sync_reload_c	Number of accesses the systems waits before it reloads the buffer after an invalidation; applies to synchronization of the entire buffer. Warning: Do not modify this parameter without prior recommendation by SAP.

Table C.5 SAP Profile Parameters for Buffer Synchronization (Cont.)

Parameter	Description
rdisp/tm_max_no	Maximum number of frontend connections in table tm_adm.
rdisp/max_comm_entries	Maximum number of CPIC/RFC connections that can be managed in the communication table comm_adm.
gw/max_conn	Maximum number of CPIC/RFC connections that can be managed by the gateway service in table conn_tbl.
rdisp/rfc_max_login	Limit for the number of RFC logon connections to an SAP instance. If this limit is exceeded, no resources are made available to the affected user.
rdisp/rfc_max_own_login	Limit for the number of individual RFC logon connections to an SAP instance. If this individual limit is exceeded, no resources are made available to the affected user.
rdisp/rfc_max_comm_entries	Limit for the number of communication entries used for RFCs. If this limit is exceeded, no resources are made available to the affected user. The number of communication entries is set via the profile parameter rdisp/max_comm_entries.

Table C.6 Profile Parameters for Interface Configurations (See SAP Note 74141)

Parameter	Description
rdisp/rfc_max_own_used_wp	Limit for the number of dialog work processes used for RFCs by an individual user. If this limit is exceeded, no resources are made available to the affected user.
rdisp/rfc_min_wait_dia_wp	Limit for the number of dialog work processes to be reserved for non-RFC users. If this limit is exceeded, no resources are made available to the affected users.
rdisp/rfc_max_wait_time	Maximum number of seconds for which a work process can receive no resources before "going to sleep."

Table C.6 Profile Parameters for Interface Configurations (See SAP Note 74141) (Cont.)

Parameter	Description
rstr/file	Name of the SQL trace file
rstr/max_diskspace	Size of the SQL trace file in bytes
abap/atrapath	Path name for the ABAP trace files
abap/atrasizeQuote	Size of the ABAP trace files
rdisp/wpdbug_max_no	Maximum number of work processes that can be run simultaneously in debugging mode

Table C.7 SAP Profile Parameters for Configuring Monitoring Tools

Performance Key Figures

You can find the most essential performance key figures (see Table C.8) under SAP CCMS MONITOR MONITOR TEMPLATES • PERFORMANCE OVERVIEW MONITOR.

Performance Overview Monitor

Entry in the Central CCMS Monitor	Explanation
DIALOG • RESPONSE TIME	Average response time of the dialog service
DIALOG • USERS LOGGED IN	Number of logged-on users

Table C.8 Performance Key Figures for the ABAP Server in the Central CCMS Monitor

Entry in the Central CCMS Monitor	Explanation
DIALOG • QUEUE TIME	Average wait time in the dispatcher queue
DIALOG • LOAD+GEN TIME	Average time for loading and generating ABAP programs
DIALOG • DB REQUEST TIME	Average time for requests to the database
MEMORY MANAGEMENT • R3 ROLL USED	Utilization of the roll area as a percentage
MEMORY MANAGEMENT • ES ACT	Utilization of the extended memory as a percentage
MEMORY MANAGEMENT • HEAP ACT	Utilization of the heap memory as a percentage
MEMORY MANAGEMENT • PROGRAM\SWAP	Number of displacements in the ABAP program buffer

Table C.8 Performance Key Figures for the ABAP Server in the Central CCMS Monitor (Cont.)

Logon load balancing monitor

For monitoring load distribution, you can use the logon load balancing monitor in the group of SAP CCMS Monitors for Optional Components.

Entry in the Central CCMS Monitor	Explanation
USERS LOGGED IN • <NAME OF INSTANCE>	Number of logged-on users.
RESPONSE TIME • <NAME OF INSTANCE>	Average response time of the dialog service.
LOGON LOAD QUALITY • <NAME OF INSTANCE>	Abstract key figure calculated for load distribution; among other things, based on the number of users and response time. New logons have a high logon quality in the instances.
LOGON LOAD STATUS • <NAME OF INSTANCE AND LOGON GROUP>	Information about the instance that is used for the next new logon.

Table C.9 Performance Key Figures for Load Distribution Between ABAP Instances in the Central CCMS Monitor

Additional interesting monitors are:

▸ **Buffers**
Shows displacements and fill levels of all buffers.

▸ **Background processing monitor**
The System Wide Free BPWP entry indicates the number of free background work processes currently available. Other key figures show the (percentage) utilization of all background processes. Moreover, several key figures on error situations are also provided.

▸ **Enqueue**
SAP locks are responsible for performance problems only in rare cases. However, if you know that your system has some "hot spots" in the special locks area, you can use this monitor.

You can track the response times of certain clients or SAP transactions with the Alert Monitor. This is of particular importance for transactions you have included in the service-level agreement. As of SAP Basis 4.6C, the Alert Monitor contains the Transaction-specific dialog monitor in the SAP CCMS Monitors for Optional Components collection (Table C.10).

Monitoring individual ABAP transactions

Entry in the Central CCMS Monitor	Explanation
Name of Transaction> • RESPONSE TIME	Average response time of the dialog service
Name of Transaction> • QUEUE TIME	Average wait time in the dispatcher queue
Name of Transaction> • LOAD+GEN TIME	Average time for loading and generating ABAP programs
Name of Transaction> • DB REQUEST TIME	Average time for requests to the database
Name of Transaction> • FRONTEND RESPONSE TIME	Response time at the presentation server

Table C.10 Performance Key Figures in the CCMS Monitor for Individual Transactions

727

C.2 Internet Communication Manager

Configuration Parameters

Parameter	Description
`icm/min_threads`	Specifies the minimum number of threads in the ICM. This number corresponds to the number of connections that can be processed simultaneously. The minimum number of threads is set at startup, and you cannot go below this number at runtime.
`icm/max_threads`	Specifies the maximum number of threads in the ICM. It corresponds to the maximum number of connections that can be processed simultaneously. When the workload is heavy, the ICM starts additional threads until the maximum number is reached. The number of threads actually needed is displayed in the ICM monitor (Transaction SMICM).
`icm/max_conn`	Maximum number of (simultaneously) open connections in the ICM. This parameter value can be greater than `icm/max_threads`, because inactive connections in the ICM do not need a thread. The maximum value of this parameter is determined by the maximum number of open file handles in the operating system. Each ICM service needs a connection. These are displayed with the open connections. The number of connections actually needed is displayed in the ICM monitor (Transaction SMICM).
`icm/listen_queue_len`	The operating system has to hold connection requests in a queue while waiting for a connection to be established. This parameter specifies the maximum number of threads that can be held in this status. If the network queue is full, additional connection requests are denied.

Table C.11 Profile Parameters for Configuring the Internet Communication Manager

Parameter	Description
icm/req_queue_len	All requests to the ICM are first saved in a queue before they are passed on to work threads. This parameter is specified by the size of the queue. The number of queue entries needed is displayed in the ICM monitor (Transaction SMICM).
mpi/buffer_size	Data transfer within memory pipes is done in blocks of a fixed length. The mpi/buffer_size parameter defines the size of these blocks in bytes.
mpi/total_size_MB	Data transfer between ICM (Internet Communication Manager) and the SAP work processes is done via memory pipes (MPI). The parameter mpi/total_size_MB gives the total size of the MPI in megabytes. This memory area is created in the shared memory of the SAP instance.
icm/HTTP/server_ cache_<xx>/memory_ size_MB	Size of the ICM server cache in the main memory in megabytes.
icm/HTTP/server_ cache_<xx>/size_MB	Total size of the ICM server cache. Main memory and file system in megabytes.
icm/HTTP/server_ cache_<xx>/ expiration	Time interval after which objects stored in the ICM server cache are automatically invalidated.
icm/HTTP/ logging_<xx>	You can use this parameter to activate logging in the ICM. Further information on how to use it is available in SAP Online Help. Warning: Activating logging can lead to serialization effects.

Table C.11 Profile Parameters for Configuring the Internet Communication Manager (Cont.)

Performance Key Figures

You can find the performance key figures on ICM under SAP CCMS MONITOR TEMPLATES • ENTIRE SYSTEM (see Table C.12). In this monitor, select your system and navigate to Application Server. Select an instance, and then select R3SERVICES • ICM • GENERAL.

Entry in the Central CCMS Monitor	Explanation
NoOfThreads	Number of currently generated ICM threads
PeakNoOfThreads	Number of maximum generated ICM threads
NoOfConnections	Number of current ICM connections
PeakNoOfConnections	Maximum number of ICM connections in the past
QueueLen	Current length of queue
PeakQueueLen	Maximum length of queue in the past
MPISizeTotal	Size of the memory area for memory pipes
MPIBufferCount	Number of available memory pipes
PeakMPIBufUsed	Maximum number of memory pipes used in the past

Table C.12 ICM Performance Key Figures in the Central CCMS Monitor

C.3 Java Virtual Machine and SAP J2EE Engine

Performance Key Figures

You can find the performance key figures for the SAP J2EE Engine (see Table C.13) under SAP CCMS MONITOR TEMPLATES • J2EE ENGINE • ENTIRE SYSTEM, or under ENGINE KERNEL and ENGINE SERVICES, which you can find under MONITOR • SAP J2EE MONITOR TEMPLATES. The key figures are given for each dispatcher and each server.

Entry in the Central CCMS Monitor	Explanation
KERNEL • SYSTEM/ APPLICATION THREADS POOL	Key figures on the threads in the system or in the application pool: initial and current number, free and occupied threads, and number of requests in queue
SERVICES • MEMORY INFO	Key figures on memory usage: memory allocated and currently in use, and memory limit

Table C.13 Performance Key Figures of the SAP J2EE Engine in the Central CCMS Monitor (JVM-Independent)

If the SAP JVM is used as the Java Virtual Machine, as of SAP NetWeaver 7.10 the following performance key figures are provided under SAP J2EE Monitor Templates • Java Instance Overview. The key figures indicated are given for each server (Table C.14). The architecture of SAP NetWeaver 7.10 does not provide dispatchers any longer; the ICM completely assumed the role of the dispatchers.

Entry in the Central CCMS Monitor	Explanation
Threads • Threads of serverX • Long Running Threads	Number of threads occupied for a long time during the processing of a request that are no longer available for new requests
Threads • Threads of serverX • Active Threads	Number of active threads
Garbage Collection • GC of serverX • Average Proportion of Total Time	Time proportion (percentage) that the JVM requires for garbage collection
Garbage Collection • GC of serverX • Object Heap Usage After Full GC	Heap memory usage (percentage) after the last full garbage collection
Garbage Collection • GC of serverX • Class Heap Usage After Full GC	Permanent memory usage (percentage) after the last full garbage collection
Garbage Collection • GC of serverX • Duration of Last Full GC	Duration of the last full garbage collection in seconds
Process Table • serverX • CPU Usage	CPU usage (percentage) of a J2EE server

Table C.14 Performance Key Figures of the SAP J2EE Engine on an SAP JVM in the Central CCMS Monitor

C.4 Java Virtual Machine Container (VMC)

You can find the performance key figures on the VMC under SAP CCMS Monitor Templates • VM Container.

C.5 Internet Transaction Server (Integrated Version)

Configuration Parameters

Parameter	Description
itsp/enable	Activation of the integrated ITS
itsp/Traces/ ... / TraceLevel *	Trace level for different ITS subcomponents
itsp/SAPjulep/ MaxHtmlPPs	Maximum number of preparsed templates in the buffer
itsp/SAPjulep/ Profiling	Performance analysis of the HTML generation
itsp/max_eg_mem_ percent	Limit of the memory area that the ITS can use in extended memory
itsp/memory_check	Activation of memory consumption monitoring
em/global_area_MB	Size of the global area in extended memory (see also the previous section on memory management)

Table C.15 Profile Parameters for Configuring the Internet Transaction Server (Integrated Version)

C.6 Internet Transaction Server (Independent Installation)

Configuration Parameters

You can change the SAP ITS using the ITS administration and monitoring tool (Table C.16).

Parameter	Description
MaxSessions	Maximum number of possible user sessions.
MaxWorkThreads	Maximum number of ITS work processes (threads).
MinWorkThreads	Minimum number of ITS work processes (normally equal to MaxWorkThreads).

Table C.16 Profile Parameters for Configuring the Internet Transaction Server

Parameter	Description
MaxAGates	Maximum number of AGate processes (operating system level processes).
MinAgates	Minimum number of AGate work processes (normally equal to MaxAGates).
StaticTemplates	A value of 1 deactivates the runtime parsing of HTML templates. The default setting is 1, so for performance reasons, changes to templates are not implemented.
CacheSize	Size of the HTML template cache.
ProductionMode	A value of 1 activates the caching of RFC function module/BAPI repository data. The default setting is 1, which means changes to RFC function modules are not identified.
Caching	A value of 1 activates the caching of ITS log files. The trace level; the default setting is 1.
TraceLevel	Trace level. The trace level; the default setting is 1.
Debug	A value of ON activates debugging. The default setting is OFF.
TimeoutPercentage	Percentage limit for the portion of timeouts for high load sessions.
~http_compress_level	Compression level (0 to 9). The default setting is 7.
~http_use_compression	A value of 1 activates data compression between the ITS and web browsers. The default setting is. 1).

Table C.16 Profile Parameters for Configuring the Internet Transaction Server (Cont.)

Performance Key Figures

Entry in the Central CCMS Monitor	Explanation
Status	Information on the initiated AGate processes
Log	AGate instance number

Table C.17 Performance Key Figures of the Independent ITS in the Central CCMS Monitor

Entry in the Central CCMS Monitor	Explanation
Heartbeat	"Sign of life" of SAP ITS
Availability	Availability of ITS instance in the past 15 minutes
Max. Threads	Total number of available ITS work processes (threads)
Used Threads	Number of used ITS work processes (percentage)
Max. Sessions	Total number of available sessions
Used Sessions	Number of used sessions (percentage)
Hits	Number of accesses (hits) per second
Hits A	Number of currently open accesses to the application server
TAT	Turnaround time: Average response time for accessing the application server and generating the HTML page
Up time	Time since ITS instance started
User time	User's CPU share on the ITS server
Kernel time	System's CPU share on the ITS server (percentage)

Table C.17 Performance Key Figures of the Independent ITS in the Central CCMS Monitor (Cont.)

C.7 Operating System

You can find the performance key figures on the operating system (Table C.18) under SAP CCMS MONITOR TEMPLATES • OPERATING SYSTEM.

Entry in the Central CCMS Monitor	Explanation
CPU • CPU UTILIZATION	CPU utilization as a percentage
CPU • 5 MIN LOAD AVERAGE	Average number of waiting operating system processes (size of the queue)
PAGING • PAGING OUT	Swapped main memory pages per second

Table C.18 Performance Key Figures of the Operating System in the Central CCMS Monitor

Entry in the Central CCMS Monitor	Explanation
PAGING • PAGING IN	Returned pages to the main memory per second
COMMIT CHARGE • COMMIT CHARGE FREE	Free physical and virtual memory in megabytes (on Windows operating systems)
COMMIT CHARGE • COMMIT CHARGE PERCENT	Used physical and virtual memory as a percentage (on Windows operating systems)
SWAP SPACE • FREE SPACE	Free swap space in megabytes (on UNIX operating systems)
SWAP SPACE • PERCENTAGE USED	Used swap space as a percentage (on UNIX operating systems)
OS COLLECTOR • STATE	Status of the operating system collector

Table C.18 Performance Key Figures of the Operating System in the Central CCMS Monitor (Cont.)

You can use the operating system monitor to monitor the status of any operating system process. A configuration step will make the process to be monitored known to the collector. You can find the monitoring results in the operating system monitor under Monitored Processes.

Monitored operating system processes

With the CCMS Alert Monitor, you can check the availability and performance of any computer in your system landscape — not only those running SAP systems. To do this, you need to install what is known as a "monitoring agent" on the computers you want to monitor.

Computers without SAP software

C.8   Database

You can find database performance key figures under SAP CCMS MONITOR TEMPLATES • DATABASE. Typically, monitored key figures are buffer quality and the up-to-date status of database optimizer statistics. The example in Table C.19 provides key figures for MaxDB, which are also valid for liveCache.

Entry in the Central CCMS Monitor	Explanation
MAXDB MONITORING • PERFORMANCE • DATA CACHE HITRATE – TOTAL	Hit ratio in the data buffer storing the data pages (percentage)
MAXDB MONITORING • PERFORMANCE • DATA CACHE HITRATE – OMS DATA	Hit ratio in the data buffer (OMS data; percentage)
MAXDB MONITORING • PERFORMANCE • DATA CACHE HITRATE – SQL DATA	Hit ratio in the data buffer (SQL data; percentage)
MAXDB MONITORING • PERFORMANCE • DATA CACHE HITRATE – HISTORY/UNDO	Hit ratio in the data buffer (History/Undo; percentage)
MAXDB MONITORING • PERFORMANCE • CATALOG CACHE HITRATE	Hit ratio of the catalog cache that stores SQL command context, especially the execution plans for SQL statements (percentage)
OPTIMIZER STATISTICS • LAST COLLECTION	Period since the last creation of optimizer statistics (in days)

Table C.19 Performance Key Figures of the Database in the Central CCMS Monitor (MaxDB)

D   Selected Transaction Codes

AL11	Display SAP Directories
AL12	Display Table Buffer (Buffer Synchronization)
BALE	ALE administration and monitoring
DBACOCKPIT	Central Database Administrator Cockpit (DBA Cockpit, as of 7.0)
DB02	Missing Database Objects and Space Requirements (as of 7.0 in the DBA Cockpit)
DB05	Table Analysis
DB12	DBA Logs (as of 7.0 in the DBA Cockpit)
DB13	DBA Planning Calendar (as of 7.0 in the DBA Cockpit)
DB20	Generate Table Access Statistics
OSS1	Log onto the SAP Service Marketplace
RSA1	BW Administrator Workbench
RSDDV	BW Aggregate Maintenance
RSRT	BW Test Environment for Queries (Query Monitor)
RSRV	BW Check Reports
LISTCUBE	InfoCube Overview
RSCUSTV14	OLAP Cache Configuration
RSRCACHE	OLAP Cache Monitor
RSDDBWAMON	BW Accelerator Monitor
RZ01	Job Scheduling Monitor
RZ02	Network Graphics for SAP Instances
RZ03	Control Panel for Operation Modes and Server Status
RZ04	Maintain SAP Instances
RZ10	Maintain Profile Parameters (by Profile)
RZ11	Maintain Profile Parameters (by Parameter)
RZ12	Maintain RFC Groups
RZ20	Central SAP Monitor

SE11	Maintain ABAP Dictionary
SE12	Display ABAP Dictionary
SE14	Utilities for ABAP Dictionary Tables
SE15	ABAP Repository Information System
SE16	Data Browser for Displaying Table Contents
SE24	ABAP Class Library
SE38	ABAP Editor
SE80	ABAP Workbench
SEU	SAP Repository Browser
SM01	Lock Transactions
SM02	System Messages
SM04	User List
SM12	Display and Delete Locks
SM13	Display Update Records
SM21	System Log
SM36	Maintain Batch Server
SM37	Background Job Overview
SM39	Job Analysis
SM49	Execute External Operating System Commands
SM50	Work Process Overview
SM51	List of Servers
SM56	Reset or Check the Number Range Buffer
SM58	Asynchronous RFC Error Log
SM59	Display or Maintain RFC Destinations
SM63	Display or Maintain Operating Modes
SM65	Execute Tests to Analyze Background Processing
SM66	Systemwide Work Process Overview
SM69	Maintain External Operating System Commands
SITSMON	Monitor the Integrated ITS
SMICM	Internet Communication Manager Monitor
SMLG	Maintain Logon Groups

SPRO	SAP Implementation Guide (IMG)
ST01	SAP System Trace
ST02	SAP Memory Configuration Monitor
ST03(N)	Workload Monitor
ST04	Database Performance Monitor (as of 7.0 in the DBA Cockpit)
ST05	SQL Trace
ST06(N)	Operating System Monitor (new as of 7.1)
ST07	Application Monitor
ST08	Network Monitor
ST09	Network Alert Monitor
ST10	Display Statistics on Table Accesses (Table Call Statistics)
ST11	Display Developer Traces
ST14	Application Analysis—Statistics Relating to Business Document Volume
ST22	ABAP Runtime Error Analysis
STAD	Single Statistics Records on the Application Server
STMS	Transport Management System
STUN	SAP Performance Menu
SXMB_MONI	Monitor for XI and WS Messages
TU02	Parameter Changes—Display Active Parameters and a History of Changes
TREXADMIN	TREX Administration

E   Review Questions and Answers

E.1   Chapter 2

Questions

1. Which of the following can cause a CPU bottleneck on the database server?

   a) External processes that do not belong to the database or an SAP instance running on the database server.

   b) The SAP extended memory is configured too small.

   c) Work processes that belong to an SAP instance running on the database (for example, background or update work processes) require CPU capacity.

   d) There are expensive SQL statements, for example, those that contribute 5% or more of the entire database load in the shared SQL area.

   e) The database buffers are set too small; therefore, data must be continuously reloaded from the hard drives.

2. Which of the following are necessary to achieve optimal database performance?

   a) Table analyses (using a program such as Update Statistics) must be regularly scheduled.

   b) The number of SAP work processes must be large enough that there are enough database processes to process the database load.

   c) The database buffers must be sufficiently large.

   d) You should regularly check whether expensive SQL statements are unnecessarily consuming CPU and main memory resources.

   e) The database instance should be run only on a separate computer without SAP instances.

3. Which points should you take into consideration when monitoring SAP memory management?

a) The total memory allocated by the SAP and database instances should not be larger than the physical main memory of the computer.

b) The extended memory must be sufficiently large.

c) If possible, no displacements should occur in the SAP buffers.

4. In the local work process overview, the information displayed for a particular work process over a considerable time period is as follows: Running, Sequential Read, and a specific table name. What does this tell you?

a) There may be an expensive SQL statement that accesses the table and can be analyzed more closely in the database process monitor.

b) There may be a wait situation in the dispatcher, which is preventing a connection to the database. The dispatcher queue should be analyzed more closely.

c) There may be an *exclusive lock wait* that can be analyzed in the monitor for exclusive database locks.

d) There may be a network problem between the application server and the database server.

5. Your JEE Engine frequently runs full garbage collections. What does this tell you?

a) The garbage collection is a background process of the Java virtual machine; as long as there is no CPU bottleneck, performance problems won't occur.

b) During a full garbage collection run, the Java applications are stopped. Consequently, frequent runs considerably impact the system. You should perform a detailed analysis of the memory consumption.

c) During a full garbage collection run, all Java applications are terminated, the main memory of the JVM is deleted, and the applications are reloaded. You should perform a detailed error analysis of the programs involved.

Answers

1. a, c, d, e

2. a, c, d

3. b, c

4. a, c, d

5. b

E.2 Chapter 3

Questions

1. Which of the following statements are correct?

    a) CPU time is measured by the operating system of the application server.

    b) Database time is measured by the database system.

    c) High network times for data transfers between the presentation server and the application server are reflected in an increased response time in the workload monitor.

    d) High network times for data transfers between the application server and the database server are reflected in an increased response time in the workload monitor.

    e) The roll-out time is not part of the response time, because the roll-out of a user occurs only after the response has been sent to the presentation server. Nevertheless, it is important for the performance of SAP components to keep roll-out time to a minimum, because during roll-outs, the SAP work process remains occupied.

2. How is the term *load* defined in this book?

    a) *Load* is defined as the amount of load on the CPU of a computer, expressed as a percentage. It can be monitored in the operating system monitor (CPU Utilization).

    b) In this book, load is the sum of response times. Therefore, total load refers to the Response Time Total, CPU load refers to the CPU Time Total, and database load refers to the DB Time Total.

c) The term *load* refers to the number of transaction steps per unit of time.

3. The workload monitor displays increased wait times for the dispatcher such that Av. Wait Time is much greater than 50ms. What does this tell you?

a) There is a communication problem between the presentation servers and the dispatcher of the application server, for example, a network problem.

b) There is a general performance problem, for example, a database problem, hardware bottleneck, or insufficient SAP extended memory; or there are too few SAP work processes. This statement does not provide enough information to pinpoint the exact problem.

c) An increased dispatcher wait time is normal for an SAP component. It protects the operating system from being overloaded and can be ignored.

4. In the workload analysis for the SAP J2EE Engine, you determine that the response times for Web Dynpro applications increase considerably, whereas the response times for JCo calls don't change very much at all. What do you have to do?

a) Because Web Dynpro applications are always linked with business-relevant applications on an ABAP server, you should carry out an analysis on the ABAP server.

b) There is a problem on the SAP J2EE Engine. Therefore, you should check whether the load distribution is unfavorable, whether there is a hardware bottleneck on the SAP J2EE Engine's computer, or whether the SAP J2EE Engine has problems with garbage collection.

Answers

1. a, c, d, e

2. b

3. b

4. b

E.3 Chapter 4

Questions

1. Which statements can be made on the basis of SAP statistics records?

   a) If a user action involves several SAP components (for example, ABAP, J2EE, ITS, etc.), an action ID (referred to as the passport) enables you to trace the user action across the components.

   b) The statistics records contain information on the response time of individual program components (function module calls, or methods in the case of ABAP, classes in the case of Java).

   c) The global statistics records contain the response time of a corresponding component (for example, ABAP, J2EE, ITS, etc.), the CPU time needed by the component, and the response time of additional components that are called by the component that writes the statistics record.

   d) On the basis of the statistics records, you can make statements on the performance of the business processes, such as cash flow in financials or delivery reliability in logistics.

2. What do you have to consider when you perform an SQL trace?

   a) There is only one trace file in each SAP system. Therefore, only one SQL trace can be created per SAP system.

   b) The user whose actions are being traced should not run multiple programs concurrently.

   c) You should perform the SQL trace on a second execution of a program, because the relevant buffers will already have been loaded.

   d) SQL traces are useful on the database server, but not on application servers, which yield inexact results due to network times.

3. When should you perform an ABAP trace?

   a) If a problem occurs with the table buffer.

   b) For programs with high CPU requirements.

   c) An ABAP trace is useful for analyzing I/O problems on hard drives.

Answers

1. a, c

2. b, c

3. b

E.4 Chapter 5

Questions

1. In an SAP ERP system, 300 users are already active in the SD area and 50 users are in the FI area. You now plan the go-live of 150 users in the MM area and 25 users in the FI area. What do you have to do for sizing?

   a) You implement the sizing with a new sizing project in Quick Sizer, where you calculate the sizing on the basis of 300 SD, 150 MM, and 75 FI users.

   b) You determine the current hardware utilization and add 50% for the load that the newly added users will cause.

   c) You determine the current hardware utilization and run a new sizing project in Quick Sizer with 150 MM and 25 FI users. You then add up the hardware requirements.

   d) You require special tools from the hardware partner to implement a delta sizing.

2. You plan to use different system components, such as ABAP server, SAP J2EE Engine, SAP liveCache, and so on. Are these components supposed to be operated on one or multiple computers?

   a) Every components should be operated on one computer. Due to displacement effects in the main memory and more context changes in the CPU, you cannot achieve good performance otherwise.

   b) Components can be operated together on computers. However, you must add the hardware requirement of every component in the dimensioning of the computer.

c) Components can be operated together on computers. In practical use, you can assume that the operation of components together on one computer results in considerable CPU and main memory savings (thanks to synergy effects because the load is usually evenly distributed for all components).

Answers

1. c

2. b

E.5   Chapter 6

Questions

1. Where should background work processes be configured?

   a) Background work processes should always be configured on the database server. Otherwise, the runtime of background programs will be negatively affected by network problems between the database server and the application server.

   b) If background work processes are not located on the database server, they must all be set up on a dedicated application server, known as the background server.

   c) Background work processes can be distributed evenly over all of the application servers.

2. How should you configure and monitor the dynamic user distribution?

   a) By setting the appropriate SAP profile parameter, for example `rdisp/wp_no_dia`

   b) By using Transaction User Overview (SM04)

   c) By using Transaction Maintain Logon Groups (SMLG).

Answers

1. c

2. c

E.6   Chapter 7

Questions

1. What is a high roll wait time?

    a) A unique indication of a GUI communication problem — for example, in the network between the presentation server and the application server.

    b) A unique indication of an RFC communication problem with SAP or non-SAP systems.

    c) A clear indication of a problem with GUI, RFC, or HTTP communication.

    d) A problem caused by an ineffective network between the application and the database level.

2. In a transaction step, a transaction is processed and controls are used, but neither an external RFC nor an HTTP target is called. Which of the following statements are correct?

    a) The GUI time is greater than the roll wait time.

    b) The RFC time is greater than the roll wait time.

    c) The roll wait time is always greater than zero.

    d) The roll wait time is normally greater than zero, although it can also be zero.

    e) The roll wait time is always zero.

3. In a transaction step, a transaction that uses no controls and no synchronous RFCs is processed, although asynchronous RFCs are called. Which of the following statements are correct?

    a) The GUI time is greater than the roll wait time.

    b) The RFC time is greater than the roll wait time.

    c) The roll wait time is always greater than zero.

    d) The roll wait time is normally greater than zero, although it can also be zero.

    e) The roll wait time is always zero.

4. A Web application that uses ITS and an SAP system is running "too slowly." What analyses do you perform?

a) Use the ITS administration and monitoring tool, or the central CCMS monitor to check if all work processes (threads) or sessions are running on the ITS, or if the CPU is constantly running.

b) In the work process overview for the connected SAP system, check if all work processes are running.

c) Using a performance trace and the single record statistics, analyze the response time of the connected SAP system, and compare it with the user-measured response time for the presentation server.

d) Using an analysis tool on the presentation server (for example, E2E trace plug-in of SAP Solution Manager), check the data transfer volume to the browser and the compilation time for an HTML page, and compare the required time with the total response time.

Answers

1. c

2. a, d

3. b, e

4. a, b, c, d

E.7   Chapter 8

Questions

1. Which SAP profile parameters determine the parts of (a) extended memory and (b) heap memory that will be held in the physical main memory or in the swap space?

a) SAP extended memory is always kept completely in the physical main memory, and the heap memory is created in the swap space.

b) None. The distribution of memory areas to the physical main memory and swap space (that is, the page out and page in) is performed automatically by the operating system. An application program (such as an SAP or database program) cannot influence this distribution.

c) The SAP profile parameter `ztta/roll_extension` determines which part of extended memory will be held in physical main memory, whereas similarly, the `abap/heap_area_(non)dia` parameter determines this for heap memory.

2. Under what circumstances might an SAP instance not start (or only start with error messages) after you have changed SAP memory management parameters?

a) The program buffer (`abap/buffer_size`) cannot be created in the preferred size because of address space restrictions.

b) The physical memory is not sufficient for the new settings.

c) The swap space is not sufficient for the new settings.

d) The extended memory (`em/initial_size_MB`) cannot be created in the preferred size because of address space restrictions.

Answers

1. b

2. a, c, d

E.8   Chapter 9

Questions

1. Which of the following factors are reasons for not activating full buffering on a table?

a) The table is very large.

b) In the SQL statement most frequently used to access the table, the first two of five key fields are contained in an equals condition.

c) The table is changed often.

2. Which of the following statements are correct with regard to buffer synchronization?

a) During buffer synchronization, the application server where the change occurred sends a message through the message server to implement the change in the buffered table on the other application servers.

b) After a transaction changes a buffered table, the transaction must first be completed with a database commit before the table can be reloaded into the buffer.

c) In a central system, the SAP profile parameter `rdisp/bufrefmode` must be set to "sendoff, exeoff."

d) In a central SAP system, the entries in the table buffer are never invalidated, because the table buffer is changed synchronously after a database change operation.

Answers

1. a, c

2. b

E.9   Chapter 10

Questions

1. Which of the following statements are correct?

a) When you set an SAP enqueue, you lock one or more tables in the database.

b) After an SAP enqueue has been placed, the corresponding database table can still be changed by an `Update` request from programs such as customer-developed ABAP reports.

c) A database lock is usually released at the end of a transaction step, whereas an SAP enqueue is usually released at the end of an SAP transaction.

d) A database lock that lasts too long can cause an SAP system *standstill*.

2. Which of the following statements are correct with regard to the ATP server?

a) The ATP server should always be configured on the database server.

b) The ATP server is an independent SAP installation with its own database on a separate computer.

c) The ATP server reduces the number of accesses to tables RESB and VBBE.

3. When buffering number range objects in main memory, which of the following considerations should you bear in mind?

a) Because buffering occurs in all SAP instances, buffer synchronization may cause some numbers to be assigned twice.

b) Gaps occur in the number assignment when you are using buffered number ranges. You must check whether these gaps are permitted by law and are acceptable from a business point of view.

c) If the quantity of numbers in the buffer is too small, performance problems will result (particularly during mass data entry using batch or fast input).

d) Sufficient physical memory must be available, because number range buffering consumes a lot of memory.

Answers

1. b, c, d

2. c

3. b, c

E.10 Chapter 11

Questions

1. Which of the following statements is correct with regard to expensive SQL statements?

a) They can lead to hardware bottlenecks (for example, a CPU or I/O bottleneck) and negatively affect the runtime of other SQL statements.

b) They can occupy a lot of space in the data buffer of the database, displace objects that are needed by other SQL statements, and negatively affect the runtime of other SQL statements.

c) They can occupy a lot of space in the SAP table buffer and displace objects, which causes unnecessary reload operations.

d) If they are performed after database locks were set by the same program, this can cause exclusive lock wait situations in the database, which can cause a brief system standstill.

e) Expensive SQL statements in programs for reporting or in background programs are not normally a problem for the database.

2. In the results of an SQL trace, you find an SQL statement that has a runtime of one second and selects only 10 records. Which of the following could be the reason for the long runtime?

a) There is a hardware (CPU or I/O) bottleneck on the database server.

b) There is a network problem between the application server and the database server.

c) The database optimizer has created an inefficient execution plan, for example, by choosing an inefficient index.

d) There is no appropriate index for the SQL statement.

e) There are exclusive lock waits in the database.

3. In the SQL statistics, you find an SQL statement with 10,000 logical read accesses per execution (indicated as Gets/Execution). Which of the following could be the reason for this high number of read accesses?

a) There is a hardware (CPU or I/O) bottleneck on the database server.

b) There is a network problem between the application server and the database server.

c) The database optimizer has created an inefficient execution plan — for example, by choosing an inefficient index.

d) There is no appropriate index for the SQL statement.

e) There are exclusive lock waits in the database.

f) A large number of records are being transferred from the database to the ABAP program.

4. Which access is faster if you don't want an SQL statement to read the entire table: a full table scan or an index range scan?

a) The full table scan is always faster; an index is only useful for a fully qualified access (index unique scan)

b) The index range scan is always faster because less data needs to be read than in a full table scan

c) If more than approximately 10 to 20% (rule of thumb) of the data in a table is supposed to be read, a full table scan is faster, because the table can be accessed sequentially, whereas an index range scan must access the database record by record.

Answers

1. a, b, d

2. a, b, c, d, e

3. c, d, f

4. c

E.11 Chapter 12

Questions

1. Which optimization potential do you see when the SAP NetWeaver BW statistics displays a high ratio of selected data records in the database to transferred data records for a query?

a) The OLAP cache has not been filled or invalidated because otherwise the selected records of the database could have been read from the OLAP cache. You should check whether the cache can be enlarged or the query can be precalculated.

b) A suitable index on the fact table can help reduce the number of records selected from the database.

   c) A suitable index on the SID table can help reduce the number of records selected from the database.

   d) A suitable aggregate can help reduce the number of records selected from the database.

2. Which tables can be compressed?

   a) Fact tables of InfoCubes

   b) Fact tables of aggregates

   c) Dimension tables

   d) Master data tables

   e) Tables of DataStore objects

3. Which statements on aggregates and indexes are correct?

   a) Indexes are almost completely replaced by aggregates in the SAP NetWeaver BW environment.

   b) Indexes and aggregates function similarly. That is, indexes are there to improve performance where the selection has been heavily restricted in a query, whereas aggregates improve performance when a large number of data records must be totaled and a minimum or a maximum must be formed.

   c) Both indexes and aggregates require memory space and resources when filling data in SAP NetWeaver BW.

   d) Aggregates are logical constructs that apart from low administrative overheads do not require any memory space or resources.

   e) The use of indexes and aggregates in queries is specified by the database optimizer. That is, he decides whether and which index or which aggregate is used to execute the query.

Answers

1. d

2. a, b

3. b, c

E.12 Chapter 13

Questions

1. Which activities are important to obtaining a good performance for TREX queries?

   a) You must ensure that no CPU bottleneck or main memory bottleneck (paging) exists.

   b) The TREX data buffer should achieve a read quality of at least 98%, or at least 99% in the SAP NetWeaver BW Accelerator scenario.

   c) In a distributed TREX installation, the distribution of indexes to the index servers may not be optimal; in this case, you should promptly initiate a redistribution of indexes to index servers (reorganization).

   d) In the SAP NetWeaver BW Accelerator scenario you must make sure that the SAP NetWeaver BW statistics for InfoCubes that are indexed in SAP NetWeaver BW Accelerator are activated so that TREX calculates the correct aggregates in the SAP NetWeaver BW Accelerator scenario.

Answers

1. a, c

F Glossary

ABAP   Advanced Business Application Programming. Object oriented, SAP-specific programming language. ABAP is one of the three SAP programming languages of SAP Business Suite (along with Java and C/C++).

ABAP Dictionary   Central storage facility for SAP-based metadata (for example, table structures).

ACID Principle   Atomicity, Consistency, Isolation, Durability. A business logic principle that a transaction (or logical unit of work [LUW]) must obey.

Address space (of a process)   Virtual storage that can be addressed by a process. The size of the addressable storage (in 32-bit architecture) ranges from 1.8GB to 3.8GB (2^{32} = 4GB), depending on the operating system.

ALE   Application Link Enabling. ALE is a technology for building and operating distributed applications. The basic purpose of ALE is to ensure distributed yet integrated SAP components. It comprises a controlled business message exchange with consistent data storage in temporarily connected SAP applications. Applications are integrated via synchronous and asynchronous communication, rather than through a central database. ALE consists of three layers:

▸   Application services

▸   Distribution services

▸   Communication services

Alert monitor   Graphical monitor for analyzing system states and events.

ANSI   American National Standards Institute.

Application server   A computer on which at least one SAP instance runs.

Background processing   Processing that does not take place on the screen. Data is processed in the background while other functions can be concurrently executed on the screen. Although the background processes are not visible to the user and run without user intervention (there is no dialog), they have the same priority as other online processes.

BAPI   Business Application Programming Interface. Standardized programming interface that provides external access to business processes and data in the SAP system.

Batch input   Method and tools for rapid import of data from sequential files into the SAP database.

Benchmark   → Standard application benchmark.

Button   Element of the graphical user interface. Click a button to execute the button's function. You can select buttons using the keyboard and the mouse. To do this, place the cursor on the button and press Enter or click the Enter button. Buttons can contain text or graphical symbols.

Browser   A GUI program based on the HTML/HTTP protocols. Alternatively, a third-party browser can be used instead of the SAP GUI program.

Business Connector   SAP Business Connector (SAP BC). Interface software: Among other things, SAP BC is used to exchange XML documents between systems over the Internet. It was replaced by SAP NetWeaver Process Integration.

CATT   Computer Aided Test Tool. You can use this tool to generate test data and automate and test business processes.

CCMS Computing Center Management System. Tools for monitoring, controlling, and configuring SAP components. The CCMS supports 24-hour system administration functions from within the SAP system. You can use it to analyze the system load and monitor the distributed resource requirements of the system components.

Client From a commercial, legal, organizational, and technical viewpoint, a closed unit (within an SAP solution) with separate master records within a table.

CO Customizing Organizer. Tool to manage change and transport requests of all types in an SAP system.

Context switch (at the operating system level) At the operating system level, there are generally more processes (SAP work processes, database processes, etc.) than available processors. To distribute the CPU capacity among all processes, the processors serve them in time frames. A context switch occurs when a processor switches from one process to another.

Context switch (at the SAP level) In the SAP system, there are generally more users logged on than SAP work processes available. The → user contexts are therefore attached only to the SAP work process when a user request is processed. A context switch at the SAP level occurs when an SAP work process switches from one user to another. Switching between user contexts consists of a roll-out and a roll-in of user context data.

Control panel Central tool for monitoring the SAP system and its instances.

CPI-C Common Programming Interface Communication. Programming interface. the basis for synchronous, system-to-system, program-to-program communication.

CTO Change and Transport Organizer. Set of tools used to manage changes and development in the SAP system and to transport these changes to other SAP systems.

Customizing Adjusting an SAP component to specific customer requirements by selecting variants, parameter settings, and so forth.

Data archiving Removing data that is no longer needed from the relational database and storing it in archives.

Database Set of data (organized, for example, in files) for permanent storage on the hard drive.

Database instance An administrative unit that allows access to a database. A database instance consists of database processes with a common set of database buffers in shared memory. There is normally only one database instance for each database. DB2/390 and Oracle Parallel Server are database systems in which a database can be made up of multiple database instances. In an SAP ERP system, a database instance can either reside alone on a single computer or along with another or possibly more SAP instances.

Database lock Like enqueues on the SAP level, database locks help ensure data consistency. Database locks are set by modifying SQL statements (UPDATE, INSERT, DELETE) and by the statement SELECT FOR UPDATE. Database locks are released by the SQL statements COMMIT (used for database commit) and ROLLBACK (used for database rollback).

Database optimizer Part of the database program that decides how tables are accessed for an SQL statement, for example, whether an index is used.

Database server A computer with at least one database instance.

DBA Database administrator.

DCL Data Control Language. SQL statements to control user transactions.

DDL Data Definition Language. SQL statements to define relationships.

Deadlock Mutual blocking of multiple transactions that are waiting for each other to release locked objects.

DIAG protocol Communication protocol between SAP GUI and dialog work processes on the SAP application level.

Dialog work process SAP work process used to process requests from users working online.

Dispatcher The process that coordinates the SAP work processes of an SAP instance.

DML Data Manipulation Language. Language commands to query and change data.

Dynpro The dynamic program that consists of a screen and the underlying process logic.

EDI Electronic Data Interchange. Electronic interchange of structured data (for example, business documents) between business partners in the home country and abroad, who may be using different hardware, software, and communication services.

Enqueue (at the SAP level) Like → database locks, SAP enqueues help ensure data consistency. An SAP enqueue is set explicitly within an ABAP program by an enqueue function and is explicitly released by a dequeue function module. SAP enqueues can continue to be in effect over several steps within an SAP transaction. Remaining SAP enqueues are released at the end of the SAP transaction.

Enterprise IMG Enterprise-specific Implementation Guide.

Entity Uniquely identifiable object — may be real or imaginary. The connections between entities are described by relationships.

EWT Easy Web Transaction. Web-ready dialog-based transaction within an SAP solution enabled via → ITS.

Execution plan A strategy created for an SQL statement by the database optimizer tool to define the optimal way of accessing database tables.

Extended memory Storage area for storing user contexts in the shared memory of the application server.

FDDI Fiber Distributed Data Interchange.

Firewall Software to protect a local network from unauthorized access from outside.

Garbage collection → Memory management.

GUI Graphical user interface. The medium through which a user can exchange information with the computer. You use the GUI to select commands, start programs, display files, and perform other operations by selecting function keys, buttons, menu options, or icons with a mouse.

GUID Globally Unique Identifier. Used by the operating system to identify components. A GUID is unique all over the world and consists of a complex calculation that includes the current time and unique address of the network interface card.

Heap memory (at the operating system level) The local memory of an operating system process. The operating system heap of an SAP work process includes both the permanently allocated and variable local memory of the SAP work process.

Heap memory (at the SAP level) Variable local memory of an SAP work process for storing user contexts. SAP heap memory is temporarily allocated by the SAP work process and released when no longer required.

High availability Property of a service or a system that remains in production operation most of the time. High availability for an SAP component means that unplanned and planned downtimes are reduced to a minimum. Good system administration is decisive here. You can reduce unplanned downtime by using preventive hardware and software solutions that are designed to reduce single points of failure in services that support the SAP system. You can reduce the planned downtime by optimizing the scheduling of necessary maintenance activities.

Hot package → Support package.

HTML Hypertext Markup Language. Language for presenting text and graphics over the Internet.

HTTP Hypertext Transfer Protocol. Protocol for the transmission of files from a Web server to a web browser over the Internet.

IAC Internet Application Component. Web-ready SAP R/3 transaction replaced by Easy Web Transaction (EWT).

IDES International Demo and Education System. IDES contains multiple model companies and maps the relevant business processes of the SAP R/3 system. Using simple user guidelines and different master and transaction data, scenarios with large data volumes can be tested. IDES is therefore well suited as a training tool to assist in instructing project teams. In addition to the SAP R/3 system, there is an IDES for other SAP components.

IDoc Internal Document. An IDoc type filled with real data.

IDoc type Internal Document type. SAP format into which the data of a business process is transferred. An IDoc is a real business process formatted in the IDoc type. An IDoc type is described by the following components:

▸ A control record. Its format is identical for all IDoc types.

▸ One or more records. A record consists of a fixed administration segment and the data segment. The number and format of the segments differ for different IDoc types.

▸ Status records. These records describe stages of processing that an IDoc can go through. The status records have the same format for all IDoc types.

IMG Implementation Guide. A tool for making customer-specific adjustments to an SAP component. For each component, the implementation guide contains:

▸ All steps for implementing the SAP component

▸ All default settings and activities for configuring the SAP component

The IMG hierarchical structure:

▸ Maps the structure of the SAP component

▸ Lists all documentation relevant to the implementation of the SAP component

Instance Instance of the ABAP server. Administrative unit that groups together processes of an SAP system and that offers one or more services. An SAP instance can provide the following services:

▸ D: Dialog

▸ V: Update

▸ E: SAP enqueue management

▸ B: Background processing

▸ S: Printing (spool)

▸ G: SAP gateway

An SAP instance consists of a dispatcher and one or more SAP work processes for each service, as well as a common set of SAP buffers in the shared memory. The dispatcher manages the processing requests. Work processes execute the requests. Each instance provides at least one dialog service and a gateway. An instance can provide further services. Only one instance can be available that provides the SAP enqueue management service. In accordance with this definition, there can be two (or more) SAP instances on an application server. This means that with two or more instances on one server, there are two or more dispatchers and SAP buffers. → Database instance.

Intranet A company-internal network that is based on Internet technology.

IPC Interprocess Communication. SAP component for calculating prices, taxes, and product configurations. This Java-based component is used both on PCs and servers, for example, in SAP Customer Relationship Management (CRM).

ITS SAP Internet Transaction Server. The interface between the SAP system and a Web server for generating dynamic HTML pages. The Web applications SAP GUI for HTML, Easy Web Transaction (EWT), and Web-RFC are enabled via ITS. It is available in two versions: external ITS, an independent installation, and the ITS integrated in the kernel of the ABAP server (Basis version 6.20).

Java Platform-independent, object- and network-oriented programming language. Java is one of the three SAP programming languages of SAP Business Suite (along with ABAP and C/C++). The home page of the "Java Community" is *http://java.sun.com*. Here you can find further information about the following terms: Java Server Pages (JSP), Enterprise JavaBean (EJB), Java to Enterprise Edition (J2EE), and Java Application Server. The website at *http://appserver-zone.com* has a list of all Java application servers.

Java Application Request Measurement (JARM) JARM statistics are runtime statistics for Java applications and are provided by SAP. The Java applications for which statistics are created are referred to as JARM components; a single measurement is called a JARM request. The measuring points for JARM measurements are uniquely defined by the SAP developers and cannot be changed after delivery. It is no longer developed by SAP.

Java Virtual Machine (JVM) Platform-dependent implementation of the runtime environment for Java programs. Different JVM implementations exist; in addition to Sun, IBM, and HP, SAP also offers an implementation that is, in turn, based on the Open Source code of Sun. The functionality of the JVM is comparable to an SAP kernel.

LAN Local area network. Network within a specific location. Ethernets or token rings are typical LANs. The typical transfer speed of a LAN is in the megabits- to gigabits-per-second range.

Local memory (of a process) → Virtual memory that is allocated to only one operating system process. Only this process can write to or read from this memory area. → Shared memory.

Locks Database locks. Enqueues at the SAP level.

LRU Least recently used. Algorithm that decides which data records (blocks, pages, files, and so on) are removed from or overwritten in the buffer if no buffer space is available for new data records. In this context, LRU is an algorithm that first deletes those data records that haven't been read or written for the longest period of time.

LUW Logical unit of work. From the viewpoint of business logic, an indivisible sequence of database operations that conform to the ACID principle. From the viewpoint of a database system, this sequence represents a unit that plays a decisive role in securing data integrity. → Transaction.

Memory management The capability of an application server to manage the main memory that users request (allocate). This also includes the capability to release memory again and protect the server from failure due to excessive memory requirements from individual programs. ABAP memory management differentiates between memory areas that are available to all programs on the application server, for example, executable program code, metadata for data structures, and selected table contents that can be buffered, and memory areas that are assigned to a user context. (This differentiation does not consider whether this data is stored in the process-local memory or in → shared memory. User context data can be stored in shared memory so that it can be used in all work processes; however, it still remains allocated logically to a user.) At runtime, ABAP memory management ensures that a context does not exceed the memory limit. It can therefore protect the server from failure due to an individual program. At the end of a transaction, ABAP memory management releases the entire user context again to prevent increasing memory use because the user accumulates greater amounts of memory (memory leak). This also happens if a program terminates or is terminated because the memory limit has been exceeded. As of SAP Basis 4.0, you can also create shared objects in ABAP that are kept in the memory over several transactions. In Java memory management, objects of all users are kept in the local memory of the → JVM. The object-oriented Java programming model ensures that objects are not clearly assigned to user contexts. Java provides a separate process to release memory that is no longer required; this process is called garbage collection, which includes a gradual check procedure to determine which objects are no longer used (referenced), which are then released again. Because Java memory management does not enable you to assign objects to user contexts in memory, you can't set any user context limit, which means a single program can occupy the entire JVM memory. Because the objects are stored in the local memory JVM, they can't easily be moved to another JVM. This particularly constitutes a problem if a JVM failure occurs due to a program memory leak; all user contexts will be lost. However, SAP JVM enables you to move user contexts and therefore transfer them to another SAP JVM after failure.

Mode   User session in an SAP GUI window.

NSAPI   Netscape Server API (application programming interface)

OLAP   Online analytical processing.

OLE   Object linking and embedding.

OLTP   Online transaction processing. Operation mode. Defined numbers and types of work processes for one or more instances in a particular time period. Operation modes can be automatically changed.

Optimizer   → Database optimizer.

OS   Operating system.

Paging (at the operating system level)   → Swap space.

Paging (at the SAP level)   Memory area used by particular ABAP statements consisting of a local roll area for each SAP work process, a roll buffer in → shared memory, and possibly an SAP paging file on the hard drive of the application server.

PAI   Process after input. Technical program processes after data is entered in a screen (for ABAP applications).

PBO   Process before output. Technical program processes before a screen is output (for ABAP applications).

Performance   Measure of the efficiency of an IT system.

Pop-up window   A window that is called from a primary window and is displayed in front of that window.

R/3   Runtime System 3.

RAID   Redundant array of independent disks. Hardware-based technology that supports disk drive redundancy via drive mirroring and related methods.

RDBMS   Relational database management system.

RFC   Remote function call. RFC is an SAP interface protocol that is based on CPIC. It allows the programming of communication processes between systems to be simplified considerably. Using RFCs allows predefined functions to be called and executed in a remote system or within the same system.

RFCs are used for communication control, parameter passing, and error handling.

Roll memory   Memory area used to store the initial part of → user contexts. It consists of a local roll area for each SAP work process, a roll buffer in → shared memory, and possibly a roll file on the hard drive of the application server.

Roll-in   Context switch at the SAP level.

Roll-out   Context switch at the SAP level.

SAP GUI   SAP Graphical User Interface.

SAP J2EE Engine   SAP implementation of the Java application server.

SAP liveCache   SAP main memory database for optimizing material resource planning on the basis of the MaxDB database; used in SAP Supply Chain Management.

SAP NetWeaver Business Warehouse (BW)   SAP software for formatting and analyzing business data to support strategic and tactical business decisions. SAP NetWeaver Business Warehouse is part of the NetWeaver technology platform.

SAP NetWeaver Business Warehouse Accelerator (BWA)   SAP software to accelerate SAP NetWeaver BW requests (queries) on the basis of TREX.

SAP NetWeaver Enterprise Search   SAP software for cross-system searches in business data and text documents on the basis of → TREX.

SAP NetWeaver Portal   SAP portal software that combines information and applications to provide users with an overview across organizational and IT boundaries (for instance, systems).

SAProuter   A software module that functions as part of a firewall system.

SAPS   → SAP Application Benchmark Performance Standard. SAP system service. Logical function in SAP Basis. The DBMS service and the application services are functions that are needed to support the SAP system. The application services are Dialog, Update, Enqueue, Batch, Message, Gateway, and Spool; not all are absolutely necessary.

Scalability (of a program)   Dependency of the program runtime on the data volume.

Scalability (of an SAP system)   The ability of an SAP system to meet the requirements of increasing load, for example, due to a growing number of users or background documents, or due to the expansion of the system, that is, additional hardware. Linear scalability is on hand if the required hardware increases linearly to the load. Vertical scalability refers to the fact that the software components on all levels can be installed either centrally on one computer (server) or be distributed over several computers. Horizontal scalability is the ability to distribute the load that occurs within a level over several logical instances, which can run on different computers.

Server   The term *server* has multiple meanings in the SAP environment. It should therefore be used only if it is clear whether it means a logical unit such as an SAP instance or a physical unit such as a computer.

Service-level management   A structured, proactive method whose goal is to guarantee the users of an IT application an adequate level of service, that is, in accordance with the business goals of the client and at optimal cost. SLM consists of a service-level agreement (SLA), an agreement between the client (the owner of a business process) and the contractor (service provider), which covers service targets and service-level reporting or monitoring (that is, regular reporting on the achievement of targets). Useful information about SLM can be found at *http://nextslm.org*.

Session manager   The tool used for central control of SAP R/3 applications. The session manager is a graphical navigation interface used to manage sessions and start application transactions. It can generate both company-specific and user-specific menus. The session manager is available as of Release 3.0C under Windows 95 and Windows NT.

Shared memory Virtual memory that can be accessed by multiple operating system processes. Where there are several SAP instances or an SAP instance and a database instance on the same computer, a semaphore management system ensures that the processes of each instance access only the shared memory of that instance, and not the global objects of other instances. The maximum size of the shared memory is limited on some operating systems. You can set the size of the shared memory using operating system parameters. → Local memory.

SID System Identifier (SAP). Placeholder for the three-character name of an SAP system.

SQL Structured Query Language. A database language for accessing relational databases.

Standard Application Benchmark Available from SAP since 1993, this is a suite of benchmarks for SAP applications, available for many business scenarios (sales and distribution, financials, retail, assembly-to-order, banking, SAP ITS, etc.). Benchmark results received from hardware partners are certified by SAP before being made widely available. Further information (for example, all published benchmark results) can be found on the Internet at *http://service. sap.com/benchmark* (SAP-specific information) and at *http://www.ideasinternational. com* (general information). The unit used in SAP benchmarks for measuring hardware efficiency is called SAPS (SAP Application Benchmark Performance Standard).

Statistics record These records contain information on response time, CPU time, the transferred quantity of data, programs called, and much more. If several SAP components are involved in a transactional step, each component writes a statistical record (the local statistics record) into local files for reasons of performance. When the individual components communicate with each other (for example, during an RFC or HTTP communication), they forward a → GUID (also referred to as the passport). This passport is used as a basis for identifying the statistical records related to a transactional step at a later stage. The evaluation transactions for the statistical records are the workload analysis (ST03N and ST03G) and the single-record statistics (STAD and STATTTRACE).

Support package Software fixes or updates provided by SAP for a specific release version of an SAP component (previously known as hot packages).

Swap space Storage area on a hard drive or other device used for storing objects that cannot currently be stored in the physical memory (also called a paging file). The processes of storing objects outside the physical memory and retrieving them is known as page out and page in, respectively.

System landscape A real system constellation installed at a customer site. The system landscape describes the required systems and clients, their meanings, and the transport paths for implementation and maintenance. Of the methods used, client copy and the transport system are particularly important. For example, the system landscape could consist of a development system, a test system, a consolidation system, and a production system.

TCP/IP Transmission Control Protocol/ Internet Protocol.

TDC Transport Domain Controller. Application server of an SAP system in the transport domain from which transport activities between the SAP systems in the transport domain are controlled.

TemSe Temporary sequential objects. Data storage for output management.

TMS Transport Management System. Tool for managing transport requests between SAP systems.

TO Transport Organizer. Tool for managing all of the change and transport requests with more extensive functionality than the → CO and → WBO.

Transaction
1. Database transaction (→ LUW): A unit of database operation that conforms to the ACID principles of atomicity, consistency, isolation, and durability.
2. SAP transaction: an SAP LUW. SAP transactions conform to the ACID principles over multiple transaction steps; for example, creating a customer order is an SAP transaction in which the ACID principles are adhered to in several successive screens up to completion of the SAP transaction at order creation. An SAP transaction may consist of several database transactions.
3. Reference to an ABAP program: for example, Transaction VA01. (See also "Transaction code.")

Transaction code Succession of alphanumeric characters used to name a transaction, that is, a particular ABAP program in the SAP system.

Transport Term from software logistics describing data export and import between development, quality assurance, and productivity systems.

Transport domain Logical group of SAP systems between which data is transported in accordance with fixed rules. The Transport Domain Controller exercises control over the transport domain.

TREX SAP component for quick search and aggregation of data.

TRFC Transactional RFC. Remote function control to which the ACID principles are applied.

URL Uniform Resource Locator. Address on the Internet.

User context User-specific data, such as variables, internal tables, and screen lists. The user context is stored in the memory of the application server until the user logs off. User context is connected with a work process only while the work process is working on the user's request (context switch on the SAP level). User contexts are stored in roll memory, extended memory, or heap memory.

Virtual memory More memory can be allocated virtually in operating systems than is physically available. Virtual memory is organized by the operating system either in the physical main memory, or in → swap space.

VM container Virtual Machine Container. The VM container is a component that enables the operation of a Java Virtual Machine (SAP JVM) within the SAP work process, along with the ABAP runtime environment. The → memory management of JVM in the VM container is basically identical to that of the ABAP runtime environment and is no longer similar to a "normal" Java runtime environment in which user data is maintained in the local memory of the JVM and can't easily be moved from one JVM to another. The benefit of the VM container is higher stability due to processing only one transaction step and one work process at the same time in the JVM.

WAN Wide area network. Network that connects widely separated locations, such as a central office with branch offices. For example, a WAN can be an ISDN line with a transfer speed of 64KB/sec.

WBO Workbench Organizer. Tool for managing change and transport requests generated by the ABAP Workbench.

Web Dynpro SAP technology for the *declarative* development of Web-based user interfaces (Web UIs) in the Java and ABAP programming languages .

WP Work process. The application services of the SAP system have special processes, for example:

► Dialog administration

► Updating change documents

► Background processing

► Spool processing

► Enqueue management

Work processes are assigned to dedicated application servers.

WWW World Wide Web. The part of the Internet that can be accessed using a web browser.

XML Extensible Markup Language. An extensible language used to create structured (business) documents. XML is one of the preferred formats for the electronic exchange of documents between systems on the Internet.

G   Information Sources

This appendix includes references to introductory and additional literature.

General

As we mentioned in the introduction, a solid understanding of SAP system administration is the prerequisite for implementing the performance analysis and optimizations described in this book. For this purpose, refer to SAP system administration books, for instance:

▶ Föse, Frank; Hagemann, Sigrid; Will, Liane: *SAP NetWeaver AS ABAP System Administration.* 3rd edition. Boston, MA, USA: SAP PRESS. 2008.

The *SAP help* provides documents on system administration and detailed information on the transactions and administration tools described in this book. You can call the SAP help either directly from your system via HELP • APPLICATION HELP or via the Internet at:

SAP help

▶ *http://help.sap.com*

You can find documents on system administration by selecting the help for an SAP NetWeaver version and then selecting the link System Administration Technical Operations Manual.

This book often quotes additional information from SAP notes. Note once again that if you implement a specific performance optimization, you should first ensure that you've carefully checked the notes on this topic and are familiar with the most current notes. For example, the following link provides access to SAP notes in the SAP Service Marketplace:

SAP notes

▶ *http://service.sap.com/notes*

This appendix also includes a summary of the most critical notes. Note that this selection is by no means complete. Rather, we selected notes that play a central role so that you can refine your research using the associated notes.

SAP Service
Marketplace

The *SAP Service Marketplace* offers not only SAP notes, but also additional official SAP documents, for instance, on sizing. Customers, partners, and SAP employees can access the SAP Service Marketplace.

▶ *http://service.sap.com*

General performance information in the SAP Service Marketplace is available at:

▶ *http://service.sap.com/performance*

SAP Developer
Network

Finally, the *SAP Developer Network* provides a variety of additional documents, for instance, how-to guides:

▶ *https://sdn.sap.com*

Performance
trainings

SAP offers the following training courses for performance optimization:

▶ Workload Analysis and Tuning (Performance Training for Administrators)

▶ ABAP Program Optimization (Performance Training for Developers)

Chapter 1

You can find information about SAP services in the performance environment at the following addresses:

▶ SAP Solution Manager: *http://service.sap.com/solutionmanager*

▶ SAP EarlyWatch Service: *http://service.sap.com/earlywatch*

▶ SAP EarlyWatch Alert Service and Service Level Management: *http://service.sap.com/ewa*

▶ SAP GoingLive Check: *http://service.sap.com/goinglivecheck*

Note Number	Title
67739	Problem Report Priorities
131030	Performance 4.0/4.5 — Collective Note
203924	Performance 4.6 — Collective Note

Chapter 2

You can find information on the monitoring infrastructure in the SAP Computing Center Management System (CCMS) at:

▸ *http://service.sap.com/systemmanagement* • SYSTEM MONITORING AND ALERT MANAGEMENT • MEDIA LIBRARY • DOCUMENTATION.

Here you can find documents on the central Alert Monitor, workload monitors, and so on.

You can find information on performance analyses using SAP Solution Manager (Learning Map for End-to-End Runtime Analysis in SAP Solution Manager including videos and presentations) at:

▸ *http://service.sap.com/rkt-solman*. Select Solution Manager 7.0. Then select the Support Organizations/Service Providers role under Technical Roles, and open the End-To-End Root Cause Analysis area. There you can find the online trainings, J2EE Memory Analysis and J2EE Thread Dump Analysis.

You will find information on Java performance topics at:

▸ *http://javaperformancetuning.com*

▸ For more information on Sun go to:

  ▸ Java HotSpot VM Options: *java.sun.com/docs/hotspot/VMOptions. html*

  ▸ Tuning the garbage collection: *http://java.sun.com/docs/hotspot/gc/ index html*

  ▸ Optimal memory usage: *java.sun.com/docs/hotspot/ism.html*

▸ For more information on garbage collection, refer to IBM at: *http:// www-106.ibm.com/developerworks/java/library/j-jtp10283/*

Note Number	Title
994025	Collective Note on the Revised Operating System Monitor
38052	System Panic, Terminations Due to Low Swap Space
78498	High Paging Rate on AIX Servers, Particularly on Database Servers

Note Number	Title
124199	ST06 Display—Paged in [KB/h]/Paged out [KB/h] for Sun/Solaris
689818	High Paging Rates During Backup
153641	Swap Space Requirement SAP 64-Bit Kernel
1112627	SAP under HP-UX: Recommendations for Swap and Pseudo Swap
570375	SAP on Sun Solaris: Swap Space and Paging
31395	System Parameters: Where Are They Defined? How Are They Defined? Documentation?
103747	Performance 4.0/4.5/4.6: Parameter Recommendations
97497	Memory Management Parameter (3.0/3.1)
146289	Recommendations for SAP 64-Bit Kernel
146528	Configuration of SAP Systems on Hosts with Substantial RAM
33576	Memory Management for Release 3.0C and Later, UNIX and NT
68544	Memory Management Under Windows NT
88416	Zero Administration Memory Management for 40A/NT and later
386605	SAP Memory Management for Linux (32-Bit)
353579	Cancelation SYSTEM_NO_ROLL
373986	Export/Import Buffer
634006	Note on Preliminary Clarification of ICM Messages
696410	Central Note for Configuration of Java Virtual Machine for EP SP2 on J2EE 6.20
552522	Java HotSpot VM Memory Parameters
634689	Central Note for Memory Issues, SAP J2EE Engine 6.20
597187	J2EE Crashes with OutOfMemory on Sun JDK
610134	Obtain Memory Profile Information
667841	J2EE Engine 6.20 on AIX: Increase the Heap Size
667711	Max. JVM Heap Size for AIX JDK 1.3.1
209834	CCMS Monitoring: Using Agents Technology

Note Number	Title
498179	Activate Monitoring of SAP J2EE Engine 6.20
418285	Installation of the ITS Plug-In for CCMS Agent
176492	Automatic Email in Case of Alert (RZ20)

Appendix B provides database-specific notes and notes on the DBA Cockpit.

Chapter 3

You can find information on performance analyses using SAP Solution Manager at:

▶ *http://service.sap.com/rkt-solman*. Select Solution Manager 7.0. The select the Support Organizations/Service Providers role under Technical Roles, and open the End-To-End Root Cause Analysis AREA. There you can find the online training, E2E Workload Analysis.

Note Number	Title
8963	Definition SAP Response Time t/Response Time/CPU Time
12103	Contents of Table TCOLL
16083	Standard Jobs, Reorganization Jobs
23984	Workload Analysis: Duration of Data Storage
143550	ST03/Workload: User Exit for Individual Analysis
364625	Interpretation of Response Time in Basis 4.6
376148	Response Times without GUI Time
1073521	Response Times without GUI Time II
992474	URL in the Transaction Profile of ST03

Chapter 4

You can find information on performance analyses using SAP Solution Manager at:

▶ *http://service.sap.com/rkt-solman*. Select: Solution Manager 7.0. Then select the Support Organizations/Service Providers role under Technical Roles, and open the End-To-End Root Cause Analysis AREA. There you can find the online training, Java Performance Monitoring/Tracing with Wily Introscope and End-to-End Trace Analysis.

For more information on Introscope go to:

▶ *http://www.wilytech.com*

The following sources provide a good introduction to the programming of internal tables:

▶ Hermann Gahm: *ABAP Performance Tuning*. Boston, MA, USA: SAP PRESS. 2009.

▶ "Scalability of the Application Server" (TechEd speech COMP270), at *http://service.sap.com/performance* • MEDIA LIBRARY.

Note Number	Title
20097, 87447	SE30: Time Measurement Error (Multi-Processor Machine), Meter for Statistics and Runtime Measurements
69455	Service Tools for Applications ST-A/PI (ST14)
543359	Code Inspector for SAP R/3 Release 4.6C
792999	Wily Introscope: Availability and Installation
797147	Installation of Wily Introscope for SAP Customers
943031	Wily Introscope Agent with JDK 1.5
1041556	Availability of the HTTP-Trace Plug-In

Chapter 5

For more information on SAP Benchmarks go to:

▶ *http://service.sap.com/benchmark* and *http//www.sap.com/benchmark* (accessible without use of SAP Service Marketplace).

You can find information on hardware sizing at:

▶ *http://service.sap.com/sizing*. From there you can navigate to the Quick Sizer and sizing documents: SIZING GUIDELINES • SOLUTIONS & PLATFORMS.

You can find further information on sizing and hardware solutions for SAP systems in:

▶ Mißbach, Michael; Gibbels, Peter; Karnstädt, Jürgen; Stelzel, Josef; Wagenblast, Thomas: *Adaptive Hardware Infrastructures for SAP.* Boston, MA, USA: SAP PRESS. 2006.

▶ Janssen, Susanne; Marquardt, Ulrich: *Sizing SAP Systems. Essentials Guide 27.* Boston, MA, USA: SAP PRESS. 2008.

Ideas International (*http://www.ideasinternational.com*) provides comprehensive documentation on benchmarks in general.

Valuable information on the topics of landscape design is available at the following pages in the SAP Service Marketplace or SDN:

▶ *https://www.sdn.sap.com/irj/sdn/landscapedesign*

▶ *https://www.sdn.sap.com/irj/sdn/adaptive*
(adaptive computing, virtualized SAP system landscapes)

▶ *http://service.sap.com/mcod*
(multiple systems on a database)

▶ *http://service.sap.com/platforms*
(released platforms for SAP software components)

▶ *http://service.sap.com/network* (network configuration)

▶ *http://service.sap.com/unicode* (Unicode)

Note Number	Title
85524	R/3 Sizing (Quick Sizer)
89305	Resource Requirements for SAP R/3 4.0
113795	Resource Requirements for SAP R/3 4.5
151508, 178616, 323263	Resource Requirements for SAP R/3 4.6
517085, 752532	Resource Requirements for SAP R/3 Enterprise 4.7
778774	Resource Requirements for SAP Enterprise Core Component 5.0
901070, 1311835	Resource Requirements for SAP ERP Central Component (ECC) 6.0

Note Number	Title
972042, 1111414	Resource Requirements for CRM 5.0, 2006s/2, 2007
79991	Overview Note for Unicode
1139642	Hardware Requirements for Unicode
790099	Parameter Recommendations for Unicode
26417	SAP GUI Resources: Hardware and Software
164102	Network Resource Requirements for SAP R/3 4.6
12825	Installation of Two R/3 Systems on one Computer
21960	Multiple Instances/Systems on One UNIX Computer
28392	Two R/3 Systems on One Windows NT Server
855534	Integrated SAP NetWeaver Components in ERP (Consolidated ERP Installation)
392852	Additional Applications on the liveCache Server
901732	SAP on HP Integrity Virtual Machines (HPVM)
1002461	Support for IBM Dynamic LPAR and Micropartitioning
1246022	Support for SAP Applications in Solaris Zones

Chapter 6

Note Number	Title
72638	Performance Problems with SQL*Net
26317	Set Up Logon Group
39412	How Many Work Processes to Configure
51789	Bad User Distribution in Logon Distribution
68544	NT: R/3 Memory Management for Release 3.1x (Section: Number of Work Processes)
44844	No Connection to a Registered RFC Program
63930	Gateway Registration of an RFC Server Program
74141	Resource Management for tRFC and aRFC
375566	Many Entries in the tRFC and qRFC Tables
854170	Activating the VM Container Component (Implementation, Primary Initial Configuration)

Note Number	Title
863354	Administration of the VM Container Component
990115, 1020539	Configuration of the Shared Pool, Memory Management in the VM Container

Chapter 7

Note Number	Title
164102	Network Load Between Application Server and Front End
679918	Front-End Network Time
158985	How to Generate an Automation Trace
332210	Performance Improvement Within the Sales Document Processing Via Transaction Variant
203924	Performance 4.6 — Collective Note
376148, 1073521	Response Times without GUI Time
834568	HTTP Analysis for the IE Plug-In
1041556	SAP HTTP Plug-In for IE
377513	Performance Analysis of Web Applications with IEMON and HTTPMON (SAP-Internal)
321426	SAP Internet Transaction Server (ITS) 4.6D: New Functionality
350646	Condensing HTML
316877, 314 530	Highest Total of Conversations Exceeded, Number of RFC/CPIC Connections for External Clients
709038	General Information on the Integrated ITS
721993	ITS Updates in Release 6.40 (SAP Integrated ITS)
678904	ITS—New Storage Structures as of SAP Web AS 6.40
722735	Debugging IAC Applications in the Integrated ITS
885580	SAP Integrated ITS: Configuration Parameter
517484	Inactive Services in Internet Communication Framework
992474	URL in the Transaction Profile of ST03

The following URLs provide information on monitoring tools (particularly tools used to monitor websites):

- *http://dmoz.org/Computers/Software/Internet/Site_Management/Monitoring/*
- *http://www.httpwatch.com/download/* (HTTPWatch)

Chapter 8

Note Number	Title
121625, 139326	AS/400: Memory Management and Buffer Sizes
146528	Configuration of R/3 on Hosts with Substantial RAM
146289	Parameter Recommendations for SAP 64-Bit Kernel
194885	End of Support of 32-Bit SAP Software on UNIX Operating Systems
308375	64-Bit mySAP Software
313347	Windows Editions and Memory Support
996600	Not Recommended 32-Bit Platform
1280759	SAP Recommends only 64-Bit Windows for Application Server
959781	SAP ITS 6.20: Restricted Support on Windows 32-Bit
622709	liveCache Use on 32-Bit Operating Systems
353579	Cancelation SYSTEM_NO_ROLL

You can find details on 64-Bit Windows and Linux systems at:

- *http://www.saponwin.com*
- *http://www.sap.com/linux*

For more information on memory management refer to the note table for Chapter 2.

Chapter 9

A good introduction to programming using shared objects is available in the document, "In-Memory Computing" (TechEd speech CD353) at *http://service.sap.com/performance* • MEDIA LIBRARY.

Chapter 10

Note Number	Title
5424	Question and Answers on Enqueue/Locking
97760	Enqueue: Performance and Resource Consumption
62077	Info: Internal Number Assignment is not Continuous
37844	Performance: Document Number Assignment RF_BELEG
23835	Buffering RV_BELEG / Number Assignment in SD
75248	Performance During Direct Input w. ALE Distribution
40904	Performance During Availability Check
24762	Blocking with Quantities and Late Exclus.
99999	ATP Server: Installation and Sizing
179224	Document Number Assignment for Unbuffered Numbering Systems

Chapter 11

Note Number	Title
706478	Measures Against Fast Growing Basis Tables
70513	Physical Block Accesses RESB for Access via MDRS
821687	FAQ: Oracle Space Utilization and Fragmentation
724545	Manual Adaptation of the CBO Statistics with DBMS_STATS
185530, 187906, 191492	Performance: Customer Developments in SD, PP, PM, MM, WM
129385	General Database Hints

Appendix B provides database-specific notes and notes on the DBA Cockpit.

Chapter 12

You can find documents on the administration and performance tuning of SAP NetWeaver BW in the SAP Developer Network at:

▶ *https://www.sdn.sap.com/irj/sdn/bi-performance-tuning*

▶ *https://www.sdn.sap.com/irj/sdn/nw-bi*

For additional expert information on performance tuning of SAP NetWeaver BW systems refer to:

▶ Schröder, Thomas: *SAP NetWeaver BW Performance Optimization Guide.* Boston, MA, USA: SAP PRESS 2006.

Note Number	Title
557870	FAQ: BW Query Performance
192658	Basis Parameterization for BW Systems
180605	Specific Parameter Recommendations for Oracle Databases
181945	Specific Parameter Recommendations for Informix Databases
302429, 546262	Specific Parameter Recommendations for DB2 for Linux, UNIX, and Windows Databases
390016	Specific Parameter Recommendations for DB2/390 Databases
307077, 501572, 541508	Specific Parameter Recommendations for DB2/iSeries Databases
327494, 28667	Specific Parameter Recommendations for Microsoft SQL Server Databases
565075	Recommendations for BW Systems under Oracle 8.1.x
1013912	FAQ: Oracle BW Performance
351163 and 428212	Create Oracle DB Statistics via DBMS_STATS, Update Statistics of InfoCubes
550669	Compressed Transfer of BW Web Applications
764394	Guidelines for Performance Improvement of Web Applications
561792	Client-Based Caching of Image/gif Files
1013912	FAQ: Oracle BW Performance
688085, 1138864	Re-Generation of Queries, Delta Procedure of the OLAP Cache
822302	OLAP Cache for Remote Providers

Note Number	Title
751402	Cache Utilization: Queries Changeable with Variables in Navigation
656060	OLAP: Cache Main Memory Displacement Doesn't Work
807967, 859456, and 1006905	Fill Cache from Reporting Agent, Performance Gain Using the Cache, OLAP Cache Entries with Reporting Agent
607164	MultiProvider: Sequential Processing Faster than Parallel Processing
130696	Performance Trace (RSDDSTAT) in BW
934848	Collective Note: (FAQ) BI Administration Cockpit

Chapter 13

Additional information on TREX is available in the technical manual in the SAP NetWeaver 7.0 library under *http://help.sap.com/nw70* • SAP NETWEAVER ENTERPRISE SEARCH.

For additional information on SAP NetWeaver BW Accelerator refer to:

► Ross, Andrew: *SAP NetWeaver BI Accelerator.* Boston, MA, USA: SAP PRESS 2009.

► *https://www.sdn.sap.com/irj/sdn/bwa*

Note Number	Title
1254901	SES for Customer Projects in the TREX Search
631390	TREX: Additional Languages
917803	Estimate the Memory Consumption of a BIA Index
1345777	FAQs Search Engine Service (SES)
1070674	Configure CCMS/GRMG for TREX 7.1 for Enterprise Search
1085844	SAP NetWeaver Enterprise Search 7.0: Solution Guideline

Index